Economic Approaches to Organizations

Fourth Edition

Economic Approaches to Organizations

Sytse Douma
Tilburg University, the Netherlands

Hein Schreuder
DSM NV and Maastricht University, the Netherlands

FT Prentice Hall
FINANCIAL TIMES

An imprint of **Pearson Education**
Harlow, England • London • New York • Boston • San Francisco • Toronto
Sydney • Tokyo • Singapore • Hong Kong • Seoul • Taipei • New Delhi
Cape Town • Madrid • Mexico City • Amsterdam • Munich • Paris • Milan

Pearson Education Limited

Edinburgh Gate
Harlow
Essex CM20 2JE
England

and Associated Companies throughout the world

Visit us on the World Wide Web at:
www.pearsoned.co.uk

———————————————

First published 1991
Second edution published 1998
Third edition published 2002
Fourth edition published 2008

© Prentice Hall Europe 1991, 1998
© Pearson Education 2002, 2008

ISBN: 978-0-273-68197-4

British Library Cataloguing-in-Publication Data
A catalogue record for this book is available from the British Library

Library of Congress Cataloging-in-Publication Data
A catalog record for this book is available from the Library of Congress

10 9 8 7 6 5 4 3 2 1
11 10 09 08

Typeset in 9.5/12.5 pt 1Stone Serif by 3
Printed and bound in Great Britain by Ashford Colour Press, Gosport, Hants

The publisher's policy is to use paper manufactured from sustainable forests.

Contents

Preface

This is the fourth edition of a book originally published in 1991. In the meantime, it has been translated into five languages – Chinese, Danish, Japanese, Korean, and Spanish.

It has been gratifying to witness the success of the book, but to us it has been even more satisfying to work on its evolution from one edition to the other. Particularly in this fourth edition, we have felt the need to expand the conceptual framework of our book, update many chapters with new developments and add three new chapters on the applications of economic approaches to organizations. This reflects the continuous fruitful developments of these approaches by many economists and organization theorists, as well as their practical relevance in wide range of situations. It is a lasting joy and challenge to present the insights that economic approaches can offer in a way that we hope is concise, illuminating and appealing.

This book is intended for students of organization and management – an important area of study for students of business administration, economics, sociology and organizational psychology. There is no shortage of textbooks on organization and/or management, but most do not include even a short introduction to the various economic approaches to organizations that have been developed in recent decades. This book takes a different approach: it has been designed as an introductory text on the analysis of organizations from an economic perspective. The book has been used successfully as a main text on organization and management courses in many universities and business schools with an emphasis on economic aspects of management (such as finance, marketing, and accounting). In other settings, the book can be used as a supplementary text in conjunction with a more conventional textbook on organization and/or (strategic) management.

No prior knowledge of economics is assumed. The economic background needed to understand the arguments made in the text is explained in the text itself, mainly in Chapter 2.

Students of economics will also find this book useful. Most textbooks in microeconomics devote little attention to the field of organization and management. This book offers students in economics a view from their own discipline into a related but usually unknown field.

The book starts by comparing markets and organizations. Why do organizations exist at all? Why are not all economic decisions coordinated by the market mechanism? Conversely, why do markets exist at all? Why is not all production carried out by one large firm?

Our answer is that information requirements play a crucial role in understanding why markets and organizations coexist. Markets and organizations offer different solutions to the information problems that are inherent in many situations. Understanding these differences leads to insights where markets are most appropriate and where we should expect organizations to perform better. The different advantages of markets and organizations also explain why we often find that a mix of market and organizational coordination is the optimal solution from an economic point of view.

The book consists of three parts. In Part I, Chapters 1 to 5, we lay the foundations for the economic approaches to organizations that are discussed in Part II. In Chapter 1, we build, step by step, a conceptual framework to explain the fundamental economic approach to organizations. In that framework, information is a concept of vital importance.

Chapters 2 and 3 explain how markets and organizations work. In particular, these chapters explain how decisions are coordinated by various mechanisms, such as the price mechanism, direct supervision, mutual adjustment and standardization. Chapter 4 then focuses on the information requirements of different types of coordinating mechanisms. How players can coordinate their decisions in different information settings is also the central theme of the discussion of game theory in Chapter 5. The first five chapters, which form Part I, thus explain the fundamental concepts and methods underlying the economic approaches to organizations.

As the title of this book suggests, there are several different but related economic approaches to organizations. These approaches are discussed and compared in Part II, which consists of Chapters 6 to 11. The approaches are:

- behavioural theory, which sees the firm as a coalition of groups of participants, each with its own interests;
- agency theory, which focuses on delegating decisionmaking to an agent, while the boss (or principal) can only partly observe the agent's behaviour;
- transaction cost economics, which focuses on the sum of transaction costs and production costs as determinants of organizational forms;
- economic contributions to strategic management from the field of industrial organization and game theory;
- evolutionary approaches to organizations, which direct our attention to the development of organizational forms in the context of their interaction with their environments.

Chapter 11 compares and evaluates these five approaches.

Part III describes three areas of the application of the theories and approaches discussed in Part II. Chapter 12 describes how managers involved in mergers and acquisitions cope with problems of information asymmetry. Chapter 13 discusses several hybrid organization forms, such as joint ventures, business groups and franchising using theories and approaches discussed in Part II. Chapter 14 treats the subject of corporate governance as a special case of the framework developed in earlier chapters.

The chapters in Part III each focus on a highly relevant practical issue and highlight that issue in relation to the framework developed in the earlier chapters of the book.

The main differences between this fourth edition and the previous edition are that:

- there is an adaptation of the basic conceptual framework of the book in this edition, which now includes the environment and institutions;
- there is more explicit attention given to institutional and evolutionary perspectives in this edition than previously;
- evolutionary game theory is included in Chapter 5 on game theory;
- there is more emphasis on the resource-based view in Chapter 9 on economic approaches to strategy than in the last edition;
- an introduction to the concept of dynamic capabilities is given in Chapter 9 and the evolution of these capabilities is described in Chapter 10 on evolutionary approaches to organizations in this edition;
- an adapted overview and comparison of economic approaches to organizations is given in Chapter 11 of this edition, reflecting recent developments in the field;
- in this edition, there are the three new chapters on mergers and acquisitions, hybrid forms and corporate governance, which together constitute the new Part III.

The field of economic approaches to organizations has been growing substantially since 1991 and this book has been growing as well. When the first edition of the book appeared in 1991, we felt like parents of a beautiful newborn baby. Now, 17 years later, the baby has developed into a young adolescent, full of energy, wanting to explore the world and make its contribution. We hope you will enjoy reading the book as much as we enjoyed writing it.

An instructor's manual containing answers to end-of-chapter questions, together with overhead transparency masters of many of the figures found in this edition, is available at no extra cost to lecturers adopting this book as a textbook. The manual is available in hard copy on application to the publishers. An electronic version is available to download at **www.booksites.net/douma**.

Sytse Douma
Hein Schreuder

Visit the Companion Website at **http://www.pearsoned.co.uk/douma** to find valuable Lecturer Resources including:

- Complete, downloadable Instructor's Manual.
- Powerpoint slides that can be downloaded and used as OHTs.

No book can be written without the assistance of others. We wish to thank first of all our fellow economists who developed and continue to develop the new, exciting field of economic approaches to organizations. We owe a heavy debt to all contributors to this new literature. Their names can be found in the References section.

We owe special thanks to Rejie George for his important contribution to Section 13.4 on business groups and to our sons, Maarten Douma and Hans Schreuder, for their contributions to the topics of incentive contracts and M&A respectively. Further, we wish to express our thanks to the anonymous referees of the subsequent editions of this book and to Paula Parish, Ellen Morgan and Pauline Gillett from Pearson Education for their support. Marie-José Barendregt and Marijke Tiggeler provided invaluable secretarial support.

Publisher's acknowledgements

We are grateful to the following for permission to reproduce copyright material:

Illustrations

Figure 8.4 by permission of Oxford University Press, copyright © 1995, O.E. Williamson (1995), 'Transaction cost economics and organization theory', in O.E. Williamson (ed.) *Organization Theory, from Chester Barnard to the present and beyond*, p. 213, all rights reserved; Figure 10.4 by permission of Harvard University Press, Organizational Ecology, by Michael T. Hannan and John Freeman, p. 239, Cambridge, MA, copyright © 1989 by the President and Fellows of Harvard College.

Text

The Conference Board for an extract from 'Corporate leadership in an uncertain world' by D.C. North from The Conference Board website www.conference-board.org; Penguin Group (UK) for an extract from *Globalization and Its Discontents* by Joseph E. Stiglitz, published by Allen Lane, The Penguin Press 2002, © Joseph E. Stiglitz 2002; W. W. Norton & Company, Inc. for extracts from *Reinventing the Bazaar: A Natural History of Markets by John McMillan*, © John McMillan 2002, and *Thinking Strategically: The Competitive Edge in Business, Politics and Everyday Life* by Avinash K. Dixit and Barry J. Nalebuff, © 1991 Avinash K. Dixit and Barry J. Nalebuff; The Economist for extracts from 'Globalisation, specialization and co-ordination', *The Economist*

2 June 2001, © The Economist 2001, 'An Insurer's Worst Nightmare', *The Economist* 29 July 1995 © The Economist 1995, 'Cheating in OPEC', *The Economist* 28 March 1998 © The Economist 1998, 'Cheating in OPEC', *The Economist* 9 September 2000 © The Economist 2000, 'Punctuated equilibrium and computer technology', *The Economist* 25 May 1996 © The Economist 1996, 'Who controls Fiat?', *The Economist* 17 March 2007 © The Economist 2007, 'In praise of rules: a survey of Asian businesses', *The Economist* 7th April 2001 © The Economist 2001, and 'The European Market for corporatism or corporate control?', *The Economist* 7th July 2001 © The Economist 2001; Oxford University Press for an extract from *Games, Strategies and Managers* by John McMillan, Oxford University Press 1991; European Communities for an extract from press release IP/07/80 'Competition Commission fines members of gas insulated switchgear cartel over 750 million euros' taken from the European Communities website http://europa.eu/pressreleases, © European Communities 2007; Princeton University Press for extracts from *The Complexity of Cooperation* by Robert Axelrod, © Princeton University Press 1997 and *The Company of Strangers* by Paul Seabright, © Princeton University Press; The Orion Publishing Group for an extract from *The Company: A Short History of a Revolutionary Idea* by John Micklethwait and Adrian Wooldridge, by Weidenfeld & Nicolson; The Corporate Strategy Board for extracts from *Changes in the Pharmaceuticals Delivery Chain* (December 1997) and *Current State of Complexity Science* (October 1998) by The Corporate Strategy Board; Scope Publishing for an extract translated from *Management Scope* October 2000; Dr Kees Cools for an extract from his article 'Ebbers Rex' published in *The Wall Street Journal* 22 March 2005; and Knight Features for an extract from 'Breaking Up Is Hard To Do' by Daniel Gross published in *Slate* 26 April 2005, © Washington Post 2005.

We are grateful to the Financial Times Limited for permission to reprint the following material:

Box 8.2 'Self-disbelieved statements in the Enron case?', © *Financial Times*, 10 February 2002; Box 8.10 'Sold on the web', © *Financial Times*, FT Weekend 2004; Box 13.1 'A clever build to Boeing', © *Financial Times*, 9 July 2007.

We are grateful to the following for permission to use copyright material:

Box 12.2 'Using IPOs to prove the value of M&A targets', *The Financial Times Limited*, 6 October 2006, © Jeffrey J. Reuer and Roberto Ragozzino.

In some instances we have been unable to trace the owners of copyright material and we would appreciate any information that would enable us to do so.

Part I

Foundations

1 Markets and organizations

1.1 The economic problem

Imagine a world of abundance – perhaps a tropical island where you are basking in the sun, with lots of food and a tribe of friendly islanders as your companions. Would you have any economic problems on this island? Well, 'No', you may say, 'I can't imagine *any* problem on such an island, let alone an economic problem.' You may be right, but you may be right for the wrong reason.

Many people associate economic problems with money. As money would be either absent or abundant on our imaginary island, they would think there would be no economic problems. An economist, however, would not be content with this reasoning. She[1] would enquire further, asking, for example, whether you felt you had enough time to enjoy all the pleasures of your island or if your needs for housing, education, culture, friendship and so on had been met. The point is that an economist would identify an **economic problem** in any situation where needs would not be met as a result of scarcity of resources – 'resources' being quite broadly conceived as meaning all factors that may contribute towards the satisfaction of human needs. So, yes, you may not have an economic problem on your fantasy island, but only if you could truly say that all your needs would be met.

Time to return to the real world, where economic problems abound, whether we apply a narrow definition or the broader one presented above. We do not have enough land to meet all our needs for cultivation as well as eco-logical preservation. We do not manage to feed the world's population properly. Many raw materials are in limited supply. Talent is always scarce and so is time. Most people, even in rich countries such as the USA, Germany and Japan, do not earn enough money to buy everything that they would like to buy. In short, scarcity is a fact of life in the real world. Given this predicament, the economic problem may be rephrased as the problem of how to make the best use of the available resources. Alternatively, in economic jargon, what is the **optimal allocation** of the scarce resources over the alternative uses that can be made of them? Resources that are optimally allocated are said to be used with **efficiency**.[2]

This book is concerned with economic approaches to organizations. Now, economics might not be the first discipline you think of when trying to under-stand organizational phenomena. Indeed, it will be argued later that

Economic problem

Optimal allocation

Efficiency

economics had for a long time hardly any contribution to make to the study of organizations. The approaches that we present in this book have been developed relatively recently, although in some cases their origins are much older. So, you are quite justified in wondering what insights economics has to offer. Our answer is that economic approaches to organizations are fruitful whenever the problem to be studied has an **economic aspect** – that is to say, whenever part of the problem deals with the (optimal) allocation of scarce resources.

Economic aspect

Note that we have carefully specified that economics deals with parts and aspects of problems. We believe that there are hardly any 'purely economic' problems. Similarly, there are hardly any purely legal, sociological or psychological problems. All these social sciences deal with aspects of real-world phenomena. All illuminate a part of social reality. Whoever believes that economics can explain entirely the 'marriage market' or, for that matter, organizational phenomena is guilty of 'economism' (which, we are informed, is a contraction of economics and colonialism). There is an equal danger of legalism, sociologism or psychologism, too, whenever the explanatory power of one discipline is exaggerated. Having said that, we do believe economics has an important contribution to make to the understanding of organizations. From the perspective outlined above, two points follow:

■ economic approaches to organizations focus specifically on the economic problem of optimal allocation of scarce resources (broadly conceived);
■ the economic contribution to our understanding of an organizational problem increases when the economic problem forms a greater part of the organizational problem that we are trying to understand.

In this book, we present the major strands of the current economic approaches to organizations. In addition, we illustrate some of the applications of those approaches to organizational problems. In doing so, we shall avoid technical expositions and, instead, concentrate on the basic concepts involved. Our aim is to provide a conceptual introduction to these novel approaches. By focusing on the basic concepts, we hope also to present a more coherent picture of organizational economics than has been provided before. In this first chapter, we build, step by step, the basic conceptual framework that we use to explain the fundamental economic approach to organizations. This framework is shown in Figure 1.1. The framework will clarify the crucial role of information and the various ways in which information can be mediated. This central role of information will be elaborated further in Chapter 4, where we argue that this is the glue that binds the various economic approaches to organizations together.

1.2 The division of labour

Adam Smith is usually credited as the founding father of modern economics. In his book *An Inquiry into the Nature and Causes of The Wealth of Nations* (1776), he accords great importance to the division of labour: 'The greatest

Figure 1.1 The basic concepts

improvement in the productive powers of labour, and the greater part of the skill, dexterity, and judgment with which it is anywhere directed, or applied, seem to have been the effects of the division of labour.'

His famous example is that of a pin factory. He showed that a tremendous increase in the productivity of the work of pinmakers could be achieved by splitting this work up into distinct tasks and having each worker perform one specific task rather than making entire pins (see Box 1.1).

Box 1.1 The pin factory

To take an example, therefore, from a very trifling manufacture; but one in which the division of labour has been very often taken notice of, the trade of the pin-maker; a workman not educated to this business (which the division of a labour has rendered a distinct trade), nor acquainted with the use of the machinery employed in it (to the invention of which the same division of labour has probably given occasion), could scarce, perhaps, with his utmost industry, make one pin in a day, and certainly could not make twenty. But in the way in which this business is now carried on, not only the whole work is a peculiar trade, but it is divided into a number of branches, of which the greater part are likewise peculiar trades. One man draws out the wire, another straights it, a third cuts it, a fourth points it, a fifth grinds it at the top for receiving the head; to make the head requires two or three distinct operations; to put it on, is a peculiar business, to whiten the pins is another; it is even a trade by itself to put them into the paper; and the important business of making a pin is, in this manner, divided into about eighteen distinct operations, which, in some manufactories, are all performed by distinct hands, though in others the same man will sometimes perform two or three of them. I have seen a small manufactory of this kind where ten men only were employed, and where some of them consequently performed two or three distinct operations. But though they were very poor, and therefore but indifferently accommodated with the necessary machinery, they could, when they exerted themselves, make among them about twelve pounds of pins in a day. There are in a pound upwards of four thousands pins of a middling size. Those ten persons, therefore, could make among them upwards of forty-eight thousand pins in a day. Each person, therefore, making a tenth part of forty-eight thousand pins, might be considered as making four thousand eight hundred pins in a day. But if they had all wrought separately and independently, and without any of them having been educated to this particular business, they certainly could not each of them have made twenty, perhaps not one pin in a day; that is certainly, not

▶

the two hundred and fortieth, perhaps not the four thousand eight hundredth part of what they are at present capable of performing, in consequence of a proper division and combination of their different operations.

Source: Adam Smith, *The Wealth of Nations*, Book I, Chapter 1, 1776

Division of labour

Division of labour, therefore, refers to the splitting of composite tasks into their component parts and having these performed separately. It is a pervasive phenomenon in modern societies.

Our primeval ancestors were much more self-supporting. They built their own houses, grew or hunted their own food, made their own tools, defended themselves from various threats and so on. Since then, gradually, these tasks have come to be divided into separate sectors in society (such as the private and the public sectors), and, within those sectors, further divided into separate entities (such as government agencies, industries and firms). An economic system has developed in which we normally buy these goods or services in exchange for money. Most of us work in organizations where we earn our money. Looking inside those organizations we can see that the division of labour occurs there as well. We usually perform but a small part of an entire organization's task. In order to accomplish its task the organization itself is split into different parts (such as divisions and departments), levels and functions. As a result, we need organization charts (see Box 1.2) as maps to guide us through the organizational territory. These charts are one reflection of the division of labour within organizations.

Box 1.2 Labtech organization chart, September 2007

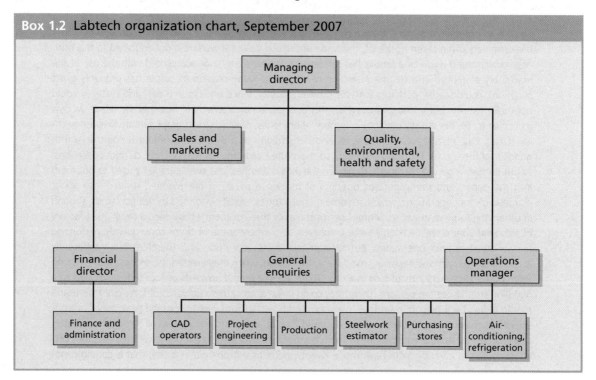

It was Adam Smith's contention that the progressive division of labour led to productivity increases that constituted the main source of the increasing 'wealth of nations'. In the next section we shall see what the basis for this contention was. Here we want to conclude by emphasizing that we take the division of labour as a fact of life in our kind of society. No matter what position we occupy, every time we interact with others to obtain goods or services we need, we may be reminded of this fact. This is what forms the starting point for our conceptual framework, which is outlined in Figure 1.1.

1.3 Specialization

Why would an increasing division of labour lead to such great productivity increases and, thus, to a growth in 'the wealth of nations'? Smith gave the following explanation:

> This great increase in the quantity of work, which, in consequence of the division of labour, the same number of people are capable of performing, is owing to three different circumstances; first, to the increase of dexterity in every particular workman; secondly, to the saving of the time which is commonly lost in passing from one species of work to another; and lastly, to the invention of a great number of machines which facilitate and abridge labour, and enable one man to do the work of many.

Economies of specialization

In our present economic terminology we say that there are **economies of specialization** to be gained. In the specialized pin factory the same amount of output can be produced with less labour effort than in the unspecialized factory. Conversely, a greater amount of output can be achieved with the same level of labour input (ten men), as Smith showed. Specialized production is thus more *efficient* than unspecialized production.

Among the reasons for this being true are the ones mentioned in the quotation above. Essentially, when work is split into specific tasks, we may select one that particularly suits our own needs and capabilities. When we specialize in that task, we can devote all our attention to improving our performance of that task. We can learn from more experience and we can use that experience to devise methods and instruments to further improve our execution of the task. For all these reasons, a specialized economic system is usually more efficient than an unspecialized one. Division of labour thus leads to specialization, which allows for efficiency gains (Figure 1.2).

This is a pervasive phenomenon in society. Let us consider some examples. In the family, household work is usually split into different tasks and the members of the family specialize in distinct tasks (while others may be shared). They become good at those tasks but not at others. Some know exactly where to shop for particular goods and get the best value for money. Some know how to operate the household appliances; perhaps others know how to fix them. Some have specialist skills in filling out the tax forms; others perhaps in monitoring the budget. Whatever the particular distribution of tasks, some degree of specialization is present in all families and, in most families, the efficiency of running the household is seriously disturbed when members have to switch to unfamiliar tasks. In that sense, there is a cost to specialization.

Similarly, in sports, specialization leads to higher performance, but comes at a cost. An individual cannot compete, let alone excel, in all sports. Choices have to be made and long, specialized training has to be undertaken. Once specialized, high performance is necessarily restricted to a narrow range of options. Even an admirable sportsman such as Tiger Woods is restricted to playing professional golf. Specialization, building on a unique talent, has allowed him to reach the top in playing golf, but even Tiger Woods would not be able to compete at the highest level in two sports (for example, in tennis and golf). In team sports such as hockey or soccer, it is usually very unproductive to switch goalkeepers and field players. Good teams make the best use of their members' specializations. Specialized skills are scarce. Good teams allocate those with these skills in an optimal manner to the tasks to be executed and, thus, are organized efficiently.

In many fields, such as medicine or transportation, it would even be disastrous to switch specialists. However much we favour variety of work, we are not willing to enter hospitals or board aircraft where the specialists take turns doing each other's work.

For the individual, then, specialization has the advantage of allowing higher levels of performance to be reached, but the disadvantage of restricting choice. At the individual level, the limits of specialization are reached when the satisfaction gained from higher performance (and the consequent rewards) is outweighed by the dissatisfaction from too narrow an area of application of one's skills (with the resulting boredom and frustration). As many organizations have learned over time, the gains from further specialization are easily offset by the costs of dissatisfaction when those individual limits are exceeded. The conveyor belt, for instance, enabled great gains in productivity, but only to the extent that the workers accepted the range of activities required of them. If such a range becomes too narrow, the gains are offset and a restructuring of activities (for example, into semi-autonomous workgroups) is called for. Individual limits are thus one boundary to increasing specialization, but there is also another boundary, which is the subject of the next section.

Figure 1.2 Division of labour leads to specialization

1.4 Coordination

In the previous paragraphs we have seen that division of labour and specialization are pervasive phenomena in society. As a result, hardly any people are economically self-reliant, in the sense that they produce all the goods and services they wish to consume. In order to obtain those goods and services, they have to acquire them from other specialized people.

Exchange

In economic terminology we say that **exchange** has to take place. Goods and services are exchanged whenever the right to use them is transferred. Much exchange takes place through markets. In a market, the right to use particular goods and services is bought (and, of course, sold at the same time). When I buy a piece of soap in my local store, I acquire the right to use the soap, while the storeowner acquires the right to use the money I have paid for it.

Exchange of goods is usually beneficial to both parties to the exchange. For example, a painter should paint and a cook should cook. They can both specialize when they exchange their products. A nice example is given in Box 1.3.

Box 1.3 Exchange of art for food

John Kay tells the story how the French hotel and restaurant Colombe d'Or acquired an extensive collection of modern art:

> For two hundred years European artists have been attracted to the bright light and brilliant scenery of the south of France. The walled village of Saint-Paul de Vence still houses a community of artists. Paul Roux, who bought a small hotel and restaurant at the entrance of the village in 1919, offered food and lodging to artists in return for examples of their work. Today, the Colombe d'Or's collection of modern French art is the envy of many galleries.
>
> Mr Roux was a talented cook and his visitors talented painters. It therefore made sense for Paul Roux to cook and for Georges Braque, one of the artists he encouraged, to paint. The exchange of food for paintings benefited both parties. It is common to think of exchange as a process in which one party wins at the expense of another, or one party makes a mistake. But the exchange between Braque and Roux, like most economic exchanges, was characterized by mutual gains from trade.
>
> The division of labour between Braque and Roux made these gains possible. By getting together each obtained a mixture of food and art. The two individuals had different capabilities. But these capabilities were, in themselves, insufficient for their needs. Braque needed to eat, and Roux did not wish to live by bread alone. Whenever there are differences in talent and a mutual desire for variety, there is the possibility of a division of labour and mutually beneficial exchange.

Source: Kay (2003)

Exchange, though, is broader than just market exchange. First, the goods involved need not be only goods that are marketable. Economists speak of goods whenever scarce resources are involved. We can indeed also exchange favours as they are very scarce and can be used to get things done. Similarly, we exchange information as soon as the right to use the information has been transferred. Second, the transfer of rights need not be mutual. When I offer you some of my time, I am offering you the right to use a scarce resource. An

Transaction

economist would regard your use of my time as an example of exchange, whether or not you reciprocate in any way.

Whenever exchange takes place, we speak of an (economic) **transaction**. Owing to the division of labour and to specialization, innumerable transactions have to occur in society. As on the one hand, we are all specialized ourselves and, on the other hand, need the specialized goods and services of others, a vast network of exchange is necessary to allocate the available goods and services. How is that accomplished? How do the parties who are willing to engage in a transaction find each other? Phrased in economic terminology,

Co-ordination

how is the **coordination** achieved within an economic system?

Specialization leads to a need for coordination (Figure 1.3). Essentially, we shall submit, there are two types of co-ordination: transactions may take place either across markets or within organizations.[3] The next section will discuss this distinction further.

Figure 1.3 Specialization entails coordination

1.5 Markets and organizations

Consider the stock market. Each day on the major stock markets of the world, millions of shares and bonds are exchanged. On the New York Stock Exchange alone, as many as 1 million transactions may be carried out on an average trading day, involving more than 100 million shares with a total value of more than $5 billion (Box 1.4 shows an extract from a London Stock Exchange listing). Buyers and sellers are not only British, but include private and institutional investors from all over the world.

How do all those parties find each other to sort out the opportunities for transactions? How, for instance, does a Japanese buyer find out who (from the USA, Germany or Hong Kong) wants to sell the stocks in which he is interested? The answer is, he does not.

He does not because the stock market comes close to that ideal type of market in which it is not necessary for buyers and sellers to have any kind of

Price system

personal contact. The reason is that the **price system** is the coordinating device that takes care of allocation.

Suppose you are a potential buyer or seller of IBM stock. All you have to do is inform yourself of the current price of IBM shares, make up your mind whether or not you want to transact at that price level and, if so, instruct your bank or broker to carry out the transaction. You will never know the party with

Box 1.4 Stock exchange prices

Stock	Price	Chng	52 week High	Low	Yld	P/e	Vol '000s
UK							
(Sep 10 / Pence)							
3i	984xd	−23	1.23k	919.13	1.6	4.6	6099
AberdAstM ♦	165.75	−3.5	225	155	3	...	2314
Admiral	879	−4.5	1.19k	741.50	3.4	19.8	1088
Aegis ♦	126.5	−25	152	123	1.6	19	5659
Alliance ♦	344.25	−3	386.25	340.75	2.2	42.6	684
Alnc&Lei ♦	946.5xd	−9.5	1.2k	946.50	5.8	10	2879
AMEC ♦	680	−4	685.50	322.75	1.9	26.1	4690
Amln ♦	296	−4.5	339.50	261	4.3	4.9	3653
AnglAmer ♦	2.73kxd	−57	3.32k	2.12k	2.3	16	8640
Antofgst	675.5	−14	763	406.14	0.5	9.4	6778
ARM	143.5xd	−2	156.50	109	1	46.4	12547
Arriva ♦	777	−10	812.50	624.50	2.7	18.4	1037
AscBrFd ♦	808.5	−28.5	948.50	801.50	2.4	18.9	6224
AstraZen ♦	2.34kxd	−28	3.53k	2.28k	4.1	12	4885
Aviva ♦	673	−9.5	854	659	4.6	7.9	10925
BAE SYS ♦♦	453	−1	466.50	373	2.6	19.9	15551
Balfour8 ♦	445.5	−6	495.25	370.50	2.2	12.5	2707
Barclays ♦	580xd	−2.5	790	580	5.5	8.7	11656
BarrtDev ♦	865	−19	1.29k	865	3.7	7.2	1863
BBA ♦	246.5	−1	292.75	222	2.9	16.7	2651
Bellway ♦	1.19k	−26	1.68k	1.16k	3.1	8.2	439
Berkeley UTS	1.53k	−41	1.94k	1.25k	...	13.6	956
BG ♦♦	791xd	−24	877.50	622.50	1	14	14313
BHP Bltn	1.41k	−24	1.55k	853	1.8	12.1	25470
BovisHme ♦	736	−7	1.2k	720.50	4.1	9.2	2684
BP ♦	558	−2	613	507.50	3.7	12.1	58828
Br Energy	476.5	+8.5	648.50	390	2.9	5.4	7023
BrAmTob ♦♦	1.59kxd	−5	1.72k	1.41k	3.7	16.5	3524
Brdford&B	335.25xd	−2.5	482.25	335.25	6	8.7	7734
BritAir	391.75	−3.5	577.50	377.75	...	10.8	14690
BritLand	1.19k	−38	1.72k	1.17k	2.5	2.3	5151
Brixton ♦	376.25	−7.5	587	348.50	2.9	2.3	3127
BSkyB ♦	668.5	+2.5	713.50	519	2.3	23.5	9169
BT Grp ♦	297.75xd	−1.5	336.75	253.25	5.1	8.8	34419
Bunzl	688.5	+5	742	623.50	2.4	17.6	1898
Burberry	582	−20.5	726.50	473.75	1.8	23.1	3476
Burren ♦	854	+6	937	725	1.6	8.9	1025
CadbSchw ♦	549.5	−7	723.50	517.50	2.5	23.6	7027
CairnEng ♦	1.79k	−22	2.13k	1.52k	...	...	1088
CaledInia ♦	2.01k	−3	2.26k	1.95k	1.5	11.3	46
Capita	717	−10	782	525.50	1.4	29.3	2431
Carnival	2.1kxd	−53	2.81k	2.06k	2.9	14.2	3694
CarphonW	328.75	+5	374.75	269	1	61.5	5977
Cattles ♦	377.5	+2.25	473	329.25	4.6	13.6	2713
Cble&Wir	161	−3.4	201.50	125.50	3.6	...	24519
Centrica ♦♦	369.75	−2.25	397	311	3.1	12.2	12410
Charter ♦	1.09k	−9	1.2k	721	...	15.6	906
CloseBrs ♦	765	−15	1.08k	700.50	4.4	9	1866
Cobham ♦	194.5	−3.5	222.50	170	1.9	16.9	4799
COLT Tel	158	...	182.50	117.25	...	...	1108
Compass ♦	307	−2	381.75	259.25	3.4	22.7	11047
Cookson ♦	754.5	+7.5	790	531	1.5	20.1	1477
CSR	645.5	+1	1.35k	404	...	17.7	1549
Daily Mail ♦	662	−2.5	865	582.50	2	24.7	2188
Diageo ♦	1.04k	−17	1.09k	927.50	3.2	21.3	15132
DSG Int.	147.2xd	−4.1	222	147.20	6	18.5	24127
easyJet	548	−4.5	732	444	...	20.7	2463
Edin Inv ♦	455.5	−6.5	514.50	426	4.1	25.1	214
Elctrcmp ♦	246.75	−4.5	311.75	234.75	7.5	19.4	4783
EMAP ♦	896	+3	911.50	701.50	3.5	27.4	1659
EMI	265	...	300.25	210.75	0.8	24.3	943
Etrplnns	605.5	−11	1.36k	565	2.3	13.1	1527
Experian	505	−1.5	633.50	483.25	1.7	8.4	8658
F&C Ast ♦	190.5	−6	222	161.25	4.7	47.7	462
FirstCh	295.75	+1	357.25	196	...	...	...
FirstGrp	640.5	−6.5	706	476	2.4	21.8	2309
For & Col ♦	293xd	−1.25	314	258.25	1.9	48.4	1258
FriendsP ♦	169.2	−2.9	227	169.20	4.7	10.4	36972
G4S	189	−2.75	236.25	162	2.4	17.3	5996
GKN ♦	347.25xd	−4	411.75	271.75	3.7	13.6	4035
GlaxoSmh ♦♦	1.3kxd	−10	1.51k	1.21k	3.8	13.5	15345
GreeneKg ♦	963.5xd	−17	1.18k	836	2.4	14.9	1172
Hammersn ♦	1.18k	−40	1.75k	1.17k	2.3	3.2	3400
Hays	147.5	−3.25	180.50	131.75	3.4	13	14515
HBOS ♦	871.5xd	−7.5	1.17k	849	5.1	8.1	17213
HomeRetail	394	−4.25	*497.50	376.75	3.3	...	8121
HSBC ♦	870xd	−3	1.03k	861.50	5.5	10.8	38963
ICAP ♦	470.5	−8.25	546.50	445.25	4	25.8	3530
ICI	632xd	−2	642	369.50	1.5	30.4	11949
IMI	574.5	−5.5	637	484	3.3	26.5	2136
ImpTob ♦	2.14k	−37	2.33k	1.76k	2.7	16.5	1883
Inchcape ♦	431.5xd	−11	593.50	431.50	3.5	12.3	2950
Informa	529.5xd	−20	623.50	438.75	2.7	20.9	2357
InterC Htls	958xd	−11.5	1.41k	920	2	12.6	3510
Intertek ♦	910	−29	1.04k	750.50	1.8	21.6	1682
IntlPowr ♦	410.75	+2.5	468.75	298	2.6	60.4	9354
Invensys ♦	336.25	+3	428.25	185.50	...	16.8	6513
Invesco	557	−21.5	665	529	1.8	15.5	1926
Investec	518.5	−9.5	769	495.75	4.4	9.5	2892
ITV	111.3	+2.2	121.50	96.75	2.8	25.7	37913
JohnsonM ♦	1.53k	...	1.83k	1.31k	2.2	19.9	1721
JohnstoP	360	−4.25	490.50	341.75	2.6	8.3	1128
JPMF Merc ♦	1.17k	−17	1.4k	1.03k	2.2	42.7	222
Kazakhmys ♦	1.27k	−15	1.43k	1.01k	1.7	7.6	2321
Kelda ♦	852	+13	1.05k	773	3.8	17.3	3649
Kesa Elect	292.5	−7	369.50	277.75	4.5	13.4	4948
Kingfshr ♦	198.6	−3.9	284	198.10	5.4	16.1	16642
Ladbrokes ♦	421xd	+2.75	459.75	366.25	3.2	13.3	8274
LandSecs ♦	1.7k	−46	2.34k	1.62k	3.1	5.6	4701
Leg&Gen ♦	132.6xd	−1.7	166.75	129.70	4.3	5.3	18464
Liberty ♦	1.68k	−18	1.41k	1.01k	3.1	2.3	3614
LloydsTSB ♦	520.5xd	−3.5	614	520.50	6.7	9.4	20334
LogicaCMG	155.5	−2.75	191.50	148.50	3.7	32.6	19526
Lonmin ♦	3.22k	−75	4.35k	2.44k	1.9	25.6	1924
LSE	1.34k	−9	1.44k	1.2k	1.3	27.2	1817
Man ♦	470.5	−7.25	633.50	415	2.3	15.5	23998
Marks&Sp ♦	602	−12	749	586.50	3	14.9	12114
Marstons ♦	359.25	−5.25	1.86k	329	3.2	16.2	943
Meggitt ♦	302.5	−3	369.75	285.25	2.5	18.2	2665
MichaelP	437.75	−8.75	595	356	1.5	17.7	2855
Misys ♦	215.5xd	−5.5	257.75	185	3.5	37.9	4892
Mitchells&B ♦	649	−11	898	554.50	2	16.2	4058
Mmm&Cth ♦	507xd	−10	773	438.75	1.7	12.2	444
Morrison ♦	272.75	−3.25	335.25	225	1.5	23.6	14854
Nation.Grid ♦♦	718.5	−3	816.50	637.50	4	13.9	7817

Stock	Price	Chng	52 week High	Low	Yld	P/e	Vol '000s
Natl Exp	1.23k	−11	1.32k	832.50	2.9	15.8	535
Next	1.86k	−18	2.44k	1.7k	2.6	12.6	3329
NorthumWtr	322.75xd	−3	349.50	247	3.5	15.3	1940
NrthnRck	646	−5	1.25k	646	6.1	6.8	7137
Old Mutl ♦	144	−2.2	187.50	144	4.5	7.4	21030
PartyGame	26.75	−.75	110.25	22.75	...	89.6	27748
Pearson ♦	729.5xd	−2	914.50	729.50	4.1	12.6	6504
Pennon	591.5xd	+9.5	699	463.75	2.9	23.1	3107
Persimn ♦	1.08kxd	−11	1.54k	1.08k	4.8	7.8	3068
Petrofac	442.75	−11.25	498	286	1.4	23.3	943
Provdnt ♦	864	−12.5	1.05k	780.99	5	13.7	1635
Prudntl ♦	669.5xd	−12	811	591	2.6	19.2	17915
Punch Tv ♦	1.02k	−8	1.4k	927.50	1.4	10.5	2625
Rank Grp	170	+2.75	278	150.50	3.5	8.8	7902
RBS ♦♦	530.5xd	−1.5	719.67	530.50	6.1	7.4	60624
ReckittB ♦	2.61kxd	−28	2.81k	2.13k	1.9	22.2	1799
Reed Els ♦	582.5	−5	689.50	554.50	2.8	25.8	3119
Regus	123	−6	153.75	99.50	0.5	12.8	6888
Rentokil	171.8	+1.5	180.50	145	4.3	23.2	19565
Reuters	633.5	−3	644	402.75	1.9	38.7	5479
REXAM ♦	512.5	−7	604.50	481.50	3.8	15.2	3041
RioTinto ♦	3.54k	−49	4.02k	2.35k	1.6	13.4	8457
RIT Cap ♦	1.03k	−11	1.13k	914	0.3	...	167
Rolls-Ryc ♦	483	−1.25	570	413.43	2	12.6	8484
RoyDtchShellA ♦♦	1.96kxd	−4	2.11k	1.62k	3.5	...	4954
RoyDtchShellB ♦	1.96kxd	−2	2.17k	1.62k	3.5	10	6296
Ryl&SunAl	134xd	−1.2	172.10	128.30	4.9	12.2	38964
SABMiller ♦	1.31k	+1	1.37k	983	2.1	24.1	4978
Sage ♦	240.25	−2.75	277.75	220.50	1.6	20.9	7510
Sainsbry ♦	544	−3	594	367.75	1.8	30.1	8368
Schroders ♦	1.28kxd	−18	1.39k	885	2.1	11.3	2793
Scot&New ♦	616	−4	653	516.50	3.5	21.9	7724
Scot&Sth ♦	1.39kxd	+8	1.5k	1.23k	4	14.2	31832
ScottMort ♦	573	−10	630	478	1.7	58.5	143
SEGRO ♦	499.5xd	−12	780.97	496.94	4.1	2.6	3117
Serco ♦	412xd	−10	514.25	342.50	0.9	26.4	4194
SevernTr ♦	1.32k	+1	1.58k	1.24k	4.7	22.2	1549
ShirePhm ♦	1.24k	−41	1.31k	830	0.3	40.6	3440
SIG ♦	1.21k	−27	1.46k	928	1.7	21	461
Signet ♦	88	+.5	127	87.50	2.4	11.2	8774
SmithNph ♦	562	−9	650	459.25	1.1	25	4898
Smiths ♦	981	+6	1.21k	888.94	3.3	16.4	4663
Soco Int ♦	2.21k	−10	2.22k	1.19k	...	...	708
St Jms Pl ♦	378.5xd	−5	484	326	1	21.7	1542
Stagech	222.25xd	−5	232.25	117.75	1.9	17.6	5688
StandCh ♦	1.45kxd	+3	1.73k	1.31k	2.8	15.9	7401
SVG Capital ♦	813.5	−11.5	944	757	0.9	49.7	113
Tate&Lyl ♦	538.5	+5	820.50	536.50	4	11.4	3091
Taylor Wmpy ♦	328.75	−3.25	518.50	290.75	4.5	6.7	10314
Telent ♦	485	−1	535	430.25	2.2	5.3	48
TemptnEm ♦	373.25xd	−5.5	409.50	255	0.8	89.7	571
Tesco ♦	415.25	−12.5	473.75	360	2.3	17.6	41939
TNS	221.75	−2.25	267.50	191	2.2	19.4	2056
Tomkins ♦	232.25	+.25	302.50	214.50	6	11.7	5469
TravsPkn ♦	1.66k	−50	2.12k	1.66k	2.4	12.5	1232
TrinityMr ♦	464.75	−6.25	574.50	442	4.7	6	1568
Tullow ♦	550	−7	562.50	349	1	30.9	5175
Unilever ♦	1.54k	−16	1.68k	1.27k	2.9	...	3003
UtdBusMd ♦	732xd	−14	867	625.23	2.7	15.4	2660
UtdUtils ♦	662.5	−1.5	799	633.50	6.8	11.7	5614
Vedanta ♦	1.81k	−17	1.91k	1.09k	1.1	11	1644
Vodafone ♦	157.8	−1.5	167.80	114.25	3.8	13	143638
Weir ♦	810	+2	828.50	440.25	1.8	19.4	2065
Whitbrd ♦	1.59k	−5	1.95k	1.28k	1.9	75.6	3408
Willm H ♦	622.5	+2.5	667.50	580.50	3.6	13	2103
Witan ♦	456.75	−3.75	506.25	418.50	2.1	41.8	555
Wolseley ♦	928	−35	1.41k	928	3.3	12.4	6723
Wood (J) Grp ♦	380.5	+6	380.50	219.50	0.8	25.3	2122
WPP ♦	675	−10	787.50	628	1.8	16.4	6289
Xstrata ♦	2.75k	−85	3.44k	2.01k	0.8	10.5	12275
Yell	428.75	−4.25	643.50	425	4	14.2	4659
NYSE							
(Sep 10 / 2:00 pm / US$)							
3M	87.96xd	−.96	91.48	71.35	2.2	15.2	1776
AbbottLabs ♦	51.75	−.11	59.43	45.65	2.5	43.6	856
Accenture ♦	39.72	−.3	43.81	28.38	0.9	19.7	633
AdvMicroD	12.88	+.27	27.38	11.64	...	...	5172
AEP	44.59xd	+.04	50.95	36.05	3.5	18.3	525
AES Corp	18.05	−.24	23.90	17.76	...	...	1041
Aetna ♦	49.81	−.43	53.27	38.32	0.1	15.2	698
AFLAC ♦	53.19	+.1	56.92	43.65	1.5	17.2	428
AgilentTec	36.19	−.09	40.40	28.86	...	23.4	666
AirProdChm	88.61	−.22	91.84	64.88	1.7	21.9	347
AlbertoCul	22.93	+.08	52.45	20.07	1	13.9	137
Alcoa ♦	33.68	−1.19	47.35	26.60	2	14	3300
Allergan ♦	61.53	+.8	65.99	52.91	0.3	43.9	446
Allstate ♦	53.4xd	−.5	65.92	51.17	2.8	6.4	878
Alltel ♦	68.77xd	+.02	69.66	53.31	0.7	30.3	1087
Altria ♦	67.39	...	72.07	53.73	4.5	14	1683
Ambac ♦	59.61	−.47	96.08	58	1.4	8	742
AmEagleOut	23.24	−.58	*34.34	22.04	1.7	13.2	122200
Amer Intl ♦	63.84	+.29	72.81	61.64	1.3	10.4	1785
Ameren Cp	50.52xd	−.1	55.12	47.54	5	16.9	304
AmerExpr ♦	58.49	+.74	65.55	52.48	1	17.5	1219
Amerip Fin	58.05	−.84	*66.95	44	1	20.4	575
AmerSbd	34.4xd	−.72	44.59	29.08	1.8	13.2	660
AmsrceBrgn	46.45	−.65	54.70	42.92	0.4	18.1	636
Anadarko ♦	49.1xd	−.67	55.33	38.63	0.7	10.1	1193
AnalogDev	36.94xd	+.37	40.56	29.14	2	23.3	829
AnheuBusch ♦	49.8xd	−.04	54.41	46.14	2.7	19	1068
Aon Cp	42.41	−.17	43.75	33.68	1.4	18.9	382
Apache ♦	77.89	−.9	88.87	60.49	0.8	11.5	720
ArcherDan ♦	32.65	−.06	39.87	30.70	1.4	9.9	819
ArchSmth	58.11	−.04	63.48	50.78	3.1	...	1076
AT&T ♦	38.76	+.03	41.85	31.41	3.7	19.6	4244
AutomData ♦	44.51	−.22	50.11	41.57	2.2	27	1213
AutoZone	110.86	−.63	140.10	94.10	...	13.6	407
AvalnbyCom ♦	111.45	+.32	148.52	106.01	3.1	47.1	355
Avaya	16.87	+.02	17.21	10.95	...	33.7	507
AveryDenn	56.67	−1.7	69.67	56.80	2.7	16.5	1058
AvonProd	32.11	−.23	41.02	29.23	2.3	27	890
Bard (C R) ♦	83.61	−1.7	89.36	62.17	0.6	24.8	366
BankNYMeln ♦	39.54	−.18	46.72	35.59	2.4	18.8	325
BkofAmeric ♦	48.91xd	−.11	54.90	47	5.2	10.3	3824
BarrPharm	52.05	−.07	56.51	46.17	...	...	175

Explanatory notes

Prices are as quoted on the individual exchanges and mostly last traded prices.

Chng is change on the day.

P/e is price to earnings ratio, where earnings are unadjusted year end earnings, except UK where the UKSIP Headline Earnings formula is used.

Yld is the dividend yield, where dividends are latest rolling 12 month figures.

k behind the values is value * 1000 (4.5k = 4500).

Highs & Lows shown relate to a period of less than 52 weeks.

Source: The Financial Times, 10 September 2007

whom you exchanged the stock. It is not necessary to know the other party. The price contains all the information you need to base your transaction on: it is a **sufficient statistic** (Hayek, 1945).

Sufficient statistic

No wonder economists marvel at the functioning of these types of markets. Through the interlinked system of stock exchanges in the world, all potential buyers and sellers of, in our example, IBM stock are connected with each other. What is more, if, globally, there are more potential buyers than sellers, the price goes up. This has the effect that some buyers are discouraged at that price level and some new sellers are interested in entering the market. This goes on until demand and supply of stock is in equilibrium. At that point, we can say that an optimal allocation of that stock has been achieved as the buyers who are most interested in that stock have been satisfied, while the sellers who were least interested have sold. This optimal allocation obtains without any personal contact being made between the transacting parties.

There are a number of such markets. Markets for raw materials often approximate ideal markets. Let us borrow an example from Hayek (1945) to emphasize how efficiently such markets operate:

> Assume that somewhere in the world a new opportunity for the use of some raw material, say tin, has arisen, or that one of the sources of the supply of tin has been eliminated. It does not matter for our purpose – and it is very significant that it does not matter – which of these two causes has made tin more scarce. All that the users of tin need to know is that some of the tin they used to consume is now more profitably employed elsewhere, and that in consequence they must economize tin. There is no need for the great majority of them even to know where the more urgent need has arisen, or in favor of what other needs they ought to husband the supply. If only some of them know directly of the new demand, and switch resources over to it, and if the people aware of the new gap thus created in turn fill it from still other sources, the effect will rapidly spread throughout the whole economic system and influence not only all the uses of tin, but also those of its substitutes and the substitutes of these substitutes, the supply of all the things made of tin, and their substitutes, and so on; and all this without the great majority of those instrumental in bringing about these substitutions knowing anything at all about the original cause of these changes.

Again, the adjustment of the price levels of tin and its substitutes is sufficient for a worldwide communication of all the necessary information to all relevant parties. As if led by the famous 'invisible hand' of Adam Smith, the individual decisions made by these parties will lead to new aggregate equilibrium levels of the supply and demand of tin.

Assuming you are now convinced of the efficiency properties of ideal markets, we may proceed to ask, why is not all exchange executed across markets? In fact, this is a rather old question. It was raised most effectively by Coase in 1937, who put it this way:

> If a workman moves from department Y to department X, he does not go because of a change in relative prices, but because he is ordered to do so ... The example given above is typical of a large sphere in our modern economic system

... But in view of the fact that it is usually argued that co-ordination will be done by the price mechanism, why is such organization necessary?

Coase went on to provide an answer along the following lines. Contrary to the standard assumptions for ideal markets, Coase maintained that usually there is a *cost* associated with using the price system. First of all, there is usually a cost (if only time) involved in finding out what the relevant prices are. Next, when important, a *contract* is usually drawn up to provide the basis for a market transaction. For instance, in the labour market, employment contracts are necessary to specify the conditions under which most exchanges take place. It is costly to draw up those contracts. Finally, there may be conditions under which it is hardly possible (or extremely costly) to reach a contractual agreement that may serve as a basis for market exchange.[4] In those cases, too, *organization* may provide an alternative.

Therefore, Coase posited markets and organizations as alternatives for the execution of transactions. For markets, the price system is the coordinating device. Within organizations, the price system is replaced by authority as a coordinating mechanism.[5] The question remains as to the circumstances under which the market will be employed for exchange transactions and the conditions under which organizations will be preferred. Coase's answer was that it is determined by the relative cost of transacting under these two alternatives. Transactions will typically be executed at the lowest cost. As a consequence, transactions will shift between markets and organizations as a function of the *transaction costs* under those two alternatives.

This last answer was taken up much later by Williamson (1975) to establish 'transaction cost economics', as we shall see in Chapter 8. Here we conclude by noting that Coase's analysis (1937) allowed standard economic reasoning to be employed in analysing both the nature and the size of the firm:

> When we are considering how large a firm will be, the principle of marginalism works smoothly. The question always is, will it pay to bring an extra exchange transaction under the organizing authority? At the margin the cost of organizing within the firm will be equal either to the cost of organizing in another firm or to the costs involved in leaving the transaction to be 'organized' by the price mechanism.

We adopt Coase's original distinction between markets and organizations as two ideal types of coordination for exchange transactions. In the next section we argue that markets and organizations differ most essentially in the way that information is communicated between the transacting parties. The argument developed above entails that an **ideal market** is characterized by the fact that prices act as 'sufficient statistics' for individual decisionmaking. If we adopt this characterization, **ideal organizations** can be characterized as all those forms of coordination of transactions that do *not* use prices to communicate information between the transacting parties. In fact, we argue in Chapter 3 that most transactions in the real world are governed by hybrid forms of coordination. Most markets are to some extent 'organized'. Most organizations do use prices (such as transfer prices) to communicate information within the

Ideal market

Ideal organizations

organization. As a summary of the argument so far, we may present the conceptual framework in its present stage of development, in Figure 1.4.

Figure 1.4 There are two types of ideal coordination: market and organization

1.6 Information

We now arrive at a decisive step in the development of our conceptual framework. We have seen that the division of labour, leading to economies of specialization, necessitates the coordination of transactions. We have seen that there are two ideal types of coordination: market and organization. We shall now argue that the actual (mix of) coordination mechanism(s) that we will observe in any situation will depend mainly on the information requirements that are inherent in that situation. Thus we present *information* as the crucial concept in our framework, explaining how coordination will take place (Figure 1.5). We introduce this concept below and elaborate on its significance in Chapter 4.

Recall that ideal markets are characterized by the operation of prices as sufficient statistics – that is to say, the price contains all the information needed for the coordination of transactions. The price mechanism is therefore a perfect channel of information to all parties potentially interested in transacting. In situations where the price mechanism is applicable as a coordination

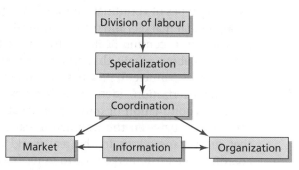

Figure 1.5 The market/organization mix depends on the particular information requirements of the situation

device, it is, therefore, hard to beat its efficiency properties. However, we have also argued that in many situations the price mechanism is complemented or substituted by organizational coordination mechanisms. There are many situations in which the price cannot absorb all the information necessary to enable the execution of transactions. When Volkswagen buys ignition systems for the Audi A6, it will probably use a long-term contract containing many details with respect to quality and quantities with one or a few suppliers. In such a situation – where Volkswagen buys ignition systems rather than making ignition systems itself – we still have market transactions, but we cannot say that price is a sufficient statistic. Rather, we have a situation in which the price mechanism (which is still important: Volkswagen will try to buy from the cheapest source) is supplemented by a form of planning not unlike the planning used within organizations.

There are also many situations in which the price mechanism is totally incapable of performing its coordination function. In Chapter 4, we delve into the reasons for this. We show there are fundamental information problems that cannot be resolved by the price system. A number of these problems can, however, be dealt with by means of organizational coordination. Thus, from the perspective developed in this book, *organizations arise as solutions to information problems*.[6] Organizations are more suited to dealing with certain information problems than are markets.

As Figure 1.5 indicates, the market/organization mix depends on the particular information requirements of the situation. Information and communication costs determine, to a large extent, the relative efficiency of the two broad coordination mechanisms (markets and organizations). This is also illustrated in Box 1.5

Box 1.5 Organizations and the Internet

We argue in this book that organizations arise as solutions to information problems. A similar line of reasoning was followed recently by *The Economist* when analysing the effects that the rise of the Internet and other new communication technologies may have on the shape of firms:

> A prime reason why economic activity is organized within firms rather than in open markets is the cost of communication. The costlier it is to process and transmit information, the more it makes sense to do things in firms; the cheaper communication becomes, the more efficient (relatively) markets will be. Because the Internet and other inventions have cut the cost of communication so much, firms ought to be able to do less in-house and to outsource more. In 1999, General Motors, a byword for vertical integration, spun off Delphi Automotive Systems, one of its supply divisions, for instance.

In Chapter 9 we shall discuss vertical integration and show that more factors are involved in General Motors' decision than just the cost of communication. However, the basic reasoning in *The Economist* is sound and well in line with the approach taken in this book:

- markets and organizations represent alternative ways to coordinate transactions;
- information will determine their relative efficiency.

Source: 'Electronic glue', *The Economist,* 2 June 2001

1.7 The environment and institutions

Finally, we want to add the *context* in which the trade-offs between market and organizational coordination are made. Broadly speaking, we will call this context the *environment*. The broad concept of the environment includes many dimensions. They are not only economic in nature, but may also be social, political, cultural or institutional. As we will show in this section, economists have particularly highlighted the importance of the institutional dimension (see Figure 1.6).

In Chapter 10 we will discuss evolutionary approaches to organizations. In those evolutionary approaches, attention is paid to the fact that organizations not only adapt to their environment, but are also shaped by pressures from the environment and may also be selected by their environment. We can best see such environmental pressures operating when we take a somewhat longer time horizon.

Consider, for instance, how environmental pressures have shaped organizations with respect to their labour practices (such as the abolition of child labour), waste management (such as reductions in carbon emissions) or internationalization (as a result of the international trade agreements negotiated by the World Trade Organization, for example).

Consider also how rapidly changing environmental conditions allowed first the creation of many new companies during the 'dot-com bubble' (see Box 1.6) of the late nineties and then the rapid selection of the few companies that survived and have become successful (such as Amazon and eBay), while others have perished. Who remembers today such companies as Boo.com, Kozmo.com or Webvan? These examples illustrate that organizations do not operate in a vacuum, but live in an *environment* that:

- provides the conditions for particular organizations to be created;
- shapes all organizations by exerting economic, social, political and other pressures;

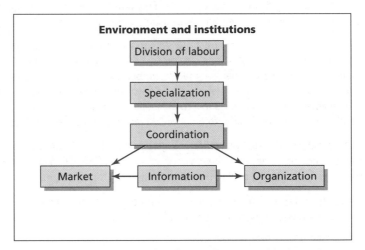

Figure 1.6 Environment as context for the market/organization mix

- is also the ultimate *selection mechanism* for determining which organizations can survive and be successful (while other organizations are 'selected out' and perish).

Box 1.6 The dot-com bubble

The 'dot-com bubble' was a speculative bubble covering roughly 1995–2001 during which stock markets in Western nations saw their value increase rapidly from growth in the new Internet sector and related fields. The period was marked by the founding (and in many cases, spectacular failure) of a group of new Internet-based companies commonly referred to as *dot-coms*. A combination of rapidly increasing stock prices, individual speculation in stocks, and widely available vernture capital created an exuberant environment in which many of these businesses dismissed standard business models, focusing on increasing market share at the expense of the bottom line. The bursting of the dot-com bubble marked the beginning of a relatively mild yet rather lengthy recession in Western nations.

Source: http://en.wikipedia.org/wiki/Dot-com_bubble, January 2007

Not only organizations but also markets are shaped and selected by environments. In 'centrally planned economies', such as the Soviet Union used to have, many markets were non-existent because the government attempted to coordinate economic activity by administrative rule. In 'market economies' too, governments have a fundamental influence on which markets are allowed to exist and how they function. Consider, for example, the government monopoly on military force, the prohibition of commercial markets for human organs for transplantation or the strict regulations on gambling. In all these cases, the government (as an important actor in the environment) determines which markets can come into being and shapes the rules by which such markets must function.

The functioning of markets will also be affected by other actors in the environment, such as trade unions, which have an impact on labour markets in many countries, or environmental pressure groups, which attempt to set standards of acceptable eco-behaviour in many markets. Moreover, markets are susceptible to more subtle environmental pressures, of social and cultural origin, for instance. In the United States of America, the market for chief executive officers of large corporations allows for them to receive much higher levels of compensation than in similar markets in Europe, where the American salary levels for CEOs are generally regarded as 'excessive'.[7]

Finally, new markets come into being as a result of environmental developments, such as advancing technology (the market for mobile phones) or ecological needs (the markets for renewable energy and resources). At the same time, 'old markets' shrink or disappear for such reasons – the market for fixed telephones or Freon (the traditional cooling agent for refrigerators, that was banned for ecological reasons). As such examples show, markets do not function in a vacuum either. Markets operate in an environment that:

- provides the conditions for particular markets to be created;
- shapes all markets by exerting economic, social, political and other pressures;

■ is also the ultimate *selection mechanism* for determining which markets can survive and be successful (while other markets are 'selected out' and perish).

Economists have paid particular attention to the environmental dimension that we call *institutional*. Institutions have been defined by Douglass North (1990), one of the most prominent 'institutional economists', as follows:

> Institutions are the rules of the game in a society, or more formally, are the humanly devised constraints that shape human interaction.

This definition includes both formal and informal rules of the game and the way those are enforced in a society. Formal rules are written laws, constitutions, regulations and the like. Informal rules are norms of behaviour, conventions and internally imposed rules of conduct – those in a company culture, for example. Enforcement of the rules can also be formal (such as through the legal courts) or informal (through peer pressure and social sanctions).

In most countries, the role of formal rules and enforcement has increased over time. As explained by Douglass North (2005b, p. 27) himself:

> Throughout most of history, exchange has been based on personal knowledge of the other party. Reputation and repeat dealings have been the basis for confidence that the exchange would be lived up to in terms of both the quantity and the quality of the good or service exchanged and that the agreement would be executed in accordance with the understanding of both parties. Transaction costs in such cases were small. But, also, markets were necessarily small.
>
> As long-distance trade expanded in the Middle Ages, the difficulties of exchange between parties that did not know each other posed fundamental transaction problems. At the champagne fairs in France in the twelfth century, one merchant was designated to collect information on the reliability of the merchants attending the fair; when contemplating an exchange that was not instantaneous, a merchant would seek advice from the designated merchant on the reliability of the other party. But extending personal knowledge by such devices has limits with respect to the size of markets. And Adam Smith, the patron saint of economists, was unequivocal in his assertion that specialization, division of labour, and the size of the markets are the source of the wealth of nations. Everything economists have learned since then reinforces this assertion.
>
> Impersonal exchange – exchange between parties with no knowledge of each other and occurring over time and space – not only runs counter to innate genetic features that evolved of the several million years that humans were hunters/gatherers; it is also simply an open invitation to fraud, cheating and corrupt practices. In fact, in the absence of the essential institutional safeguards, impersonal exchange does not exist, except in cases where strong ethnic or religious ties make reputation a viable underpinning.[8]
>
> What is required is a political institutional structure that will put in place the rule of law and the necessary enforcement structure. Such a framework must substitute effectively for the 'trust' that comes with personal exchange. The failure to create the essential institutional base is the central problem of economic development.

Indeed, the creation of appropriate institutions has not only been the central problem of economic development in historical times but also remains so today. Box 1.7 illustrates this for the recent development of Russia. In Chapter 14, Corporate Governance, we will provide modern-day examples of the importance of institutions.

Box 1.7 The importance of institutions

Consider the problems facing Russia (or the other countries) in 1989. There were institutions in Russia that had names similar to those in the West, but they did not perform the same functions. There were banks in Russia, and the banks did garner savings; but they did not make decisions about who got loans, nor did they have the responsibility for monitoring and making sure that the loans were repaid. Rather, they simply provided the 'funds,' as dictated by the government's central planning agency.

There were firms, enterprises producing goods in Russia, but the enterprises did not make decisions: they produced what they were told to produce, with inputs (raw material, labour, machines) that were allocated to them. The major scope for entrepreneurship lay in getting around problems posed by the government: the government would give enterprises quotas on output, without necessarily providing the inputs needed, but in some cases providing more than necessary. Entrepreneurial managers engaged in trades to enable themselves to fulfill their quotas, in the meanwhile getting a few more perks for themselves than they could have enjoyed on their official salaries. Those activities – which had always been necessary to make the Soviet system merely function – led to the corruption that would only increase as Russia moved to a market economy. Circumventing what laws were in force, if not breaking them outright, became part of the way of life, a precursor to the breakdown of the 'rule of law' which was to mark the transition.

As in a market economy, under the Soviet system there were prices, but the prices were set by government fiat, not by the market. Some prices, such as those for basic necessities, were kept artificially low – enabling even those at the bottom of the income distribution to avoid poverty. Prices for energy and natural resources also were kept artificially low – which Russia could only afford because of its huge reservoirs of these resources.

Old-fashioned economics textbooks often talk about market economics as if it had three essential ingredients: prices, private property, and profits. Together with competition, these provide incentives, coordinate economic decisionmaking, ensuring that firms produce what individuals want at the lowest possible cost. But there has also long been a recognition of the importance of institutions. Most important are legal and regulatory frameworks, to ensure that contracts are enforced, that there is an orderly way of resolving commercial disputes, that when borrowers cannot repay what is owed, there are orderly bankruptcy procedures, that competition is maintained, and that banks that take depositors are in a position to give the money back to depositors when they ask. That framework of laws and agencies helps ensure securities markets operate in a fair manner, managers do not take advantage of shareholders nor majority shareholders of minority shareholders. In the nations with mature market economies, the legal and regulatory frameworks had been built up over a century and a half, in response to problems encountered in unfettered market capitalism. Bank regulation came into place after massive bank failures; securities regulation after major episodes in which unwary shareholders were cheated. Countries seeking to create a market economy did not have to relive these disasters: they could learn from the experiences of others. While the market reformers may have mentioned this institutional infrastructure, they gave it short shrift. They tried to take a shortcut to capitalism, creating a market economy without the underlying institutions, and institutions without the underlying institutional infrastructure. Before you set up a stock market, you

▶

have to make sure there are real regulations in place. New firms need to be able to raise new capital, and this requires banks that are real banks, not the kinds of banks that characterized the old regime, or banks that simply lend money to government. A real and effective banking system requires strong banking regulations. New firms need to be able to acquire land and that requires a land market and land registration.

Source: Stiglitz (2002)

If we regard institutions as the rules of the game, imposed by the environment, then we can see how the economic 'game' played is fundamentally shaped by the institutional framework of a particular country. The government is, of course, a particularly important actor in the environment of markets and organizations. Market processes may, by themselves, leave many people with too few resources to survive. In countries that have been most successful, government has stepped in and compensated for such 'market failures', providing a safety net for the poor. Governments provided a high-quality education to all and furnished much of the institutional infrastructure, such as the legal system, which is required for markets to work effectively. They regulated the financial sector, ensuring that capital markets worked more in the way that they were supposed to. They fought against fraud and corruption. They promoted technology, for example, by setting up technological institutes and public research programmes. Sometimes they intervene directly in the operation of markets, as Box 1.8 illustrates for the market of mobile phone calls in Europe.

Box 1.8 Market intervention by the European Union

Europeans will save up to 70 per cent on the cost of using their mobile phones while abroad under a landmark deal agreed yesterday. The fees for making and receiving calls while in another European Union country will be slashed from mid-August following the vote by the European Parliament in Strasbourg. The decision to impose price caps on what the European Commission describes as 'exorbitant roaming charges' is a significant intervention by the EU in the market and comes despite fierce opposition from operators such as Vodafone.

Source: 'EU to cap price of mobile calls', *The Economist*, 24 May 2007

There is much debate about the appropriate roles of government and the desirable extent of a government's reach in the economy. Among economists, however, there is 'broad agreement that government has a role in making any society, any economy, function efficiently – and humanely' (Stiglitz, 2002, p. 218).

Next to the government, many other actors and factors play a role in shaping economic activities in markets and firms. Think of the legal system, trade unions, consumer groups, non-governmental organizations (NGOs), often acting as pressure groups for specific causes and so on. Add to this the many informal institutional rules that countries develop over time – traditions, norms of (non-)acceptable behaviour – and specific codes of conduct.

Together, all such actors and factors constitute the specific environmental context and institutional framework in which economic activity is carried out in organizations and markets. Given the many different choices that can be made in those dimensions in different countries, the context will also vary from country to country.[9] We will highlight some such differences in forthcoming chapters – for instance, in Section 13.4, Business groups, and Chapter 14, Corporate Governance.

All in all, it should be clear by now that we have to complete our basic conceptual framework by showing how markets and organizations are embedded in an environmental context and, particularly, an institutional framework. Environmental and institutional factors codetermine which markets and organizations are allowed to exist and also exert pressure on how they function. Those factors are not static, but evolve over time as governments change, laws are amended, social norms develop, and new issues and challenges have to be addressed by societies.

For the economic problems in society, markets and organizations are appropriate responses. The choices between these two coordination mechanisms will be driven primarily by the information requirements of the situation, but will also, to some extent, depend on the environmental and institutional context in which the choice is made.

That concludes the basic conceptual framework we use to explain the economic approaches to organizations. We take the division of labour in society as our starting point, leading to specialization, which allows efficiency gains. However, with increasing specialization, there is a corresponding need for coordination. Coordination can be achieved via markets or organizations. Information is a crucial element in the trade-off between market and organizational coordination. In this section, we have shown that the trade-offs between markets and organizations are not made in a vacuum, but are embedded in an environment that shapes and selects the market/organization mix in various ways, particularly through the institutional context (see Figure 1.7).

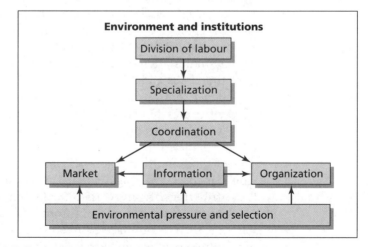

Figure 1.7 Environmental pressure and selection codetermines market/organization mix

1.8 Historical perspective

One may wonder why the economic approaches to organizations have been only fairly recently developed. Why did it take so long, for instance, to pick up on the fundamental question raised by Coase in 1937 – why do we observe so many organizations if markets are so efficient? The main reasons, as we see them, are summarized by the following two statements:

■ until recently, most (but not all) economists focused their attention on how the market achieves coordination *between* organizations (and individuals);
■ most (but not all) organization theorists studied coordination *within* organizations.

We shall briefly illustrate these statements below.

While the older economic writers, such as Adam Smith and Alfred Marshall, still had a lot to say about the functioning of organizations, over time, economists' fascination with the functioning of markets led them to study market coordination almost exclusively. The mainstream economists of the twentieth century elaborated a theory of markets. That theory is now highly developed. Meanwhile, however, there were some exceptional economists, such as Ronald Coase, who recognized that an important and growing share of the economic transactions within society were executed not across markets but within organizations. It was only fairly recently that more economists became interested in these economic processes and the resulting allocation within organizations, such as business firms. One of the reasons was that new theoretical approaches were developed that were more satisfactory than the older ones. It is the purpose of this book to introduce these approaches.

Organization theory, on the other hand, was interested primarily in what goes on within organizations. The first writers on organization focused on 'scientific management' – that is, discovering principles of work organization that would enhance productivity. Many of these early writers had a technical or engineering background and management experience to draw on. Later on, social and psychological considerations were introduced by writers in the 'human relations' school. Many of the early contributions to the field of organization studies attempted to formulate the 'one best way to organize'. Only since the 1950s and 1960s has it been recognized that the best way to organize is dependent on the particular situation the organization is in. The 'contingency theories' of organization were developed. These theories emphasized the technological and environmental factors that were important in shaping the organization. Still later, since the 1970s, organization studies have become even more multidisciplinary. Some would maintain that the subject has become increasingly fragmented. Diverse perspectives and approaches coexist. Contributions are made from the disciplines of sociology, psychology, political science, management, anthropology and so on. Perhaps it is inevitable that such a multifaceted phenomenon as organizations is studied from many different angles and backgrounds (see, for example, Morgan, 1997, or Clegg et al., 1996).

To these various contributions an economic perspective has been added since the 1970s. Initially, this occurred because economists became interested in organizations and exported their newly developed theories into the field of organization studies. As such, the economic perspective simply came to coexist alongside the other disciplinary perspectives on organizations. Organization theorists, however, became interested in those theories, too.

One reason for their interest was that some of the economic approaches incorporated concepts that had been borrowed by economists from earlier work within organization theory. Transaction cost economics, for example, makes extensive use of the concept of *bounded rationality*, developed in organization theory. Through such common use of concepts the integration of economic theories within organization studies is facilitated.[10] Another reason for the growing interest in economic perspectives on organizations is that they allow the analysis of organizational problems that are different from those studied in the other disciplines. As mentioned in Section 1.1, these problems always deal with the economic aspect of organizations – how to allocate the scarce organizational resources efficiently.

We conclude this section with a final introductory observation: there is currently a *family* of economic approaches to organizations. The family is bound together by their focus on the economic aspect of organizations. This identifies them as *economic* theories of organization. Within this common family resemblance, however, the various theories to be introduced differ in many respects. They differ, for instance, in the problems identified and in their basic modes of analysis, as will become clear when they are introduced. In the following chapters, therefore, the differences within the family may stand out more clearly than the similarities. In Chapter 11, we return to this observation and discuss the question of how tightly knit the family currently is and what the prospects are for its members' future development.

1.9 Summary: the conceptual framework of this book

This chapter has introduced the basic conceptual framework we use to explain the fundamental economic approach to organizations (Figure 1.1). The framework takes the division of labour in society as its starting point. The division of labour leads to specialization, which allows efficiency gains to be made. With increasing specialization, however, there is a corresponding need for coordination. Coordination is necessary in order to arrange the vast network of exchange between specialized economic actors. This is illustrated in a modern, international context in Box 1.9.

Box 1.9 Globalization, specialization and coordination: the case of Li & Fung

In this chapter we have used Adam Smith's original example of a pin factory as an illustration of the concepts of division of labour, specialization and coordination. These forces play not only at the local level of a factory, however, but also at the global level. This is shown by the case of Li & Fung, a Chinese firm that was called 'a surprising world leader in supply-chain management' by *The Economist:*

> Li & Fung used to introduce Western retailers of clothes, toys and the like to the sweatshops of China. As such, it was no different from countless Chinese firms . . . But when Victor and William Fung, the brothers who today run the family business, sat down to think about globalization and what it means for Asia, they came up with a winning new strategy for their company.
>
> To them, globalization meant above all *specialization,* and specialization brings complexity. If supply chains of companies once consisted of five links, they might soon have dozens, or even hundreds, they surmised. 'Somebody's got to pick up the pieces and bring them back together' says William Fung, the younger brother – which is what Li & Fung is now doing, to all appearances better than its rivals in the West.
>
> It works like this. Say, a European clothes retailer wants to order a few thousand garments. The optimal *division of labour* might be for South Korea to make the yarn, Taiwan to weave and dye it, and a Japanese-owned factory in Guangdong Province to make the zippers. Since China's textiles quota has already been used up under some country's import rules, Thailand may be the best place to do the sewing. However, no single factory can handle such bulk, so five different suppliers must share the order. The shipping and letters of credit must be seamless, and the quality assured. *Coordinating* all this is the challenge of globalization . . . And this requires knowledge. Village women with sewing machines in Bangladesh are not on the Internet. Finding the best suppliers at any given time, therefore, takes enormous research – so much, indeed, that companies are increasingly deciding that it no longer pays to do it in-house. Instead, they outsource the knowledge gathering to Li & Fung, which has an army of 3600 staff roaming 37 countries ('a machete in one hand, a laptop in the other', as Victor Fung likes to caricature them) for the purpose. In this sense, Li & Fung is itself a product of *specialization*. A company that focuses entirely on optimizing supply chains for other companies is a recent phenomenon.

Source: The Economist, 2 June 2001

We have argued that there are two ideal types of coordination of exchange transactions: markets and organizations. Markets use the price system as the coordinating device, while organizations use non-price systems, such as authority. In practice, both ideal types of coordination are usually mixed. We have argued that the actual mix found in any situation will depend mainly on the information requirements of that situation. Markets and organizations are different solutions to information problems that are inherent in (economic) transactions. From an economic perspective, they have different efficiency properties. They are efficient coordination mechanisms for different sets of transactions, depending on the information requirements involved.

Finally, we have argued that markets and organizations are embedded in an environmental context and an institutional framework. Therefore, environmental and institutional factors will codetermine the trade-off between market and organizational coordination. This basic perspective is further elaborated and illustrated in this book.

1.10 Outline of the book

This first chapter has introduced some basic concepts in a preliminary way. They will be elaborated in Chapters 2 to 10. Equipped with this further knowledge, we return to the common perspective in Chapter 11. There we discuss it more thoroughly and contrast various ways of highlighting the similarities and the differences in the economic approaches to organizations. Finally, we apply the economic concepts to the topics of mergers and acquisitions, hybrid forms and corporate governance in Chapters 12 to 14. These chapters illustrate the broad range of the applicability of the approaches introduced in this book.

In Chapters 2 to 4, the general ideas introduced so far are explored in more depth. Chapter 2 focuses on markets. Standard microeconomic theory is used to explain how coordination is achieved in an (ideal) market. This theory illustrates the role of the price mechanism in equating demand and supply for goods and services. The chapter serves two purposes: first, to introduce some basic economic concepts and modes of analysis and, second, to serve as a benchmark against which other economic approaches can be measured. If you are already familiar with standard microeconomics, you can either glance quickly through Chapter 2 or skip it entirely.

To conclude this introductory chapter, we borrow from the economist A. C. Pigou (1920, p. 3) the following quotation: 'When a man sets out upon any course of inquiry, the object of his search may be either light or fruit – either knowledge for its own sake or knowledge for the sake of good things to which it leads.' On your 'course of inquiry' through this book, we wish you occasional light and fruit, as well as some fun along the way. To this end, Box 1.10 introduces you to some typical fun that economists enjoy – lightbulb jokes.

Box 1.10 A Russian lightbulb

There are many lightbulb jokes in economics, including these.

Q: How many economists does it take to change a lightbulb?
A: Two: one to assume the existence of a ladder and one to change the bulb!

An alternative answer to this question is:

A: Eight: one to change the bulb and seven to hold everything else constant!

John McMillan tells the following version from Russia.

In Russia in 1992, amid the ruins of communism, the State abruptly ceased controlling the economy. A few years later, when the country's progress toward a market economy had bogged down and the country was in a sorry state, a joke circulated on the streets of Moscow:

Q: 'How many people does it take to change a lightbulb under communism?'
A: 'Five: one to hold the lightbulb, four to rotate the table he is standing on.'
Q: 'Under capitalism, how many does it take?'
A: 'None, the market will take care of it.'

> The Russian sarcasm underlines a key point. While markets can do a lot, they do not work automatically. Unaided, the market will not take care of things.
>
> *Source:* McMillan (2002, p. 14) (For more jokes on economics and economists see: http://netec.mcc.ac.uk/JokEc.html)

Questions

1 Suppose you are a Saudi prince and studying economics at Oxford University in the UK. Your family sends you a very large monthly allowance to cover tuition and other expenses. In fact, this allowance is more than ten times the average allowance of the other students. Do you think that you would still have an economic problem? Why?

2 Suppose you are an American student and you are about to obtain your MBA and start looking for a job. An economist would say that you are about to enter the job market. Compare this market with the tin market that is described in the text. Is the job market for MBAs also an example of an ideal market? Is price a sufficient statistic for this market? Discuss the latter question from the point of view of both employers and those seeking employment.

3 What might be the economic aspect of (partner matching in) the 'marriage market'?

4 Box 1.9 describes the success of a company named Li & Fung. What exactly is Li & Fung's business? Who are Li & Fung's customers? After having read Chapter 1, including Box 1.9, what do you think is the main point that the case brings forward?

5 In Box 1.5, it is argued that the rise of the Internet has cut the cost of communication so much that firms will be inclined to outsource more than before. Do you think this is true? Do you see an implicit assumption, made by the journalists of *The Economist*, that is highly relevant but which is not mentioned in Box 1.5? Discuss.

Suggested further reading

Barney, J. B. and Ouchi, W. G. (eds) (1986), *Organizational Economics*, San Francisco, CA: Jossey-Bass.

FitzRoy, F. R., Acs, Z. J. and Gerlowski, D. A. (1998), *Management and Economics of Organization*, Harlow: Prentice Hall.

Kay, J. (2003), *The Truth about Markets: Their genius, their limits, their follies*, London: Penguin.

McMillan, J. (2002), *Reinventing the Bazaar: A natural history of markets*, New York: W. W. Norton.

Milgrom, P. and Roberts, J. (1992), *Economics, Organization and Management*, Englewood Cliffs, NJ: Prentice Hall.

Putterman, L. (ed.) (1986), *The Economic Nature of the Firm: A reader*, Cambridge: Cambridge University Press.

Roberts, D. J. (2004), *The Modern Firm*, Oxford: Oxford University Press.

Seabright, P. (2004), *The Company of Strangers: A natural history of economic life*, Princeton, NJ: Princeton University Press.

Notes

1   We use he and she interchangeably in this book.
2   Strictly speaking, we introduce here the concept of *static efficiency* or *allocative efficiency*. Another question is how resources should be (re)distributed over time to adapt an economy or an organization to changing circumstances and keep it efficient. This is a question of *dynamic efficiency*. See further Section 11.3.2.
3   These two types of coordination should be regarded as ideal types in the Weberian sense. That is to say, they are theoretical notions that are hardly observable in the real world in any 'pure' form. This is discussed further in Section 1.5.
4   This is further elaborated in Chapter 8.
5   As we argue in Chapter 3, authority (or direct supervision) is only one of several coordinating mechanisms employed within organizations.
6   We consider it fruitless to discuss the question whether 'in the beginning there were markets' (as Williamson has posited as an analytical device) or organizations 'came first' (as an historical analysis would probably reveal). We are concerned here with the explanation of present-day phenomena.
7   See, for instance, John Kay, 'A Star Executive does not make a Company', *The Financial Times*, 15 February 2005, or John Plender, 'It pays to simplify boardroom compensation', *The Financial Times*, 5 January 2007. We return to the topic of executive compensation in Chapter 7.
8   One modern institutional arrangement to foster impersonal exchange between strangers can be observed on the Internet: the concept of 'feedback', as used by eBay. After each transaction, buyers and sellers get to rate each other – positive, negative or neutral. In that way, every eBay member builds a reputation. We return to this topic in Chapter 8.
9   On the other hand, such differences have likely become smaller in recent decades as globalization and economic integration of the world has progressed (see Stiglitz, 2002).
10 In this book we use the terms 'economic theories of organization' and 'economic approaches to organizations'. Examples of economic theories of organization are the behavioural theory of the firm, agency theory and transaction cost economics (Chapters 6, 7 and 8 respectively). 'Economic approaches to organizations' is a broader term, encompassing also the economic contributions to strategic management that are described in Chapter 9.

2.1 Introduction

When the weather is bad in the summer, the price for foreign holiday breaks goes up, but domestic hotels start cutting their prices. When political tensions rise in the Middle East, the price of oil increases, but the cost of purchasing a used car that consumes a lot of petrol decreases. If a luxury good, like a Rolex watch or a Gucci bag, fetches a high price, counterfeited articles (copies) usually start entering street markets at a lower price. Governments in many countries try to discourage drinking and smoking by slapping hefty taxes on alcohol and cigarettes. At the same time, many governments would like to create a market for 'emission trading rights' to combat climate change.

What do these examples have in common? They all refer to situations where:

1 there is demand and supply for certain goods or services
2 a market can match demand and supply at a certain price.

In this chapter we examine how standard microeconomic theory explains the functioning of such markets.

Standard microeconomic theory focuses on how economic decisions are coordinated by the market mechanism. Economic decisions have to be made by both consumers and producers. Consumers can choose from a large number of goods. For each good, they must decide how much they are going to consume. Producers must decide how much they are going to produce and how they are going to produce. Consumers and producers meet each other in the market. Coordination between the total quantity demanded by consumers and the total quantity supplied by producers is achieved through interaction in the market. Thus, the quantity of tomatoes shipped to London on a certain day is determined not by a planning authority but by **the process of market interaction** (see Box 2.1). This process of market interaction is explained in Section 2.2. In competitive markets, prices are determined by the process of market interaction, not by individual buyers or sellers.

The process of market interaction

Box 2.1 The London vegetable market

In rich countries, markets are too familiar to attract attention. Yet a certain awe is appropriate. When Soviet planners visited a vegetable market in London during the early days of *perestroika*, they were impressed to find no queues, shortages, or mountains of spoiled and unwanted vegetables. They took their hosts aside and said: 'We understand, you have to say it's all done by supply and demand. But can't you tell us what's really going on? Where are your planners, and what are their methods?'

Source: The Economist, 17 February 1996

How does an individual consumer choose between different goods when the prices of those goods are given? That is the central question of the theory of demand that we discuss in Section 2.3.

How does an individual producer decide how much to produce? How does the producer decide how to produce that quantity? Those are the central questions of the theory of production that we discuss in Section 2.4.

Having thus outlined the main characteristics of standard microeconomic theory, Section 2.5 concludes this chapter with a number of comments on the theory. Here we highlight important assumptions underlying the models of standard microeconomics and give a preview as to which of these assumptions will be relaxed in subsequent chapters.

2.2 Market interaction: analysis of demand and supply

The total demand for a certain good depends on the price for that good. Take, for example, TV sets. When the price of a TV set is €500, total demand in the European Union (EU) market may be 10 million sets annually. If the price of TV sets goes down (and nothing else changes), some families that now have only one set may decide to buy a second one. Other families may decide to replace their existing set with a new one. Hence, we would expect total demand to go up if the price goes down. This is the **law of demand**. The relation between price and quantity demanded is shown in Figure 2.1. The **demand curve** D in Figure 2.1 is presented as a straight line only for the purposes of simplicity – there is no reason to expect a linear relationship between price and quantity demanded. From the demand curve we can read, for every price, the quantity demanded. For a price of €500, the quantity demanded is 10 million sets.

Television sets are supplied to the market by TV manufacturers. The total quantity supplied also depends on the price. If prices go up (and everything else remains the same), then TV manufacturers will find it more profitable to make TV sets and they will supply more sets in order to take advantage of increased profit opportunities. Therefore we expect supply to go up as the price goes up. This is the **law of supply**. The **supply curve** S in Figure 2.2 depicts the relationship between price and quantity supplied. For example, if the price is €500, all manufacturers will together produce 24 million sets. The supply curve need not be a straight line, as it is shown in the figure.

Law of demand

Demand curve

Law of supply

Supply curve

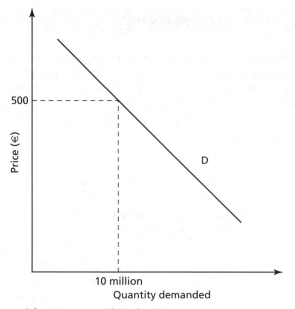

Figure 2.1 Demand for TV sets within the EU

Market equilibrium

Market equilibrium occurs where the demand curve D and the supply curve S intersect. The equilibrium price is €400 per set (see Figure 2.3). At that price, total supply is 14 million sets, while total demand is also 14 million sets. At the equilibrium price of €400 per set, all sets manufactured by producers are sold to consumers. Moreover, all consumers who want to buy at €400 per set actually buy a set.

Figure 2.2 Supply of TV sets to the EU market

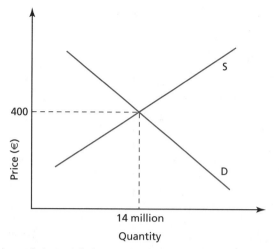

Figure 2.3 Supply and demand

Suppose there is an increase in the demand for TV sets in the EU. This may occur as a result of population growth or because of an increase in per capita income. It will result in a new market equilibrium. Box 2.2 illustrates how an increase in the demand for tin leads to an increase in price and an increase in the quantity supplied.

Box 2.2 An increase in the demand for tin

In Chapter 1, we quoted Hayek (1945): 'Assume that somewhere in the world a new opportunity for the use of some raw material, say tin, has arisen . . .'. A new opportunity for the use of tin means an increase in the demand for tin, which will lead to higher prices. This in turn will encourage users of tin to economize on the use of tin. In terms of the analysis presented in Section 2.2 an increase in the demand for tin is simply a shift in the demand curve, as is illustrated in Figure 2.4. The fact that a new opportunity for the use of tin is discovered means that the demand curve shifts from D_1 to D_2. As a result, the price of an ounce of tin increases from p_1 to p_2 and quantity supplied (and used) increases from q_1 to q_2.

2.3 The theory of demand

How does an individual consumer choose between the goods he or she can buy? Suppose a consumer is confronted with several different baskets of goods. Standard microeconomic theory assumes that each person can rank these baskets in the order that reflects his or her preferences. These preference rank-

Transitive

ings are assumed to be **transitive**. This means that if a person prefers basket A to basket B and prefers basket B to basket C, then he also prefers basket A to basket C. Finally, it is assumed that each person prefers more of a certain good to less of it.

Indifference curves

With these assumptions about consumers' preferences it is possible to represent the preferences of a certain consumer by a set of **indifference curves**.

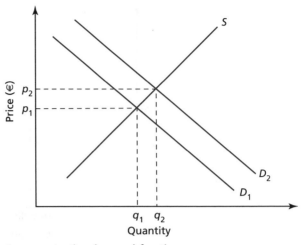

Figure 2.4 An increase in the demand for tin

Figure 2.5 shows the indifference curves for a consumer who can choose between baskets containing different quantities of apples and pears.

The consumer whose preferences are depicted in Figure 2.5 is indifferent about baskets B_1 and B_2. Basket B_1 means having X_1 kilograms of apples per week and Y_1 kilograms of pears per week; basket B_2 means having X_2 kilograms of apples and Y_2 kilograms of pears per week. Points B_1 and B_2 lie on curve U_1. A curve like U_1 is called an indifference curve: this consumer is indifferent about the baskets represented by points on U_1. He is not indifferent about baskets B_1 and B_3: on the contrary, he prefers B_3 over B_1. This is represented in Figure 2.5 by the fact that B_3 lies on an indifference curve that is further from the origin. This consumer prefers all baskets represented by points on indifference curve U_2 to all points on indifference curve U_1.

 Utility

The satisfaction that consumers derive from having goods is usually called **utility** by economists. Instead of saying that a consumer is indifferent about

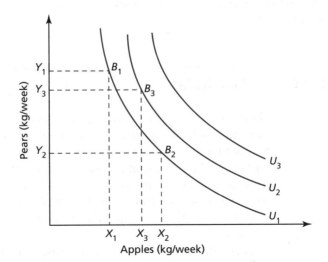

Figure 2.5 Indifference curves

baskets B_1 and B_2, we can say that this consumer derives the same utility from both basket B_1 and basket B_2. Thus, an indifference curve is a curve that represents points with the same level of utility. Curve U_2 represents all points that give our consumer a level of utility equal to U_2, whereas curve U_1 indicates all points that give him a level of utility U_1.

It is not possible to measure utility. Standard microeconomic theory assumes only that consumers can rank different baskets of goods. Therefore the assumption is that our consumer can indicate that he prefers basket B_3 to basket B_1, but not that he can indicate how great the difference in utility is between these two baskets.

The amounts of apples and pears that our consumer will buy depend not only on his preferences as given by his set of indifference curves, but also on his budget. Suppose that this consumer has €3.00 per week available for buying fresh fruit and that apples are €1.00 per kg and pears €1.50 per kg (for simplicity, assume that it is possible to buy every quantity you want, such as 0.683 kg).

Budget line

The quantities of apples and pears that our consumer can buy with this budget are given by line l in Figure 2.6. Line l is called the **budget line**.

We assume that every consumer wants to maximize his level of utility, so our consumer will choose the point on line l that gives him the highest possible level of utility. This is point P on line l, where line l is tangential to indifference curve U_2. Point P represents a basket of 1.68 kg of apples and 0.88 kg of pears.

Looking at the set of indifference curves, we see that some indifference curves (such as U_1) intersect with line l, while other indifference curves (such as U_3) do not. There is one, and only one, indifference curve that is tangential to the budget line: it is U_2. The point of tangency indicates the basket that the consumer will actually buy, given the budget constraint set out above. This basket provides him with the highest attainable utility.

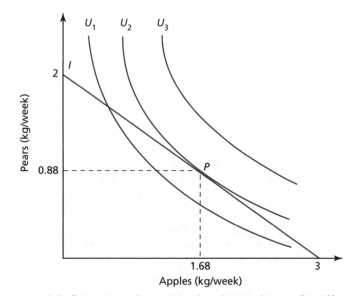

Figure 2.6 A model of consumer choice: a budget line and a set of indifference curves

2.4 The theory of production

How does a producer of a certain good decide *how much* she is going to produce? How does she decide *how* she is going to produce that quantity? These are the two main questions of the theory of production in standard microeconomic theory. In order to answer them we need a description of the firm.

In standard microeconomics the firm is described as an entity that maximizes an **objective function**. The objective function of a firm describes the goal(s) that the firm pursues (usually profit or the value of the firm on the stock market). The objective function can be maximized only within the constraints given to the firm by its production function.

Objective function

Here, we shall first describe the concept of a production function, then discuss how the firm, in trying to maximize profits, decides how much and how to produce.

2.4.1 The production function

Production function

A **production function** describes the relationship between any combination of inputs and the maximum output that a firm can produce with those inputs. As an example, consider a firm producing pencils. In order to make pencils, the firm needs machines, labour and raw materials. Assume, for the sake of simplicity, that the firm needs only one kind of machine, only one kind of labour and only one kind of raw material. This assumption is not very realistic, but it has no influence at all on what follows. Standard microeconomic theory can easily handle several kinds of machine, several kinds of labour and several kinds of raw materials – it just makes the mathematics a little bit more complicated.

Let K be the amount of capital, L the amount of labour and M the amount of raw material the firm has at its disposal. K may be measured as the number of machines, L as the number of labour hours per period (number of employees times the number of hours worked per period) and M as the volume or weight of raw material. Let Q be the maximum quantity of pencils that the firm can produce for a given combination of K, L and M. The production function is the relationship between Q and K, L, M and is expressed as:

$$Q = Q(K,L,M)$$

The production function describes how much output can be achieved with any combination of inputs. For given values of K and M, Q generally increases when L is increased. This implies that, for a factory with a given number of machines and a given amount of raw materials, output can be increased by hiring more employees or working overtime. However, output cannot be increased indefinitely in this way: either the amount of raw materials available per period or the amount of capital goods will prevent a further increase in production by adding more and more labour.

To increase or decrease the inputs that are available for production takes time. It is useful to make a distinction between the *short run* and the *long run*.

In the short run, only some inputs can be varied. In the long run, all inputs can be varied. In most cases it is fairly easy to vary the amounts of raw materials that the firm buys per period. This means that M can be varied in the short run. To build a new factory usually takes more time, so it seems reasonable to assume that K can vary only in the long run. Labour may fall somewhere between, depending on how easily employees can be hired and fired or induced to work overtime. Whether or not it is possible to vary the amount of labour may also depend on the type of labour: perhaps it is easier to hire and fire unskilled workers at short notice than highly skilled workers.

The distinction between input factors that can be varied in both the short run and the long run and input factors that can be varied only in the long run is an important one. In fact, we need only two kinds of input to develop the theory further:

- those inputs that can be varied in the short run as well as in the long run
- those inputs that can vary only in the long run.

It is customary to denote input factors that can be varied in the short run by L and input factors that can be varied only in the long run by K, so, from now on, L stands for all input factors that can vary both in the short run and in the long run, such as raw materials and perhaps certain kinds of labour, while K stands for all inputs that can vary only in the long run, such as capital goods and other kinds of labour. Despite this new interpretation of L and K we shall still refer to L as labour and to K as capital, so labour now means those inputs that can be varied in the short run as well as in the long run, while capital means those inputs that can be varied only in the long run.

The production function with two inputs is:

$$Q = Q(K,L)$$

This production function is depicted in Figure 2.7.

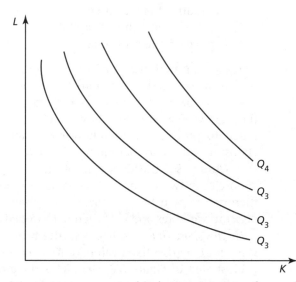

Figure 2.7 An isoquant map as a graphical representation of a production function

The curve Q_1 in Figure 2.7 represents all possible combinations of K and L that the firm can choose from if it wants to produce quantity Q_1. The points on Q_1 thus represent combinations of K and L leading to the same volume of output. The curves Q_1, Q_2, Q_3 and Q_4 are called **isoquants**. In Figure 2.7 the four iso-quants are such that $Q_4 > Q_3 > Q_2 > Q_1$.

Isoquants

2.4.2 Profit maximization in competitive markets

Suppose we have a firm with a given production function. How does this firm decide how and how much to produce? In order to answer these questions we need to make an assumption about the firm's objective function. In standard microeconomics it is usually assumed that the firm wants to maximize profits.

How can a firm with a given production function maximize profits? It depends on whether or not the firm has some freedom to determine the price of its products. In a competitive market – that is, a market with many sellers and buyers and with free entry and exit of firms – the firm cannot set its own prices. In competitive markets, prices are determined by the process of market interaction. The price resulting from this process is then given for each individual firm. In what follows, we discuss only profit maximization in competitive markets.

We first need a definition of profit. *Profit* is defined as revenue minus total cost, or:

$$\pi = pQ - KP_K - LP_1$$

where:

π = profit
p = market price of the firm's product pQ = total revenue
Q = quantity produced (and sold)
K = amount of capital used
L = amount of labour used $KP_K + LP1$ = total cost
P_K = price of one unit of capital
P_1 = price of one unit of labour

Here, Q is a function of K and L (remember that profit can be maximized only within the constraint of the firm's production function), $Q = Q(K,L)$.

We now have all that we need in order to discuss the two main questions of the theory of production: how much to produce and how to produce. How much to produce means choosing a value for Q. How to produce means choosing values for K and L. The two questions are not independent as $Q = Q(K,L)$. So, the firm cannot choose Q, K and L independently: it can choose only two of those three variables independently. The third variable is then determined by $Q = Q(K,L)$. We shall assume that K and L are the two decision variables and Q is then determined by $Q = Q(K,L)$.

In the *short run*, K is fixed, so the firm can choose only L. By choosing a value for L (with a fixed value for K), Q is also determined by $Q = Q(K, L)$. This is illustrated in Figure 2.8. Here K^* is the amount of capital that the firm has installed. In the short run it cannot add or scrap capital goods, so it can choose only values for K and L that lie on the vertical line l. If the firm chooses a value for L, say L_1, then it has also decided to produce quantity Q_1 (Q_1 is the isoquant through point (K^*,L_1)).

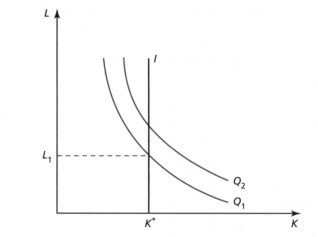

Figure 2.8 In the short run, K is fixed. By choosing a level of L, the firm also
chooses a level Q

We can now formulate the problem of short-run profit maximization in mathematical terms. Total profit as a function of L is:

$$\pi = pQ(K,L) - KP_K - LP_1$$

For a maximum, the first-order derivative with respect to L must equal zero, so we have:

$$p\frac{dQ}{dL} - P_1 = 0$$

or, alternatively:

$$\frac{dQ}{dL} = \frac{P_1}{p}$$

Solving this equation gives a value for L. Quantity Q is then determined by $Q = Q(K,L)$. This procedure can be illustrated by an example.

Suppose, again, that the firm is producing pencils. The market price of pencils is 25 cents per item and the rate of pay is $20.00 per hour. So, we have $p = 0.25$ and $P_1 = 20$.

Suppose, further, that the production function is such that its first-order derivative with respect to L is a decreasing function of L. In Figure 2.9 we have sketched dQ/dL, which is called the **marginal productivity of labour**, as a function of L. The economic interpretation of dQ/dL is the additional quantity of pencils that the firm can produce if it adds one hour of labour.

Marginal productivity of labour

Given this interpretation, it is quite reasonable to assume that dQ/dL is a decreasing function of L. In our example, the firm will choose that value of L for which:

$$\frac{dQ}{dL} = \frac{P_1}{p} = \frac{20}{0.25} = 80$$

This is L_{opt} in Figure 2.9.

We can summarize this discussion on profit maximization in the short run as follows. In the short run, the firm can choose only L. By choosing a value for L, Q is also determined. The firm will choose L such that the marginal productivity of labour (dQ/dL) is equal to P_1/p.

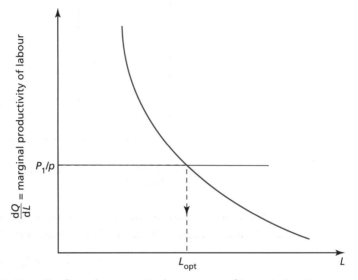

Figure 2.9 How the firm chooses L in short-run profit maximization

In the *long run*, however, both K and L can be varied. The problem of profit maximization now is one of working out how to maximize the expression

$$\pi = pQ(K,L) - KP_K - LP_1$$

with respect to both the decision variables K and L.

For a maximum, both partial derivatives $\partial\pi/\partial K$ and $\partial\pi/\partial L$ must equal zero. This gives:

$$p\partial Q/\partial K - P_K = 0$$

or, alternatively:

$$\frac{\partial Q}{\partial K} = \frac{P_K}{p}$$

and:

$$p\partial Q/\partial L - P_1 = 0$$

or, alternatively:

$$\frac{\partial Q}{\partial L} = \frac{P_1}{p}$$

Solving these two equations gives the optimal values for K and L. With $Q = Q(K,L)$, Q is also determined. The firm will choose K and L such that the marginal productivity of capital, $\partial Q/\partial K$, is equal to the ratio P_K/p, and the marginal productivity of labour, $\partial Q/\partial L$, is equal to the ratio P_1/p. The interpretation of this result is analogous to the interpretation given above for the short-run case.

We can summarize these results as follows.

■ In the short run, the firm can only decide how much labour to use. This is equivalent to deciding how much to produce. Once L and, thus, Q have been determined, the firm has no freedom left. So, the firm can, in the short run, decide only how much to produce, not how to produce. It decides how much to produce by choosing L, such that the marginal productivity of labour equals P_1/p.

■ In the long run, the firm can decide how much to produce *and* how to produce. This is equivalent to choosing both K and L independently. It will choose K and L such that the marginal productivity of capital equals P_K/p and the marginal productivity of labour equals P_1/p.

2.4.3 The paradox of profits

In a competitive market (that is, a market with large numbers of sellers and buyers and with free entry and exit of firms) the firm can earn no economic profit in the long run. Here, economic profit means profit in excess of normal profit, where normal profit is defined as the profit that a firm needs to make in order to stay in business. Normal profit is equal to the opportunity cost[1] of the equity capital provided by the owner(s) of the firm. If profit is lower than the opportunity cost of equity capital, the owners will decide to take their capital out of this firm and employ it elsewhere (in a competitive market there is free – that is, costless – exit). In the long run, no firm can earn an economic profit in a competitive market. It is easy to see why this is true: if there were economic profits, entry would occur, supply would increase, price would go down and economic profits would vanish. Hence, while each firm tries to maximize profits, no firm can make any economic profit in the long run.

2.5 Comments on standard microeconomic theory

The model of a competitive market is an important benchmark for understanding how markets operate. It shows how coordination between quantities demanded by buyers and quantities supplied by sellers is achieved by the price mechanism. It introduces some basic concepts and techniques of economic analysis. It also shows that, although every firm has maximization of profits as its objective, no firm can earn an economic profit in the long run.

If all industries were adequately described by the model of perfect competition, we should live in a maximally efficient world. The result of free

Pareto-optimal
allocation of resources

competition would then be an allocation of resources in the economy that is called Pareto-optimal. A **Pareto-optimal allocation of resources** is such that no one can be made better off by changing the allocation of resources without anyone becoming worse off. It does not mean that everyone's wants are satisfied to the same extent. Some people may be able to buy many more goods than others, depending on the initial distribution of wealth and talents. A Pareto-optimal allocation of resources means only that there is no other allocation of resources that can make someone better off while making no one worse off.

This result of the model of competitive markets has led economists and policymakers alike to the conclusion that competition between firms should be encouraged. This is the general idea behind antitrust policy.

Perfect competition

While recognizing the importance of the model of **perfect competition**, we should also point out some of its limitations. We should start by summarizing the basic assumptions on which the model of perfect competition is based. There are three assumptions that, when relaxed, lead to other models within the context of standard microeconomics:

- There is a *large number of small buyers and sellers*. That is, each seller and each buyer is so small that their decisions do not affect the market price. This assumption is relaxed in other models of standard microeconomics, such as models of monopoly and oligopoly.
- There is *free entry and exit of firms*. That is, there are no barriers to entry and no barriers to exit. This assumption is also relaxed in other models of standard microeconomics, such as models of monopoly and oligopoly.
- Each industry is characterized by *standardized products*. That is, consumers do not care whether they buy from firm A or firm B. The products of firms A and B are perfect substitutes in the eyes of the consumer. This assumption is relaxed in the model of monopolistic competition. This is another extension of standard microeconomics.

We shall not discuss these other models of standard microeconomics here. If you would like to know more about them, you should consult a textbook on microeconomics (see the suggested further reading list at the end of this chapter). Instead, we want to point out five other assumptions underlying all models of standard microeconomics:

Holistic entities

- Firms are viewed as **holistic entities**. This means that a firm is considered to be a single unified entity. There is, in fact, no difference in standard microeconomics between the concept of a producer (one person working alone) and a firm (several people cooperating to produce outputs). When, for example, profit maximization is the firm's objective, then it is assumed that everyone inside the firm makes all decisions solely with that objective in mind. In standard microeconomics, the firm is really no more than a production function with an objective function (profit maximization). When the purpose of the analysis is to explain how competitive markets work, this may be an adequate description of a firm. When, however, the purpose of the analysis is to explain how a firm makes decisions to coordinate the work of its employees, we need another description of the firm.

Single objective

■ Firms are supposed to have a **single objective**. Standard microeconomics assumes that this is so. Usually it is assumed that the objective is to maximize either profits or the value of the firm on the stock market. Now, imagine a firm having two objectives: to maximize profits *and* maximize employee satisfaction. Suppose it is impossible to measure profits and employee satisfaction with the same yardstick: there is no common *numéraire*, no unit for expressing both objectives. In standard microeconomics this situation can be handled in one of two ways: one can assume that the firm's objective is to maximize profits and introduce a minimum level of employee satisfaction as an additional constraint *or* one can assume that the firm's objective is to maximize employee satisfaction and introduce a minimum profit level as an additional constraint. Suppose now, for the sake of argument, that all producers are able to say, 'for me, every unit of employee satisfaction is worth €3.00 of profits'. It would then be possible to combine both objectives into one single objective: profits in € + units of employee satisfaction × €3.00. Standard microeconomics can handle firms with two objectives only when these two objectives can be combined into a single one. With objectives such as maximization of profits and maximization of employee satisfaction, this seems unlikely.

Perfect information

■ There is **perfect information**. Another important assumption of standard microeconomics is that everyone has perfect information: everyone knows everything. Here, 'everything' means everything that is relevant to making decisions about how much and how to produce (producers) and how much to buy of each finished consumer good (consumers). Hence, each producer is assumed to know the production functions of all goods and prices of all finished consumer goods, component parts, raw materials, wages and capital goods, while all consumers are supposed to know all the prices of all consumer goods. In modern microeconomics, that assumption of perfect information is relaxed. In Section 4.2 we illustrate this by discussing the market for health insurance. Here, an individual considering whether or not to take out a policy has more information about his risk profile than the insurance company does. We show that such a market cannot exist (that is, no transactions in health insurance policies can take place) unless there is a solution to this information problem. Another example is the market for the services of a travelling salesperson. Here, the salesperson has more information about the level of effort exerted than does the boss back in the office. As we explain in Section 4.3, the problem now is how to write a contract that gives the travelling salesperson a strong incentive to put in a real effort without allocating all the risk to him. This is an example of an agency relation. Agency theory is discussed in Chapter 7.

Maximizing behaviour

■ Behaviour of producers and consumers is described as **maximizing behaviour**. Producers are assumed to maximize a given objective function, usually profit. The essential assumption is that producers know all the alternatives (for example, they know the complete isoquant map we saw in Figure 2.7), such that they are able to compare all the alternative decisions and choose the one that maximizes the objective function. For some types of decision, such as how much to produce in the short run, that assumption may not be very unrealistic. For other types of decision, for example decisions concerning which new products to develop, it does seem unrealistic. Such decisions can be so complex that it is difficult or costly to evaluate fully even one alternative. Moreover, ideas for new products do not all come along at the same time. Firms have to decide on one idea without knowing what other ones may come up the next day. Therefore, not all the alternative decisions may be known at the time a decision must be made.

Markets function in isolation

- Finally, standard microeconomics examines markets as if they **function in isolation** – 'on their own' – disregarding the environmental context. However, as we argued in Chapter 1, markets function in an environment. They are shaped by their social, political, cultural and institutional context. Markets are 'embedded' in that context. Standard microeconomics abstracts from that environmental context to focus on the functioning of markets as such. It is useful as an analytical approach. To understand the functioning of markets in the real world, however, it will often be necessary to add the environmental factors. We will return to this theme in subsequent chapters as well.[2]

2.6 Summary: how economic decisions are coordinated by the market

In a competitive market, economic decisions are coordinated by the laws of supply and demand. The law of supply states that supply will increase as the price of a product goes up. The law of demand states that demand will decrease as the price of a product goes up. This means that there is only one price at which total demand equals total supply. This is the market (or equilibrium) price. The market price is determined by the point of intersection of the supply curve and the demand curve. Let us take another look at Figure 2.3. The supply curve for TV sets and the demand curve for TV sets intersect at a price of €400. At that price, all manufacturers of television sets in the EU will together produce exactly 14 million sets without any planning authority telling them how many to produce. Each manufacturer of television sets will take the price of €400 as given. Given this price, it will determine how many sets to produce. There are many manufacturers of TV sets in the EU. With a price of €400, total production by all these manufacturers is 14 million sets. Also, with a price of €400, total demand by all consumers in the EU is equal to 14 million sets. This means that all sets will be sold and that every consumer who wants to buy at €400 can do so. The quantity of sets to be produced is determined not by a planning authority but by the laws of supply and demand.

Consumers buy not only TV sets but also many other products. Consider a consumer who likes apples as well as pears. Given a certain budget, how many apples and how many pears will he buy?

That depends on his tastes and on the prices of apples and pears. In order to explain how a consumer makes this type of decision, economists use the rather abstract concept of utility. Consumers act as if they are maximizing their utility. This enables us to draw indifference curves like those in Figure 2.6. All points on the same indifference curve give the consumer the same level of utility. The concepts of utility and indifference curves belong to the standard toolbox of a microeconomist. These tools are used again in Chapter 7.

How does a manufacturer decide how much to produce? Here we have to make a distinction between the short run and the long run. In the short run (days or weeks), the manufacturer cannot add another assembly line or close one of the existing assembly lines. The firm can add labour, however, by, for example, working overtime or hiring temporary employees (perhaps students).

It is standard economic theory to assume that, as the firm adds more and more labour, the output will not increase linearly. That is because employees get tired if they work long hours and the factory becomes crowded as the number of employees increases. The additional output as a result of an additional hour of labour decreases as the firm adds more and more labour. In the language of economists, the marginal productivity of labour decreases as the amount of labour increases. Given a market price, the firm will choose the amount of labour in such a way that its profits are maximized.

In the long run, the firm can vary both capital *and* labour. For example, the firm can invest in additional assembly lines and hire additional employees. The firm has more freedom in the long run than in the short run. In the long run it can decide not only how much to produce but also how to produce it – that is, how much capital and labour to use in order to produce a given quantity.

The standard microeconomic theory that is explained in this chapter is based on five assumptions.

- **Firms are holistic entities** This means that a firm is assumed to be a single, unified entity. The result is that, in standard microeconomics, one does not consider what goes on inside the firm: it is as if the firm is simply a black box that we cannot look into. This first assumption is relaxed in more modern approaches that are discussed in subsequent chapters. It is quite obvious that, if we want to discuss organizations, we have to look inside them.

- **Firms have a single objective function** such as to maximize profit or the value of the firm. That assumption means the objectives of the owner(s) of the firm are the only objectives that matter. In later chapters, especially in Chapters 6 and 7, that assumption is relaxed.

- **Everyone has perfect information** That is a very important assumption underlying standard microeconomics. As we have stated in Chapter 1, however, organizations arise mainly as solutions to information problems. If we want to understand why not all economic decisions are coordinated by the price mechanism of standard microeconomics, then we have to relax that crucial assumption, which we do in all subsequent chapters.

- **The behaviour of producers and consumers can be described as maximizing behaviour** This assumption typifies the 'homo economicus', who knows everything and makes decisions solely on the basis of calculating the solution to some maximizing problem. This **homo economicus** reappears in Chapters 5 and 7. In several other chapters, however, we assume that human beings may try to maximize something, but they are unable to calculate the optimal solutions in all circumstances.

■ **Standard microeconomics examines the market independent of its environmental context** While this is useful as an analytical approach, the functioning of many markets in the real world cannot be fully understood without including the environmental factors. In Chapter 1 we highlighted some of these factors and will continue to add illustrations in subsequent chapters.

Questions

1 Prove that two indifference curves can never intersect. *Hint:* sketch a situation in which two indifference curves do intersect and show that this leads to a contradiction.

2 Prove that two isoquants can never intersect.

3 Box 2.2 illustrates the increase in the demand for tin as a result of the fact that a new opportunity for the use of tin has arisen. As you can see in Figure 2.4, the quantity supplied increases (from q_1 to q_2) as a result of the shift in the demand curve. Does this contradict Hayek's conclusion that a new opportunity for the use of tin will cause existing users of tin to economize on the use of tin?

4 Consider Figure 2.9. This figure gives the marginal productivity of labour, dQ/dL, as a function of L. According to the text, the firm should choose L such that dQ/dL equals P_1/p, where P_1 is the price of labour and p is the price of pencils. In the example given in the text, $P_1 = \$20$ and $p = \$0.25$, so L must be chosen such that $dQ/dL = 80$.

Show that the firm can increase profits by adding labour when $dQ/dL > 80$. Also show that the firm can increase profits by reducing the amount of labour when $dQ/dL < 80$.

5 Consider a very large firm such as Royal Dutch/Shell. Do you think that it is realistic to treat such a firm as an holistic entity? Can you give an example of a situation in which conflicts between different parts of such a firm can arise?

Suggested further reading

Bowles, S. (2004), *Microeconomics: Behavior, institutions, and evolution*, Princeton, NJ: Princeton University Press.
Katz, M. L. and Rosen, H. S. (1998), *Microeconomics*, Boston, MA: Irwin/McGraw-Hill.
Kreps, D. M. (2004), *Microeconomics for Managers*, New York: W. W. Norton.
Perloff, J. M. (2001), *Microeconomics*, Boston, MA: Addison-Wesley.

Notes

1 If you are unfamiliar with the notion of opportunity cost, consider the following example. Suppose a dentist decides to take a day off in order to fish. Suppose that, on a normal working day, he earns €1800. The opportunity cost of his day off is then

€1800. To put it in more general terms, the opportunity cost of a resource (a dentist's day, an amount of capital) is equal to the revenue that could have been generated by the best alternative use.

2 A useful introduction to microeconomics building on new behavioural foundations and incorporating the environmental (institutional) context – as elaborated later in this book – is provided by Bowles (2004).

We live in a world of organizations. Think about it for a moment. When you were born, it was perhaps in a hospital – a healthcare organization. Growing up, you attended school – an educational organization. In your adult life, you will probably earn your living in a work organization. You may be a member of one or more recreational organizations. You may belong to a religious organization. You buy the goods and services you need from a variety of organizations. You pay your taxes to government organizations. Culture is preserved in organizations such as museums and libraries. Communication is made possible by organizations such as publishers, television networks and telecom services. Discovery is enabled by research laboratories and universities. Resocialization is arranged in psychiatric hospitals and prisons. Finally, when you die, your funeral will probably be supervised by an undertaker's business.

A moment's reflection will make it clear that organizations are a pervasive phenomenon in the contemporary world. So pervasive are they that some people will be surprised (or even mildly shocked) by the realization of their ubiquity. Organizations perform many of the pleasant and unpleasant tasks that we usually take for granted in our societies. They are the main vehicles by which individuals can collaborate in the pursuit of specified goals. As a well-known sociologist has observed, 'the development of organizations is the principal mechanism by which, in a highly differentiated society, it is possible to 'get things done', to achieve goals beyond the reach of the individual' (Parsons, 1960, p. 41).

If we state this in the terms introduced in our opening chapter, in a world characterized by a high level of division of labour, in which we are all specialized, organizations are the principal means by which we coordinate for collective action. We can hardly imagine a world in which individuals would have only the market mechanism to coordinate their actions. Even people working 'alone' from home, say as a 'power seller' on eBay, depend on organizations to get things done. They depend on eBay, of course, itself an organization, but they also depend on a Web-enabled, standardized (hence, organized) way of working with other people, as argued in Box 3.1. Also, finally, they depend on the Internet itself, which – contrary to popular belief – needs to be managed and organized as well (see Box 3.6 at the end of this chapter).

Box 3.1 Specialization and organization via the Internet

The Internet allows people to work in what seems a quite individual way: on their own behind a PC. It even enables us to work from home or 'on the road'. However, behind this appearance of individuals working on their own is a reality of highly sophisticated interdependency. Internet has in fact spurred new, Web-enabled ways of working and organizing:

This, then, is a fundamental paradox at the heart of modern economies: The more highly educated and specialized we become, the more we need other people to perform. The Internet, which allows so many people to work as individual contributors and to think of themselves as free agents or independent professionals, underscores this interdependency but, ironically, also makes it less immediately apparent. We think we live in worlds of our own and can contribute as individuals, but this is only possible because some form of organization makes the specialized work we do productive.

Source: Magretta (2002, p. 7)

How is organizational coordination achieved? How does it differ from market coordination by the price mechanism, as introduced in the previous chapter? That is the subject of the next section, where six coordination mechanisms will be identified. In Section 3.3, we build on this distinction to identify six ideal types of organization. Then we relax somewhat the sharp distinction between organizational and market coordination in Sections 3.4 and 3.5. In the concluding section, we summarize the argument so far.

3.2 Organizational coordination

Let us first examine what economists have had to say about organizational coordination. When Coase (1937) posited organizations and markets as alternative coordination devices, he assumed that, within organizations, **authority** directed the allocation of resources instead of the price mechanism:

Authority

> Outside the firm, price movements direct production, which is coordinated through a series of exchange transactions on the market. Within a firm, these market transactions are eliminated and in place of the complicated market structure with exchange transactions is substituted the entrepreneur/coordinator, who directs production ... We may sum up this section of the argument by saying that the operation of a market costs something and by forming an organization and allowing some authority (an 'entrepreneur') to direct the resources, certain marketing costs are saved.

Similarly, when Hayek (1945) praised the virtues of the market, he compared a market system with a central planning authority for an entire economic system:

> The various ways in which the knowledge on which people base their plans is communicated to them is the crucial problem for any theory explaining the economic process. And the problem of what is the best way of utilizing knowledge

initially dispersed among all the people is at least one of the main problems of economic policy – or of designing an efficient economic system. The answer to this question is closely connected with that other question which arises here, that of *who* is to do the planning. It is about this question that all the dispute about 'economic planning' centers. This is not a dispute about whether planning is to be done or not. It is a dispute as to whether planning is to be done centrally, by one authority for the whole economic system, or is to be divided among many individuals.

We show in this section that Hayek's problem diagnosis was right: the best use of dispersed knowledge is indeed one of the main problems in economic coordination. However, by comparing a market system with a central planning system, Hayek overlooked the fact that there are various other ways to communicate knowledge and coordinate economic activities than through prices or authority. It is to these alternatives that we now turn.

Mintzberg (1979, 1989) has synthesized the organizational literature on the structure of organizations. He has shown how the various elements of the structure of organizations (such as the size of its parts or the extent of decentralization) 'configure' with determinants of organizational structure (such as **Organizational configurations** the type of environment). He has thus developed a typology of **organizational configurations**. This typology is described in the next section. For now, we focus on the basis of this typology: a distinction between various types of coordination mechanism. These six mechanisms are reproduced in Figure 3.1. Here is a description of each of them (based on Mintzberg, 1989, p. 101).

Mutual adjustment

- **mutual adjustment**, which achieves coordination by the simple process of informal communication (as between two operating employees);

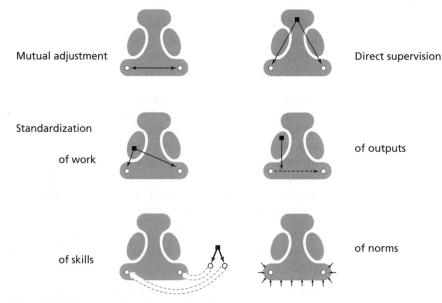

Mutual adjustment — Direct supervision

Standardization

of work — of outputs

of skills — of norms

Figure 3.1 The co-ordinating mechanisms
Source: Mintzberg (1989, p. 102)

Direct supervision	■ **direct supervision**, in which coordination is achieved by having one person issue orders or instructions to several others whose work interrelates (as when a boss tells others what is to be done, one step at a time);
Standardization of work processes	■ **standardization of work processes**, which achieves coordination by specifying the work processes of people carrying out interrelated tasks (those standards usually being developed in the technostructure[1]; to be carried out in the operating core, as in the case of the work instructions that come out of time-and-motion studies – see Box 3.2 for an example of the standardization of work processes);
Standardization of outputs	■ **standardization of outputs**, which achieves coordination by specifying the results of different work (again, usually developed in the technostructure, as in a financial plan that specifies subunit performance targets or specifications that outline the dimensions of a product to be produced);
Standardization of skills	■ **standardization of skills** (as well as *knowledge*), in which different pieces of work are coordinated by virtue of the related training the workers have received (as with medical specialists – say, a surgeon and an anaesthetist in an operating room – responding almost automatically to each other's standardized procedures);
Standardization of norms	■ **standardization of norms**, in which it is the norms determining the work that are controlled, usually for the entire organization, so that everyone functions according to the same set of beliefs (as in a religious order).

Box 3.2 Standardization of 'operating procedures' at Aravind Eye Hospital

India's Aravind Eye Hospital is a mission-driven organization, the success of which illustrates the kind of impact that can be achieved when the lines of organization are drawn in support of strategy. Aravind has made smart choices about scale, scope and structure since its founding in 1976 by a retired eye surgeon, Dr Govindappa Venkataswamy. He started small, with a 20-bed private, non-profit hospital. Within 25 years, Aravind has become the largest provider of eye surgery in the world, performing 180,000 cataract operations a year, 70 per cent of them for free.

Dr V's vision and his methods owe a lot to Henry Ford. (Dr V himself credits McDonald's as his inspiration; the principles are the same). In India, millions of people suffer from blindness due to cataracts. Most can be cured with a simple operation. The management challenge is to make that operation affordable. Dr V's dream, in a sense, was to build an eye hospital for the multitude.

Cataract surgery is Dr V's Model T. Focusing on this one 'product', Aravind has designed an extraordinarily efficient, high-volume, assembly-line process to produce it. Every step has been standardized, from patient screening and registration to the surgery itself. The operating theatre is designed to maximize the productivity of the surgeons. While a surgeon operates on one patient, the next is being prepped on a second table. When the first operation ends, the surgeon can turn immediately to start the next one, and so on, back and forth.

Yes, the surgeons have given up some autonomy in order to follow, step by step, a standardized operating procedure. We may dismiss Henry Ford's command and control style as a throwback to the industrial age, but standardization as a design principle is alive and well and still works miracles of productivity. According to one recent report, it costs Aravind about $10 to perform a cataract operation that costs a typical United States hospital $1650.

Source: Magretta (2002)

The six mechanisms listed above are all ways in which work is coordinated within organizations. They are thus also the ways in which people in organizations can communicate knowledge and expectations. Conversely, they are the ways in which people in the organization may learn from others what they need to know to carry out their tasks as well as what is expected from them. In short, all six mechanisms are alternatives to the price mechanism for communicating information and coordinating economic activities. Authority (direct supervision by an entrepreneur or a boss) is but one of these organizational coordinating mechanisms.

Only in relatively small organizations can authority be used as the primary coordination mechanism, as we emphasize in the next section. Almost all large organizations use a variety of coordination mechanisms, including mutual adjustment and standardization of work processes, skills, outputs and norms. Standardization of work processes, skills, outputs and norms may be fostered by training. Box 3.3 explains how Disney uses training of new employees at Disney University to standardize norms.

Box 3.3 Disney training: the standardization of norms

The Disney company is well known for the rigorous training it offers to every new employee. The courses are taught by the faculty of Disney University, the company's own training organization. The introductory course is called 'Disney Traditions' and is designed so that 'new members of the Disney team can be introduced to our traditions, philosophies, organization, and the way we do business' (company brochure). The trainers drill new employees with questions about Disney characters, history and mythology. They also constantly emphasize the values and norms that Disney holds dear:

> **Trainer:** What business are we in? Everybody knows that McDonald's makes hamburgers. What does Disney make?
>
> **New hire:** It makes people happy.
>
> **Trainer:** Yes, exactly! *It makes people happy.* It doesn't matter who they are, what language they speak, what they do, where they come from, what colour they are, or anything else. We're here to make them happy...

In the University textbooks the values and norms are reinforced:

> At Disneyland we get tired, but never bored, and even if it's a rough day, we appear happy.
> You've got to have an honest smile. It's got to come from within ... If nothing else helps, remember that you get paid for smiling.

The culture even comes with its own language, which is designed to convey that work at Disney should be seen as 'play', a theatrical performance:

employees	=	cast members
customers	=	guests
a crowd	=	audience
a work shift	=	performance
a job	=	part
a uniform	=	costume
on duty	=	onstage
off duty	=	backstage

Sources: Collins and Porras (1998); Tom Peters Group, *In Search of Excellence* – video

To illustrate how organizations use a variety of coordinating mechanisms, let us take an example from our own experience. When we have moved to new universities, we have learned, in various ways, how to coordinate our work with that of others. First, we received several rule books, such as computer manuals, administrative procedures, regulations and library instructions. These told us the formal rules that govern the coordination of work (standardization of work processes). However, although universities are definitely bureaucracies, they are not so bureaucratic that all work is coordinated 'by the book'. Some of the formal rules are not upheld (they might, for instance, be outdated and nobody has bothered to update them). Moreover, much coordination is not formalized, so we negotiated with coworkers how to work with each other (mutual adjustment). With our fellow professors we coordinated our courses, with the administrative staff we scheduled them and, with the secretaries, we negotiated to have them typed. In our research work we looked for coworkers who understood our type of work and had complementary knowledge or skills. On the doctoral courses, we taught the skills required of future colleagues (standardization of skills). Finally, we tried to find out what was regarded as really important at our new institutions: how important research was versus teaching, how important the fulfilment of administrative duties or the rendering of community service was, how sociable we were expected to be and so on (standardization of norms). In all of these ways and more we learned how to coordinate our work with that of our new colleagues.

Similar accounts could be given about learning to deal with other types of organization. The point is that each organization has an array of communication and coordination mechanisms available. Through these mechanisms, knowledge and information are transported. In certain types of organization, certain mechanisms dominate, but hardly any organization uses just one mechanism – and we shall see in the next section that it is only in relatively small, entrepreneurial organizations that authority (direct supervision) is dominant. Therefore, it is too simple a view to assume that authority is substituted for the price mechanism when markets give way to organizations. The price mechanism is certainly substituted when we move away from ideal markets, but the alternatives are manifold.

In concluding this section, let us restate what we indicated by way of a preview in Chapter 1. If we adopt the definition of an ideal market as the coordination device that uses the price mechanism *only*, then we may define ideal organizations as the coordination devices that do *not* use the price mechanism at all for (internal) coordination. This leaves, however, a number of organizational forms, each defined by which mechanism it uses primarily for coordination purposes. The next section is devoted to these forms.

3.3 Types of organizations

We have introduced six alternative coordination mechanisms to the price system. The descriptions of these six mechanisms are based on Mintzberg's

(1979, 1989) work, which integrates much previous organizational research into a typology of organizational configurations. The purpose of this section is to introduce the organizational configurations that correspond to the dominant use of any one of these six mechanisms. As real organizations are often hybrid forms of these six 'pure' types, this section provides an overview of the variety of organizational forms we are dealing with that operate as alternatives to market coordination.

The six coordination mechanisms introduced in the previous section correspond with six organizational configurations, as presented in Figure 3.2. That is to say, when, for instance, direct supervision is the prime coordinating mechanism, we are dealing with a configuration called the **entrepreneurial organization**.[2] This type corresponds well to the firm that Coase envisaged as substituting for market coordination. In this firm, an entrepreneur directs production and the allocation of resources. The firm is simple enough for the entrepreneur to control personally the organizational activities through direct supervision. Its structure is thus flexible, informal and not elaborated. It operates in environments that are simple and dynamic – simple enough for one person at the top to be able to coordinate activities; dynamic enough to require organizational flexibility and not turn into a bureaucracy. Think of retail stores or young computer companies as good examples of this type.

Take the Apple Computer Company. In the early stages of its existence, it was an entrepreneurial organization under the direct supervision of Steve Jobs. Jobs was a charismatic leader with a clear vision of the company that he wanted Apple to be. Under his personal leadership and supervision, Apple developed the Macintosh and became a credible, aggressive player in the market for personal computers. As the company grew, however, coordination solely from the top became problematic – one man could no longer oversee all the operations. Choices had to be made about how to reshape Apple in order to allow it to develop further. Jobs appointed a manager, John Sculley. At first, the two sought solutions together, but, over time, their differences of opinion grew and, in the end, Jobs was forced to leave the company (see Sculley, 1987).[3]

From a configuration point of view, the dilemmas could be described as follows. Apple had grown too large to be run as a simple entrepreneurial organization. Direct supervision broke down as the prime coordinating mech-

Entrepreneurial organization

CONFIGURATION	PRIME COORDINATING MECHANISM
Entrepreneurial organization	Direct supervision
Machine organization	Standardization of work processes
Professional organization	Standardization of skills
Diversified organization	Standardization of outputs
Innovative organization	Mutual adjustment
Missionary organization	Standardization of norms

Figure 3.2 The six configurations

anism. The organization should have been taken through a transition phase in which one or more of the alternative coordinating mechanisms shown in Figure 3.2 would have become more prominent. Which one(s) would have depended on the circumstances. To the extent that Apple's environment had stabilized, standardization of work processes would have been the most feasible. If, for instance, technological developments had slowed down and basic technical designs had been developed, more routinization of production would have been possible than in the early stages when no one really knew what technological horse to bet on. Once production is routinized, other functions can be standardized, too. Standard products generate standard purchasing requirements, standard packaging instructions and so on. The more Apple standardized its work processes, the more it would turn into a **machine organization**.

Machine organization

This is not the only possibility, though. Also important is the amount of professional work in the company's operations. Professional work (such as R&D and systems design) cannot be standardized: all an organization can do is standardize the skills required for executing this work by, for instance, demanding a certain type of training. The more professional work an organization requires, the more it has to rely on well-trained individuals to execute their work with considerable discretion and coordinate it through the professional standards acquired during their long training. Universities and hospitals are examples of **professional organizations**, but certain parts of Apple would probably show these features as well.

Professional organization

Similarly, the other three coordinating mechanisms listed in Figure 3.2 could be employed. If the company wanted to diversify into other markets or market niches, it could aim for standardization of outputs, in terms of both product specifications and financial results of its divisions. It would then move towards the **diversified organization**, which specifies the output expected from its divisions and then leaves them considerable autonomy as to how they attain these goals. Many of the large corporations in the world, such as General Electric, Unilever and Mitsubishi, are diversified organizations, which operate on diverse markets with different families of products.

Diversified organization

It is important to remain innovative in the computer market, which requires the collaboration of hardware and software specialists, marketing and production people through mutual adjustment. Organizations that rely primarily on this coordination mechanism are called **innovative organizations**.[4] As organizations grow larger, it becomes harder to retain mutual adjustment as the dominant coordination mechanism. This point is illustrated in Box 3.4 about Hewlett-Packard (HP). HP has found it difficult to maintain the entrepreneurial and innovative spirit that brought the company enormous growth and success.

Innovative organization

Box 3.4 The HP Way

In 1939, Bill Hewlett and Dave Packard, two engineers aged 26, founded the Hewlett-Packard company in a garage in Palo Alto, California. That garage is regarded by many as the birthplace of Silicon Valley. The founders instilled an entrepreneurial, innovative spirit into their company. HP became a symbol of inventiveness. It also became well known for its business principles, encoded in 'the HP Way'. The HP way of doing business emphasized:

- making a technological contribution to society
- respect and opportunity for its employees
- being a responsible citizen in its communities
- profitable growth as a means to achieve these other values and goals.

The HP Way brought the company enormous success. Its famous products included hand-held calculators and printers. By the end of the century, it was approaching $50 billion in revenue and employed 80,000 people. However, as our organizational framework predicts, HP had found it increasingly difficult to maintain its entrepreneurial and innovative spirit as it grew to this huge size. New product development was disappointing, growth was faltering and profitability was decreasing rapidly. Moreover, it had developed the image of a slow, stumbling giant and was dubbed the Gray Lady of Silicon Valley.

In 1999, the HP Board took the radical step of looking outside the company for a new president and CEO. It appointed Carly Fiorina, the first woman to head a company listed on the Dow Jones Industrial Average. She found a company that still lived up to 'the core values of the firm: respect, integrity, teamwork, contribution', but one that had also become 'a gentle bureaucracy of entitlement and consensus', consisting of 'a collection of tribes'. In order to revitalize this company, she launched the slogan 'preserve the best, reinvent the rest'. Reaching back to its origins, HP issued new 'Rules of the Garage', including the following.

- Believe you can change the world.
- Share tools, ideas. Trust your colleagues.
- No politics. No bureaucracy. (These are ridiculous in a garage.)
- Radical ideas are not bad ideas.
- Make a contribution every day. If it doesn't contribute, it doesn't leave the garage.
- Believe that together we can do anything.

Fiorina streamlined the company, slashing the number of product divisions from 83 to 16. In addition, she cut costs and jobs (5 per cent of the workforce) and reorientated the company to become a service-centred company rather than a hardware-centred company.

On 4 September 2001, Fiorina announced that HP would acquire Compaq, a large maker of personal computers, for $19 billion. 'For the first time in a very long time, IBM will have a competitor that is strong enough to take it head-on', she said. Analysts, however, dubbed this step 'a classical defensive move in a consolidating industry'. For the next few years, HP struggled to integrate Compaq well, Dell was still increasing its market share (see Box 10.6), HP's share price suffered and a bitter feud broke out between Fiorina and Walter Hewlett, the son of Bill and a Board member of HP. In 2005, Fiorina was fired. It was clear once again how difficult it is for successful firms to retain their success – a theme we shall return to in Chapters 10 and 11.

Sources: Collins and Porras (1998); 'The HP Way forward', interview with Carly Fiorina in *Worldlink*, magazine of the World Economic Forum, Jan/Feb 2001; 'Rebuilding the HP way', *Information Week*, 23 July 2001; 'Hewlett-Packard and Compaq: sheltering from the storm', *The Economist*, 8 September 2001; 'Can anyone save HP?', *Business Week*, 21 February 2005

Smaller organizations, though, such as consultancy firms or architectural practices, can rely on mutual adjustment as the main coordination mechanism and thus maintain a spirit of innovation. For larger organizations such as Apple and HP, the challenge is to combine mutual adjustment – which is especially suited to bringing together specialists collaborating under dynamic and complex circumstances – with other coordination mechanisms.

Finally, Apple could rely on the standardization of norms (or ideology), to the extent that members of its workforce share a common system of values and beliefs that direct their activities. A strong sense of mission, esprit de corps or ideology, which individuals share, tells them how to act together and dispenses the need for other forms of coordination. Religious orders may depend to a large extent on standardization of norms – they are prime examples of **missionary organizations** – but other organizations often have their own cultures, too. If those cultures are strong and tell organizational members what to do in certain situations, they act as a coordination mechanism.

Missionary organization

Which course(s) Apple takes depends on the actual circumstances at the time. In all cases, however, the pressures of the situation would force it to replace direct supervision as its prime coordinating mechanism. One or more other mechanisms would take over. To the extent that Apple would, after some time, show a new *prime* coordinating mechanism, it would transform into a new configurational type. If it were to employ a mixture of these mechanisms, with no single one being prominent, it would be a hybrid of the relatively 'pure' types. That is common – most organizations combine several types of coordination mechanisms. An example is given in Box 3.5.

Box 3.5 An insurance brokerage firm

Real organizations are often a mixture of two or more of the six pure organizational configurations described above. As an example, consider an insurance brokerage firm. Such a firm is often a combination of a professional organization and a machine organization.

An important element that characterizes an insurance brokerage firm as a professional organization is the extensive training that insurance brokers receive before they are allowed to work independently. As a result, standardization of skills is an important coordinating mechanism in these firms.

Administrative procedures also tend to be very much standardized in an insurance brokerage firm. When a client requires a certain type of policy, all brokers within the firm use exactly the same administrative method and routing for that type of policy. This is an example of standardization of work processes and, as mentioned earlier, standardization of work processes is the prime coordinating mechanism for a machine organization.

Figure 3.3 summarizes the space available for organizational forms. The relatively pure configurations are located toward the corners of the pentagon. Within the pentagon, all kinds of hybrid forms are possible. What form a particular organization will tend to take is a complex issue. For a discussion of the forces involved, you are referred to Mintzberg (1989). For our purposes, it is sufficient if the main point has come across: when markets are replaced by organizations, coordination by the price mechanism gives way to coordination by a set of other mechanisms. Organizations can take many forms and each one is specifically adapted to particular circumstances – it can handle different types of transactions. No wonder we see so many organizations and that such a large part of economic life is conducted within them.

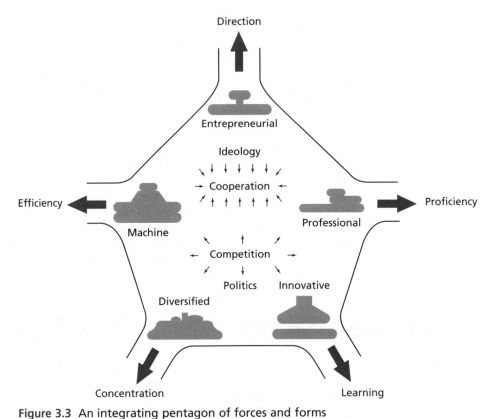

Figure 3.3 An integrating pentagon of forces and forms

Note: in this figure you do not see the missionary organization, which is the organizational form relying primarily on the standardization of norms or ideology.

Source: Mintzberg (1989, p. 256)

3.4 Organizational markets

Until now, we have argued as though market coordination and organizational coordination were mutually exclusive – that is, as if these two types of coordination cannot be combined. We now take the argument one step further and show that markets may exist within organizations as well. In the next section, we briefly show that markets may be organized to some extent, too. Hence, in practice, market and organizational coordination may often be found in combination.

Take the example of a large, diversified organization such as Exxon. Within that organization, transactions between divisions may take place, such as when the oil division delivers oil to the petrochemical division, which processes it further into commodity chemicals. Within the petrochemical division, similar exchanges may occur, such as when the commodity chemicals are produced by one business unit and delivered to the next to be processed further into specialized chemicals. Often such transactions are effected against an internal price, the transfer price. In such a case, Exxon may be said to have an **internal market for goods**. Decisions on whether to sell or procure internally will be based on the transfer price as compared with external prices.

Internal market for goods

Similarly, Shell has an **internal capital market** as corporate management allocates its funds to the divisions on the basis of those divisional plans that fit best with corporate policy and generate the highest returns. Internally, Exxon's corporate management takes over the function of the external capital market by directing financial resources to their best use. The internal and external capital markets remain linked. Management may decide not to invest all its available resources internally if the internal returns are insufficient. It may then seek temporary outside investment for its superfluous funds, perhaps in anticipation of the acquisition of another firm. Alternatively, it may want to attract new (external) capital when it can meet the required external conditions and earn an additional profit.

Internal capital market

Similarly, an **internal labour market** may be said to exist where divisions compete for the best human resources and may also bid up their potential salaries.[5] Members of an organization may seek career advancement by applying internally for better positions with higher salaries. If the allocation of human resources is primarily an internal affair, the function of the external labour market is taken over by the organization. Again, the internal and external markets remain linked, however. New people enter the organization through its ports of entry. Others leave the organization and seek new employment in the external labour market.

Internal labour market

Within organizations, then, several types of market may operate. This implies that market and organizational coordination may be mixed. It further implies that there is no sharp demarcation between markets and organizations. In our conceptual framework we distinguish between the two ideal types: 'pure' market coordination (solely by the price mechanism) and 'pure' organizational coordination (solely by other mechanisms). Most real cases fall between these two pure types and will be characterized by mixed coordination systems. This is shown below for the operation of most markets.

3.5 Organized markets

Pure market coordination – solely by means of the price mechanism – is an exceptional case. Let us return to the example of the stock market, discussed in Section 1.5, Chapter 1. That example was used because it conforms closely to the model of perfect competition. The numerous buyers and sellers of IBM stock individually have no effect on the stock price. IBM's common stock is standardized: there is no product variation. The market for IBM stock has no barriers to entry or exit. That market therefore meets the main assumptions specified in Chapter 2 for the operation of perfect competition.

Yet, when we look more closely at the operation of that market, we see at least two organizational coordination mechanisms operate as well. First, the market is regulated. It is regulated by both governments (through Securities Acts) and stock exchange boards (through conditions for listing). Those regulations specify the rules with which the various market parties must comply. For example, in most countries, buyers are prohibited from acquiring a controlling interest in listed firms without prior notification of their intentions. Similarly, IBM has to comply with a number of regulations and restrictions before it is permitted to issue new stock. Such regulations standardize the work processes of the market parties. The Securities Acts and the stock exchange regulations function just as operating manuals do in organizations. The market parties can use them to see what behaviour is required in particular situations. The stock market is organized in that sense. It is organized in the further sense, too, that direct supervision is operative. The stock markets are supervised by bodies such as the Securities and Exchange Commission in the USA and stock market boards. Those bodies have the power to interfere with free market interaction, for instance, by suspending the listing of a firm when there are strong indications of irregularities or misconduct. These examples illustrate that markets do not operate in isolation: they are embedded in an institutional environment that sets the 'rules of the game' (see Section 1.7).

Let us take another of the six organizational coordination mechanisms: mutual adjustment. As explained above, this mechanism achieves coordination through the process of informal communication. Such informal communication is a common feature in many markets. One pernicious form

Collusion

of it is called **collusion** by economists. It refers, for example, to conspiracies by the few suppliers in oligopolistic markets to set prices higher than would result under free market interaction. Alternatively, informal cartels may divide markets between them and thus collude to restrain competition.

Tacit collusion

Collusion may be rather overt or it may be tacit. **Tacit collusion** is a prime example of mutual adjustment as it involves the informal development of rules regulating market behaviour. One such rule may be that a particular supplier acts as price leader. If that supplier changes its price level, the other suppliers follow. No formal communication is required to organize an oligopolistic market in that way.

Finally, consider two examples of the influence of culture (standardization of norms) on the operation of markets. First, the Islamic prohibition on charging interest. The prohibition derives from the Koran. As a result, the Islamic banking system has to organize some of its transactions differently from those customary in the Western world. Second, take the common Asiatic practice of charging a different price to the 'in group' of family, friends and long standing business associates from that charged to outsiders. These examples illustrate how economic transactions are embedded in cultural norms.[6]

If some foreign practices seem strange to us, we should realize that our norms, too, are standardized to allow us to engage in economic transactions with roughly the same expectations of what is fair and what is not. One illustration of this is provided by Stewart Macaulay (1963, p. 61):

> One purchasing agent expressed a common business attitude when he said, 'if something comes up, you get the other man on the telephone and deal with the problem. You don't read legalistic contract clauses at each other if you ever want to do business again. One doesn't run to lawyers if he wants to stay in business because one must behave decently.

These few examples suffice to show that combining market and organizational coordination is the rule rather than the exception.[7] Analytically, it is necessary to distinguish carefully between the price system as the market coordination device and the six organizational mechanisms. We shall continue to do so in the following chapters. Only by means of a clear, analytical separation can we examine which device is most efficient under what circumstances. The foregoing discussion will have made it clear, however, that, when we move from the analytical world (with its sharp distinctions) to the messy real world, we often find bundles of coordination mechanisms operating together. This is illustrated in Figure 3.4.

3.6 Summary: how organizations achieve coordination

Market and organizational coordination are the two ideal types of coordination device for economic transactions. Pure market coordination is effected by the use of the price mechanism only. Pure organizational coordination is characterized by the use of non-price mechanisms only. In this chapter, we introduced six of those non-price mechanisms. All six mechanisms can communicate the knowledge necessary for organizational members to engage in economic transactions. All six may substitute for the price mechanism in coordinating economic action.

Associated with the dominant use of each of these six mechanisms are six pure types of organizational configuration, such as the entrepreneurial organization in which direct supervision is the prime coordinating mechanism. The

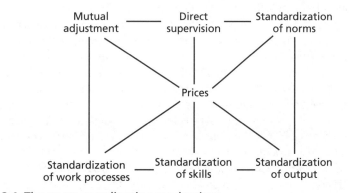

Figure 3.4 The seven coordinating mechanisms

entrepreneurial organization thus conforms closely to the type of organization that Coase had in mind when he posited authority as the alternative to the price mechanism in coordinating economic transactions. However, organizational theory shows that four types of standardization (of work processes, skills, outputs or norms) and mutual adjustment can act as coordinating mechanisms as well. If organizational coordination is dominated by one of these six mechanisms, we shall observe one of the relatively 'pure types' of organizational configuration. It was shown, however, that most organizations use a combination of those mechanisms. In the real world, therefore, we usually encounter hybrid types of organization. Moreover, it was shown that many organizations (such as business firms) also use the price mechanism to some extent for internal purposes. Within those firms, market and organizational coordination are then combined.

Finally, it was briefly shown that the opposite occurs frequently as well – that is, markets are often organized to some extent. Market coordination by the price mechanism is often combined with one or more of the organizational mechanisms. We conclude, therefore, that, in practice, we often find economic transactions are coordinated by a bundle of coordination mechanisms. It is the exception when one mechanism suffices; it is the rule where two or more are combined. Box 3.6 illustrates this for the Internet.

Box 3.6 Management and organization of the Internet

According to computer entrepreneurs Sharon Eisner Gillett and Mitchell Kapor (the founder of the software giant Lotus Development Corporation), 'Contrary to its popular portrayal as total anarchy, the Internet is actually managed.' It is not fully decentralized. While 99 per cent of the Internet's day-to-day operations, according to a guesstimate by Gillett and Kapor, are handled without any direction, central authorities are needed for the remaining 1 per cent, consisting of various non-routine activities. In addition, central authorities were needed to set up the system initially and continue to be needed to integrate new activities into it.

Some of the Internet's central decisions come from organizations run from the bottom up. Technical management and standard-setting is the responsibility of ad hoc voluntary groups such as the Internet Engineering Task Force, with open membership and democratic procedures. Self-regulation has not been the only form of central decisionmaking, however – the government has also played a role. The Internet did not arise spontaneously. It was built by the government. With the Internet, for once the government picked a winner.

Subsidies from the State got the Internet started: the US government spent about $125 million building the Internet's predecessors. In the 1960s and 1970s, the US military sponsored research into how to link computers so as to allow the sharing of data and that research led to a network of university computers. Crucial technological advances were also made at the European Laboratory for Particle Physics (known by its French acronym CERN), a cooperative effort by European governments. The National Science Foundation, the US government's science agency, also provided substantial funding after it took over responsibility for the computer network from the military in the 1980s. It was not until 1995 that the US government ceased to have direct control over the Internet.

Not only was government funding crucial but so was government decisionmaking. The very fact that the Internet was so decentralized is, ironically enough, the result of a decision made centrally. The US military imposed the modular structure in the early 1980s for the sake of flexibility of use.

Another decision by the military – the adoption of the Internet Protocol – solved the problem that, to be able to talk to each other, different kinds of computers needed a common language. Incompatibilities between networks could have arisen, otherwise making it hard to send documents and read web pages. Without a modicum of central management, the Internet would not have grown into the flexible, easy-to-use tool we experience now.

Some management continues to be needed – in particular regarding domain names or dot-com addresses. For the network to be able to function, each name must be unique, which could not be ensured without coordination. The domain name servers bring an unavoidable element of centralization. Each of these servers, one or a few for each address ending, for example, '.com' or '.edu', acts like a telephone directory, maintaining a master list of addresses and ensuring communications are routed accurately. The system of assigning names to Internet users is also unavoidably centralized. Names must be in step if they are to be usable.

Initially, the US government assigned names itself or through a subcontractor. In 1998, it established a private, non-profit corporation to do it – the Internet Corporation for Assigned Names and Numbers (ICANN). ICANN became controversial among those who saw the Internet as free and informal because it could prevent them from picking whatever domain names they felt like, but coordination of some sort was needed. 'Like it or not, you really do need a single root to make it all work,' says Vinton Cerf, an Internet pioneer who became chair of ICANN. 'There should be common ground rules. That's what ICANN strives to achieve.'

For contracting and intellectual property protection, Internet commerce has relied on the existing State-supplied legal system. The regulatory apparatus of antitrust has shielded Internet firms from predatory competition, just as it has shielded traditional firms. The State prosecutes those who spread computer viruses.

The Internet offers us, then, a conflicting pair of lessons. Its vigour lies in its decentralization. The initiative and imagination of hundreds of thousands have pushed it forward. Decentralization has limits, however. A crucial aspect of the Internet's success lies in its central management.

Source: McMillan (2002, pp. 157-9)

Questions

1 Did you see the film *A Few Good Men*? It is a film about an American élite corps of marines. What do you think is the main coordinating mechanism in such an élite unit? What other coordinating mechanisms will probably be employed?

2 Section 3.4 gave two examples of internal markets – an internal capital market and an internal labour market. Read the two examples again carefully. Do you feel that the example of the internal labour market is a better example of an internal market than the internal capital market? Discuss the possible differences between the internal capital market and the internal labour market.

3 Linklaters & Alliance is a large international law firm with more than 1900 lawyers, including 429 partners based in 26 offices in Europe, Asia and North and South America. The firm is headed by a senior partner, who is elected by the partners for a five-year term. Lawyers who are not (yet) partners work under the supervision of one of the partners, often as a member of a client team. The firm also has 16 key practice areas, such as EU and competition law, litigation and arbitration, intellectual property

and corporate and M&A, as well as a number of business groups, drawing together lawyers from across the firm specializing in certain sectors of the economy.

Which type(s) of coordination mechanism(s) is/are likely to be used by Linklaters? Would you say that Linklaters corresponds closely to one of Mintzberg's six configurations or that it corresponds more closely to a hybrid form?

4 SNCF is the French, State-owned railway company, comprised of the parent company SNCF and over 500 consolidated subsidiaries. In 1999, it employed 211,265 employees, 178,893 of whom were working for the parent company. More than 70 per cent of its annual income is from the railway itself. SNCF's ambition is to become the model for public service companies in Europe. It is firmly committed to guaranteeing a high level of traffic safety, punctuality, reliability, security of people and goods and cleanliness.

Which type(s) of coordination mechanism(s) is/are likely to be used by SNCF? Would you say that SNCF corresponds closely to one of Mintzberg's six configurations or that it corresponds more closely to a hybrid form?

Suggested further reading

Mintzberg, H. (1983), *Structure in Fives: Designing effective organizations*, Englewood Cliffs, NJ: Prentice Hall.

Mintzberg, H. (1989), *Mintzberg on Management*, New York: Free Press.

Schreuder, H. (1993), 'Coase, Hayek, and hierarchy', in S. Lindenberg and H. Schreuder, *Interdisciplinary Perspectives on Organization Studies*, Pergamon Press.

Notes

1 The technostructure is that part of the organization where the analysts are located. They are the staff, outside the hierarchy of line authority, who plan and control the work of others. Examples are work-study analysts, schedulers, quality control engineers, planners, budgeters, accountants and operations researchers.

2 In Mintzberg (1979), called the simple structure. In Figure 3.2 we show only the correspondence between the prime coordinating mechanism and the organizational configuration. For other elements of each configuration (such as the key parts, the type of decentralization, contextual variables and so on), see Mintzberg, 1979, 1989. The political organization has been left out of Figure 3.2 as it is characterized by lack of coordination and absence of clear structure.

3 In 1997, Steve Jobs returned to be CEO of Apple when the company was at the brink of failure. He led it to a new era of success, diversifying its product base to include iTunes, the iPod and the iPhone, among others.

4 Formerly called the adhocracy by Mintzberg (1979).

5 Interestingly, from an economist's perspective, internal labour markets are characterized by the existence of formalization (see Doeringer and Piore, 1971). However, given that we are dealing with markets that are internal to organizations and organizations are generally characterized by some degree of formalization, for an organization theorist, the distinguishing characteristic of internal markets is that competition is allowed, partly by price.

6 On the embeddedness of economic behaviour, see Granovetter (1985).

7 As also argued by Imai and Itami (1984) and Schreuder (1993a).

4 Information

4.1 Coordination and information

In Chapter 1, we developed a basic conceptual framework that represents a fundamental economic approach to organizations. This approach starts from the division of labour within society, which necessitates coordination between specialized economic entities. We have argued that there are two ideal types of coordination mechanism for economic transactions: markets and organizations. We have also indicated that the information requirements present in any situation will determine the actual (mix of) coordination mechanism(s) we observe in that situation.

In this chapter, we explore those information requirements, indicate some fundamental information problems and discuss how organizations may be seen as solutions to such problems. In the first section, we explore some differences between information requirements in various situations and show how they are related to market and organizational coordination. The purpose is to give you a feel for those situations. In the course of this chapter, we gradually use more precise language and distinctions, thus introducing the main concepts involved in the economic analysis of information problems.

Let us again take an ideal market as a point of departure. Hayek's example of the tin market (see Chapter 1) may come reasonably close. In the tin market, numerous buyers and sellers operate. Let us assume that each one of them has no appreciable effect on the market price for tin as all buyers and sellers are small. That is to say, their individual transactions will not have an effect on the market price as there is such a huge volume of transactions that no individual transaction can make a difference. Only the collective (in economic terms, aggregate) effect of all those individual transactions becomes noticeable as changes of the market price. As discussed in Chapter 2, we say that, under these circumstances, *perfect competition* exists. With perfect competition, each individual economic entity is necessarily a **price-taker**: it has to accept the prevailing market price and cannot hope to influence the price level. Only in such circumstances can we say prices act as sufficient statistics that convey all the necessary information to the market parties.

Prices act as sufficient statistics under conditions of perfect competition because the decisions that the economic entities can make are really very limited. Given the prevailing market price, each seller can only decide *how much* to (produce and) sell. Each buyer can only decide *how much* to buy.

Price-taker

Hence, each party can only make decisions as to *quantities* of tin. Under conditions of perfect competition, many other types of decision are irrelevant, owing to the assumptions that underlie the model of perfect competition. One of those assumptions is indeed that there are numerous buyers and sellers – so many, in fact, that we are always assured of a counterparty when we want to transact at the market price. Another crucial assumption is that we are dealing with a **homogeneous good** – a good that comes in only one standardized form. Therefore, we do not have to be concerned what variety of the good to make or buy. There are no quality differences: it does not matter to whom we sell or from whom we buy. Moreover, as buyers of those goods, we can easily observe if we have obtained what we expected as all we have to do is check the quantity delivered. As we shall see, such conditions (numerous buyers and sellers, homogeneous goods) are not met in most situations in the real world. As Samuelson (1976, p. 43) notes in his well-known introduction to economics:

> A cynic might say of perfect competition what Bernard Shaw said of Christianity: The only trouble with it is that it has never been tried.

The price mechanism, then, is a sufficient coordination mechanism only in circumstances where the economic entities involved have quite limited information requirements. Essentially, only when all the necessary information can be 'absorbed' in the price can we rely on the price mechanism as the sole communication device. Let us examine some situations in which the price mechanism is *not* sufficient to communicate all the necessary information, taking situations that are quite close to the model of perfect competition as a starting point.

First, let us have a look at retail markets – for instance, groceries and supermarkets. Have you ever wondered why the various products are displayed so differently? Some products are packaged, others are not. Some have brand names, others do not. Some can be inspected by the customer, others cannot. We submit that a major reason for these differences is the variation in *quality* that may be expected of these different goods. Sugar, for instance, is such a standardized product that most people are interested only in its price per kilo. They have no desire to inspect the product before purchasing it and do not care much about brand names. Now compare sugar with, for instance, fruit. Fruit is normally on display for customers. Often they are also able to inspect the fruit and even choose the particular pieces that they would like to buy. The major reason for this, we submit, is that fruit quality varies (with season, region, delivery time and so on). The customer wants to be able to form a first-hand judgment about its quality before purchase. The price is insufficient as a communication device to transmit the quality dimension. A higher price should reflect a higher quality, but not many of us trust the operation of that mechanism to be flawless.

For many retail products, an intermediate solution is to standardize quality as much as possible. Soup, for example, is a product that may also vary in quality. It is difficult, however, to give the potential buyers a first-hand experience of the product before purchase. The solution to that information problem

Homogeneous good

is usually the creation of *brand names* that are supposed to reflect the quality class of particular soups. Through advertising, the accumulation of consumer experience and joint use of common brand names for different products (soups and sauces), we learn to identify certain brand names as signals of particular quality classes. We may rely on that signal as an accurate indicator of quality, at least for the first purchase of a particular soup. If our quality expectation is met, our confidence in the accuracy of the brand name signal is increased. Brand names can thus be seen as solutions to information problems. Those solutions are available to organizations that are willing to invest in the creation and maintenance of their brand name reputations.[1]

The above examples assume that there is one true quality of the product and the information problem is one of communicating the true quality to the consumer. Suppose, however, that the quality of the product is not yet known (to anyone). That might be the case for a supermarket wanting to be assured of a good supply of next year's crop of fruit. In such a situation, the supermarket might contemplate a long-term contract with a supplier. The quality of next year's crop, however, is dependent on the future weather, which is unknown to both the supermarket and the supplier. In that case, we say there is *uncertainty* as to the quality of the fruit.

Markets can deal with uncertainty, at least to some extent. In our example, the supermarket and the supplier will have difficulty agreeing on a contract that specifies only the quantities of fruit to be delivered next year (at a certain price). Both will want to feel assured that the price is fair given the quality of next year's fruit. They have opposing interests in setting a particular price level, given the uncertainty involved. They might agree, however, on a specification of quality levels and prices that are dependent on the actual quality

Contingent claims contract

levels of next year's fruit. Such a contract is called a **contingent claims contract**. The specific terms of the contract are made contingent on the uncertainty involved. Note, such a contract is possible only if there is a way to determine next year's fruit quality that is acceptable to both parties. If such quality measurement is not possible, the transaction will probably not come to pass.

If parties can negotiate a contract covering all possible future contingencies, they can agree to that *complete contract*. However, in reality, we will often

Incomplete contracting

observe **incomplete contracting** in situations of uncertainty. Reasons for incomplete contracting include the following:

- It is usually difficult to foresee and plan for all possible contingencies.
- It may be expensive to fully negotiate contracts. Parties may make a trade-off between such expenses and the risks of leaving contingencies (with a low probability of occurrence) open.
- Language limitations may prevent the totally unambiguous description of terms and situations. Thus, after-the-fact interpretations may remain necessary.

In such circumstances, we may see that incomplete contracts cover some, but not all, uncertainty. In Chapter 12 we will discuss further incomplete contracts in the M&A context.

While markets may handle some uncertainty in such ways, they are not able to handle very much of it. The simple reason is that it is not possible for human minds to juggle with very many uncertain factors simultaneously. That is why we are unable to write contingent claims contracts for situations with numerous uncertain factors.

Suppose the fruit supplier wants to research and develop a new strain of fruit – say, a cross between apples and pears: appearls. Imagine that to do so requires large sums in investment, for a laboratory and specialized biologists, for example. If the supplier wanted to cover part of that investment by offering the supermarket a contract for the delivery of appearls (for an advance payment), it is questionable whether the supermarket would take it.

The reason is that there are so many uncertain factors (the technology required, the mass production possibilities, consumers' tastes and so on) that it would be almost impossible to specify all the possible (combinations of) contingencies. Hence, the contract for it could not be written and the basis for the transaction would not be there.

One organizational solution might be vertical integration of the supermarket and the fruit supplier – the one taking over the other. That organizational solution would remedy the fact that the price mechanism and, hence, market coordination cannot absorb all the uncertainty involved (we return to this issue in Chapter 8).

Finally, let us explore the situation where information is available but it is unevenly distributed – there is an **information asymmetry**. Say the supplier has developed his appearls in the laboratory, but is unable to grow them on a scale large enough by himself. Then, there would be two routes he could follow. One would be to sell his knowledge in the market – for instance, to other suppliers. However, there is a fundamental difficulty here. Those other suppliers would want to know what exactly they were buying. How are appearls grown? What steps are to be followed in the appearl-growing process and which investments are necessary for each step? How sensitive are appearls to weather conditions? Are they resistant to the common apple and pear diseases? All such questions would have to be answered before potential buyers would be able to determine the value of the new appearl-growing recipe they were being offered. If, however, all these questions were answered, they would have all the information they would need to grow appearls themselves. That is the **fundamental paradox of information**: the value of information can only be realized by revealing it to another party, but such disclosure destroys its value.

The second route the appearl-grower could take would also be an organizational route. He could, for example, enter into joint venture agreements with other producers. Such agreements can be efficient risk-sharing arrangements, as we discuss further in Section 7.6.

We have now discussed situations in which:

- the price cannot reflect all the dimensions of the good;
- uncertainty is present; and
- information asymmetries exist.

It is especially in situations where there are information asymmetries that all kinds of interesting problems occur. The reason is that such asymmetries may give rise to *opportunistic behaviour*. The notion of opportunistic behaviour (also

Information asymmetry

Fundamental paradox of information

called *strategic behaviour*) is more fully described in Chapter 8. Here, though, we shall illustrate it by means of an example derived from Milgrom and Roberts (1987, p. 184). The example also introduces the distinction between information (in)completeness, uncertainty and asymmetry:

> To get an idea of the role of informational asymmetries in strategic behavior, consider three simple card games. In the first, each player is dealt five cards face up, the players make any bets they want, and then the best hand wins. In the second, each player receives five cards, some of which are dealt face up and the rest face down. Without looking at their hole cards, the players make their bets, then the cards are turned face up and the best hand wins. Finally, the third game is like the second except that the players can look at their hole cards. Again there is betting, the hidden cards are revealed, and the best hand wins.
>
> The first game is one of complete (and perfect) information. Everyone knows everything, and as long as we assume that people prefer more money to less, it is fairly trivial to figure out what will happen: there will certainly be no betting, and probably no one will bother to play! . . .
>
> The second game has uncertainty/informational incompleteness, but no information asymmetries . . . Games of this sort are useful models for studying such issues as insurance, risky investments, and learning (especially if we revise the game to have the hole cards revealed one at a time, with betting after each is shown). However, its play would not generate any interesting forms of strategic behavior.
>
> The third game involves informational asymmetries: while there is some publicly available information, each player is privately informed of his or her hole cards . . . The existence of this private information can obviously lead to interesting strategic play: bluffing, signaling, reputation building, etc. It is also the reason why poker is of enduring popularity.

In the next sections, we continue the exploration of the consequences of information problems, particularly of information asymmetries. From the examples above, we hope that you have gained the intuition that information problems might be significant in explaining the type of coordination that is appropriate for particular transactions.

All coordination requires information. When two parties wish to enter into a transaction, they must both be able to receive the necessary information. Markets and prices are able to transmit certain types of information, but often not all the necessary information. Through organizational coordination, other types of information can be communicated. In the following sections, we shall develop this basic notion further by introducing some concepts from the economics of information.

4.2 Hidden information

The economics of information is a young branch of economics. It studies the implications of information problems and characteristics for economic theory. Some of its main inspirations have come from the analysis of insurance problems. We shall use some of these classic examples to introduce the concepts of *hidden information* (or *adverse selection*) and *hidden action* (or *moral hazard*) below and in Section 4.3.

First, let us look at hidden information. To illustrate, imagine a country with no health insurance. Let us call the country Riskaria. You have emigrated to Riskaria and have determined that no health insurance coverage is yet available, so you decide to go into the insurance business to fill that market niche. How do you proceed? The normal course of action is to employ an actuary.[2] The actuary will determine the health risks of the population of Riskaria. She might come up with a bell-shaped curve (a normal distribution), as shown in Figure 4.1.

We can observe from Figure 4.1 that the population of Riskaria includes people with very low health risks (represented towards the left of the figure) as well as people with high risks (on the right). Older people will tend to be located on the right as health risks increase with age. Also, people with, for instance, hereditary health risks or who smoke will be located further to the right than one would expect just from their age. There will also be older people who are in good shape and thus represent lower health risks than is average for their age group. In Riskaria, most people know more or less what risk class they belong to.

On the basis of risk distributions such as Figure 4.1, an actuary can calculate the insurance rate you would have to set in order to be able to provide the specified coverage. Say this rate was calculated on the basis of Figure 4.1, which represents the entire population of Riskaria. In essence, the rate then reflects the average risk.

You now enter the market and offer your new product – a health insurance policy. Which members of the population of Riskaria will buy it? The prediction is that members of the population with higher than average risks will be particularly keen to take out a policy. The reason is simple: at a rate reflecting average risks, your product is attractive to those with higher risks. Very few people with lower-than-average risks will take out your insurance policy. For them, the required rate is unattractive.

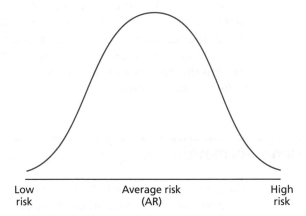

Low
risk

Average risk
(AR)

High
risk

Figure 4.1 The health risks in the population of Riskaria

Adverse selection

The phenomenon described is called **adverse selection** in insurance economics. It refers to the expected outcome of the above scenario, which is that you will end up with a set of clients in which the high-risk part of the population is over-represented. The high-risk clients have self-selected themselves in response to your product offer. They alone have been offered an attractive incentive to apply for health insurance.

As a consequence of such adverse (client) selection, you will be forced to raise your rates, but that has an adverse effect as well. At the higher rate, the insurance policy has become unattractive even to those in the average-risk group. They will cancel their policies and you will be left with an even worse selection of clients. Driven to the extreme, adverse selection could become a self-reinforcing mechanism that would make a health insurance policy an impossible product to offer in the market.

Before delving into the possible solutions to this problem, let us first consider the basic characteristics of the adverse selection phenomenon.

Hidden information

Essentially, adverse selection is a type of information asymmetry. It is a problem of **hidden information** (Arrow, 1985), which means that one party in a potential transaction (here, the population of Riskaria) is better informed about a relevant variable in the transaction (the individual member's health) than the other party (your insurance company). It is an information problem that already exists *before* the insurance contract is written. In the language of the economics of information, it is an **ex ante information problem**.

Ex ante information problem

The problem for your insurance company is how to determine the actual risks that your potential clients represent: you will want to know whether your potential clients are indeed a fair representation of the Riskaria population. If not, you may want to adjust your rates or introduce risk-dependent rates (for instance, partly dependent on age). To some extent, the company can use available information, such as age, to determine such risks. Those seeking insurance, however, will still have better knowledge about risk factors, such as hereditary risks and smoking habits, than the insurance company. They have no *incentive* to reveal this knowledge truthfully if it could be harmful to them. On the contrary, those who have private knowledge that they are higher risks than is observable have an incentive to both apply for the insurance *and* keep quiet about their private information. The company has hardly any means of finding out what this knowledge is without the cooperation of the potential clients.

In its information structure, this example corresponds with the third card game discussed in the previous section. The adverse selection phenomenon arises because one party has *private information* that is relevant to a potential transaction. That private information is unobservable to the other party. It is that *unobservability* of the private information which constitutes the essence of the information problem and introduces the risks for the other party.

Adverse selection problems abound in society. One example is given in Box 4.1. Another example comes from the market for used cars, as analysed by Akerlof (1970). Akerlof set out to explain why there is such a large price difference between brand new (that is, unregistered) cars and those that have just left the showroom. Suppose you have just bought a new car (say, a Ford) and have driven it for only a short time when you find out that you have won a Mercedes in a lottery. You decide to sell the Ford. Then you will normally have to accept a loss of up to 20 per cent of the original purchase price of the Ford. Why is this?

Akerlof's answer starts from the assumption that there are good cars and bad cars. The latter may have been assembled on a Monday morning. Such cars are referred to as 'lemons'. When buying a new car, we all run the risk of buying a 'lemon'. All parties involved are unaware which of the new cars is a lemon. Your Ford dealer was unaware whether he sold you a good car (the normal case) or a lemon (the exception). Similarly, you, as a buyer, cannot tell the difference after just one test drive. So, we all face the same probability of ending up with a new car that is a lemon.

After owning the car for some time, however, the owner can form a revised opinion about the quality of his automobile. He may have become aware of some (potential) problems. An information asymmetry develops: the sellers of used cars now have more knowledge about the true quality of their vehicles than the potential buyers. The buyers, however, have no way to discriminate between good and bad used cars. As they are unable to tell the difference, good cars and bad cars must sell at the same market price. However, at this price, there is little incentive for owners of good used cars to sell their vehicles. For owners of lemons, however, selling is attractive. As a consequence, the probability of buying a lemon is much higher in the used car market than the new car market. That risk is reflected in the market price. Even if your Ford has given you no problem at all, its selling price will reflect the higher probability of used cars being lemons.

Again, the basic problem is the unobservability of the true quality of the used cars for the buyers. Sellers have private information and they have no incentive to share bad news with the buyers. Bad risks self-select into the used car market. Buyers have few means at their disposal to identify bad risks. If there were no means at all, the market for used cars would conceivably not exist.

The 'lemon effect' can also occur in the labour market, as illustrated in Box 4.2.

Box 4.1 Blood donorship

In various parts of the world, there is a serious shortage of good-quality blood that can be used for blood transfusion purposes. As a potential recipient of such blood, you can imagine that you want it to be of the best quality – that is, totally uncontaminated (by hepatitis or HIV viruses, for example). It would be very beneficial if more people could be convinced to donate such blood. In principle, it could command a high price, yet we observe that most blood collection is still organized on a voluntary basis. The problem of increasing the blood supply, therefore, is one of finding more voluntary donors. Why do we not observe more commercial transactions? Why is blood collection not governed by the price mechanism?

One reason is the adverse selection problem introduced by offering money for blood. The incidence of hepatitis and HIV among drug addicts is high because they tend to infect one another by sharing needles. At the same time, their need for cash is high. For those individuals, then, 'cash for blood' is a particularly attractive offer.

Any attempt to purchase blood in the market, therefore, is likely to attract a relatively large proportion of carriers. Such adverse selection is unacceptable if we cannot be 100 per cent certain that our blood-testing procedures will capture all contaminations, including possible new strains of viruses.

Conversely, a voluntary system presents no incentive whatsoever to people who know or suspect that they are carriers to volunteer for blood donation (Titmuss, 1971). Another reason is given in Box 8.4.

Box 4.2 Layoffs and lemons

Suppose you are working for a company fiercely threatened by international competition. During the imminent company restructuring, about 10 per cent of all white-collar workers are to be fired. However, it is also possible that the company will go bankrupt and, if that happens, every worker will lose his or her job. Do you think that it will make any difference to you whether you lose your job as a result of a restructuring or a bankruptcy?

In a world of asymmetrical information, it is reasonable to assume that your current employer has better information on your productivity than potential future employers. If you were to be fired as a result of restructuring, then future employers would probably think that, in the opinion of your current employer, you belong to the 10 per cent of workers with the lowest productivity. It would not be easy for you to find a new job and you may be forced to accept a level of pay that is much lower than you currently earn. The fact that you have been fired is a negative signal to future employers. There is no such negative signal if the company goes bankrupt as all workers would then have to leave. So, it should be easier for you to find a job if the company were to go bankrupt than if you were fired.

This effect has been confirmed in statistical research: the earnings of white-collar workers who have been displaced by lay-offs are significantly lower than those who have been displaced by plant closings. Also, white-collar workers displaced by lay-offs endure longer unemployment spells than those displaced by plant closings (Gibbons and Katz, 1991).

Hence, you are probably better off when you are fired as a result of bankruptcy rather than as a result of restructuring.

Fortunately, in many cases there are some solutions to the problems of hidden information, although they are often only partial solutions. As the essential problem is one of unobservability, we could try to increase its observability. In the case of health insurance, we may require applicants to undertake a medical examination. That would at least reveal already observable problems, but it would not reveal hereditary risks. Similarly, a used car buyer may insist on an inspection of the vehicle. Such an inspection can be carried out by a qualified dealer, although he has some interest in an active used car market for his brand of cars. In some countries, automobile associations arrange for independent inspections. In these countries the consumers have thus organized to try and overcome the information problem. Even then, an inspection can reveal apparent problems, but still cannot guarantee that the car is not a lemon.

Signalling

If we cannot directly improve the observability of the hidden information, perhaps we can do so in an indirect way. That is the idea behind the concept of **signalling**, pioneered by Michael Spence for job markets. Consider an employer looking to recruit a person who can absorb new information fast in a business context. Of course, all potential applicants will say that they possess this skill and only they will know their true level of skill. Thus, there is an information asymmetry between employer and applicants.

Spence proposed that going to a business school and getting an MBA can serve as a *signal* of that skill. The reason is that if the education signal is really correlated to the skill, employers are better off recruiting those who have have invested in that (costly) signal. In our chapter on mergers and acquisitions we will look at the example of start-up firms using the costly process of filing for an initial public offering (IPO) to signal their credibility as acquisition targets.

There are other strategies for dealing with hidden information. A number of them aim at the risk involved. For the adverse selection problem in health insurance, one solution is to pool the risks. If the insurance policy can be made a collective one for *all* inhabitants of Riskaria, the asymmetry problem is dealt with as the actuarial rates would reflect the true risks of the population. That, of course, is the solution adopted in the case of mutual insurance companies or insurance provided by the State.

An alternative strategy is to redistribute the risks involved. In a used car transaction, all the risk that the car is a lemon is located with the buyer. Part of that risk can be relocated if the seller can provide a warranty specifying risks that will remain with the seller for some period of time. Often, garages will provide such a warranty. The credibility of that arrangement is strongly dependent on the type of organization that provides it. You will not believe the junkyard garage as easily as an approved dealer, which has more of a *reputation* to protect (we return to this subject and trust in Chapter 8).

Finally, risks can sometimes be *segmented* (if only crudely) and dealt with in separate ways. In many countries, health risks are segmented into one portion that is dealt with privately and another that is covered collectively (by social security). In the used car market, you indeed have a choice between buying from another individual, the junkyard garage or approved dealers. You know that the risk characteristics of these market segments as well as the terms of trade will differ from each other.

To conclude this section, it is probably useful to emphasize that hidden information is a problem that may be manifest across markets as well as within organizations. It can prevent the development of a market for health insurance as well as the establishment of a mutual insurance company. Private information, unobservable to other parties, may preclude transactions across markets as well as within organizations. It does not matter whether you, as an individual, are trying to sell your Ford to another individual or whether you are acting in your capacity as the head of a department trying to sell a car, a person or an idea to another department. Hidden information, or only the suspicion of it, may hinder all such transactions.

From the examples above, however, we hope you have gained the insight that markets and organizations do differ in the kinds of solution they may provide for particular problems of hidden information. For some types of problem, the market has an appropriate solution, such as market segmentation. For other types, we need organizations such as mutual insurance companies or consumer associations. Hence, problems of hidden information lead us to the basic perspective of this book: markets and organizations provide differential solutions for the information problems involved in economic transactions. Which (mix of) coordination mechanism(s) is most appropriate depends on the kinds of information problems involved and the kinds of solutions offered by both mechanisms. We develop this perspective further in the next section, which deals with problems of hidden action.

4.3 Hidden action

Hidden action

Hidden action (or moral hazard) is another kind of information asymmetry that can develop in both market and organizational settings. It is, however, not an ex ante but an ex post phenomenon. That is to say, it refers to actions that parties in a transaction may take *after* they have agreed to execute the transaction. If those actions are unobservable to the other party in the transaction and if they may harm that other party's interest, then they may prevent the successful completion of the transaction. Worse still, the *anticipation* that such hidden actions are possible may prevent the transaction altogether. We illustrate these ideas with some examples, first from the insurance field once again.

Take fire insurance. In the Netherlands, personal fire insurance policies used to extend to damage to personal belongings from contact with burning objects, such as cigars and cigarettes. The latter coverage has been terminated now. The reason is that the insurance companies were confronted with a rising tide of claims for such coverage. An increasing amount of damage to, for instance, clothes and furniture was claimed to be the result of accidental contact with cigarettes and so on. Interestingly, the clothes tended to be not brand new, but last year's models.

Here we have a typical problem of hidden action. Once insurance is provided for such accidents, there is an *incentive effect* on the behaviour of the insured. They may start to behave with less caution, perhaps with some sloppiness or, in extreme cases, even with malicious intent. Examples of this kind

Moral hazard

gave rise to the term **moral hazard**. For the insurance company, it is impossible to observe whether the damage has indeed been caused by uncontrollable accidents or whether the behaviour of the insured had something to do with the damage. When, as a result, the number of claims becomes too high, the coverage cannot be continued.[3]

Travel insurance is a similar case in point, which also indicates one type of organizational solution. Under travel insurance, we may claim personal belongings that we have lost while travelling abroad. Such claims have also risen enormously. It is hard to believe that we have collectively become much more accident-prone. Some degree of deception and fraud must be present.

Apparently, a growing number of those insured try to finance their trip partly by making false travel insurance claims. In order to counter this trend, Dutch insurance companies have set up a joint venture that supervises a collective databank to register such claims. In addition, they have agreed on measures to take against possible fraud, such as joint exclusion of people who make an exceptionally high number of claims. Through a databank, they share information and may prevent some frauds, such as those involving one lost item being claimed twice under different policies and people with fraudulent behaviour going unnoticed as long as they 'hop' from one company to another. It will be clear that these organizational arrangements are (partial) countermeasures against the problem of the unobservability of hidden action.

When we leave the field of insurance, we find that problems of hidden action are plentiful elsewhere, too. Take the travelling salesperson as an example. One such person may be assigned by his company to a particular new region. Assume that he returns with a disappointing number of orders. Perhaps he has not put in enough effort and has chosen to pursue other interests. Perhaps, also, the competition is stiffer in that region, consumer tastes are different, the time of year is not right and so on. The point is that the company is unable to differentiate between these reasons because of a lack of observability.

One strategy to overcome such a lack, as discussed above, is to increase observability. This can be done by rotating the salespeople or conducting market research. Another strategy is to consider risk-sharing arrangements. If our salesman is paid a fixed salary, the risk is entirely on the company. Whatever amount of effort the salesman puts in, he always receives the same salary. So, he bears no risk in this transaction.[4] At the same time, there is little incentive for him to put in the required effort, let alone that extra bit of work. As a consequence, the entire risk of disappointing outcomes is on the company. If, instead, the salesman is paid an entirely variable salary (say, on a percentage basis), all the risk is on him: no orders, no salary. That will probably not be acceptable to him. Hence, the company may negotiate a salary with him that contains fixed as well as variable elements. The mix of these elements determines the specific allocation of risks (and incentives). In Chapter 7 we return to these kinds of solutions when we discuss agency theory.

As a final example, assume that you cannot even determine whether or not actions are correct, even if you observe them. The relation between a physician and a patient is a case in point. The very basis of the relation is the superior knowledge of the physician in medical affairs. Even if the physician were to disclose every step she took when treating you as a patient, you would normally not be able to determine whether her actions were as diligent and as responsible as they could be. There is a fundamental information asymmetry owing to the existence of professional knowledge. You simply do not have the knowledge to correctly interpret the signals regarding the physician's actions. You will want some assurance that this asymmetry is not being exploited against your best interests: you want the best treatment possible. In this case, the medical associations try to provide you with some such assurance by the development of professional codes of conduct, requiring the continuous education of their members and reviewing complaints that are brought to their attention (with sanctions in case of professionally substandard behaviour). While those organizational arrangements may give you some assurance, they are not able to guarantee high performance in all cases. In the end, professional ethics and individual responsibility are the only solutions with regard to the considerable discretion that the doctor has as a consequence of this fundamental information asymmetry (Arrow, 1963, 1973).[5]

To summarize this section, we may list some similarities and some differences between the concepts of hidden information (adverse selection) and hidden action (moral hazard). One basic similarity is that they are both a consequence of problems of unobservability. If, at any time, all parties in a transaction were able to observe all the information they needed to prepare and execute the transaction, both concepts would be irrelevant. A second similarity is that the information is unevenly distributed. One party has private information that is unobservable to the other party. That private information is valuable, in the sense that it could affect the terms of trade in the transaction. As the information is private, the owner can decide whether to disclose it or not. There is no incentive to do so when disclosure would harm the owner's private interest. A final similarity is that both problems may occur in both market and organizational settings. However, markets and organizations offer different solutions for these problems, albeit often partial ones.

Hidden information

Hidden action

Differences between both concepts are the following. **Hidden information** is an ex ante concept – it refers to private information that exists before parties agree on a transaction. **Hidden action** is an ex post concept – it pertains to private information that may develop during the execution of a transaction. Moreover, it denotes a particular type of private information – information about the unobservable behaviour of one of the parties in the transaction. Again, the behaviour is valuable in the sense that it affects the terms of trade in the transaction. If an insurance company knows negligence or fraud is involved, it will provide no coverage. There is no incentive for the insured party to disclose such information. The similarity and the differences between the concepts of moral hazard and adverse selection are also illustrated in Box 4.3. Both concepts are extensively applied in Chapter 12 on mergers and acquisitions.

Box 4.3 An insurer's worst nightmare

Insurance can reduce the devastating financial fallout from accidents, but it can also increase the risk of them happening.

Aeroplane crashes, oil spills and product failures are generally unpredictable events, but they are not totally random. Their occurrence can sometimes be influenced by human actions, and, although insurance can help to protect people from the financial impact of accidental misfortune, it may also inadvertently make them more accident-prone.

Insurance works on the principle of pooling risks and charging each customer a premium based only on the average risk of the pool. This approach has much appeal, but it also presents two problems, which economists call 'adverse selection' and 'moral hazard'.

▶

Customers who have the greatest incentive to buy insurance are likely to be those who pose the worst risk for insurers, hence adverse selection. A person will be keener to buy health insurance, for example, if he is already ill. This increases the odds that insurers will have to pay out claims and so may drive up premiums for healthier people. It should not, however, increase a society's total risk.

Moral hazard does. The term describes the temptation for a customer, once she has bought insurance, to take greater risks than she otherwise might have done. Moral hazard can take different forms. A customer might, for instance, increase the chances that he will incur a loss, so somebody with car insurance may drive more recklessly than he would if he were uninsured. Even though an insured person may try to reduce the odds of a mishap, he may do so in a way that increases the size of the potential loss. A firm that discovers it has a defective product, for example, may withhold its findings to avoid early lawsuits it has to settle itself, while raising the risk of a huge later payout that falls on its insurance company.

Source: The Economist, 29 July 1995

Assuming that these concepts have now been sufficiently clarified by the use of examples, we proceed to introduce the basic concepts in the economics of information somewhat more formally. This will help to define their exact meaning and will also allow us to use them in subsequent chapters in these precise terms.

4.4 The value of information

In a world where everybody knew everything, the economics of information would have no place. Information would not be scarce, so economics would have nothing to say about it. The *economic aspect* of information pertains to its scarcity and the value that scarce information may have.

We illustrate this first with the example of an individual decisionmaker who has to choose an action in the face of uncertainty. In the language of game theory (the subject of the next chapter) this is the situation of an individual playing against Nature. In this section we show how the value of information can be determined in such a game.

You are the marketing manager of Standard Breakfast Corporation. A new product has been developed and you have to decide whether or not to introduce it. If the new product is a success, you gain 8 (million dollars). If it is a failure you lose 2 (unfortunately also million dollars). Your estimate that the new product will be a success is 0.3, that it will be a failure 0.7. What do you decide? Figure 4.2 summarizes the situation.

If you are risk-neutral, you should simply calculate the expected value of introducing the new product:

$$0.3 \times 8 + 0.7 \times (-2) = 1 \text{ (million dollars)}$$

The result is positive, so you should introduce the new product.

Decision tree

Another way to describe the situation is by using a **decision tree** (Figure 4.3). A decision tree may have two kinds of node: nodes where an individual has to

STATES OF NATURE

		Success	Failure
ACTS	Introduce	8	-2
	Do not introduce	0	0
Probabilities of states		0.3	0.7

Figure 4.2 An individual decision under uncertainty: whether or not to introduce a new product

choose an act (represented by squares) and nodes where Nature chooses her moves by means of a random process (represented by circles). Working backwards (that is, from right to left), we can calculate the expected value for each node. In Figure 4.3, the expected value for node A is:

$$0.3 \times 8 + 0.7 \times (-2) = 1$$

For node B it is 0. Therefore, in node C you will choose A rather than B. The expected value for node C is 1 (million dollars). That is the expected value of this game against Nature.

Now, suppose that you could do test marketing. Suppose, first, that test marketing gives you **complete information**. By complete information we mean information that removes all uncertainty. So, by test marketing first, you will know for sure whether or not the new product will be a success.

How valuable is complete information in this case? There is a probability of 0.3 that test marketing will tell you the new product will be a success (see Figure 4.2). As you now know for sure that it will be successful, you introduce the new product. Without test marketing, you also introduce the new product. So, there is a probability of 0.3 that test marketing will not alter your decision. There is a probability of 0.7 that test marketing will show the product to be a failure. You then decide not to introduce the new product, in which case you save 2 (million dollars). So, by test marketing you have a 0.7 probability of saving 2. The value of the information from test marketing is:

Complete information

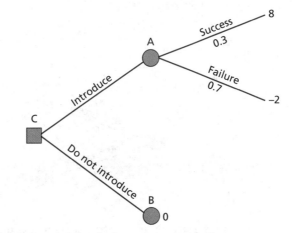

Figure 4.3 Decision tree: introducing a new product

$$0.3 \times 0 + 0.7 \times 2 = 1.4 \text{ (million dollars)}$$

If test marketing costs you less than that amount, it is rational to test market your product.

In practice, test marketing seldom gives you complete information. In most cases there will be some uncertainty left. For example, if test marketing is successful, your estimate that the new product will really be a success may be revised to 0.8. If test marketing is a failure, your estimate that the new product will really be a failure may be 0.9. The situation is summarized in Figure 4.4. The information in the figure would be complete if the first and the second row each contained one 1 and one 0. As it is, the information is incomplete.

		THE NEW PRODUCT WILL REALLY BE	
		a success	a failure
TEST MARKETING IS	a success	0.8	0.2
	a failure	0.1	0.9

Figure 4.4 Incomplete information from test marketing

In order to determine the expected value of this incomplete information, consider Figure 4.5. Working backwards, we calculate the expected value for each node as follows. For node A, the expected value is:

$$0.8 \times 8 + 0.2 \times (-2) = 6$$

In node C, you will choose A, so the expected value for node C is also 6. For node B the expected value is:

$$0.1 \times 8 + 0.9 \times (-2) = -1$$

In node D, you decide not to introduce, so the expected value for node D is 0.

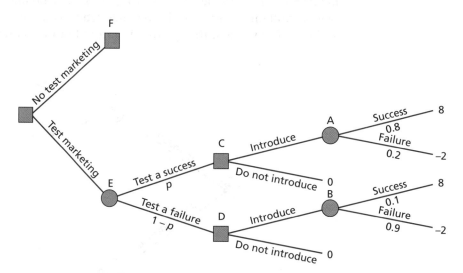

Figure 4.5 Decision tree: introducing a new product with test marketing

To find the expected value in node E, we need the probability, p, that test marketing will be successful. We can calculate p as follows. The probability that the new product will really be a success is equal to:

$$p \times 0.8 + (1 - p) \times 0.1$$

This expression must be equal to 0.3, which is the known probability that the new product will be a success. So, we have:

$$p \times 0.8 + (1 - p) \times 0.1 = 0.3$$

Hence:

$$p = 2/7$$

The expected value in node E is $2/7 \times 6 = 12/7$.

The value of information from test marketing can now be calculated by comparing the expected value in node E with the expected value in node F, which we know is 1. So, the value of the information from test marketing is:

$$12/7 - 1 = 5/7 \text{ (million dollars)}$$

which is about $714,000. Again, if test marketing costs you less than this amount, you should test market your product.

4.5 Summary: information problems for markets and organizations

In this chapter, information has been examined from an economic viewpoint. It has been shown how information can be seen as an economic good, deriving its value from its scarcity.

The chapter took an ideal market with perfect competition as its point of departure. Under perfect competition, prices act as sufficient statistics for conveying all the necessary information to the market parties. It was shown that perfect competition can work only under conditions of very limited information requirements. If goods are not homogeneous, for instance, it may be necessary to signal a quality dimension to potential buyers. The price mechanism is often insufficient for conveying such information. Also, under conditions of uncertainty, the price mechanism may break down as a coordination device. Particular attention has been paid to situations of information asymmetry. In such situations, information is unevenly distributed. This introduces the risk that some economic players will use their informational advantage to gain an economic advantage in executing transactions.

In the economics of information, a fundamental distinction is made between ex ante and ex post information problems. Adverse selection (or hidden information) is an ex ante information problem. It arises when one party has private information that is relevant to a potential transaction. Private information is unobservable to the other party. In the case of adverse selection, the private information already exists *before* parties agree to execute a transaction. We have used the examples of setting up health insurance in

Riskaria and selling used cars to illustrate the concept. Hidden information, or only the suspicion of it, may hinder transactions across markets as well as within organizations. Markets and organizations offer different solutions, however, to the information problems inherent in adverse selection.

Moral hazard (or hidden action) can also develop in both market and organizational settings. This concept refers to an ex post information problem. It applies *after* parties have agreed to execute a transaction. Hidden information and hidden action both pertain to private information that one of the parties in a transaction may possess. In the case of hidden action, this information concerns unobservable behaviour of one of the parties in executing the transaction. This information is valuable as it would affect the terms of the trade, if the other party were aware of it. However, the party with private information has no incentive to disclose it. Again, markets and organizations offer different solutions for overcoming the problem of hidden action.

Finally, we illustrated one approach to determining the value of information. It was shown how we should distinguish between decisions where complete information can be obtained (removing all uncertainty) and decisions under conditions of remaining uncertainty (with incomplete information). In both cases we made use of a decision tree to sketch the decision context. The decision tree depicted a game of one individual playing against Nature. In the next chapter, we explore more complicated games, involving two or more players.

Questions

1 There are many jokes about the laziness of civil servants. Do you think that those jokes contain an element of truth? Let us, for the sake of argument, suppose that government officials are lazier than employees working for a business firm. Can you explain this phenomenon by using the concepts of hidden information and hidden action?

2 Section 4.2 discussed the market for 'lemons'. The large price difference between new (unregistered) cars and ones that have just left the showroom can be explained by the information asymmetry between buyers and sellers of used cars: the seller knows if the car is a 'lemon' but the buyer does not. Do you see another explanation for the large price difference between new cars and cars that have just left the showroom?

3 Suppose you are the negotiator for I.G. Metall, an important union in Germany. You expect that, in the next four years, many companies will have to reduce their labour force substantially. You know that if a company fires 10 per cent of its employees, there might be a 'lemon effect'. What would you demand from employers in order to eliminate that effect?

4 Mutual insurance companies exist in most European countries, together with insurance companies owned by investors. Most mutual insurance companies were founded by farmers and many today still have close ties with the agricultural sector. In the first decades of the eighteenth century in countries such as Belgium, France, Germany and the Netherlands, a class of very small farmers owning the land and the farm they tended emerged (in previous centuries many farms had been owned by the nobility). These

farmers were quite poor. They produced their own food and sold the rest in local markets. Their farmhouses were usually thatched with straw or hay. Fire brigades did not exist in the countryside. If a farm caught fire, the farmer lost everything he owned, including his means of subsistence. Investor-owned insurance companies existed in those days, but most refused to insure these small farms. Can you explain why mutual fire insurance companies arose in those days in the agricultural sector?

Suggested further reading

Arrow, K. J. (1985), 'The economics of agency', in J. W. Pratt and R. J. Zeckhauser (eds), *Principals and Agents: The structure of business*, Boston, MA: Harvard Business School Press.

Birchler, U. and Bütler M. (2007), *Information Economics*, London: Routledge.

Raiffa, H. (1968), *Decision Analysis: Introductory lectures on choices under uncertainty*, Reading, MA: Addison-Wesley.

Notes

1 Brand names are thus organizational solutions to such information problems. The property rights of a brand name usually belong to an organization. They are sometimes sold on the market, for instance through takeovers, then becoming the property of another organization.

2 An actuary is an expert in the determination of insurance risks. A well-known alternative description of an actuary is 'someone who found life as an accountant too exciting'.

3 A sociologist would rightly point to the importance of norms regulating this behaviour. Of course, the fact that such coverage used to be possible and now no longer is, has to do with a deterioration of norms regarding use of insurance. All economic transactions are embedded in a set of norms regulating behaviour, as discussed in Chapter 3.

4 In the longer term, he may, of course, risk being fired. For the time being, we consider transactions one at a time.

5 Of course, we could conclude this example by pointing towards the insurance implications again, certainly in the context of the 'litigation culture' in the USA. However, there are huge international differences in dealing with potential medical malpractice through the legal system. These differences show the importance of the environmental context, including the social embeddedness of such transactions (Granovetter, 1985).

5.1 Introduction

In the previous chapter we discussed the value of information. As an example, we used the decisionmaking process involved in choosing whether or not to introduce a new product. As we saw in Section 4.4, that situation can be modelled as a game against Nature. We saw how an individual can make up his mind what to do in the face of uncertainty.

In this chapter, we introduce game theory. Game theory is concerned with situations in which there are two or more players. Moreover, these players have to make interdependent decisions. By that we mean any player in the game is affected by what the others do. Each player in making his or her decision has to take into account the other players' decisions. We assume in Sections 5.2 to 5.5 that players are rational decisionmakers who act only in their own interest. Moreover, we assume that each player knows that other players are rational.[1] These are the assumptions of 'classical' game theory. In Section 5.6, we move on to 'evolutionary' game theory, which studies the development of populations rather than the rational decisionmaking of individuals.

There are several types of game. Two important characteristics of games are the number of:

- players involved;
- stages in the game.

Combining these two characteristics in Figure 5.1, we can distinguish the types of game we discuss in this chapter.

	2 players	N players (N > 2)
1 stage	Coordination game (Section 5,2) Single-stage prisoner's dilemma (Section 5.5.1)	Auctions (Section 5.4)
M stages (M > 1)	Entry game (Section 5.3)	Iterated prisoner's dilemma for many players (Section 5.5.2) Evolutionary game theory (Section 5.6)

Figure 5.1 Six types of game in this chapter

The purpose of this chapter is to acquaint you with some important insights from game theory. Game theory has become an increasingly important tool in a number of sciences, including economics. By introducing game theory here, we hope to give you a feel for the different types of setting in which economic decisions can be made. An important message in this chapter is that different settings (different structures of games) provide different incentives for players and allow different strategies of play. It is therefore important to discern the basic features of any economic game in theory or practice.

5.2 The coordination game

Coordination game

Simultaneous and sequential games

We start with an example of a game between two players. The game is played in one stage. The main point to note in this game is how players can coordinate their actions. Therefore, we call it the **coordination game**. The coordination game introduces the important distinction between **simultaneous and sequential games**.

There are many situations in which two or more players have to coordinate their decisions in order to reach the outcome that is best for all of them. An example is the standardization of a new technology. Suppose that Philips and Sony have to decide on the standard specifications of a new piece of electronic technology – say, a combination of video and compact disc technology called VIDISC (see also Box 5.1). Both have been working on this breakthrough.

There are two types of system both can choose. If they choose the same type of system, the pay-offs for each of them will be larger than if they choose different systems. The reason is that, with different systems, they have to compete not only in terms of the brand chosen by consumers, but also in terms of the system chosen.[2] The VI technology (video technology with added CD facilities) promises larger pay-offs for both than the DISC technology (CD technology with added video facilities). VI is twice as attractive for both players as DISC. Figure 5.2 gives a handy summary of the main game theory features of this story.

The numbers in Figure 5.2 indicate the pay-offs to both players. The first number always gives the pay-off for the row player (Philips in this example), the second, the pay-off to the column player. The pay-off is the reward enjoyed by a player at the end of the game. For example, if Philips and Sony both choose VI, they would both gain $400 million.[3] If both choose DISC, they will

		SONY	
		VI	DISC
PHILIPS	VI	4,4	−2,−2
	DISC	−2,−2	2,2

Figure 5.2 Philips and Sony with the VIDISC technology

Box 5.1 Philips, Sony, Toshiba and video disc in the real world

The example of VIDISC technology was included in the first edition of this book, which appeared in 1991. Meanwhile, it has become clear that the 'game' of video disc technology has played out in the real world as well. Here are some of the features of this real-world game.

■ More players are involved than just Sony and Philips. At least ten electronics firms have an interest in setting the standard for digital video discs (DVDs). DVDs have a much higher data storage capacity than CDs and are expected to replace them in the future.
■ Initially, there were two camps of players, Philips/Sony versus Toshiba/Matsushita/Time Warner. Both camps tried to set the standard for DVDs on their own, thus risking a 'standards war', as observed for videos but not for CDs.
■ In September 1995 the two camps reached an agreement to form one consortium in order to set a joint technology standard.
■ However, within that consortium, the haggling over each other's contributions continued. This focused on the licence fees that individual players could require for their contributions to the common standard. The lengthy haggling could jeopardize a rapid and successful introduction of the new technology.
■ In 1996, Philips and Sony threatened individually to sell their licences to other hardware and software firms interested in DVDs. That did not undermine the common standard, but required other interested firms to obtain the necessary licences from two separate camps again.
■ In 1997, Philips, Sony and Pioneer (the three main DVD patent holders) announced their cooperation. Other firms wishing to produce DVDs would be required to pay a 3.5 per cent royalty fee (on the sales price) to these three firms.
■ For the next generation of DVDs, however, a 'standards war' broke out again between Toshiba (High Definition DVD) and Sony (Blu-ray technology). At the time of writing this fourth edition of our book, it was unclear which standard would prevail in the market.

This real-world 'game' illustrates some features that we introduce in this chapter. We move from two-player to N(>2)-player games. We discuss the potential benefits of cooperation, such as in consortia or cartels, as well as some inherent difficulties. In particular, we show that, for individual players, the central question often is whether to cooperate or defect.

---

both gain $200 million. The worst situation would be if one company chooses VI while the other chooses DISC. In that case both would incur a loss of $200 million. Which of these results will come about?

That depends on the way the game is played. If both players have to choose simultaneously, without any information on the other's preferences, no prediction can be made.[4] The reason is that it is not clear what each player will assume the other player will do. If Philips, for example, expects Sony to choose DISC, Philips may be tempted to choose DISC, too. However, if one player is allowed to move *after* the other, we can predict that both companies will choose the same technology. That is because, for the second player, it is always the most advantageous choice to follow the first player's move.

Suppose Philips has to move first and Sony can observe Philips' move. We can now represent the game by drawing a **game tree** (Figure 5.3). A game tree is similar to a decision tree, as introduced in Chapter 4, except that in a game

Game tree

tree there are two rational players acting in their own interests, while in a decision tree there is only one. At the end nodes of a game tree, two pay-offs are given. The first pay-off is for the player who moves first, the second pay-off for the other player.

Philips has to move first. What should Philips do? Assuming that the required information is available, the Philips manager who has to make the decision could look at the game tree in Figure 5.3. The Philips manager will see immediately that Sony will choose VI in node B and DISC in node C. So, the Philips manager sees that whatever she chooses, Sony will choose, too. So, Philips chooses VI and Sony follows. Both players receive $400 million.

In this game, it is important that one player be allowed to move first. In the sequential game, it is easy to coordinate the choices made by both players. In a simultaneous game, it is not at all obvious how coordination between the two players' choices can be obtained.

Simultaneous game

When is a game a **simultaneous game**? Is it really necessary that both players make their choices at exactly the same time? No, of course not. Both companies may make their choices at different dates. The point is that, when Sony has to make its choice, it does not know what Philips has chosen or will choose. It is that lack of information which distinguishes the simultaneous game from the sequential game.

In this game, it is in Philips' interest to tell Sony about its choice as soon as it has made a final decision. For Sony, there is no reason not to believe the message it receives from Philips. So, in this game, it is quite likely that reality is represented better by a sequential game than by a simultaneous game.

A sequential game can be represented by a matrix specifying the pay-offs or by a game tree. So, Figure 5.2 can represent both a simultaneous game and a sequential game. If the matrix represents a sequential game, we also need to know who moves first before we can draw the game tree.

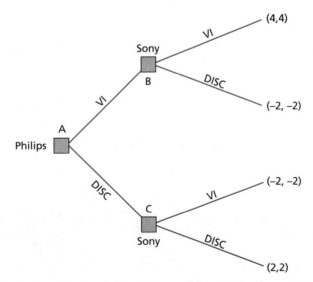

Figure 5.3 Game tree for the sequential coordination game

A simultaneous game can be represented by a matrix giving the pay-offs and by a game tree. The game tree for the simultaneous coordination game is given in Figure 5.4. Figure 5.4 is quite similar to Figure 5.3, except for the oval around Sony's two decision nodes. That oval represents Sony's information set. It indicates the fact that Sony cannot distinguish between the two nodes at the time it has to make its decision. Sony's manager simply does not know whether he is in node B or in node C at the time he has to make his choice. Because of that lack of information, the game has no predictable outcome.

The coordination game is a very simple game. If there are only two players, the best solution is reached if the players can communicate (Philips and Sony will simply agree to choose VI). If the number of players is large, it may be necessary to establish a rule. An example is on which side of the road to drive.

In a country with only two car-owners, the government need not establish a rule – the two car-owners can simply agree to drive either on the right or on the left. If the number of car-owners is very large, it is difficult and costly for all of them to make an agreement. In such a case we see that the government establishes a rule.[5]

In a duet for violin and piano, the two players must play at the same tempo. The pay-off for both of them (in terms of their satisfaction or the number of CDs they sell) is zero if they play at different tempos. However, they can easily agree on the tempo to use. If the number of players becomes large, as in a symphony orchestra, it becomes much more difficult to agree on a tempo (that is one of the reasons for a symphony orchestra needing a conductor).

Philips and Sony, the two car-owners and the two musicians can reach the best solution to the coordination game through mutual adjustment (see Chapter 3). A large number of car-owners or the members of a symphony orchestra, however, may need another coordination mechanism, such as standardization or direct supervision, to reach the best solution.

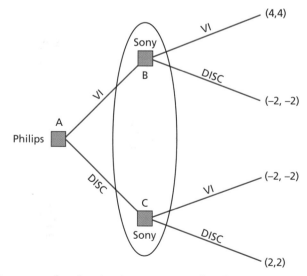

Figure 5.4 Game tree for the simultaneous coordination game

This section has illustrated two features of games that are important in the context of economic approaches to organizations.

1 The distinction between simultaneous and sequential games. It was shown that in sequential games, where the moves of the first player can be observed by the second player, coordination is easily achieved. The second player has *information* to base a decision on. In contrast, simultaneous games lack such information and, hence, have no predictable outcome.

2 How co-ordination between two (or a small number of) players can be achieved through mutual adjustment. Because of the interdependence of the players' decisions, however, this coordination mechanism breaks down as the number of players increases. It then has to be replaced with other coordination mechanisms (see Chapter 3).

5.3 The entry game

Two-stage games

In this section, we move from one-stage games to **two-stage games** by considering the entry game. The entry game is a sequential game between a monopolist and a potential entrant. Suppose, first, that the monopolist restricts output and keeps prices high. That gives a potential entrant the opportunity to enter the industry. We analyse that situation first as a one-stage game and then as a two-stage game.

Suppose that a telecommunications company – let us call it National Telecom – has a legal monopoly in the market for mobile telecommunications. The firm knows, however, that the legal protection it now enjoys will not last for ever and predicts that, within a few years, other companies will be allowed to enter the market.

Suppose, next, that there is a potential entrant, Mobicom, which possesses the know-how and resources to enter that market. Will Mobicom enter the market? Is there anything National can do to prevent entry by Mobicom? These are the questions considered in the entry game.

In a sequential game like the entry game, it is known which player moves first. Let us suppose that Mobicom moves first. Mobicom has to decide whether or not to enter the market. It knows that National charges relatively high prices. Mobicom knows that it will make a nice profit if National maintains that price level after it enters the market. If National lowers its price substantially after entry, however, Mobicom will not be able to make a profit. What should Mobicom do? We suppose that Mobicom knows exactly what National will earn in each situation. The game tree representing the choices is given in Figure 5.5 (overleaf).

Mobicom's decision depends on the price level that National will choose after its entry. Mobicom will have to put itself into National's shoes in order to predict what National will do after its entry. It is quite easy to predict what National will do if Mobicom stays out. National's pay-off with high prices is 16; with low prices it is only 7. Therefore, National will choose high prices if Mobicom stays out.

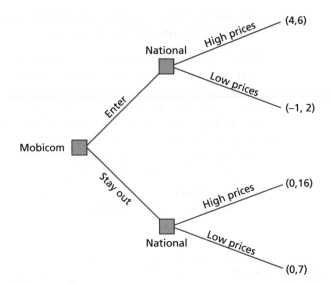

Figure 5.5 Game tree for an entry game

Much more relevant for Mobicom is predicting what National will do after its entry. It is easy for Mobicom to see that, with high prices, National will earn 6 and with low prices only 2. Mobicom knows that National is a rational player, acting only in its own interest, so predicts that National will choose high prices after its entry. Thus, Mobicom enters and knows that it will earn a profit of 4. This illustrates an important principle for solving sequential games. It is the **principle of looking ahead and reasoning backwards**. By looking ahead and then reasoning backwards, Mobicom is able to predict that entry will be profitable.

Principle of looking ahead and reasoning backwards

Is there anything that National can do to deter entry? Suppose that, before Mobicom makes its decision, National threatens to choose low prices after its entry. If Mobicom believes that National will carry out its threat, it will not enter because with low prices, it will incur a loss. It is quite likely, however, that Mobicom will not believe National will actually carry out its threat. After all, if entry has in fact occurred, it is no longer in National's interest to lower its prices. National's threat is not a **credible threat**.

Credible threat

Suppose that National already has a large network in place before Mobicom makes its decision. The result of having that large network is National faces higher fixed costs and, thus, earns a smaller profit. However, if entry occurs, National already has a large network in place. It can now lower its prices and attract many new customers for very low additional costs. Indeed, if entry occurs, National is now better off with low prices than with high prices. Figure 5.6 shows the revised pay-offs that result from having that large network. Mobicom will now predict low prices if it enters. Mobicom knows that it will incur a loss in case of entry and decides not to enter. If National now threatens to lower prices after entry, Mobicom will believe this. National's threat is now a credible threat.

We have seen what happens if National has a small network and what happens if National has a large network. If National can choose first between

Figure 5.6 Game tree for another entry game

having a small and a large network, which should it choose? It is a two-stage, sequential game in which National chooses first between a small and a large network, then Mobicom decides whether or not to enter and, finally, National chooses between high and low prices. The game tree for that sequence is given in Figure 5.7, which combines the two game trees in Figures 5.5 and 5.6 into one larger tree.

Should National choose a small or a large network? How should Mobicom react to National's choice concerning the size of its network? How should

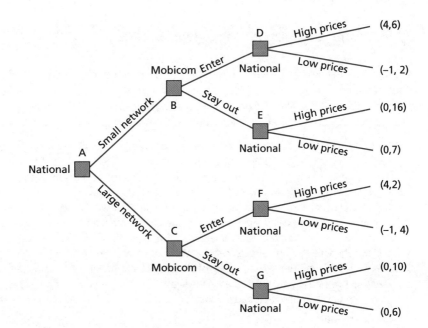

Figure 5.7 An entry game with commitment

National react to Mobicom's decision? Those three questions can be answered by applying the principle of looking ahead and reasoning backwards through the two stages of the game tree. In nodes D and E, National will choose high prices. So, in node B, Mobicom will decide to enter. In node F, National will choose low prices and, in node G, it will choose high prices. Mobicom knows this, so, in node C, it decides to stay out. Now National knows that, with a small network, Mobicom will enter. The result for National is a profit of 6. It also knows that when it decides to build a large network, Mobicom will not enter. The result is that it will enjoy a profit of 10. So, National decides to build a large network in order to prevent Mobicom's entry.

The point of this example is that, by building a large network, National can commit itself to lower its prices if entry occurs. In the language of game theory, **commitment** is the process whereby a player irreversibly alters the pay-offs in advance so that it will be in his own interest to carry out a threat. In this example, by building a large network, National alters the pay-offs in such a way that, after Mobicom's entry, it is in National's self-interest to carry out the threat of lowering prices. Hence, such commitment makes National's threat credible.

Commitment

From this section you can infer the following.

- In a sequential game, you should *anticipate your rival's response*. You can do so by applying the principle of looking ahead and reasoning backwards through the game tree. If the game tree shows more than one stage, the principle also applies.
- A threat can be made credible by showing commitment. By undertaking actions that demonstrate commitment, one player can show another that it is in his own interest to carry out the threat. In order to be effective, commitments must be *observable* and *credible*. Box 5.2 illustrates the dangers of making threats that are not credible because they are not backed up by binding commitments.[6]

Box 5.2 Commitment in labour negotiations

Labour negotiations can be viewed from the perspective of game theory as well. In any negotiation, one party may attempt to formulate a 'take it or leave it' offer at a certain stage. In order for such a strategy to be effective, the 'or leave it' part must be credible. If the other party does not believe that is the final offer, the negotiations may be seriously disturbed, as the following story illustrates.

For a time, General Electric in its labour negotiations used a strategy known as Boulwarism (named after Lemuel R. Boulware, the GE vice-president of employee and public relations who introduced it in the 1950s), under which its initial offer, chosen after careful research into wages and working conditions in GE and its competitors, was its final offer. Although this take-it-or-leave-it offer was intended to be fair and acceptable to the workers, the union strongly opposed this technique – understandably, given . . . the amount of bargaining power to be gained from commitment. One union response was likewise to present a set of demands and announce they were inflexible. Another was to behave disruptively during negotiations. Another was to strike. Yet another was to complain to the National Labor Relations Board, which found that GE was guilty of an unfair labour practice; the adjudicator considered the lack of real concessions by GE during negotiations as evidence that GE was not bargaining in good faith. By 1970, the union's opposition had induced GE to cease using the commitment strategy.

Source: McMillan (1991)

5.4 Auctions

We now turn to a situation involving more than two players in a single-stage game. A prototypical example is the auction.

Auctions come in various shapes and forms. An important distinction is between the **open auction**, in which the bids of all parties are observable, and the **sealed bid auction**, in which that is not the case. Again, we shall see that the observability of information plays a crucial role.

Imagine that, as a manager, you are attending the open auction of a piece of land that is adjacent to your factory. As you are contemplating an expansion that exceeds the boundaries of your current acreage, you are strongly interested in this additional piece of land. You think the land should be worth more to you than to competing bidders, but are not sure. Several people you do not know are attending the auction. What should your bidding strategy be? How should the seller set up the auction in order to extract the highest possible price from the audience? As we shall see, the answers to those questions are not unrelated.

If the seller sets up the auction as an 'increasing bid' competition, the optimal strategy for you as a potential buyer is straightforward. It is to remain in the bidding competition until the price rises to your own valuation of the land and drop out of the competition as soon as the price moves beyond your own valuation. If all bidders are rational and execute the same strategy, the land will be transferred to the buyer with the highest private valuation of the land.[7] Note that during the bidding process you will also thus be informed of the other players' private valuations of the land. As the bidding process unfolds, you are able to observe what those private valuations are by noticing who remains in the competition and who drops out. The bidding process forces the players to reveal their preferences.

Such an increasing bid competition is, however, not entirely optimal from the seller's point of view. In order to grasp this point, imagine that you are among the last two bidders for the property. One of the two must have the highest private valuation – say it is you. However, the other player will then be the first to drop out of the competition. He drops out as soon as the price rises just beyond his own private valuation. That may still be far below your own private valuation, however. Hence, there is good news for you: you acquire the land at a price substantially below the level you were willing to pay. Conversely, it is bad news for the seller: her land could have fetched far more than it did.

There are several strategies the seller could employ to counter that risk. One of the most interesting is to use a **Dutch auction** instead of an increasing bid competition. In a Dutch auction, the auctioneer starts with a very high price (a price that is, in the auctioneer's opinion, well above the highest private value of all bidders). The auctioneer cries out loudly prices that slowly decrease. This process stops when one of the bidders cries out 'mine'.

In a Dutch auction you have to make your bid (that is, you have to cry out 'mine') without knowing what other bidders might be willing to bid. So, if the piece of land is worth \$1 million to you and you estimate that it is worth \$700,000 to the second highest bidder, then your best strategy would seem to be to cry out 'mine' when the price is \$701,000. That, however, is risky because your estimate may be too low. If you think that the private value of the second highest bidder is somewhere between \$650,000 and \$750,000 with an expected value of \$700,000 your best strategy is probably to cry out 'mine' at a price level somewhere between \$751,000 and \$701,000.

In a Dutch auction, the seller probably receives at least a part of the difference between the private values of the highest and the second highest bidders. For the seller there is also a risk, however. In an increasing bid auction the auctioneer can start with a minimum price. In a Dutch auction there is no such minimum.

In order to establish a minimum the seller can convert the auction from a one-stage to a two-stage game. In the first stage, the game is played as an increasing bid competition. The winner of the first stage gets a financial reward (a fixed fee or a small percentage of his bid), but not the land. The land is subsequently auctioned in a second stage, which takes the form of a Dutch auction. If, in the second stage, no one cries out 'mine' before the first-stage price is reached, the winner of the first stage has to buy the land for the first-stage price. The bidders in the first stage are usually professional bidders who bid in order to obtain the fee for winning the first stage. They usually do not want the land for themselves.

Notice several interesting features of the open auction game:

- it is a game with private information: each bidder's private valuation of the land;
- most of this private information is revealed as the game is played, but in the increasing bid case, only the winner's private information can ultimately remain private;
- the design of the game determines the incentives for players to reveal their private information and, by adding a second-stage Dutch auction, the seller attempts to induce potential buyers above the first-stage price to reveal their private information;
- the private information is valuable – the seller is prepared to pay the first-stage winner a price (the fee or percentage) in order to participate in this design.[8]

Sealed bid (one-stage) auction

In a **sealed-bid (one-stage) auction**, all bidders have to submit their bids in a sealed envelope at the same time. The most striking difference between it and the open auction is that you do not learn about the private information of the other bidders during the auction process. You get only one chance to place your bid under conditions of uncertainty about the other players' private valuations.

What is a good strategy for bidders when sellers design the game as a sealed-bid, one-stage auction? To derive the answer, first consider the case where you, as a bidder, have full information on all the other bidders' valuations. If your valuation is the highest, what should you bid? It seems clear that you should bid just above the second highest valuation. If you bid lower than that, you risk losing the competition. However, bidding much higher makes no sense as you would pay more than needed (colloquially, you would leave money on the table).

The full information case gives a clue as to how to proceed in the more realistic case in which none of the bidders knows the competitors' valuations. Say you are contemplating submitting a bid for a business unit that is divested by its parent company. The parent has solicited the help of an investment banker to set up a one-stage sealed bid auction.

First, you have to determine the likely competition. Which other companies may be interested in acquiring that particular business unit? Which companies are bidding only because they think that they can run the business unit better (financial bidders)? Which other companies, in addition, believe that they could realize *synergies* by combining the business unit with their current operations (strategic bidders)?

As a potential bidder, you must determine that there is a reasonable chance your valuation is the highest of all (you are the most strategic bidder). If so, the prescription is to estimate what the second highest valuation is most likely to be and submit a bid slightly above that level.

To illustrate, assume that the value of the business unit on sale is €100 million at its current performance level. That performance level can already be raised on a standalone basis, however. If the performance level is raised to 'best practice level', the value increases to €120 million. That means €120 million represents the maximum amount the best financial bidder should be willing to submit. However, strategic bidders can go beyond that level if they can also raise the performance level of the unit and, in addition, realize synergy benefits. If the combined effects of those two factors are more than €20 million, then strategic bidders can win over financial bidders. If you are the most strategic bidder, the rule is to submit a bid just above the valuation level of your best competitor.

The example above highlights the fact that the value of the bid you, as the most strategic bidder, submit depends on a number of estimates:

- the performance level to which you can raise the acquired unit;
- the synergies to be gained by combining this unit with your own operations;
- the private valuation of your best competitor in the auction.

It is possible that you will make one or more mistakes in these various estimates as it is highly unlikely all your estimates will be correct. Some will be too pessimistic; some too optimistic. In circumstances of intense competition by many bidders, however, it is quite likely that the winner turns out to have made the most optimistic estimates. If you are the winner, there may therefore be good news as well as bad news in that outcome. The good news is that you have acquired the business unit. The bad news may be that you have based your calculations on the most optimistic calculations of all the competitors. That phenomenon is called the **winner's curse** in game theory. It refers to situations where winners obtain the prize not because the value is truly highest for them, but because of their optimistic expectations.

Winner's curse

The main difference between open and sealed bid auctions pertains to the uncertainty about other players' private valuations. In open auctions, most of the players' private valuations become observable as the process unfolds. Only the winner's private valuation may remain unobservable. Sellers who wish to extract more value for their property may therefore wish to design the auction process differently – by for instance, adding a second-stage Dutch auction. However, because of the open nature of the auction, a rational winner will never pay more than his private valuation. In sealed bid auctions, though, the private valuations of all players remain unobservable. In situations of uncertainty regarding the true value of the auctioned object, all private valuations must be based on estimates (in our example of a divested business unit, on three estimates). In such situations, it is possible that the winner is inflicted with the 'winner's curse', obtaining the prize as a consequence of making the most optimistic estimates – Box 5.3 relates an example. We return to the winner's curse in Chapter 12, on mergers and acquisitions, where we also examine a potential cause of the phenomenon in the M&A context.

Box 5.3 The winners curse in the classroom

To demonstrate the winner's curse, Bazerman and Samuelson (1983) held a series of auctions in an MBA classroom. The object was a glass jar filled with $8-worth of coins. The value of the jar was not revealed, but students could look at it and make their own estimates. Thereafter, they submitted their sealed bids.

Over a large number of such auctions, the average bid was $5.13, while the average *winning* bid was $10.01. On average, the winner therefore lost $2.01, a clear example of the winner's curse.

Source: Bazerman and Samuelson (1983)

While the winner's curse is a potential problem for buyers in an auction, there is also a potential problem for sellers: *collusion* between buyers. We encountered collusion in Chapter 3 as an example of *mutual adjustment* between economic actors – for instance, in cartels. It can also occur in auctions, particularly if there is only a small number of potential buyers (and it is known who these are). Buyers can secretly agree not to drive prices up. Alternatively, they can agree how to divide the auction's objects between them. Sometimes it is even possible for bidders in 'increasing bid' auctions to use the early rounds to *signal* their intentions. Box 5.4 gives examples. Needless to say, collusion between buyers may prevent the seller from obtaining the full value for the items in the auction. Clever auction design needs to mitigate the risk of collusion (see Klemperer, 2004).

Box 5.4 Signalling and collusion in auctions

Ascending-bid auctions, particularly when they involve only a few bidders, are often susceptible to collusion, since participants can use early rounds to signal their intentions.

In 1999, Germany sold some mobile phone spectrums by auction, with one rule specifying that any new bid had to exceed the previous high bid by 10 per cent. Two serious bidders were involved.

One company bid 18.18 million marks on blocks 1 to 5 and 20 million on blocks 6 to 10. Why the difference? Note that 18.18 million plus 10 per cent is just about 20 million. The first company was sending the second a message: 'We think 20 million is the right price: let's not compete to push it up.' The signalling strategy worked: the auction ended after two rounds, and each bidder got half the blocks at the same low price.

Source: H. R. Varian, 'Tales of manipulation and design flaws from the crypt of auction history', *The New York Times*, 1 August 2002

In concluding this section, we want to stress that the way an auction is designed determines the result to a large extent. We have discussed only the most fundamental forms: a single-stage increasing bid auction, a Dutch auction (which is just one example of a two-stage auction) and a single-stage sealed bid auction. The outcome of an auction is further determined by the number of bidders, number of items to be sold and rules allowing or forbidding the formation of alliances. All these factors can have important consequences for the outcome of the auction, as illustrated in Box 5.5.

Box 5.5 The 3G mobile spectrum auctions in Europe

In 2000, many European governments were contemplating how to allocate a new and scarce good: third-generation (3G) mobile phone licences. 3G mobile phones would use the Universal Mobile Technology Standard (UMTS), which offers much more bandwidth than previously, allowing applications such as high-speed Internet and video on your mobile phone. The governments owned the rights to the radio spectra necessary for UMTS. How should they allocate these rights to the interested telecom companies?

Some governments (Finland, Poland, Spain, Sweden) chose to distribute the 3G licences on the basis of a *beauty contest*. In such a contest, the interested parties compete by demonstrating their qualifications against criteria set by the government. An advantage of a beauty contest may be that governments can set any criteria they deem politically relevant. A disadvantage may be that this invites favouritism by the governments – for instance, towards the incumbent national telecom companies.

Economic theory suggests that an *auction* could allocate the new licences efficiently – that is, to those who value them most, not those whom regulators favour. Governments interested in obtaining the highest prices for the new licences should therefore consider using an auction.

In fact, the UK government was the first to use an auction in April 2000. There were nine telecom companies wishing to enter the UK market. Those new entrants bid strongly against the four incumbents to obtain one of the five available licences. As a result, the UK government collected an astonishing £22.5 billion. Finance ministers across Europe started grinning at the prospect of their own auctions.

The next auction was held in the Netherlands. There were five incumbents and five new licences available. The Dutch government anticipated that, again, many new entrants would compete. In fact, many of them formed alliances with the incumbents: BT-Telfort, KPN-NTT Docomo and Ben–Deutsche Telekom. On the morning before the auction, two of the three last new entrants withdrew from the auction, leaving only six players – the five incumbents and one weak new entrant, Versatel. As a result, the Dutch government collected only €12.7 billion, less than a third of what they hoped on the basis of the UK experience.

▶

Revenue from European 3G mobile spectrum auctions in 2000

	Euros per capita
Austria	100
Germany	615
Italy	240
Netherlands	170
Switzerland	20
UK	630

As the table illustrates, revenue from 3G auctions has varied widely. The revenue was high again in Germany, but very low in Austria and Switzerland. Reasons for these differences include the experience that players acquired over time and the changing market sentiment about the high sums paid initially. A comparison of the auctions shows that it has also been tremendously important how auctions were designed. Important design features include the following:

- Increasing bid only or also a second-stage Dutch auction?
- Were there incentives for new entrants to compete (such as a special lot reserved for them)?
- What were the rules for forming alliances and 'collusive behaviour' during the auction?

Many game theorists were employed by governments to advise on optimal auction design and by companies on optimal bidding strategies. They have had a spectacular opportunity to test their theories (see Klemperer, 2001). Moreover, the practical value of a good training in game theory was evident for many in the public sector and the business world. Indeed, *The Financial Times* quoted a telecoms analyst as saying, 'All these people who thought that they wasted their first year at university listening to boring game theory lectures are now running around the City feeling really grateful.'

Sources: Klemperer (2001, 2004); 'Best bids guaranteed', *The Financial Times*, 8 November 2000; 'The price is right', *The Economist*, 29 July 2000; www.paulklemperer.org/index.htm

5.5 The prisoner's dilemma: single-stage and iterated

We now introduce a famous class of games: the prisoner's dilemma.[9] We start with the single-stage prisoner's dilemma (for two players) to show its basic structure. We then proceed to play the prisoner's dilemma game repeatedly with two or more players in order to show the difference between single-stage and iterated games.

5.5.1 The single-stage prisoner's dilemma

Two men, Robber and Thief, are being accused of a bank robbery. They are interrogated separately. They know that, if they both confess, each will be sentenced to five years in prison. If neither of them confesses, each will be sentenced to three years for illegal possession of arms. However, if Robber confesses while Thief holds out, Robber will be sentenced for only one year and Thief will receive six years. If Thief confesses and Robber holds out, the situation will be reversed. The pay-offs for this game are given in Figure 5.8.

Robber will now reason as follows. If Thief holds out, then my best choice is to confess (one year in prison is better than three years). If Thief confesses,

THIEF

		Do not confess	Confess
ROBBER	Do not confess	–3,–3	–6,–1
	Confess	–1,–6	–5,–5

Figure 5.8 The prisoner's dilemma

then my best choice is to also confess (six years in prison is worse than five years). So, whatever Thief does, my best choice is to confess.

Dominant strategy

In the language of game theory we say that Robber has a **dominant strategy** – that is, one which is best whatever the other player does. Robber's dominant strategy is to confess.

Thief will follow the same line of reasoning, so he will also confess. The result is that both will confess, while both would be better off if they were to hold out.

Suppose that Robber and Thief are allowed to communicate before being interrogated. Perhaps they have been held in the same cell, but they are now interrogated in separate rooms. Suppose Robber and Thief have promised each other not to confess. Will they stick to their promise?

If we suppose that each is completely selfish and rational, then we must predict that they will not. It is in Robber's interests to promise Thief that he, Robber, will cooperate (by not confessing) if Thief promises the same. Having made that promise, however, it is in Robber's interests to break that promise. Whether or not Thief keeps his promise, Robber will always be better off breaking his promise.

The problem is that if the prisoners are dishonest and disloyal (as we would expect bank robbers to be) they cannot make binding commitments. Because they cannot make binding commitments, they have no way to achieve cooperation. If they could make binding commitments, cooperation could be achieved.[10]

Looking at the dilemma in that way, it is logical to relabel the actions the players can choose as 'cooperate' (which for the prisoners is equal to 'do not confess') and 'defect' (which for the prisoners is the same as 'confess'). The general form of a prisoner's dilemma is given in Figure 5.9.

The game represented in Figure 5.9 is a prisoner's dilemma if there are certain relations between the four pay-offs that each player can receive. Those relations are:

$$N < P < R < T$$

where

COLUMN PLAYER

		Cooperate	Defect	Key:
ROW PLAYER	Cooperate	R,R	N,T	R = reward for cooperation / N = pay off for being naive
	Defect	T,N	P,P	T = temptation to defect / P = penalty for mutual defection

Figure 5.9 General form of the prisoner's dilemma

$N < P$ means that, for the row player, it is better to defect if the column player defects;

$P < R$ means that the pay-off for mutual defection is less than it is for mutual cooperation;

$R < T$ means that, if the other player cooperates, then it is better to defect (there is a temptation to defect).

Note that the pay-offs given in Figure 5.8 for the two prisoners satisfy these inequalities.

In Box 5.6 we offer an example of how government authorities may offer incentives to increase the temptation to defect for conspirators in a cartel.

Box 5.6 Leniency policy as an incentive to defect

The lessons of game theory can be applied in many contexts. One of them is the antitrust policy of governments, aimed at illegal secret (cartel) agreements between competitors to fix prices, restrict supply or divide up markets. The authorities have learned from the prisoner's dilemma that it can pay to increase the incentive for players to defect from such cartels. Increasingly, they have adopted a 'leniency policy' to stimulate companies to defect from cartels. Under the leniency policy of the EU, adopted in 2002, the first company to 'blow the whistle' on a cartel is granted immunity from the (rather stiff) fines that the European Commission can impose.

The leniency policy works well. For instance, the Swiss company ABB blew the whistle on a cartel for gas insulated switchgear (GIS) projects:

The Commission concluded that the companies had participated in an illegal cartel on the basis of numerous documents and corporate statements provided by the immunity applicant (including two detailed written agreements concluded in 1988), together with documents discovered by the Commission during on-site inspections . . . From at least 1988, when a written agreement between the members was adopted, GIS suppliers informed each other of calls for tender for GIS and coordinated their bids in order to secure projects for the cartel members according to their respective cartel quotas. Alternatively, they would agree to respect minimum bidding prices. The companies agreed that the Japanese companies would not sell in Europe, and the European companies would not sell in Japan. European tenders were usually allocated according to the cartel rules and the European projects won by cartel members outside their home countries were counted into the agreed global cartel quotas. Thus the Japanese companies have also been fined, despite their nearly total absence from the market for GIS in Europe, because their agreement to abstain from bidding contributed directly to the restriction of competition on the EU market.

As a result, the European Commission imposed fines of, in total, €750 million on 10 members of the cartel, while ABB was granted immunity for its fine, which would otherwise have amounted to €215 million. The largest fine was imposed on the German company Siemens (€396 million).

Source: http://europa.eu/rapid/PressReleasesaction.do?reference=IP/07/80&guiLanguage=en (IP/07/80), 24 January 2007

The fundamental problem in the prisoner's dilemma is that, for each player, the dominant strategy is to defect, while they would both be better off if they chose mutual cooperation.

There are many situations in which a prisoner's dilemma arises. Consider the following situation. Suppose there are only two oil-producing countries in the world. Let us call those countries Arabia and Russia. Both countries have to choose an output level. If each chooses a low output level, then oil prices will be high and both will make a profit of 3 (billion dollars). If each chooses a high output level, oil prices will be low and each will make a profit of 1 (billion dollars). If Arabia chooses a low output level and Russia a high output level, then oil prices will be moderately high. Now Russia, with its high output level, will make a large profit of 5 (billion dollars) while Arabia, with its low output level, will earn nothing. If Russia chooses a low output level and Arabia a high one, then the situation is reversed. The pay-offs for each country are given in Figure 5.10.

RUSSIA

		Cooperate	Defect
ARABIA	Cooperate	3,3	0.5
	Defect	5,0	1,1

Figure 5.10 Two oil-producing countries facing a prisoner's dilemma

In this example, to cooperate means to choose a low output level and to defect means to choose a high output level. If oil-producing countries form a cartel, then each country promises to maintain a certain price level and restrict output. Having made such a promise, however, it is in each country's interest to produce and sell more oil than its quota, even at a slightly lower price. As each country will do this, the cartel will break down.

In reality, we see that OPEC was able to raise oil prices effectively in the 1970s (the oil crises), but has suffered from defection at other times. In particular, certain countries have repeatedly tried to benefit from the lack of observability of actual output levels, as illustrated in Box 5.7 (overleaf). Furthermore, availability of non-OPEC oil (which increases when oil prices are high) has helped to keep OPEC 'honest'.

That shows our model does not (yet) incorporate all the relevant aspects of reality. One important and relevant aspect in many prisoner's dilemmas in the real world is that the game is played many times instead of only once. In the next section we find that makes a big difference.

5.5.2 The iterated prisoner's dilemma for many players

Suppose that two selfish and rational players play the prisoner's dilemma many times. That is the iterated prisoner's dilemma.

In the iterated prisoner's dilemma, each player has to choose to either co-operate or defect in each round of the game. In making that choice, each player can take into account what the other player did in previous rounds. In the repeated game, a strategy is defined as a set of rules that specify what action to take given the history of the game so far. To illustrate the concept of a strategy for an iterated game, we give a few examples.

Box 5.7 Cheating in OPEC

Cheating has been a persistent problem in the OPEC cartel, regardless of whether the oil price has been high or low. After the oil shocks of the 1970s and 1980s, when oil prices reached levels of above $50, the price level had come down again to around $20. However, in the late 1990s, the oil price slid towards a level of $10, which caused a lot of turmoil within OPEC, with various members blaming each other:

> After criticising each other from afar for several weeks, Saudi and Venezuelan oil officials got into the same room and glared at each other: the Venezuelans blinked. As recently as early March, Erwin Jose Arrieta, Venezuela's energy minister, had declared that he was too busy to attend a proposed OPEC meeting and vowed not to cut production 'even by one barrel'. Coming from OPEC's biggest cheater, that attitude was regarded as unhelpful. Oil prices had dropped by 55% since January 1997, to hit a low of $11.27 a barrel, and had been sinking by 50 cents a week for months. Now, under a deal brokered by Mexico, its great non-OPEC rival in the hemisphere, Venezuela has agreed to cheat somewhat less flagrantly, and Saudi Arabia to match cuts by the two big Latin American producers. Ten other producers are having their arms twisted to follow suit. By removing between 1.1m and 2m barrels a day from world markets, the producers hope to 'stabilize' prices.

Oil prices recovered and, by the year 2000, they were above $30 again. High oil prices are a threat to economic growth in many regions, so the OPEC countries had, in principle, agreed to keep oil prices in a target band of $22–28. If the price remained above $28 for 20 trading days, the cartel was supposed to raise production by 0.5m barrels a day. That 'automatic' increase did not happen in June 2000, however, when the price had sailed past the 20-day upper trigger. *The Economist* analysed the situation as follows:

> Various confused and contradictory explanations surfaced from ministers, but not the oil. Only at their next officially scheduled meeting did they come up with a meagre quota increase. Even if ministers agree to lift quotas by the magic 500,000 barrels per day (bpd) figure, very little oil may actually reach the markets. That is because this figure does not allow for cheating. At the moment, the cartel's official quotas total about 25.4m bpd, whereas its actual production last month topped 26m bpd. A quota increase of 500,000 bpd will serve merely to legitimize existing cheating. Countries will try to cheat once again on whatever new quotas are agreed.

Sources: The Economist, 28 March 1998 and 9 September 2000

Tit-for-tat

- **Tit-for-tat** is the strategy consisting of the following decision rules: in the first round, choose cooperate, in the following rounds choose whatever the other player did in the previous round.
- *Permanent retaliation*: in the first round, choose cooperate; if the other player defects in any round, choose defect in all subsequent rounds.
- *All D*: always choose defect no matter what the other player does.
- *All C*: always choose cooperate no matter what the other player does.
- *Random*: choose randomly (by tossing a coin) between cooperate and defect.
- *Tit-for-tat plus*: in the first round, choose cooperate; in the following rounds, if the other player cooperated in the previous round, choose cooperate with probability $1-\varepsilon$ and defect with probability ε; if the other player defected in the previous round, choose defect.

- *Tit-for-two-tats*: in the first two rounds, choose cooperate; in the following rounds, choose defect if the other player defected in the last two rounds, otherwise choose cooperate.
- *Uneven*: in the first round and in all subsequent uneven rounds, cooperate; in the second and in all subsequent even rounds, defect.

Now suppose that you belong to a group of, say, ten people. You will successively play the iterated prisoner's dilemma against each of the other members of the group. That is the iterated prisoner's dilemma for many players. What is your best strategy? The answer depends on many factors:

- the pay-offs – if T (the temptation to defect in Figure 5.9) is very large, then an occasional unexpected defection could be part of your best strategy;
- the strategies of the other players – tit-for-tat-plus will perform very nicely against tit-for-two-tats, but probably not very well against permanent retaliation;
- the way you discount future pay-offs.

The iterated prisoner's dilemma has been investigated by Axelrod (1984). Axelrod invited scientists from several disciplines, from mathematics to psychology, to submit strategies for the prisoner's dilemma with pay-offs given in Figure 5.10. Note that with these pay-offs permanent mutual cooperation is better than taking turns at exploiting each other (permanent mutual cooperation gives each player 3 in each round; taking turns at exploiting each other means receiving 5 and 0 in two consecutive rounds, an average of 2.5). In most real-world situations it is better to cooperate than take turns at exploiting each other. In the iterated prisoner's dilemma, that is equivalent to assuming that $0.5(N + T) < R$.

With the pay-offs given in Figure 5.10 and no discounting, Axelrod organized two computer tournaments between the strategies he had received. In each tournament, each strategy was paired with each other strategy, with itself and with random. Both tournaments were won by tit-for-tat.

Tit-for-tat has several characteristics that may explain its success. First, tit-for-tat is *nice*. That means it is never the first to defect. If tit-for-tat is paired with itself, with tit-for-two-tats, permanent retaliation or all C, then it will receive 3 in each round.

Second, tit-for-tat is *forgiving*. That means, if the other player defects once but then starts to cooperate again, tit-for-tat will punish him only once. Thus, unlike permanent retaliation, tit-for-tat is able to restore cooperation after a single defection.

Third, tit-for-tat is *retaliatory*. If the other player defects, he is punished immediately. For that reason, it is difficult to exploit tit-for-tat.

Axelrod's results show quite nicely how two selfish and rational players in the iterated prisoner's dilemma can achieve cooperation even if they cannot make binding commitments (they cannot trust each other not to break promises). That has important consequences for the way members of an organization cooperate. Suppose the two players are Arabia and Russia and each country can choose its production level each week. The two countries then play the iterated prisoner's dilemma. Suppose, further, that they agree to have production levels observed. That mutual cooperation can arise, based on such an agreement, is not surprising. Now suppose the two players are two large firms that have formed a joint venture. To cooperate means giving your partner full access to all relevant know-how; to defect means giving away as little knowledge as possible. If both firms expect to set up similar joint ventures in the future, cooperation is likely to arise. For those firms, it now pays to invest in their *reputation* as trustworthy partners. Building a reputation is one way to show a commitment (see Box 5.8). In single-stage games it is not possible to build a reputation as the game is over after the first move. In repeated games, however, players may invest in building reputations. Reputations for trustworthiness and cooperativeness help to establish cooperation even in the adverse conditions of a prisoner's dilemma.

Box 5.8 Reputation as commitment

Dixit and Nalebuff (1991) explain the building of reputation as being a form of commitment as follows:

If you try a strategic move in a game and then back off, you may lose your reputation for credibility. In a once-in-a-lifetime situation, reputation may be unimportant and therefore of little commitment value. But, you typically play several games with different rivals at the same time, or the same rivals at different times. Then you have an incentive to establish a reputation, and this serves as a commitment that makes your strategic moves credible.

During the Berlin crisis in 1961, John F. Kennedy explained the importance of the US reputation: 'If we do not meet our commitments in Berlin, where will we later stand? If we are not true to our word there, all that we have achieved in collective security, which relies on these words, will mean nothing.'

Source: Dixit and Nalebuff (1991)

Similar situations arise when two people have to work together to accomplish a task. They can both choose between a high level of effort (which is equivalent to cooperating) and a low level of effort (defecting). If they have to work together many times, cooperation is more likely to arise than if they work together only once. If the players meet only once, then we predict mutual defection.

What happens if they know that they will meet each other 1000 times? In the last round they will surely both defect as there is no future from there on in which the other player can punish defection. In round number 999, they will also both defect as they know they are both going to defect in the last round anyway. That logic, taken to the extreme, leads inevitably to the conclusion that both players will defect in the first round. Of course, instead of 1000, any other finite number will yield the same result. Only if both players are to meet an infinite number of times or they do not know how often they will meet can we expect mutual cooperation.

What is the lesson we can learn from Axelrod's results? Does it mean that, in reality, it is always best to play tit-for-tat? Not necessarily. An important difference between the real world and a computer tournament concerns the possibility of mistakes. In computer tournaments, errors do not occur, unless programed. In reality, mistakes are a fact of life. Therefore, we have to allow for the possibility of errors if we want to increase the usefulness of game theory's recommendations.

Suppose that the heads of two Mafia families, Antara and Brizi, are both tit-for-tat players. Suppose, too, that mistakes are possible. Thus, it is possible that, while Antara and Brizi both cooperated in a certain round (round n), Brizi incorrectly thinks Antara defected in round n. Brizi will then defect in round $n + 1$. Antara will react by defecting in round $n + 2$, which means that Brizi will defect in round number $n + 3$. That is called the **echo effect**, as the echo of a mistake can go on indefinitely. It is illustrated in Table 5.1.

One mistake provokes a chain reaction of punishments. Antara and Brizi now take turns at exploiting each other, which is worse than mutual cooperation. When mistakes are possible, tit-for-tat may be too aggressive. In game theory, such random errors are called **noise**. When we allow for noise in the iterated prisoner's dilemma game, we can show that it is better to play an amended tit-for-tat strategy with, for example:[11]

- **generosity**: make the response to a defection somewhat less than the provocation, so retaliation diminishes over time and a new basis for cooperation can be established;
- **contrition**: show 'remorse' if you realize that you have defected by accident, which you can signal by, for instance, not responding to the other's retaliation with yet another defection, so the vicious circle of retaliations by defection can be broken.

So, introducing noise into the system requires the tit-for-tat strategy to be more forgiving than it already was. It is, however, a fine balance in an environment where other strategies may be seeking opportunities to benefit from such forgiveness. As summarized by Axelrod (1997, p. 31): noise calls for forgiveness, but too much forgiveness invites exploitation.

Tit-for-tat can be observed in real-world situations, such as the trade policies pursued by various countries and regions. Box 5.9 (overleaf) gives an example. You may ask yourself if President Bush made a mistake in the example. You may also ask yourself if there are examples of forgiveness and retaliation.

Echo effect

Noise

Generosity

Contrition

Table 5.1 Two tit-for-tat players with the possibility of making a mistake

Round	Antara	Brizi
1	Cooperate	Cooperate
2	Cooperate	Cooperate
⋮	⋮	⋮
n	Cooperate	Cooperate
$n + 1$	Cooperate	Defect
$n + 2$	Defect	Cooperate
$n + 3$	Cooperate	Defect

Box 5.9 **Tit-for-tat between the EU and the USA**

Countries, such as the USA, and regions, such as the EU, cooperate in the World Trade Organization (WTO) to establish a 'level playing field' of common rules for international trade. In spite of the WTO rules, every now and then a 'trade war' may erupt with tit-for-tat characteristics:

- early in 2002, President Bush slapped tariffs of up to 30 per cent on imported steel, hurting European exports, and the EU contested the tariffs before the WTO – the wait for the final WTO ruling could take two to three years;
- the EU published a list of retaliatory tariffs on such products as citrus fruit, clothing and sunglasses to be imposed in mid-2002 – the products were clearly chosen to inflict electoral pain on President Bush in states viewed as key political battlegrounds, with Senate elections foreseen in November 2002;
- moreover, the EU drew up its own steel restrictions 'to prevent cheap steel diverted from the US flooding the European market';
- the EU delayed the imposition of the retaliatory tariffs in anticipation of a WTO ruling, which was promised in a 'fast track' process; in late autumn of 2003, the WTO came out against the steel tariffs, saying that they represented an illegal barrier to free trade;
- after receiving the verdict, Bush declared that he would still maintain the tariffs; under WTO rules, the EU threatened to now counter with the retaliatory tariffs;
- faced with this credible threat, the USA backed down and withdrew the tariffs in December 2003.

In the context of international trade, tit-for-tat can be observed between two players (as above), between multiple players (as in the trade rounds aimed at expanding the reach of WTO rules) and in multiple rounds (the trade rounds continue over time). As we move to situations involving many players in many rounds, a branch of game theory becomes relevant, called 'evolutionary game theory'. We introduce that branch briefly in the next section by examining three types of questions that can be answered by the evolutionary game theory approach. That brief introduction will also serve to make a useful link between this chapter and Chapter 10 on evolutionary approaches to organizations.

In Sections 5.2 to 5.5 we assumed that players are rational decisionmakers who act only in their own interests. That is exactly what homo economicus would do. Consider, however, Box 5.10 for a result that is not really consistent with this view of human behaviour.

Box 5.10 **The ultimatum game**

Before we leave classical game theory, we want to discuss one other game that is rapidly becoming just as famous as the prisoner's dilemma. It is the one-stage *ultimatum game*, in which two players interact anonymously.

The first player (the 'proposer') has a sum of money available and is asked to propose to the second player (the 'responder') how to divide the money. If the responder accepts the proposal, the sum is divided accordingly. However, if the responder rejects the proposal, both players receive nothing.

The full rationality assumption of the homo economicus model would imply that any offer to split the money should be accepted by the responder as receiving some money is better than getting nothing. Anticipating such rational behaviour from the respondent, a proposer should be able to get away with offering very low amounts of money.

In fact, across many cultures and with varying amounts of money involved, proposers offer very substantial amounts of money (the modal offer is 40–50 per cent) and responders frequently reject proposals below 20–30 per cent. Apparently, a notion of 'fairness' is implied in the behaviour of proposers as well as responders. Moreover, that notion is shared by the players in the ultimatum game.

These experimental results are generally interpreted to mean that the homo economicus model is incomplete. The model is useful to approximate human behaviour with respect to the 'economic aspect' of decisions, but it is not sufficient as a model of real-life decisions involving more than 'purely economic' aspects. Besides (full) rationality, human behaviour is also determined by notions such as reciprocity and fairness. We return to this discussion in Chapter 8 (see Box 8.3).

Sources: Güth, Schmittberger and Schwarze (1982) and Gintis (2000)

5.6 Evolutionary game theory

The iterated prisoner's dilemma is a dynamic game involving multiple players. In Axelrod's computer tournaments, different strategies were submitted and tit-for-tat came out as the overall winner. Imagine that the whole population of players in the tournament over time adopts tit-for-tat. Would that population now be immune from attack by alternative strategies?

That is one of the oldest questions in evolutionary game theory. It is asking if an 'evolutionary stable strategy' has evolved. We examine that question first below then move on to situations of strategies competing for success in populations. How can we structure the analysis of competing strategies in evolutionary game theory? That second question will be addressed using an example of the *Hawk–Dove* game.

Note that our first two questions deal with the success of strategies that are fixed in the sense that they do not evolve over time. Our third question will address what happens when we allow the evolution of strategies in our game theoretic models. We will see that evolution introduces innovation and the outcome of such games is much less predictable than in the first two situations.

Evolutionary stable strategy (ESS)

Our first question concerns evolutionary stable strategies. A behaviour is defined as an **evolutionary stable strategy (ESS)** if a population adopting that behaviour cannot be invaded by any competing alternative strategy. Consider an entire population playing the tit-for-tat strategy and a group of newcomers who prefer the 'always defect' strategy (they try to cheat everyone they meet) entering the population. Then, the tit-for-tat strategy will prove more successful and the defectors will either be converted or lose out. Tit-for-tat is therefore an ESS with respect to the strategy 'always defect'. Note that, in the branch of evolutionary game theory that examines evolutionary stable strategies, the strategies are fixed. Because of its superior performance, tit-for-tat comes to dominate the population.

Now imagine that we have two (fixed) strategies competing in the population, but neither of them can become dominant. That would be the case in the Hawk–Dove game depicted in Figure 5.11. Originally developed to analyse 'the logic of animal conflict',[12] the game refers to two types of birds (or players) competing for food (or resources):

- *hawks* initiate a fight, not stopping until exhausted or the opponent backs down;
- *doves* retreat immediately when the opponent initiates a fight.

In the game specified in Figure 5.11, the hawk wins most of the food when it meets a dove. The latter has to be content with leftovers. When two hawks meet, however, they will use more energy fighting than the food can replenish. When two doves meet, they share the food.

If better-fed birds breed more, how will the bird population evolve over time? We can start by observing that any population consisting entirely of doves is not 'evolutionarily stable' as they can be successfully invaded by a hawk mutant. Initially, such a hawk invader will have an easy time winning each fight for food. The hawk proportion of the bird population will grow as the initial hawks spend their time feeding and breeding. Increasingly, however, they will be confronted with other hawks putting up a fight for their food. The end result of a population totally dominated by hawks is not attainable as they will all fight each other to starvation (each fight costing more energy than the food gives back). Each dove, however, always gains something (either 1 or 5) in its food encounters. As a result, the dove population will always have some breeding success. Doves will have higher breeding success than hawks when the hawk numbers are reaching the point where they fight each other to death. Thus, it can be seen that the bird population settles into an equilibrium of doves and hawks. If the population swings out of that equilibrium towards one type of strategy, the other strategy will become slightly more advantaged and its proportion in the population will increase to bring the balance back.

In business environments, the Hawk–Dove game may play out in aggressive environments, with fierce competition for projects. Powell (2003) gives the following example:

> some buyers demand 'fly-offs' when contracting larger projects. In a 'fly-off' bidders have to make huge risky investments to develop prototypes which are then trialed against each other with the winner taking full control of the project.

		BIRD B	
		Hawk	Dove
BIRD A	Hawk	-1,-1	9,1
	Dove	1,9	5,5

Figure 5.11 Hawk–Dove game – pay-offs to Birds A and B respectively

One response is to put investment into this highly uncertain bidding process and take the competitors head-on. Another response is to look for small work-shares from the resulting winners, taking a smaller return, but using much less resource in the process. Contractors in these environments can be clearly seen to fall into two groups – those who fight aggressively for leadership (i.e. majority work-share) and those who act as substantial subcontractors for, say, production or specialized contributions. Often these *Doves* are as large and successful as the *Hawks* but their core competencies are very different, the latter having highly developed bidding teams skilled in fighting the *Hawk–Hawk* game.

Note that the two questions above relate to the success of *fixed* strategies in a population. If we relax that assumption and allow the strategies to evolve over time, evolutionary game theory takes us a step further. What will happen if we model gradual change (evolution) of strategies? How much learning would we observe? Would new strategies emerge?

Such questions are addressed in a younger branch of evolutionary game theory. It allows strategies to develop over time by using the evolutionary mechanism (or genetic algorithm) of:

- **variation** (or mutation) of strategic behaviour or response to the environment;
- **selection**: testing for success (or fitness) of the variations;
- **retention** (or heredity) of successful variations.

That is the same mechanism we will encounter in Chapter 10, where we introduce evolutionary approaches to organizations. It is the mechanism operating in our genes bringing about the evolution of humankind. It is a mechanism that can also be modelled using a computer to operate on strategies (represented as strings of bits). That is exactly what Robert Axelrod did in cooperation with John Holland.

Instead of humans proposing strategies for the prisoner's dilemma, he started with a population of strictly random strategies. He then allowed strategies to evolve on the computer and slug it out in a 'survival of the fittest'. Essentially, the genetic algorithm enables *learning*.

First, he held the environment constant by playing the evolving strategies against fixed proportions of competitor strategies. What were the results? Well, quite remarkable. From a strictly random start, the genetic algorithm evolved populations the *median* member of which was just as successful as the *best* rule in the tournament – tit-for-tat. Most strategies actually resembled tit-for-tat: 95 per cent of the time they would make the same choice as tit-for-tat in the same situation. However, the effective strategies had evolved certain variations, such as (Axelrod, 1997, p. 21):

> very effective rules evolved by breaking the most important advice developed in the computer tournament, namely, to be 'nice', that is, never to be the first to defect. These highly effective rules always defect on the very first move, and sometimes on the second move as well, and use the choices of the other player to discriminate what should be done next. The highly effective rules then had responses that allowed them to 'apologize' and get to mutual cooperation with

most of the unexploitable representatives, and different responses that allowed them to exploit a representative that was exploitable.

So, in a fixed environment, it pays to learn which competitors are exploitable and which are not. Maximum effectiveness is then reached by maximizing cooperation with cooperating strategies and maximizing exploitation of the exploitable strategies. Note that that outcome crucially depends on the environment being structured as fixed proportions of competing strategies: the exploitable strategies retain their proportion despite being taken advantage of.

Then, Axelrod relaxed the assumption of a constant environment. Instead of playing against fixed proportions of competitor strategies, the environment now evolved itself. That is called an **ecological simulation**. A selection process using the average game pay-offs of the various strategies as fitness criterion determines the evolution of the population. The more successful strategies increase their proportion in the population and the less successful ones decrease their proportion. What happens now?

Ecological simulation

Typically, cooperation first decreases and then increases:

> From a random start, the population first evolves away from whatever cooper-
> ation was initially displayed. The less cooperative rules do better than the more
> cooperative rules because at first there are few other players who are responsive
> – and when the other player is unresponsive, the most effective thing for an
> individual to do is simply defect ... However, after about ten or twenty gener-
> ations the trend starts to reverse. Some players evolve a pattern of reciprocating
> what cooperation they find, and these reciprocating players tend to do well
> because they can do very well with others who reciprocate without being
> exploited for very long by those who just defect ... As the reciprocators do well,
> they spread in the population, resulting in more and more cooperation and
> greater and greater effectiveness.

So, in an ecological simulation, where the proportion of strategies in the population varies with their success, 'not nice' strategies destroy the basis of their initial success because the exploited (unsuccessful) strategies become a decreasing proportion of the environment. Now, the evolving ability to discriminate between those who will reciprocate cooperation and those who will not allows reciprocators to jointly do well and increase their proportion of the population.

Coevolution

If all strategies in a population can evolve, we are simulating **coevolution**. Strategies can learn and evolve. Their success depends on the speed of their learning versus that of the others in the population. Success is never guaranteed as new mutations continuously arise, either through random variation or recombination (when two strategies combine in a novel way).

While most of these will fail, a few will represent successful *innovations*.[13] Successful innovations will spread in the population, until they meet the boundaries of their success or new competition. To get an impression of the coevolution of such populations, have a look at Figure 5.12. Without getting into the details of this simulation,[14] it is essentially a coevolutionary simulation over 26,000 generations of strategies for the prisoner's dilemma, allowing the development of memory (longer strings have longer memories).

So, in the simulation, strategies develop from simple to more complex. Notice the progression in the simulation:

1 initially, a few simple strategies fight it out (with 01 being most successful);
2 then, evolution creates longer memory strategies and a period of turbulence sets in (with 1101 being the most successful, but with many competitors);
3 in a next stage, two strategies emerge that coexist and together wipe out almost all competition in a period of relative stability, until;
4 a new mutant strategy develops with an even longer memory (16) that rapidly becomes dominant but the success of which already starts to fade towards the end of the simulation.

This example of a simulation allowing the evolution of strategies shows how a population may develop over time, never reaching any stable equilibrium, with increased learning and new innovations popping up continuously, and periods of relative stability alternating with high levels of turbulence.[15]

Let us sum up some of the lessons we have learned from applying the genetic algorithm to the iterated prisoner's dilemma.

■ *Evolution can be a better designer than humans* The genetic algorithm produced strategies that can be more effective than tit-for-tat in specific environments. Allowing agents to be *adaptive* (as in evolutionary game theory) can be more effective than only allowing them to be *rational* (as in classical game theory).

■ *Cooperation can emerge from reciprocity* That is now confirmed not only for human entries to the tournament but also emergent strategies in fixed and evolving environments.

■ *There is often an optimal balance between cooperation and exploitation* Already in the tournament setting, the introduction of noise calls for forgiveness, but too much forgiveness invites exploitation. If the environment contains exploitable strategies, it usually pays to learn how to identify them and take advantage of their exploitability.

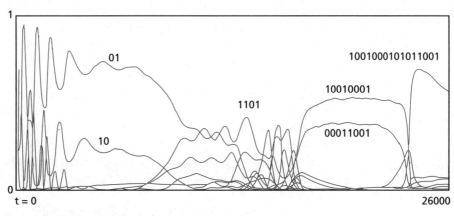

Figure 5.12 Coevolution of strategies
Source: Lindgren (1997)

■ *Strategies and environments interact and coevolve* Depending on the specifications of strategies, the environment can come to be dominated by one (environmentally stable) strategy, into a (dynamic) equilibrium between strategies (as in the Hawk–Dove game) and become highly turbulent as strategies continually learn and evolve (as in Figure 5.12). Alternatively, the properties of the environment determine the relative success of strategies. In Chapters 10 and 11 we will further explore how organizations and environments can coevolve.

We will not delve further into the exciting new field of evolutionary game theory here (see Gintis, 2000, for an introduction). We will, however, build on its foundations when we discuss *evolutionary approaches to organizations* in Chapter 10 and *complex adaptive systems* in Chapter 11. To summarize, evolutionary game theory primarily studies the development of **populations** rather than the rational decisionmaking of an individual. In those populations there is a variety (N≥2) of strategies to survive and compete. Interactions between players (or agents) are simulated by having the computer organize chance encounters (random pairing). In many rounds, the strategies of the different players are tested for success (or fitness). Successful strategies increase in the population and unsuccessful ones are 'selected out'. If an entire population adopts a strategy and cannot be invaded by a competing alternative strategy, we say that an 'evolutionary stable strategy' has been selected. Alternatively, two strategies may come to a (dynamic) equilibrium, as in the Hawk–Dove game. If strategies are allowed to evolve (through mutation), such an equilibrium may prove to be elusive as new innovations are continuously tested and successful ones are selected for further replication (and mutation). This latter representation of evolutionary dynamics may be close to our real-world development of organizational populations over time – a topic that we will return to in Chapters 10 and 11.

Populations

5.7 Summary: insights from game theory

In this chapter we have given an introduction to game theory. Game theory is, first of all, a powerful tool for analysing situations in which two or more people have to make interdependent decisions.

Several types of game have been discussed. In the one-stage game for two players we distinguished between sequential and simultaneous games. In a sequential game, one of the players moves first and the other player can observe that move. In a simultaneous game, each player has to make her decision not knowing what the other player has decided or will decide. The difference between a sequential and a simultaneous game has to do with lack of information. Without observable information, coordination is difficult to achieve.

The main principle to remember in sequential games is 'look ahead and reason back'. We saw how a potential entrant can use that principle in the entry game. A threat by the incumbent firm to lower prices after entry is an empty threat if, after entry has occurred, it is in the incumbent's own interest to not lower prices.

The incumbent can make its threat credible by making a commitment that irreversibly alters the pay-offs so that, after entry, it is in the incumbent's interest to execute the threat. By applying the principle of looking ahead and reasoning back, we saw how the incumbent firm can determine whether or not it is in its interest to change the pay-offs (and, thus, pose a credible threat). Of course, it is again a necessary condition that the information about the commitment is available to the entrant. If it is, the entrant can apply the same principle of looking ahead and reasoning back to determine whether profitable entry will be possible or not. By changing the structure of the game, the incumbent can thus influence the incentives for the entrant and, thereby, the likely outcome of the game.

The role of observable information became even more apparent in the discussion of different types of auction. In open auctions, the private information of most bidders is gradually revealed. Only the winner can still possess private information that would have led him to bid substantially higher, if he were forced to. We saw how the seller may therefore consider changing the design of the auction to a two-stage process with a Dutch auction as a second stage. That was another example of when one party may change the structure of the game, the incentives for the other party and, thus, the likely outcome.

In sealed bid auctions, no information about the private valuations of bidders is revealed during the auction. In the face of this uncertainty, winners run the risk of suffering the winner's curse – that is, obtaining the prize as a consequence of making the most optimistic estimates.

For simultaneous games (such as the prisoner's dilemma), we explained the concept of a dominant strategy. A dominant strategy is one that is best whatever the other player does. In the prisoner's dilemma, each player has a dominant strategy. That strategy is to defect. Hence, if the game is played only once, we would expect both players to defect. Mutual cooperation is better for both of them, however. If they can trust each other – that is, if they can both make binding commitments – then surely they will agree to cooperate.

The problem in the prisoner's dilemma is that, after such an agreement has been made, each party has an incentive to cheat. That is a problem, too, for the stability of cartels. After an agreement has been made to restrict output by cartel members, each member has an incentive to increase output. Another problem for cartels is that governments may offer incentives to defect by adopting a 'leniency policy'.

Finally, we explored the consequences of playing a game repeatedly. We saw that cooperation between individual players may then evolve even in the adverse conditions of a prisoner's dilemma. In the iterated prisoner's dilemma, a strategy consists of a set of rules that specify what action to take given the history of the game so far.

In computer tournaments, tit-for-tat has proven to be a good strategy. That is probably because tit-for-tat is nice (it is never the first to defect), forgiving (it is able to restore cooperation after a defection by the other player) and retaliatory (the other player is punished immediately for defection). However, when mistakes are possible, tit-for-tat may be too aggressive. As the strategy now includes the history of the game so far, players may invest in building reputations. It was shown that reputations can be considered to be assets that reflect commitment.

When games are played for many rounds, and the focus is more on populations than on individuals, we enter into evolutionary game theory. We examined several questions that can be addressed by evolutionary game theory, including the following.

- What is an 'evolutionary stable strategy' (ESS) – that is, one immune to the invasion of the population by another strategy?
- How can we model the mix of strategies in a population when there is not one ESS (using the Hawk–Dove game)? We saw how a population may tend towards an equilibrium balance between competing strategies.
- What happens when we relax the assumption that strategies are fixed and, instead, allow for evolution of strategies (through application of the genetic algorithm)? We saw that learning and innovation enter into the picture and the population may not tend towards equilibrium. Instead, it may be in continuous evolution and flux, just like our own human evolution, as well as the evolution of organizations, to which we will turn in Chapter 10.

This chapter completes the set of Chapters 2–5 in which we have explained the fundamental concepts and methods underlying the economic approaches to organizations. In Chapters 6–10, we will build on that knowledge to introduce five economic approaches to organizations. As you will see, the approaches differ in terms of the problems addressed, concepts and language used and modes of analysis. This introduction to game theory will help you discern, first, the basic features of the settings in which the players make their decisions in each of the subsequent chapters and, second, distinguish between different levels of analysis – individual players and populations of players – that we will both further explore in subsequent chapters. In the final chapter, we return to the common perspective in these approaches and highlight their similarities and differences.

Questions

1 When corporations want to divest individual business units, they often employ the services of an investment banker, such as Goldman Sachs or Morgan Stanley. Such investment bankers often use an auction process to find the most suitable buyers for the business. It is customary that these auctions are two-stage and sealed bid.

- The first stage consists of soliciting non-binding bids from a wide range of potential buyers on the basis of general information distributed in a bid book.

- The second stage consists of a 'due diligence' procedure in which a limited set of potential buyers may investigate the acquisition candidate in depth as a basis for their final (binding) bid.

Discuss the advantages of this procedure for the corporation selling the business unit.

2 Suppose you are a competitor of the business unit to be sold under the conditions sketched in Question 1. You have no interest or not enough money to acquire the divested company, but you would like to obtain the private information that will be available for inspection in Round 2. You contemplate the possibility of making a sufficiently high (non-binding) bid in Round 1 in order to be admitted to Round 2, only to decline making a final, binding bid in round 2.

Apart from legal reasons (you would not be negotiating in good faith), which economic reason could deter you from this course of action?

3 Look at the list of strategies against which tit-for-tat competed in Axelrod's tournament (Section 5.5.2). It varies from permanent retaliation to uneven. Against which individual strategies do you expect tit-for-tat to win, tie and lose? Why did tit-for-tat win the tournament?

4 Can you explain why tit-for-tat is an 'evolutionary stable strategy' in Axelrod's tournament?

Suggested further reading

Axelrod, R. (1984), *The Evolution of Cooperation*, New York: Basic Books.

Axelrod, R. (1997), *The Complexity of Cooperation*, Princeton, NJ: Princeton University Press.

Dixit, A. and Nalebuff, B. (1991), *Thinking Strategically*, New York: Norton.

Ghemawat, P. (1997), *Games Businesses Play*, Cambridge, MA: MIT Press.

Gintis, H. (2000), *Game Theory Evolving*, Princeton, NJ: Princeton University Press.

Klemperer, P. (2004), *Auctions: Theory and practice*, Princeton, NJ: Princeton University Press.

Powell, J. H. (2003), 'Game theory in strategy', in D. O. Faulkner and A. Campbell, *The Oxford Handbook in Strategy* (Vol. 2), Oxford: Oxford University Press.

Rasmusen, E. (1989), *Games and Information: An introduction to the theory of games*, Oxford: Basil Blackwell.

Notes

1 By rational we mean that players decide on the basis of their utility functions (or objective functions) only. Game theory usually assumes that players act only in their own interests. That implies their utility functions include no variables pertaining to the other players' welfare.

2 In fact, with video technology, no agreement was reached on standard specifications, leading to long and intense competition regarding systems. With CD technology, such agreement was reached and all parties adhered to the set specifications. See Box 5.1 for the developments in DVDs.

3 This $400 million can be interpreted as the expected net present value from all future cash flows if both companies choose VI.

4 Rasmusen (1989, p.35) concludes a similar example by saying, 'The question is really one of psychology rather than economics.'

5 Once a rule has been established, it is difficult to change, especially if there are increasing returns (see Box 10.8) or 'network effects'. Economists speak of (institutional) lock-in. A

famous example is the QWERTY keyboard (see David, 1985, but also Liebowitz and Margolis, 1990) and the rule to drive on the right or left. One-third of the world's population drives on the left, mostly in Great Britain and its former colonies. It is rumoured that an official of the EU once proposed that Great Britain should *gradually* change over to right-hand side driving, by first requiring this of trucks and only later of passenger cars!

6 Credible threats and binding commitments can be made in various ways. Dixit and Nalebuff (1991, chapter 6) discuss eight such ways. See also Ghemawat (1991). We return to the subject of commitment in Chapter 9.

7 In economic terms, that outcome would be considered efficient as it is Pareto-optimal (see Chapters 1 and 2).

8 In addition, it could be mentioned that different designs allow for different types of strategic behaviour. Consider the use by the seller of a 'straw man' in the bidding or the 'signalling' of a buyer's intentions in the first phase of a two-stage auction. For an excellent overview of auction design see Klemperer (2004) and www.paulklemperer.org/index.htm.

9 Notationally, there is some confusion in the literature as to whether to refer to these games as the prisoner's dilemma or the prisoners' dilemma. As will become clear, each prisoner has a dilemma (favouring the singular notation) and all prisoners have the same dilemma (favouring the plural). If you want to identify with more than one prisoner, please feel free to mentally adjust the apostrophe.

10 One way such binding commitments are made in criminal practice is to take hostages. If both prisoners know that their families are threatened if they confess, they will think twice before confessing.

11 Wu and Axelrod (1995). See also Axelrod (1997, Chapter 2) on coping with noise. Overall, generous tit-for-tat seems to perform best when the players it meets have not adapted to noise. If the other players have adapted to noise, a contrite version of tit-for-tat is even more effective at quickly restoring mutual cooperation without the risk of exploitation.

12 See Maynard Smith and Price (1973). Biological games often concern the Four 'F's that preoccupy living beings, according to biologists – feeding, fighting, fleeing and mating. Hawk–Dove games can be generalized by introducing V (value of the resource) and C (the cost of conflict). The outcomes can then be examined for different values of V and C. In this section we use the specific example provided by Powell (2003).

13 Innovation through successful recombination reminds economists of the Schumpeterian definition of innovation: 'new combinations' in a process of 'creative destruction' of hitherto successful solutions.

14 It is taken from Lindgren (1997). See also Beinhocker (2006) for a discussion.

15 The latter aspect resembles 'punctuated equilibrium', as we will discuss in Chapter 11.

Part II

Economic Approaches

6 Behavioural theory of the firm

6.1 Introduction

How does a business firm make economic decisions? That is the central question of the behavioural theory of the firm developed by March, Simon and Cyert (March and Simon, 1958; Cyert and March, 1963). Examples of economic decisions include those regarding price, output, advertising levels and investments in machinery.

In standard microeconomics it is assumed that firms are holistic entities seeking to maximize their profits. By contrast, the behavioural theory of the firm postulates the firm as a coalition of (groups of) participants, each with their own objectives. Such a coalition of participants need not have maximization of profits as its sole objective. In fact, the process of defining the goals of the organization is the first step in describing actual decision processes within the firm. The second step is to describe how the organization forms expectations on which the decision processes are based. The third and last step is to describe the process of organizational choice.

6.2 The firm as a coalition of participants

The behavioural theory of the firm postulates that it is a coalition of participants. Each participant receives from the organization *inducements* and, in return, makes *contributions* to the organization. Each participant will continue to participate only as long as the inducements offered are as great as or greater than (measured in terms of the *individual's* values and the alternatives open to him) the contributions he is asked to make. Hence, the organization will continue to exist only so long as the contributions are sufficient to provide inducements in large enough measure to draw forth these contributions.

Participants in the firm are employees, investors, suppliers, distributors, consumers and possibly others. **Contributions** made by employees include not only the labour hours they put in but also their ideas for improvements, intelligence and so on. **Inducements** offered to employees include monetary payments (pay, pensions and so on), but also non-monetary benefits, such as self-achievement and job satisfaction. The relationship between the firm and

Contributions

Inducements

its employees is illustrated in Figure 6.1. A similar figure can be sketched for any other group of participants. The figure suggests that the firm is more than just one group of participants (here the employees). It also suggests that employees have other roles outside the firm, such as where they live, in their families, churches and so on.

In order to illustrate the differences between the behavioural theory and standard microeconomics, we discuss the decision of an employee to continue participation. In our description of standard microeconomics, employees receive pay in return for a number of hours of work. In behavioural theory, employees receive several different inducements, including monetary and non-monetary payments. In mathematical terms we would say that they receive a vector of inducements (that is, several inducements of different types). They also make a vector of contributions. That, however, is not a fundamental difference as standard microeconomics can also handle a vector of inducements and contributions. The fundamental difference lies in the *information* that employees have concerning alternative job opportunities.

In standard microeconomics we assume that each employee knows exactly what he could earn elsewhere. As soon as an employee sees more can be earned elsewhere, he will take the other job. So, for the same work, all companies must pay the same – in a competitive labour market there can be only one price for labour of a particular type. In the behavioural theory we assume that each employee has an **aspiration level** concerning the rate of pay. He will be content and not start looking for another job so long as the pay received is greater than or equal to that aspiration level. If the pay received continues to be higher than that aspiration level, then the aspiration level is slowly adjusted upwards. Thus, it takes some time before the aspiration level will reach the pay she regularly receives. The aspiration level is also adjusted upwards if the employee hears that another company pays more than the aspiration level for the same work. That adjustment also occurs slowly, so it takes some time before he becomes dissatisfied.

If after some time there is a large enough gap between the employee's aspiration level and the pay received, he will start to look for another job. If the employee finds another job that pays significantly more than the current job,

Aspiration level

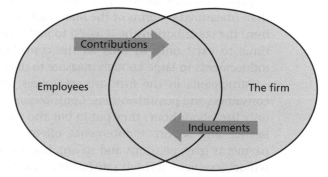

Figure 6.1 The firm and its employees in behavioural theory

he will leave. This process of adjusting one's aspiration level and looking for another job may take a considerable amount of time.

The situation is even more complicated than described above because inducements contain not only monetary payments but also various other benefits. Information about these other benefits may be even harder to obtain than information about levels of pay. It is, for example, usually very hard to find out what the atmosphere among colleagues in another organization is really like. The harder it is to obtain information about inducements and contributions that other firms make and demand, the slower is the process of adjusting aspiration levels. In behavioural theory the labour market is not a market of perfect competition. Differences in levels of pay and other working conditions can exist for long periods of time because workers cannot compare the inducements offered and the contributions demanded by other firms. They simply lack that information.

For other participants we can sketch a similar picture concerning the decision to stay with the coalition or leave. Consider consumers. In the model of perfectly competitive markets, price is all that matters for a consumer (remember that in the model of a perfectly competitive market, products are homogeneous: there are no differences between the products of different producers). Moreover, we assume that consumers know exactly what prices quoted by different producers are. Naturally they buy only from the cheapest source. Thus, in the model of a competitive market, all prices must be equal. If producers quote different prices, only the one with the lowest price will sell anything; all others will cease to exist.

In behavioural theory we assume that consumers do not know exactly what prices are quoted by other producers. A consumer continues to buy from the same producer so long as the price is less than or equal to his aspiration level. If a consumer gets more information on lower prices quoted by other producers he will slowly adjust the aspiration level downwards.

This picture becomes more realistic if we allow quality differences between products from different producers. Then a consumer also has an aspiration level with respect to quality. It seems quite reasonable to assume that a consumer has only vague information about quality levels of products offered by other producers. Thus, aspiration levels with respect to quality will be adjusted only slowly.

For every group of participants we can sketch a picture like that in Figure 6.1. If we do so and combine all those pictures we arrive at a picture like that in Figure 6.2. It shows that the firm is a coalition of groups of participants and each group of participants has other roles and interests outside the firm.

The groups of participants in Figure 6.2 are often referred to as *stakeholders* (each group has a 'stake' in the firm). Stakeholders include the investors (the shareholders) as well as employees, suppliers and customers. According to standard microeconomics, managers should serve only the interests of the shareholders. According to behavioural theory, however, a firm can survive only if its managers take care of the interests of all stakeholders, not just the shareholders (Box 6.1 develops this point further).

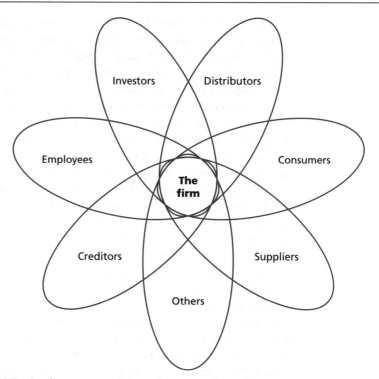

Figure 6.2 The firm as a coalition of groups of participants

Box 6.1 Stakeholders and shareholders

One of the liveliest current debates in the management field focuses on the question of which interests the management of a company should serve: those of the shareholders (only) or of the broader set of 'stakeholders' (which includes the employees, customers, suppliers and the community as well as the shareholders)?

Economic theories give different answers to this question. In Chapter 7 we see that agency theory tends to view the shareholders as the owners of the firm. In this view the managers should act as agents of the owners of the firm, maximizing the owner's wealth. In everyday management language, this view implies that the management of a company should maximize shareholder value.

Behavioural theory of the firm has a different perspective. It views the firm as a coalition of groups of participants. In this view, management's task is not to maximize the wealth of any particular group of participants, such as shareholders; rather, it is to enhance the firm's wealth by serving all interests of participant (= stakeholder) groups well. (Behavioural theory leaves the question unanswered as to what should happen with any economic surplus (profit) that is left after all participants have received their necessary inducements. In agency theory, this residual value belongs to the shareholders.)

The flavour of this debate can be tasted from the following excerpts of an interview by *Fortune* magazine with economist John Kay, who is introduced by *Fortune* as 'Britain's leading management thinker'.

> *FORTUNE: While the recent trend in the US and elsewhere is to give priority to shareholders' interests, you argue that managers need to balance all stakeholders' interests. Why should managers focus more on the interests of stakeholders like customers, employees, suppliers, and the local community?*

JOHN KAY: Let's turn this around and ask instead: why should managers give priority to shareholders' interests? The most compelling answer I hear is that it's because the shareholders own the business. Now if the business consisted purely of its physical assets, then I would find that fairly persuasive, but I don't think that is true. A company is its history, its structure of relationships, its reputation. These are the things that allow the company to add value, which creates shareholder wealth, and to say that shareholders own these things is kind of bizarre. They don't and they couldn't.

FORTUNE: *Is the primary purpose of management to maximize shareholder wealth?*

JOHN KAY: Economists tend to believe that everyone acts to maximize something. But in our everyday lives, we aren't maximizing any particular thing: rather, we are balancing different and conflicting concerns. I think the same is true of companies, and therefore I don't think companies are there to maximize shareholder value – or social welfare. Managers of companies work to balance several different interests. That is the reality of how companies function.

FORTUNE: *What is a company's purpose, if it is not to maximize shareholder value?*

JOHN KAY: Producing goods and services people want. Business is about providing employment, providing value for customers, for developing skills of employees, for developing capabilities of suppliers – as well as earning money for shareholders.

Source: Fortune, 17 February 1997, p. 61. See further: Donaldson & Preston (1995) and Freeman (1984)

It is clear from the discussion that in behavioural theory there is competition between firms in the labour market, the market for final products, the capital market and so on. However, behavioural theory focuses not on competition between firms, but on the process of decisionmaking within the firm. The competitive context in various markets is further taken as given.

6.3 Organizational goals

6.3.1 Bargaining and organizational slack

The process of decisionmaking within the firm starts with the definition of its goals. In standard microeconomics we assume that the firm has a single goal – usually profit maximization. In behavioural theory the firm is viewed as a

Coalition of participants

coalition of participants. Each participant has his or her own goals. Ordinarily, those goals will not coincide. In general, we expect a conflict of goals from different participants. Consumers cannot be offered lower prices and employees higher pay without lowering profits (the inducements for the providers of equity capital).

In behavioural theory it is postulated that the goals of a firm are arrived at through a bargaining process. During that bargaining process both the compo-

Bargaining power

sition and the general goals of the coalition are established. The **bargaining power** of each potential participant depends on how unique the contribution is that he can offer to the coalition. So, an unskilled worker in a country where unskilled labour is plentiful does not have much bargaining power (unless there are strong labour unions). Someone possessing a highly specialized skill that is essential to the success of the coalition has much more bargaining power. For the providers of equity capital, profit maximization or maximization of the value of the firm is an important objective. The extent to which they succeed in realizing their objective depends on the relative bargaining power of the various groups of participants.

The upshot of this discussion is that a real firm ordinarily has no single goal or clearly defined objective function. Only individual participants have goals. Those goals are in the form of aspiration levels. The real achievement of the particular goal of a certain participant can be only temporarily below his aspiration level. For all participants, achievement levels will be at least equal to their aspiration levels most of the time. For some they will be above their aspiration levels.

Organizational slack

The difference between total resources and the total payments necessary to preserve the coalition is termed **organizational slack**. Participants' aspiration levels adjust to actual payments and alternatives external to the organization. Hence, in the long run, we would expect aspiration levels to be equal to actual payments *and* alternatives external to the organization. If this were the case, there would be no organizational slack. The rate of payments made to coalition members would then be analogous to factor prices in a perfectly competitive market. However, behavioural theory states that markets are imperfect. The basic reason is that information about levels of goal achievement participants can realize if they join another organization is difficult to obtain, especially concerning non-monetary payments, so aspiration levels adjust only slowly. In a world without change, aspiration levels would, after some time, equal actual payments and external alternatives. In a changing world – for example, in a world with technological progress – we normally expect to have organizational slack.

6.3.2 Operational subgoals

Operational subgoals

In a real firm, an overall goal such as profit maximization needs to be translated into several **operational subgoals**. It is often impossible to avoid a conflict between those operational subgoals.

As an example, imagine a firm making soap noodles. Soap noodles are little pieces of soap in the form of noodles. They are made in a chemical plant that uses animal fat as a basic raw material. They are sold to soap manufacturers, who press soap noodles into tablets and give the soap a colour, a scent and a brand name.

Suppose you are in charge of the soap noodle firm. You have two managers reporting to you – a production manager and a sales manager. You know that the number of soap noodles sold depends on price, level of effort of your sales manager and a random factor. You also know that the real production costs per unit depend on the number of units sold per year, number and size of changes in production levels during the year and level of effort of your production manager. The sales manager makes decisions on prices quoted to individual customers; the production manager decides how much to produce each week.

Assume for the moment that soap noodles can be stored on site at no cost. You want to give each manager an operational subgoal that is consistent with your overall goal of profit maximization. You can do this by specifying the following operational subgoals.

For the sales manager:

$$\text{maximize } N \times (P - SC)$$

where

N = number of units sold
P = price
SC = standard unit cost

For the production manager you can specify the following goal:

$$\text{minimize } RC$$

where

RC = real unit cost

This is equivalent to maximizing $(SC - RC)$ as SC is fixed.

Now, for simplicity, assume that the production cost per unit does not depend on the number of units sold (that is, assume there are no scale economies to be had in production). The production manager's goal is then equivalent to:

$$\text{maximize } N \times (SC - RC)$$

We can now combine the goals of the two managers thus:

$$\text{maximize } [N \times (P - SC)] + [N \times (SC - RC)]$$

That is equivalent to:

$$\text{maximize } N \times (P - RC)$$

As we assume inventory costs are zero, that is equivalent to profit maximization. If inventories can be stored without cost, the sales manager and the production manager can make their decisions independently. In reality, inventories cannot be stored without cost. If inventory costs are not negligible, you cannot specify operational subgoals for your two managers without creating a conflict of interests between them.

Who should be responsible for inventory costs? The inventory level depends on the decisions made by both the sales manager and production manager. If you make the production manager responsible for inventory costs, you create a conflict. The production manager will want to keep the inventory levels as low as possible, but that imposes the risk of stock-out on the sales manager. She would prefer safe levels of inventory in order to be able to satisfy customer demand at all times. However, if you make the sales manager responsible for inventory costs, you also create a conflict. Now the sales manager will want to keep inventory levels as low as possible. She will try to achieve that by frequently ordering very small lots. That means very small lots in manufacturing. The production manager would prefer large lots in order to minimize production costs. If you introduce an inventory manager, what subgoal can you specify for her? You would surely create a conflict between your inventory manager and your sales manager as well as one between your inventory manager and your production manager.

This example demonstrates that it is difficult, and often impossible, to specify operational subgoals that are consistent with profit maximization and do not lead to conflicts between managers of functional departments.

In behavioural theory we assume that operational subgoals are specified and given to managers of functional departments. With each subgoal goes an aspiration level. Managers are rewarded if they at least reach those aspiration levels. This does not eliminate conflict between managers of functional departments – it is *quasi-resolution of conflict* rather than *complete* resolution of conflict.

6.4 Organizational expectations

An important assumption of standard microeconomics is symmetrical information: everyone has the same information. In behavioural theory that assumption is relaxed: everyone does not have the same information.

In the soap noodle firm, you have a production manager and a sales manager reporting to you. The production manager decides how much to produce each week. To make that decision, he needs information on future sales. He can make a sales forecast by extrapolating historical data on shipments made. He can also ask the sales manager to make a sales forecast. It is likely that the sales manager can make the better forecast: the sales manager can make the same extrapolation as the production manager, but she can improve on it because of her knowledge of recent changes in market situations.

Suppose the sales manager makes a sales forecast each week. Will the production manager now use that sales forecast only? Empirical evidence shows that many production managers do not – they continue to make their own sales forecast. The reason is that they know:

- the sales manager is more often than not too optimistic (maybe people with an optimistic nature tend to become sales managers);
- the sales manager has an incentive to make an optimistic sales forecast in order to reduce the probability of a stock-out.

The above example demonstrates the use of expectations in decisionmaking within the firm. Expectations are the result of drawing inferences from available information. Decisionmakers within the firm may have different information. In addition, they may draw different inferences from the same set of information. Hence, even if two people within the same firm have the same information, they may still have different expectations.

6.5 Organizational choice

Another important assumption made in standard microeconomics is that behaviour of firms can be adequately described as maximizing behaviour. That itself makes two assumptions:

- at the moment of decisionmaking, firms know all the decision alternatives;
- firms are able to compare all alternatives and choose the one that maximizes the objective function.

Behavioural theory rejects both assumptions. In the real world, firms have to make decisions under conditions of partial ignorance. That is, they have to make a decision on a proposal (to accept or reject a proposal to develop a new product, for example) without knowing what alternatives will turn up the next day. Of course, they can also decide to devote resources to search for alternatives before deciding on the present proposal.

In the context of standard microeconomics we would have to assume that firms are able to calculate the expected marginal revenue from searching for an alternative and the expected marginal cost of searching for an alternative. Firms would then, presumably, continue searching until the marginal cost of additional searching equalled the marginal revenue of additional searching. If many alternatives were potentially available, firms would invest a lot of time (and resources) in searching. So much, in fact, that other firms could realize significant advantages in deciding more quickly. Moreover, in the real world, firms cannot possibly hope to evaluate all potential new products against each other.

In behavioural theory we therefore assume that alternatives are evaluated one at a time. Firms do not maximize an objective function. Instead, they make a rough estimate of several consequences of a decision alternative. For example, for a proposal to develop a new product, they try to estimate:

- the size of the market;
- their expected market share;
- the price and production cost of the new product;
- the development cost.

There are perhaps other variables as well. They have aspiration levels for all of these variables. If the market is 'large enough', if their expected market share is 'sufficient', if the margin between price and production cost is 'reasonable' and if the development cost is 'not too high', then they accept the proposal. They do not maximize in the sense of evaluating all possible proposals for new products at the same time. Their behaviour is better described as **satisficing** – that is, searching for a solution that meets aspiration levels and is therefore acceptable.

Satisficing

In behavioural theory, then, we assume that firms satisfice rather than maximize. One reason for this is that decision alternatives come one at a time. Another reason is that human decisionmakers are simply unable to make all the calculations necessary to compare all the alternatives. The calculations often are too complex. To put it another way, the capacity of the human mind to make all the necessary calculations is often too small. In behavioural theory, therefore, we assume **bounded rationality** – we assume that human decisionmakers may try to maximize but are not always able to do so. We return to the notion of bounded rationality in Chapter 8 on transaction cost economics. It has proven to be an important concept. Therefore, we sum it up here in the words of James March (1994, pp. 8–9) and describe further developments in Box 6.2:

Bounded rationality

'Studies of decision making in the real world suggest that not all alternatives are known, that not all consequences are considered, and that not all preferences are evoked at the same time. Instead of considering all alternatives, decision makers typically appear to consider only a few and to look at them sequentially rather than simultaneously. Decision makers do not consider all consequences of their alternatives. They focus on some and ignore others. Relevant information about consequences is not sought, and available information is not used. Instead of having a complete, consistent set of preferences, decision makers seem to have incomplete and inconsistent goals, not all of which are considered at the same time ... Instead of calculating the 'best possible action', they search for an action that is 'good enough' ... The core notion of limited (or bounded) rationality is that individuals are intendedly rational. Although decision makers try to be rational, they are constrained by limited cognitive capabilities and incomplete information, and thus their actions may be less than completely rational in spite of their best intentions and efforts'.

Box 6.2 Bounded rationality: further developments

Herbert Simon and James March were concerned with the limits to the 'full rationality' model of homo economicus. They maintained that most decisionmakers were *intendedly* rational, but only *limitedly* so. Later research revealed that may be still a somewhat too generous description of human decisionmaking. Further limits on rationality were uncovered in the work of Amos Tversky and Daniel Kahneman. They found that many decisions, made in conditions of uncertainty, are subject to cognitive biases (distortions) and are taken with heuristics (simple rules of thumb), such as the following.

■ *Availability* People base their prediction of an outcome on the vividness and emotional impact of recent information rather than on actual probability. For example, most people overrate the probability of airplane crashes versus car crashes, because plane accidents are reported more frequently and vividly.

■ *Anchoring* The tendency to rely too heavily on one (early) piece of information when making decisions. That specific piece of information then becomes an 'anchor', an initial value from which people make their adjustments to arrive at the outcome. For instance, when you ask a group of people 'is the success rate of acquisitions higher or lower than 50 per cent?', you will get higher values than if you had set the anchor at 30 per cent. That is because most people adjust from the anchor given.

■ *Representativeness* Basing your prediction not on an individual case but the class of cases you think that individual case belongs to (or is representative of). That bias leads you to 'jump to conclusions' about the individual case, which may deviate from the class of cases you assigned it to.

Such heuristics and biases pose further limits on rationality. They have given rise to a separate field of *behavioural economics* based on observed decisionmaking behaviour of economic actors rather than on assumed (full) rationality.

See further: Bazerman (2006); Kahneman (2002); Tversky and Kahneman (1974)

Finally, there is a third reason for firms satisficing rather than maximizing. The firm is seen as a coalition of participants, each having his own objectives. If a firm has no single objective function, how can it maximize? Instead, organizational choice is described as a process of deciding on alternatives one at a time. As soon as an alternative is found that meets the aspiration levels of all coalition members, it is accepted.

Suppose a firm wants to buy a new software package for order processing. Suppose, further, that the sales manager, production manager and controller form a three-person committee that has to make the decision. Behavioural theory assumes that each may have a different criterion for choosing the software package. For example, the sales manager wants to buy a package that provides information on inventories available for sale in real time, the production manager wants one that allows him to make a reliable sales forecast and the controller one that produces invoices as soon as the order is shipped. The three-person committee cannot maximize as their three criteria cannot be translated into a single criterion (see Box 6.3). Instead, they start to look for a package that meets certain minimum standards (aspiration levels) for each of those three criteria. As soon as they have found a package that is acceptable to all of them, they stop searching for another package.

Box 6.3 Decisionmaking by a committee

Consider a three-person committee. Suppose each person wants to maximize his or her own objective. Suppose, further, that all objectives are quantifiable and you denote them as C_1, C_2 and C_3. The three-person committee can maximize only if these three objectives can be combined into a single objective function, as follows:

$$C_0 = \alpha C_1 + \beta C_2 + \gamma C_3$$

That requires the three-person committee to

- accept each other's objectives;
- agree on the weights (α, β, γ) assigned to each objective.

Only if the members of the committee are able to meet both conditions, can they jointly maximize an overall objective function (C_0). If either of the two conditions is not met – as will often be the case in real life – satisficing is a ready alternative procedure. It requires only that each member of the committee is able to specify his or her own aspiration level. If an alternative is found that meets all three aspiration levels, a unanimous decision can be made.

6.6 Summary: goals and decisionmaking within the firm in behavioural theory

In behavioural theory, the firm is postulated as a coalition of (groups of) participants, such as shareholders, employees, managers, suppliers and customers. That is a major way in which it differs from standard microeconomic theory, which sees the firm as a holistic entity. Each participant receives inducements from the firm in return for the contributions he or she makes to the firm. A participant will remain within the coalition if, in his own opinion, the value of the inducements received is greater than the value of the contributions made.

In behavioural theory we assume that not all people have the same information. For example, an employee may not know exactly how much he could earn with another employer or what the atmosphere between colleagues is really like in another firm.

In behavioural theory we also assume that human beings are boundedly rational. That means human beings are unable to make all sorts of difficult calculations in a split second, nor can they process all the information they receive. It does not mean that humans do not want to maximize something, only that they are not always able to do so. The behaviour of human beings is better described as satisficing than maximizing. For example, an employee will have an aspiration level with respect to the level of pay he wants to receive. As long as the pay earned is above that aspiration level, the employee is content. Owing to lack of information he may even be content with a lower level of pay than is offered elsewhere.

In behavioural theory concerning the firm, each participant or group of participants has his own goals, usually in the form of aspiration levels. Those goals will generally not coincide. The result is that the firm will generally have several goals, which are arrived at through a bargaining process between the (groups of) participants.

The overall goals of the firm need to be translated into operational subgoals in order to be of practical value. That is usually quite complicated, even if the firm has only one goal, such as profit maximization.

Consider a firm owned and managed by one person, the entrepreneur. Why is it impossible for the entrepreneur to hire only people who just do as they are told? In a very small firm, it may be possible. Direct supervision is often the most important coordinating mechanism in a very small firm, as we saw in Chapter 3. In a larger firm, however, the decisions that have to be made become so numerous the entrepreneur has to delegate some of them. For example, one person cannot make all the decisions concerning marketing, production and inventory management. It is simply inefficient to transmit all information to a single person so that he can make all the decisions. So, we have a decisionmaking process in which two or more people participate. Those people bring their own goals to the organization.

Suppose the goal of the entrepreneur is profit maximization. If he appoints functional managers, it is impossible to specify operational subgoals without creating a conflict of interests between them. So, managers of functional departments are given an operational subgoal with a target level. Their task is to reach their target level, not to maximize or minimize something. By giving managers of functional departments a target level, the entrepreneur leaves some room for mutual adjustment. Mutual adjustment is then used in conjunction with direct supervision as a coordinating mechanism (see Chapter 3).

There are four fundamental differences between behavioural theory and standard microeconomic theory. Behavioural theory:

- postulates the firm as a coalition of participants;
- does not assume that the firm has a single objective;
- assumes that information cannot be transmitted without cost;
- assumes that human decisionmakers are boundedly rational.

As we shall see in the following chapters, several of these characteristics of decisionmaking within firms have been incorporated in various economic approaches to organizations, which were developed later. That was recognized by Cyert and March when they wrote a preface to the second edition of their classic book *A Behavioral Theory of the Firm* in 1992:

> We had an agenda in 1963. We thought that research on economics and research on organizations should have something to say to each other. We thought that the theory of the firm should be connected to empirical observations of firms. We thought that empirical observations of what happens in firms should be connected to interesting theoretical ideas ... The agenda and the first steps we proposed were somewhat deviant from dominant ideas in both economics and organization theory when the book first appeared. In the years since 1963 ... a number of the ideas discussed in the book have become part of the received doctrine. In particular, a perspective that sees firms as coalitions of multiple, conflicting interests using standard rules and procedures to operate under conditions of bounded rationality is now rather widely adopted in descriptions and theories of the firm.

Questions

1 In a period of economic recession, most companies are able to increase production efficiency by reducing their workforce without any decrease in the level of output. Apparently, firms take action to reduce costs only when profit rates are declining. Many firms seem to be able to restore previous profit levels by taking this kind of action. Why do firms not minimize production cost in the first place, before the recession sets in?

2 Reread Box 6.1. We assume you agree with John Kay, that managers should serve the interests of all stakeholders in the firm, not just those of the shareholders. Somehow it seems morally right to do so. Now, suppose that you meet a proponent of standard microeconomic theory who tells you: 'Yes, I do agree with you that the interests of the employees are very important. That is exactly why managers should take into account only the interests of the shareholders. If they do just that, the result will be a Pareto-optimal allocation of resources in the economy. That is the major result of standard microeconomic theory. There can be no doubt about the correctness of that statement. The result is that the employees will be better off when the managers do not take into account the interests of their employees explicitly than when they do. If they were to do so, they would make decisions resulting in an allocation of resources in the economy that is not Pareto-optimal. For example, managers may be tempted to postpone a plant closure because by closing that plant employees would lose their jobs. The result would be that employees would have to continue working in their present job, but, if managers were to constantly close inefficient plants, people would always work in the most modern plants where they can earn the most.'

Suppose that you are invited to debate with this proponent of standard microeconomics. What would your main arguments be?

3 In behavioural theory regarding the firm, management's task is not to maximize shareholder value, but to achieve a balanced satisfaction of all the firm's stakeholders, including employees, customers, suppliers and shareholders. In the real world, a firm's top management team has a choice. It can emphasize shareholder value in its policy statements and use shareholder value as the main objective in strategic decisionmaking or it can emphasize stakeholder interests in its policy statements and use a variety of objectives, including satisfaction of major stakeholders, in strategic decisionmaking. Can you give arguments as to why firms choosing the second option might end up creating more shareholder value than would firms choosing the first?

4   Goliath Ltd is a company manufacturing bicycles. It is located in Hemel Hempstead, England. The Goliath product offering includes 20 different models with names such as Goliath-Sport, Goliath-Tourist, Goliath-City and so on. Each type comes in versions for men and women and is available in several colours and sizes. In total, Goliath's product range consists of about 600 different bicycles. It is quite difficult to make reliable demand forecasts for each of the 600 types.

Goliath sells its bicycles mainly through servicing retailers. These are quite small outlets. On average these outlets have no more than 30 bicycles in store. Very often, a potential buyer will choose a bicycle of a certain model, but in a colour or size that is not directly available in the store. In such a case, the retailer can check online whether or not the desired bicycle is available in Goliath's central warehouse in Hemel Hempstead. If it is, the retailer can order the desired bicycle with one mouse click and it will be delivered within 72 hours to any retailer in England. If the desired bicycle is not available, Goliath is likely to lose the sale.

Mrs Prime is Goliath's sales manager. She is responsible for making a new sales forecast every four weeks. She has considerable freedom in setting prices and spending money on promotions and campaigns. A substantial part of her compensation is tied to the results of her sales department. Those results are defined as sales minus cost of sales (at standard cost prices) minus selling costs (such as advertising).

Mr Griffin is production manager at Goliath. He is responsible for planning and scheduling production runs. A large part of his compensation is in the form of a bonus, which is determined by manufacturing costs per bicycle. Small production runs are extremely expensive and so Mr Griffin is very reluctant to plan them.

Mr Robbins has been recently appointed as managing director. He soon finds out that Mrs Prime and Mr Griffin have many conflicts. Very often, certain bicycles are out of stock, so Mrs Prime complains bitterly to Mr Robbins about Mr Griffin's refusal to adjust to what the market demands. In turn, Mr Griffin complains to Mr Robbins that Mrs Prime's sales forecasts are very unreliable.

What do you think Mr Robbins should do in order to improve cooperation between Mrs Prime and Mr Griffin? Discuss.

Suggested further reading

Bazerman, M. H. (2006), *Judgment in Managerial Decision Making*, New York: John Wiley.

Cyert, R. M. and March, J. G. (1963), *A Behavioral Theory of the Firm*, Englewood Cliffs, NJ: Prentice Hall. (Second edition 1992.)

March, J. G. (1994), *A Primer on Decision Making: How Decisions Happen*, New York: Free Press.

March, J. G. and Simon, H. A. (1958), *Organizations*, New York: John Wiley.

7 Agency theory

7.1 Introduction

Agency theory, in its simplest form, discusses the relations between two people – a principal and an agent who makes decisions on behalf of the principal. Here are a few examples of agency relations:

- the owner of a firm (principal) and the manager of a firm (agent), who makes decisions affecting the owner's wealth;
- the owner of an estate (principal) and her steward (agent), who makes decisions affecting the owner's wealth;
- a manager (principal) and his subordinate, who makes decisions affecting the manager's reputation;
- a patient (principal) and her physician (agent), who makes decisions affecting the patient's health;
- an insurance company (principal) and a person holding a fire insurance policy (agent), who makes decisions affecting the insurance company's cash flows;
- a lessor (principal) and a lessee (agent), who makes decisions affecting the lessor's property.

Agency relations can be found both within firms (manager and subordinate) and between firms (for example, licensing and franchising). In this chapter we shall take the agency relation between the shareholder(s) and the manager of a firm as our main example.

Within agency theory two streams of literature can be distinguished: the positive theory of agency and the theory of principal and agent.

Positive theory of agency

In the **positive theory of agency**, the firm is viewed as a nexus of contracts. The main research questions in the positive theory of agency are how do contracts affect the behaviour of participants and why do we observe certain organizational forms in the real world? In general, it is assumed in the positive theory of agency that existing organizational forms are efficient. If they were not, they would not continue to exist. The positive theory of agency thus sets out to explain why organizational forms are as they are. The theory is not (yet) expressed in the form of mathematical models.

Theory of principal and agent

In the **theory of principal and agent**, the central question is how should the principal design the agent's reward structure? That question is dealt with in formal mathematical models.

Both streams of literature – positive agency theory and theory of principal and agent – have their antecedents in the literature on the separation of ownership and control (see Section 7.2).

The remainder of this chapter is organized as follows. Sections 7.3–7.5 discuss three different but strongly related contributions to the positive theory of agency. Two important organizational forms in Western societies are the entrepreneurial firm and the public corporation. The entrepreneurial firm is a firm owned and managed by the same person. The public corporation is a corporation with publicly traded shares and widely dispersed ownership. In the entrepreneurial firm there is no separation of ownership and control, while in the public corporation there is.

How ownership structure affects managerial behaviour is discussed in Section 7.3. Then, in Section 7.4, we explain how team production might explain the existence of entrepreneurial firms. In Section 7.5 the existence of both entrepreneurial firms and public corporations is explained by focusing on decision processes in conjunction with residual claims. The theory of principal and agent is then discussed in Section 7.6. A summary is provided in Section 7.7.

Applications of agency theory can be found in Section 12.10 and in Chapter 14.

7.2 Separation of ownership and control

Adam Smith recognized the problem resulting from the separation of ownership and control: 'Negligence and profusion ... must always prevail, more or less, in such a company' (see quote from *The Wealth of Nations* in Box 7.1).

Box 7.1 The joint stock company

The trade of a joint stock company is always managed by a court of directors. The court, indeed, is frequently subject, in many respects, to the control of a general court of proprietors. But the greater part of those proprietors seldom pretend to understand any thing of the business of the company; and when the spirit of faction happens not to prevail among them, give themselves no trouble about it, but receive contentedly such half yearly or yearly dividend, as the directors think proper to make to them. This total exemption from trouble and from risk, beyond a limited sum, encouraged many people to become adventurers in joint stock companies, who would, upon no account, hazard their fortunes in any private copartnery. Such companies, therefore, commonly draw to themselves much greater stocks than any private copartnery can boast of ... The directors of such companies, however, being the managers rather of other people's money than of their own, it cannot well be expected, that they should watch over it with the same anxious vigilance with which the partners in a private copartnery frequently watch over their own. Like the stewards of a rich man, they are apt to consider attention to small matters as not for their master's honour, and very easily give themselves a dispensation from having it. Negligence and profusion, therefore, must always prevail, more or less, in the management of the affairs of such a company. It is upon this account that joint stock companies for foreign trade have seldom been able to maintain the competition against private adventurers. They have, accordingly, very seldom succeeded without an exclusive privilege; and frequently have not succeeded with one.

Source: Adam Smith (1776) *The Wealth of Nations*, Book V, Chapter 1

The issue of separation of ownership and control did not receive much attention from other early economic writers. The situation changed when, in 1932, Adolf Berle and Gardiner C. Means published *The Modern Corporation and Private Property*. In that book, Berle and Means describe the **separation of ownership and control** in the typical twentieth-century corporation. The large corporation, they say, is owned by so many shareholders that no single shareholder owns a significant fraction of the outstanding stock. Therefore, no single shareholder has the power really to control the actions of the officers of the corporation.

The officers themselves, in general, also own a very small part of the stock of their corporations. Hence, the situation may be characterized as follows:

■ the bulk of the dividends goes to the outside shareholders;
■ all the major decisions are made by the corporate officers;
■ the outside shareholders are unable to control the corporate officers.

In that situation, Berle and Means say, the interests of the officers and shareholders diverge widely. The officers are in search of power, prestige and money for themselves, while the shareholders are interested only in profits. Senior managers, in the view of Berle and Means, are in a position to enrich themselves at the expense of the shareholders and, they fear, sometimes engage in corporate plundering.

In most but not all large corporations, the officers own only a very small percentage of all shares. In some large corporations the officers' portion is significant. Those corporations might be called owner-controlled and the corporations with widely dispersed shareholdings manager-controlled. If the argument of Berle and Means is true, we expect a significant difference in profitability between owner-controlled and manager-controlled companies. Owner-controlled companies should be much more profitable than manager-controlled companies. That is a direct implication of the work by Berle and Means. In empirical work, however, little or no support for that implication has been found.

Why do managers of manager-controlled corporations perform as well as managers of owner-controlled corporations? If they have the opportunity to enrich themselves at the expense of shareholders, why do they not do so? When we want to improve or discuss the way in which large public corporations are governed, that is certainly one of the key questions. In Chapter 14 on corporate governance we shall deal with the question in greater detail than we can do now. Here we want to say that, yes, of course, managers can and should refrain from excessive on-the-job consumption because of ethical considerations. Moreover, managers do not work in isolation but in an environmental and institutional context, consisting of company law, auditing, antitrust authorities and public opinion. Here we want to stress that, in addition to those factors, there are powerful mechanisms that prevent managers from engaging in excessive on-the-job consumption. Let us examine some of those potential mechanisms.

First, there is the *stock market*. If a corporation performs badly because the managers of that corporation are incompetent, lazy or not really interested in running the corporation as well as they can, the market price of that company's stock will decline. If, moreover, it becomes clear why the market price of that company's stock is so low, a determined outsider can try to acquire a majority of the shares at a low price. The outsider can then oust the managers, install new managers and control them more tightly. Therefore, managers who perform poorly must always fear that their company can be taken over. There is a market not only for individual shares but also for whole corporations. To put it differently, there is a market for the rights to manage corporations. That market is usually called the **market for corporate control**. Competition between management teams in the market for corporate control increases the pressure on managers to perform well.

Market for corporate control

Second, there is a *market for managerial labour*. The top position in a large company usually gives a manager more power, more prestige, more money and more job satisfaction than the top position in a smaller company. Hence, we expect some competition between managers to obtain those few top positions in the largest firms. All managers, therefore, have to worry about their reputations. If they acquire a reputation for pursuing their personal interests instead of profit opportunities, it is likely that their chances of being offered a better position are small.

Third, there are *markets for the company's products*. The more intense the competition in those markets, the less opportunity there is for managers to pursue their own interests. If they do so, the company will have higher unit costs than its competitors or it will turn out products of a lower quality than those of its competitors. It will lose market share and, ultimately, cease to exist. Therefore, competition in product markets also restricts managers from pursuing their own interests. How markets can discipline managers of public companies is discussed more extensively in Section 14.6.

Finally, even if the officers of a company do not own shares in their company, their *pay package* may still include a bonus related to annual profits, an option to buy stock at a later date and so on. This can also bring the interests of top managers more in line with those of the shareholders. The role of reward structures is the key issue in the theory of principal and agent. The theory is discussed extensively in Section 7.6. The question of how to design compensation packages for managers is discussed in more detail in Section 14.3.

7.3 Managerial behaviour and ownership structure in a world with certainty and symmetrical information

The preceding section discussed the separation of ownership and control in quite general terms. Here we discuss the issue in more precise terms. How does the ownership structure of the firm affect the behaviour of managers in that firm? To answer that question, Jensen and Meckling in 1976 developed a theory that is explained in this section.

On-the-job consumption

Consider, first, a manager who owns all the shares of the company she manages. That owner-manager has two conflicting objectives. She is interested in maximizing both the value of the firm and **on-the-job consumption**. The latter may take various forms, such as buying a company jet, furnishing the office in a luxurious way or spending fewer hours on the job (and more in expensive restaurants). This is not to say that buying a company jet is always a matter of on-the-job consumption. In order to make the point clear, consider what a manager interested only in maximizing the value of a company would do. Such a manager would first calculate the following:

- the present value of the managerial time saved by buying a company jet (a);
- the present value of buying tickets for regular airlines (b);
- the present value of the cash outflows from buying and operating a company jet (c).

A manager interested in maximizing the value of the firm would buy a company jet if and only if:

$$c - a < b$$

Now define d as $d = c - a - b$ and suppose that d is greater than zero. A manager interested in not only maximizing the value of the firm but also in prestige and personal comfort might still buy a company jet. If so, d is the amount spent as on-the-job consumption.

On-the-job consumption does take place in the real world, although not often in a way that is as conspicuous as the example given in Box 7.2.

Box 7.2 **The agency costs of Casey Reginald Williams**

Sometimes the agency costs of on-the-job consumption are not only substantial but also hilarious. Below are some excerpts from the interrogation of Raymond R. Williams, founder and former CEO of the Australian firm HIH Insurance Limited, about the bankruptcy of the firm.

Mr Williams was interrogated by Mr Wayne Martin, QC as follows.

Martin: *Could you tell us please if, on your frequent first-class trips to London, you booked the seat next to you for your briefcase?*
Williams: *I don't recall specifically. But that may have been the case, on some occasions.*
Martin: *That your briefcase was also travelling first class?*
Williams: *That may have been the case.*
Martin: *Did you express the view to Qantas that this briefcase should be eligible for frequent flyer points?*
Williams: *I can't recall that.*
Martin: *And were you subsequently informed that said briefcase would not be eligible for such points on the grounds that it was not, in fact, a person?*
Williams: *That may have been the airline's position on that issue.*
Martin: *Was that briefcase, from that point on, booked under the name of Casey Williams?*
Williams: *Yes, Casey Reginald Williams, AM.*

Source: HIH Royal Commission, Day 131, Wayne Martin QC examining Raymond Reginald Williams, AM (founder/former CEO of HIH) as reported in Nederlandse Corporate Governance Stichting, *Corporate Governance in Nederland 2002*, p. 63.

From that example it is clear, if managers engage in on-the-job consumption, they are not maximizing the value of their firm. The more that is spent as on-the-job consumption, the lower the value of their firms. If a manager spent $1 million as on-the-job consumption (in our example, $d = \$1$ million), he would lower the value of the firm by $1 million.

In Figure 7.1, the present value of on-the-job consumption, C, is plotted against the value of the firm, V. It is now clear that the sum of the two variables – value of the firm and present value of on-the-job consumption – is constant. If the manager decides to consume C_4, the value of the firm will be V_4. If he decides to consume C_5, the value of the firm will be V_5. The line V_0C_0 represents all possible combinations of V and C. That line gives the set of combinations of V and C the manager can choose from and is called the **budget constraint**. In Figure 7.1, the budget constraint V_0C_0 has slope -1. Note that a manager who is interested only in maximizing the value of the firm, not in any form of on-the-job consumption, would not consume anything on the job. The value of the firm then would be V_0.

Budget constraint

The values of C and V chosen by the manager depend on his utility function. In Figure 7.1, all points on curve U_3 represent points of equal utility to the manager. All points on curve U_1 also represent points of equal utility to the manager. Points on curve U_1, however, represent a higher level of utility than points on curve U_3. Points on curve U_2 represent a still higher level of utility, but there is no way the manager can reach that level. The manager maximizes his utility by choosing point P_1, where his consumption is C_1 and the value of

Figure 7.1 Value of the firm (V) and present value of on-the-job consumption (C). The manager owns all the shares in the firm

the firm is V_1. At that point, the marginal utility of an additional dollar of on-the-job consumption is equal to the marginal utility of an additional dollar of wealth.

The curves U_1, U_2 and U_3 in Figure 7.1 are called *indifference curves* because they represent points of equal utility to the manager.[1] Thus the manager is indifferent about the points lying on the same indifference curve. As we are still dealing with a manager who owns all the shares in the firm, we need only the information in Figure 7.1 to determine his trade-off between the value of his firm and his on-the-job consumption.

Now suppose the manager sells a fraction $(1 - \alpha)$ of his shares to outsiders. The manager then owns a fraction α of the shares himself. For example, α could be equal to 0.7, which would mean that the manager sells 30 per cent of the shares to outsiders and retains 70 per cent himself. If he decides to spend an additional $1 on on-the-job consumption, the value of the firm will be reduced by $1. Now, however, the personal wealth of the manager will be reduced by only 70 cents and the wealth of the outside shareholders by 30 cents. The manager will now spend an amount on consumption such that the marginal utility of an additional $1 of on-the-job consumption is equal to the marginal utility of an additional 70 cents of personal wealth. So we know that he will now spend more money on on-the-job consumption.

How much more the manager will spend on on-the-job consumption depends on the set of possible combinations of personal wealth and on-the-job consumption he can choose from. That set depends on the price he can achieve for the shares he sells to the outsiders, which depends on whether or not the outsiders know beforehand that the manager will spend more on on-the-job consumption after he has sold the shares.

Suppose they do *not* know the manager will do that. Such naïve outsiders will be willing to pay 30 per cent of V_1 for 30 per cent of the shares. The budget constraint now facing the manager must have a slope of -0.7 as the manager can trade $1 of consumption for 70 cents of personal wealth. The budget constraint must also pass through point P_1. At that point the manager consumes C_1 and his personal wealth is V_1 (he will have 30 per cent of V_1 in cash and the other 70 per cent of V_1 in shares). So, the budget constraint now facing the manager must be line L in Figure 7.2 (see overleaf). Line L passes through point P_1 and has a slope of -0.7.

At point P_2 there is an indifference curve (U_2 in Figure 7.2) tangential to the budget constraint L. At that point the manager consumes C_2. The value of the firm is reduced to V_2. Thus, the outside shareholders, who paid 30 per cent of V_1 for their shares, now find that their shares have a value of 30 per cent of V_2 only.

Suppose now that the outsiders were not so naïve as to assume the manager would not increase his on-the-job consumption. Suppose, instead, that they expected the manager to increase his consumption as soon as he sold the shares. Suppose, moreover, that the outsiders knew the exact shape of the manager's indifference curves. They would have a look at Figure 7.3 (overleaf) and try to find a point P_3 such that P_3 lies on V_0C_0 and the indifference curve passing through P_3 has, at point P_3, a slope of $-\alpha$ – that is, the indifference curve is tangential at P_3 to a line through P_3 with slope $-\alpha$.

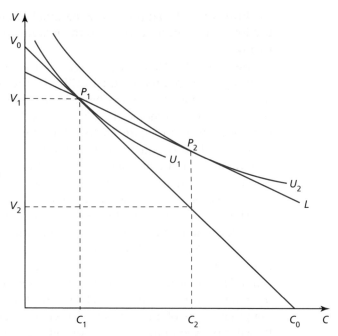

Figure 7.2 Value of the firm (V) and present value of on-the-job consumption (C). The manager owns a fraction α of the shares. The outsiders expect no increase in on-the-job consumption after the manager has sold a fraction $(1 - \alpha)$ of the shares

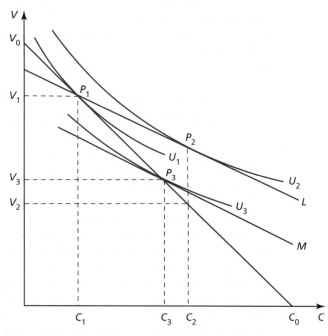

Figure 7.3 Value of the firm (V) and present value of on-the-job consumption (C). The manager owns a fraction α of the shares. The outsiders know the exact shape of the indifference curves of the manager and adjust the price they are willing to pay accordingly

The outsiders will soon find out that there is one, and only one, such point P_3. Thus, they will know that at P_3 the marginal utility for the manager of spending an additional \$1 on on-the-job consumption is equal to the marginal utility of 70 cents of personal wealth. Therefore, they are willing to pay only 30 per cent of V_3 for the shares, not 30 per cent of V_1. If they pay 30 per cent of V_3, the manager's budget constraint becomes line M with a slope of -0.7. The manager will then decide to consume C_3. The value of the firm will be V_3 and the outsiders will neither gain nor lose from buying the shares.

The personal wealth of the manager is now V_3. Of this amount he has a fraction $(1 - \alpha)$ in cash and a fraction α in shares. His wealth has reduced by $V_1 - V_3$ and the present value of his on-the-job consumption has increased by $C_3 - C_1$. The result is a decrease in his level of utility: he is now on indifference curve U_3, having started on indifference curve U_1. So, it is clear that no manager would ever sell a fraction of the shares of his company unless there were something else, not included in the analysis presented above, that would make him do so. Three such possibilities are:

- the manager prefers to have a portion of his wealth in cash instead of shares because he can then use the cash for other things;
- the manager wants to diversify company-specific risk;
- the manager sees an opportunity for investment that he cannot finance out of his own personal wealth.

7.3.1 Monitoring and bonding

Monitoring

In the above analysis, we have ignored the potential for the outsiders of **monitoring** the behaviour of the manager. In practice, it is usually possible for outsiders to observe the behaviour of managers to a certain extent. For example, they could have the books audited by an external auditor or install a board of directors.

Monitoring the behaviour of a manager is not without cost. By spending money on monitoring, however, the outsiders could reduce the manager's on-the-job consumption. The more they spend on monitoring, the better they can observe the manager's behaviour and the more they can reduce his on-the-job consumption.

We know from the analysis of Figure 7.3 that the manager bears the full cost of his increase in on-the-job consumption. If the manager can convince the outsiders before selling the shares that he will consume less than C_3, he will be able to sell the shares for an amount greater than 30 per cent of V_3. If he consumes less, the value of the firm increases and it is the manager who captures that increase, not the outsiders. Hence, it is in the interests of the manager to **Bonding** bind himself – called bonding. **Bonding** and monitoring are almost the same thing. *Bonding* means that the manager takes the initiative to bind himself and be monitored; *monitoring* means that the outsiders take the initiative.

Like monitoring, bonding is not without cost. It involves the same kinds of activities as monitoring: the manager takes the initiative to have the books audited or install a board of directors. Monitoring costs and bonding costs are borne by the manager. By consuming less than C_3, he increases his level of utility. By spending money on monitoring and bonding, he decreases the value of the firm. For this reason his budget constraint is no longer shown by the line V_0C_0. Rather, his budget constraint now is curve S in Figure 7.4.

Somewhere there is an optimal amount of money to spend on monitoring and bonding. That is indicated in Figure 7.4 by point P_4. At that point, the manager spends an amount MB (equal to the distance P_5P_4) on monitoring and bonding costs. His level of utility is U_4 – higher than U_3, but still lower than U_1.

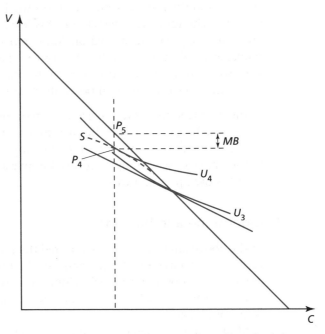

Figure 7.4 Value of the firm (V) and present value of on-the-job consumption (C) with monitoring and bonding costs

7.4 Entrepreneurial firms and team production

Entrepreneurial firm

Why do entrepreneurial firms exist? By an **entrepreneurial firm** we mean one that is owned and managed by the same person. That person (the entrepreneur) coordinates and monitors the work of several others (the employees) and receives the residual funds after fixed contractual payments (such as wages and interest payments) have been paid.

Direct supervision is the most important coordination mechanism in such a firm. An alternative organizational form is a workers' cooperative, in which the workers cooperate as peers. Then, mutual adjustment is the prime coordination mechanism. In manufacturing industries, few workers' cooperatives exist. Alchian

Team production

and Demsetz (1972) explain this by using the concept of **team production**.

Team production is a situation in which two or more people can produce more when they are working together than when they are working separately. The classical example is two people loading heavy cargo on to a truck. Suppose two people have to load heavy cargo on to two trucks. They can organize their work in one of two ways. Either each person can load one truck, working on his own, or they can work together, first loading one truck and then the other. If the second arrangement is more efficient, you have team production. Some goods or services cannot be produced by one person working alone. Examples are the music made by a symphony orchestra and open heart surgery. These are also examples of team production.

In mathematical terms we can express the situation as follows. Let $q(x_1, x_2)$ be a production function: q is the quantity produced; it is a function of two different inputs x_1 and x_2. There is team production if and only if:

$$\frac{\delta^2 q}{\delta x_1 \, \delta x_2} \neq 0$$

The production function $q = 3x_1^2 + 7x_2 + x_2^2$ does not represent team production; the production function $q = 3x_1^2 + 5x_1x_2 + 2x_2^2$ does. The first example of a production function is separable – that is, it can be written as a sum of terms such that some terms contain only x_1 and the other terms only x_2. The second production function is not separable. To say that a production function is separable is equivalent to saying that the second partial derivative with respect to x_1 and x_2 is unequal to zero, as in the second case.

Self-employed people receive the fruits of their efforts alone. If they put in more effort, they produce more and earn more money. How much effort they put in depends on their utility function. In equilibrium, the marginal utility of having an additional unit of leisure is equal to the marginal utility of earning an additional unit of money as income. Now, suppose that n people form a team and share the earnings from their production activities. Then, each person knows that if he puts in an extra unit of effort, he will receive only $1/n$th part of the additional earnings generated by his additional effort. For that reason each person will be strongly tempted to put in a much lower level of effort.

We know, then, that people working in a team and sharing the proceeds of their work will put in a lower level of effort than people who are self-employed.

Shirking

The phenomenon is called **shirking**. Every team member will be tempted to engage in shirking. With everybody shirking, the total output of the team will be much lower than if there was no shirking. Every member of the team is willing to put in more effort, provided that everybody else also puts in more effort.

The members of a team can discuss this issue. Suppose the result of such a discussion is that everyone promises not to shirk. If shirking by one of the team members is easily detected by the other team members, such mutual promises can work. A team member who shirks could then be expelled. If, however, it is difficult to detect shirking, such mutual promises will not be effective. Here again we see that the unobservability of the effort put in by the team members causes an information problem.

Do you think shirking occurs in the real world? Box 7.3 gives the results of a survey examining people's propensity to shirk.

Box 7.3 What people say about shirking

In 2000, a national telephone survey was conducted with adult members of the workforce in the USA to determine their work attitudes. Slightly over 1000 interviews were completed. The survey examined people's propensity to shirk by asking the following question:

Suppose that it is almost impossible for your employer to check up on you. Would you say that you are very likely, somewhat likely, somewhat unlikely or very unlikely to work hard if you agreed to?

Of the respondents, 82.7 per cent answered that they were 'very likely' to work hard, 12.1 per cent 'somewhat likely', 1.9 per cent 'somewhat unlikely' and 1.6 per cent 'very unlikely'.

What do you think? Do those results corroborate or refute the potential problem of shirking?

Source: Minkler (2004)

Monitor

Suppose that it is difficult for other team members to detect shirking but not very difficult for someone whose only task is to detect shirking. Let us call that person a **monitor**. A team with a monitor would produce more than a team without a monitor. If the value of the additional output from having a monitor is sufficiently high, it is in the interests of all team members to have a monitor.

How should the monitor be rewarded for his effort? Suppose that the monitor just shares in the proceeds on an equal basis with the other team members. The monitor then also has an incentive to shirk. The question then becomes, who monitors the monitor? If there is a second monitor to monitor the first monitor, who will monitor that second monitor? There is only one solution: give the monitor title to the residual funds after the other team members have been given a fixed level of pay. If the monitor receives the residual funds, he will have no incentive to shirk as a monitor.

If the monitor is to be effective, he must have the power to revise the terms of the contracts of individual team members, without having to negotiate with all the other team members. The monitor must have the right to terminate contracts, attract new members and adjust the rates of pay of every team member to reflect the marginal productivity of each person. Finally, the monitor must also have the right to sell his rights as monitor. Some of the monitor's activities – for example actions to alter the composition of the team – will pay off only after a certain period of time. There would be no incentive to engage in those kinds of activities unless he sooner or later would receive the rewards of such activities. If the monitor has the right to sell his or her rights as monitor, that will be a strong incentive to build an effective team.

Thus we have the entrepreneurial firm. The monitor is the owner of the firm, who receives the residual funds, has the right to sell the firm, has the right to hire and fire team members and adjust their pay on an individual basis. The monitor is the entrepreneur and the other team members are his employees.

The classical entrepreneur emerges in this theory as the solution to the problem of shirking within teams. The theory rests on two vital assumptions:

- there is team production;
- monitoring by someone specializing in that function can reduce shirking.

The second assumption really means that, for the other team members, it is more difficult or costly to monitor other team members than it is for someone who specializes in being the monitor. If the team members can see quite easily who is shirking and who is not, they can adjust team membership without having a monitor. Therefore, the monitor must be able to detect shirking more easily than the other team members.

7.5 The firm as a nexus of contracts

In Sections 7.3 and 7.4, ownership of the firm is a concept of vital importance – it restricts on-the-job consumption and shirking by managers. How, then, can we explain the existence of large corporations, shares in which are publicly traded and the managers of which do not own (a significant portion of) the shares?

The answer is that separation of security ownership and control can be an efficient form of economic organization. Note that here we introduce separation of *security ownership* and control. In the theory explained here, ownership of the firm is an irrelevant concept. A shareholder in a large public corporation owns just a number of shares. With ownership of the shares go certain well-defined rights, but that does not mean a shareholder (or all shareholders jointly) own the corporation in any meaningful sense. They just contract to receive the residual funds, just as workers contract to receive a fixed rate of pay. Shareholders are just one party in a group of many parties bound together in a nexus of contracts. Box 7.4 gives an illustration of a company that may be not much more than a 'nexus (bunch) of contracts'.

Box 7.4 Monorail Corporation as a nexus of contracts

In an excellent small book on the evolution of 'The Company', Micklethwait and Wooldridge (staff members of *The Economist*) discuss different perspectives on its future.

One perspective – particularly popular in antiglobalization circles – holds that giant corporations will come to dominate the world (economy). Empirical evidence shows, however, that big companies have been losing ground.

A second view argues the opposite – that companies are becoming ever less substantial:

for a glimpse of the future, its proponents recommend the Monorail Corporation, which sells computers. Monorail owns no factories, warehouses, or any other tangible asset. It operates from a single floor that it leases in an office building in Atlanta. Its computers are designed by freelance workers. To place orders, customers call a toll-free number connected to Federal Express's logistics service, which passes the orders on to a contract manufacturer that assembles the computers from various parts.

FedEx then ships the computers to the customers and sends the invoices to the Sun Trust Bank, Monorail's agent. The company is not much of anything except a good idea, a handful of people in Atlanta and a *bunch of contracts* (emphasis added).

A third perspective holds that the company will be increasingly replaced by networks – boundaryless firms operating together in loose-fitting alliances. Micklethwait and Wooldridge conclude that:

none of these three futures looks inevitable. Yet, the last two visions seem more plausible than the first. The trend at the moment is for the corporation to become ever less 'corporate': for bigger organizations to break themselves down into smaller entrepreneurial units. The erosion of Coasian transaction costs will make it ever easier for small companies – or just collections of entrepreneurs – to challenge the dominance of big companies; and ever more tempting for entrepreneurs to enter into loose relationships with other entrepreneurs rather than to form long-lasting corporations.

In Chapter 13 on hybrid forms we will explore the network perspective further.

Source: Micklethwait and Wooldridge (2003)

Fama and Jensen (1983a, b) use this perspective to explain the existence of both entrepreneurial firms and public corporations. They see the organization as a nexus of contracts, written and unwritten, between owners of factors of production and customers. The most important contracts specify the nature of residual claims and the allocation of steps in the decision process of agents. Most agents receive a fixed promised payment or an incentive payment based on a specific measure of performance. The residual risk is the risk of the difference between stochastic inflows of cash and promised payments, which is borne by the residual claimants or residual risk bearers.

The decision process has four steps:

Initiation

1 **initiation**, which is the generation of proposals for resource utilization and structuring of contracts;

Ratification

2 **ratification**, which is the process culminating in choosing which of the initiatives is to be implemented;

Implementation

3 **implementation**, which is the execution of the ratified decisions;

Monitoring

4 **monitoring**, which is the measurement of the performance of decision agents and implementation of rewards.

Decision management

Decision control

Initiation and implementation are usually allocated to the same agents. These two functions are combined within the term **decision management**. Likewise, **decision control** includes ratification and monitoring.

Fama and Jensen now posit two complementary hypotheses about the relations between risk-bearing and decision processes of organizations:

■ the separation of residual risk-bearing from decision management leads to decision systems that separate decision management from decision control;

■ combining of decision management and decision control in the work of a few agents leads to residual claims that are largely restricted to those agents.

Fama and Jensen call an organization *non-complex* if specific information relevant to decisions is concentrated in one or a few agents. 'Specific information' is detailed information that is costly to transfer between agents. Most small organizations tend to be non-complex, while most large organizations tend to be complex, but the correspondence is not perfect.

In small, non-complex organizations it is efficient to allocate both decision management and decision control to those agents who have the specific information. When decision management and decision control are combined, residual claimants have no protection against the opportunistic actions of decision agents. Hence, in small, non-complex organizations, residual claims are also allocated to the important decision agents. An example is the small entrepreneurial firm, owned and managed by the same person. Such an example conforms to the second hypothesis.

Now, suppose that the small entrepreneurial firm (we shall call it company E) is acquired by a larger firm (company L). The managers of company E are now no longer the residual claimants of the company. It is likely, however, that they still possess the specific knowledge relevant to making decisions for company E. It is now efficient to delegate decision management to the managers of company E. Decision control, however, is exercised by the manager(s) and corporate staff of company L. The separation of residual risk-bearing from decision management makes it necessary to separate decision management from decision control. This conforms to the first hypothesis.

In the large public corporation there are many shareholders. Having many shareholders has advantages because the total risk to be shared is large and there are large demands for capital in order to be able to make fixed promises to other agents. It is very costly for all of the shareholders to be involved in decision control, so they delegate decision control to the Board. While decision management is diffused within a large public corporation, decision control is exercised by the Board on behalf of shareholders.

7.6 Theory of principal and agent

In Section 7.3, the agency relation between the outside shareholder and the manager was analysed in a deterministic way – risk did not play a role in the analysis. Moreover, neither principal (outside shareholder) nor agent (manager) had private information. In the theory of principal and agent, risk is introduced into the analysis. In addition, we relax the condition of symmetrical information for our discussion in this section.

The theory of principal and agent is developed in mathematical models that, even in their simplest form, are already quite complicated. The essentials of such models can be explained by giving an example.

Take the relationship between the owner of a piece of land and someone who is willing to use that land to grow strawberries. The owner is the principal and the other person the agent. The principal is willing to give the agent the right to use her land to grow strawberries for one summer. The principal's problem is that of designing the agent's reward structure.

The quantity and the quality of strawberries that are available for sale at the end of the summer depend on two factors: how well the agent cares for the strawberries and the weather. In the language of the theory of principal and agent, the pay-off (the amount of money realized from the sale of the strawberries) depends on two variables – the level of effort exerted by the agent and a random variable (the weather).

A crucial question in the theory of principal and agent is how well the principal can observe the agent's behaviour. In this respect, three cases will be discussed:

- Case 1: the principal can observe the agent's behaviour;
- Case 2: the principal has no information about the agent's behaviour;
- Case 3: the principal cannot observe the agent's behaviour directly, but can obtain a signal concerning the level of effort being put in by the agent.

In Case 1, there is symmetrical information, but in Cases 2 and 3, there is asymmetrical information. In Cases 2 and 3, the agent knows his own level of effort, but the principal does not. The agent has *private information* (about his level of effort; see Chapter 4 for more on the concepts of asymmetrical and private information).

7.6.1 The principal can observe the agent's behaviour (symmetrical information)

Assuming that the principal can observe the level of effort being exerted by the agent, what is the optimal reward structure from the principal's point of view?

The agent's compensation can be based on his level of effort. We know that the agent does not like effort. He is willing to put in more effort only if his compensation is also higher. In Figure 7.5, curve I represents one of the agent's indifference curves. The graph plots the agent's level of effort against his income. The higher his level of effort, the more additional income he demands for an additional unit of effort.

Curve I is really one of a *set* of indifference curves. Assume, however, that the agent cannot obtain a contract anywhere that gives him a positive income if his level of effort is zero. Curve I then represents the minimum level of utility that the agent is willing to accept. He need not accept a contract giving him a lower level of utility as he is free not to work. So, he can always choose the point at the origin, which puts him at the utility level given by curve I.

The higher the agent's level of effort, the higher the expected pay-off. This relation is given by line m in Figure 7.5 (for simplicity, we have assumed that this relation is given by a straight line).

The principal now must choose a reward structure for the agent. Before dealing with that issue, let us try to find out what, from the principal's point of view, is the optimal level of the agent's effort. For the principal, the optimal level of the agent's effort is e_0. At that point, the expected pay-off is Ey_0 The agent must receive an amount W_0 and the principal receives the difference:

$$Ey_0 - W_0 = R_0$$

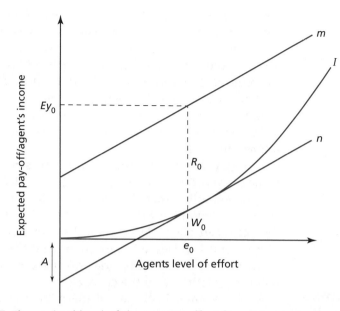

Figure 7.5 The optimal level of the agent's effort from the principal's point of view

At any other point, the vertical distance between line m and curve I is smaller than R_0. So, the principal wants to select a reward structure that induces the agent to choose a level of effort e_0, which also gives him a payment of W_0 if he chooses that level.

Forcing contract

A very simple contract that solves the principal's problem is a **forcing contract**.

Under a forcing contract, the principal promises to pay an amount e_0 if the agent's level of effort is at least e_0 and to pay nothing if the agent's level of effort is smaller than e_0. Under such a contract, the agent is forced to bring his level of effort up to e_0, otherwise he will not be paid. He will not increase his level of effort any further, however, as he receives no extra reward for doing so. Hence, the agent is forced to work at level e_0.

Another solution would be to give the agent the reward structure represented by line n in Figure 7.5. Under this reward structure, the agent would have to pay an amount A to the principal if his level of effort was zero. For every additional unit of effort, the agent receives an amount given by the slope of line n. In order to obtain the highest utility level achievable under that reward structure, the agent will again choose effort level e_0.

The point of this whole discussion is that, if the principal can observe the agent's level of effort, the principal can, first, determine which level of effort, from his own point of view, is optimal and, second, give the agent a forcing contract that obliges him to choose that level. As the principal can observe the actual level of effort chosen by the agent, she will pay W_0 only if the agent works at level e_0.

The set of Pareto-optimal solutions

In the discussion above, we have assumed that curve I represents the minimum level of utility that the agent is willing to accept. Let us call that level of (expected) utility EUA_1. EUA_1 represents the expected utility that the agent can obtain elsewhere. The principal maximizes her own expected utility by designing a reward structure, given the constraint that the agent will not accept a contract giving him an expected utility lower than EUA_1. Let EUP_1 be the principal's maximum level of utility, given EUA_1.

Now suppose that the agent perceives an opportunity to obtain a level of utility $EUA_2 > EUA_1$ elsewhere. Let EUP_2 be the principal's maximum level of utility, given EUA_2. As the principal is now faced with a tighter constraint, it follows that $EUP_2 < EUP_1$.

In Figure 7.6, the horizontal axis represents the agent's expected utility, while the vertical shows the principal's expected utility. If the minimum level of expected utility that the agent is willing to accept is EUA_1, then the principal's maximum level of utility is EUP_1 – point 1 in Figure 7.6. If, elsewhere, the agent can obtain EUA_2, then the principal's maximum level of utility is EUP_2 – point 2 in Figure 7.6. By choosing different values for EUA, we can calculate for each value of EUA the principal's maximum level of utility, EUP. All points thus found form the curve cs.

Pareto-optimal solution   A **Pareto-optimal solution** of the principal's problem is defined as one in which it is impossible to increase one person's expected utility without decreasing the other person's. Point 1 in Figure 7.6 represents a Pareto-optimal solution as the principal can obtain more than EUP_1 only if the agent receives less than EUA_1, while the agent can obtain more than EUA_1 only if the principal receives less than EUP_1. Point 2 is also a Pareto-optimal solution. In fact, curve cs gives the set of Pareto-optimal solutions.

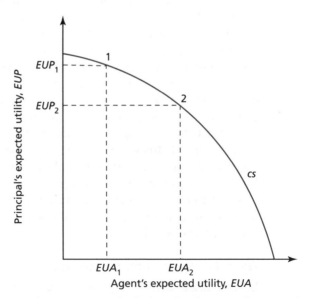

Figure 7.6 The set of Pareto-optimal solutions for the case of symmetrical information

7.6.2 The principal cannot observe the agent's level of effort (asymmetrical information)

Let us now assume that the principal has no way to observe the level of effort exerted by the agent and, after the summer, she also has no detailed information about weather conditions during the summer. All she can observe is the pay-off – the amount of money made by selling the strawberries. If the pay-off is high, it can be the result of a high level of effort on the part of the agent and average weather conditions or an average level of effort by the agent and good weather conditions.

The principal cannot tell what contributed more to a good result – the agent's effort or the weather conditions. Those are now the conditions under which the principal must specify, at the beginning of the summer, a reward structure for the agent. How should she do that? There are two extreme solutions.

The first of these is to set a fixed salary for the agent, independent of the pay-off. Such a reward structure may be called a **wage contract**. It is like an employment contract with a fixed rate of pay. The problem with a reward structure like that is the agent has no incentive whatsoever to do a good job. In the theory of principal and agent it is assumed that the agent likes to receive more money and dislikes delivering more effort,[2] so the agent will choose a level of effort equal to zero if his income does not depend on the pay-off.

The second extreme solution is that the agent receives the pay-off minus a fixed amount to be agreed at the beginning of the summer. Such a structure may be called a **rent contract**. The agent rents the land from the landowner for a fixed amount. The rent is not dependent on the pay-off. The agent grows the strawberries and receives whatever he can make for the strawberries after he has paid the rent to the landowner. With such a reward structure, the agent has a maximum incentive to do his very best.

The wage and rent contracts differ not only in terms of how the rewards are distributed, but also in the distribution of risks imposed on agent and principal. Under the wage contract, the principal bears all the risk. For instance, if weather conditions ruin the strawberry crop, she still has to pay the agent, but receives no reward herself. Under the rent contract, the situation is reversed. The agent now bears all the risk. He has to pay the rent, whether or not the proceeds from selling the strawberries permit him to do so. Hence, we can see that the reward structure determines the distribution of risks between principal and agent.

What reward structures are acceptable to both parties will depend on their attitudes to risk. They may be risk-neutral, risk-averse or risk-loving. In most agency models, the principal is assumed to be risk-neutral and the agent either risk-neutral or risk-averse.

If both principal and agent are risk-neutral, the best reward structure is a rent contract. It gives the agent maximum incentive. It also imposes all the risk on the agent, but, as he is risk-neutral, he does not care about risk. To be more precise, a risk-neutral agent does not demand **compensation for risk-bearing** as he does not care about risk. As risk can be imposed on the agent without

Wage contract

Rent contract

Compensation for risk-bearing

cost, a rent contract (giving maximum incentives) is the best reward structure for the agent.

Suppose that the principal is risk-neutral and the agent is risk-averse. With a rent contract, the agent has maximum incentive to put in a high level of effort, but he also has to bear all the risk. As we are now assuming that the agent is risk-averse, the agent cares about the amount of risk he has to bear. He, therefore, is willing to accept more risk only if it is offset by a higher expected income. This is illustrated in Figure 7.7. Curve U is the agent's indifference curve. It is also assumed that the agent has an alternative opportunity to accept another job. It is a job without risk and an income of W. W is the agent's **reservation wage**.

Reservation wage

If the principal wants to engage the agent, she can offer a wage contract for amount W. The principal can also offer a contract where the agent's income depends on the pay-off. The agent is willing to accept such a contract provided he remains on the same indifference curve.

The relation between the expected pay-off and the amount of risk borne by the agent is illustrated in Figure 7.7 by line I (we assume that this relation can be shown as a straight line). The higher the level of risk borne by the agent, the more incentive the agent has to do a good job and the higher the expected pay-off will be. If the agent bears no risk (a wage contract), the expected pay-off is Ey_3. As the agent will not accept a pay contract if his pay is lower than W, the maximum amount the principal can receive is R_3. If the agent bears all

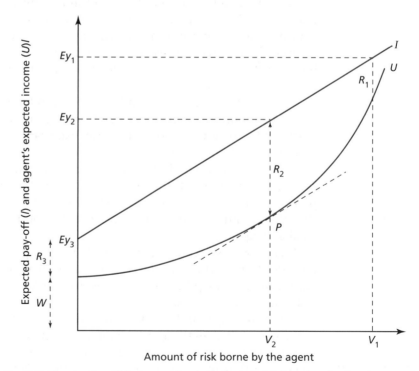

Figure 7.7 The trade-off between incentives and risk-bearing in the theory of principal and agent

the risk (a rent contract), the expected payoff is Ey_1. The principal can then charge a rent equal to R_1. If the principal charged a higher figure for rent, the agent would not accept the contract. The principal thus maximizes her expected income by choosing point P on the agent's indifference curve U, such that the slope of the indifference curve at point P is equal to the slope of line I. At that point the agent bears some risk (V_2) but not all of it (V_1).

Figure 7.7 portrays the fundamental trade-off that the principal must make. The principal wants to give the agent incentives in order to make him put in more effort, but, in order for this to occur, the agent must *also* bear risk. The agent is willing to accept risk only if he is compensated in the form of a higher expected income. So, the principal must make a trade-off between giving the agent incentives (the more incentives, the higher the expected pay-off) and having the agent bear more risk (the higher the level of risk borne by the agent, the more the principal has to pay him in the form of expected income).

As we can see in Figure 7.7, the optimal contract for the principal involves risk-sharing between agent and principal. The agent bears an amount of risk equal to V_2 and the principal bears an amount of risk equal to $V_1 - V_2$. The result is true if the principal is risk-neutral and the agent is risk-averse.

Why does the theory of principal and agent assume that the principal is risk-neutral while the agent is risk-averse? If both the principal and the agent are risk-neutral, the optimal contract is a rent contract. The theory then is not very interesting. It also seems reasonable to assume that the principal is risk-neutral and the agent risk-averse if the situation is such that the principal can diversify while the agent cannot. If, for example, the principal is the landowner and the agent the farmer, the principal may own several pieces of land in countries with different climates. The principal can then make contracts with several agents and, in so doing, diversify away most of the risk. The agent, however, can work on only one piece of land, so cannot diversify his risk. If the principal is the owner of a company and the agent is the manager of that company, we have the same situation: the principal can diversify (by owning shares in several companies) while the agent normally cannot.

In situations in which the model discussed here represents reality, there is no doubt that for the principal it is best to design a reward schedule based in part on the agent's performance. As shareholders can be regarded as risk-neutral and the top manager (the CEO) as risk-averse, we would expect to find performance-related pay packages for top managers. That is indeed what we find in the real world (see Section 14.3 and Box 14.3 for more details).

First-best and second-best solutions

All points on curve U in Figure 7.7 give the agent the same expected utility. Let us call that level of utility EUA_1. Associated with EUA_1 is EUP_1 – the principal's maximum level of utility given EUA_1. For each level of EUA we can calculate the associated level of EUP. That gives curve ca in Figure 7.8 (overleaf). Curve ca represents the set of Pareto-optimal solutions.

Curve cs in Figure 7.8 is the same as curve cs in Figure 7.6. That is, curve cs represents solutions to the principal's problem for the case of symmetrical

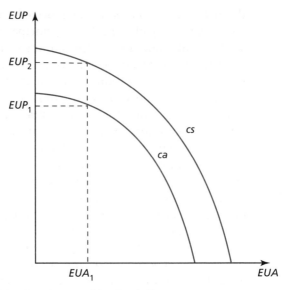

Figure 7.8 First-best and second-best solutions

information (the principal can observe the agent's level of effort). Curve *ca* represents solutions to the principal's problem in the case of asymmetrical information (the principal cannot observe the agent's level of effort).

First-best solutions

Second-best solutions

The solutions represented by curve cs are called **first-best solutions** and those represented by curve *ca* are **second-best solutions**. If EUA_1 is the minimum level of utility the agent is willing to accept, then the principal can obtain EUP_1 if she cannot observe the agent's behaviour and EUP_2 if she can. The distance $EUP_2 - EUP_1$ represents the principal's loss of expected utility because of non-observability. Moral hazard is also involved, however. Recall that moral hazard refers to the ex post information problem owing to private information (Chapter 4). In such a case, the agent has private information on his effort level and may exploit that information asymmetry.

To see that is so, suppose for a moment the principal cannot observe the agent's level of effort and the principal can trust the agent's word. We then have the situation shown in Figure 7.5. The optimal level of effort from the principal's point of view is e_0. The principal simply asks the agent to deliver that level of effort and the agent promises to do so. There is no need for the principal to observe the agent's level of effort if she can trust him. So, the difference between a first-best and a second-best solution is caused by non-observability of information in the presence of moral hazard.

7.6.3 The principal can observe a signal concerning the agent's level of effort

Signal

Now suppose that the principal cannot observe the agent's level of effort directly but, instead, the principal can observe, without cost, a **signal** concerning the agent's level of effort. For example, the principal can observe how many hours the agent spends on his job. The number of hours worked by the agent gives the principal an indication about the agent's level of effort. The true level of effort, however, remains unobservable for the principal. This may be the case, for instance, if the agent is required to clock in when he begins work and to clock out when he stops. His real level of effort, however, still remains unobservable.

In formal agency models, one can show that the agent's reward structure should be based on such a signal if and only if the agent is risk-averse. To make this result intuitively clear, assume first that the agent is risk-neutral. The agent then does not care about risk-bearing, so he does not demand compensation in the form of a higher expected income if more risk is imposed on him. Therefore, there is no cost to the principal for imposing risk on the agent, if the agent is risk-neutral. In such a case, it is better for the principal to give the agent incentives by letting him bear all the risk (through a rent contract) than by giving him a reward structure based on an imperfect signal concerning his level of effort.

Suppose now that the agent is risk-averse. In that case, there is a cost to the principal of letting the agent bear more risk. In such a situation a reward structure based on both the signal concerning the agent's level of effort and the pay-off is better from the principal's point of view than a reward structure based only on the pay-off.

Hence, the information contained in the signal concerning the agent's level of effort is valuable to the principal if and only if the agent is risk-averse.

Consider next the situation where the principal can observe a signal through monitoring and that monitoring is not free. Assume, further, that the quality of the signal (the correlation of the signal with the agent's real level of effort) increases as the principal spends more on monitoring. Assume, too, that the principal is risk-neutral and the agent is risk-averse. In that situation the principal has to determine the optimal level of monitoring and the reward structure simultaneously.

7.6.4 Extending the model

In this section we have given an introduction to the theory of principal and agent. In its simplest form the theory concerns the relations between one principal and one agent. Moreover, that relationship is analysed in a one-period model. What happens to our conclusions, however, when we examine the relations between one principal and several agents? What happens if we analyse the relations between one principal and one agent in a model with more than one period?

One principal and several agents

Consider first one principal with several agents. As an example, think of our landowner again who divides her land into several plots. Now there are several agents who want to grow strawberries on adjacent plots. The weather conditions are the same for all the plots. The principal does not know in detail about the weather conditions either before or after the summer, but she does know that the weather conditions are the same for each plot. That gives the principal the opportunity to make comparisons between the pay-offs of the agents.

Assume that the principal is risk-neutral and some agents are risk-averse and others risk-neutral. Consider, first, agents who are risk-neutral. Those agents do not demand compensation for bearing risk, so it is best to give them a rent contract. The principal can now give the other agents a forcing contract: 'If your pay-off is not lower than the pay-off of the risk-neutral agents, who have a rent contract, your compensation will be the same as theirs; if, however, your pay-off is lower, then you will get nothing.'

Assume now instead that all the agents are risk-averse. In that case, it is still possible to make comparisons between agents by comparing the pay-off of a certain agent with the average for all the agents. Any difference between the pay-off of a particular agent and the average pay-off for all the other agents can be due only to that agent's level of effort. For the principal, that is a signal concerning the agent's level of effort. From the principal's point of view, an optimal reward structure should be based on both the pay-off and the average pay-off for all the agents.

Several periods

Consider next one principal and one agent in a setting with several periods. Assume further that the principal cannot observe the agent's behaviour and the agent is risk-averse (if the agent is risk-neutral, the best contract is, again, a rent contract). The principal can now base the agent's reward structure on the pay-off of the present period and on that of all previous periods. From the principal's point of view, such a reward structure is better than one based only on the pay-off of the present period.

7.6.5 Applying agency theory

In the previous sections, various agency models have been described. We, the authors, hope that you have enjoyed reading about this fascinating field. In this final section on agency theory, we want to stress that care should be taken when applying agency theory to practical situations. We will discuss some factors that impede a straight 'translation' of agency concepts and solutions into the real world.

As an example, consider a corporation with several business units. It is a situation with one principal and several agents: the CEO is the principal, the managers of the business units are the agents. Suppose the CEO engages you as a consultant to devise incentive contracts for the business unit managers. How useful is the theory explained in previous sections to you in that situation? If you do not fully understand the theory's limitations, there is a real danger that the theory will be misapplied. There are several reasons for that.

First, the models we have discussed in Sections 7.6.1, 7.6.2 and 7.6.3 are one-period models. That is why we have used the example of growing strawberries during one summer. However, you are asked to advise in a situation where the business unit managers will be reviewed periodically by the CEO. That requires a multiple-period model. Multiple-period models have been described only very briefly in Section 7.6.4.

Second, you are being asked to advise on a situation with one principal and several agents. In Section 7.6.4 we briefly discussed a situation with one principal and several agents. In that model we saw several agents growing strawberries on adjacent plots of land. The weather conditions were the same for each plot, so we could assume that each agent faced the same random factor (the same weather conditions). In a setting with several business unit managers, each business unit may be affected differently by such random factors as the exchange rate or the fortunes of important customers. Another complication is that different business units may be affected by different random factors.

Third, the CEO will probably be able to collect several signals concerning the effort levels of business unit managers. As monitoring reduces the information asymmetry problem, it is quite likely that it will reduce the principal's loss of expected utility (see Figure 7.8). Monitoring is costly, however, so the real issue is not whether or not to monitor, but how and how much. It is a very complicated issue with no easy solutions. Most CEOs will evaluate the performance of a business unit manager on several financial and non-financial indicators and compare the manager's performance against those indicators with his and his colleagues' previous performance against those indicators. Those quantitative evaluations may be used to determine bonus payments. When it comes to promoting a business unit manager to a position of more responsibility, most CEOs will be reluctant to rely exclusively on such quantitative evaluations. Instead, they will tend to supplement them with a qualitative judgment of a business unit manager's qualifications and performance.

Finally, alignment of business unit managers in the real world is not only affected by their contract and pay packages but also the company culture and opportunities for promotion. There are more factors at play than mere monetary compensation!

Applying agency theory to practical situations is by no means easy. It is, however, very useful for shaping our thinking regarding, for example, the way in which public companies are (or should be) governed. The subject is discussed extensively in Chapter 14 on corporate governance.

7.7 Summary: agency relations between owners, managers and employees

Within agency theory we distinguish between the positive theory of agency and the theory of principal and agent. The positive theory of agency views the organization as a nexus of contracts. It tries to explain why organizational forms are as they are. Two important questions in this respect are how does the ownership structure of a firm affect managerial behaviour and why do we observe certain organizational forms in the real world?

In order to explain how the ownership structure of a firm can affect managerial behaviour, let us consider first an entrepreneurial firm. An entrepreneurial firm is one that is owned and managed by the same person. In such a firm there is no conflict of interests between owner(s) and manager(s).

A public corporation is one with shares that are traded on a stock market. In a public corporation there may be a real conflict of interests between the (outside) shareholders and the manager(s). Usually, shareholders are interested in a high return on their investment (in the form of dividends and appreciation of the share price on the stock market), so they would like to see managers maximizing the value of the firm on the stock market. The managers, however, may have other interests. Some of them like to have a luxury car, or travel and stay in expensive hotels, as long as the bill is paid by the company. In other words, managers may engage in on-the-job consumption that decreases the value of the firm. Even in an entrepreneurial firm, the manager will engage in such consumption. If he sells (part of) his shares to outsiders, he will increase his on-the-job consumption, thus reducing the value of the firm. The outsiders expect such behaviour and it is reflected in the price they are willing to pay for the shares.

In most manufacturing industries there are entrepreneurial firms and public corporations, but very few cooperative firms (a firm owned by the workers). Why do we observe so many entrepreneurial firms and so few cooperative firms in the real world?

The answer may have to do with the existence of team production. Team production is a situation in which two or more people can produce more when they are working together than when they are working separately. A problem with team production is that it leads to shirking. A member of a team who receives only a portion of the team's output will work less hard than a person working alone. The result is that the output of the team is greatly reduced. Thus, team members want to reduce shirking.

One solution may be to have a monitor who specializes in observing shirking. In a cooperative firm, the monitor would share in the proceeds with other team members. That would give the monitor an incentive to shirk as a monitor. If the monitor is the owner of the firm, however, he has no incentive to shirk. That may explain why entrepreneurial firms are more efficient than cooperative firms. As we would expect the most efficient organizational forms to survive, we are not surprised to see many small manufacturing firms organized as entrepreneurial firms and very few as cooperatives.

The theory of principal and agent forms the core of modern agency theory. In the theory, risk is introduced into the analysis. In its simplest form, the theory focuses on the relations between one principal and one agent. The agent performs a task and, in so doing, has to choose a level of effort. The output is determined by the level of effort, but also by a random factor, such as the weather. The problem for the principal is one of determining a reward structure for the agent. If the principal can observe the level of effort of the agent, he can specify a minimum level of effort. The agent will receive nothing if he does not meet that minimum level of effort. If his level of effort exceeds the minimum, he will receive a fixed level of pay.

The principal's problem is much more interesting if he cannot observe the agent's behaviour. In that case, the agent's attitude towards risk becomes important. If the agent is risk-neutral, he or she is willing to take on risk without asking compensation for bearing it. The best solution then is simply to give the agent a rent contract. It allocates all risk to the agent, but also gives the agent a very strong incentive to increase his level of effort. If the agent is risk-averse and the principal risk-neutral, the principal has to make a trade-off between giving the agent incentives and having the agent bear more risk. The best solution in that case is to give the agent a reward structure that depends to some extent on the pay-off but also contains a fixed element independent of it. Such a contract involves risk-sharing between principal and agent.

In summary, we want to stress that:

1 the agency problem is a very real one in many settings;
2 economists have started to conceptualize and model the agency problem, which has led to some insightful results;
3 there is still a gap between rather 'pure' agency models (focusing on one or a few variables only) and the rather 'messy' real world, in which many factors are at play.

Questions

1 Your car has been making a strange noise lately. You don't know what it is, but you don't feel comfortable with it, so you take your car to the garage. You take it in the morning and return in the evening to collect it. Is the relation you have with your garage an example of an agency relation? Who is the principal and who is the agent? Which kind of action is taken by the agent? Can the principal observe the actual action taken by the agent? Why do the agent's decisions or actions affect the principal's assets broadly defined?

2 Consider, in the theory of principal and agent, the case in which the principal can observe the agent's behaviour. Does the optimal reward structure from the principal's point of view depend on the agent's attitude towards risk? Explain your answer.

3 Fama and Jensen (1983a, b) describe decision processes as consisting of four steps – initiation, ratification, implementation and monitoring. Further, they introduce the terms 'decision management' and 'decision control'. Consider a small company (S) operating as a subsidiary of a larger company (L). Suppose that the managers of S are contemplating a major investment. Who will exercise decision management and who will exercise decision control? Why? Does it conform to one of Fama and Jensen's hypotheses? If yes, how did Fama and Jensen phrase that hypothesis?

4 Consider, in the theory of principal and agent, the situation in which the principal cannot observe the agent's behaviour and in which both principal and agent are risk-neutral. What is the optimal contract from the principal's point of view?

5 A definition of team production has been given on pages 140–1. Which of the following situations represents team production? Explain your answer.
   a A violin quartet playing Mozart.
   b Eighteen people working in a factory that produces grandfather clocks (see Box 8.1 in the next chapter).
   c Twenty engineers working on the design for a new car.

6 Ummels Services BV is a Dutch company with limited liability offering maintenance services for chemical processing plants. Ummels Services BV was founded in 1984 by Mr Stef Ummels. The company was owned and managed by Mr Ummels until he died in 1995. Since then, 50 per cent of the shares of Ummels Services BV have been owned by his son, Paul Ummels, while the other 50 per cent are owned by his daughter, Lara Ummels. Since his father's death, Paul Ummels has managed the company. Lara Ummels is a medical student and intends to become a urologist.

   In March 2002, Paul and Lara talk about Lara selling her shares in the company to her brother. Lara would like to cash them in because she has little affinity with the company. Paul is interested in buying because he likes the idea of becoming sole owner. Paul is sure that he can borrow the money he needs to buy Lara's shares. Paul and Lara engage Mr Schlösser, an independent financial consultant, to estimate the value of Lara's shares.

   Mr Schlösser calculates the present value of all future cash flows of the company. In estimating future cash flows, he uses the historical cash flows for the last five years. This results in a value of €4.6 million for the company. He recommends that Lara sells her shares to Paul for €2.3 million.

   Lara is now asking you for a second opinion on Mr Schlösser's calculation. Do you see anything that Mr Schlösser may have neglected? How can Lara justify a price higher than €2.3 million? Do you think Paul will be interested in buying at a price higher than €2.3 million? Why?

7 Mr Howard Rothey owns an ice-cream bar at the beach in Bournemouth. He has been running it for several years. Ice-cream sales at the beach are highly seasonal: almost all sales take place in the period of May to September. For that reason, Mr Rothey has never taken a holiday during the peak season. Now, however, he wants to visit his son and daughter-in-law in Alaska in July, so wants to engage someone to run his ice-cream business during a period of three weeks in July. Alex Waterman, a 22-year-old student from Bath University, is looking for a summer job. Mr Rothey is contemplating the kind of contract that he should offer. Mr Rothey is well aware of the fact that ice-cream sales depend, to a large extent, on the way Alex will treat customers (in the language of the theory of principal and agent, we would say that ice-cream sales depend on Alex's level of effort). Of course, the weather is quite important, too. For the English south coast, the weather in July can be very nice with lots of sun, but it can also be rainy and cold for several weeks.
   a Should Mr Rothey offer Alex a forcing contract?
   b Should Mr Rothey offer Alex a wage contract? If he does and Alex accepts, what will be Alex's level of effort?
   c What other types of contract can Mr Rothey offer?
   d What is the best contract for Mr Rothey if he and Alex Waterman are both risk-neutral?
   e Now suppose that Mr Rothey is risk-neutral and Alex Waterman is risk-averse. Figure 7.9 gives the trade-off between providing incentives and the cost of risk-bearing for that situation.

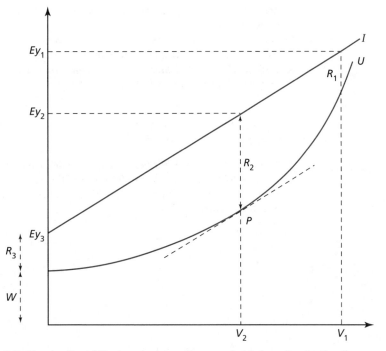

Figure 7.9 The trade-off between incentives and risk-bearing in the theory of principal and agent

- Which variable is indicated on the horizontal axis?
- What does line I stand for?
- What does curve U in this figure stand for?

f Figure 7.9 also indicates the optimal solution for Mr Rothey. Indicate in the figure how much money Alex Waterman receives in the optimal solution.

8 Large multinational companies have many foreign subsidiaries. The relationship between the manager of one of those foreign subsidiaries with company headquarters is an agency relation, with the manager of the foreign subsidiary as agent and headquarters as principal. Managers of the foreign subsidiaries can receive a bonus payment related to the financial results of their subsidiary. There is considerable variation, however, in terms of the relative importance of such financial incentives.

One factor that might explain part of the variation is industry volatility (the degree to which conditions in the foreign subsidiary's industry fluctuate: some industries are relatively stable, others show large fluctuations in levels of demand and customer preferences). How would you expect industry volatility to influence the use of financial incentives?

Which other factors could possibly explain the variation in the use of financial incentives?

Suggested further reading

Holmstrom, B. R. and Tirole, J. (1989), 'The theory of the firm', in R. Schmalensee and R. Willig (eds), *Handbook of Industrial Organization*, Vol. 1, Amsterdam: North Holland.

Jensen, M. C. (1998), *Foundations of Organizational Strategy*, Cambridge, MA: Harvard University Press.

Jensen, M. C. (2000), *A Theory of the Firm: Governance, residual claims, and organizational forms*, Cambridge, MA: Harvard University Press.

Roberts, J. (2004), *The Modern Firm: Organizational design for performance and growth*, Oxford: Oxford University Press.

Notes

1 The concept of the indifference curve is explained in Section 2.3
2 To be more precise, the utility function of the agent is such that the first partial derivative with respect to income is positive and the first partial derivative with respect to effort is negative.

8 Transaction cost economics

8.1 Introduction

In Chapter 1 we laid the framework for this book, which was summarized in Figure 1.1. Essentially, the argument is that division of labour creates opportunities for specialization, which necessitates the coordination of economic decisions. There are two ideal types of coordination mechanism: markets and organizations.

In transaction cost economics the fundamental unit of analysis is the transaction. Transactions can take place across markets or within organizations. Whether a particular transaction is allocated to the market or an organization is a matter of cost minimization. Transaction cost economics emphasizes that transaction costs as well as traditional production costs should be taken into account. The term 'transaction costs' includes costs of both market transactions and internal transactions.

According to the argument we have developed so far, firms exist because, in some cases, the costs of internal coordination are lower than the costs of market transactions (see Box 8.1). That is almost a tautology. If there is a firm, then, apparently, the costs of internal coordination are lower than the costs of market transactions. That is not much of a theory. Such a 'theory' can never be empirically tested. If we really want to develop a theory, we should specify beforehand in which cases we expect the costs of market transactions to be high compared with the costs of internal coordination. If we can do that, we can hope to derive hypotheses that are suitable for empirical testing.

Oliver Williamson has almost single-handedly developed such a theory in numerous publications. This chapter is based primarily on Williamson's work, especially on his two books *Markets and Hierarchies* (1975) and *The Economic Institutions of Capitalism* (1985).

Box 8.1 A factory making grandfather clocks

Why do firms exist? Why is not everyone self-employed?

Consider a factory employing 18 people making grandfather clocks. Five of the employees specialize in sawing the wooden parts that together form the clocks' cases. Two of them assemble the wooden parts to form the cases. Another two spray the cases with paint. Two paint faces. Four

▶

assemble cases, faces and movements to form complete clocks. There are two salespeople and one general manager. The general manager is also the owner of the company.

Why are the first 17 people working as employees? Why is not everyone self-employed? The answer is transaction costs. Consider the following three situations:

- *Situation 1* 17 self-employed people working at geographically dispersed locations;
- *Situation 2* 17 self-employed people all working under the same roof;
- *Situation 3* 17 people employed by the owner of the factory.

Compare, first, Situations 1 and 2. In Situation 1, the costs of transporting semi-finished goods is high compared with 2. In Situation 2, the costs of market transactions between the 17 self-employed people may be high because of the small numbers bargaining. For example, if the two people spraying cases with paint collude, they can try to lower the prices of unpainted cases and raise the prices of painted cases. That may result in frequent interruptions of the workflow. In Situation 1, the two sprayers may have to compete with numerous other sprayers, which would restrict their bargaining power.

Compare now Situations 2 and 3. In Situation 3, there is no costly haggling over prices of semi-finished goods (no interruptions of the workflow because parties cannot reach agreement over prices of semi-finished goods). The quantities of semi-finished goods that each must produce are determined by the general manager, not negotiation between the self-employed people.

The general manager must also evaluate each person's level of effort. The three situations can be summarized as shown in the table below.

	(1) Self-employed workers in geographically dispersed locations	(2) Self-employed workers under the same roof	(3) Employeees working for an employer
Transportation costs	High	Low	Low
Costs of market transactions	Low	High	Low
Costs of internal coordination	Low	Low	High

In a market economy, only the most efficient organizational form can survive in the long run. Therefore, if we observe, in reality, there are only grandfather clockmaking factories like Situation 3, then, apparently, that is the most efficient type of organization.

Transaction cost economics as developed by Williamson is based on the assumption that human beings are *boundedly rational* and sometimes display *opportunistic behaviour*. These two behavioural assumptions are discussed in Section 8.2. Whether transaction costs for a particular transaction will be high or low depends on the *critical dimensions* of that transaction. Critical dimensions of transactions are discussed in Section 8.3. These two sections lay the basic foundations for transaction cost economics.

In the subsequent sections, we apply transaction cost reasoning. First, we discuss several organizational forms – peer groups, single-stage hierarchies and multistage hierarchies. Then we discuss internal markets within firms. We examine the role of reputation and trust as countervailing forces against opportunistic behaviour in Section 8.8. In Section 8.9 we round off by paying attention to the (meso) level of analysis at which the governance of transactions is located and the interplay with the macro (institutional) and micro (individual) levels.

8.2 Behavioural assumptions: bounded rationality and opportunism

8.2.1 Bounded rationality

Bounded rationality

The concept of bounded rationality was introduced in Chapter 6 on behavioural theory. **Bounded rationality** means that the capacity of human beings to formulate and solve complex problems is limited. A good example is the game of chess. A chess player has all the information she needs to make her decisions: the positions of the white and black pieces at the moment that she is contemplating a move are all the information she needs. In order to evaluate a certain move, she needs only to analyse what moves her opponent can possibly make and evaluate all possible moves that she could make in answer to each possible countermove. The problem in chess is simply that the number of alternative sequences of moves and countermoves is too great even for the world's best chess players. It is not that a chess player does not want to make fully rational decisions. She does want to make fully rational decisions, but her capacity to evaluate fully the consequences of all the possible decisions is limited. So, bounded rationality refers to human behaviour that is 'intendedly rational, but only limitedly so' (Simon, 1961).

From the discussion it is clear that bounded rationality poses a problem in chess because chess is a complex game. A game such as bridge is characterized by both complexity and uncertainty. In bridge the players do not know the hands of their opponents. If they did, then the game would be much less interesting. In bridge, bounded rationality is a problem because of the combination of uncertainty and complexity.

Uncertainty/complexity

Now let us return to transactions. Bounded rationality will pose a problem only in environments that are characterized by **uncertainty/complexity**. When you buy petrol for your car, there is not much complexity or uncertainty. You know the product quite well, you do not have to worry about aftersales service and the seller does not need any information about you provided you pay directly. To buy petrol you do not need to write and sign a contract.

Now consider the case of a government that wants to buy a new weapon system. In that case it *is* necessary to write and sign a contract. Such a contract is very complicated. Product specifications should be clearly defined in the contract, but that can be quite difficult because of uncertainty about the technology. Is it feasible to develop a new weapon system that meets some clearly defined specifications? How much will it cost to develop such a system? How much will it cost to manufacture those systems? These are elements of uncertainty/complexity in the case of buying new and complex weaponry. It is likely that bounded rationality in conjunction with uncertainty/complexity makes it costly to write a contract for buying a new weapon system.

8.2.2 Opportunism

Opportunism

In Williamson's view, human beings are not only boundedly rational but they also sometimes display opportunistic behaviour. Williamson describes **opportunism** as 'self interest seeking with guile' and as making 'self-disbelieved statements' (see Box 8.2). In plain English, trying to exploit a situation to your own advantage.

Box 8.2 **Self-disbelieved statements in the Enron case?**

Enron was one of the world's leading electricity, natural gas, pulp and paper and communications companies, with claimed revenues of $111 billion in 2000 and 21,000 employees. *Fortune* named Enron 'America's Most Innovative Company' for six consecutive years.

It caused a scandal at the end of 2001 when it was revealed that its reported financial condition was sustained mostly by systematic accounting fraud. The US Congress held hearings on the Enron scandal. *The Financial Times* reported that some Congressmen felt that the former CEO of Enron, Jeffrey Skilling, made 'self-disbelieved statements' to them during these hearings:

> US lawmakers leading the congressional investigations into the collapse of Enron said on Sunday they believed Jeffrey Skilling, former chief executive, was lying when he testified last week that he knew nothing of transactions made by subordinates to inflate profits and conceal liabilities at the energy giant. The statements came from the bipartisan group of Congressmen including Democrat Ernest Hollings, chairman of the Senate commerce committee, and Republican James Greenwood, who chaired last Thursday's hearing at which Mr Skilling appeared. They said testimony by other Enron employees and documents uncovered by investigators contradict his claims that he was unaware of any wrongdoing. 'Nobody thinks he was telling the truth,' Mr Hollings told CBS. 'I don't believe he thinks so.'

Source: 'Leaders of Enron probe say Skilling lied to them', *The Financial Times*, 10 February 2002

Williamson does not assume that everybody behaves opportunistically. He assumes only that some people might display opportunistic behaviour *and* that it is difficult or impossible to distinguish ex ante (that is, before you make a deal) honest people from dishonest people. Even those who behave opportunistically need not do so all the time. Williamson assumes only that those who might display opportunistic behaviour do so *sometimes* and that it is difficult or costly to tell ex ante when they do or do not.

Sometimes people blame Williamson for having too pessimistic a view of human nature. It somehow does not seem right to build a theory on such a gloomy assumption. If that is your first reaction, too, consider the following examples.

Suppose you would like to spend your summer holiday in Greece. You go to a travel agent and find that almost everyone wants to go to Greece this year. You have to decide on the spot and book a holiday that is a little bit too expensive and not exactly what you want. The next day you see the perfect holiday at another travel agent – it is exactly what you want *and* much cheaper. Would you not be tempted to cancel the first reservation if you could?

Suppose travel agents did not make their customers sign contracts that were legally binding, would you not agree that sometimes some customers would deny they had already booked the first expensive holiday? Apparently, travel agents think so – that is why they have their customers sign a contract.

Consider also the following example. Suppose you want to buy a second-hand car from someone you do not know. The seller tells you that the car has no defects. Do you believe him? Suppose you can have the car inspected by an independent expert. Would you pay the cost of the inspection before buying? If you are prepared to pay the inspection cost, it means that you do not believe everyone.

Suppose you can choose between two secondhand cars (A and B) from two different sellers (A and B). You can detect no difference between the two cars themselves. There is only one difference: car A has been inspected by an independent expert, who tells you that it has no defects. Car B has not been inspected. Seller B tells you that car B has no defects. Would you prefer car A? That means you do not rule out the possibility of opportunistic behaviour by seller B.

From those two examples it is clear that travel agents and buyers of second-hand cars must spend a little amount of money (on drawing up a contract or having a car inspected), not because they expect all their trading partners to behave opportunistically all the time, but because *some people* might display opportunistic behaviour *sometimes*.

Box 8.3 The evolution of exchanges between strangers

Paul Seabright has written a beautiful book entitled *The Company of Strangers: A natural history of economic life* (2004). In the book he examines the evolutionary economic history of mankind. Specifically, he enquires how we have been able to build such a complex, interlinked economy in a relatively short period of time (a mere ten thousand years – equivalent to about two and a half minutes on an evolutionary clock that began ticking when our evolution diverged from the rest of the animal kingdom). Seabright shows the most remarkable feature of that evolution to be the enormous amount of (economic) interaction we have with strangers:

Homo sapiens is the only animal that engages in elaborate task-sharing – the division of labour as it is sometimes known – between genetically unrelated members of the same species. It is a phenomenon as remarkable and uniquely human as language itself. Most human beings now obtain a large share of the provision for their daily lives from others to whom they are not related by blood or marriage.

This is what Seabright has to say about the behavioural underpinnings of that evolution:

Two kinds of disposition have proved important to our evolution: a capacity for rational calculation of the costs and benefits of cooperation, and a tendency for what has been called *reciprocity* – the willingness to repay kindness with kindness and betrayal with revenge, even when this is not what rational calculation would recommend. Neither disposition could support cooperation without the other. People given to calculation without reciprocity would be too opportunistic, so nobody would trust them. People given to reciprocity without calculation would be too easily exploited by others. It seems likely that natural selection favored the evolution of a balance between these two dispositions in our ancestors. It did so because such a balance was important to the development of social life even before these ancestors ever began to deal with strangers in any systematic way. But once these dispositions were there, they could be put to work to make exchange between strangers possible.

▶

Note that Seabright's argument is in line with Williamson's: not all people are opportunistic all of the time, but this 'disposition' does exist in the population. Particularly as many of our dealings are with 'strangers', we have a hard time sorting out who can be trusted (when) and who not. Note also the link with evolutionary game theory (Section 5.6), showing how cooperation can evolve from reciprocity, but that it usually also pays to learn where exploitation may be applied. We return to the topics of trust, reciprocity and reputation later in this chapter.

From the two examples above, it is also clear that opportunistic behaviour can occur ex ante (a seller might not tell you about defects before you buy) or ex post (after you have booked a holiday you might want to back out of it). Ex ante opportunistic behaviour leads to adverse selection, a concept that was introduced in Section 4.2. Ex ante opportunistic behaviour can occur only when there is asymmetrical information: the seller of a used car has information that potential buyers do not have.

Now suppose that there are large numbers of sellers and buyers who trade with each other on a regular basis. Suppose that in a certain town there are ten dealers in secondhand cars. Suppose you buy a secondhand car. If you have a negative experience with one of the dealers, you do not want to buy from her a second time. A dealer who behaves opportunistically will damage her reputation. The dealers know that and you know the dealers know that, so you tend to believe a dealer when he says that a car has no defects. In that way, the problem of opportunism is attenuated because there are many sellers and because reputations matter.[1] You can therefore save the inspection costs. (Note that you can save the inspection costs only if reputations are important and information about reputations is freely available.)[2] There is a problem only if opportunism occurs in conjunction with small numbers of trading partners, which is termed **small numbers exchange**. If there is only one seller, he does not have to worry about reputation because you do not have an alternative. In that case you would want to have the car inspected, so you have to pay transaction costs.

Small numbers exchange

The argument so far is illustrated in Figure 8.1. There are two human factors and two environmental factors. Bounded rationality in conjunction with uncertainty/complexity and opportunism in conjunction with small numbers exchange lead to transaction costs.

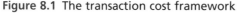

Figure 8.1 The transaction cost framework

8.2.3 Atmosphere

Atmosphere

The mode of a transaction (that is, whether a transaction is governed by the market or an organization) is determined by minimization of the sum of production and transaction costs.[3] There is another factor that also determines the mode of a transaction, however. It is called **atmosphere** (see Figure 8.1).

The atmosphere factor refers to the fact that participants in a transaction may value the mode of the transaction. Consider, for example, the workers making grandfather clocks in Box 8.1. Maybe they derive satisfaction from being self-employed. If that is true, they would be willing to work as an employee only if higher income compensated for the loss of atmosphere. For that reason, an employer with 17 employees might not be able to compete against a group of 18 self-employed people even if the transaction costs of the former arrangement were lower than those of the latter.

Sometimes people prefer to give away something for free. In that case, they derive more satisfaction from the act of giving than from the money they could receive. That indicates most people value the nature of a transaction. As an example, read Box 8.4 about donating blood.

In the framework of transaction cost economics, the atmosphere factor refers to the *local environment* in which the transaction takes place. Just as in our conceptual framework (see Figure 1.1), it acknowledges the fact that economic exchange is embedded in an environmental and institutional context with formal and informal 'rules of the game'. As elaborated in Section 1.7, the informal rules of the game are norms of behaviour, conventions and internally imposed rules of conduct, such as those of a company culture. Williamson (1998) relates the atmosphere factor to the concept of 'informal organization'. He acknowledges the importance of such informal rules, but admits that both the concept of informal organization and the economics of atmosphere remain relatively underdeveloped.

Box 8.4 Blood donorship

As described in Box 4.1, there is a serious shortage of good-quality blood that can be used for blood transfusion purposes. Clearly there is a demand for blood. Good-quality blood should command a high price, yet we observe that blood collection is still organized on a voluntary basis. Blood donors give their blood for free. Why are blood donors not paid?

One reason, explained in Box 4.1, is adverse selection, but there is a second reason: if blood donors were to receive payment, then that would fundamentally change the nature of the transaction. As it is, blood donors derive satisfaction from the idea that they give their blood for the common good. They voluntarily give to those who are so unfortunate as to need a transfusion. To pay blood donors would transform the act of giving blood into an ordinary commercial transaction. Titmuss (1971) argued that it would be quite likely that the result would be fewer (good-quality) donors instead of more. This is an example of 'atmosphere' being disturbed by transforming blood donation into a commercial transaction.

See, however, Gary Becker's work for arguments in favour of markets being allowed for blood and organ donation.[4] The main reasons given are an expected (sharp) increase in the supply and the curtailing of current 'black markets' in blood and organs.

8.2.4 The fundamental transformation

Suppose that an automobile company invites bids from a large number of potential suppliers for a certain part for a new automobile. Suppose that the automobile company signs a contract with one of the original bidders for a five-year period. During that five-year period the supplier learns how to produce the component efficiently. After five years, when the contract must be renewed, the original winner of the contract has a significant advantage over other potential suppliers. Williamson (1975) refers to this situation as **lock-in**. Through learning by doing, the original situation involving a large number of bidders is transformed into a situation of monopoly: the experience gained by the supplier puts the firm in the position of a monopolist. However, the supplier can use that experience only in the manufacturing of a part for which there is only one buyer. So, the situation is again one of bilateral monopoly.

Lock-in

When learning by doing occurs, an original situation of large numbers exchange is transformed into a situation of small numbers exchange. That is termed the **fundamental transformation**.

Fundamental
transformation

8.3 Dimensions of transactions

Critical dimensions of
transactions

Transaction costs for a particular transaction depend on the critical dimensions of that transaction. There are three **critical dimensions of transactions**:

- asset specificity
- uncertainty/complexity
- frequency.

8.3.1 Asset specificity

Asset specificity

Transaction-specific
assets

The **asset specificity** of a transaction refers to the degree to which the transaction needs to be supported by **transaction-specific assets**. An asset is transaction-specific if it cannot be redeployed to an alternative use without a significant reduction in the value of the asset. Asset specificity may refer to physical or human assets. To illustrate the concept, consider the following example, which refers to physical assets.[5]

Imagine a town located in the centre of a very thinly populated area. Let us call the town Appropria. At present there is no local newspaper in Appropria, but there is a publisher, Mr P, who wants to start a local newspaper.

The new newspaper must be printed locally in Appropria because of transportation costs. Mr P does not have printing know-how, so he must rely on that of one of the local printers. There are several printers in Appropria but none of them has a press suitable for printing newspapers.

One of the printers in Appropria, Mrs Q, considers buying a press for printing newspapers. If she buys such a press, it will be a transaction-specific asset: she can use the press only for the transaction with Mr P as there is no other newspaper in Appropria and it is very costly to transport newspapers to other towns. To put it in the language of transaction cost economics, the transaction between Mr P and Mrs Q is characterized by asset specificity and lock-in.

For transactions with high asset specificity, the costs of market transactions are high. To see why that is true, let us return to Appropria. Suppose that the new press has an economic life of five years. Mrs Q will want a five-year contract with Mr P before she buys the press. At first glance it may not seem very difficult or costly to write and sign a five-year contract. To illustrate the difficulties in writing such a contract, however, we use a numerical example.

Assume fixed costs are $3500 per day, if the new press is depreciated over five years. Assume, further, that variable costs for operating the new press are $1500 per day. Mrs Q cannot sell the services of the press to another publisher, nor can she sell the press.

Suppose Mrs Q obtains a five-year contract from Mr P for $5000 per day and, on that basis, orders the new press. As soon as Mrs Q has committed herself, Mr P has an incentive for opportunistic behaviour. Even though Mrs Q has a legally binding contract with Mr P, he can come back to her. Suppose he tells her, 'Look, this new newspaper is not really the success I expected it to become. With a contract for $5000 a day I will go bankrupt and then your press will have no value at all. If you can help me a little by agreeing to lower the price to $4000 a day, I will be able to manage. I am very sorry that I have to say this, but really I see no other solution.'

If Mrs Q believes his story, she has no other choice than to accept the lower price. In fact, she must accept any price higher than $1500 a day. In business language, we would say that, for a price higher than $1500, there is still a positive contribution margin. In the language of economics, we would say that, for a price higher than $1500, there is still a positive **quasi-rent**. By making self-disbelieved statements, Mr P tries to appropriate (a part of) that quasi-rent. In Appropria trying to appropriate someone else's quasi-rent is a great sport. If someone else can try to appropriate your quasi-rent, economists refer to the danger of **hold-up**. Box 8.5 gives another example of the threat of hold-up (and the solution applied in that situation).

Quasi-rent

Hold-up

Box 8.5 Hold-up in The *Lord of the Rings*

When television series become successful, the lead actors can often renegotiate their compensation before shooting the next season. A similar threat of hold-up may occur with films – for example, when a trilogy is foreseen:

> all three movies in the *Lord of the Rings* series were made before the first was released to avoid just this problem. The studio clearly wanted to avoid a situation in which Elijah Wood, who played central character Frodo Baggins, could negotiate a new and highly lucrative contract on the strength of the success of the first film before completing the final part of the trilogy, *Return of the King*.

Source: Gilson et al. (2006)

If Mr P cannot go bankrupt under any circumstances, there is no problem. In that case, a legally binding contract protects Mrs Q against post-contractual opportunistic behaviour by Mr P. If, however, Mr P can go bankrupt, Mrs Q will not buy the press on the basis of a simple five-year contract. What she needs is a guarantee from Mr P's bank that, in the event of bankruptcy, the bank will pay her the fixed costs ($3500 a day, assuming no salvage value) for the rest of the five-year period. Now, though, the bank will be vulnerable to Mr P's post-contractual opportunistic behaviour. Mr P can go to his banker and say, 'Look, if you pay me $1000 a day, I will not go bankrupt and you can save your contractual obligation to pay Mrs Q $3500 a day.' So, the guarantee does not solve the problem, but transfers it to someone else.

In reality, Mrs Q might be willing to sign a contract with Mr P, but, before doing so, she needs much more information about Mr P's business plan, his character, his personal wealth and so on. To acquire such information is costly. In addition, she will demand the right to have Mr P's books inspected by an independent auditor, which is costly, too. Finally, as her money will still be at risk, she will demand compensation for risk-bearing. That compensation may come in the form of a price higher than $5000 a day or a share in Mr P's profits.

Another solution to these contractual difficulties is a merger between the firms of Mr P and Mrs Q. Then, the transaction between publisher and printer would be taken out of the market and allocated to an organization. After a merger, Mr P and Mrs Q jointly own the assets and share the profits, so Mr P no longer has an incentive to behave opportunistically towards his partner.

In our example, the degree of asset specificity is so high that a series of sequential spot contracts (say, contracts for one day only and daily negotiations on the price for the next day) is not feasible (Mrs Q can never accept this, so she will not buy the press). So, there are only two options left: a merger between Mr P and Mrs Q or a five-year contract specifying in detail Mrs Q's right to inspect Mr P's business. Such a long-term contract is an intermediate form between market and organization. In the language of transaction cost economics, it is termed **relational contracting**.

Relational contracting

By the way, there may be another asset that is highly transaction-specific in the example above. A new newspaper normally suffers start-up losses during the first few years. By financing those start-up losses, Mr P invests in an intangible asset. Let us call it goodwill. That goodwill is also a transaction-specific asset. Mrs Q now also has an incentive for post-contractual opportunistic behaviour. For example, she might say, 'Look, I made a mistake in calculating the price of $5000 a day. You really must pay me $5700 a day. If you don't, I will go bankrupt and the value of your investment in goodwill will be zero.' That would pose a problem for Mr P if other printers would need at least a few months before they could start printing newspapers.

So, Mr P and Mrs Q both have to invest in a transaction-specific asset. That means, after they have invested, they will be locked into a bilateral monopoly: they both have a monopoly position towards the other with respect to certain assets.

In the introduction to this section we distinguished between physical and human asset specificity. Box 8.6 gives a somewhat finer distinction.

Box 8.6 Different types of asset specificity

Transaction cost economics has filtered through to the managerial literature. Consider the following discussion of several types of asset specificity from the *McKinsey Quarterly:*

There are three principal types of asset specificity ... *Site specificity* occurs when buyers and sellers locate fixed assets, such as a coalmine and power station, in close proximity to minimize transport and inventory costs. *Technical specificity* occurs when one or both parties to a transaction invest in equipment that can only be used by one or both parties and that has low value in alternative uses. *Human capital specificity* occurs when employees develop skills that are specific to a particular buyer or customer relationship.

The upstream aluminum industry has high asset specificity. The industry has two principal stages of production: bauxite mining and aluminum refining. Mines and refineries are usually located close together (site specificity) because of the high cost of transporting bauxite, relative to its value, and the 60 to 70 per cent volume reduction typically achieved during refining. Refineries are tailored to process their own bauxite, with its unique chemical and physical properties; switching suppliers or customers is either impossible or prohibitively expensive (technical specificity). Consequently, mine-refinery pairs are locked together economically.

Source: Stuckey and White (1993)

8.3.2 Uncertainty/complexity

The second dimension of transactions, uncertainty/complexity, needs no further explanation: we learned earlier that bounded rationality is a problem only for transactions with a high degree of uncertainty/complexity (remember the examples of buying petrol and ordering a new weapon system).

8.3.3 Frequency

When asset specificity is high, we expect transactions to be carried out within organizations rather than across markets. However, to set up a specialized governance structure (such as a vertically integrated firm) involves certain fixed costs. Whether the volume of transactions conducted through such a specialized governance structure utilizes it to capacity is then the remaining issue. The costs of a specialized governance structure are more easily recovered for high-frequency transactions. Hence, frequency is the third relevant dimension of transactions.

8.3.4 Competition between organizational forms

Transaction costs for a particular transaction depend on the critical dimensions of that transaction. For transactions with a high degree of asset specificity, a high degree of uncertainty/complexity and a high frequency, the costs of market transactions are extremely high – much higher than the costs of internal transactions. Such transactions tend to be carried out within organizations, at least in the long run.

In the real world, we might see certain market transactions and, at the same time, similar transactions taking place within organizations. That can indicate the costs of transacting under the two modes are about equal. If the costs of transacting under the two modes differ significantly, then the most efficient form will ultimately prevail. It might take quite a long time, however, as is illustrated in Box 8.7.

Box 8.7 Why are dairy firms organized as farmers' cooperatives?

Dairy firms are often, though not always, organized as farmers' cooperatives. Why is that?

Before trying to answer this question, let us give you some details about the emergence of the first dairy cooperatives in the Netherlands or, more specifically, in two provinces of the Netherlands: Friesland and North Holland.

In the middle of the nineteenth century, there were only three dairy products: cheese, butter and fresh milk. In those days, farmers made cheese and butter at the farm (that was usually done by women). In 1878, a centrifuge for separating cream from milk was developed. The invention provided economies of scale and led to the emergence of dairy factories.

In Friesland, the first dairy factory was established in 1879 by a private entrepreneur. Seven years later, in 1886, Friesland had seven dairy firms owned and operated by entrepreneurs. In that same year, a dairy factory was established by a group of farmers as a cooperative firm.

A dairy firm organized as a farmers' cooperative does not have shareholders, so maximizing profit is not its main goal. A farmers' cooperative has members and tries to pay its members as high a price as possible for the milk its members supply.

In Friesland, the number of dairy factories set up by farmers' cooperatives grew rapidly, but so did the number of dairy firms run by entrepreneurs. In 1898, Friesland had 46 dairy factories run by entrepreneurs and 66 run by farmers' cooperatives. In the first 25 years of the next century, however, dairy firms run by farmers' cooperatives grew faster in size and number, while some of the entrepreneurial dairy firms failed. As a result, the farmers' cooperative has been the dominant organizational form of dairy firms in Friesland since 1925.

In the northern part of North Holland, dairy firms developed in the same way as in Friesland: around 1900 there were entrepreneurial as well as cooperative dairy firms, but the cooperatives grew faster. As a result, cooperatives came to dominate that region as well.

In the southern part of North Holland, there were no farmers' cooperatives around 1900. That area is close to the cities of Amsterdam, Haarlem, Leiden and Utrecht. Milk from the area was sold primarily as fresh milk to consumers in those cities by distributors. The distributors were private entrepreneurs.

Why did the cooperative dairy firm overtake entrepreneurial dairy firms in Friesland and the northern part of North Holland? Why did cooperative dairy firms not emerge in the southern part of North Holland?

The answers to those questions have much to do with the fact that milk is a perishable product. In the nineteenth century, milk could not be stored for more than a day (cooling was not available) and transporting milk over long distances was not feasible. Milk had to be processed into cheese and butter within a short time and not far from the farm. As a result, farmers who sold their milk to an entrepreneurial dairy firm were in a situation where they had only one customer. Their investment in cattle is a transaction-specific investment. The farmers had no alternative for their milk but to resume the old way of processing milk at the farm. In the early days of the dairy factories, it was probably a feasible alternative because farmers still had the equipment and the know-how for making butter and cheese. However, as economies of scale became more pronounced and farmers' equipment for making butter and cheese was no longer in a good condition, making butter and cheese at the farm ceased to be a realistic alternative. Farmers were powerless against opportunistic behaviour from entrepreneurial dairy firms, especially as butter and cheese are much less perishable than fresh milk. That prompted more and more farmers who initially sold their milk to entrepreneurial firms to become members of the nearest farmers' cooperative. It explains the developments in Friesland and the northern part of North Holland, where almost all milk was used for making butter and cheese.

In the southern part of North Holland, the situation was different: the distributors of fresh milk were as dependent on the farmers as the farmers were dependent on them. The investment by the farmers in cattle is transaction-specific, but so is the investment by the distributors in their customer base and their means of distribution. As fresh milk could not be stored for more than a day, the distributors needed a daily supply of fresh milk. That made opportunistic behaviour by distributors towards their suppliers unlikely.

The main difference between a distributor of fresh milk and an entrepreneurial dairy firm making butter and cheese seems to be that the former needs a daily supply of fresh milk while the latter does not. That explains why cooperative dairy firms did not emerge in the southern part of North Holland.

The example in Box 8.7 also illustrates how organizational forms compete. There was competition between cooperative dairy firms and entrepreneurial dairy firms. That points to a fundamental assumption in transaction cost economics: there is always competition between organizational forms and, in the long run, only the most efficient organizational form will survive.

8.4 Peer groups

In Sections 8.2 and 8.3 we have laid the foundations for transaction cost reasoning. In the next sections we apply transaction cost reasoning to explain the existence of different organizational forms.

Peer group

The first organizational form to be discussed is the peer group. A **peer group** is simply a group of people working together without hierarchy. In a peer group, the most important coordinating mechanism is mutual adjustment. There is no boss, so there can be no direct supervision. The peer group sells its output, the proceeds of which are shared among the members of the peer group according to some sharing rule. Examples of peer groups are small partnerships, such as lawyers, auditors and doctors.

8.4.1 Advantages of peer groups

Why do peer groups arise? For example, why do most management consultants work as partners in a partnership instead of working independently? What are the advantages of a peer group over a group of independent self-employed people?

First, *economies of scale* may be obtained. Suppose two dentists form a partnership. The partnership may then buy equipment for X-ray photography that each dentist uses for perhaps not more than half an hour per day. However, an alternative arrangement would be two dentists working independently (without pooling revenue) in the same building. They could still jointly own or lease the X-ray equipment.

In the examples, economies of scale arise because the workers (the dentists) need the services of expensive equipment on a part-time basis only. Joint ownership (as farmers sometimes have of harvesting machines) is then a viable arrangement for obtaining such economies. It may also be possible to obtain the services of such indivisible specialized physical assets by renting (harvesting equipment that can be moved easily from one farmer to the next provides an example).

Economies of scale may also arise in *information-gathering*. Imagine two consultants who specialize in marketing studies for pharmaceutical companies. Both need background information on developments in the pharmaceutical industry on a continuous basis. Suppose they both employ a young economist for desk research. By forming a partnership, they can economize on desk research.

Suppose the two consultants decide to remain independent, but still want to economize on desk research. Could one of them stop doing desk research and buy the information he needed from his competitor/colleague? Without going into details now, it seems plausible that this would be more difficult than buying the services of specialized equipment. In general, it is difficult to trade information because of the fundamental paradox of information (see Section 4.1). So, economies of scale in information-gathering are difficult to obtain for two independent consultants.

Second, a peer group may have *risk-bearing advantages* over a group of independent people. Consider a group of ten independent marketing consultants. A major risk for each of them is to have no assignments for an extended period. Forming a partnership is one way to obtain pooling of that risk. Alternatively, it is useful to ask if such risk-pooling could be obtained through a market, in this case the insurance market.

It may be possible but difficult to obtain insurance for the risk of having no assignments. Those consultants who are weak in selling their services will be especially eager to take out such an insurance policy. Also, after having obtained one, it may be quite difficult for the insurance company to check whether or not the consultant really tried hard enough to get assignments. Thus, adverse selection and moral hazard would be severe problems for the insurance company.

The partners forming a peer group may be able to mitigate against adverse selection if they can screen potential partners better than an insurance company can. It also seems plausible that a partnership can avoid the problem of moral hazard as observability of effort is less of a problem for colleagues than it is for an insurance company.

Third, a peer group may offer *associational gains*. That is, consultants may be more productive when working as member of a partnership than when working independently. If they belong to a partnership, they may feel a responsibility to do their fair share, but, working alone, they may slack off. Also, they may value being a partner and working with peers. That is an example of atmosphere: people may simply prefer one organizational form over another.

8.4.2 Limitations of peer groups

In a small peer group (for example, two authors writing a book on economic theories of organization), shirking may not be a problem at all. On the contrary, each may take pride in doing more than his fair share. In a large peer group, however, shirking often becomes a severe problem. Very large partnerships (in auditing and/or consulting) do exist, but then some of the partners are elected managing partners. It is their duty to restrict shirking by evaluating the performance of other partners and adjusting the income-sharing rules accordingly. Such large partnerships are, therefore, more accurately described as simple hierarchies than peer groups.

8.5 Simple hierarchies

Simple hierarchy

A **simple hierarchy** is a group of workers with a boss. The boss has the right to adjust rates of pay, alter the composition of the group and tell the workers in the group what to do. Most small manufacturing firms (such as the factory making grandfather clocks) are organized as simple hierarchies, not peer groups.

In a peer group, all members are equal: they receive the same income and have the same decision rights. In a hierarchy, some people can tell other people what to do, so direct supervision is an important coordinating mechanism. Also, in a hierarchy, a person's income usually has a relationship to his or her performance – either past performance or expected future performance.

Why do we observe so few peer groups, especially in manufacturing industries? What advantages do simple hierarchies have over peer groups?

8.5.1 Team production

In Section 7.4 we explained how, in the view of Alchian and Demsetz (1972), team production leads to the emergence of a simple hierarchy. Team production, they say, will induce people to shirk. A monitor has to be brought in to reduce shirking. To avoid shirking by the monitor, the monitor must be the residual claimant.

Williamson (1975, Chapter 3) disagrees with Alchian and Demsetz's view. Most production processes consist of several stages, he says, which are technologically separable. As an example, consider again the factory making grandfather clocks. There are several stages of production, such as sawing, assembling and painting. Those stages can be separated by intermediate product inventories, so the work of the sawyers and assemblers can be separated. There is no team production in this example, yet we see most such firms organized as simple hierarchies rather than as peer groups.

8.5.2 Economies of communication and decisionmaking

In a peer group, every member participates in decisionmaking. In a simple hierarchy, decisions are made by the boss. Now, suppose that information relevant for decisionmaking originates with each member. In a peer group, each member must communicate with all the other members. In a simple hierarchy, that person need only communicate with the boss. Thus, in a peer group the number of communication channels is $\frac{1}{2}n(n-1)$, while in a simple hierarchy it is $n-1$, where n is the number of individuals in the group (Figure 8.2). Transfer of information is costly because of bounded rationality (it takes time to explain things to other team members; information may become distorted when transferred). Thus, for $n > 2$, a simple hierarchy can realize **economies of communication** over a peer group.

Economies of communication

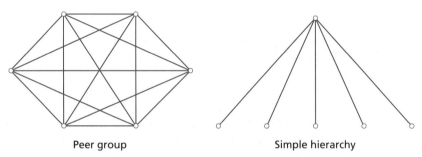

Peer group   Simple hierarchy

Figure 8.2 Number of communication channels in a peer group and in a simple hierarchy

Economies in decisionmaking

A simple hierarchy can also realize **economies in decisionmaking**. Where, in a peer group, decisions are reached after discussions in the whole group, in a simple hierarchy the boss alone makes decisions, so less time is needed for decisionmaking.

8.5.3 Monitoring

As indicated in Section 8.4, shirking becomes a severe problem in a large peer group. Thus, in such a group it is not uncommon to see one or a few members designated to perform productivity audits and given the power to adjust the compensation of group members accordingly. That, however, violates the essence of a peer group. Whatever its legal form (partnership or mutual corporation), it has now been transformed into a simple hierarchy.

For the reasons explained above, we observe relatively few peer groups in the economy. Williamson stresses hierarchy as the alternative to mutual adjustment within peer groups. Most organizations are of a more complex type, involving more coordination mechanisms than mutual adjustment and direct supervision (see Chapter 3).

8.6 Multistage hierarchies: U-form and M-form enterprises

In a simple hierarchy, there is only one manager who coordinates the work of the other team members. Suppose that economies of scale are such that the size of the group is large. Then, because of bounded rationality, a single manager can no longer coordinate the work of all team members. Several managers are now needed. That creates an opportunity for division of managerial work so that each manager can specialize. One manager, for example, may specialize in managing the factory, another in managing the marketing and salespeople and so on. Thus, within the firm, departments are created along functional lines and each functional department has a manager. The work of those functional managers is coordinated by a general manager. This organization form is used widely by medium-sized firms. Williamson calls it the *unitary form*, or, *U-form enterprise*. Within a **U-form enterprise** there are at least two layers of managers. It is a **multistage hierarchy** as opposed to a single-stage or simple hierarchy.

U-form enterprise

Multistage hierarchy

Now suppose that a U-form firm expands by adding several new products. Alfred D. Chandler (1966) studied the history of several large American companies and found that, in the late nineteenth century, most of them were involved in a single activity (for example, steel, meatpacking, tobacco, oil) and were organized along functional lines.

In the early twentieth century, however, many of the large companies diversified into new products. At first, most of them continued as U-form enterprises, but, after some time, they found out that, for the large, multiproduct firm, the U-form has severe disadvantages. The disadvantages are of two kinds.

First, in a large U-form firm, there are several layers of management. Coordination of two functional departments (say marketing and production) occurs mainly at the top level. Thus, information has to be transmitted across several layers before it is used for decisionmaking. As information is transmitted, some of it is usually lost. Data are summarized and interpreted as they move upwards and instructions are operationalized as they move downwards, which leads to **cumulative control loss**, the corporate board losing control of day-to-day operations as the number of management layers increases. Cumulative control loss is a result of bounded rationality. Only because of bounded rationality do data have to be summarized and interpreted before they reach the top manager, and only because of bounded rationality is the top manager unable to give detailed, operationalized instructions.

Cumulative control loss

Second, as the U-form firm grows, the character of the strategic decision-making process alters. The top manager is involved in day-to-day operational coordination to such an extent that long-run, strategic decisions receive little attention. That is another manifestation of bounded rationality. Suppose that a management committee is formed consisting of the general manager and the top managers of the functional departments. In a large U-form firm, the top manager of a functional department may be interested more in furthering the local interests of her department than the overall goals for the enterprise. As explained in Section 6.3, it is very difficult to translate an overall goal such as profit maximization into operational subgoals for functional departments. Conflicts of interest between functional departments cannot be avoided. In a small U-form firm such conflicts of interest are mitigated because the general manager is still in a position to judge how much functional managers care for and contribute to overall goals. In a large U-form firm, the top manager may find herself to be the only person attending to overall companywide goals. Thus, the tendency to pursue operational subgoals simply becomes too strong. Departmental interests voiced by functional managers enter the strategic decisionmaking process.

To summarize, the large, multiproduct U-form firm faces two problems: cumulative control loss and corruption of the strategic decisionmaking process. The solution to these two problems is to introduce the *multidivisional*,

M-form enterprise

or, **M-form enterprise**. In the 1920s, the multidivisional structure was a major organizational innovation that occurred first in the USA. Most large American multiproduct firms adopted this structure before World War II. Most large European multiproduct firms followed in the 1950s and 1960s.

The M-form firm is divided at the top level into several quasi-autonomous operating divisions, usually along product lines. Top management is assisted by a general office (corporate staff). The main characteristics and advantages of the M-form are as follows (Williamson, 1975, p. 137):

- the responsibility for operating decisions is assigned to more-or-less self-contained operating divisions that operate as quasi-firms;
- the corporate staff attached to the general office performs both advisory and auditing functions, which have the effect of securing greater control over operating division behaviour;
- the general office is principally concerned with strategic decisions, including the allocation of resources to the operating divisions;
- the separation of the general office from operations provides general office executives with the psychological commitment to being concerned with the overall performance of the organization rather than becoming absorbed in the affairs and subgoals of functional departments.

Compared with the U-form organization of the same activities, the M-form serves to economize both on bounded rationality and opportunism. Bounded rationality is less a problem in the M-form than in the U-form firm because information needs to be transferred less often. Opportunism is attenuated in the M-form firm because goal congruence is easier to obtain: it is easier to translate an overall company goal (such as profit maximization) into operational subgoals per division (such as profit maximization for each division).

8.7 Organizational markets

8.7.1 Markets for intermediate goods and services

Within M-form enterprises, division managers are evaluated primarily on the basis of indicators of financial performance, such as return on sales, return on assets and so on. Between divisions, numerous transactions of intermediate goods and services take place. There are internal markets within the M-form enterprise for intermediate goods and services. The financial results of each division are affected by the prices (usually called transfer prices) at which those internal transactions take place. Transfer prices may be either set by corporate headquarters or negotiated between divisions. If divisions are left free to negotiate transfer prices for internal transactions, then one advantage of organizations over markets (reduction of transaction costs due to costly haggling and workflow interruptions) is seriously impaired.

Transactions can also occur between corporate headquarters and an operating division. As an example, consider a group of internal management consultants belonging to the corporate staff. Suppose the internal management consultants do not have to charge the operating divisions for their services, but are paid out of corporate funds. In that case, the marginal cost to operating divisions of an additional consulting hour is zero, so the operating divisions will demand more services until the marginal revenue to the division of an additional consulting hour is zero. The result is an oversized group of internal management consultants at the corporate level.

Now, suppose that the management consultants do have to charge the operating divisions for the full cost of their services. If operating divisions are not allowed to hire external consultants, the internal consultants have a monopoly for consulting services. The result will be monopoly pricing and shirking by the internal consultants.

Such a situation can be avoided by giving the operating divisions freedom to engage external consultants. The internal consultants now have to compete with external consultants and an internal market for consulting services with several suppliers has been created.

When, in addition, the internal consultants are allowed to offer their services in the external market, the difference between the internal and external market virtually disappears. There is then simply one market for consulting services with several suppliers (one of which is the group of internal consultants) and several customers (operating divisions and numerous other companies).

8.7.2 Internal labour markets

Internal markets also exist for human resources. Two ways to organize the internal managerial labour market will be considered.

First, managers may be rotated, working in the various divisions according to a plan devised by a corporate personnel department. Operating divisions notify the corporate personnel department if there is a vacancy and the corporate personnel department then selects a person to fill that vacancy.

Second, operating divisions may simply compete for the best managers in the internal managerial labour market. If there is a vacancy, they advertise in a corporate newsletter or on the Intranet. Managers from other divisions who are interested may apply. If they have to compete with candidates from outside companies, there is really no difference between the internal managerial labour market and the external one.

8.7.3 Internal capital market

Finally, there is an internal capital market. Three ways to organize the internal capital market will be discussed.

- *Case 1* The operating divisions are not allowed to reinvest automatically the cash flow they generate. Instead, the general office reallocates the entire corporate cash flow to the divisions. Moreover, operating divisions are not allowed to raise equity capital or debt capital in the external capital market.
- *Case 2* The operating divisions are allowed to reinvest the cash flow they generate. Moreover, operating divisions are free to raise debt capital in the external capital market, but not equity capital.
- *Case 3* The operating divisions are allowed to reinvest the cash flow they generate. Moreover, they are allowed to raise both equity capital and debt capital in the external capital market.

Case 1 is the normal situation for most M-form enterprises. The general office reallocates cash flows to divisions to high-yield uses. That is a fundamental attribute of the M-form firm.

Williamson (1975) argues that the general office in an M-form enterprise is in a better position to allocate capital to the highest-yield uses than is the external capital market. His argument is as follows. Compare an M-form enterprise with, say, five operating divisions with a set of five independent comparable companies. The general office has an advantage over the external capital market in monitoring the performance of the division managers: there exists an internal relation with the division and, thus, better access to information than external investors have to independent companies. Also, the general office is in a better position to evaluate investment proposals. The manager of an operating division can provide sensitive internal information to the general office, while the disclosure of such information to outsiders (including competitors) might jeopardize the project.

In Case 2, the general office is, in essence, reduced to a clerical agency for the preparation of financial reports. The role of the general office is simply that of a large shareholder. As long as financial results of an operating division are satisfactory the general office does not interfere. Only when results of an operating division are deteriorating would the general office take steps to replace the division manager or sell the division. Williamson calls this organization form a **holding company, or H-form**.

In Case 3, the operating divisions are really autonomous companies forming a loose federation. An example is the Belgian Société Générale. There

Holding company, or, H-form

is a central holding company, holding majority as well as minority interests in numerous operating companies. Also, between operating companies there are several interlocking shareholdings. Other examples are venture capital companies that have majority as well as minority shareholdings in several operating companies.

8.8 Markets and organizations: are these all there is?

In the conceptual framework of this book (see Figure 1.1) markets and organizations are seen as two alternative ways to coordinate economic decisions. Markets are coordinated by means of the price mechanism; organizations by any (combination) of the six mechanisms we introduced in Chapter 3. To refresh your memory, those organizational mechanisms are repeated in Figure 8.3, together with the organizational configurations they are associated with.

In Chapter 3 we also argued that, in practice, those organizational coordinating mechanisms will often be combined. While we can distinguish the six pure types of organizational configuration that are mentioned in Figure 8.3, in practice we often observe that bundles of coordination mechanisms will govern specific transactions. Moreover, we showed in Chapter 3 that market coordination and organizational coordination often operate in conjunction – that is, within organizations markets exist and markets are always more or less organized.

Markets and hierachies paradigm

So far in this chapter, organizations have been analysed from a narrower perspective. Williamson's transaction cost economics is also called the **markets and hierarchies paradigm**. In this view, markets are replaced by hierarchies when price coordination breaks down. In that sense, Williamson's ideas are direct descendants of Coase's, who also argued that organizations are characterized primarily by 'authority' (in our terminology, direct supervision). Within organizations, however, there are other coordinating mechanisms, such as mutual adjustment and standardization of norms. Mutual adjustment is the main coordinating mechanism in a small peer group (for example, a partnership of a few consultants). It is also very important in larger organizations and occurs between departments (such as marketing and product

PRIME COORDINATING MECHANISM	CONFIGURATION
Direct supervision	Entrepreneurial organization
Standardization of work processes	Machine organization
Standardization of skills	Professional organization
Standardization of outputs	Diversified organization
Mutual adjustment	Innovative organization
Standardization of norms	Missionary organization

Figure 8.3 The six organizational coordination mechanisms

development) in a U-form firm and between divisions in an M-form firm. Mutual adjustment can also occur between two organizations, such as a supplier and a buyer.

It is hard to see how mutual adjustment can work smoothly between parties who display opportunistic behaviour. For that reason it is not surprising Williamson's version of transaction cost economics has evoked several critical comments. These critical comments pertain to two points.

- Transaction cost economics relies too much on the assumption of opportunistic behaviour. In the real world, people often cooperate because they trust one another. Many commercial transactions cannot occur without a certain level of trust between the parties to that transaction. That is especially true for transactions that are conducted over a period of time.
- Markets and hierarchies should not be viewed as two mutually exclusive governance structures. In the real world, we also see organizational forms such as long-term relations between buyers and suppliers, joint ventures and various forms of network organizations. They are examples of intermediate or **hybrid organizational forms** – organizational forms that fall somewhere between markets and hierarchies. In Chapter 13 we will discuss hybrid forms in some detail.

Hybrid organizational forms

That hybrid organizational forms exist has also been recognized by Williamson. For him, they occur for intermediate levels of asset specificity. Other scholars have argued that some hybrid forms can be understood only if the assumption of opportunism is relaxed. For them, those two critical comments above are very much related.

We shall first discuss an approach in which the assumption of opportunism is partly replaced by allowing for trust. In that approach clans are defined as organizations that rely to a great extent on mutual trust. Also, a distinction is made between markets, bureaucracies and clans as three alternative ways to coordinate economic decisions and that is explained in Section 8.8.1. In Section 8.8.2, we explain in more general terms the role of trust.

8.8.1 Markets, bureaucracies and clans

One of the earliest extensions of the markets and hierarchies framework was provided by William G. Ouchi. A professor of management, he drew on organizational theory to suggest that a more appropriate framework would encompass markets, bureaucracies and clans (Ouchi, 1980; Ouchi and Williamson, 1981). In that extension, hierarchies were substituted for bureaucracies and clans were added as a third way to coordinate economic transactions.

The substitution of hierarchies for bureaucracies is in accordance with mainstream organizational sociology. It was the German sociologist Max Weber (1925) who proposed that, in modern organizations, personal authority had been replaced by organizational authority. While older organizations had relied on the personal authority of the ruler, modern organizations had acquired the legitimacy to substitute organizational rules for personal authority. Such modern organizations were described by Weber as bureaucracies.[6] Ouchi therefore argued that, in organizational coordination, prices were replaced by rules. The rules contained the information necessary for coordination. The essence of that type of coordination was therefore not its hierarchical but its bureaucratic nature.

Moreover, Ouchi argued that there was a third way of coordinating transactions. That third way relies on the socialization of individuals, which ensures that they have common values and beliefs. Individuals who have been socialized in the same way have common norms for behaviour. Such norms can also contain the information necessary for transactions. By way of example, Ouchi (1980) pointed to Japanese firms that rely to a great extent on socializing their workers to accept the company's goals as their own and compensating them according to length of service and other non-performance criteria. For those firms it is not necessary to measure the performance of their employees as the employees' natural inclination (thanks to socialization) is to do what is best for the firm.

Thus, Ouchi argued that Williamson's framework did not acknowledge the richness of organizational coordination, as summarized in Figure 8.3. The markets and hierarchies paradigm pays too little attention to the role of rules and norms. However, Ouchi's proposal of markets, bureaucracies and clans does not capture that full richness either. In our view Ouchi's proposal is subsumed in Mintzberg's typology, displayed in Figure 8.3. Ouchi's emphasis on the importance of rules corresponds with the standardization of work processes, standardization of skills and standardization of output, while socialization is equivalent to standardization of norms. For that reason, in this book we have not adopted Ouchi's proposal to distinguish between three governance structures. Rather, we argue that markets are replaced by neither hierarchies nor bureaucracies but *organizations* when the price mechanism starts to fail. Organizations do not rely on authority (direct supervision) only but employ the full set of six coordination mechanisms identified by Mintzberg.

8.8.2 The role of trust

Williamson's version of transaction cost economics is built on the assumption of opportunism. As explained in Section 8.2.2, Williamson does not assume that everyone behaves opportunistically all the time. Rather, he assumes that some people might behave opportunistically sometimes *and* that it is difficult to tell ex ante (that is, before you enter into a transaction) whether or not your partner will behave opportunistically. That means you don't know up front who you can trust (especially if you haven't dealt with the person before).

Several scholars have attacked that assumption. It has been argued (Goshal and Moran, 1996) that the tendency of a certain person to behave in an opportunistic way depends on two things: the immediate net benefits of such behaviour and 'disposition toward the transaction partner'. This recognizes that many people will not cheat their partner in a transaction simply because they would not have a good feeling when they do so. If you like your trading partner and feel that he trusts you, you will probably not cheat on him even if that would bring you some financial gain. Also, if you trust your trading partner and he trusts you, you can develop a long-term mutually profitable relationship. Thus, many economists now recognize that trust is an important concept and several have tried to investigate under which circumstances trust is likely to develop. Box 8.8 presents some of the results.[7]

Box 8.8 Economic research on trust

Economists have begun to measure trust in order to establish when it is present and explore the circumstances in which it increases or decreases over time. Some of the early research outcomes indicate the following.

- *Different people behave differently* That has been established in experimental games such as iterated prisoner's dilemmas (see Chapter 5) in which they have to decide whether to cooperate or defect during several rounds of play. For instance, in a game set up by Clark and Sefton (2001) the first mover began by trusting 57 per cent of the time and, in 35 per cent of those cases, the second mover reciprocated by trusting also. In the other instances, the players decided to defect, thus undermining the best (trusting) outcome.
- *To a certain extent, these differences can be traced to their personality traits* For instance, people differ in their attributions of causes for their success or failure. Some people tend to point towards external, environmental causes. Others attribute their successes and failures more to their own choices and behaviour. The former tend to prefer cooperative strategies while the latter favour competitive strategies. Other personality traits, such as sensation seeking, also help to explain individual variations in players' behaviour (Boone, de Brabander and van Witteloostuijn, 1996, 1999).
- *Culture may matter, too* A striking example is in the study by Henrich (2000), who showed that the Machiguenga Indians of the Peruvian Amazon strongly deviate from Western game theory predictions in a bargaining game.
- *Over time, levels of trust can increase or decrease* In Clark and Sefton's (2001) game, the percentage of first movers trusting their counterparts went down from 57 per cent in the initial rounds to 32 per cent in the tenth round. Trust is fragile and prone to break down altogether in the event of negative experiences.
- *Incentives matter* If, for instance, the rewards for solitary confessors are increased in the prisoner's dilemma game, defections tend to increase.
- *Already knowing each other helps* Glaeser et al. (2000) designed a game in which the first player received $15, of which he could give any part to a second player. The amount sent to the second player was then doubled by the researchers and the second player could decide how much to send back to the first player. The trusting outcome is that the first player sends all of the $15 to the second and the second sends half of the doubled sum back. That allows both players to walk away with $15. In the game, however, the first players sent an average of $12.41 to their partners, who returned an average of 45 per cent of the doubled sum. The existence of a previous acquaintance helped, however: both the amount initially sent, and the percentage returned by the second player, rose in proportion to the length of time the players had known each other.
- *Belonging to the same 'group' helps* In the game set up by Glaeser et al. (2000), the ratio of money returned was much lower when players were of different races or nationalities. Alesina and La Ferrara (2002) found that members of racially mixed communities were less likely to trust each other than members of racially homogeneous communities.

- *Seemingly unrelated, personal experiences play a role, too* Alesina and La Ferrara (2002) report that respondents who had recently suffered a personal setback – for instance, serious illness or financial problems – also reported lower levels of trust.

Overall, these first studies show that trust is prevalent in many situations and can then help towards achieving the best collective outcome. However, trust cannot be taken for granted and people differ in the trust they have when dealing with others. Moreover, trust is fragile and can be destroyed more easily than built. Economic research thus supports both the view that trust is an important foundation for many economic transactions and Williamson's admonition that opportunism cannot be excluded from the outset.

Trust

Trust plays a role both *between* and *within* organizations. Between organizations very often long-term trading relations develop. Such relations are, to a large extent, based on mutual trust and often of crucial importance for the organization's success.

Within organizations it is very important that employers place a certain level of trust in their employees. Employees who feel that they are being trusted by their employer will be more inclined to 'act in good faith' than employees who feel they are not. Employees might see very close monitoring by their boss as a sign that they are not being trusted. That will have a negative effect on their 'disposition' towards their firm and, thus, increase rather than attenuate opportunistic behaviour. An employer who installs close monitoring on the assumption that employees will behave opportunistically will indeed find that they behave opportunistically. Opportunistic behaviour thus becomes a self-fulfilling prophecy!

8.8.3 Impersonal trust: institutions and reputation

As argued above, trust is important as a condition for economic exchange. Throughout most of economic history, trust was built up in personal exchange. Repeat dealings in small groups and personal contexts allowed transaction costs to remain relatively small. As the economy expanded, however, personal exchange was increasingly replaced by exchange between 'strangers' (see Box 8.3). As a consequence, more fundamental transaction problems arose. 'Personal trust' needed to be complemented by other means of a more impersonal nature.

Two important forms of such 'impersonal trust' are the following.

- *In institutions* (See Section 1.7.) We have to be able to trust the rule of law and its enforcement. Similarly, we have to trust the Central Banks to maintain the value of our money. To return to the quote from Douglass North in Section 1.7, such an institutional framework 'must substitute effectively for the 'trust' that comes with personal exchange. The failure to create the essential institutional base is the central problem of economic development'.
- *Reputation* As economies evolve, someone's reputation as a trustworthy partner for exchange transactions may increasingly involve an impersonal

element as well. Originally, a trader's reputation would be built up solely in small groups. Small groups are usually able to enforce standards of behaviour via peer group pressure. When you cheat in a small group, the word will spread and your reputation will be undermined, affecting the willingness of other parties to deal with you – see Box 8.9 for an impressive example. As exchange takes place in larger and larger groups, however, it becomes increasingly difficult to rely on small group pressure and sanctions. In our modern economy, many transactions take place with 'strangers'. Consider, for instance, the many transactions over the Internet. When you participate in an eBay auction, you may not even know the real name of the seller. How can you trust that person? Interestingly, eBay has found a way to provide you with information about sellers by using the 'feedback system' to build a reputation. By giving feedback on previous transactions, buyers collectively allow eBay to communicate a seller's reputation to prospective buyers – see Box 8.10. As a consequence, the reputation of a seller is no longer restricted to small group settings; it has become public.

Box 8.9 Enforcing honesty in diamond trading

In the New York wholesale diamond trade, dealers pass among themselves bags of diamonds worth millions of dollars, without written contracts. A handshake with the words mazal u'brache – 'with luck and a blessing' – creates a binding agreement. The oral contracts work in part because the dealers are mostly Hassidic Jews, sharing a common outlook. With such large sums at stake, however, individual relationships would not provide a weighty sanction. The diamond marketplace is designed so that anyone who breaches a contract loses the future business not only of the person cheated but also of all the other diamond traders. The Diamond Dealers Club organizes the sanctioning. On joining, a new member agrees to submit all disputes to the club's arbitration. Members who breach contracts may be fined or excluded from trading up to 20 days. Unpaid fines are posted for all to see. In the extreme, a member may be expelled from the club and thus from diamond dealing. To last in the business, a diamond trader must be honest.'

Source: McMillan (2002, p. 57)

Box 8.10 Reputation on eBay

In 1995, computer programmer Pierre Omidyar founded AuctionWeb, which was to become eBay. Ten years later, it had become a phenomenal success, partly because of its culture and philosophy, but surely also because of the inventive way in which it makes reputations publicly available:

So much for the warm and fuzzy side of eBay, which is surely not enough to explain $8bn in cold cash changing hands in the latest quarter alone. For that, you need not only fellow-feeling, but rock-solid trust. And that, in the end, is the true genius of eBay: not just that it resurrects the market stalls of the Middle Ages, but that it rebuilds a pre-industrial system of trust. Everybody in the ancient souk knew who was a crook and who was honest: eBay has done its best to build that same certainty into the cybersouk. The secret is the eBay system of 'feedback': after each transaction, buyers and sellers get to rate each other – positive, negative or neutral. In that way, every eBay member builds a reputation.

Beside every member's auction ID is their feedback score: mine is 786, and it is 100 per cent positive. A reputation like that is invaluable. Some day I may put it on my résumé.

Feedback explains the fundamental mystery of eBay: why strangers buy from strangers. Buyers must pay for goods before receiving or inspecting them – without feedback, it is hard to believe they would be so foolish. In some ways, feedback is just a very old solution to a timeless problem, writes Chrysanthos Dellarocas – an academic who has studied the phenomenon of trust among strangers online. It guarantees 'good conduct in communities of self-interested individuals who have short-term incentives to cheat one another'. The eBay system is different from the reputation systems evolved over thousands of years to guarantee trust in the marketplace, however. Paul Resnick, a professor at the University of Michigan, says that, offline, we buy goods because we can see them and squeeze them and learn about the seller from our neighbours – or because we have dealt with that seller in the past or he knows our brother-in-law. Online, we cannot buy by these rules. There is much less information about merchants – eBay sellers do not even use their real names. What information there is, says Resnick, is distributed more efficiently.

As power seller Wood points out: 'When you walk into a store, you don't have comments from the last 600 buyers to go by!' On eBay, everyone will know if you cheat your customer.

Source: E. Waldmeir, 'Sold on the web', *FT Weekend,* 2004

To sum up this section, let's first return to Paul Seabright's account of the evolution of economic transactions in humankind, as summarized in Box 8.3.

Seabright was particularly impressed with how we have learned to deal not only in personal networks but also increasingly with 'strangers'. He argued that two 'dispositions' must be present in the population to enable such an evolution: the capacity for rational calculation and reciprocity. Williamson's opportunism refers to rational calculation without any regard for another person's interest. Let us emphasize again that Williamson does *not* argue that this is a universal characteristic of all human beings. He *does* argue that it is present among the population and that it is hard to tell ex ante where and when you will encounter it. As a result, economic institutions have to arise that are robust against opportunism.

In this section, we have examined the role of trust and the transfer of trust from personal to impersonal settings. We have also summarized what economic research has so far uncovered as factors increasing or decreasing trust.[8] We believe that the arguments show Seabright is right: economic transactions take place in an environment that is characterized by *both* rational calculation (including outright opportunism) *and* reciprocity and trust.

In this section, we have also started to examine hybrid organizational forms, using Ouchi's introduction of 'clans' as a third way to coordinate transactions. We have contrasted it with our perspective in this book that all non-price coordination is organizational in nature. We have adopted Mintzberg's rich description of six such organizational mechanisms. As a consequence, all non-market coordination is organizational by definition in our framework. We have thus maintained Williamson's bipolar distinction between markets and 'something else'. For Williamson that 'something else' consisted of *hierarchies* (vertical coordination based on authority); for us it is *organizations* in all their possible variations.

Organizational theorists were right to argue that Williamson took too narrow a view on organizations, seeing only one form of non-market coordination: hierarchy. By allowing for rules (standardization) or trust to develop between parties to a transaction we can adopt the full set of six organizational mechanisms proposed by Mintzberg. Our bipolar distinction in this book is between markets and organizations. As repeatedly stressed, the bipolar distinction refers to ideal types of coordination. In practice, we shall encounter many mixed cases or hybrid forms. Chapter 13 discusses several examples of hybrid forms.

8.9 Governance in a three-level schema

Transaction cost economics is mainly concerned with the governance of contractual relations. It is, however, recognized that governance does not operate in isolation. It is embedded in the wider institutional environment (the macro level) on the one hand and the individual attributes of economic actors (the micro level) on the other hand. Williamson (1995) therefore proposes a three-level schema, as depicted in Figure 8.4.

In the schema, the institutional environment is seen as the context from **Shift parameters** which **shift parameters** originate. Shift parameters cause changes in the comparative costs of governance. The macro institutional environment defines the 'rules of the game' for governance. If changes in, for example, property rights,

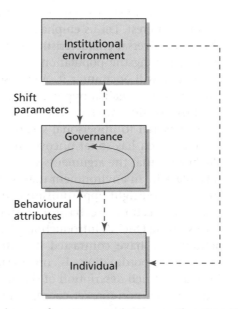

Figure 8.4 A layer schema of governance in Transaction Cost Economics
Source: Williamson (1995 , p. 213)

contract laws or social norms induce changes in the comparative costs of governance, then usually a reconfiguration of the economic organization is triggered.

Behavioural attributes

Transaction cost economics operates with **behavioural attributes** that are drawn from the individual level. They are the assumption of bounded rationality and the possibility of opportunism.

Finally, Williamson recognizes that there may be feedback effects. For instance, economic actors may attempt to change the rules of the game, as defined in the institutional environment. Think of all the groups lobbying in the political capitals of the world. Similarly, they may try to influence individuals by, for example, advertising. Also, the individual is, of course, influenced by developments and opinions in the wider environment. These three kinds of feedback effects are shown as dotted lines in Figure 8.4. It is fair to say, however, that they are underdeveloped in the TCE framework, which is focused on governance as the central concept, with shift parameters and behavioural attributes 'imported' from the other two levels.

In Chapter 11, we will give an overview of the economic approaches to organizations as presented in this book. There, we will also distinguish (more) levels of analysis at which the various approaches operate. That allows us to compare the 'reach' of the economic approaches to organizations across the various levels of analysis (see Figure 11.4).

8.10 Summary: effect of transaction costs on choosing between markets and organizations and organizational forms

Transaction cost economics attempts to explain the governance of transactions. Which transactions will be executed across markets and which transactions will take place within organizations? Transaction cost economics is based on two assumptions with respect to human behaviour:

1 human beings are boundedly rational;
2 human beings can be opportunistic.

In comparison, behavioural theory also assumes bounded rationality but not opportunism, while the theory of principal and agent assumes full rationality and opportunism.

Choosing between markets and organizations depends on three critical dimensions of transactions: asset specificity, uncertainty/complexity and frequency. Transactions are said to have a high level of asset specificity when they need to be supported by assets that can be used only in those specific transactions. The higher the levels of asset specificity, uncertainty/complexity and frequency, the higher the costs of executing the transaction across a market. Thus, transactions with high levels of asset specificity, uncertainty/complexity and frequency tend to take place within organizations rather than across markets.

Transaction cost economics can also be used to explain why we observe different organizational forms, such as peer groups, simple hierarchies, U-form firms and M-form firms in different circumstances.

Providers of professional services – such as management consultants, accountants, lawyers and doctors – frequently form partnerships. They do so because forming a partnership offers advantages (economies of scale in information-gathering, pooling of risk) that are difficult to obtain through market transactions between independent professionals.

A small partnership can function as a peer group – that is, a group of equals cooperating without hierarchy. In a large peer group, however, communication and decisionmaking become quite complicated and time-consuming. That is why large partnerships usually have a managing board and thus a form of hierarchy. Hierarchy in a large partnership also helps to reduce shirking.

Small manufacturing firms are usually organized as a simple hierarchy: a group of workers with a boss. That happens mainly because a simple hierarchy offers advantages in communication and decisionmaking. If there is team production, these benefits can explain why a simple hierarchy is an efficient form of organization.

Suppose that, because of economies of scale, an efficient firm needs to employ 100 workers. Such a firm needs at least two levels of managers because one manager cannot direct the work of so many workers. In a firm of that size, it is usually efficient for the workers to specialize in one type of activity, such as manufacturing, sales or billing. That leads to the formation of functional departments, with managers also specializing in the functional activities of those departments. That is the unitary or U-form firm.

Now suppose that the firm grows by adding more and more product lines. If the firm continues to use the U-form, its top managers will experience cumulative loss of control. The firm may also face a corruption of the strategic decisionmaking process because functional top managers may display too much loyalty to their department. The solution to those problems is to create a multidivisional (M-form) firm in which the divisions are responsible for manufacturing and marketing of a more limited product range. The divisions operate as quasi-autonomous firms, responsible for all day-to-day decisions. In an M-form firm, there is a general office responsible for strategic decisions and allocating cash flows to divisions.

A major criticism of transaction cost economics is that it ignores the role of social relations and culture. Many relations between human beings are built on trust. Without trust it is difficult to understand how people can cooperate within a firm or build lasting commercial relations.

We have examined the role of trust and the factors that increase or decrease the level of trust. We have also seen that the modern economy requires trust in 'strangers' for the execution of most transactions.

Clans, built on shared norms and trust, have been proposed as a third governance structure besides markets and hierarchies. On closer inspection, we believe that clans correspond closely to organizations relying heavily on standardization of norms as their main coordinating mechanism. That is why we argue that markets are replaced not by hierarchies but by organizations.

Organizations use various coordinating mechanisms. In practice, there are also many hybrid forms that combine market relations with coordinating mechanisms used within organizations (see Chapter 13).

Another criticism is that transaction cost economics is static: in comparing different organizational forms, it simply assumes that the most efficient forms have survived. That ignores the dynamic process of competition between different organizational forms, which takes centre stage in the next chapter.

Questions

1 Suppose you are Spanish and living in Sevilla. You have bought a car from a garage in Sevilla and bring it back regularly to the garage for ordinary maintenance.

Now imagine that you are on holiday in the Netherlands. Your car has been making a strange noise lately, so you decide to go to a local garage. You bring your car in the morning and return in the evening to collect it.

There is, of course, the problem of the possibility of opportunistic behaviour by the garage: the garage can misrepresent the amount of time spent on fixing your car. Do you expect that the problem will be more severe or less severe than when you take your car to the garage in Sevilla? Why?

2 Mayer GmbH is a small German company involved in car body repair. Mayer GmbH employs ten people: Gert Mayer, who owns all the shares in Mayer GmbH, and nine other people working as employees. The production process involves three stages: parts repair, painting and assembly. Four people are working in parts repair, two in painting and three in assembly. Mr Mayer takes care of marketing, sales, bookkeeping, and general management.

Autofix is one of Mayer's competitors. Autofix is a workers' cooperative and has recently been set up by ten people. Four people are working in parts repair, two in painting, three in assembly and one in marketing, sales and bookkeeping. All decisions within Autofix are being made by the general assembly, consisting of all ten worker-members. The general assembly is chaired each week by a different worker-member.

a How would you characterize Mayer GmbH in Mintzberg's typology of organizational configurations? What is the main coordinating mechanism in that configuration? Now answer the same questions for Autofix.

b How would you characterize Mayer GmbH in the language of transaction cost economics? What about Autofix? Compare, using transaction cost economics, the organizational form of Mayer GmbH with that of Autofix in terms of efficiency advantages and disadvantages.

c Suppose that competition in the car body repair industry becomes very intense. Which of the two companies is more likely to survive that competitive battle? Why?

3 In some industries, private firms compete with non-profit organizations. An example is the hospital industry in the USA, where hospitals owned and run by private companies compete with hospitals owned by foundations, charities and local governments. Private hospitals and public hospitals face the same make-or-buy decisions: services such as laundry, maintenance, restaurant, physical therapy, laboratory and pharmacy can be bought from outside suppliers or supplied inhouse.

Transaction cost economics predicts that transactions with high levels of asset specificity, uncertainty/complexity and frequency will be supplied inhouse, while transactions with low levels of asset specificity, uncertainty/complexity and frequency will be bought from outside suppliers. A recent study examined if that was really the case. The study also examined whether or not the prediction from transaction cost economics was true for both private and non-profit hospitals. Do you expect the prediction to be equally true for private and non-profit hospitals? Why?

4 Rock bands emerged in the late 1950s and early 1960s in coastal areas of the UK (Liverpool, for example) as very informal partnerships of young males. Originally bands performed in dance venues, did not produce their own songs and did not make much money. That changed with the meteoric rise of The Beatles, a band built on original songs written by the band's members. The example of The Beatles was soon followed by other bands who also integrated writer and performer functions. This created income disparities between band members according to their writing royalties.

Most rock bands were organized as partnerships. However, some were organized as hierarchies, with one band member acting as entrepreneur and the other members receiving pay as workers. What do you think are the advantages and disadvantages of partnerships versus hierarchies in the case of rock bands?

5 Renata Girndt holds a degree in business administration from a well-known Swiss university. She has three years' experience working for a major Swiss pharmaceutical firm. Her main task for the firm has been to investigate ways to enter eastern European markets.

Annamaria Schalke holds a degree from the same university as Renata and has five years' experience working for a major international consulting firm based in Frankfurt, Germany. Her main experience is in designing joint ventures between German and eastern European firms.

Renata has been considering starting her own business as a self-employed consultant. So has Annamaria. When they meet during an alumni day, a plan to form a partnership begins to emerge. In the partnership they will share all revenue and expenses. The partnership will focus on German companies willing to enter eastern European markets through strategic alliances.

For Renata, one of the main risks of starting to work as a self-employed consultant is that of having no consulting assignments during a certain period of time. As she sees it, one of the advantages of forming a partnership with Annamaria is to share that risk.

Do you think Renata would be able to buy an insurance policy for that risk from an insurance company? What kinds of problem(s) might occur for an insurance company offering such a policy? Do they occur when Renata and Annamaria share the risk by forming a partnership? Do you see other advantages of forming a partnership instead of Renata and Annamaria each setting up their own business independently?

Suggested further reading

Thompson, G., Frances, J., Levacic, R. and Mitchell, J. (1991), *Markets, Hierarchies and Networks,* London: Sage.

Williamson, O. E. (1975), *Markets and Hierarchies: Analysis and Antitrust Implications,* New York: Free Press.

Williamson, O. E. (1985), *The Economic Institutions of Capitalism,* New York: Free Press.

Williamson, O. E. (1995), *Organization Theory: From Chester Barnard to the present and beyond,* expanded edition, Oxford: Oxford University Press.

Williamson, O. E. (1996), 'Economics and organization: a primer', *California Management Review,* vol. 38, pp. 131–46.

Williamson, O. E. (1998), 'Transaction cost economics: how it works; where it is headed', *De Economist,* vol. 146, pp. 23–58.

Notes

1 As discussed in Chapter 5, reputations matter in multiperiod games.
2 In Section 4.2 we discussed the used car market as an example of a market with adverse selection. As a solution to the problem of adverse selection we suggested relocation of the risk that a car is a lemon from the buyer to the seller through a warranty. The problem for the seller is to make a credible promise to the potential buyer. For a qualified dealer it is easier than for a junkyard garage. The main reason is that a qualified dealer risks losing more (his qualification) if he does not provide the services specified in the warranty.
3 We do not mean to say that human beings always make explicit comparisons of the production and transaction costs of alternative governance structures. They probably cannot do so because of bounded rationality and complexity. However, in a world with competition between governance structures, it is likely that the most efficient governance structures will survive in the long run. Thus, the governance structures we observe in the real world are probably close to the cost-minimizing solution.
4 See, for example, Becker and Elias (2003) for a detailed argument in favour of allowing such markets. A summary of those arguments can be found at www.becker-posner-blog.com/archives/2006/01
5 We have borrowed the idea for this example from Klein et al. (1978).
6 For Weber, the bureaucracy was a modern phenomenon, enabling stable and efficient organizational arrangements. He emphasized the improvements that bureaucracies brought over the more traditional forms of organization. It was only later that 'bureaucracy' also acquired more pejorative meanings, related to the stifling of individual freedom and initiative by excessive rules.
7 See the collection of contributions in the reader on *Trust* by Khalil (2003), who discusses trust as strategy, taste and trait.
8 See also Hurley (2006) and Galford and Drapeau (2003) for a discussion of trust in an organizational setting.

9.1 Introduction

In Chapters 6–8, three different but closely related economic theories of organization (behavioural theory, agency theory and transaction cost economics) have been discussed. This chapter focuses on economic contributions to the field of strategic management. As you will see, those contributions do not (yet) form one integrated theory, although they have much in common.

There are two levels of strategy in a multibusiness firm: competitive strategy
Competitive strategy (also termed business strategy) and corporate strategy. A **competitive strategy** is a strategy for a single business unit: it specifies *how* the business unit's managers compete in a given industry.[1] A **corporate strategy** is a strategy for a
Corporate strategy portfolio of business units: it specifies *where* (that is, in which industries and in which countries) a multibusiness firm competes.

The field of strategic management has a normative and a descriptive part (as do many other empirical fields). Normative questions deal with what firms *should* do. Descriptive questions deal with what firms *actually* do. The literature on strategic management may be further divided into contributions that focus on the *process* and the *content* of strategic management (see Table 9.1). Economics attempts to analyse the content of firms' strategies. To see whether the analysis has explanatory power, it is compared with the actual behaviour of firms. If the analysis does correspond to real firms' behaviour and, furthermore, indicates which choices are best, then we have a basis for normative recommendations. That is why it is hard to divide economic contributions to the content of strategic management into normative and descriptive contributions.

The early literature on strategic management (for example, Ansoff, 1965) emerged out of a need to help practitioners with the process of strategic planning.
Strategic planning **Strategic planning** is the component of strategic management that aims at the formulation of a firm's strategy.[2]

Table 9.1 The literature on strategic management

	Process	Content
Normative	Normative models of strategic management processes	Economic contributions to strategic management
Descriptive	Description of actual strategic management processes	

An important issue in that literature is how the process of strategic planning should be structured. It is argued that the process of strategic planning should consist of a logical sequence of steps, such as the seven steps indicated in Figure 9.1. The figure is an example of a normative model of strategic planning. You might wonder why that sequence of steps is the most logical one or whether it leads to the best results. Economics has little to say on that question. As we want to focus on economic contributions to strategic management, we shall not try to answer it.

You may also wonder if, in real firms, the process of strategic planning is always as neatly structured as Figure 9.1. Descriptions of actual strategic planning processes show that it is usually not, but, again, this issue falls outside the scope of this chapter.

The economic contributions to strategic planning and strategic management focus mainly on issues of content, not of process. Economics deals with the actual information that firms need and the actual choices they have to make when formulating their strategies but hardly at all with the process they may use to arrive at those choices and implement their chosen strategy.[3] Important economic contributions have been made to the content of steps 2–5 in the diagram; very few economic contributions have been made to the other

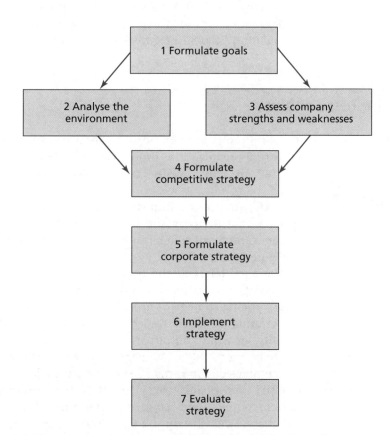

Figure 9.1 The process of strategic planning in a multibusiness firm

three. As the focus of this chapter is on economic contributions to strategic management, we concentrate mainly on steps 2–5, although we touch on step 6 in Section 9.6.

This chapter follows the sequence of steps outlined in Figure 9.1. Section 9.2 discusses the economic contributions to industry analysis. This concerns step 2 in the strategic planning process as the industry in which a firm operates is an important part of its environment.

Section 9.3 discusses the economic contributions to competitor analysis, which is a way to assess a company's strengths and weaknesses relative to its competitors' (step 3). The economic contributions to competitor analysis also come from the field of industrial organization.

Another way to describe a company's strengths comes from the resource-based view of the firm. That is the subject of Section 9.4, which discusses the formulation of competitive strategy (step 4) in a static context and relies again on industrial organization. According to the resource-based view of the firm, a competitive advantage is sustainable if it is based on the possession of resources that other firms cannot easily obtain. That is explained in Section 9.5 and extended in Section 9.6 by introducing the concept of dynamic capabilities.

Section 9.7 discusses the formulation of competitive strategy in a dynamic context, drawing on concepts from game theory.

Sections 9.8–9.10 discuss vertical integration, diversification and multinationalization. Those three issues form the core of corporate strategy formulation (step 5 in Figure 9.1). A summary is provided in Section 9.11.

9.2 Industry analysis

The economic contributions to industry analysis stem from the field of industrial organization. Industrial organization emerged as an academic discipline in the 1950s and 1960s. Its main paradigm was the **structure–conduct–performance (or S–C–P) paradigm**. 'Structure' refers to characteristics of the industry, such as the number, size and distribution of firms in that industry and the barriers that impede other firms entering it. Other examples of characteristics that determine industry structure are given in Figure 9.2.

> **Structure–conduct–performance (S–C–P) paradigm**

'Conduct' refers to the behaviour (or strategies) of firms in the industry. Aspects of firm conduct are collusion (that is, the extent to which firms cooperate), pricing strategy of firms in the industry and product strategy.

'Performance' refers to performance of the industry in such terms as profitability, growth in output and employment.

According to the S–C–P paradigm, the structure of an industry determines the conduct of the firms in that industry and, in turn, conduct determines industry performance (see Figure 9.2). As an example of how structure determines conduct and conduct determines performance, consider the US automobile industry during the 1960s.

Figure 9.2 The structure–conduct–performance paradigm

There were only four firms – General Motors (GM), Ford, Chrysler and American Motors (AM). General Motors and Ford were much bigger than Chrysler or American Motors. There were many buyers (dealers), so sellers were few and unequal in size, while buyers were numerous. Moreover, barriers to entry into the automobile industry were high. In this industry economies of scale are very important: you can produce cars efficiently only if you produce on a large scale. If a new competitor were to consider entering the industry, it would have to enter on a large scale. That would create overcapacity in the industry, prices would fall and no one would make a profit. Hence, in the automobile industry, economies of scale constitute a barrier to entry.

Another barrier to entry is the technological know-how required to develop a new car. In the automobile industry in the USA during the 1960s, GM and Ford were the most efficient producers, so they could set prices, while Chrysler and AM followed GM's and Ford's pricing strategy. Although the four firms probably never coordinated their pricing strategy as such, the result was

Tacit collusion

coordination of prices. Such **tacit collusion** is greatly facilitated if there are only a few sellers of unequal size and there are significant barriers to entry. In the Internet era, tacit collusion may be facilitated by the way websites, such as business-to-business (B2B) marketplaces are designed (Box 9.1 gives an example).

Box 9.1 Collusion on B2B exchanges?

Above, we have used the example of the automobile industry in the USA in the 1960s to explain the risk of (tacit) collusion in a concentrated industry. At the beginning of this millennium, the industry had become even more concentrated: General Motors, Ford and DaimlerChrysler formed the surviving Big Three. The risk of collusion had not lessened in the Internet age. To illustrate this point we use a report by J. P. Morgan on business-to-business (B2B) exchanges – marketplaces where business suppliers sell to business customers.

The first wave of such B2B marketplaces consisted of independent companies that saw an opportunity to broker between buyers and sellers. However, in many industries, large companies buying many components from a large number of suppliers soon struck back by creating their own marketplaces, often forming an alliance to do so. An example is Covisint, a B2B marketplace created by the Big Three automakers, that collectively represents about 85 per cent of the industry's purchasing power in the USA.

A B2B marketplace can come quite close to the pure or ideal market we described in Chapter 1 if two conditions are met. First, there are many buyers and sellers and, second, there are no information asymmetries. If there are only a few buyers, however, B2B marketplaces can form a vehicle to aggregate demand from those few buyers, thus enhancing their purchasing power even further. If those few buyers design the website, they have an opportunity to create information asymmetries that work to their advantage.

Covisint is a very ambitious enterprise. It has the potential to shift tens of billions of dollars in annual procurement transactions to the Internet. Because its founders were competitors in the marketplace, its early development has been scrutinized by both the Federal Trade Commission (FTC) and the Bundeskartellamt (BKA), the antitrust authorities in the USA and Germany. Covisint received clearance from them in 2000. However, the FTC and BKA will continue to monitor the structure and procedures of such Internet sites for evidence of collusion, just as it evaluates other business alliances and arrangements.

Source: J. P. Morgan, *B2B Marketplaces: The Third Wave,* New York, 5 September 2000; http://en.wikipedia.org/wiki/Covisint

---

Structure (number and size distribution of sellers and buyers, barriers to entry) therefore determined conduct (pricing strategy). Pricing strategy, of course, directly affects profitability. Thus, an element of conduct (pricing strategy) affects performance (profitability). These relationships are indicated by the solid arrows flowing from the top to the bottom of Figure 9.2.

In the S–C–P paradigm, the direction of causation runs, therefore, from structure to conduct and from conduct to performance. However, it is now increasingly recognized that the conduct of firms can also affect industry structure and the performance of an industry can also affect the conduct of firms in that industry. For example, firms can try to erect barriers to entry. They may, for instance, protect their product and process innovations by means of patents. If such patents are awarded, the firm can prevent competitors from using the latest technology. Patents are an example of strategic barriers to entry. The conduct of firms (their patenting behaviour) thus affects an industry's structure. In addition, performance may affect conduct, as when industry profitability affects the amount of R&D carried out. These relationships are indicated by the dotted 'feedback' arrows in Figure 9.2.

A crucial view in many early empirical studies was that, as structure determined conduct and conduct determined performance, one could ignore conduct and look directly at industry structure to try to explain performance. Thus, many studies sought to explain an indicator of industry performance (such as industry profitability) by using elements of structure as determinants. By comparing several industries in the same time period it became clear that, first, not all industries are equal in terms of profitability and, second, differences in profitability between industries can be explained in large measure by the elements of structure indicated in Figure 9.2. As a result, the profitability of a multibusiness firm is determined, to a certain extent, by the choice of which industries to compete in.

Five forces driving industry competition

These findings from industrial organization inspired Michael Porter's well-known model of **five forces driving industry competition** (Figure 9.3). Intensity of rivalry between existing firms depends inter alia on the number, size and distribution of firms, level of product differentiation and cost structures. The threat of new entrants depends on barriers to entry. The bargaining power of buyers depends inter alia on the number, size and distribution of buyers and level of product differentiation. A similar statement can be made regarding the bargaining power of suppliers. Therefore, in Porter's five-forces model, the industry's structure determines the intensity of competition and, thus, the industry's profitability.[4]

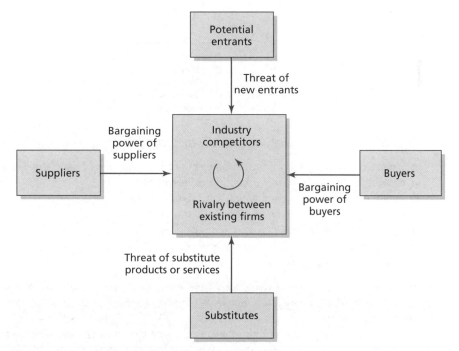

Figure 9.3 Five forces driving industry competition
Source: Porter (1980, p. 4), Porter (2008)

Porter's **five-forces model** has proved to be a valuable tool for analysing present and future levels of an industry's level of competition and profitability. Box 9.2 provides an illustration.

Box 9.2 Porter's five-forces analysis applied to the pharmaceutical industry

In the pharmaceutical industry, patents play an important role. Proprietary drugs are drugs that are protected by patents. Patents offer protection for a limited number of years only. After the expiry of a patent, other companies are free to offer low-cost copies (generic drugs).

Application of Porter's five-forces model to the pharmaceutical industry in 1997 shows that competition comes mainly from rivalry between industry competitors. That may change, however, as biotechnology companies enter the industry or as buyers organize themselves into more powerful purchasing groups.

The intensity of the rivalry between industry competitors is characterized by several factors:

■ global competition is concentrated between a limited number of very large companies;
■ competition is based mainly on product differentiation;
■ patent protection limits competition between incumbent firms;
■ most companies focus on particular types of disease therapy;
■ government intervention increases and puts pressure on prices;
■ rivalry focuses on developing blockbuster drugs and decreasing the time-to-market, resulting in sharply rising R&D costs.

The threat of new entry is low because there are large economies of scale in R&D and high risks inherent in developing new drugs. However, biotechnology firms can enter the industry on their new technology platform.

The threat of substitutes comes mainly from generic drugs. As buyers become more cost-conscious, consumption of generic drugs is growing.

The bargaining power of suppliers to the pharmaceutical industry is low.

The bargaining power of buyers is moderate, but growing, as buyers tend to aggregate demand (that is, hospitals forming alliances, concentration of drug distributors, rise in numbers of managed care organizations).

Source: The Corporate Strategy Board, *Changes in the Pharmaceuticals Delivery Chain*, Washington DC, December 1997

9.3 Competitor analysis

In the S–C–P paradigm discussed in Section 9.2, the unit of analysis is the industry. In this paradigm, industry structure determines the firm's conduct, which, in turn, determines the industry's performance. If industry structure were to completely determine a firm's conduct, there could be no differences between the conduct of firms in the same industry. For example, if industry structure determines a firm's pricing strategy, all firms in the industry should follow the same pricing strategy. If, moreover, all firms in the industry have the same unit cost (they employ the same technology, are of the same size and so on), profitability differences between firms in the same industry can be attributed only to random disturbances. However, the firms in an industry are clearly not all alike. The result is that there are usually differences in profitability between firms in the same industry.

How important are differences between industries relative to differences between firms in the same industry? That important question has been examined by Rumelt (1991). He studied a large sample of business units from large (Fortune 500) firms over a period of four years and found that differences between firms in the same industry are far more important than differences between industries.

Firms belonging to the same industry can still differ in many respects. They differ along dimensions such as pricing strategy, advertising levels, R&D levels, degree of vertical integration, breadth of product line, cost position and so on. Such disparities may be due to differences in information. Firms may perceive different profit opportunities when they enter an industry, for example. So, firm A may decide to heavily advertise a high-quality product and firm B to pursue a high-volume line because they do not have the same information.

Once firms A and B have made such decisions, they become committed to a strategy. Firm A invests in building a brand name; should firm A decide to change its strategy, then its past advertising expenditures would lose most of their value. As long as it sticks to its present strategy, those past expenditures constitute an intangible asset. Similarly, firm B has to invest in facilities for high-volume production. If firm B changes its competitive strategy, its high-volume production facilities are likely to decline in value. So, both firms A and B have to invest in assets that probably decline in value if the firms change their strategies.

That is one reason firms' strategies are likely to be 'sticky' and difficult to alter radically. Another explanation is that firms use organizational routines to make strategic decisions. As long as profit performance is satisfactory, firms tend to follow the same rules of thumb (in setting advertising levels, R&D levels and so on) that they have used in the past.[5]

Firms do not maximize but satisfice, as explained in Chapter 6. That is to say, as long as their routines lead to satisfactory results, firms have few incentives to search for better routines. In some industries (for example, those with many small firms and very low entry barriers), rivalry may be so intense that only one strategy can survive. In other industries (for example, those with a few large firms and high entry barriers), two or more different strategies may turn out to be sufficiently profitable to allow survival.

Strategic dimensions

It seems likely, then, that firms in the same industry differ along certain key variables. Those key variables are the **strategic dimensions** of that industry. In addition, it seems likely that those differences persist for several years because there are **mobility barriers** between the strategic groups.[6] If both propositions are true, then an industry can be viewed as being composed of groups of firms, each group consisting of firms following similar competitive strategies.

Mobility barriers

The competitive strategy of a firm is that firm's choice with regard to the strategic dimensions of its particular industry. Strategic dimensions can vary with the industry studied. Examples of strategic dimensions are advertising levels, R&D levels, cost position, product differentiation, breadth of product line and degree of vertical integration.

Strategic groups

Groups of firms following similar competitive strategies are called **strategic groups**. Firms within a strategic group closely resemble one another. Profitability differences between firms in the same strategic group are likely to be small. However, profitability differences between firms in different groups (firms pursuing different strategies) may be large.

Following this line of reasoning, two empirical questions have to be answered.

- Do differences in strategies persist over time? (If they do not, the concept of strategic groups has little meaning.)
- Are profitability differences between strategic groups significant?

Several studies have examined these questions. Most have come to the conclusion that strategic groups can be identified in many industries. Moreover, they tend to be stable over time. Significant profitability differences between strategic groups are found less often. Hence, in many industries there appear to be several roads to (roughly the same kind of) success. Thus, strategic planners can use the concept of strategic groups to construct a map showing the competitive strategies of their own company and those of their competitors. As an **Strategic map** example, consider Box 9.3, which describes a **strategic map** of the European brewing industry in 2001.

Box 9.3 The European beer industry

The European beer industry consists of a large number of companies.

In Germany, there are many (several hundred) small breweries, each serving a small regional market.

Small breweries with only one brand serving a local or national market can be found in many other European countries. Heineken sells beer under a variety of brand names: Heineken, Amstel and Murphy's (which are sold in almost all countries in Europe) and a large number of national brands (for example, Moretti and Dreher in Italy).

Interbrew also uses a variety of brand names: Stella (its most international brand) and a large number of local or regional brands.

SAB (South African Breweries) has acquired several European breweries, each with its own brand name, but SAB does not have a pan-European brand.

Finally, the American brewers Anheuser-Bush and Miller are active in Europe with their flagship brands (Budweiser and Miller respectively).

Thus, on the basis of brand strategy and market share, four strategic groups emerge (Figure 9.4).

See further: McGee (2003)

Figure 9.4 Strategic map of the European brewing industry

The strategic map shown in Figure 9.4 uses brand strategy (one local brand, several local brands, several local brands plus at least one international brand, one international brand only) and market share as strategic dimensions. Other strategic dimensions that may be important in the brewing industry (such as level of diversification, level of advertising or level of vertical integration) cannot be shown on the same map.

9.4 Competitive strategy

A competitive strategy reflects the firm's choices concerning the strategic dimensions of its industry. As there are many strategic dimensions and different industries may have different strategic dimensions, many competitive strategies are possible. In many industries, however, two successful competitive strategies can be identified: cost leadership and product differentiation. Both strategies can be applied industry-wide or to a few segments only. Such so-called **generic competitive strategies** have been discussed extensively by Michael Porter (1980, Chapter 2; 1985, Chapters 3 and 4).

Generic competitive strategies

Strategy of cost leadership

Under a **strategy of cost leadership**, the firm tries to manufacture and distribute products at the lowest possible unit cost. Quite often, cost leadership can be attained only through large-scale production (economies of scale) or experience. Both economies of scale and experience are easier to obtain if the firm has a large market share.

Strategy of product differentiation

Under a **strategy of product differentiation**, the firm competes by offering a product that the customers perceive as more valuable than the competitors' products. It can do so by offering a product that differs from other products in quality, safety, design, reliability, ease of repair, durability, taste or whatever. If buyers recognize the additional value, the firm can charge a higher price. For a strategy of product differentiation, brand name recognition is usually very important. Thus, advertising levels tend to be high for firms using that strategy.

As discussed above, firms' strategies are likely to be sticky as a result of the necessary commitment to a chosen strategy and because of the development of successful routines. Once a firm has chosen to pursue one of Porter's generic strategies, it is likely to continue along that path for quite some time. That may be dangerous, however.

A firm committed to a strategy of cost leadership must be aware that its customers compare the standard low-cost products with differentiated products offered by its competitors. As income levels rise or demand patterns change, customers may increasingly demand a number of differentiating features, forcing the low-cost producers to incorporate these into their product offerings. The Model T Ford and the VW Beetle are examples of very successful low-cost products. In both cases, the more differentiated cars offered by GM and others finally forced Ford and Volkswagen to develop new more differentiated cars. Similarly, firms pursuing a strategy of product differentiation cannot remain complacent about their costs. Buyers do not simply seek high value; they seek value for money. Hence, care should be taken not to overemphasize Porter's useful distinction in generic competitive strategies.

9.5 Resource-based view of the firm

In the preceding section, two competitive strategies – cost leadership and product differentiation – have been discussed. A firm may attain cost leadership through large-scale production (economies of scale) or through experience. According to the resource-based view of the firm, a competitive advantage is always based on the possession of (or, at least, the access to) certain resources, such as a large-scale plant or experience. The extent to which a competitive advantage is sustainable depends on how difficult or costly it is for other firms to obtain the same resources.

Resource-based view of the firm

In the **resource-based view of the firm** (RBV), resources are defined quite broadly. They include human, financial, tangible (such as plants, equipment, buildings) and intangible resources (such as patents, know-how, brand names, experience and organizational routines). Some resources are easily bought and sold in (nearly) perfect markets. That is true of most financial assets, such as marketable securities. Other assets are much more difficult to buy and sell, however. For example, there are active markets for new and secondhand cars and trucks, but there is no market for 'organizational routines' (the concept of organizational routines is explained in Section 10.5).

According to the resource-based theory of the firm, a resource can be the basis of a competitive advantage *only* if that resource has certain properties. First, it must be difficult to buy and sell. In order to understand what that means, consider a market with five firms of equal size, each having a market share of 20 per cent. Suppose that firm A has more modern equipment than the other firms and, thus, enjoys a cost advantage. If the other firms can easily buy the same equipment, then firm A's advantage will be short-lived. However, if firm A has developed its own equipment and the development of that type of equipment demands special skills or experience only firm A's employees possess, then firm A's competitive advantage is sustainable. In the latter case, firm A's competitive advantage is, in the final analysis, based on an intangible resource (the skills and experience of its employees) rather than on a tangible asset (the equipment itself). It is, generally speaking, much more difficult to 'buy' intangible resources such as skills or experience than it is to buy tangible assets such as equipment.

For intangible resources, it is useful to make a distinction between resources for which property rights are well defined (such as patents, brand names and copyrights) and intangible resources for which property rights are ill defined (such as technological know-how not protected by patents, organizational routines and the know-how and experience of the top management team). It is quite difficult to trade in know-how that is not protected by patents because of the fundamental paradox of information (see Section 4.1). That type of know-how can be the basis of a sustainable competitive advantage. If several competing firms obtain a licence to use the same patented know-how in return for a royalty payment, the use of that know-how is unlikely to be the source of a competitive advantage.

Second, the resource must be difficult to replicate. Some resources, such as point-of-sale systems in retailing, can be replicated fairly easily by competitors. By contrast, highly complex organizational routines are much more difficult to replicate.

Third, it must be difficult to substitute the resource with another resource. For example, pipelines and tankers are substitutes for shipping oil. The possession of a pipeline will give a firm a competitive advantage only if it is more costly or impossible to use tankers.

Finally, the advantage that the resource may yield must not be competed away by ex ante competition. Suppose that the government announces that it will allow only one firm to use a radio frequency for mobile telecom services. Surely the concession to use that frequency has a value. If, however, the government organizes an auction to sell that frequency to the highest bidder, a (large) part of its value will be cashed by the government. If all bidders make the same estimates concerning future sales and costs and those estimates are correct, then each bidder will bid the same. The winner will then have to be chosen at random, but will not make any economic profit (that is the paradox of profits described in Section 2.4.3). If the winner obtains the concession based on overly optimistic expectations, however, that is an example of the winner's curse (see Section 5.4)

In summary, the original formulation of the RBV pointed to four conditions that resources have to satisfy in order to contribute towards competitive advantage. They have to be:

- valuable
- rare
- inimitable
- non-substitutable.

VRIN-framework

Those conditions are sometimes thus referred to as the **VRIN-framework** of competitive advantage.[7] We will return to the question of competitive advantage in the next section, but first wish to make some remarks evaluating the contribution of the RBV to economic approaches to organizations.

Note first that the RBV of the firm argues that the competitive advantage of a firm depends on the resources at its disposal. For a sustainable competitive advantage, it must be difficult or costly for other firms to obtain similar resources. Sustainable competitive advantage should lead to superior economic performance over a period of time. On this reasoning, there is a direct causal chain from a firm's resources to its performance. It is therefore very important to know which resources can lead to such superior economic performance.

In standard economic theory, the resources at the firm's disposal were traditionally classified as follows:

- land (including natural resources);
- labour (human resources);
- capital (financial and physical resources).

A debate in economics is whether or not *information* should be included as a fourth type of resource (also called a 'factor of production').[8]

As noted in Chapter 2, in standard microeconomics, the factors of production come together in firms seen as *holistic entities*. That is to say, economic theory did not look *into* firms: they were regarded as black boxes.

RBV is an economic theory that *does* look inside firms. It tries to identify which resources are the basis of sustainable competitive advantage. As noted above, it defines resources much more widely. It then examines which conditions those resources must meet in order to serve as a basis for sustainable competitive advantage.

As an economic approach to organizations, the RBV of the firm is a clear improvement over standard microeconomics. However, it had to deal with two criticisms that were levelled against its original formulation.

- RBV is to a certain extent *tautological*. It attempts to explain superior performance in terms of the use of particular valuable resources. At the same time, the question as to whether or not resources are valuable has to be answered by reference to the performance they enable. In other words, the argument is circular. What is missing is an independent selection mechanism that explains which resources are valuable and which are not.
- RBV is *static*. It assumes that resources simply 'exist' and the firm's task is to choose from among the existing resources. RBV in its original formulation neither asked where these resources came from nor how they were developed and maintained over time.

As a response to those criticisms, the RBV has been further developed. We deal with that further development in two steps.

In the next section, we introduce the concept of *dynamic capabilities*. As the terminology already implies, the concept of dynamic capabilities addresses the development of a firm's capabilities as the basis for sustainable competitive advantage. While it therefore addresses the second criticism above, it also enquires deeper into the nature of the resources and capabilities that generate competitive advantage.

At the end of the next chapter, on evolutionary approaches to organizations, we return to the concept of dynamic capabilities. There we will show that the selection mechanism introduced to address the first criticism, is evolutionary selection. Thus, dynamic capabilities provide a bridge between strategic and evolutionary approaches to organizations.

9.6 Dynamic capabilities

Dynamic capability

A **dynamic capability** can be defined as 'the capacity of an organization to purposefully create, extend, or modify its resource base'.[9] The 'resource base' of an organization includes tangible, intangible and human assets (or resources), as in the RBV. However, it also includes capabilities that the organization owns, controls or has access to on a preferential basis. An example could be the process of new product development. A start-up company may have the tangible assets (plant), intangible assets (intellectual property) and human assets (researchers) to come up with good product inventions, but it may have to draw on the resources and capabilities of a partner to commercialize them. If it has preferential access to such complementary resources and capabilities through an alliance, we may say that it has extended its resource base by creating that alliance.

Operational capabilities

Dynamic capabilities can be distinguished from **operational capabilities**, which pertain to the current operations of an organization. Thus, operational capabilities are any type of capability that the organization uses in its effort to earn a living in the present. Current production methods, existing marketing policies and customary HR recruiting campaigns are all operationally orientated. Dynamic capabilities, by contrast are aimed at change. They alter the resource base of an organization. Forging alliances or making acquisitions are typical examples. The capabilities of Starbucks to open new outlets at an amazing rate, also in foreign markets, is another example. Note, further, that through dynamic capabilities the organizational resource base is *purposefully* created, extended or modified. That means there must be some degree of intent, either on the part of top management or at lower levels in the organization (such as the country managers in the Starbucks organization). In our alliance example, there must be a search and selection process to identify the right alliance partner. Furthermore, there must be a capability to work with an alliance partner. The firm must therefore have some alliance management skills that can be deployed in such a situation. From this perspective, the strategic management of the organization therefore entails the purposeful application of dynamic capabilities to change the resource base of the organization.

The extension of RBV with the concept of dynamic capabilities also allows for the possibility of delving deeper into the nature of the resources and capabilities that generate sustainable competitive advantage. Economic researchers have uncovered specific factors and circumstances that contribute to dynamic capabilities being valuable, rare and/or inimitable. Some of the features identified include the following.

Co-specialization

- **Co-specialization** Consider our example of a start-up company above. Let's say that it is involved in the development of new biotech-based drugs. It has created special-purpose laboratories and manufacturing facilities. It has recruited researchers at the cutting edge of a particular branch of biotechnology. It has also filed for patents that give it the exclusive rights to its new findings. We can say that all of its assets and resources are specialized. What is more, the plant, patents and researchers are *co-specialized*, meaning that they are uniquely valuable only when used in combination. It may cost a considerable amount of time and/or investment to build such a complementary combination of assets. Outside of that combination, any individual asset loses a significant amount of value.[10] Co-specialization may therefore contribute to the value of assets.

Asset orchestration

- **Asset orchestration** If capabilities are dependent on co-specialized assets, it makes the coordination task of management particularly difficult. Managerial decisions should then take the optimal *configuration* of assets into account. The term 'asset orchestration' is used to denote the managerial search, selection and configuration/coordination of resources and capabilities.[11] The term attempts to convey that, in an optimal configuration of assets, the whole is more valuable than the sum of its parts.[12]

Tacit knowledge

- **Tacit knowledge** If the capability is partly based on tacit knowledge, it is impossible to make it fully explicit. The capability can therefore not be fully articulated. It partly resides in people's heads and behaviours. That makes it difficult for competitors to fully imitate it. We return to tacit knowledge in Chapter 10.

Firm specificity

- **Firm specificity** Dynamic capabilities are often dependent on the firm's historical development and unique circumstances. They are usually developed in practice through learning-by-doing. Therefore, there is an element of *path dependence* – that is, the particular paths taken by a firm have shaped the opportunities for its specific learning-by-doing. As a consequence, its dynamic capabilities have become firm-specific. Firm specificity makes a dynamic capability rare and imitation difficult.

Isolating mechanisms

- **Isolating mechanisms** A dynamic capability is also inimitable if it is surrounded by effective 'isolating mechanisms'.[13] Such mechanisms are to a firm what an entry barrier is to an industry: they prevent other firms competing away the profit that a firm earns from its capability. If capabilities are highly firm-specific and partly depend on tacit knowledge, there may be significant 'causal ambiguity' as to the exact way in which they contribute to competitive advantage. It may then already be difficult for the firm's managers to articulate the causal connection between capability and competitive advantage, let alone for outside managers to copy the capability easily.

The discussion in this section shows that the concept of dynamic capabilities is a useful extension of the RBV. It effectively addresses the earlier critique that RBV provided only a static perspective. Dynamic capabilities are aimed at change in the resource base of organizations. They are developed over time and may require significant managerial effort to maintain and extend. Management's task is to not only choose from among 'existing' resources but also engage in active search, selection, configuration and orchestration of resources and capabilities. The objective remains sustainable competitive advantage.

The concept of dynamic capabilities has allowed a deeper understanding of factors that may contribute to resources and capabilities generating sustainable competitive advantage. If resources and capabilities are co-specialized and configured well, that may contribute to their value. If they are (in part) dependent on tacit knowledge, firm-specific and surrounded by isolating mechanisms, that makes them rarer and more difficult to replicate than resources and capabilities without such features. Potentially, they can therefore contribute to resources and capabilities meeting the requirements of Barney's VRIN-framework. However, the discussion so far has only highlighted the *internal* organizational context of dynamic capabilities. If they are to have value and generate sustainable competitive advantage, an *external* dimension is required as well. The capabilities have to be applied in a competitive environment.

Competition is an environmental selection mechanism. Only dynamic capabilities that survive competitive environmental selection have value. Therefore, we return to the concept of dynamic capabilities in the next chapter, after having introduced environmental selection.

9.7 Move and counter move

In the discussion in the preceding section we have ignored the fact that, in the real world, companies choosing a competitive strategy usually take into account how competitors are likely to react.

When a firm chooses a competitive strategy, it chooses values for the strategic dimensions of its industry. For example, it chooses its levels of expenditure on advertising, R&D and so on. When a firm makes such choices, it should (and usually does) take into account how competitors will react. If it does not, it is like a chess player who, when considering a move, does not analyse the possible counter moves an opponent will make. If you have ever played chess, you will know that you will probably lose the game if you play that way.

In this section we want to show how a company, when considering a strategic move, can take into account possible counter moves by a competitor. We shall do this by discussing how a monopolist can impede entry into its industry by a potential entrant. It is a complicated subject as many moves and counter moves are possible. To make things as simple as possible we shall use a particular industry to illustrate moves by the monopolist and counter moves by the potential entrant: the ice-cream-selling business. After our analysis of the ice-cream-selling industry, we shall translate our main findings for other industries.

9.7.1 The ice-cream-selling industry

Imagine a beach with a length of 480 metres. Potential customers are evenly distributed along the beach. There are two companies that consider setting up ice-cream stands on the beach. Let us call them Mr Sun and Mrs Orange. There is another company, Rent-a-Stand, that specializes in letting ice-cream stands. Rent-a-Stand is not interested in selling ice-cream. Ice-cream stands can be rented for $140 a day. Both Mr Sun and Mrs Orange can rent as many ice-cream stands as they want.

The price of an ice-cream is $1.00. The price has been determined by the municipality and neither Mr Sun nor Mrs Orange is allowed to sell ice-creams at any other price. Mr Sun and Mrs Orange both have to buy ice-creams from a distributor at $0.90 apiece, so, for each ice-cream they sell, they make a gross margin of $0.10.

The number of ice-creams sold by an ice-cream stand depends its location and the locations of other ice-cream stands, as illustrated in Figure 9.5.

In diagram a, for example, there is only one ice-cream stand located in the middle of the beach. The stand is indicated by the small dark blue box and the distances from each end of the beach (240 m) are also indicated. We assume that, per metre of beach, a maximum of 10 ice-creams per day can be sold, generating sales of $10.00. As you can see in diagram a, sales decrease linearly with distance: no potential customer is prepared to walk more than 240 m for an ice-cream. That is why in diagram b, sales are only half those in diagram a.

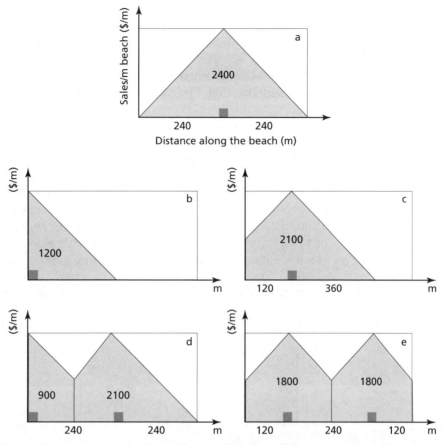

Figure 9.5 Ice-cream sales dependent on location of the ice-cream stands

Total ice-cream sales for a can be calculated as follows. If no potential customer should have to walk a single step in order to reach an ice-cream stand, then total sales would be $480 \times \$10.00 = \$4800$.[14] That total ($4800) corresponds to the area of the rectangle. If there is one ice-cream stand in the middle of the beach (diagram a), sales are half as much, $2400 (the shaded area in diagram a).

Following the same logic, we can calculate the sales for the other diagrams. In diagrams d and e, there are two ice-cream stands, with a distance of less than 480 m between them. All customers walk to the nearest ice-cream stand.

9.7.2 Number of ice-cream stands

Mr Sun arrives at the beach one day. He has to decide how many ice-cream stands to place on the beach and also where to locate them. As soon as Mr Sun has placed his stands, Mrs Orange arrives. Mrs Orange then has to decide where to place her ice-cream stands on the beach. That, of course, is an entry game (see Section 5.3 for another example of an entry game).

Let us return to Mr Sun deciding how many stands to place on the beach. Suppose, first, that he chooses to have only one stand. By looking at the diagrams in Figure 9.5, it is clear that he should locate his stand in the middle of the beach. If Mrs Orange decides to stay out of the ice-cream-selling business, then his sales will be $2400, his gross margin $240 and his net profit $240 − $140 = $100.

Will Mrs Orange enter if Mr Sun locates one stand in the middle of the beach? Suppose, first, that Mrs Orange locates one stand to the left of Mr Sun's stand.

Diagrams a, b and c in Figure 9.6 show what her sales would be for three different locations: a at one end of the beach, b in the middle of the beach just left of Mr Sun's stand, and c 96 m to the left of Mr Sun's stand (a little calculation shows that this last is the optimal location given Mr Sun's location).[15]

In diagram a, Mrs Orange's gross margin is only $90, which is not enough to cover the rent of $140. In diagram b, Mrs Orange's gross margin is $120 – again, not enough to cover the rent. In c, Mrs Orange generates a gross margin of $144, so, after paying the rent, her net profit is $4. So, Mrs Orange enters by placing a stand 96 m to the left of Mr Sun's stand.

Mrs Orange can, of course, also place a new stand 96 m to the right of Mr Sun's stand. There Mrs Orange will also make a net profit of $4 a day. Mr Sun's

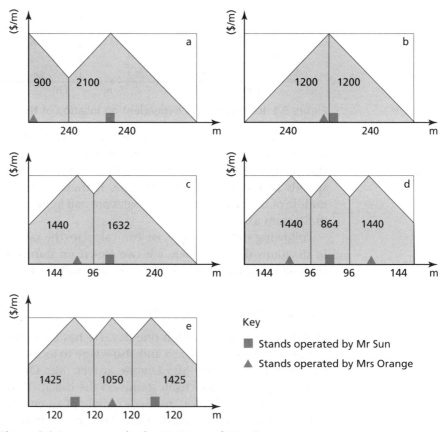

Figure 9.6 Ice-cream sales by Mr Sun and Mrs Orange

gross margin will then drop to only $86.40 a day. As a result, his net profit will be negative ($86.40 − $140.00 = −$53.60).

Now, suppose that Mr Sun decides to place two stands on the beach (diagram e in Figure 9.5). If Mrs Orange stays out, Mr Sun's sales will be $3600, his gross margin $360 and his net profit $360 − $280 = $80.

Will Mrs Orange enter after Mr Sun has placed two stands on the beach? If she does, the best place she can choose is the middle of the beach (diagram e in Figure 9.6). She will then generate sales of $1050, a gross margin of $105. That is not enough to cover the rent of $140, however, so she will not enter.

The results of this analysis are indicated in the game tree shown in Figure 9.7. If Mr Sun applies the principle of looking ahead and reasoning back, he will decide to have two stands. Notice two interesting features of this game.

- Mr Sun would choose to have only one stand if he had a legal monopoly. By choosing two stands instead of one he can effectively deter entry. The essence of this strategy is to *blanket* potential demand for ice-cream, leaving no room for Mrs Orange to enter. We will come back to blanketing strategies in Section 9.7.6, in the context of product competition.
- It is a great advantage for Mr Sun that he arrives on the beach before Mrs Orange. As a consequence, he can make the first move in the game and deter Mrs Orange from entering. If Mrs Orange had arrived first, she could have blocked Mr Sun and she would have pocketed all ice-cream profits. Hence, this game illustrates a situation with a significant **first mover advantage**. In Section 9.7.7, we will explore this concept more generally.

First mover advantage

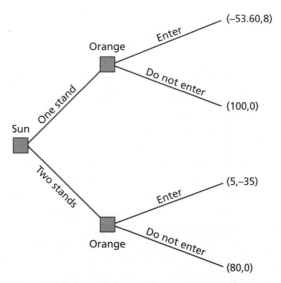

Figure 9.7 Game tree for the ice-cream-selling game. Mr Sun can move first to determine the number and location of his stands

9.7.3 Commitment

In Section 5.3 we introduced the idea of commitment. There we discussed a situation in which the incumbent firm can commit itself to lower prices after entry has occurred. The ice-cream example offers an opportunity to illustrate another form of commitment.

Suppose that there are now two types of ice-cream stand – movable stands (on wheels) and immobile stands (on legs). Movable stands can be moved along the beach without cost. Both types of stand can be rented from Rent-a-Stand for $150 a day.

Mr Sun has to decide how many stands to place on the beach, whether to choose stands on legs or wheels and where to locate the stands on the beach. Then Mrs Orange has to decide whether to enter, how many and what type of stands to choose and where to locate her stands on the beach. Finally, if Mr Sun has one or more stands on wheels, he has to decide whether or not he wants to move those stands along the beach.

Suppose, first, that Mr Sun locates one stand on legs in the middle of the beach. If Mrs Orange does not enter, he makes a profit of:

$$\$240 - \$150 = \$90$$

If Mrs Orange decides to enter, the best she can do is place a stand 96 m to the left (or right) of Mr Sun's stand. At that location, Mrs Orange will generate sales of $1440 (diagram c in Figure 9.6), realizing a gross margin of $144. That is not enough to cover the rent of $150, so she will make a loss of $6.

Now suppose that Mr Sun employs a stand on wheels in the middle of the beach. Mrs Orange can now place a stand on legs next to Mr Sun's stand. Mr Sun then has to decide whether or not to move his stand along the beach (he can move his stand without cost).

Given that he now has a stand on legs next to his own stand, the best he can do is to move 96 m to the right or left. By doing so, he increases his sales from $1200 to $1440 and his gross margin from $120 to $144. The result is a loss of $6 if he moves and a loss of $30 if he does not move.

If Mr Sun moves 96 m away, Mrs Orange's sales increase from $1200 to $1632. If Mr Sun does not move, she makes a loss of $30, but if Mr Sun does move, she makes a profit of $13.20.

This results in the game tree shown in Figure 9.8. If Mrs Orange applies the principle of looking ahead and reasoning back, she will not enter if Mr Sun employs a stand on legs. However, she will decide to enter if Mr Sun employs a stand on wheels. After all, she knows that if she locates next to him, Mr Sun will move away because it is in his own interests to do so. Now Mr Sun knows that he must choose a stand on legs. From looking ahead and reasoning back he sees that with a stand on legs he will make a profit of $90, but with a stand on wheels he will lose $6.

In this example, one stand on legs is enough to deter entry. One stand on wheels will not deter entry. If Mr Sun uses a stand on legs, he cannot move. Mrs Orange then sees that Mr Sun cannot move, so Mrs Orange will not enter. By using a stand on legs rather than a stand on wheels, Mr Sun can deter entry.

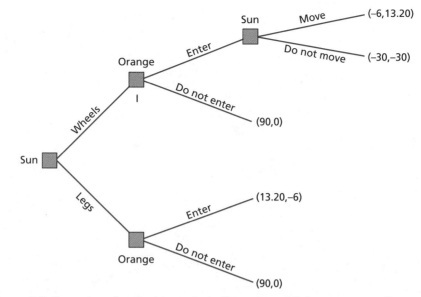

Figure 9.8 Game tree for the ice-cream-selling game. Mr Sun can move first to choose between a stand on wheels and a stand on legs

This is another example of an entry-deterring strategy. Mr Sun shows that he is committed to his place on the beach. That *spatial commitment* deters Mrs Orange from entering.

Thus far we have ignored the time dimension. We have assumed that the future consists of only one day. Suppose now that both Mr Sun and Mrs Orange have a time horizon of one week rather than one day. Suppose that Mr Sun can choose between two types of rental contract: a fixed contract and a flexible contract. A fixed contract is a contract for one week that cannot be cancelled by Mr Sun. If Mr Sun chooses a fixed contract, he has to pay the rent ($150 a day) for seven days even if he does not sell a single ice-cream. A flexible contract is one that gives Mr Sun the option to cancel the contract after one day. After Mr Sun has signed a rental contract with Rent-a-Stand, Mrs Orange has to decide whether or not she wants to rent a stand. For simplicity, we shall assume that Mrs Orange can choose only a fixed contract.

To analyse this situation, suppose, first, that Mr Sun decides to choose a flexible contract. He rents one stand and places it on the middle of the beach. Suppose Mrs Orange decides to enter and also places one stand on the middle of the beach. Then both will make a loss of $30 during the first day.

After the first day, Mr Sun will have to decide whether to cancel the rental contract with Rent-a-Stand. If he does not cancel the contract, he will make a loss of $30 for each of the remaining six days – $210 for the whole week. If he cancels the contract, his loss during the whole week will be only $30. Mrs Orange will then make a profit of $90 during each of the remaining six days – $510 for the whole week.

This results in the game tree shown in Figure 9.9 (we have explained how the pay-offs are calculated if Mr Sun chooses a fixed contract, so you should be able to do those calculations yourself). Assuming that both Mrs Orange and

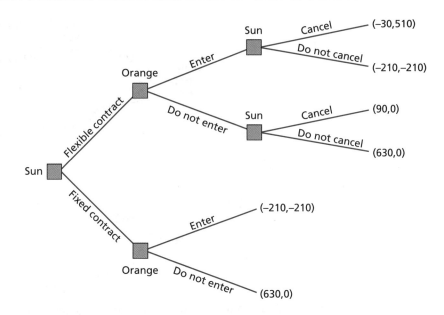

Figure 9.9 Game tree for the ice-cream-selling game. Mr Sun can move first to choose between a fixed and a flexible contract

Mr Sun apply the principle of looking ahead and reasoning back, it is easy to see that Mr Sun should choose a fixed contract. In that case, Mrs Orange will not enter. That is an example of *temporal commitment*. By signing a contract for a week rather than for a day, Mr Sun commits himself to the ice-cream-selling business and so deters entry.

9.7.4 Lessons from the ice-cream example

Two important lessons emerge from the ice-cream example. First, from Section 9.7.2, we see that Mr Sun can block entry by employing two stands rather than one. That finding has an important analogy in product competition, as we shall explain below (in Section 9.7.6).

Credible commitment

Second, from Section 9.7.3, we know that Mr Sun can deter entry by making a **credible commitment**. If Mr Sun has to choose between a stand on wheels and a stand on legs, he can deter entry by using a stand on legs. Suppose Mr Sun uses a stand on wheels and then simply tells Mrs Orange that he will not move if Mrs Orange locates next to him. If he does that, however, Mrs Orange may not believe him. The problem for Mr Sun is one of convincing Mrs Orange that he will not move. Mr Sun must make a credible threat not to move, which he can do by using a stand on legs.

If Mr Sun has to choose between a contract for a day and a contract for a week, he can make a credible commitment by signing a contract for a week with Rent-a-Stand. Suppose Mr Sun does not make a long-term contract with Rent-a-Stand but, instead, simply tells Mrs Orange that he will not leave the ice-cream business. Again, Mrs Orange may just not believe him. Mr Sun must make a credible threat not to leave the ice-cream business. By binding himself to a long-term contract and making this known to Mrs Orange, he makes such a credible threat.

The lesson from the games in Figures 9.8 and 9.9 is that Mr Sun must make a credible threat. The simple but important point is that it is easier to convince someone of something that is true than of something that might not be true. By using a stand on legs or by signing a long-term contract Mr Sun really cannot move along the beach or leave the ice-cream business. Mr Sun's threat is credible because he has committed himself. See Box 9.4 for more on commitments.

It is often thought that strategic flexibility is always an advantage. In Section 9.7.3, we analysed situations where flexibility (the ability to move the stand along the beach or leave the industry) was a disadvantage rather than an advantage.

Box 9.4 Commitments are essential to strategic management

Commitments are essential to management. They are the means by which a company secures the resources necessary for its survival. Investors, customers and employees would likely shun any company the management of which refused to commit publicly to a strategy and back its intentions with investments.

Commitments are more than just necessities, however. Used wisely, they can be powerful tools that help a company to beat the competition. Pre-emptive investments in production capacity or brand recognition can deter potential rivals from entering a market, while heavy investments in durable, specialized and illiquid resources can be difficult for other companies to replicate quickly. Sometimes, just the signal sent by a major commitment can freeze competitors in their tracks. When Microsoft announces a coming product launch, for instance, would-be rivals rethink their plans.

Source: D. N. Sull, 'Managing by commitments', *Harvard Business Review,* June 2003, pp. 82–91

Flexibility is always an advantage when you play against Nature, however. Nature's moves are determined by a random process: they are not determined by whether or not you are committed to a certain strategy. If, however, you play against a human opponent, it may be better to commit yourself rather than retain flexibility. To use a military analogy, burning the bridges behind you signals a credible commitment that you are willing to fight.[16]

9.7.5 Spatial competition

Selecting locations for ice-cream stands on a beach is an example of spatial competition.[17] A clearer example of **spatial competition** is the competition between supermarket chains for new locations. It differs from our ice-cream example in the following respects:

- it is spatial competition in two dimensions instead of one (our beach could be represented by a line and, thus, has only one dimension; an area has two dimensions: north/south and east/west);
- zoning regulations and existing buildings exclude parts of the total area as possible sites for a new supermarket;
- customers tend to shop at the nearest supermarket, but not everyone always shops at the nearest supermarket;
- population, and thus demand, need not be evenly distributed over the area;
- population shifts may occur – to be able to forecast population shifts correctly is an important competitive weapon.

9.7.6 Product competition

Spatial competition has an important analogy in product competition. Imagine two companies selling different brands of cola drink, which differ along one dimension – let's say, sweetness. If sweetness can be expressed as a number, the position of a brand can be given by a number.

To introduce a new product is then the equivalent of opening an ice-cream stand on our beach. Potential customers have different tastes. The distribution of tastes is the parallel of the distribution of potential customers along the beach. Each customer will buy the brand that comes closest to his or her taste preference.

Of course, products can differ in more than one dimension and consumer preferences may change over time. Under these conditions the game of introducing new brands is analogous to the game of selecting new supermarket sites.

In most real-life cases, firms compete in several dimensions. For example, Coca-Cola and Pepsi compete not only in terms of the taste of their products, but also branding, distribution channels, price and so on. The importance of those dimensions may vary per region and change over time, which adds further complexity to the competitive game of move and counter move in the 'cola wars'.

By the way, do you think Coca-Cola or Pepsi was the first to market cola drinks? Which company pioneered diet colas? Would it be an advantage to be the 'first to market' with such products? What would determine success? These questions are explored in the next section (where we will also answer those cola questions).

9.7.7 First mover advantages

In Section 9.7.2, we saw that Mr Sun enjoyed a great advantage – he was the first to arrive at the beach. In this section, we explore under which circum-

First mover advantages

stances such **first mover advantages** can be expected. We will also examine why it is not always an advantage to be the first and why many pioneering firms that are 'first to market' fail to take advantage of their lead.

First mover advantages may arise in the following situations.

■ *The first mover is able to capture a resource that gives competitive advantage* That is the situation in our ice-cream example. Mr Sun is able to monopolize the beach, by means of either a blanketing strategy of putting up two stands first or making credible commitments. Mr Sun's location on the beach is a valuable resource that is rare, inimitable and non-substitutable (VRIN). A location on the beach thus conforms to the VRIN conditions for competitive advantage (see Section 9.5). That advantage is temporary, however, if the game is repeated after expiry of the rental contract. Mrs Orange will have learned that it pays to get to the beach first. Mining companies acquiring the best locations to find natural resources, however, are building the resource base for sustainable competitive advantage. Similarly, a unique patented technology provides such a basis.

■ *The first mover is able to 'lock in' customers or suppliers* An example may actually be Coca-Cola, which was invented and first marketed in 1886 (Pepsi followed in 1898). Coca-Cola was originally positioned as one of many medicinal drinks, offering the beneficial effects of the coca leaves and kola nuts used to make it.[18] It may well have been that Coca-Cola's initial formulation was mildly addictive for consumers (containing cocaine, until it was removed in 1903) – a very literal route to lock-in. More generally, we saw in Section 8.2.4 that lock-in may occur when large numbers exchange is transformed to small numbers exchange as a result of learning-by-doing. If Mr Sun is able to strike an exclusive long-term deal with the rental company letting the ice-cream stands, he may be able to achieve lock-in with his supplier (locking out Mrs Orange).

■ *The first mover is able to benefit from learning* In many industries, the production costs per unit decrease over time as a result of learning. The first mover may therefore have lower costs per unit than followers.

■ *The first mover is able to appropriate increasing returns* Normally, economics works with decreasing returns: demand curves are downward sloping. The first product is able to fetch a higher price than later copies. Sometimes, however, products exhibit increasing returns – namely, if your product becomes more valuable as more copies of it are sold. An example is the fax machine. The first fax machine was essentially worthless as it could not send faxes to anyone else, but each additional fax machine increases the value of all other fax machines. This is called a **network effect** (or, more formally, a **positive network externality**). Other examples are the creation of *standards* (the Windows standard for computer operating systems, for example) or *dominant designs* (such as Intel has established for microprocessors). We will come back to these concepts in Chapters 10 and 11. Suffice it to say here that it is usually very difficult for a first mover or pioneer to start a process of increasing returns *and* appropriate those returns.

Network effect, or, positive network externality

Is it, then, *always* an advantage to be the first mover, to come to market with your products first? The answer is no. In fact, it is much more often the case that 'first to market' is 'first to fail'.[19] Among the reasons for that are the following two.

- The pioneer has to gain acceptance of the new product. That process is known to be subject to high failure rates and, even in the case of a success, to long time delays. Often, those hurdles are too high for pioneers to overcome. In the next chapter, we will see that there is a 'liability of newness', causing high mortality among firms in the early stages of establishing new markets.
- The skills and competences necessary for *invention* (discovery) are rather different from those necessary for *innovation* (commercial success of inventions). Entrepreneurial firms that are good at idea generation and prototyping (making the first version of a product) often already have difficulties working towards market adoption of those products. When they succeed in building a market, it often remains a *niche* market. They lack the competences to really build a *mass* market. To do that requires marketing and distribution skills as well as manufacturing competences and a low cost mentality, which are usually difficult to reconcile with the entrepreneurial culture. Large, established firms on the other hand, usually have difficulty combining sufficient **exploration** with their competences in **exploitation** of existing concepts and products (see also Chapters 10 and 11)

Exploration

Exploitation

As an illustration of the last point, consider the market for 'diet coke'. Which one of the large, established cola companies (Coca-Cola or Pepsi) created the market? The answer is neither of them. The pioneer was Kirsch with a 'No-Cal Cola' in 1952, creating a niche market. The mass market was, however, developed by Coca-Cola with its Diet Coke (1982, notice the time lag!) That is only one example among very many of an established company making an innovation success out of an invention and niche market developed by another, pioneering firm. Markides and Geroski (2005) therefore shift the original meaning of *first mover advantages* (for pioneers) to the *first movers into the mass market*, as follows:

> First mover advantages are almost permanent competitive advantages that early movers can realize and use to protect themselves against the competitive threats of later-moving, imitative entrants. They come from being first to the *mass* market, but, as we have just seen, this is not the same as being first in the market.

Fast second

Their recommendation for established firms is to follow a **fast second** strategy in the case of radical innovations – that is, allowing early movers to establish a niche market and then being the first to consolidate it into a mass market. In fact, such a strategy need not be very 'fast'. Research by Tellis and Golder (2002) showed an average time lag of 19 years between the (niche) market entry of pioneers and the (mass) market entry of consolidators.

Consolidators then leverage their existing resources (such as brands and distribution networks) and their established lock-ins (with retail chains and suppliers) to realize first mover advantages in the mass market. In that process of consolidation, the early movers into the niche market usually (but not always) lose out.

It is fair to say that the literature on first mover advantages is still in its infancy. We expect that our insights into when it is advantageous to move first and when it is better to be (fast) second will be further developed in years to come.

9.7.8 Moving lessons

Let's summarize some of the main lessons we have learned in this section on moves and counter moves.

- Given a (potential) demand for a certain product, firms may deter entry by blanketing that demand – that is, leaving no room for other firms to enter profitably. If, however, they leave certain niches open for potential entrants, they may be profitably exploited. Niches may be of a geographical or product differentiation nature.
- Incumbents may also deter entry by showing that they are committed to their (place in the) industry. In order to be an effective deterrent, the commitment needs to be observable by and credible to the potential entrant.
- As a corollary, flexibility is not always the strategic advantage it is usually assumed to be. If potential entrants interpret an incumbent's flexibility as the likelihood that it will accommodate new entries, entry may in fact be encouraged.
- Similarly, moving first can be an advantage in certain circumstances. It may be less often the case than usually presumed, however. Sometimes, it is more beneficial to wait and be (fast) second. That is specifically the case if the competences for invention/exploration are very different from the requirements for innovation/exploitation. We return to this theme in Chapters 10 and 11.

9.8 Vertical integration

Sections 9.2–9.7 discussed competitive strategies. Now we shift our focus to corporate strategy. As indicated in Section 9.1, the main question when formulating a corporate strategy is *where* (that is, in which industries and in which countries) to compete?

The profitability of a multibusiness firm depends, to a certain extent, on the set of industries in which it operates. There are three ways in which a company can extend its portfolio of business units – through vertical integration, diversification, and multinationalization. This section deals with vertical integration. Diversification and multinationalization are discussed in the next two sections.

Every production process consists of several technologically separable stages. The production of automobiles, for example, consists of assembling an automobile from components such as the body, engine, gearbox, wheels and so on. Each of those components consists of several other components.

Vertical integration means moving into the production of previous stages (backward integration) or subsequent stages (forward integration).

It is easy to see that no firm can be *fully* integrated. For example, for a text-book publisher to be *fully* integrated would mean that it would have to not only undertake printing, bookbinding and operating bookstores but also producing paper, ink, computers, printing presses, bookbinding equipment and all the inputs for producing paper, ink, computers and so on. So, the question is not whether or not to be fully integrated, but, rather, in *which stages* of the production process do you want to be involved? For example, an automobile company may or may not produce its own gearboxes or ignition systems, but it is unlikely to consider producing tyres or lightbulbs.

In order to analyse vertical integration, we can directly apply transaction cost economics, discussed in Chapter 8. An automobile company making its own seats and a small building contractor buying nails from a hardware shop rely on different governance structures. The first uses a managerial hierarchy, while the latter relies on the market. Between the two extremes are long-term contracts, such as a five-year contract between an automobile company and a seat manufacturer. Such long-term contracts are sometimes called *quasi-vertical integration*. Other examples of quasi-vertical integration involving long-term contracts between firms are franchising and licensing contracts.

9.8.1 Technological interdependence

It is sometimes thought that technological factors determine whether or not two subsequent stages in a production process will be vertically integrated. As an example, consider steelmaking.

Steelmaking involves two stages. First, iron is produced by heating iron ore in a blast furnace. Then, the iron is used to produce sheet steel in a rolling mill. Significant energy savings are realized when these two stages are located next to each other. Then, the molten iron need not cool and be reheated, but is used directly as input for the rolling mill. Thus, it is sometimes argued that the production of iron and steel should be vertically integrated because of their technological interdependence.

Williamson (1975, section 5.1.1; see also Box 8.3 earlier) argues that technological interdependence alone does not necessarily lead to vertical integration. The blast furnace and the rolling mill could be owned and operated by two independent firms. Of course, they should still be located next to each other in order to capture the energy savings.

9.8.2 Critical dimensions of transactions

In order to explain why, in practice, we observe integrated iron and steelworks instead of two separate firms, we need a transaction cost argument in addition to the technological factors.

What factors determine the choice made between vertical integration, quasi-vertical integration through long-term contracts and a series of spot contracts? As discussed in Chapter 8, three dimensions of transactions are important:

■ asset specificity
■ uncertainty/complexity
■ frequency.

Asset specificity and uncertainty/complexity are more important than frequency, so, for simplicity, we shall ignore frequency for the moment.

Asset specificity can be low for both parties to a transaction or it can be high for one party and low for the other party or it can be high for both parties. If asset specificity is high for one party but low for the other, the party with highly transaction-specific assets is vulnerable to opportunistic behaviour by the other party. If, however, asset specificity is high for both parties to a transaction, they are in the same position as two enemies holding hostages. If one party hurts the hostages it holds, the other party can retaliate. Such a situation encourages both parties to be careful. In military terms, there will be an incentive to aim for a truce. In economic terms, two parties with mutually high asset specificity may aim for a long-term contract. If either party violates the contract, both will be hurt. Under such conditions, a long-term contract may work quite well, provided that not too many contingencies need to be included in it.

If we say that asset specificity can be low for both parties, high for one party and low for the other or high for both parties and that uncertainty/complexity can be low or high, we have six different situations (see Figure 9.10).

We discuss each of these six situations below and analyse which governance structures are efficient in each case.

Case 1: Asset specificity low on both sides, uncertainty/complexity low

An example of such a situation is a building contractor buying nails. Spot contracts are very efficient in such cases.

Case 2: Asset specificity high on both sides, uncertainty/complexity low

As an example of this situation, consider again the relationship between a newspaper publisher and a printer in an isolated town discussed in Section 8.3.

Figure 9.10 Six different cases with regard to asset specificity and uncertainty/complexity

For the printer, the press is transaction-specific as there is only one newspaper publisher in that town. The printer cannot sell the services of the press to newspaper publishers in other towns because of transportation costs. For the publisher, his investment in goodwill with subscribers and advertisers is transaction-specific because there is only one printer. Hence, asset specificity is high for both parties: they are dependent on each other for a transaction to occur.

The major source of uncertainty/complexity would seem to be whether or not the publisher will be able to pay. If the printer has no doubts concerning the publisher's ability to pay (either because she knows that the publisher has ample financial resources or because she knows that the newspaper will generate enough cash flow), a long-term contract will work quite well.

Case 3: Asset specificity high on one side, uncertainty/complexity low

As an example, consider the relations between an auto component manufacturer and an automobile company. If the component manufacturer has to invest in specialized tooling for components that can be sold to one automobile company only, asset specificity is high for the component manufacturer, but not for the automobile company. The component manufacturer would be vulnerable to opportunistic behaviour by the automobile company. Even if uncertainty/complexity is low, vertical integration will probably be the preferred solution.[20]

Case 4: Asset specificity low on both sides, uncertainty/complexity high

As an example of such a situation, consider the relations between an oil company and a management consulting firm. The potential transaction might be advice about the oil company's organizational policies. Asset specificity is low on both sides: the oil company can turn to many other consulting firms for advice; the management consulting firm has many other potential clients. It may be quite difficult, however, to specify in a contract the services of the management consulting firm. Often, the specific problems that have to be dealt with only become clear as the consultancy work progresses, so uncertainty/complexity may be quite high. In that case, frequency may become an important dimension.

If frequency is very low (if the oil company seeks that type of advice only very rarely), vertical integration cannot be the solution. Somehow the two parties must agree on a contract, even in the face of high uncertainty/complexity. Perhaps the consultancy work will be split into phases, with the oil company retaining the right to reconsider the transaction after a pilot study by the consulting firm. If, however, frequency is high (if the oil company needs such advice regularly), vertical integration might be a good solution. The oil company then builds an internal group of management consultants. Such a solution becomes even more efficient when asset specificity is not totally absent. That may be the case if some organization-specific knowledge is necessary. Then, we would say that the preferred solution depends primarily on frequency.

Case 5: Asset specificity high on both sides, uncertainty/complexity high

Consider again our steelmaking example. Suppose the two stages in steel-making (blast furnace and rolling mill) were organized in two separate firms. In order to realize energy savings, the blast furnace and the rolling mill should be located next to each other. The blast furnace would have only one customer for its molten iron and the rolling mill would have only one supplier of molten iron. That implies, for both the blast furnace and the rolling mill, most of the physical assets would be transaction-specific.

Uncertainty/complexity would also be high. One source of complexity may be the fact that the quality of the different grades of steel depends to a large extent on the quality of the molten iron, while the quality of molten iron is hard to measure. As the quality of the molten iron depends on the quality of the iron ore used by the blast furnace, and grades of iron ore differ in quality and in price, the owner of the blast furnace has an opportunity to behave opportunistically. Under such circumstances, it is very difficult to write and enforce a contingent claims contract.[21] In this case, vertical integration is the most efficient solution.

Case 6: Asset specificity high for one party and low for the other, uncertainty/complexity high

Consider a component manufacturer who has to invest a large sum in the development of a component for which there will be only one customer. The investment in development is then highly transaction-specific. Uncertainty/complexity may come from two sources: the development costs may be uncertain and/or demand for the final product (and thus for the component) may be uncertain. If uncertainty from either source is high, it is very difficult to write and enforce a contingent claims contract. Vertical integration is the most efficient solution here.

The six cases discussed above are summarized in Figure 9.11.

Figure 9.11 How asset specificity and uncertainty/complexity determine governance structure

9.9 Diversification

Related diversification

A firm can also extend its portfolio of businesses through diversification. It will be useful to make a distinction here between *related* and *unrelated diversification*. **Related diversification** occurs when the new business is in some way related to the firm's existing business. Examples of related diversification are a coffee firm diversifying into coffee creamer (market-related), a dairy firm currently producing only cheese, butter and fresh milk products that diversifies into coffee creamer (input-related) and a commercial aircraft company diversifying into military aircraft (technology-related).

9.9.1 Related diversification

Economies of scope

An important reason for related diversification is the existence of **economies of scope**. Economies of scope exist when the joint production of two goods is less costly than the cost of producing those two goods separately.[22] As an example, consider the joint production of fruit and sheep.[23]

A fruitgrower must have space between fruit trees in order to facilitate adequate growth of the trees and the movement of farm machinery between the trees. That land can be used as pasture, where sheep can graze.

As the land can be used as a common input, the joint production of fruit and sheep on one piece of land is less costly than the production of fruit and sheep separately on two different pieces of land.

A more industrial example is the joint use of a physical distribution system for beer and soft drinks.

The existence of economies of scope does not imply that both goods should be produced by the same firm, as has been pointed out by Teece (1980). The fruitgrower can diversify into sheep and thus realize economies of scope. As an alternative, however, he may lease the land to a sheepfarmer. In the latter case, a market transaction in the common input factor (land) occurs. Thus, the fruitgrower can choose between two governance structures: the firm (if he diversifies) or the market (if he leases his land to a sheepfarmer).

Teece's argument here is analogous to Williamson's discussion of vertical integration of iron and steel production (see Section 9.8.1). In both cases a market arrangement can be used to capture the economies of scope or the energy savings. The actual choice made between these two arrangements will thus be driven by the transaction costs involved.

Economies of scope can always be traced to a common production factor. If market transactions in this common production factor are relatively costly, joint production of the two products in one firm may be the least costly solution. Common production factors leading to economies of scope are:

- specialized indivisible physical assets;
- technological know-how;
- organizational know-how;
- brand names.

Specialized indivisible physical assets

The services of **specialized indivisible physical assets** may be difficult to sell (exactly because the assets are specialized). As an example, consider once again a newspaper publisher in an isolated town. Suppose the publisher prints his own newspaper. The press is used for this purpose six days a week. One day a week, then, the press is idle. Suppose that idle capacity can be used to print a Sunday paper. The newspaper publisher can start a Sunday paper or can write a contract for printing a Sunday paper with someone else who wants to start such a paper. Both solutions would seem feasible (see our earlier discussion in Section 9.8).

Technological know-how

Technological know-how may also lead to economies of scope. Technological know-how may be difficult to trade across markets for two reasons:

- property rights may be ill defined;
- transfer of know-how within a firm may be easier than across markets.

Not all technological know-how is patentable. Also, firms often choose not to patent technological findings, even if patents could be obtained. One reason is that they have to register their findings at the patent office. By registering, they reveal their knowledge, which is not always strategically advantageous. It is usually difficult to sell technological know-how if property rights are not protected by patent law, however. Thus, a seller must try to convince a potential buyer of its value and, in doing so, must reveal some of his know-how. A potential buyer can assess the real value of the know-how only after she has received it, but then she already possesses the know-how, so will refuse to pay for it. That is the fundamental paradox of information, as described in Section 4.1: its value can only be revealed to another party by disclosing the information, while such disclosure destroys its value.

The paradox emerges because potential buyers may behave opportunistically. Suppose a buyer agrees to pay in advance for technological know-how. Now the seller may behave opportunistically by transferring only a minor part of the know-how. Thus, the possibility of opportunistic behaviour by both buyers and sellers leads to the fundamental paradox of information.

Suppose now that property rights to know-how are protected by patent law. Then a potential buyer knows what he buys. Opportunistic behaviour by buyer and seller is less of a problem.

Transfer of know-how within a firm may still be easier (and thus cheaper) than between firms. If a recipe or a blueprint is all that needs to be transferred, it is easy to realize the transfer both between firms and within a firm. Frequently, however, more than a recipe or blueprint needs to be transferred: if the know-how contains an element of learning-by-doing, then training and consulting are part of the transfer. If engineers working for the same firm have received similar training, the transfer between engineers working for the same firm may be easier than that between engineers working for different firms. In such a case, related diversification may again be efficient.

Organizational know-how

Organizational know-how is the third production factor giving rise to economies of scope. The term refers to the fact that organizations 'know' how to respond to external events. Organizations use *routines* to respond to external events. An important characteristic of routines is that they are to a large extent *tacit*: organization members find it difficult to articulate why they respond to a stimulus in a particular way. Yet, organizations seem to 'remember by doing'.

The concept of organizational routines (developed by Nelson and Winter, 1982) is discussed more fully in Section 10.5. Here, we want to state that organizational know-how is often *fungible* – that is, organizational know-how often has several kinds of application (Teece, 1982). For example, automobile companies can also use their organizational know-how to make tanks (as they did during World War II) and breweries can use their organizational know-how to produce soft drinks and so on.

It is nearly impossible to trade organizational know-how across a market. If one manager is transferred from one firm to another, she must learn the organizational routines of her new firm. Organizational routines are more difficult to transfer. Through diversification, organizational know-how can be exploited across different applications. Thus, organizational know-how is a fundamental reason to diversify.

Brand names

Brand names can also lead to economies of scope. That is because it is usually cheaper to introduce a new product under an established brand name than under a new one (suppose DaimlerChrysler were to diversify into motorcycles; it would then be cheaper to use the Mercedes brand name than it would to use a new name). Brand names can also be traded across markets. We shall say more on this subject in Section 9.10.

Sometimes economies of scope can be quite important. In food retailing, for example, there seem to be important economies of scope between traditional supermarkets and 'e-tailing' (food retailing using the Internet), as is illustrated in Box 9.5.

Box 9.5 Retailing versus e-tailing

With the advent of the Internet, many companies (dot-coms) were set up to challenge incumbents in various industries. One example is from retailing. The idea was that many consumers would eventually rather order their groceries over the Internet and have them delivered at home (or at a convenient place such as the office) than do their laborious shopping in their sparse time off. This idea was the basis of new business models in 'e-tailing', pursued by start-up companies such as Kozmo, Streamline, Peapod and Webvan. Webvan, for instance, collected $1.2 billion in financing in 1999 and built 26 enormous distribution centres with the latest Web-enabled inventory management systems and a huge fleet of delivery vans. Nevertheless, it went bankrupt in mid 2001. Similarly, many other e-tailers did not survive: they also folded or were taken over.

The incumbent retailers were at first rather slow to react. However, in the endgame they may be the eventual survivors in e-tailing by blending it with their conventional 'bricks-and mortar' approach (sometimes the blend is referred to as 'clicks-and-mortar'). Ahold, the Dutch retailer, has taken over Peapod and is now keen on acquiring the employees and customers of Webvan. On 25 June 2001, Tesco, Britain's biggest grocer, announced a deal with Safeway, California's biggest food retailer, to bring its successful Internet shopping service to the USA. Tesco has worked hard to perfect its so-called 'store-picking' system, under which orders placed online are plucked from the shelves of existing stores. It is now the world's biggest Internet grocer, with a turnover of over $420 million.

Sources: The Economist, 30 June 2001; Het Financieele Dagblad, 11 July 2001

The argument so far can be summarized as follows. An important reason for related diversification is the existence of economies of scope. Economies of scope always rest on use of a common production factor. Four such factors have been identified:

- specialized indivisible physical assets
- technological know-how
- organizational know-how
- brand names.

Economies of scope can be exploited through market arrangements or organizational arrangements. The actual choice between the two – and thus the choice for related diversification – depends on the transaction costs involved.

9.9.2 Unrelated diversification

Unrelated diversification

As we have argued above, related diversification may be the most efficient way to realize economies of scope. In the case of **unrelated diversification**, economies of scope cannot arise in R&D, production, marketing or distribution. However, as Williamson has submitted, a firm with several unrelated business units (a conglomerate firm) may still have an advantage as it may be more efficient in allocating cash flow to high-yield uses than is the external capital market. If a conglomerate firm adopts an M-form structure, it can realize all the advantages of the M-form (see Section 8.6). The general office of such a conglomerate evaluates investment proposals from the business units and allocates cash flow to the most profitable proposals. Thus, the general office performs the task of the capital market. In comparison with the capital market, the general office of a conglomerate has two advantages. First, business unit managers are subordinates, so the general office can demand much more information from them than can outside investors. Second, business unit managers will be prepared to share with the general office confidential information that they would not like to give to a large number of external investors. Hence, again, the conglomerate organization arises as a solution to an *information problem*.

The benefits of unrelated diversification must be balanced against the costs. As conglomerates grow larger and older, the general office tends to grow and corporate overhead costs tend to rise. Thus, without substantial economies of scope, the financial performance of conglomerates is, on average, not impressive (Goold et al., 1994; Rumelt, 1974, p. 94).

It is not always easy to classify a firm's portfolio as either related or unrelated. Perhaps it is better to speak about degrees of relatedness. As an example, consider Gillette's product portfolio, described in Box 9.6.

Box 9.6 Gillette's product portfolio

Gillette was an American company based in Boston, Massachusetts, with three major product divisions: grooming, portable power and oral care. Grooming includes products for male shaving, such

▶

as razors – manual and electrical – razor blades, shaving preparations and aftershaves. Gillette's grooming business also includes hair removal products for women. Gillette's portable power business consists mainly of Duracell, a company offering alkaline batteries for use in a wide variety of consumer products. Duracell was acquired by Gillette in 1996.

Gillette's oral care products include manual toothbrushes and a variety of oral care appliances sold under the Braun brand name.

At first glance, there appears to be little possibility for economies of scope for Gillette's three divisions. If one division, say the grooming business division, has unused manufacturing capacity, then it is highly unlikely that capacity can be used by another division, simply because razor blades, batteries and toothbrushes require highly different manufacturing facilities. Thus, specialized indivisible physical assets cannot be the source of economies of scope. The same is true of technological know-how (batteries are quite different from razor blades and toothbrushes) and brand names (batteries are sold under the Duracell brand name, oral appliances under the Braun brand name).

It is possible, however, that economies of scope may be obtained by using one sales organization for the products of all three divisions, especially in certain developing countries (Gillette's products are sold in over 200 countries). In that case, economies of scope would be based on organizational know-how (local marketing know-how in countries such as China and India).

Gillette's product portfolio may be classified as related (economies of scope from the joint use of marketing and sales operations in certain countries), but only distantly related.

In 2005, Gillette was acquired by Procter & Gamble and became one of its business units.

9.10 Horizontal multinationalization

Horizontal multinationalization

In Sections 9.8 and 9.9 we discussed why a firm may extend its portfolio of business units through vertical integration and diversification. A firm can also extend its portfolio through horizontal multinationalization. By **horizontal multinationalization** we mean becoming involved in the same activities in another country. An example is the acquisition of an American truck company by a German truck company.

Consider a firm operating two different plants in two different countries (say the USA and Germany). Suppose, further, that both plants produce the same product (trucks) and that there are no shipments of intermediate goods between the two plants (if there were, we would have a case of vertical integration, which was discussed in Section 9.8). Suppose, also, that transportation costs or import duties make it efficient to operate two plants (in the USA and Germany) instead of one. What advantage can be realized by bringing the US plant and the German plant under one managerial hierarchy?

As there are no shipments of intermediate goods or finished products, the reason must be the realization of economies of scale through the joint use of intangible assets. Three types of asset are relevant here:

- technological know-how;
- organizational know-how;
- brand names.

These three types of asset have also been mentioned in the preceding section. There we discussed economies of scope; now we discuss economies of scale.

There is a strong similarity between related diversification (which is one way to exploit economies of scope) and horizontal multinationalization (which is one way to exploit economies of scale). For that reason, the discussion here closely resembles that of the preceding section.

- *Technological know-how* As an example, suppose that the German firm has an excellent capability for designing aerodynamic trucks. There are two ways in which it can exploit its technological know-how in the USA. It can try to sell that capability to US truck manufacturers or it can acquire a US truck manufacturer and transfer the know-how to the new subsidiary. Again, a market arrangement or an organizational arrangement can be used to exploit the economies of scale from technological know-how. The difficulties involved in trading technological know-how were discussed in Section 9.9.1.
- *Organizational know-how* Suppose a Dutch brewery, such as Heineken, has expert knowledge in the marketing of premium beers. Through horizontal multinationalization that know-how may be applied in other countries. See also Section 9.9.1 for the difficulties involved in selling organizational know-how across markets.
- *Brand names* Suppose an American hotel chain (Hilton or Sheraton) has invested heavily in developing a brand name. Suppose, further, that the hotel appeals especially to business people who also travel a great deal abroad. Clearly, a hotel in Beijing, New Delhi or Amsterdam would be in a better position to attract American businesspeople if it could use the Hilton brand name. Hilton now has three alternatives: it can start its own hotels in other countries (or buy existing ones), it can sell the Hilton brand name once and for all or it can employ franchising.

Suppose Hilton wants to continue to use the Hilton name in the USA but decides to sell the right to use the Hilton brand name in the Netherlands once and for all to a Dutch firm. For Hilton, that would entail a big risk: the Dutch firm may, after the sale, behave opportunistically by charging high prices (customers would book because of the Hilton name) and not delivering quality. The American Hilton hotels would, in time, be hurt because the value of the brand name would decline owing to the opportunistic behaviour of the Dutch firm.

Franchising, however, is a feasible alternative. Through franchising, the Dutch firm acquires the right to use the Hilton name for a limited period of time only. The franchisor (the American Hilton) has the right to inspect the franchisee's (the Dutch) hotel during that period. If the franchisee does not comply with specified quality standards, he loses the right to use the Hilton name in the next period.

Of course, instead of franchising, horizontal multinationalization is a feasible alternative for Hilton.

By way of a summary we can now state that three types of intangible asset – technological know-how, organizational know-how and brand names – may lead to economies of scale when used outside the firm's home country. In principle, both market arrangements and organizational arrangements may be used to realize those benefits. The actual choice depends on the transaction costs of the arrangements.

9.11 Summary: how economic analysis can contribute to the formulation of competitive and corporate strategies

In a multibusiness firm, there are two levels of strategy: at the business and corporate levels. Each business unit needs to have a competitive strategy that specifies how that business intends to compete in its given industry. At the corporate level, there is a need for a strategy that specifies where – that is, in which industries and in which countries – the company intends to compete.

If a firm or a business unit wants to formulate a competitive strategy, it should first analyse its environment and assess its strengths and weaknesses. Porter's five-forces model, which is based on the results of several studies in the tradition of the structure–conduct–performance paradigm, has proved to be a useful tool for assessing the attractiveness of the industry in which the firm operates. The concept of strategic groups provides a foundation for analysing differences in performance between companies (or business units) belonging to the same industry. That gives the strategic planner a tool with which to assess a business unit's strengths and weaknesses.

In formulating a competitive strategy, the firm has many options. The options that are available depend on the industry and the firm's position within that industry. However, two successful strategies – those of cost leadership and product differentiation – have been identified in many industries. Any firm should at least consider these so-called generic competitive strategies.

The objective of a competitive strategy is to create a competitive advantage over rival firms. Preferably, that competitive advantage should be as sustainable as possible. The resource-based view (RBV) of the firm examines which resources may form the basis of such a competitive advantage. It has concluded that resources should be valuable, rare, inimitable and non-substitutable (the VRIN-framework). The RBV has been extended with the concept of dynamic capabilities, denoting the capacity of an organization to purposefully create, extend or modify its resource base. That has allowed us to delve deeper into the factors enabling resources and capabilities to provide competitive advantage. Factors noted in this chapter include co-specialization, asset orchestration, tacit knowledge, firm specificity and isolating mechanisms. In the next chapter we will examine the evolution and selection of dynamic capabilities.

In formulating a competitive strategy, a firm should take into account how its competitors will react. That is true especially in an oligopolistic industry – an industry consisting of a few large companies. For example, when Philips decides to develop a new product standard for a digital videodisc it has to take into account how its competitors (Sony and Matsushita, among others) will react. Game theory (discussed in Chapter 5), can help in that respect. The game of selling ice-cream on a beach shows, first, how companies can try to prevent entry by other firms by offering several competing brands and, second, that by making a credible commitment to an industry, a company can discourage other firms from entering that industry.

At the corporate level, the firm needs to decide in which industries and in which countries it wants to operate. There are three ways in which a firm can extend its scope: vertical integration, diversification and horizontal expansion.

Vertical integration means that the firm moves into activities that were previously performed by its suppliers or its customers. Transaction cost economics (discussed in Chapter 8), can usefully be employed to analyse when it will pay to integrate vertically. The important dimensions of transactions to be included in the analysis are asset specificity and uncertainty/complexity. Two polar cases stand out. First, if asset specificity is low and uncertainty/complexity is also low, then spot contracts are efficient. Vertical integration is not warranted in such cases. Second, if asset specificity is high and uncertainty/complexity is also high, then vertical integration is desirable.

Diversification means that the firm enters another industry. It may be related or unrelated. Related diversification occurs when the *new* business is related to the firm's *existing* business. Through related diversification the firm may realize economies of scope. Economies of scope arise when the joint production of two products is less costly than the production of each product separately. Such instances may occur when the firm can use one input factor to produce two different products. When it is difficult or impossible to sell the services of those input factors in the market for input factors, related diversification is an efficient way to realize the economies of scope. Examples of input factors that may lead to economies of scope and are also difficult to trade are specialized machinery, technological know-how, organizational know-how and brand names. A firm that has these types of input factors and sees an opportunity to employ them in another industry may be well advised to take this opportunity. It will then lead to related diversification.

Unrelated diversification occurs when there is *no* relation between the new business and the firm's existing business(es). A firm engaging in unrelated diversification cannot hope to realize economies of scope. However, it may reap the benefits of an internal capital market. An internal capital market can be more efficient than the external capital market in allocating cash flows. Such an advantage should be weighed against the costs of corporate overheads.

Horizontal expansion occurs when the firm extends its activities within the same industry. When, in doing so, it crosses national borders, it engages in horizontal multinationalization. A firm operating plants that produce the same products in different countries may realize economies of scale if those plants share the use of intangible assets, such as technological know-how, organizational know-how and brand names. As such intangible assets are generally difficult to sell across markets, horizontal multinationalization may be the only way to capture those benefits.

Questions

1 Consider an industry that you know well – for example, the industry consisting of the bars in the town where you live. Use Porter's model of the forces driving industry competition to describe the intensity of competition in that industry.

2 You are managing director of a small, young electronics firm. One of your engineers has developed a specialized kind of memory chip. The new chip can be manufactured in one of two ways – by buying highly specialized equipment or buying less specialized equipment. The specialized equipment can be used to produce only the new chip. The less specialized equipment can be used to produce the new chip but could, with a minor additional investment, also be used to produce a variety of other chips. Demand for the new chip is highly uncertain. The new chip could turn out to be a bestseller or a complete failure in the market. Also uncertain is whether or not other firms are already working on the development of a similar chip. You know that it is impossible to protect the new chip by patents.

   Do you see an advantage in buying the specialized equipment? Assume that the amount to be invested and unit cost for the specialized equipment are the same as for the less specialized equipment.

3 Electricité de France (EDF) is the French State-owned power utility. Although its main source of energy is nuclear power, it also generates electricity from coal. For this purpose it has several riverside-based power plants fuelled by coal. Most plants use coal from France, delivered by rail, but also coal imported from overseas. Demand for coal for each power plant is very stable. Imported coal is delivered to the power plants by barges. In France, there are three rivers that can be used by the barges – the Loire, Seine and Rhône. The rivers differ considerably in depth and sluice size. Two types of barge can be used to transport coal on the rivers: general-purpose barges, which can be used to transport a variety of goods and can be used on all rivers, and special barges, which can be used to only transport coal and can be used on only one river. The special barges have been adapted to the circumstances of one particular river. Moreover, they require special unloading facilities that have been built by EDF. The special barges are much more efficient than general-purpose barges as they use the depth and sluice size of each river to the maximum.

   Coal is imported into France by independent suppliers. On each river, there is only one supplier. Although EDF is State-owned, it is driven very much by efficiency considerations.

   a Do you think that general-purpose barges will be used to a great extent or that most of the coal will be transported by the special barges?

   b Suppose, first, that general-purpose barges are used. Do you think that it is important who owns the barges? Supposing the supplier owns the barges, do you expect long-term or short-term contracts between EDF and the supplier in question?

   c Now suppose that special barges are used. Do you think that it is important who owns the barges? Supposing the supplier owns the barges, do you expect long-term or short-term contracts between EDF and the supplier in question?

4 Norwegian salmon is farmed all along the Norwegian coast by fish farmers. They sell their fish mainly to exporters, who sell the fish fresh to importers in the UK, Germany, France, Spain, the USA and Japan. Because of the cold and pure water along the Norwegian coast and strict quality standards at all levels of the industry, Norwegian

salmon is a high-quality product. Given its high quality, most of the fresh salmon ends up in gourmet restaurants. The duration of the relations between the Norwegian exporters and the importers varies from one occasional transaction to several years. In your opinion, which factors determine the duration of those relationships?

5 Box 9.5 described how Tesco, Britain's largest food retailer, successfully entered the Internet-based food retailing business, while companies such as Webvan failed. What explains the superiority of Tesco's business model? Do you see potential economies of scope for traditional food retailing and Internet-based food retailing? Which production factors will probably lead to economies of scope in this case?

6 During the last two decades, the big global auditing firms (such as KPMG, PricewaterhouseCoopers and Ernst & Young) have diversified into areas such as consulting, IT services, legal advice and headhunting (also called executive recruiting). The reasons for that are discussed in an article in *The Economist* (7 July 2001). According to *The Economist*, the auditing firms themselves see two reasons for transforming into professional services conglomerates.

The first reason is risk reduction. The risk that auditors worry most about today is the risk of being sued. Expensive settlements of shareholder lawsuits are increasing. According to *The Economist*, the best way to reduce that risk is not to offer more services, but seek incorporation as a limited liability company.

The second reason given by professional services firms, according to *The Economist*, is that their corporate clients want it. Again, *The Economist* is sceptical – many large global businesses use several different consulting firms.

The Economist suggests a third reason: networking:

In professional-service conglomerates, old-fashioned networking is a powerful influence on business. The addition of legal (and other) services to the big firms' menu of offerings will expand their networking potential considerably. At a time when there is downward pressure on fees for professional services of all kinds, that could help explain their enthusiasm for diversification.

Compare the three reasons given above with the logic underlying related and unrelated diversification as given in the text. On the basis of your analysis, can you come up with a list of other possible reasons? In order to be able to get an idea of the relevance of those reasons, what kind of additional information would you need?

Suggested further reading

Barney, J. B. (1997), *Gaining and Sustaining Competitive Advantage*, Reading, MA: Addison-Wesley.

Besanko, D., Dranove, D., Shanley, M. and Schaefer, S. (2004), *Economics of Strategy*, New York: John Wiley.

Grant, R. M. (2005), *Contemporary Strategy Analysis*, Oxford: Blackwell.

Johnson, G., Scholes, K. and Whittington, R. (2005), *Exploring Corporate Strategy: Text and Cases*, Harlow: FT Prentice-Hall.

Kay, J. (1993), *Foundations for Corporate Success: How business strategies add value*, Oxford: Oxford University Press.

Porter, M. E. (1980), *Competitive Strategy: Techniques for analyzing industries and competitors*, New York: Free Press.

Porter, M. E. (1985), *Competitive Advantage: Creating and sustaining superior performance*, New York: Free Press.

Porter, M. E. (2008). 'The five competitive forces that shape strategy', *Harvard Business Review*, vol. 861(1), Reprint R080IE, pp. 1–17.

Notes

1 The term 'strategy' may be used in a normative or descriptive sense. If we say that a competitive strategy specifies how the business unit's managers should compete in a given industry, we are using the term in a normative sense. We can also say that a competitive strategy specifies how the business unit's managers actually compete in a given industry. We are then using the term in a descriptive sense.

2 In terms used by Mintzberg, strategic planning is directed towards the formulation of a *deliberate* strategy that the firm intends to pursue and implement. In addition, firms have *emergent* strategies: patterns of strategic behaviour that develop over time in the absence of, or even in spite of, deliberate intentions. See Mintzberg and Quinn (1991).

3 If you are interested in this issue, see, for example, Mintzberg and Quinn (1991). In this chapter we only touch on strategic process and implementation when we discuss dynamic capabilities in Section 9.6. There we discuss management's task of 'asset orchestration'.

4 For a detailed discussion of Porter's five-forces model, see Porter (1985), Chapter 1 and his recent update in Porter (2008).

5 The concept of organizational routines has been introduced by Nelson and Winter (1982). See Section 10.5 for an exposition of the concept.

6 Mobility barriers between strategic groups are roughly equivalent to entry barriers around industries – that is, those investments that raise the cost of strategy imitation to non-group members. See McGee (2003) for an excellent discussion of the theory and practice of strategic groups.

7 See Helfat et al. (2007). The major developer of this framework has been Jay Barney. In Barney (1997), the additional question is raised as to whether or not the firm is organized to exploit the full competitive potential of its resources and capabilities.

8 Related to the discussion of information as a economic factor of production is the knowledge-based view of the firm. See Grant (2003).

9 This is the definition presented in Helfat et al. (2007), which is the best summary of the dynamic capabilities literature so far. See also Tallman (2003).

10 As discussed in Chapter 8, specialized assets can lead to a situation of lock-in. They also introduce the potential problem of hold-up.

11 The term 'asset orchestration' has been proposed by Helfat et al. (2007).

12 Note that the terminology of configuration corresponds very well with Mintzberg's concept of *organizational configuration* (see Section 3.2). Helfat et al. (2007) argue that asset orchestration involves much more than coordination and adaptation. We would say that their judgment is predicated on too narrow a concept of organizational coordination. If all six organizational coordination mechanisms are taken into account (see Section 3.2), we would be inclined to view asset orchestration as a manifestation of organizational coordination.

13 The term 'isolating mechanisms' was introduced by Rumelt (1984). See also Besanko et al. (2004) and Peteraf (1993) for an extensive discussion.

14 That, however, would leave hardly any room on the beach for customers, so it does not seem a very practical strategy.

15 If Mrs Orange's stand is x metres to the left of Mr Sun's stand, then Mrs Orange's gross margin (the shaded area around her stand in Figure 9.6 c) is:

$$120 + \frac{1}{2}x - \frac{5}{8} \cdot \frac{x^2}{240}$$

This expression reaches its maximum value for $x = 96$ – its value is then 144.

16 For a further discussion of strategic commitment, see Ghemawat (1991).

17 Our model of ice-cream stands on a beach is a very simple model of spatial competition. In our model, price is not a decision variable as we assumed that price was determined by the municipality. In more general models, demand depends on both distance and price. Firms then have two decision variables: location and price. See, for example, d'Aspremont et al. (1979), Hotelling (1929) or Rasmusen (1989, pp. 269–73).

18 Coca-Cola was advertised as offering 'the valuable tonic and nerve stimulant properties of the coca plant and kola nuts'. Pepsi was named after the beneficial effects its creator, Caleb Bradham, claimed it had on dyspepsia (an upset stomach).

19 'First to market, first to fail' is the title of an interesting article by Tellis and Golder (1996), later expanded into a book (2002).They examined 66 product categories and found that the pioneer had become the market leader in only 6 of those categories. On average, most pioneers failed (64 per cent). Surviving pioneers held, on average, only 6 per cent market share. For this section we have also relied on Geroski (2003), Lieberman and Montgomery (1998) as well as Markides and Geroski (2005).

20 Another solution may be to have the automobile company own the specialized tooling. Then, however, the automobile company has to invest in transaction-specific assets, which makes it vulnerable to opportunistic behaviour by the component manufacturer. That problem may be mitigated, however, if the automobile company can transfer the assets to another component manufacturer. For a further discussion of this issue, see Masten et al. (1989).

21 The term contingent claims contract was introduced in Section 4.1.

22 This can be expressed more accurately in a mathematical formula. Let $c(x_1, x_2)$ be the cost of producing x_1 units of good 1 and x_2 units of good 2. Economies of scope exist if and only if:

$$c(x_1,x_2) < c(x_1,0) + c(0,x_2)$$

for all positive x_1 and x_2.

23 We have borrowed this example from Teece (1980).

10.1 Introduction

While the preceding chapters dealt mainly with the explanation of current organizational forms, the perspective now shifts to the *development* of organizational forms over time. In economic terms, we shift from a static to a dynamic perspective. In organization theory, such dynamic, developmental perspectives are usually called *evolutionary*. We already encountered such an evolutionary perspective when we discussed evolutionary game theory in Chapter 5. A biological example (the long necks of giraffes) introduces the perspective further in the next section. Then we move on to consider the usefulness of evolutionary ideas when explaining organizational phenomena in Section 10.3.

Two examples of evolutionary approaches represent the core of the chapter. One of them is decidedly economic in nature; the other is presented as sociological. They are introduced in Sections 10.4 and 10.5 and compared in Section 10.6.

In Section 10.7, we come back to the concept of dynamic capabilities, as introduced in the previous chapter. We can now delve into the evolution of dynamic capabilities and the question of how they are selected for providing sustainable competitive advantage. These broad linkages (economics, sociology, strategy) demonstrate that the evolutionary perspective transcends the boundaries of several scientific disciplines and has the potential to integrate the contributions of various disciplines into the study of particular organizational phenomena. That potential is outlined in the final section.

10.2 Giraffes

Our biological example is a famous one: why do giraffes have such long necks? That simple question allows us to separate creationist and evolutionary arguments and, within the evolutionary strand, Darwinist and Lamarckian arguments.

The creationist answer to the question why do giraffes have such long necks is quite straightforward: because they were made that way. *Creationist* arguments involve deliberate design. Giraffes were designed with long necks. That characteristic gave them an advantage and allowed them to survive when in competition with other species. Only giraffes could reach for the leaves at the top of trees. That monopoly among the leaf-eating species guaranteed them a continuing food supply.

Cumulative adaptation

Evolutionary arguments, however, emphasize **cumulative adaptation**. Giraffes were not designed with long necks, but gradually acquired them. It was a process involving many generations of giraffes. The evolutionary process consists of small steps that, over time, may make a large difference. Moreover, evolutionists argue that the cumulative effect of these changes over time amounts to adaptation of the species to its environment. It is a particular type of adaptation to its environment that allows the species to survive when in competition with other species. Giraffes survive because they occupy the 'niche' of 'high leaf eaters'. In that niche there is hardly any competition from other species.

Within the evolutionary perspective, there are several explanations that account for the process of cumulative adaptation. One explanation can be traced to Lamarck, another to Darwin.[1]

Lamarckian explanation

Inheritance of acquired characteristics

Principle of use and disuse

The **Lamarckian explanation** is based on two principles: the **inheritance of acquired characteristics** and the principle of use and disuse. The **principle of use and disuse** states that those parts of an organism's body that are used grow larger. Those parts that are not used tend to wither away. For individual giraffes, that principle translates into a lengthening of the neck due to continuous striving for higher leaves.

The second Lamarckian principle takes care of the intergenerational effect. Characteristics acquired by individuals can be inherited by future generations. The longer necks acquired by father and mother giraffes can be passed on to their offspring. Each generation thus ends up with a slightly longer neck than its predecessor and passes that feature on to the next generation. Such evolutionary advancement continues until giraffes can reach the highest leaves.

Darwinian explanation

Natural selection

The **Darwinian explanation**, emphasizes the role of cumulative **natural selection**. A Darwinist explains the giraffe's long neck as being the result of the cumulative selection, step by step, over many generations, of small mutations (or variations) in giraffe genes. Consider a stage in their development where giraffes had medium/long necks. They could reach halfway up the tallest trees. At that stage, all kinds of small mutations in the genes of that generation of giraffes would have occured. Only one or a few of those mutations would have caused longer necks. The giraffes that embodied that mutation had better survival chances in the environment (other things being equal) – they could reach just a bit higher for their food. Put differently, given competition for food resources, the environment will tend to select giraffes with longer necks. The reason is that the selected animals are better adapted to their environment. Over time, mutations that cause longer necks will be increasingly passed on in the gene pool of the giraffe species. Hence, while the individual mutation is a chance process, the cumulative selection is not. Over generations of giraffes, natural selection will favour the growth of necks and will cause a better adaptation of the species to its environment. Individual (chance) **variations**, natural **selection** as a result of environmental conditions and **retention**

Variation

Selection

Retention

(in the gene pool) of the adaptive characteristics thus form the causal chain of the Darwinist explanation. In Chapter 5 we already encountered this as the evolutionary mechanism (or genetic algorithm) at work in evolutionary game theory.

Why bother with giraffes in a book on organizations? The reason is that such a biological example serves as a useful analogy for contemplating possible explanations for the evolution of organizational forms. In the next section, we consider to what extent biological explanations can be transposed to the organizational field. To conclude this section it should be emphasized that, while the analogy is useful, there is no reason to expect that it is perfect. In biology, the Darwinist explanation appears to have the best scientific credentials (although not everyone is convinced – see Box 10.1),[2] but organizations are different beasts from the species examined by biologists. Perhaps creationist or Lamarckian arguments (or still other explanations) should carry greater weight in the organizational field. Indeed, we shall see that competing explanations currently run neck and neck.

Box 10.1 Darwin in Germany and the USA

Darwin published his evolution theory in *On the Origin of Species* in 1859. One of its implications is that humans descended from apes. That implication has been hard for people all over the world to accept, and some incredulity remains even today.

In spite of the theory of evolution set out by Charles Darwin nearly 150 years ago, one in five Germans remains unconvinced that humans descended from apes. At least, that was the finding of the Allensbach Institute for Opinion Research, which surveyed a test group of 1112 Germans in 1996. Of the group, 62 per cent said that they believed apes and humans shared common ancestors, while 21 per cent said that they did not believe this; 17 per cent did not know. Overall, however, the percentage of those believing in evolution is increasing. A similar survey in 1970 found that 40 per cent disagreed with Darwin.

Darwin has had a more difficult time being accepted in the USA. Figure 10.1 shows the percentages of Americans who believe in creationism (the top line), intelligent design (the middle line) and evolution (the bottom line).

Source: Holland Herald, August 1996.

10.3 Organizations and giraffes

First of all, let us repeat that we are now dealing with a different set of questions from those in the previous chapters. We are now interested in explanations of the development of organizational forms over time. Of course, we may take as a starting point the question why do we observe so many different organizational forms in the present?[3] The explanation of current forms will, however, necessarily involve arguments that address their development over time, if we are to regard them as dynamic or evolutionary.

Which of the following statements comes closest to your views on the origin and development of human beings – (human beings have developed over millions of years from less advanced forms of life, but God guided this process, human beings have developed over millions of years from less advanced forms of life, but God had no part in this process, (or) God created human beings pretty much in their present form at one time within the last 10,000 years or so)?

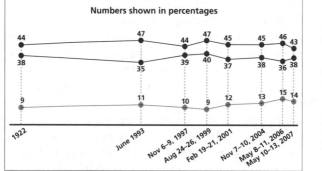

Figure 10.1 Percentages of Americans believing in creationism, intelligent design and evolution

Source: www.galluppoll.com (2007)

Second, the analysis now explicitly deals with populations of organizational forms (our equivalent of biological species). It is not the individual organization in which we are interested, but the class of similar organizational forms.

Third, the development of organizational forms is not analysed in isolation from the environments in which the organizations operate. Environmental selection plays a prominent role in both of the evolutionary approaches outlined in the following sections.

What use can we make of our biological analogies? What are some obvious differences and similarities between organizational forms and biological species? We briefly discuss one cluster of differences and one cluster of similarities.

Human constructs The differences relate to the fact that organizations are **human constructs**. To denote organizations as human constructs has two kinds of implication. The first is that organizations are created and constructed by human actors. Entrepreneurs create small firms, governments create their agencies, management teams regularly redesign organizations and human decisionmakers are similarly involved in the merger or discontinuance of organizations. Giraffes cannot (re)design themselves. Organizations are, to some extent at least, purposively created and designed. Of course, they often turn out differently from how they were originally intended – organizations can lead a life of their own, to continue the biological analogy – but the element of purposive human behaviour and rational construction is always there (Scott, 1992). That means creationist arguments, emphasizing purposive design, will probably play a greater role in the organizational field than they do in the biological one.

The second implication follows from the term 'construct'. Organizations are not only constructed in the real sense of deliberate design but are also constructs in the more philosophical sense that they are products of human mental activity. That can perhaps be best illustrated by means of the anecdote of the three baseball umpires being interviewed about how they call balls and strikes. They answered as follows.

- *The first:* I call them as they are.
- *The second:* I call them as I see them.
- *The third:* They are nothing until I call them.

The first umpire assumes that there are balls and strikes 'out there' and that he sorts them out correctly. The second acknowledges that there may be a difference between reality and his perception or judgement. The third shows that it is nothing but his judgement that makes them balls and strikes. The third is right, of course – in the sense that baseball rules dictate that it is only his judgement that counts. In philosophical terms, the first umpire is a realist, the third an idealist or constructionist. In the constructionist view, reality has to be constructed through human mental activity.

What about organizations and giraffes? Without delving too much into philosophical issues, it may be said that many organizational theorists would regard organizations as much more constructional in nature than giraffes. Consider the following questions.

- What do organizations/giraffes consist of?
- What are the boundaries of organizations/giraffes?

There is more room for differences in judgement about organizations than about giraffes. Organizations are much less 'out there': we have first to construct them in our minds before we find them. This delicate philosophical point has important consequences. One of those consequences is that it is harder to agree on the delineation of organizational forms than of biological species. Another consequence is that it is much less clear what exactly is being 'selected', 'reproduced' in the next generations and so on. There is room for choice and the choices made will depend partly on who makes them. The two approaches discussed later in this chapter also take different viewpoints here.

The cluster of similarities evolves from the recognition, first, that organizations, whatever they are, have environments and, second, that environments will play a role in explaining the development of organizational forms. In some of the previous chapters, we examined organizational phenomena without much reference to the environmental context. Agency relationships, for instance, are analysed rather 'context-free'. In transaction cost analysis, the environment is represented as two variables: uncertainty/complexity and small numbers exchange.

In industrial economics and strategy, the environment begins to play a more prominent and complex role. That role is extended in the present chapter. It is extended in two ways. First, we explicitly analyse the development of organizational forms rather than the development of individual firms (as in most of the strategy literature). Second, the concept of the environment is broader. It includes any dimension of the environment that may influence selection processes. Those dimensions are not only economic in nature, but may also be social, political, cultural or institutional. As we shall see, the concept of legitimacy of an organizational form is important in the next section. Thus, this chapter provides the most extensive illustration of the role of the environmental context – including environmental pressure and selection – in our conceptual framework, as introduced in Chapter 1 (see Section 1.7).

By using the biological analogy, our attention is directed towards *selection* processes rather than *adaptation* processes. Most organizational theory focuses on the adaptation of individual organizations to environmental circumstances and change. Yet, it cannot be denied that selection processes are important, too. There is such a thing as organizational mortality. Organizations go bankrupt, are abandoned by their members or cease to exist in other ways (such as due to prohibition). Organizational forms also have their lifecycles: new forms come into being (often as a result of new technology), old forms die. In many professions and industries, the medieval guilds gave way to more modern forms of organization. So, there is no question that selection, birth and death, replacement and other such phenomena are important objects of organizational study as well. The approaches to be outlined in the following sections illustrate the usefulness of the biological analogy.

10.4 Organizational ecology

Organizational ecology

The first approach is labelled *population ecology* or, more appropriately, **organizational ecology**. It has been elaborated by a relatively small number of authors over the past decade, foremost among whom are Michael T. Hannan and John Freeman.[4] In the exposition that follows, their work will feature most prominently.

Hannan and Freeman present their work as sociological, but, as will become clear, their approach uses economic concepts, such as competition, and is often likened to economic analysis.[5] We, too, believe that this approach intersects with economic analysis and can be fruitfully integrated with it (see Section 10.6). Hence, it is included in this overview of economic approaches to organizations.

Organizational ecology distinguishes between three levels of complexity of the analysis. The first level deals with the *demography* of organizations. At that level, various rates of change in organizational populations are the central interest. Foremost are founding rates and mortality rates.

The next level concerns the *population ecology* of organizations and attempts to link vital rates between populations. How are the founding and mortality rates of organizational populations interlinked?

The third level is the *community ecology* of organizations. At that level, the central question is how the links between and among populations affect the likelihood of persistence of the community as a whole.

It is fair to say that much of the work done so far concerns the first (demographic) level. Some studies are located at the second level – for instance, the studies comparing the survival rates of generalist and specialist restaurants in different environmental situations.[6] Hardly any studies could aspire to be located at the third level of analysis.

Ecological studies use data on individual organizations. Those data are used, however, to analyse developments at the population level. Ecologists are not so much interested in explaining the founding, growth, decline and death of individual organizations, but, rather, want to find out what the aggregate rates are at the population level. We therefore need a definition of populations and a procedure to separate one population of organizational forms from another.

For biologists, the main criterion for distinguishing populations of different species is interbreeding. A biological species is a collection of forms that can interbreed – that is, constitute a gene pool. No such operational definition exists for organizational analysis. An analogy of interbreeding is probably not very useful as we observe mergers and joint ventures between all sorts of firms in the real world. What should we do, for example, with conglomerate firms?

Theoretically, that is a difficult issue.[7] In practice, most ecological studies focus on populations that are readily acceptable as distinct, such as newspapers, restaurants and labour unions. As a working definition (adopted from Carroll and Hannan, 1995), we can say that an **organizational form** summarizes the core properties that make a set of organizations ecologically similar. Thus, organizations with the same form depend in a common way on the material and social environment. A set of organizations possesses the same form in that sense if environmental changes affect them similarly.

An **organizational population**, then, consists of the set of organizations with a specific form within a particular time and space. A public bureaucracy and an investment bank are examples of organizational forms. The set of public bureaucracies in Japan from 1946 to 1997 and the set of investment banks in the USA during the same period are examples of interesting organizational populations.

An important assumption in organizational ecology is that organizations are characterized by **relative inertia**. They are rather slow to respond to changes in their environment. It is not claimed that organizations never change; rather it is argued that, if radical change is required, organizations are hard pressed to implement it. Such changes are infrequent, subject to serious delays and often unsuccessful. Therefore, organizations tend to be inert, relative to changes in the environment. That is an important assumption as it separates organizational ecology from many other organizational approaches that emphasize adaptability. Below, we explore the assumptions that form the basis of organizational ecology and indicate how the assumption of relative inertia fits into that foundation.

Organizational form

Organizational population

Relative inertia

Box 10.2 Inertia and change: outsider versus insider CEOs

There is a large, anecdotal body of literature on 'heroic CEOs' who are appointed from outside a troubled company and subsequently have successfully turned their new companies around and transformed them. Indeed, sometimes that appears to be the case, as Lou Gerstner showed at IBM.

There is, however, relatively little systematic evidence that such outsider appointments and 'heroic CEOs' are in actual fact generally effective. Research by Jim Collins points towards other conclusions, including slow change and relative inertia, as summarized in *The Financial Times* as follows:

> Research by Jim Collins, formerly of Stanford Business School, found turnarounds were usually the work of insiders. In his book *Good to Great*, Mr Collins identified 11 US companies that, after 15 years of underperformance, had produced shareholder returns at least three times the market average over the next 15 years. Of the 11 chief executives responsible, 10 came from inside the company.
>
> Most of these turnaround bosses were people we have never heard of: Darwin Smith of Kimberley-Clark, for example, and Jim Herring of Kroger, the US retailer.
>
> The source of their success was not the advice of outsiders but an instinctive feel for and deep knowledge of their companies and industries.
>
> Organisations are difficult to budge. Most people resist change. Sacking their colleagues may frighten them into working harder but will not win their enthusiasm or commitment. Producing improved performance comes from a detailed knowledge of the market and a feel for the company's culture. It also comes from knowing who in the organisation wields influence.
>
> Mr Collins' chief executives often changed their companies substantially but they took their time thinking about it. 'We're a crawl, walk, run company', said one. Stories of heroic action and speedy deliverance appeal to something deep within us. We should not always believe them.

Source: Michael Skapinker, 'Slowly does it', *The Financial Times*, 27 March 2002, p.11; Collins (2001). See also, Collins and Porras (1994) and Gerstner (2002).

Why *are* organizations assumed to be inert? In most of the approaches discussed so far, efficiency arguments are used. Efficiency drives organizations to change or else they are replaced by more efficient organizations. Hannan and Freeman take a different route. They argue that organizations have different

Reliability competences. The first of these is **reliability**. Theoretically, organizational products and services could often be produced just as well by ad hoc groups of skilled workers. Compared with such ad hoc groups, however, organizations will tend to produce more reliably – that is, they will do so with less variance in the quality of performance, including its timeliness. Given uncertainty about the future, the potential members, investors and clients might value reliability more than efficiency. That is, they may be willing to pay a relatively high price for the certainty that a product or service of a minimum quality will be available when needed. Therefore, they transact with organizations.

Routines Within organizations, **routines** develop that direct the activities. Such routines can be retained within organizations, but not in ad hoc groups of varying composition. The routines play an important role in ensuring the reliability of performance.[8] To empathize with that argument, imagine yourself as a businessperson travelling to an unfamiliar country and needing a rented car. Would you book your car with an international chain (such as Avis or Hertz) or with a local individual who has dropped a leaflet through the letterbox? Indeed, international hotel chains, car rental agencies and financial services may thrive more as a result of our need for reliable services than as a result of their being the low-cost alternative in any specific case.[9]

Accountability Organizations are not only more reliable than ad hoc groups but they can also be held accountable more easily. **Accountability** is an important property in the modern world. Sociologists argue that norms of (procedural) rationality are pervasive. Decisions and actions must be explained in rational terms. For instance, investors expect reasonable and consistent accounts of the allocation of resources. The profession of accountants arose in response to such desires. Employees demand rational explanations for hiring and firing practices and will evaluate those explanations against widely held social standards (such as equal opportunities legislation). Consumers demand rational justifications of product performance. This can be seen most clearly in the case of litigation. If taken to court regarding product liability, producers must be able to argue their case convincingly based on full documentation of their procedures, decisions and actions.

Hannan and Freeman argue that organizations can produce such rational accounts of their decisions and actions more readily than can ad hoc groups. An important factor is the existence of appropriate rules and procedures within organizations. Just like the production routines, such rules and procedures are also more easily developed and retained within organizations than within other collectives (such as ad hoc groups). The plethora of information that they collect and file means that they can document how resources have been used and reconstruct the sequences of decisions, rules and actions that produced an outcome. In a world that increasingly demands procedural rationality, such accountability gives organizations an advantage over ad hoc groups.

Hannan and Freeman (1989a, p. 74) summarize the present stage of the argument as follows:

> The modern world favors collective actors that can demonstrate or at least reasonably claim a capacity for reliable performance and can account rationally for their actions. So it favors organizations over other kinds of collectives and favors certain kinds of organizations over others, since not all organizations have these properties in equal measure. Selection within organizational populations tends to eliminate organizations with low reliability and accountability ... Thus we assume that selection in populations of organizations in modern societies favors forms with high reliability of performance and high levels of accountability.

From this summary to the conclusion that organizations exhibit high levels of inertia requires one more step. That step is the recognition that organizational reliability and accountability require that organizational structures are highly

Reproducible

reproducible. The routines, rules and procedures that determine reliability and accountability must stay in place. The organizational structure – the structure of roles, authority and communication – must therefore be very much the same today as it was yesterday. That is to say, it must be reproducible from day to day. Indeed, it will be (very nearly) reproduced from day to day to ensure reliability and accountability. As one executive of a large financial services company put it (Box 10.3), that requires a tight organization.

Box 10.3 Reproducibility in the ING Group

The ING Group is a large banking and insurance group with its roots in the Netherlands. It was one of the first corporations to combine banking and insurance (*bancassurance*) in one group on a large scale. It globally employs more than 100,000 people. It is well known for its Internet daughter ING Direct. Below are excerpts from an interview with one of its former board members, Alexander Rinnooy Kan:

> Our activities are characterized by very high process requirements in terms of reproducibility and documentation. That is true globally, across all distribution channels and across the full range of financial products. Regulatory bodies also require this, both on the banking and on the insurance side. Those tight process requirements are a necessary condition to be active in this sector. They are not easily compatible with an environment that is primarily focused on creativity, flexibility, and improvization. In the financial world, today's whim is not tomorrow's product.
>
> We may not lose sight of which products the ING Group offers. Concepts such as trust, predictability and solidity are crucial. Particularly in the current hectic environment, people need dependability of financial services. Look what happens when electronic banking [*initially*[10]] turns out to be less reliable than everybody thought. We therefore have the task to retain that trust, also in times of turbulent change. It is an important part of the value we can add. That is only possible by meticulously safeguarding the quality of all processes enabling our services. This requires a tight organization.

Source: Management Scope, October 2000 (translated by authors)

Selection pressures will work in this direction. The conclusion that organizational structures will be (very nearly) reproduced is equivalent to saying that they will be (relatively) highly *inert*. Selection pressures will thus favour organizations that have structures with high inertia. Structural inertia, according to Hannan and Freeman's argument, is a *consequence* of selection rather than a precondition.

The preceding argument can be represented diagrammatically to show the interrelationships between the various basic assumptions (Figure 10.2).

We shall not attempt to spell out the entire theoretical structure that is built on these basic assumptions of organizational ecology. Rather, we shall move on to some of the more solid empirical results. They apply to the founding and death rates within organizational populations. Specifically, the ecological perspective has convincingly shown that these vital rates are dependent on the

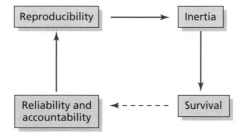

Figure 10.2 Interrelationships between the four basic assumptions
Source: derived from Young (1988)

density of the population. Below, we first focus on the theoretical reasoning underlying the empirical work, then summarize some results.

What determines the size of an organizational population? In other words, how many individual organizations do we expect to find within a certain population? The answer depends on various factors. First of all, we have to know in what environmental **niche** the population resides. A niche expresses the population's way of earning a living, its role and function in a community.[11] The niche is assumed to have a particular **carrying capacity**. There are social and material limits to the extent to which we need particular roles and functions to be performed in society. There is only so much 'written news' that we can absorb, for instance. As a consequence, the environment will allow only a certain volume of newspapers. That volume can, however, be filled by a few large newspapers or many small ones. Thus, the carrying capacity of an environmental niche only represents an upper bound on the aggregate levels of activity performed by a certain organizational form.

The actual number of organizations inhabiting a certain niche will then depend on the founding rate, mortality rate and merger rates over time. Assume, for instance, we observe a particular population that remains constant in number over a certain period of time (Figure 10.3). How can that phenomenon be explained? If we were dealing with biological populations, there would be two answers:

■ over that period of time, the population consisted of exactly the same individuals; or
■ the birth rate equalled the death rate.

For organizational populations, the second explanation would remain valid in the absence of mergers. Otherwise, it should be amended to read:

■ the birth rate equalled the death rate + merger rate.

In addition, the interpretation of the term 'birth rate' has to be slightly changed for organizations. It includes not only new foundings but also migrations of organizations into the population. Animals cannot change population, but organizations can. For example, the 3M Corporation was originally called the Minnesota Mining and Manufacturing Company. Whereas

Niche

Carrying capacity

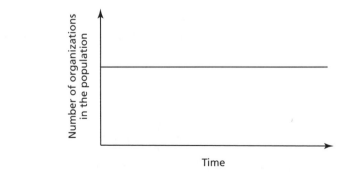

Figure 10.3 A hypothetical population over time

mining was its initial activity, now it is strong in the bonding and coating business. By changing its major activities, it can be said to have migrated to a new population.

How do *actual* organizational populations develop over time? Hannan and Freeman argue that two forces mainly account for actual developments: *competition* and *legitimation*. These two forces will both affect the **density of the population** (the number of organizations in the population), but they have opposite effects. The force of **competition** is, of course, familiar to economists. If resources within the niche are scarce, there will be competition within the population for those resources. Moreover, there may be competition between populations. Think of the competition between all sorts of shops for the best locations in shopping areas.

The force of **legitimation** is less familiar to economists; it is a sociological concept. Essentially, it refers to the social 'acceptance' of the organizational form. New forms have low legitimacy. As they perform reliably and accountably over time, they may acquire greater legitimacy. However, if they do not conform to social norms over time, they may not acquire the legitimacy that is necessary for them to survive.

Roughly, organizational ecology assumes that both legitimacy and competition increase with the age of the organizational form. As stated above, a new form has low legitimacy. It has to acquire it over time. As the form acquires legitimacy, it becomes easier to found organizations of that form. In addition to increasing legitimacy, a variety of other factors may contribute to the self-reinforcement (or positive feedback) of the early growth of an industry.[12] Those factors include changes in consumer tastes and habits, the development of markets, collective gains in efficiency from learning-by-doing and the emergence of supporting institutions. Hence, we expect the founding rates to increase, with the age of the form (at least initially), but competition will increase too. As more organizations come to inhabit the niche, competition within the population will increase. Competition will have a negative effect on founding rates. It will be harder to found a new organization or migrate into a more competitive environment.

In the language of organizational ecology, the vital rates of an organizational population – the rates of founding and mortality – show **density dependence**. Legitimacy processes produce positive density dependence in *founding rates* and competition produces negative density dependence. Using similar reasoning, it is assumed that the *mortality rate* is high at first (owing to insufficient legitimacy, there is a **liability of newness**), then falls with increasing density up to a point (the neighbourhood of the carrying capacity) and then rises with increasing density (owing to competitive effects). All in all, then, organizational ecology expects:

- the relationship between density and mortality rates to have a U-shape;
- the relationship between density and founding rates to have an inverted U-shape.

The empirical work that has been done to date has largely borne out these expectations (see Carroll and Hannan, 1995). The observed densities of organizational

Density of the population

Competition

Legitimation

Density dependence

Liability of newness

populations produce a figure like Figure 10.4. While it charts the number of newspapers in the San Francisco Bay area, such graphs have been produced for other newspaper populations, unions and restaurants, for example. The organizational ecology approach has given us empirical insight into the density dependence of founding and mortality rates. It has, therefore, also given us an approximation of 'typical' developments of populations over time. The results are encouraging.[13] In the following sections they are compared with another evolutionary approach, developed by the economists Nelson and Winter.

10.5 An evolutionary theory of economic change

In their book *An Evolutionary Theory of Economic Change* (1982), the economists Richard Nelson and Sidney Winter outline another evolutionary perspective. That perspective shares a number of features with organizational ecology, including:

■ an emphasis on organizational routines and limits to organizational adaptability;
■ the population or system level of analysis;
■ the importance of environmental selection.

Nelson and Winter's theory is different from Hannan and Freeman's in several respects as well. One important difference is that Nelson and Winter attempt to provide an alternative to what they label orthodox economic theory. By that they mean standard micro- and macroeconomic theory and, specifically, the standard concepts of maximizing behaviour by firms and equilibrium out-

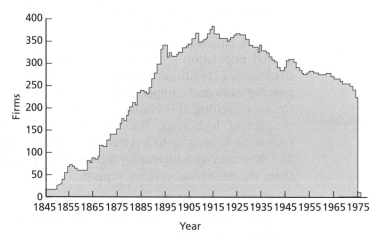

Figure 10.4 Density of newspaper publishing firms by year (1845–1975) in the San Francisco Bay area

Source: Hannan and Freeman (1989a, p. 239)

comes in markets. Instead, their alternative view stresses *routine* behaviour by firms and *development* of economic systems.

Nelson and Winter provide an alternative 'microfoundation' of macroeconomics. Their models show, for instance, the effects of technological change on macroeconomic growth. In this section we concentrate on the main features of their microfoundation: their modelling of firm behaviour and the selection process. That allows us to compare the two evolutionary approaches in Section 10.6.

Nelson and Winter conceive of organizations as being typically much better at the tasks of self-maintenance in a constant environment than they are at major change and also much better at changing in the direction of 'more of the same' than they are at any other kind of change. Their primary concept to

Routines

denote organizational functioning is routines. **Routines** refer to all regular and predictable behaviour patterns of firms. There are production routines, advertising routines, hiring and firing routines and strategic routines. Routines rather than deliberate choice determine, in large part, how an organization functions. They explain why organizations are resistant to change. They are the organizational analogue of biological genes. In 'organizational genetics', routines are selected by the environment. Let us examine how these ideas are introduced and developed.

Organizational routines may be understood by comparison to individual

Skills

skills, such as riding a bicycle, playing tennis or operating a computer. Such skills have two features in common. First, they require exercise. It is not enough to read how to ride a bike, it must be practised; learning-by-doing is involved. At the outset, the learning is very conscious – every detail of the performance is observed. During practice, however, the conscious attention to the performance is gradually transformed into a behaviour programme. Riding a bike becomes a capability that can be exercised automatically. Individual skills, such as organizational routines, can be usefully regarded as such automatic behaviour programmes.

Second, it is ordinarily very difficult to fully articulate the programme. It is, for example, impossible for most people to express fully in words how to ride

Tacit knowledge

a bike. There is **tacit knowledge** involved – a concept introduced in Section 9.6 (see also Box 10.4). Similarly, it is often impossible in organizations to explain fully particular behaviour programmes, such as the selection of job candidates. Skills and routines share this tacit component, which may vary in importance. Skills such as computer operation and routines such as production schedules can probably be articulated more fully than the examples given above. However, such articulation is often not necessary for correct execution, is difficult to reproduce when called for and is almost never complete.

Box 10.4 Tacit knowledge

Michael Polanyi (1962, 1967) developed the concept of 'tacit knowledge'. The importance of tacit knowledge is nowadays widely recognized, as can be seen from the following excerpt from the magazine published by the consultancy company Arthur D. Little:

▶

When Banc One decided to grow through acquisitions, its learning challenge was at the *process* level: how to create a particularly effective process for making many successful acquisitions – identifying, acquiring, and integrating companies that would be a good strategic, operational, and cultural fit.

When Mercedes-Benz opened a new factory to produce its cars in India, the Indian organization needed to learn at the *procedures* level: to acquire and use explicit knowledge from Mercedes to produce Mercedes cars.

The distinction between process and procedure is essential. Procedures contain only *explicit* knowledge. Processes embed procedures in *tacit* knowledge of both the expert and the social kinds. Many of the problems of re-engineering can be traced to the treatment of processes as though they were procedures – i.e. as though people's tacit knowledge didn't matter.

Source: Nayak et al. (1995)

Organizational routines

Organizational routines are thus the analogue of individual skills. In executing those automatic behaviour programmes, choice is suppressed. When riding a bike, we normally do not consider all the choice options when we approach a red light. Instead, we automatically slow down and come to a halt, if necessary. Similarly, many behaviours in organizations are evoked automatically. The clock tells people when it is time for lunch or the weekly meeting. The calendar marks the date for closing budgets. One activity automatically leads to the next, as when a person reacts to mail in their inbox, or products reach the next stage in the assembly line. Responses to external signals can be nearly automatic, such as the prescription to match price cuts by the competition. Numerous examples can be added. In all cases, behaviour is governed largely by routine-like programmes and the role of deliberate choice is much less pronounced than 'orthodox' economic theory would have it.

Routines thus abound in organizational life. Before categorizing organizational routines, it is useful to point out two other aspects. One is that routines

Organizational memories

serve as **organizational memories**. Organizations remember largely by doing, according to Nelson and Winter. Routines that are not used for some time wither away. The organization loses the capability to perform such routines. Individuals lose the required skills to perform the routines and play the organizational role required of them. Routine-like coordination is disturbed. Memories are further endangered when there is individual turnover. Turnover is one cause of mutations in routines, as we observe later.

Organizational truce

The second aspect is that routines also serve as an **organizational truce**. By this metaphor, Nelson and Winter refer to the behavioural foundations of their concept of organizations (see Chapter 6). Satisficing takes the place of maximizing and the existence of organizational conflict is not assumed away. Routines may be seen as a stabilizing force in organizations: in that sense they represent a truce in intraorganizational conflict. Changes in routines will upset existing political balances (Nelson and Winter, 1982, pp. 111–12):

> The result may be that the routines of the organization as a whole are confined to extremely narrow channels by the dikes of vested interest . . . fear of breaking the truce is, in general, a powerful force tending to hold organizations on the path of relatively inflexible routine.

Three broad classes of organizational routines can be distinguished:

- *operating characteristics*, which relate to what a firm does at any time, given its prevailing stock of plant, equipment and other factors of production that are not readily augmented in the short run;
- the predictable patterns in the period-by-period changes in the firm's *capital stock* (those factors of production that are fixed in the short run);
- routines that operate to *modify over time* various aspects of the firm's operating characteristics.

The last category represents 'higher-order' routines that may act occasionally to modify lower-order ones. Thus, it may be customary in a firm to review the R&D policy from time to time or change advertising agencies or make a competitive analysis. Nelson and Winter argue that such 'strategic' behaviours are often also subject to quite stringent rules within a firm. Thus, the routine-changing processes are themselves routine-guided (or guided by dynamic capabilities, as Sections 9.6 and 10.7 argue). In Nelson and Winter's terminology, organizational search is itself routine-like.[14] It may lead to mutations in organizational routines. Just as in biological species the genetic make-up partly determines the potential mutations, so the routine make-up of firms partly determines the outcomes of their search.

Mutations of organizational routines can thus come about by chance or as a result of deliberation. An example of a chance process is the turnover of individuals in the firm. A deliberate mutation may result from organizational search. Deliberate mutations will, however, first be sought in the neighbourhood of existing routines. In that respect, Nelson and Winter again use ideas from the behavioural school ('local search', see Chapter 6). Whatever change takes place, it is expected to follow the path of least resistance. Staying close to prevailing routines minimizes the disturbance of the organizational truce. Moreover, it enhances the probability of success as firms will be able to draw largely on the (tacit) knowledge and experiences they have collected.

Environmental selection will favour successful routines. For firms, that translates into higher profit levels. If an existing routine is a success, replication of that success is likely to be desired. The point emphasized by evolutionary theory is that, when a firm is already successful in a given activity, it is a particularly good candidate for being successful if it attempts to apply its routine on a larger scale. From one period to another, that implies successful routines will be increasingly incorporated in the 'routine pool' of the particular industry concerned (Nelson and Winter, 1982, p. 19):

> Search and selection are simultaneous, interacting aspects of the evolutionary process: the same prices that provide selection feedback also influence the directions of search. Through the joint action of search and selection, the firms evolve over time, with the condition of the industry in each period bearing the seeds of its condition in the following period.

In their models, the distribution of routines is carried over from one period to the next by means of a stochastic (Markov) process. While the technicalities of such modelling do not interest us here, the basic idea is clear. It is the basic idea of all evolutionary approaches: *variations* (or mutations) of routines, environmental *selection* (according to the value of the routine for the survival chances of the firms in the population) and cumulative *retention* of successful routines.

The original contribution by Nelson and Winter has given rise to a growing body of economic literature employing such evolutionary approaches. Surveying that literature, Nelson (1991) remarked, the common element is a focus on firm-specific dynamic capabilities. Comparing *An Evolutionary Theory of Economic Change* (1982) with the current state of the literature, Nelson observed that, 'with the vision of hindsight, it is clear that our writing then was handicapped by insufficient study of the writings of Chandler, particularly his *Strategy and Structure* [1966]'.

He went on to point out that there are 'three different if strongly related features of a firm that must be recognized if one is to describe it adequately: its strategy, its structure, and its core capabilities'. The evolving insights into those three features together constitute an 'emerging theory of dynamic firm capabilities'. In that theory, the concept of *strategy* connotes a broad set of commitments made by a firm that define and rationalize its objectives and how it intends to pursue them. Some of the strategy may be formalized and written down, but some may also reside in the organizational culture and the management repertoire. Strategy tends to define a desired firm structure in a general way, but not in its details. *Structure* involves the way a firm is organized and governed and the way decisions are actually made and carried out. Thus, the organization's structure largely determines what it does, given the broad strategy. Changes in strategy may require changes in structure, but the latter are difficult to carry out. The reason is that structure involves not only the organization chart but also, much more basically, the routines governing the operating-level decisions. Changing them is time-consuming and costly, so it is a major task to get the new structure into shape and operating smoothly.

The reason for contemplating a change in the organization's structure is to change, possibly augment, the things that a firm is capable of doing well: its **core capabilities**. Strategy and structure call forth and mould organizational capabilities, but what an organization can do well also has something of a life of its own. Nelson and Winter (1982) had already proposed that firms working well can be understood in terms of a hierarchy of practised organizational routines that define lower-order organizational skills and how those are coordinated as well as higher-order decisionmaking procedures for choosing what is to be done at lower levels. This notion of a **hierarchy of organizational routines** is the key building block of Nelson and Winter's concept of core organizational capabilities (see, further, Section 10.7 for how this line of thinking was further developed in the literature on dynamic capabilities).

This summary of the developments in the evolutionary approaches in the economic literature illustrates how influential this line of thought has been. While most people would, for instance, believe that the concept of core capabilities or core competences was developed by Prahalad and Hamel and popularized by them in their very successful book *Competing for the Future*

Core capabilities

Hierarchy of organizational routines

(1994), in fact, the origins of this line of thought can be traced much further back. Similarly, just as the organizational ecologists provided a fresh, dynamic approach to the organizational literature, so the evolutionary economists have provided a healthy antidote to too much (comparative) static and equilibrium thinking in economics.

In conclusion, we therefore want to summarize the basic process of economic change that is incorporated in Nelson and Winter's models. That change starts with firms characterized with behaviourist notions. They satisfice rather than maximize, they would rather not upset intraorganizational balances and, if they have to change, they search locally for solutions (that is to say, they start searching as near to their current routines as possible). That search is modelled probabilistically, by assuming that the probability of finding a superior technique – by innovation or imitation – is a function of the amount invested in the search. The search may be induced by adverse conditions or may itself be a routine – firms often have routinized R&D and strategic planning.

Selection by market forces will favour firms that happen to find better techniques or to use better search rules than the others. Their features – the techniques or search rules that make them successful – will spread in the population of firms, partly by expansion and partly by imitation. In that process, however, new mutations of routines will be generated. Replication of routines by successful firms will often already be less than perfect, imitation by other firms probably involves a higher mutation rate and innovation will occur.

Innovation is modelled by Nelson and Winter as a routinized activity, consisting in a large part, of new combinations of existing routines[15] (but discontinuous, radical innovation is not excluded). Through all these sources, the economic system is continually injected with new mutations of routines. It is thus in continuous flux, so equilibrium will be the exception rather than the rule. The changing economic system, however, constitutes an evolving environment for firms and routines, with corresponding change in selection pressures over time. New routines impact the economic system and the economic system impacts the selection of (old and new) routines. In Section 5.6, we introduced the concept of **coevolution** to denote this feature of Nelson and Winter's approach.

Coevolution

10.6 Comparison

As a starting point for a comparison of the two evolutionary approaches, let us return to the introductory comments we made on the biological strands of arguments. We distinguished between evolutionary and creationist arguments and, within the evolutionary branch, between Darwinism and Lamarckianism. How do the approaches discussed in this chapter relate to those distinctions? The answer is quite straightforward: Hannan and Freeman's perspective is Darwinistic, while Nelson and Winter's is Lamarckian. (We would add that both leave room for creationist arguments to play a role.)

Nelson and Winter (1982, p. 11) classify themselves as follows:

It is neither difficult nor implausible to develop models of firm behavior that interweave 'blind' and 'deliberate' processes. Indeed, in human problem solving itself, both elements are involved and difficult to disentangle. Relatedly, our theory is unabashedly Lamarckian: it contemplates both the 'inheritance' of acquired characteristics and the timely appearance of variation under the stimulus of adversity.

Hannan and Freeman (1989a, pp. 20–2) take the following position:[20]

> our work approximates a Malthusian–Darwinian position on the nature of change in organizational populations over time. We think that the current diversity of organizational forms reflects the cumulative effect of a long history of variation and selection, including the consequences of founding processes, mortality processes, and merger processes ... The line of theory we develop builds on the assumption that change in core features of organizational populations is more Darwinian than Lamarckian. It argues that inertial pressures prevent most organizations from radically changing strategies and structures.

Both approaches leave room for not only organizational members to make rational plans for change but also the possibility that organizations may be founded with a rational design. In the latter sense, they both allow creationist elements. They further agree that organizations show intrinsic rigidities that hamper change. Finally, both view organizational adaptability not as an all-or-nothing proposition, but in relation to environmental change. That said, Hannan and Freeman subsequently argue that the original organizational 'imprint' will, essentially, remain intact. Inertial pressures will prevent major change and cause a major gap between individual intentions for change and organizational (inertial) outcomes (see Box 10.5). Ecologists generally regard successful adaptation as unlikely for two reasons (Carroll and Hannan, 1995). First, organizations frequently cannot make good forecasts about future states of the environment. Second, it is uncertain whether or not designed organizational adaptations will have their intended effects (if not, the cure may be worse than the disease).

The ecologists' position, therefore, in essence, states that adaptation is random with respect to the future.[16] Nelson and Winter, on the other hand, allow for more learning, imitation and conscious adaptation through search. However, they also argue that prevailing routines will seriously constrain such processes and organizations are therefore much less adaptable than other organizational theories would have it. We will return to this important issue of relative inertia versus relative adaptability in the concluding section of this chapter (as well as in the next chapter).

Box 10.5 Changing Auntie

The launch of digital broadcasting services in Britain by Rupert Murdoch's BskyB was expected to boost the number of TV channels from 30 to 200 plus in 1997. As a result the BBC's forecasts showed that audience share for the four traditional channels – BBC 1, BBC 2, ITV and Channel 4 –

could have fallen from 90 per cent to 65 per cent within 10 years. That led the BBC's director-general to propose a major reorganization:

> It's a tricky business trying to change 'Auntie'. That's the nickname for the 74-year-old British Broadcasting Corp., and it rightly conveys the affection most British have for the publicly funded broadcaster. John Birt, director-general of the BBC, discovered in June how quickly the public would rush to Auntie's aid when he announced dramatic plans to merge the TV and radio operations – including the revered World Service. A roar of protest arose from BBC reporters, ordinary viewers, and government officials, all fearful that the BBC's standards would be hopelessly compromised. One Member of Parliament denounced Birt for acting like some tyrannical czar.

Source: *Business Week*, 12 August 1996, p. 25

Care should be taken to not overemphasize the biological analogy. In both approaches, the authors are very explicit about that. Nelson and Winter (1982, p. 11) state:

> We are pleased to exploit any idea from biology that seems helpful in the understanding of economic problems, but we are equally prepared to pass over anything that seems awkward, or to modify accepted biological theories radically in the interest of getting better *economic* theory.

Hannan and Freeman (1989b, p. 428) explain things in much the same manner:

> we did not seek to use biological theory to explain organizational change. Nor did we propose to develop metaphors between biotic populations and organizational populations ... We relied on models from population ecology because these models appeared to clarify the social processes of interest ... We have adapted ecological models to sociological uses and have changed them in the process.
>
> Therefore, it is inappropriate to judge these approaches on the basis of the (too) simple question, What does biology have to say about organizational or economic phenomena? The appropriate question is indeed whether the imported and adapted ideas contribute to our understanding of these phenomena. To this latter question we would suggest an affirmative answer.

We indicated earlier the main similarities between the two approaches, namely, first, the emphasis on organizational routines and limits to organizational adaptability, second, the population or system level of analysis and, third, the importance of environmental selection. It is now useful perhaps to point out some differences.

One major difference concerns the question of what it is that is selected by the environment. In organizational ecology, it is the 'organizational form'. Although a precise definition of organizational forms is lacking, it is clear that forms are collections of core properties of organizations. It is the entire collection of properties of, say, newspapers or labour unions that is selected.[17] In contrast, Nelson and Winter propose that specific characteristics of organizations (particular routines) are selected: theirs is a 'routines as genes' approach (Winter, 1990).[18] Owing to their Lamarckian perspective, those specific characteristics may change, while the form remains intact in other respects. Furthermore, their approach allows the possibility that particular competences are 'inherited' by other organizations – by acquisition or sharing in an alliance, for example.[19]

A second major difference is closely related to the first. It is the observation that Nelson and Winter have more to say about intraorganizational processes. Both approaches are interested in phenomena at the population level, but only Nelson and Winter provide a microfoundation for changes at the population level. They explicitly incorporate a number of behavioural features into their models of organizations. As a result, we have an idea of the forces at the micro level that contribute to stability and change. In comparison, the organization is a relatively empty box in organizational ecology. The emphasis there is more on the external demands on organizations (demands of reliability and reproducibility) than on internal processes. Organizational ecology has relatively little to say about what goes on *inside* organizations.

A third and final difference pertains to the description of organizations and their relative success. Organizational ecology generally treats all organizations in a particular population as alike: it relies heavily on counting numbers of organizations. This research strategy tends to disregard differences between the members of that population. Evolutionary economics, however, accords particular significance to the organizations' size and their success. The two are, of course, interrelated: successful organizations are assumed to grow. The economic approaches tend to focus on the *firm* as the particular subject of interest. Hence, they can model success with a profit measure and capital accumulation. Organizational ecology, however, aspires to be a more general organization theory and empirically examines non-firm types of organization as well, such as labour unions. That makes a general approach to the modelling of success much more difficult.

10.7 The evolution of dynamic capabilities

In the preceding section, we introduced the seminal work of Nelson and Winter, as incorporated in their book *An Evolutionary Theory of Economic Change* (1982). In that context, we noted Nelson's remark in 1991 that a 'theory of dynamic firm capabilities' was emerging. Indeed, in Section 9.6 we introduced you to the concept of dynamic capabilities as an extension of the resource-based view (RBV) of the firm. As mentioned at the end of that section, we concentrated in the previous chapter on the internal organizational context of dynamic capabilities. We had to refrain there from introducing the external context, notably environmental (competitive) selection, until we had the chance to introduce environmental selection more generally in this chapter. We can now proceed to adding the external context. More specifically, we will focus in this section on the question of environmental selection of *valuable* dynamic capabilities of firms.

Dynamic capabilities

Recall first that **dynamic capabilities** have been defined as 'the capacity of an organization to purposefully create, extend or modify its resource base'.

Operational capabilities

They are geared towards change in an organization's resource base. This aspect distinguishes dynamic capabilities from **operational capabilities**, which pertain to the *current* operations of an organization. How does the concept of capabilities compare with Nelson and Winter's original concept of organizational routines?

Some of the main similarities and differences are as follows.

- Both routines and capabilities only continue to exist if practised. They are remembered by doing. If not practised, a routine or capability withers away. Consider a research capability – in semiconductor development, for instance. If Intel would consider halting R&D for several years, it would seriously erode the firm's competitiveness. Such capabilities are subject to the adage 'use it or lose it'. In that sense, both Nelson and Winter's routines and the concept of dynamic capabilities are decidedly Lamarckian: they are acquired characteristics, that need to be maintained by active use.

- Both routines and dynamic capabilities generate 'patterned activity'. When confronted with a problem, there is a 'normal way' to seek the solution. They do not start from scratch or engage in ad hoc problem solving (see Winter, 2003). Rather, they start from 'the way we do things around here'. For example, some firms have developed their own 'best practices' for integrating acquisitions. When making a new acquisition, the assumption will be that the best practice will be applied, perhaps with some variation to allow for the particularities of the new acquisition. In Chapter 12, on mergers and acquisitions, we will refer to evidence that firms making acquisitions quite often (serial acquirers), have a higher acquisition success rate. Part of the explanation may be that they have developed well-honed acquisition routines or dynamic capabilities.

- As noted by Nelson (1991; see also Section 10.5), with hindsight he would have liked to link the concept of organizational routines more closely to Chandler's work *Strategy and Structure*. It is fair to say that the concept of dynamic capabilities is more closely linked to the strategy literature, in particular the resource-based view (RBV). Therefore, we already introduced the concept in Section 9.6 as a further development within RBV. We will now proceed to elaborate on the environmental context and, particularly, the selection of dynamic capabilities in the remainder of this section. Thus, the concept of dynamic capabilities serves as a link, connecting evolutionary theory with strategic management.

- The reason that dynamic capabilities can serve as such a link is that they emphasize more the necessity of strategic management of the firm. While routines can also involve deliberate choice, it is much less pronounced. The literature on dynamic capabilities seeks to explicitly ground this concept in a view on the strategic management of organizations (Helfat et al., 2007, pp. 20–1):

executive management performs several distinctive and important roles, which help the economic system overcome special problems, problems that might otherwise result in 'market failures'. That is, but for the actions of astute managers, competitive markets wouldn't function very well. Moreover, business organizations couldn't function either. Seven particular classes of economic functions can be assigned in economic theory to management. They are: 1) orchestrating co-specialized assets; 2) selecting organizational/governance modes and associated incentive systems; 3) designing business models; 4) nurturing change (and innovation) processes/routines; 5) making investment choices; 6) providing leadership, vision, and motivation to employees; and 7) designing and implementing controls and basic operations ... Managers are needed to make markets work well, and to make organizations function properly.

■ Nelson and Winter introduced the notion of a *hierarchy of organization routines*, which was already the basis for core capabilities thinking. The distinction between dynamic and operational capabilities can be regarded as a further elaboration on this approach. Operational capabilities are the basis of a firm's ability to survive and compete in present circumstances. Dynamic capabilities provide the (higher-order) capacity for change by purposefully altering the organization's resource base. The linkage to the RBV enables the concept of dynamic capabilities to be much more specific in terms of the reasons for some changes enhancing competitive advantage and other changes not. In Section 9.6 we examined specific factors and circumstances that contribute towards dynamic capabilities being valuable, rare and/or inimitable. If resources and capabilities are co-specialized and configured well, that may contribute to their value. If they are (partly) dependent on tacit knowledge, firm-specific and surrounded by isolating mechanisms, that makes them rarer and more difficult to replicate. Potentially, such features help dynamic capabilities to meet the requirements of Barney's VRIN-framework to generate sustainable competitive advantage. If, on the other hand, dynamic capabilities can be easily bought and sold in the market or simply imitated, they will most likely not contribute much to sustainable competitive advantage. Best practices that can be acquired from consultancy firms, for example (such as state-of-the-art IT systems), will spread rapidly through the population of competing firms if they contribute to competitive advantage. Such advantages will be short-lived, however, as they will be eroded by rapid imitation. A firm with a unique innovation culture (such as Apple), though, that attracts unusually talented people and is able to protect its innovations by patents, will likely maintain its competitive advantage for a significantly longer period of time.

So far, we have compared the notion of dynamic capabilities with Nelson and Winter's original concept of organizational routines. We hope to have shown, first, that it is more firmly embedded in a strategic management view of the firm and, second, provides a better basis for understanding the potential basis for competitive advantage than their original concept. However, competitive advantage is necessarily an externally orientated concept: it has to be gained in the external competitive environment. In the language of the present chapter, environmental selection will ultimately determine which dynamic capabilities are valuable in the external context (and, hence, can provide a sustainable competitive advantage). Therefore, we now turn to the environment to examine how the external selection of dynamic capabilities that do or do not contribute to competitive advantage, takes place.

Consider the evolution of Dell, as summarized in Box 10.6. Michael Dell created a company in 1984 that succeeded to become the market leader in the USA 15 years later and the worldwide leader soon thereafter. That success was due to an innovative business model offering personal computers for an unprecedented low cost.

In terms of our discussion so far, Dell was initially successful in building up the *operational capabilities* of his firm to run a low-cost direct-to-consumer business model. Later success was based on Dell's *dynamic capability* to adjust the business model (and its required resource base) with a continuous focus on remaining the lowest-cost supplier, by for instance, taking early and full advantage of the rise of the Internet.

So far, so good. We also know, however, that many more attempts at building new business models fail than succeed. Sometimes they fail for internal reasons, but Dell obviously got that part right.

More often, they fail for external reasons. What explains the success of Dell from the external perspective? Why was Dell's new business model successful in its relevant environment? Why did it succeed against the competition? Why was it not 'selected out', like so many other attempts?

We suggest that, in the case of Dell, the explanation involves a combination of the following three factors.

- The new business model offered many consumers sufficient functionality for dramatically lower costs. In more general terms, we can say that the model had excellent 'technical fitness' (see further below).
- In the fast-growing market for personal computers, there was a large and growing demand for such relatively standardized low-cost products.[20]
- The competitive environment was rather 'soft' as the established producers (IBM and HP) had difficulties matching the low-cost proposition of Dell. There were four main reasons for that:[21]
  - the established firms were themselves vertically integrated, covering the value chain from R&D to manufacturing and sales, whereas Dell focused just on assembly and direct sales;
  - they covered inhouse the full scope of chips, operating systems, computer hardware and application software;
  - they had difficulty switching to a direct-to-customer model because of the inherent conflicts with their prime sales channel through retailers;
  - they were slow to realize that the innovation-driven industry they had competed in successfully for many years had been maturing and personal computers had developed into rather commodity-like products for many customers.

Box 10.6 The evolution of Dell Inc., Part 1

In 1984, Michael Dell founded a company selling personal computers from his student room at the University of Texas. In 1999, his company had become the largest seller of personal computers in the ▶

USA and, in early 2006, it had the largest share (some 18–19 per cent) of the worldwide personal computer market. How did Dell achieve such phenomenal success?

There are several important elements.

■ While most large computer manufacturers, such as IBM and Hewlett-Packard, sold via retailers or their own stores, Dell developed a direct-to-consumer sales model – initially mainly by telephone, later via the Internet. In that way, Dell 'cut out the middle man', shortened the supply chain and saved itself the retailer's margin.

■ The Dell computers are assembled from standard components, but customers can order their own configuration of those components. That allows Dell to capture the benefits of standardization (of components), while offering its customers choice (of computer configurations). Dell can therefore very closely match its product offerings to consumer demand.

■ Dell practises just-in-time assembly by building the computers only after customers have ordered them and taking the components from suppliers as needed. It is a pull system of lean production that economizes significantly on inventory (of both components and end products).

■ As a consequence, Dell receives payment for its computers from the customers before it has to pay its suppliers for the necessary components. That is called a negative cash conversion cycle. Together with the low inventories, that means Dell needs only very low levels of working capital.

■ Dell has captured the benefits of the Internet faster than its rivals – for example, economizing on ordering procedures. It has also led the way in establishing call centres for customer support and outsourcing.

In all these ways, Dell has been able to build a low-cost business model that offers consumers a range of choices for an unprecedented low cost. As the Internet became available to more and more households across the world, the target market for Dell expanded accordingly. Moreover, it was also able to penetrate the market of corporate customers and expand its range of products to include servers, printers and televisions.

Source: Dell (1999); http://en.wikipedia.org/wiki/Dell

The case of the rise of Dell Inc. illustrates that the answer to the question of whether or not capabilities can offer competitive advantage is context-dependent. We cannot give such an answer without considering the nature of the environment in which the capabilities are executed. We need a measure of success for capabilities that accounts for that context-dependence.

External fit

For operational capabilities, that measure is **external fit**, as developed in the so-called 'contingency theories of organization'.[22] External fit measures the match between organizational and environmental characteristics at any moment in time – hence, it measures in a *static* way.

Evolutionary fitness

For dynamic capabilities, the measure is **evolutionary fitness**. It is a dynamic concept. Evolutionary fitness refers to how well a dynamic capability enables an organization to make a living by creating, extending or modifying its resource base. It depends on the external selection environment: evolutionary fit dynamic capabilities enable a firm to survive and perhaps grow, as well as prosper in the marketplace (in changing circumstances). In line with our example of Dell, Helfat et al. (2007) suggest that evolutionary fitness is affected by three important influences.

Technical fitness
- **Technical fitness** How effectively a capability performs its intended function when divided by its costs. In shorthand, it can be denoted as quality per unit of cost. In our example of Dell, the ability of Dell's business model to consistently deliver sufficient functionality to the customers at absolute lowest cost is evidence of its technical fitness.

Market demand
- **Market demand** The (derived) demand for a capability, depending on the demand for the end product or service to which that capability contributes. The market demand for Starbuck's ability to open new stores at amazing speed is derived from the ultimate demand for espressos, cappuccinos and café lattes in various countries.

Competition
- **Competition** Finally, the competitive environment – including competition and cooperation with other firms – impacts on the evolutionary fitness of dynamic capabilities. As the case of Dell illustrated, relatively 'soft' competition from the incumbents allowed Dell to build and expand its business model rather rapidly. That contributed to its sustainable competitive advantage for a period of over 20 years (see, however, Box 10.7 for the second part of the story). Greater competition makes it more difficult for firms to survive and prosper.

Capturing the argument so far, we should first recall that we discussed in Section 9.6 a number of 'internal' factors that may contribute to resources and capabilities offering sustainable competitive advantage. Those factors include co-specialization, asset orchestration, tacit knowledge, firm specificity and isolating mechanisms. To those internal factors we have now added external factors. They are the technical fitness to deliver the required quality per unit of cost, sufficient market demand and the ability to survive competition. Together, these external factors determine the evolutionary fitness of firms' dynamic capabilities. Evolutionary fitness results in the survival and growth of companies and their production of economic value.

As an overall summary, we can now answer the question 'when do dynamic capabilities lead to competitive advantage?' The answer is as follows.

- There must be differences in the technical fitness of dynamic capabilities of competing organizations.[23] The technical fitness of our capabilities should allow us to survive the actions of competing organizations.
- There must be market demand for the end products or services to which the capability contributes. Hence, there is derived demand for the capability itself.
- The capability must be relatively rare in relation to that demand. This conforms to standard economic reasoning: value comes from scarcity.

In order for the competitive advantage to be *sustainable*, several further conditions should be met.

- The capability should be inimitable and non-substitutable by the competition.
- It should be able to cope with the rate of change in the external environment. Hence, it should not become obsolete as a result of environmental change that it cannot accommodate.

■ The capability should be maintained by continued good asset orchestration (as an element of strategic management).

Hence, sustainable competitive advantage arises from the interplay of internal and external factors. It is the outcome of both adequate strategic management and evolutionary environmental selection.[24] Box 10.7 illustrates that sustainable competitive advantage can never be taken for granted. Internal and external factors can, similarly, work together to undermine even the strongest capabilities and best business models. After 20 years of uninterrupted success, Dell has more recently experienced difficulties as well.

Box 10.7 The evolution of Dell Inc., Part 2

In 2004, Kevin Rollins took over as CEO from Michael Dell, who remained chairman of the Board of Dell Inc. In February 2005, *Fortune* magazine awarded Dell first place in its annual ranking of 'Most Admired Companies', but soon thereafter cracks were appearing in its business model:

■ by the second quarter of 2005, Dell was missing revenue and earnings targets and that remained the case in subsequent quarters;

■ operational problems surfaced, such as faulty capacitators on the motherboards of some models, costing over $300 million to address;

■ customer complaints doubled in 2005, mainly about levels of service received from Dell's customer support;

■ Dell started losing market share in personal computers as of 2006 and was overtaken as market leader by Hewlett-Packard;

■ similar problems became manifest in other parts of the product range, such as servers and televisions.

Commentary on Dell's problems suggested that internal as well as external factors played a role. Competitors had reacted to Dell's success: Hewlett-Packard had taken over Compaq and IBM had sold its PC business to Lenovo, a Chinese company. Other low-cost rivals had emerged, such as Acer. As a result, Dell was increasingly facing stronger and equally low-cost competitors. As a reaction, it may have cut costs further in ways that compromised customer service and, possibly, product quality. As *Business Week* quoted some observers, 'They are a one-trick pony. It was a great trick for over ten years, but the rest of us have figured it out and Dell has not ploughed any of its profits into creating a new trick' and 'This is when they have to be imaginative, but Dell's culture only wants to talk about execution'.

In January 2007, Kevin Rollins abruptly resigned and Michael Dell returned to the CEO role. He demonstrated his willingness to re-examine the Dell business model by signing an agreement with Wal-Mart to launch two Dell Dimension desktops through 3500 Wal-Mart stores. At the time of writing this fourth edition of our book, it was too early to tell whether the return of Michael Dell would lead to the revival of Dell's fortunes (like the return of Steve Jobs led to a turnaround of Apple) or Dell's competitive advantage had been decisively eroded.

Sources: 'It's bad to worse at Dell', *Business Week*, 1 November 2005; 'Dark days at Dell', *Business Week*, 24 August 2006; 'Dude, you're getting a Dell – at Wal-Mart', *Business Week*, 24 May 2007.

The more recent problems at Dell are an illustration of a theme that we will elaborate on further in the next section and Chapter 11. It is the theme of the sustainability of success. Firms such as Dell, which are on a successful strategic trajectory, will want to build on that success and expand it further. Following the standard evolutionary pathway of variation–selection–retention, they will therefore want to select, retain and extend successful capabilities. In the case of Dell, that entailed the further development and refinement of the low-cost direct-to-consumer business model. On the one hand, it is exactly what was needed to reinforce its competitive advantage. On the other, there is the threat that firms will myopically invest according to their 'dominant logic' only, which may come to haunt them when environmental conditions change. We saw in Chapter 5 how evolutionary game theory can model such changes in environmental conditions, including the learning by competitors and emergence of innovative strategies (see Section 5.6). Evolutionary approaches offer great potential to understand the basic tensions involved in those strategic choices more fundamentally. It is with a sketch of this potential that we want to conclude this chapter.

10.8 Further developments

In conclusion, we should like to observe that there appears to be great potential for the further development and integration of the evolutionary approaches we have described. The evolutionary perspective is still young in our field and is attracting increasing numbers of researchers. As a result, it is to be expected that the perspective will be developed and refined. In that process, it is to be hoped that a more integrative framework for the evolutionary analysis of organizational phenomena will emerge. Ecological and evolutionary models have great potential to incorporate insights from various disciplines. For a multidisciplinary field such as organization studies, it is to be hoped that this potential will be realized.

As an illustration of its potential, we can speculatively point to two fields of interest. The first is the further analysis of organizations as 'bundles of routinized competences' or 'bundles of dynamic and operational capabilities'. Particularly in the learning perspective of evolutionary economics, the conceptualization of the firm as a bundle of competences/capabilities may provide a unitary framework for a number of theoretical and empirical observations, including the following.

Increasing returns

- The finding that firms which have a head start (or, more formally, a *first mover advantage*) along a competence-building pathway that eventually turns out to be a success often experience significant **increasing returns** (Arthur, 1994b, 1996). Again, Microsoft is an example, as are all the electronics firms competing for dominance in the area of HD-DVDs. The firm that can set the standard for the development of such new environmental niches will reap a disproportionate share of the resources that the niche will provide (see Box 10.8).

Box 10.8 An example of increasing returns (or positive feedback)

The history of the videocassette recorder furnishes a simple example of positive feedback.

The VCR market started out with two competing formats selling at about the same price: VHS and Betamax. Each format could realize increasing returns as its market share increased. Thus, large numbers of VHS recorders would encourage video outlets to stock more prerecorded tapes in VHS, thereby enhancing the value of owning a VHS recorder, leading more people to buy one. The same would, of course, have been true for Beta-format players. In that way, a small gain in market share would improve the competitive position of one system and help it to further increase its lead.

Such a market is initially unstable. Both systems were introduced at about the same time and so began with roughly equal market shares. Those shares fluctuated early on because of external circumstance, 'luck' and corporate manoeuvring.

Increasing returns on early gains eventually tilted the competition towards VHS. It then accumulated enough of an advantage to take virtually the entire VCR market. Yet, it would have been impossible at the outset to say which system was going to win, which of the two possible equilibria would be selected.

Source: Arthur (1994b)

- One reason for success breeding success in such firms is the early accumulation of resources, which allows them to pursue dominance of their niche more aggressively. Another organizational reason may be that its early start increases the possibility that the firm will also develop the necessary supporting competences earlier. Eventually, it will need to arrive at a 'configuration' of competences that allows it to exploit the possibilities of the niche to the optimum. Think of the various competences that allowed IBM to dominate the niche of mainframe computers for several decades or, alternatively, of the competences that McDonald's needed to acquire in order to, first, dominate the US market in its niche and then internationalize successfully.
- Such successful configurations often contain the seeds of their demise. Miller (1990, 1994) has shown how successful corporations can become simple over time, focusing exclusively on the successful repertoire of routines and becoming intolerant of deviation or variation. It is well documented how IBM underestimated the potential impact of the personal computer and has had great difficulty in catching up. Similarly, former dominant players in their industries such as Steinway pianos or Singer sewing machines have lost their dominance or even ceased to exist. Large corporations, such as ITT and Texas Instruments, have also floundered.

  Icarus paradox
  Miller has labelled this phenomenon the **Icarus paradox** after the Greek saga of Icarus, who suffered a fatal fall after achieving great success.[25]
- Successful firms may find it hard to adapt for the following reasons, among others.
  - as discussed in Chapter 8, firms may invest in specific assets to demonstrate their commitment to a strategy. However, the more such specific investments are made, the more *lock-in* occurs (see Section 8.3) Lock-in is thus a two-edged sword: it demonstrates commitment, but reduces flexibility. In the terminology of this chapter, it contributes to relative inertia.

Cannibalization

– Relative inertia may be further increased in incumbent firms by the threat of **cannibalization** of their existing products. An outsider firm with no stake in the current market may expect to reap the full benefits of an innovation. An incumbent firm, with existing products that threaten to be replaced by the innovation, will also consider the lost profits from existing products. Thus, the incentives for the outsider firm to introduce the innovation, will be higher.

– success may generate a feeling of complacency (see Tellis and Golder, 2002, Chapter 7). For example, the potential of external innovations may be underestimated as a result of a 'not invented here' attitude. Sometimes companies may focus excessively on providing ever more functionality for their products, thus increasing their vulnerability to 'disruptive innovations' that offer basic functionality at a much lower cost (Christensen, 1997, 2003).

Exploitation

Exploration

– In many ways, then, success fosters a focus on **exploitation** rather than **exploration** – that is, on fully exploiting the current pathway to success and to underinvesting in the exploration of new pathways.[26]

■ Many firms, however, do live a long life. Some are able to persist as industry leaders during decades of economic and social change – General Motors and Shell, for example. Others completely transform themselves along the way, such as STORA, a Swedish company that has gone from copper mining to forestry operations, paper production and power generation in the 700 years of its existence to date (see Box 10.9).

Box 10.9 The history of STORA

STORA is probably the world's oldest company. It was officially founded in 1288, when Bishop Peter signed a deed of exchange. That was the document on which the 700th anniversary of the founding of STORA was based in 1988. The company brochure, *STORA's world*, describes its history as follows:

The world's oldest company

STORA's history commences with a copper mine, which in the 14th century produced approximately 200 tons of crude copper per year. Some 300 years later, the mine entered its golden era, producing an ore that was richer in copper content than at any time previously. During the 17th century, the mine was generating about 1500 tons of crude copper per year. In 1687, the great cave-in occurred, which signalled the end of the golden era. Operations continued after the collapse, however, with the extraction of new products, such as sulphur, vitriol, and pigment for red paint. This latter product continues to be used today to decorate many homes throughout Sweden.

The mining of copper ore based on a 'fire-setting' process required substantial quantities of wood. And to obtain wood, forests were required. Towards the end of the 18th century, the company's operations shifted increasingly towards forestry and the production of iron. In the middle of the 1870s a large iron mill and one of the largest sawmills in Europe were built near the copper mine.

At the end of the 19th century, a sulphate (kraft) and sulphite pulp mill was constructed in Skutskar in central Sweden. Around this time, the first paper mill was also built in Kvarnsveden, not far from Falun. In 1972, Kvarnsveden produced approximately 300,000 tons of newsprint and magazine paper. At the end of the 1970s, the mining and steel operations were gradually phased out.

▶

During the next decade, the Swedish companies Billerud, Papyrus and Swedish Match were acquired and incorporated within the STORA Group. Following the acquisition of Germany's Feldmühle group in 1990, STORA could without doubt be ranked as one of the world's leading forest products companies. In 1998 STORA merged with Enso, a Finnish forest products company, to become STORA Enso.

Further development of the evolutionary approaches will, it is hoped, lead to more systematic insights into the organization/environment interplay that gives rise to such pathways and the triggers of its various episodes. As will be evident from the above, a key theme will be the relative importance of *inertia versus adaptability* in various circumstances. As Boone and van Witteloostuijn (1995) have noted, this theme shows close correspondence with the 'commitment versus flexibility' theme in industrial organization and strategic management we encountered in Chapter 9. It is therefore very likely that cross-fertilization of these various approaches offers ample opportunities to increase our understanding of these important phenomena.

As noted above, organizational ecology is rather silent about what goes on *within* the organization. Evolutionary economics has more to say about processes within the firm. In particular, the behavioural concept of a local search near existing routines is incorporated into this theory. In terms of organizational change, the concept implies that firms will prefer to stay close to current competences. Organizational change, then, will be predominantly *incremental* (see Quinn, 1982). Such change will allow a firm to keep up with slow to moderate environmental change. It does not seem to explain how firms can survive in the midst of turbulent change, however. Nor does it seem to allow for complete transformations of firms, such as in the example of STORA above.

Intraorganizational ecology and evolution

A promising avenue of enquiry that may contribute to our understanding of these phenomena relates to **intraorganizational ecology and evolution**. The basic idea here is that selection takes place *within* the organization as well as outside it. Various worldviews may exist among the organization's members; different analyses of the organization's challenges may vie for prominence; too many requests for resource allocations may compete for scarce resources; different strategies may be propagated and so on (see Bettis and Prahalad, 1995). How do the internal selection processes of the organization operate under such circumstances?

Induced strategic processes

Burgelman (1990, 1991, 2002) has proposed a distinction in strategic processes that may contribute to an intraorganizational ecology of strategy formation: induced processes versus autonomous processes.[27] **Induced strategic processes** fit with the current strategy, as propagated by top management, and are compatible with current routines and competences. Induced processes serve to ensure that organizational actions will remain consistent with top management preferences as incorporated in the current strategy. In that vein, induced processes are within the current strategic domain and, hence, also demarcate what the organization will *not* do. Burgelman thus identifies such processes as *variation-reducing*.

Autonomous strategic processes

Autonomous strategic processes refer to strategic initiatives outside the current strategic domain. They arise 'bottom up', from the managers who are directly in contact with new technological developments and changing market conditions and have some budgetary discretion. Such autonomous initiatives are expected to emerge unpredictably, but not completely randomly as they are rooted in and constrained by the evolving competence set of the organization (including newly acquired and perceived competences at lower levels of the organization). Hence, such processes tend to be *variation-enhancing* rather than variation-reducing.[28] An important task of top management is to nurture such operational-level strategic initiatives as they spur continuous strategic renewal.

Burgelman has more recently summarized his perspective in his book *Strategy is Destiny* (2002). The book explains how Burgelman's conceptual framework was developed in close association with his work at Intel and its CEO, Andy Grove.[29] In his own words, Burgelman's (2002, pp. 20–1) integrated view of strategy-making and organizational ecology is as follows:

> Almost all companies start small and are subject to liabilities of newness (they are unknown, untested, lacking legitimacy, and so on). The major force faced by small, new companies is environmental selection. Most do not survive external selection pressures. Organizational ecology provides a useful framework within which the evolutionary dynamics of small companies can be more clearly understood. Some companies, however, do survive and become large and established. Although large, established companies continue to remain subject to the selection force of the external environment – and many succumb to it in the long run – these companies have gained the opportunity to substitute internal for external selection. Analogous to external selection, internal selection is concerned with a company's entering new businesses and exiting from failing ones over time.

In other words, Burgelman argues that, as companies grow from small to large and established, the question of corporate strategy is added to the question(s) of business strategy. The ecological approach to corporate strategy adds the internal selection environment of firms to the external selection environment (the issue of 'external fit'). In the internal selection environment:

- *Induced* strategy processes emphasize the familiar environment of the firm, current competences, fit with the prevailing strategy, and 'alignment'. Induced processes thus favour exploitation rather than exploration and contribute to strategic inertia.
- *Autonomous* processes involve new combinations of competences that are not currently recognized as distinctive or important to the firm. They are aimed more at emerging environments than the firm's familiar environment. They do not 'fit' the current corporate strategy well, but may achieve recognition over time and then be incorporated in the new corporate strategy, almost 'after the fact' of their emerging success.

All in all, Burgelman's perspective is that the long-term survival of firms is enhanced by the balancing of variation-reducing and variation-enhancing mechanisms. One process leads to relative inertia and incremental adjustments;

the other expands the organization's domain and renews its competence base. Likely propositions are that:

- the appropriate balance of the two will depend on environmental conditions;
- the episodes of organizational success and failure observed above depend on the appropriateness of the actual choices made by firms, given the then prevailing environmental conditions.

In the latter statement, our two 'speculative fields of interest' are coming together. Conceptualizing the firm as a bundle of competences allows us to analyse whether or not it makes *competent* choices with regard to its environmental challenges. That is no coincidence. We see the evolutionary perspectives as being capable of integrating theoretical and empirical contributions from various disciplines.

10.9 Summary: the evolutionary perspective

This chapter has presented two original strands of the evolutionary perspective on organizations as well as some more recent developments.

We started out by exploring the biological analogy and examining different biological explanations for the long necks of giraffes. That allowed us to distinguish creationist and evolutionary arguments and, within the latter, Lamarckian and Darwinist explanations. Those distinctions are also helpful in the organizational field. We were careful, however, to point out that there are both differences and similarities between organizational forms and biological species. The differences imply that successful biological explanations do not necessarily translate to the organizational field. While the Darwinian perspective currently has the strongest scientific credentials in biology, creationist or Lamarckian (or still other) arguments may be much more important for organizational evolution.

We saw that Nelson and Winter's evolutionary theory of economic change is decidedly Lamarckian in nature, while Hannan and Freeman's organizational ecology is Darwinist. Both, however, employ the basic process of variation–selection–retention as their main explanatory device for evolution, with competition (and legitimation in organizational ecology) as the external selection mechanism.

Evolutionary perspectives direct our attention to the development of organizational forms in the interaction with their environments. Such perspectives therefore accord more importance to environmental selection processes than most of the other organizational theories, which tend to emphasize organizational adaptability. In organizational ecology, it is assumed that organizations are relatively inert. That is to say, they have a hard time responding to changes in their environments. The reasons for this relative inertia are sought in the demands on organizations for reliability, accountability and reproducibility. Selection pressures will favour organizations with structures exhibiting relatively high inertia. Therefore, organizational ecology sees inertia as a consequence of selection. The empirical work within this approach has tended to concentrate on the vital rates for organizational populations: the rates of founding and mortality. Those rates have been found to be density-dependent.

Nelson and Winter's evolutionary theory of economic change focuses on organizational routines as being the primary concept when describing organizational functioning. Routines refer to all regular and predictable behaviour patterns of firms. They often contain a component of tacit knowledge. Routines explain why organizations are resistant to change and, therefore, again, relatively inert.

In this approach, routines are the organizational analogue of biological genes. Successful routines are those that have survived environmental selection. They serve as organizational memories. In addition, they may be seen as a stabilizing force in organizations, representing a truce in intraorganizational conflict.

Nelson and Winter clearly build on the foundations of the behavioural theory of the firm. Their emphasis on organizational routines has been extended to encompass firm-specific dynamic capabilities. Thus, the organization itself has increasingly come to be studied through the evolutionary lens. From the evolutionary perspective, the organization may be seen as an ecology of patterned activity.

We discussed two examples of the increasing attention on evolutionary processes within organizations. The first example pertained to the research into dynamic capabilities. These were introduced in the previous chapter as an extension of the resource-based view (RBV) relating to strategy. There, the focus was on the internal context of dynamic capabilities and the strategic management tasks required to build and maintain such capabilities. In this chapter, we have added the external context. We have shown how technical fitness, sufficient market demand and the ability to survive competition determine the evolutionary fitness of dynamic capabilities. Thus, we were able to specify the internal and external conditions for dynamic capabilities to provide sustainable competitive advantage. Competitive success arises from the interplay of internal *and* external factors: it is the outcome of adequate strategic management *and* environmental selection.

As a second example, Burgelman's analysis of the internal selection environment of companies was presented. Burgelman explicitly analyses *intraorganizational* processes through the evolutionary lens of variation–selection–retention, with competition as the selection mechanism.

Variation exists within firms as, usually, a variety of strategic initiatives exist at any moment. Induced strategy processes are variation-reducing due to their emphasis on alignment with the prevailing strategy. Autonomous strategy processes, on the other hand, are variation-enhancing as they lead to strategic initiatives outside of the current strategic focus.

There is *internal competition* between the different strategic initiatives to obtain the resources necessary to grow and increase in importance in the firm. *Selection* works internally through the managerial processes that regulate the allocation of resources and attention to the various initiatives.

Retention operates on those initiatives that survive the internal and external competition. Those initiatives are enabled to grow and become more important in the company.

The evolutionary approaches to organizations thus shed light on the dynamics of organizational functioning. They also give insights into the long-term evolution of organizations. They show that, in the interactions between populations of organizations and their environments, conditions may change over time. Organizational ecology shows how the forces of competition and legitimation develop with the density of the population. That has an effect on the founding and mortality rates. All in all, the conditions for survival change substantially over the lifetime of a population.

Similarly, the analysis of firms as bundles of routinized competences or capabilities illuminates a number of formerly disparate theoretical and empirical observations. It shows how firms may have initial success by building competences along a new pathway. Success will reinforce the routinization of those competences. As competences become more routinized, the relative inertia of the firm increases. Thus, success breeds not only success but also its own demise when environmental conditions change and organizational adaptation is called for. Many firms do live a long life, however, and succeed in adapting when necessary.

A deeper understanding of the conditions leading to relative inertia on the one hand and relative adaptability on the other is one of the greatest challenges for current organizational theory. We return to this theme in the closing section of the next chapter.

Questions

1 In evolutionary approaches to organizations, biological analogies play an important role. It is argued that populations of organizational forms develop over time as a result of environmental selection, just as populations of giraffes do. Yet, a major difference between organizations and giraffes is that organizations are human constructs. That difference has two kinds of implication for the analogy between populations of organizations and populations of giraffes. Explain the two implications.

2 Skills and routines are two important concepts in the evolutionary theory of economic change developed by Nelson and Winter.
   a Give an example of a skill.
   b Name two characteristic features of skills.
   c Give an example of a routine.
   d What is the major difference between a skill and a routine? What are the major similarities between skills and routines?
   e What are the differences and similarities between routines and dynamic capabilities?

3 In a number of countries there has been experimentation with a new form of pharmacy: mail-order pharmacy. This new distribution form would allow patients to receive their regular prescriptions by post. In the Netherlands, the early experiments with this new form of pharmacy were set up by entrepreneurs. They were not successful. Many of the entrepreneurial firms failed (the experiments continue, but now under the auspices of

health insurance companies). What could explain the early failures, if you adopt the perspective of organizational ecology?

4 Read Box 10.9, on the 700-year history of STORA, again. If you look at its history from the perspective of Nelson and Winter's evolutionary theory of economic change, what may be the factors contributing to STORA's remarkably long survival as a company?

5 In 1959, almost all petrol in major Canadian cities was sold by service stations. Service stations provided simple car repair services and sold tyres, batteries and car accessories as well as petrol. They also employed 'pump jockeys', who filled up the tanks and perhaps provided other services, such as washing the windscreen. Thirty years later, that situation had changed dramatically. Less than 30 per cent of all petrol sold was sold by traditional service stations – the rest being sold in roughly equal proportions by 'gas bars' (outlets selling petrol only), convenience stores (petrol sales plus convenience retail) and car washes (petrol sales and automated carwashes). Table 10.1 provides data for the city of Edmonton in Alberta, Canada.

Using population ecology, how would you explain the transition that occurred in Edmonton between 1959 and 1988? Which information would you need in order to know whether or not your explanation is correct from the point of view of population ecology?

Table 10.1 Number of outlets selling petrol in Edmonton, Alberta, Canada

Year	1959	1988
Service stations	262	104
Gas bars	1	73
Convenience stores	0	73
Carwashes	1	84
Other outlets selling petrol	15	40

Source: Usher and Evans (1996)

Suggested further reading

Arthur, W. B. (1996), 'Increasing returns and the new world of business', *Harvard Business Review*, July/August, pp. 100–9.

Barron, D. N. (2003), 'Evolutionary theories', in D. O. Faulkner and A. Campbell, *The Oxford Handbook of Strategy*, Oxford: Oxford University Press.

Baum, J. A. C. (1996), 'Organizational ecology' in S. R. Clegg, C. Hardy and W. R. Nord, *Handbook of Organization Studies*, London: Sage.

Burgelman, R. A. (2002), *Strategy is Destiny*, New York: Free Press.

Carroll, G. R. and Hannan, M. T. (1995), *Organizations in Industry: Strategy, structure, and selection*, Oxford: Oxford University Press.

Carroll, G. R. and Hannan, M. T. (2000), *The Demography of Corporations and Industries*, Princeton, NJ: Princeton University Press.

Geroski, P. A. (2003), *The Evolution of New Markets*, Oxford: Oxford University Press.

Hannan, M. T. and Freeman, J. (1989a), *Organizational Ecology*, Cambridge, MA: Harvard University Press.

Helfat, C. E., Finkelstein, S., Mitchell, W., Peteraf, M. A., Singh, H., Teece, D. J. and Winter, S. G. (2007), *Dynamic Capabilities: Understanding strategic change in organizations*, Oxford: Blackwell.

Nelson, R. R. (1991), 'Why do firms differ and how does it matter?', *Strategic Management Journal*, Vol.12 (special issue), pp. 61–74.

Nelson, R. R. and Winter, S. E. (1982), *An Evolutionary Theory of Economic Change*, Cambridge, MA: Harvard University Press.

Winter, S. G. (1990), 'Survival, selection, and inheritance in evolutionary theories of organization', in J. V. Singh, *Organizational Evolution: New directions*, Newbury Park, CA: Sage.

Notes

1 The following account is based primarily on Dawkins (1986). As is argued in Section 10.3, his rejection of the Lamarckian explanation for biological evolution does not transfer to the organizational field.

2 See Dawkins (1986) for a popular overview, which also discusses some other strands of evolutionary arguments, such as salutationism and punctuationism. The second author's eldest son advanced a new hypothesis for the long necks of giraffes. According to him, giraffes were created when a baby dromedary had difficulty leaving its egg. This led its parents to pull it out. As the little dromedary was really stuck in the egg, the parents had to pull so hard that a giraffe with a long neck was born.

3 As, for instance, Hannan and Freeman (1989a) do. Their approach is outlined in the subsequent section.

4 Others are Aldrich (1979, for example) and Carroll (1987 and 1988, for example).

5 For instance, by Pfeffer (1982) and Young (1988). Hannan and Freeman (1989a, p.10) also recognize the potential fruitfulness of more integration between ecological and economic studies.

6 Some studies are located between these two levels of analysis, such as the studies that use environmental variables as 'proxies' for competition by other organizational forms.

7 Hannan and Freeman (1989a) attempt to solve it by arguing, first, that there is a fundamental duality between niches and forms – 'niches define forms and forms define niches' (p. 50) – and, second, by focusing subsequently on boundaries around populations: 'boundaries should be drawn in organizational space to produce uniformity within populations in terms of observable attributes and relations' (p. 53). That still does not give us theoretically satisfactory definitions and procedures. Hannan and Freeman (1989a, p. 63) are frank enough to admit that they themselves have relied in large part on 'the conventional wisdom of participants and observers'.

8 In Section 10.5 we shall see that Nelson and Winter also stress the role of routines.

9 An economist would probably point out, in addition, that, for international chains, making such a choice economizes on search costs, particularly if the problem occurs frequently (that is, you often have to find rented cars in unfamiliar countries). In this sense, individual routines in decisionmaking can be efficient, as the behavioural school has argued (see Chapter 6).

10 Added by the authors as Rinnooy Kan is referring to some early breaches in security in Internet banking.

11 Ecologists distinguish between the 'fundamental niche' (roughly, the maximum potential space a particular form can occupy in its environment) and the 'realized niche' (the restricted environmental space in which a population can be sustained in the presence of competing populations). As only the realized niche can be observed, that is the concept used in most studies.

12 Interestingly, these ideas bear close resemblance to the 'increasing returns' argument that has more recently received recognition in economics (see Arthur, 1994a, 1994b, 1996). In this strand of the economic literature it is argued that industries can be subject to self-reinforced growth and particular firms in the industry can realize substantial 'first-mover advantages' if they set the new standards. Microsoft is often mentioned as a case in point.

13 See Carroll and Hannan (1995) for further elaborations of organizational ecology, including density delay, resource partitioning and segregation.

14 Again, this conforms to ideas of the Carnegie school. See Cyert and March (1963, Chapter 6).

15 In that sense, they are decidedly neo-Schumpeterian. Schumpeter (1934) also identified innovation as the 'carrying out of new combinations'.

16 Again, this corresponds closely to the Darwinian point of view, where mutations are also random. Many organization theorists would, however, regard this as an extreme position.

17 See Carroll and Hannan (2000, Chapter 4) for a discussion on the definitions of 'organizational forms' and 'organizational populations'.

18 By analogy to biology, Hannan and Freeman thus represent the original Darwinian position that species (= forms) are selected. Nelson and Winter hold the now common position that selection operates on the gene level. It goes without saying that the analogy to biology represents no arguments for or against particular *organizational* theories.

19 In that respect, of course, organizational theories are decidedly different from biological theories, where only offspring can inherit. An interesting strategy-orientated answer to the question of what is selected is provided by Beinhocker (2006, pp. 282–5): modules of business plans. Notice that this answer also allows 'inheritance' by imitation.

20 Christensen (1997, 2003) describes 'disruptive innovations' in much the same way. Often, an industry can be obsessed with providing ever more functionality in its products, while a large and growing market segment would be happy with a product providing basic functionality at low cost. That fact offers opportunities for entry to outsiders not bothered by the prevailing industry mindset and 'legacy' investments and commitments.

21 See Grove (1996) for a description of how the computer industry changed from a vertical structure in 1980 to a horizontal structure in 1995 – a relatively short period of time – causing great upheaval for many 'established' firms.

22 As mentioned in Chapter 1, the contingency theories of organization emphasize that there is no 'one best way' to organize and organizational success hinges on the match between the organization and its environment. 'External fit' is the yardstick used to measure that match.

23 In economic jargon, there must be heterogeneity in the technical fitness of dynamic capabilities of the same type. If all organizations had the same technical fitness of their capabilities, there would be no basis for competitive advantage.

24 In Section 9.5, we noted the criticism of RBV that it is tautological. One cannot argue that resources are valuable because they allow competitive performance and at the same time regard competitive performance as the evidence for resources being valuable. Note that the circularity has been broken in two ways: specification of conditions for (lasting) resource value and specification of competitive environmental selection as the independent selection mechanism.

25 In Greek mythology, Icarus found that he could attach wings to his arms with wax and fly. Unfortunately, he was too successful and flew higher and higher towards the sun, thus provoking the gods. His success turned to disaster when the heat from the sun melted the wax, leaving Icarus to plummet back to Earth.

26 See March (1994; Section 6.2) for a fuller discussion of exploitation and exploration, including how both can become a trap. Axelrod and Cohen (1999) provide a perspective on this trade-off in the framework of complex, adaptive systems (see also Chapter 11).

27 Note that we are now discussing strategic processes – the left side of Table 9.1 – which we could not deal with in the previous chapter.

28 Burgelman's description of strategic processes corresponds closely to Mintzberg's view of intended/deliberate and emerging strategies – the realized strategy usually being a mix of the two. See Mintzberg and Quinn (1991). Burgelman (2002, p. 15) discusses some nuances of both sets of terms.

29 Andy Grove's own learning from his episode as CEO of Intel (and his association with Robert Burgelman at Stanford) is captured in his book *Only the Paranoid Survive* (1996).

11 All in the family

11.1 Introduction

You have now been introduced to the main economic approaches that are currently available. You are familiar with the problems addressed by each approach, the basic concepts used and the particular mode of analysis. Our task in this chapter is to provide you with an overall perspective on the various approaches included in this book.

First, we return to the basic conceptual framework laid out in Chapter 1. Having thus refreshed your memory, we proceed to discuss, in Section 11.3, what the similarities are between our family of economic approaches to organizations. In Section 11.4, we turn to the family differences. Together, these two sections should provide a balanced view of our family. Do they quarrel a lot? Are there any clear family traits? Do they have the same views or hobbies? Can we discern a family structure? Section 11.5 summarizes our findings and Section 11.6 sketches a concluding perspective before we move on to look at the applications of these approaches in the final three chapters.

11.2 The basic conceptual framework

In Chapter 1, we developed a basic conceptual framework, which is reproduced in Figure 11.1 (overleaf). The framework took as its starting point the division of labour in society. That division of labour allows economies of specialization to be gained. It is only one side of the coin, however. The other side is that coordination is necessary in a specialized economy. Without some kind of coordination, no exchange transaction could take place between specialized economic actors. Specialization and (the need for) coordination are thus the inseparable consequences of division of labour.

We argued that markets and organizations offer alternative solutions for the coordination of exchange transactions. We characterized markets and organizations by means of the coordination mechanisms they employed. Markets use the price mechanism. Organizations use any of six alternative mechanisms. We argued that pure market coordination and pure organizational coordination are rare. In practice, we often find a mix of coordination mechanisms. The actual mix that we find in any one situation will depend mainly on the

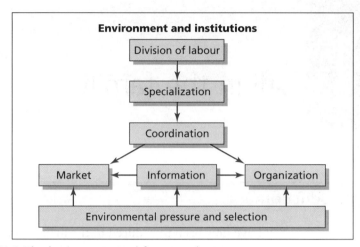

Figure 11.1 The basic conceptual framework

information required to execute the transaction. Thus, information is the pivotal element of our basic conceptual framework, determining which (mix of) coordination mechanism(s) will prevail. Finally, we placed our framework in an environmental and institutional context, highlighting the environmental pressure and selection operating on both markets and organizations.

In Chapter 1, too, we showed how the basic economic perspective expressed in Figure 11.1 could be traced to some founding fathers of modern economics. Division of labour and its consequences was a main theme of Adam Smith, the efficiency of market coordination by the price system was vigorously expounded by Friedrich Hayek and the idea that organizational coordination could arise as a remedy to flaws in market coordination was first systematically addressed by Ronald Coase. Now that we have surveyed more recent economic approaches to organizations, to what extent can we say that this basic conceptual framework underlies the spectrum of approaches that are currently available?

'To some extent', would be our answer. If anything has become clear in the preceding chapters, it should be the diversity of the approaches surveyed. In Section 11.4, we chart that diversity in more detail. Notwithstanding such diversity, we also see a common foundation to the economic approaches to organizations. Three of the common elements included in our framework are discussed below.

11.3 Family resemblances

11.3.1 Organizations and markets

The first common element in the economic approaches to organization is indeed that economists always tend to compare organizations to markets. Their background leads economists to think of markets as natural benchmarks for the appraisal of organizations. That is probably most obvious in Chapter 8, where we discussed transaction cost economics. Williamson's initial formulation of that approach in terms of markets and hierarchies brings it out clearly.

The leading question in transaction cost economics is how to explain the relative occurrence of markets and firms as governance structures for economic transactions. It represents an extension of Coase's fundamental question, why do we observe so many firms (with internal governance of transactions) if the market functions so efficiently? Both Coase and Williamson take the market as their point of departure and explain that organizations exist as a result of 'market failure'.

Another, perhaps more implicit, way to compare organizations with markets is to analyse the boundaries of organizations. Consider the corporate strategies discussed in Chapter 9. Vertical integration, horizontal multinationalization and corporate diversification all extend the boundaries of an organization. Under a vertical integration policy, the firm absorbs a supplier or a customer firm. If multinationalization or diversification is effected by mergers and acquisitions, again, two firms are integrated into one.[1] In all these cases we now find one firm instead of two. The relevant comparison is between one integrated firm and two firms with a market relation between them. Again, this boils down to a comparative assessment of organizational versus market coordination of transactions.

Consider also the agency explanation for the existence of firms. As elaborated in Chapter 7, this explanation involves the concept of team production. Team production denotes the situation where two or more people can be more productive when they join forces than when they operate separately. Again, the (implicit) comparison is between an organizational arrangement and a market arrangement. Organizational arrangements come into being when market arrangements would be inferior.

Finally, the evolutionary approaches to organizations direct our attention to the environment in which the organization operates. A significant part of that environment will consist of markets: markets for the products and services produced by the organization, but also markets for the resources they require and even a 'market for corporate control' (see Chapter 7). In all those markets, the force of *competition* operates as an external selection mechanism. Organizations only survive if they are able to withstand such competitive market pressures and selection. In that sense, a market versus organization perspective can be discerned in the evolutionary approaches to organizations as well.[2]

11.3.2 Efficiency

By what standards would the market arrangement be inferior? That question leads us to the second common element in the economic approaches to organization. It is the observation that the primary economic criterion for evaluating market versus organizational coordination is *efficiency*.

Efficiency

As broadly defined in Chapter 1, the **efficiency** criterion refers to the optimal allocation of scarce resources. That is to say, resources are efficiently allocated if they are directed towards their most productive use or, alternatively, if a given amount of production is achieved with a minimum of resources. If, moreover, all resources can be expressed in money terms, it translates into the 'least cost' condition that most people would intuitively associate with the term 'efficiency'. Bear in mind, however, that the economic definition of resources encompasses *all* means that may contribute to the satisfaction of human needs, broadly conceived (see Chapter 1).

Efficiency considerations abound in the preceding chapters. In the behavioural theory, organizational participants weigh up the contributions they have to make against the inducements they are offered. They compare that ratio with the alternatives available elsewhere. They strive for the most efficient allocation of their resources. A manager, according to agency theory, will wonder about the effects of buying a company jet on the objective of maximizing her utility (her utility depends on the value of the firm and on her on-the-job consumption). Will the company's resources be spent efficiently if they are spent on a jet? The strategist in another firm will consider moving from a cost leadership position to a differentiation strategy. He will conclude that this is feasible only if the increase in revenue outweighs the increase in costs.

Hence, efficiency considerations are, in part, manifest in the assumed thoughts and behaviour of economic actors. Economists tend to presume that people are not totally unaffected by the expected efficiency of the resources at their disposal. However, efficiency considerations play an additional and more important role in economic analysis. Efficiency is the economic selection mechanism. It is our main criterion for assessing which coordination arrangements have the highest survival value when selection pressures are operative. Economists usually assume that the least efficient arrangements will tend to be selected out (after some time).

That assumption is evident in Nelson and Winter's evolutionary theory of the firm. Environmental selection favours successful routines. Successful routines are indicated by the higher profit levels of the firms incorporating them. Profit is an indicator of efficiency. Hence, efficient firms will tend to be selected by the environment and inefficient firms (with less successful routines) will tend to be selected out. Similarly, in transaction cost economics, the governance structure that economizes on production and transaction costs (and is thus more efficient) supersedes the less efficient alternative. These examples refer, strictly speaking, to the commonest use of the efficiency concept – that

Static efficiency

is, **static efficiency** or *allocative efficiency*. Another question is how should resources be (re)distributed over time to adapt an economy or an organization to changing circumstances and keep it efficient and growing? That is a ques-

Dynamic efficiency

tion of **dynamic efficiency**.

In Chapter 10, we introduced the concept of 'evolutionary fitness'. We noted that dynamic capabilities that are evolutionarily fit, enable a firm to survive, and perhaps grow and prosper in the marketplace (in changing circumstances). Thus, evolutionary fitness and dynamic efficiency are conceptually related criteria.

Efficiency, therefore, is the second common element that binds the various economic approaches to organization together. It is partly implicit in the basic conceptual framework of Figure 11.1. As discussed above, it is the primary economic criterion that determines the selection of either markets or organizations as coordination devices for particular transactions.[3] We have also made it explicit, however, by focusing on one specific source of efficiency: informational advantages.

11.3.3 Information

The focus on information is the third and final common element that we want to discuss here. An important impetus to both agency theory and transaction cost economics was provided by the development of the **economics of information**. It was increasingly recognized that information itself was a scarce resource that could be unevenly distributed. Uneven distributions of information present opportunities for strategic behaviour. Whether the relevant information is observable to all players or not is a prime distinction in the games that people (and organizations) play, as we saw in Chapter 5. There is economic value in the possession of private information. Informational asymmetries can be exploited, whether opportunistically or not.

Economics of information

Agency theory and transaction cost economics share a concern for such situations. Both maintain that such informational problems pervade (economic) life and both seek efficient contractual arrangements to deal with such problems. As markets and organizations differ in the types of information problem they can handle (efficiently), a good part of the choice between them will be explained by the information requirements of particular transactions.

Although less clearly at first sight, information is a central concept in most other economic approaches to organizations as well. The behavioural theory of the firm, for instance, departs from standard microeconomics in the assumptions that, first, information is often imperfectly available to economic actors and, second, these actors are only boundedly rational in processing the information that is available.

Those behavioural assumptions spurred later developments in organizational economics, as we have seen, and have often been incorporated in later approaches. In the evolutionary approach, much information is stored in the organizational routines and capabilities. They embody **tacit knowledge**. Tacit knowledge is difficult to articulate and, therefore, communicate. It is, consequently, also difficult for third parties to acquire. In that sense, tacit knowledge embodied in organizational routines and capabilities represents a well-protected form of private information for the organization. A fundamental information asymmetry exists between firms with and without successful routines and capabilities. Just like DNA stores our (coded) genetic information, routines and capabilities store the information necessary for organizations to function and grow. As Beinhocker (2006, p. 12) has noted:

Tacit knowledge

> Evolution is an *algorithm* ... Evolution can perform its tricks not just in the substrate of DNA, but in any system that has the right information-processing and information-storing characteristics.

We do not want to overemphasize the commonality between the economic approaches to organizations. Each common element discussed above is probably to some extent debatable.[4] Together, however, they represent the main binding features, as we see them. In the next sections, some important differences between these approaches are discussed and summarized, together with the similarities. Taken together, these sections should provide a balanced overall picture.

11.4 Family differences

Let us now turn to the differences between our family members. You will have noticed abundant differences while reading through Chapters 6–10. Our purpose here will not be to enumerate all those differences. Rather, we shall attempt to provide some structure by ordering the various approaches along some dimensions that we believe are particularly instructive. Three such dimensions are discussed below.

11.4.1 Process versus content approaches

The first dimension refers to the subject matter of the various approaches, which is the problems that they deal with. Here, we borrow a distinction from the strategy literature in order to classify our approaches. It is the distinction between *process theories* and *content theories* of strategy.

Process theories deal with the processes that enable strategies to come into being.[5] *Content theories* deal with the content of those strategies: the firm's strategic posture and positioning in the market.

Process and content approaches to organizations

Similarly, we shall distinguish here between **process and content approaches to organizations**. The former deal with organizational processes, but hardly inform us about the likely outcomes of those processes. The latter focus on substantive outcomes without being very informative about the processes that lead to these outcomes.

To illustrate this dimension, let us contrast two of our approaches. The behavioural theory of the firm is a process approach. It explains the internal functioning of the firm when seen as a coalition of participant groups. It highlights the potential conflicts between those groups as well as the organizational processes that may lead to quasi-resolutions of such conflicts, such as satisficing and sequential decisionmaking. It does not tell us, however, what the specific outcome of those processes will be. That is completely dependent on the detailed decisions and behaviours of the organizational participants involved.

Contrast this with principal/agent theory. How do the principal and the agent arrive at making a choice between, say, a wage contract and a rent contract for growing strawberries (see Section 7.6)? Is it a matter of intense dispute with fierce bargaining on both sides? Is one party in a better bargaining position, maybe because of a lack of alternatives for the other party? Is it only a bilateral exchange situation or perhaps what Williamson would call a large numbers exchange situation (ex ante)?

Principal/agent theory is silent on such process and content issues. It presents the expected outcomes, given the variables on which it focuses (utilities, reservation pay, effort levels and so on) and the efficiency criterion it employs.

Figure 11.2 presents our ordering of the various approaches along the process versus content dimension. Behavioural theory is a fairly pure process theory. Organizational ecology is only somewhat more content-orientated. 'Content' here refers to the expected development of the population over time and the density dependence of founding and exit rates.

Nelson and Winter's evolutionary theory started out as a rather pure process theory. However, as discussed in Chapter 10, subsequently they came to realize that the theory could have benefited from the incorporation of some insights from the strategy literature. That led them to, first, explore links with Chandler's work, *Strategy and Structure*, and later contribute to the literature on *dynamic capabilities*. Winter in particular has been personally active in further developing the literature on this subject (see Winter, 2003, and his contribution to Helfat et al., 2007). As a result, evolutionary theory has strengthened its micro-foundations and acquired the possibility to conduct content research – into the nature of dynamic capabilities that provide sustainable competitive advantage, for example. Such research is starting to come on stream now (see Helfat et al., 2007). Therefore, we now classify evolutionary theory (with the incorporation of dynamic capabilities) as a process theory with more ability to generate substantive outcomes than we found in previous editions of this book.

At the other end of the spectrum, positive agency theory is slightly more process-orientated than principal/agent theory because it is occasionally more explicit about the mechanisms that produce particular outcomes, such as the operation of a market for corporate control. It roughly shares this position with transaction cost economics. The latter is explicit about one particular process: the fundamental transformation that may occur as a result of

Figure 11.2 Process and content approaches

increasing asset specificity (see Section 8.3). Transaction cost economics leaves the selection process, which is assumed to lead to efficient outcomes, open, however.

Finally, we turn to the classification of economic approaches to strategy. As explained in Chapter 9, traditional industrial organization is clearly a content theory. It attempts to explain the structure, conduct and performance of (firms within) an industry. In so far as industrial organization is the basis of our approach to strategic management, we are therefore applying a content theory. It informs us about the posture and positioning of firms within and across industries. Our discussion of move and counter move is only partly more process-orientated, to the extent that the development of strategies over time is considered. The economic contribution to strategic management originally left the internal processes of strategy formation and development undiscussed. However, with the development of the resource-based view (RBV) and, particularly, the extension to dynamic capabilities, process considerations are entering into the economic contributions to strategy. The concept of dynamic capabilities allows a link between economic contributions to strategy and evolutionary theories, which offers exciting opportunities to narrow the gap between content and process theories. We show this link as a dotted line in Figure 11.2.

Figure 11.2 makes it clear that there still remains a gap between process- and content-orientated approaches. While this is true of economic theories of organization, it also reflects the more general tendencies in the field of organization studies. A fully integrated content and process model of organizational behaviour and development is still a challenge.

11.4.2 Static versus dynamic approaches

The second dimension we use to order our economic approaches to organizations is not unrelated to the first one discussed above. It is, however, sufficiently different to merit a separate discussion. It is the distinction between static and dynamic theories. This distinction allows us to make some observations about the various modes of analysis used in our theories. It also allows some remarks on the timeframe that is inherent in each theory.

In Figure 11.3, the vertical axis corresponds to that in Figure 11.2 and represents the process versus content dimension. We have now added the static versus dynamic dimension as a horizontal axis. Each axis is divided into three parts, which define regions of the figure.

Following the vertical axis, we find that the process approaches are in the top region and the content approaches in the bottom region. The rather empty middle region illustrates the absence of integrated process and content theories (but we have indicated the potential of the dynamic capabilities literature to start filling this gap).

The horizontal axis is also divided into three parts. The regions defined by the horizontal axis are discussed in turn below.

Comparative-static analysis

To the left we find the agency theories. They employ a mode of analysis that is known as **comparative-static** in economics. A comparative-static analysis

Figure 11.3 Static and dynamic approaches

compares one (static) situation with another. For instance, the principal/agent situation under a wage contract is compared with the situation under a rent contract. The analysis is aimed at discovering whether or not one of these situations is superior to the other (given the variables included in the analysis and the criterion of efficiency). What the analysis reveals, therefore, is a ranking of alternative situations, given the (efficiency) criterion employed. It will not tell you how the present situation may evolve or how to get from here to there if you are now in an inferior situation.

To the right, we find the ecological and evolutionary theories that are characterized by their long-term perspective. The cumulative selection and adaptation processes that are required for the theories to work clearly indicate their long-term dynamic character.

Behavioural theory and strategy occupy a middle position between these two extremes. They usually take the present situation as a starting point for the analysis and may then ask, what's next? In behavioural theory, we might analyse the effects of the rise in aspiration levels. In strategy, we may contemplate a strategic move. While, therefore, these approaches are partly dynamic in character, they certainly do not share the long-term timeframe of their neighbours to the right.

That leaves transaction cost economics to be classified. As is evident from Figure 11.3, it is not possible to classify it completely in just *one* of the three boxes along the static versus dynamic dimension. The reason is that transaction cost economics employs a mode of analysis that can be characterized as **comparative-institutional**. It compares the functioning of one institutional arrangement (such as markets) with the functioning of another (such as hierarchies).[6] The criterion for comparison is, again, efficiency (now including transaction costs, of course). In that respect it is analogous to a comparative-static approach com-

Comparative-institutional analysis

paring one situation with another. It also answers some 'what's next?' questions, however. The progression of hierarchical forms – from peer groups via simple hierarchies to more complex hierarchies – is one case in point. Another is fundamental transformation (see Section 8.3). These elements of transaction cost theory belong in the middle column. That is why we have placed this approach in both the left and middle regions of the static versus dynamic axis.

11.4.3 Levels of analysis

Level of analysis

Our third and final dimension refers to the level(s) of analysis the theories are addressing. A **level of analysis** denotes the level at which the problems that a theory is attempting to analyse is located. Psychological theories, for example, are directed mainly at the individual level of analysis: they attempt to explain individual behaviour.

Which level(s) of analysis are the economic approaches to organization addressing? A surprisingly large number, we submit. We feel obliged to distinguish the following seven levels of analysis:

- *person dyad* a pair of individuals in an exchange relationship;
- *group* a (relatively small) number of individuals bound together by a community of purpose, interest or function;
- *intergroup* the relations between organizational groups with different purposes, interests or functions;
- *organization* the nexus of contracts, the coalition of participant groups and/or the administrative structure that forms a unity and is usually legally recognized as such;[7]
- *organizational dyad* a pair of organizations in an exchange relationship;
- *population of organizations* all organizations of a particular type or form;
- *system* the entire set of organizational populations, environmental characteristics and their interrelationships that are relevant to the analysis of aggregate phenomena.

These seven levels form the vertical axis in Figure 11.4. The figure shows which levels of analysis are covered by the approaches included in this book. The position of each approach is discussed in turn below.

Agency theory spans the person dyad to organizational levels of analysis, while *principal/agent theory* is specifically geared to the person dyad level. That is because the latter theory formally examines agency relationships between two people. Although attempts are made to extend principal/agent theory to multiple agent and/or multiple principal settings, it proves to be very difficult. The formal analysis soon poses intractable problems when heterogeneity of principals or agents is introduced. The insights gained from principal/agent analysis, therefore, strictly apply only to the one principal, one agent level of analysis. Often they are used, however, as a paradigm for analyses at a higher level. It should be clear that considerable caution is in order when such inferences are made.[8] At the group level, all kinds of heterogeneities and group interactions may already start to play a major role. At higher levels of analysis many environmental and institutional factors will come into play.

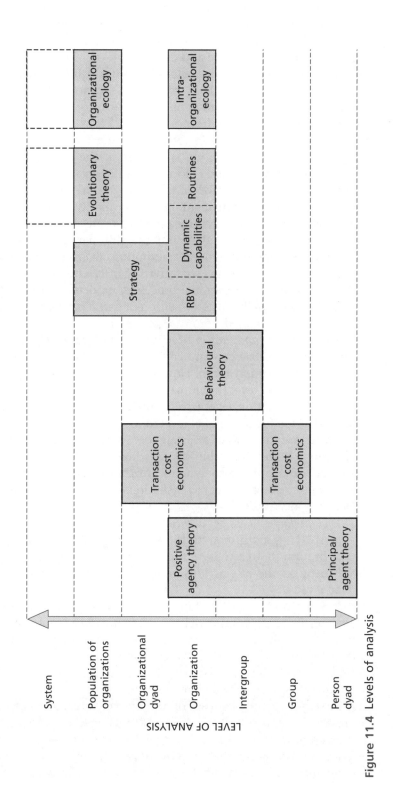

Figure 11.4 Levels of analysis

Positive agency theory takes the analysis up from the group to the organizational level. An example at the group level might be the analysis of the managerial reward structures. For instance, how should managerial reward packages at the corporate and divisional levels differ? The intergroup level of analysis is reached when potential conflicts between, for instance, shareholders and bondholders in public corporations are analysed. The organizational level of analysis pertains to, for example, takeovers and the market for corporate control.

Transaction cost economics focuses at the group level when it analyses peer groups. Most of its attention is directed at the organizational level (e.g. the comparison of U-, M- and H-forms) and the organizational dyad level (such as vertical integration), however. Interestingly, the intergroup level of potential conflicts between participant groups is hardly analysed.[9] Transaction cost analysis focuses on governance and has a rather holistic view of organizations. As discussed in Section 8.10, it 'imports' shift parameters from the institutional environment and behavioural assumptions from the individual level.

It is, of course, a major characteristic of *behavioural theory* that it explicitly deals with intraorganizational processes, particularly intergroup conflict. The organization is analysed as a coalition of participant groups and organizational behaviour is explained from that perspective.

The *economics and strategy* literature spans three levels of analysis. It analyses individual organizations and contemplates their strategic development (such as the diversification issue). However, it also studies competition and rivalry, both at a dyadic level (the moves and counter moves of two strategic players) and at a population level (rivalry within an industry). The RBV is primarily located at the organizational level. It looks inside the firm to determine which resources are the basis of a sustainable competitive advantage. As discussed in Sections 9.6 and 10.7, the RBV has been extended to incorporate not only (static) resources but also dynamic capabilities. That extension has allowed for a very interesting 'bridge' to evolutionary theory, as originally developed by Nelson and Winter.

Evolutionary and ecological theories are both located at the population level of analysis. They both analyse the population of organizations of a particular type or form. Both also have the potential to extend to the system level. Both are silent on the interactions between two organizations, the organizational dyad level.

Nelson and Winter's evolutionary theory originally already contained some analyses at the organizational level, as the firm is conceptualized as a hierarchy of routines. Those routines can be subject to development and change, such as through learning, imitation and conscious adaptation through a (local) search. However, such change is seriously constrained by prevailing routines. Hence, evolutionary theories strongly emphasize the relative inertia of firms. Interestingly, the extension of the concept of routines with dynamic capabilities, which has provided a 'bridge' to the strategy (RBV) literature, implies that evolutionary theories now allow for more *purposeful adaptation* than in their original formulation. It also means that there is more recognition of the managerial task to build, maintain and modify the resource and capability base of an organization.

Organizational ecology, in its original formulation by Hannan and Freeman, treated organizations as rather inert 'black boxes' (see also Section 10.6). The reason is that in their approach the 'organizational form' in its entirety was subject to selection (while Nelson and Winter selection operated at the intra-organizational level of routines). For Hannan and Freeman there was, therefore, much less reason to look inside the firm. However, in subsequent research, the ecological perspective has also been applied to the organization itself. Burgelman (2002, p. 7) conceptualizes a company as 'an ecology within which strategic initiatives emerge in a patterned way'. As a consequence, he is able to add the force of *internal selection* to the external selection forces operating on the firm. Through such contributions, the box of *intraorganizational ecology* in Figure 11.4 has become a fully fledged research stream of its own.

We may make three final observations about the levels of analysis addressed by economic approaches to organizations. The first is that they vary widely. That is probably due to the fact economics has something to contribute as soon as there is an economic aspect involved in the phenomena that interest us (see Chapter 1). At all levels of analysis – from the two-person to system levels – economic aspects are involved.

The second, related, observation is that the various approaches tend to address quite different problems. That is, in part, due to the different levels of analysis. The evolution of organizational forms over long periods of time is a very different sort of problem from that of the short-term strategic moves that a company may make in a strategic battle. Each level of analysis has its own particular characteristics: groups are more than a collection of dyads; organizations are more than a collection of groups. Care should be taken to specify clearly the level of analysis at which certain findings apply and not make any undue inferences to other levels.

Third, even if we stay with one level of analysis, different theories tend to see different problems. Take the organizational level, to which nearly all theories apply (not surprisingly in this book). Agency theories tend to see an organization as a nexus of contracts; transaction cost economics see it as a governance structure of transactions, behavioural theory as a coalition of participant groups and evolutionary theory as a collection of routines or capabilities. Different theories look at the world through different lenses. The image of the organization that underlies any particular theory strongly shapes the kinds of problems observed and the importance attached to them.[10]

11.5 Summary: all in the family?

We have now discussed the three major similarities we observe between the economic approaches to organizations as well as the three major dimensions of their differences. These are summarized in Table 11.1. The final question remains as to whether the similarities outweigh the differences or not. Are the approaches included in this book members of a family?

In the final analysis, we should like to leave that question for you to answer. We have presented the approaches themselves, as well as our view on their

Table 11.1 Family resemblances and differences

Major similarities	Major differences
Organizations versus markets	Process versus content approaches
Efficiency	Static versus dynamic approaches
Information	Levels of analysis

resemblances and differences, in some detail. That should enable you to form a judgement. Obviously, our judgement is that they belong together in this book and, yes, we do regard them as a family. We pursue this metaphor below, offering some observations on the structure of the family as we see it.

Agency theory, transaction cost economics and industrial economics-cum-strategy and game theory are the members of the *nuclear family*. They represent the hard core of the present economic approaches to organizations. They are the fields where most of the current attention is focused and most of the research work in organizational economics is presently done.

The other approaches belong to the *extended family*. We may think of behavioural theory as being at the grandparent level. It has generated work in many areas and, within organizational economics, its strongest influence has been on transaction cost economics and evolutionary theory. There are other siblings, too, in microeconomics as well as in theories of organizational behaviour.

Evolutionary theory might be a cousin (perhaps once removed). One familial link is through the behavioural foundations of its concept of organizations, which connects it to organizational theory. Moreover, it has become recently engaged to the RBV member of the strategy clan. Last but not least, it has a clear lineage in economics. Such a family tree leaves no doubt about its inclusion in the family of organizational economics.

Organizational ecology, finally, may be regarded as the 'odd one out' in the family. It is clearly a relative of evolutionary theory and it is also a member of the family of organizational theories. Its links to the economic family are tenuous, however. Its clearest connection with economics is through the concept of competition, but, as that concept is not well developed in organizational ecology, doubts remain. Our reasons for including organizational ecology in this book were two-fold:

1 its relation to evolutionary theory
2 our expectation that it will develop more links with economics over time (see Sections 10.6–10.8). In fact, it is already quite attracted to industrial organization, with which it shares some basic interests (see, for example, Barron, 2003; Boone and van Witteloostuijn, 1995; Schreuder and van Witteloostuijn, 1990).

That rounds off our picture of the family structure. For us, the similarities discussed in Section 11.3, as well as our perception of the family structure, led us to include these approaches in the book. Some judgement is involved, however. What is more, the family structure is not static; it develops over time. As with human families, new offspring may be generated and the family may redefine its structure as its members are perceived to grow either closer together or further apart. That's all in the family.

11.6 New developments: organizations as complex, adaptive systems

In this section, we want to sketch a theoretical perspective that we expect will have a significant impact on the future development of our family of economic approaches to organizations. It is the perspective of complexity. The **complexity perspective** spans several scientific disciplines and it is being developed by a truly interdisciplinary set of scholars.[11] In this section we want to focus on potential implications of this perspective for the study of organizations.

Complexity perspective

As a starting point, look back to Figure 11.4. It describes a hierarchy of levels of analysis. Individuals may form dyads, dyads may cluster into groups, various groups may constitute organizations, organizations have relations with other organizations and belong to populations, populations together form a community system. At each level of analysis, the phenomena we study are usually complex. At the lowest level of our analysis, the dyad,[12] the people concerned may already have complex relationships with one another. Organizations certainly represent complex systems.

Complexity has no generally accepted definition (Gell-Mann, 1994), but usually refers to systems in which numerous agents are interacting with each other in a great many ways (Waldrop, 1992, p. 86):

> Whenever you look at very complicated systems in physics or biology, ... you generally find that the basic components and the basic laws are quite simple; the complexity arises because you have a great many of these simple components interacting simultaneously. The complexity is actually in the organization – the myriad possible ways that the components of the system can interact.

When scientists from different backgrounds came together to compare notes on such complex systems, they found that (Waldrop, 1992, p. 88):

> every topic of interest had at its heart a system composed of many, many 'agents'. These agents might be molecules or neurons or species or consumers or even corporations. But whatever their nature, the agents were constantly organizing and reorganizing themselves into larger structures through the clash of mutual accommodation and mutual rivalry. Thus, molecules would form cells, neurons would form brains, species would form ecosystems, consumers and corporations would form economies, and so on. At each level, new emergent structures would form and engage in new emergent behaviors.

Emergence

Emergence is thus a central concept in the science of complexity (see Holland, 1998, and Johnson, 2001). It denotes the common finding that the properties, behaviours and structures of systems cannot simply be deduced from the properties, behaviours and structures of the constituent agents. Complex systems 'lead a life of their own'. Knowledge of their parts is helpful, but knowledge of the whole requires more than knowledge of all the parts. In other words, applying this thinking to organizations, we cannot hope ever to understand organizations fully by dissecting them and examining all their parts. The reason is that the interaction of the parts and the interaction of the organization with the environment codetermine the organizational evolution.[13] In the language of complexity, complex systems self-organize.

Self-organization

The exact form of that **self-organization** emerges from the evolution of the system. Remember Box 10.8 on the evolution of competition between Betamax and VHS in the market for videorecorders? As Brian Arthur told the story, the outcome could have gone either way. In the language of complexity, the competitive outcome emerged from the self-organization of the market.

In Chapters 3 and 8 we argued that within large organizations we often see markets for intermediate goods and services. Self-organization and decentralized decisionmaking are often superior to direct supervision and centralized planning in large complex organizations.

Insights from complexity theory can be usefully applied in that context, as illustrated in Box 11.1. The examples in Box 11.1 show that, in large complex systems, detailed top-down planning may be inferior to self-organization of the system.

That insight, in turn, corresponds well to Mintzberg's (1985) empirical observation that strategies arise in organizations in (a mix of) two ways: delib-

Deliberate strategies

erate and emergent. In **deliberate strategies**, pre-existing intentions or plans

Emergent strategies

are realized over time. In **emergent strategies**, a strategic pattern of behaviour develops in the absence of intentions or plans (and sometimes even in spite of other pre-existing intentions or plans). Emergent strategies are thus one manifestation of the self-organization of organizational systems.[14]

Box 11.1 Complexity science in business

Complexity science has attracted the interest of the business community in recent years. The Corporate Strategy Board prepared an overview document entitled 'Current state of complexity science' in 1998. It contains an overview of complexity science from a business perspective as well as a number of illustrative cases. Some of those cases describe how companies have moved away from centralized control of their operations – for instance, in their production scheduling. Recognizing that such centralized control is vulnerable to breaking down in circumstances of high uncertainty, companies have been experimenting with models that allow a solution (to a scheduling problem, for example) to 'emerge' from the interaction of organizational units acting as free agents. Here are two cases in point.

General Motors
In 1992, Dick Morley, one of the creators of the floppy disk, developed a factory control system based on complexity theory principles.

Morley's computer system was put to the test in the paint section of a GM assembly plant in Fort Wayne, Indiana. Morley enabled ten paint booths, previously routed by a centralized controller, to act as free agents with a simple goal: paint as many trucks as possible using as little paint as needed. Each booth electronically 'bids' for the right to paint a certain truck based on colour and the queue in front of the booth. A central computer then compares the bids and assigns a 'winner'.

This system saved $1 million per year in paint alone.

Cemex

The problems Cementos Mexicanos faces in delivering ready-mix concrete to its customers involve many constantly changing variables. A limited window for delivery, congested traffic and work stoppages create an environment that defies linear, command-and-control optimization and is not conducive to top-down scheduling.

The complexity approach to this scheduling dilemma included revamping the systems with global positioning satellite equipment to pinpoint the location of every concrete truck at a very low cost and almost in real time.

Manipulation of the data and other information about truck cargo, plant conditions and construction allows trucks to become independent agents within a network of plants, rather than appendages of a particular plant held to fragile, centrally controlled schedules.

With the help of a complex adaptive systems approach, Cemex's delivery window dropped from the industry average of within approximately 2 hours of a request to within 30 minutes and the company is now moving towards a 10-minute window.

Source: The Corporate Strategy Board, 'Current state of complexity science', Washington DC, October 1998

In such self-organization, small factors may make a huge difference. The reason is that complex systems can behave in a way that mathematicians describe with non-linear dynamics.[15] One of the most striking non-linear

Chaos

phenomena has come to be known as **chaos** (Gleick, 1987): under the right circumstances, tiny perturbations and slight uncertainties may grow until the system's future becomes utterly unpredictable. Moreover, patterns of regularity and chaos seem to alternate in the evolution of most complex systems (Waldrop, 1992, p. 66):[16]

> researchers began to realize that even some very simple systems could produce astonishingly rich patterns of behavior. All that was required was a little bit of nonlinearity. The drip-drip-drip of water from a leaky faucet, for example, could be as maddeningly regular as a metronome – so long as the leak was slow enough. But if you ignored the leak for a while and let the flow rate increase ever so slightly, then the drops would soon start to alternate between large and small: DRIP-drip-DRIP-drip. If you ignored it a while longer and let the flow increase still more, the drops would soon start to come in sequences of 4 – and then 8, 16, and so forth. Eventually, the sequence would become so complex that the drops would seem to come at random – again, chaos. Moreover, this same pattern of ever-increasing complexity could be seen in the population swings of fruit flies, or in the turbulent flow of fluids, or in any number of domains.

Sensitive to initial conditions

The non-linear, dynamic behaviour of complex systems implies that their evolution can be very **sensitive to initial conditions**. Small variations in the circumstances at the start of their development may have large consequences for their direction and outcome (see again Box 10.8). An organizational example may be the 'imprint' that founders leave on their companies, even long after they have retired. Sam Walton's impact on Wal-Mart and Walt Disney's lasting influence on the Disney Corporation are cases in point.

Path dependence

A related characteristic of non-linear, dynamic systems is **path dependence**. Path dependence means that history matters. Consider again the development of STORA over more than 700 years, from coppermining to a forest products company (see Box 10.9). If the 'fire-setting' process for coppermining had not required substantial quantities of wood, STORA would not have acquired forests. Having acquired the forests, it made sense to use the forest products more widely, including the construction of paper mills. There is, thus, a 'chain of events' that explains the transformation of STORA from a mining company to a paper company. Any changes in that chain of events could have yielded a very different outcome. The sensitivity to initial conditions, together with the path dependence of non-linear, dynamic systems, makes it notoriously difficult to predict their development.

Another property of complex systems is that they seek to adapt to their environment. They do so by constantly revising and rearranging their building blocks as they gain experience. The brain will continually strengthen or weaken myriad connections between its neurons as an individual learns from experience in the world. A firm will promote individuals who do well, attempt to transfer best practice across its units and occasionally reshuffle its organization chart.

A particular set of building blocks are the internal models from which complex systems anticipate and predict the future. From bacteria upwards, every living creature has an implicit prediction encoded in its genes. Every creature with a brain has numerous predictions encoded in what it has learned. As we have seen in Chapters 3 and 10, organizations have routines that serve as internal models for prediction. Such organizational routines guide organizational behaviour. In the perspective of complexity, such routines are not passive blueprints but subject to continuous testing, refinement and rearranging as the organizational system gains experience. It is through this process of readjustment of its internal models that a complex system learns to adapt its predictions and, consequently, its behaviour. Hence, we speak of complex, *adaptive* systems.

We can model their behaviour with the tools of evolutionary game theory, as introduced in Section 5.6. You may recall the model of Lindgren (1997) in which he allowed agents (strategies) to develop memory. As a result of learning, the strategies develop from simple to complex. The interactions between agents, similarly, develop from simple to complex. The population, consisting of all strategies at any point in time, continually evolves. Sometimes it shows periods of relative stability, but then it suddenly 'tips' into turbulence. New innovations pop up and upset any seeming stability achieved for some time. Those new innovations thus also change the environment for all other strategies, thereby shifting selection pressures. As a consequence, strategies and environments coevolve.

When selection pressures are strong, success spreads rapidly as the most successful strategies are copied. The disadvantage is that variety is reduced in the population. Such variety can be required when new, better strategies need to be explored as the environment develops further. Weak selection pressure encourages such variety. Thus, the strength of selection pressures impacts the trade-off between exploitation (of success) and exploration (of innovations).

These ideas correspond closely to insights in organization theory about organizational learning (and unlearning), managerial repertoires and dominant logics. We want to illustrate the potential of applying 'complexity theory' to organizations with one example, which we borrow from Bettis and Prahalad (1995). We have chosen it because it sheds additional light on the inertia versus adaptability theme that we raised at the end of Chapter 10.

As noted in Section 10.8, successful firms can become 'simple' over time, focusing exclusively on their successful repertoire of routines (or competences) and becoming intolerant of deviation or variation. Bettis and Prahalad refer to the **dominant logic** of such a firm. Its dominant logic serves an organization well so long as its predictions about the environment are largely borne out. When the environment is turbulent and conditions change rapidly, however, the organization may need to 'unlearn' its dominant logic.

Complexity theorists have shown that complex systems can achieve such unlearning when they move far from (the previous) equilibrium.[17] Bettis and Prahalad visualize these notions with the three graphs shown in Figures 11.5–11.7. All three figures show organizational stability plotted against a composite environmental variable, which is assumed to be composed of the major environmental variables combined in some fashion. Hence, different points on the horizontal axis represent different environmental conditions.

The organization is shown as a small marble at rest in Figure 11.5 in one of the 'valleys', or equilibria, of the stability function. That particular equilibrium corresponds to the current dominant logic that is matched to the environment facing the firm.

Figure 11.6 shows how small displacements from a state of equilibrium, corresponding to small changes in the environment, will result in the firm 'rolling back' into its previous repertoire, called forth by the dominant logic. That is the situation described by organizational ecology when it argues that organizations tend to be relatively inert.

Under such circumstances, the match between dominant logic and environment may deteriorate, but, because of the small differences, the current dominant logic may continue to be useful. If, however, there are large enough changes in the environment (Figure 11.7), organizations may be sufficiently shaken up to roll over an adjacent hill into a new equilibrium, based on a newly developed dominant logic.

Dominant logic

Figure 11.5 Organizational stability

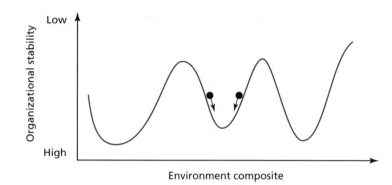

Figure 11.6 Small fluctuations return to original equilibrium

Figure 11.7 Moving far from equilibrium allows firms to establish new equilibrium

This last proposition corresponds closely with the empirical observation that organizations often develop such new logics only in response to crises – or fail (Schreuder, 1993b). It may also suggest why firms that recognize they must do something completely different increasingly locate new activities far away from their current activities. When IBM struggled to catch up with developments in the PC field, for example, it established a separate unit that was geographically and managerially insulated from the 'old IBM' with its mainframe mentality. Similarly, when General Motors wanted to build its new Saturn model with innovative production techniques, it established a separate organization for the purpose.

Finally, this proposition may explain why new competitors often displace experienced incumbents in an industry when major structural change occurs (see Box 11.2 on the software industry). The new entrants are, in essence, starting with a clean sheet and do not have the problem of having to climb up an unlearning curve (the 'hills' in Figures 11.5–11.7) before being able to run down a new learning curve.

If the steepness of the hills and/or their height were to depend on the strength of the dominant logic, we would have an explanation of the Icarus paradox discussed in Chapter 10. Continuous success would have the effect of reinforcing the dominant logic of the incumbent firm, deepening the 'valley' of its current position and, thus, making it harder to migrate over the

Box 11.2 Punctuated equilibrium and computer technology

The birth of a new species

About 570m years ago, in the ancient oceans of the early Earth, something odd happened. In the space of just a few million years, the seas, which had previously held only microscopic organisms, exploded with a huge variety of life, from a metre-long armoured slab of a fish with a mouth like a rubbish disposal chute to a bizarre beast that walked on 14 stilts and had 7 mouths on stalks. For the next few hundred million years, evolution progressed at its usual stately pace. Then, 225m years ago, something else odd happened. Perhaps an asteroid hit the planet; scientists cannot agree. Whatever it was, it caused 96% of marine species to disappear and dinosaurs to appear. There followed another uneventful interval, until 65m years ago it was suddenly out with the dinosaurs and in with the large mammals, including, eventually, man.

This sort of progression, described beautifully in Stephen J. Gould's *Wonderful Life*, is called 'punctuated equilibrium'. Over millions of years species adapt to fill every imaginable niche. Then along comes some external force – a volcano, an asteroid, an ice age – that changes all the niches and launches a mad scramble for survival. Evolution favours new forms of life that, through a sort of biological lateral thinking, can find a whole new way to thrive. Wings, legs, lungs: all were revolutionary mutations once. Life down the ages has tended to evolve in sudden great leaps, separated by periods of slow change.

The same is true for technology, though the timescale is a little more compressed. In the past half-century, computer technology has evolved in three large jumps, each one followed by an explosion of new companies, a period of rapid change and then the gradual emergence of a few dominant species that rule until the next digital disturbance ... Start around 1950, with the IBM mainframe, when the term 'data processing' entered the language. The next big upheaval came in the mid-1960s, when the minicomputer arrived to open the computing market to a host of upstarts such as Digital Equipment ... Then, in 1981, IBM introduced the personal computer, causing a market explosion from which emerged some of today's strongest companies: Intel, Microsoft, Compaq.

Now the time has come for another shock, duly delivered in the shape of the Internet, which has emerged practically overnight from 25 years of boffin obscurity into the light of mass-media ubiquity. It was made possible by the serendipitous convergence of three technological developments: the spread of PCs and computer networks in offices; a rapid drop in communication costs; and the appearance of the World Wide Web, a brilliantly simple way of linking multimedia documents around the world over the Internet.

Source: The Economist, 25 May 1996

---

unlearning curve to a new and more appropriate position when external change would demand so.

Competency trap

March (1994) refers to this situation as a **competency trap** – a type of lock-in produced by prolonged positive feedback on a successful competence. All in all, such a perspective explains why success carries the seeds of its own demise and successful companies so often fail after some time.

Interestingly, an analogous story can be told about the evolution of new markets. Geroski (2003) tells of markets based on new technologies. Those new technologies are often pushed to markets from the supply side – that is, the technology has not yet developed in a way that is user-friendly. That opens up space for entrepreneurs to offer many different adaptations or applications to the market. Sometimes entrepreneurial established firms can occupy that new space (think of Apple with its iPod in the space of portable music carriers), but often it attracts many new entrants as well (think of all the new Internet-based businesses in the dot-com bubble of Box 1.6).

In fact, most new markets cannot sustain the whole population of firms that enter early or the wide range of different product variants. As a consequence,

Shakeout

Dominant design

there is often a **shakeout**, of both the product variants and the firms that supply them. What emerges is a well-defined product with a **dominant design**. That dominant design is then the basis for the development of a mass market for the product.

In the shift from a new market to a mass market, the basis of the competition changes. Where, initially, the competition is between different designs, the emergence of a dominant design implies that competition shifts to differentiation within the dominant design and price. With the maturing of the market, the product becomes more of a commodity. For a totally commoditized product, only price competition remains.[18]

Our discussions of the *dominant logic* of organizations and the emergence of a *dominant (product) design* that causes the shift from new to maturing markets are, of course, closely interrelated. The dominant logic of firms competing successfully in new markets should focus on creating the dominant product design. An example of this is the competitive battle between retailers and the new Internet-based e-tailers, as recounted in Box 9.5. Another example is the 'standards wars' that have raged in videorecorder markets (see Box 10.8) and DVD markets (see Box 5.1) between firms trying to establish their standard as dominant for these new technologies. Box 11.3 illustrates the case of the then small Haloid Corporation, which introduced the dominant design of xerography printing and was transformed into the global Xerox corporation as a result.

As soon as a dominant design has been established, however, the basis of the competition shifts and firms then need to focus more on, for example, distribution power and cost competitiveness. Thus, their dominant logic has to shift as well.

Young start-up firms often find it difficult to achieve such changes. They may continue to emphasize exploration and flexibility, thus showing insufficient commitment to the emerging dominant design.[19]

Incumbent firms, which have enjoyed success with a particular dominant logic for a long time, find it just as difficult to adjust their modus operandi when radically new technologies emerge that have the potential to erode their basis of competition. Again, Box 11.3 illustrates this point. Xerox found that it was unable to compete against the Japanese dominant design developed for the low-cost segment of small business and home office copying. In effect, the Japanese split the copying market in two, with different firms competing on the basis of different competences in the two segments.

Coevolution

All these examples show that there is **coevolution** between markets and firms.[20] As markets change (in their structure and basis of competition), organizations have to adapt. Conversely, successful innovations and adaptations by firms change the market conditions.

Box 11.3 Xerox: dominant designs and dominant logic.

In the 1930s, Chester Carlson invented a new technology for copying: xerography. It promised much better performance than the prevailing technologies ('wet' photographic methods or 'dry' thermal processes), but initially also at a much higher price.

Carlson took his invention to many of the leading American technology firms of his day, including IBM, Kodak, General Electric, but none was interested. In the end, only the Haloid Corporation, a small manufacturer of photographic paper, was willing to develop the xerography technology further.

It took Haloid Corporation 14 years of research, at a cost of $75 million, to develop the invention into an innovation. In 1960, the first commercial model, named the Xerox 914, was shipped.

To overcome the problem of its still relatively high cost, Haloid offered customers a lease contract at $95 per month. That lease cost included service and 2000 free copies. Additional copies cost 4 cents each. The revenue from leasing alone would not be sufficient for Haloid: the Xerox 914 would have to lead to greatly increased volumes of copying for this business model to pay off.

The Xerox 914 was a huge success. Once it was installed, customers made an average 2000 copies per day, not per month, generating enormous additional revenue for Haloid by each second day of the monthly lease. Haloid's revenues started growing at an average of 41 per cent over the next 12 years. The company changed its name to The Xerox Corporation. By 1966, Xerox held 61 per cent of the copier market. The little $30 million Haloid Corporation turned into the global Xerox Corporation with $2.5 billion revenue in 1972.

Its success was built on developing the dominant copier design of that age – the Xerox 914. That design not only radically altered the market for office copying, sweeping the older technologies away, but also vastly expanded the market (the new design triggering a coevolution of company and market).

Its enormous success shaped the dominant logic of Xerox for many years to come. The 914 business model generated more revenue as more copies were made. As a consequence, Xerox was motivated to develop ever-faster machines that could handle very high copy volumes, with maximum uptime and availability. As a later Xerox CEO said, 'If a copier was slow in generating copies, that was money plucked out of our pocket.'

The dominant logic of Xerox led it to focus on large companies and governmental organizations needing high volumes of high-quality copies. It was not suited to serving the needs of small businesses and individuals, requiring lower outputs and willing to trade off quality against price. Japanese firms later attacked that segment of the copier market with low-cost machines, in effect establishing a new dominant design for that particular segment.

Xerox wanted to fight for that segment, but faced great challenges. It had to ask its engineers, who excelled in developing ever-faster machines, to now focus on simpler products that cost less. It had to build a distribution network to reach the home office and small business market. It had to retrain its sales force to propagate a different business model and manage sales channel conflicts. Xerox attempted all of that for over a decade. In 2001, under pressure across its copier business, Xerox abandoned that part of the market and refocused on its dominant logic.

Sources: Chesbrough (2003) and Tellis and Golder (2002). Both books also discuss how the strong dominant logic of Xerox prevented it from benefiting from many computer technology inventions in its Palo Alto Research Centre (PARC) that did not fit its prevailing business model. Only inventions, such as laser printing, which did fit its dominant logic and business model, were exploited by Xerox.

All in all, complexity theory allows us to see the organization as a complex, adaptive system that has several levels of analysis. Each level acts as a building block for the next, higher level. At the same time, each level cannot be completely explained by understanding the lower levels. In that sense, each level leads a life of its own. Each is subject to internal as well as external selection. For instance, in organizations, there is internal selection of competing views, routines, proposals and so on and there is external selection (by the environment) acting on the resulting organizational configuration of strategy, structure and capabilities.

Organizations and their relevant environments (including markets) co-evolve. Organizations can adapt, but it is a process that can lead as often to failure as it does to success. We are beginning to see some of the mechanisms that underly those processes. A better understanding of these phenomena is of utmost theoretical as well as practical significance.

Questions

1 Which definitions of the firm have been given in this book? Indicate for each definition how coordination between several (groups of) people within the firm is achieved.

2 Consider Boxes 11.2 and 11.3. What relevance do these extracts have for the discussion in the text of Bettis and Prahalad's view on dominant logics and organizational adaptability (through learning)?

Suggested further reading

Axelrod, R. M. and Cohen, M. D. (1999), *Harnessing Complexity: Organizational implications of a scientific frontier*, New York: Free Press.

Beinhocker, E. D. (2006), *The Origin of Wealth*, Boston, MA: Harvard Business School Press.

Gould, S. J. (1989), *Wonderful Life*, New York: Norton.

Milgrom, P. and Roberts, J. (1992), *Economics, Organization and Management*, Englewood Cliffs, NJ: Prentice Hall.

Roberts, J. (2004), *The Modern Firm*, Oxford: Oxford University Press.

Scott, W. R. (2003), *Organizations: Rational, natural and open systems*, 5th edn, Englewood Cliffs, NJ: Prentice Hall.

Slater, M. (2003), 'The boundary of the firm', in D. O. Faulkner and A. Campbell, *The Oxford Handbook of Strategy*, Oxford: Oxford University Press.

Stacey, R. D. (2007), *Strategic Management and Organisational Dynamics: The challenge of complexity*, 5th edn, Harlow: Prentice Hall/Financial Times.

Notes

1 If the policies are pursued by internal growth (instead of mergers and acquisitions), the analytical benchmark from an economic point of view remains that a separate entity could have been created and a (cooperative or competitive) market relation established.

2   We thus leave behavioural theories out of our discussion here. We believe, however, that the markets versus organizations perspective applies to these as well, albeit probably to a lesser extent than to the other approaches (see also Section 11.5). Behavioural theories arose in opposition to the view of firms as holistic entities responding automatically to market changes.

3   Observing that efficiency is the primary economic criterion determining selection implies that it is not the only criterion recognized in economics. Monopolistic tendencies, for instance, are recognized as well. Furthermore, it is an empirical question, to what extent does efficiency explain selection in the real world (and how important is the economic aspect of the phenomenon we are studying)? Sociologists may be quite right that, for example, schools or parts of the public sector are not primarily subject to efficiency selection pressures. Most economists, however, would agree that a large part of the world of economic transactions is subject to important efficiency pressures. Exceptions are noted, for instance, in the 'increasing returns' literature (see Section 10.8).

4   In particular, our emphasis on the centrality of the information concept may be regarded as too strong by some economists.

5   Strategies may, for instance, be deliberately formulated and subsequently implemented. Alternatively, they may emerge from the firm's current operations and be formulated only afterwards. Recall Burgelman's distinction between autonomous and induced processes of strategy formation (Section 10.8). We discuss this further in Section 11.6.

6   Davis and North (1971) distinguished between the *institutional environment* and *institutional arrangements*. In Section 1.7, we introduced the institutional environment, which produces the 'rules of the game' for both markets and organizations. When we describe transaction cost economics as comparative-institutional in this chapter, we refer to the comparison of two different governance structures (or *institutional arrangements*) for economic transactions. See also Ménard (1995).

7   It is perhaps ironic to observe that the level of analysis for organizations is hardest to define. The reason is that each approach has its own image of the organization – for example, the nexus of contracts view in agency theory versus the hierarchical view in transaction cost economics. Again, this is representative of a more general characteristic of organizational theory (see Morgan, 1997).

8   We saw in Chapter 5 how games with more than two players (and/or more than one stage) differ from two-player, one-stage games.

9   One exception is the analysis of potential interdepartmental conflict within the U-form firm (see Section 8.6).

10 See, for images of organizations, Morgan (1997). As Weick (1979) has observed, we should be very careful that, as a consequence, 'I believe it when I see it' and 'I see it when I believe it' do not become too intermingled.

11 See, for instance, Waldrop (1992) or Lewin (1995) for popular introductions to complexity.

12 The dyad is not the lowest conceivable level of analysis. Dyads consist of individuals who, in turn, represent complex systems with several levels of analysis (down to genetics and biochemistry). Those levels fall outside the scope of a book on organizations.

13 For those with a philosophical bent, that implies reductionism is not a viable approach to the study of complex systems.

14 In Burgelman's (2002) terminology, it is the interplay of variation-reducing induced strategic processes with variation-enhancing autonomous processes that produces the pattern of strategic behaviour.

15 Non-linear refers to the fact that if you plot a non-linear equation on a graph paper, it is curvy. That implies cause and effect are not proportional: a large cause may have a small effect and vice versa. As systems must be described with various such equations, they can exhibit very unexpected behaviour.

16 Notice that this description is analogous to the results of ecological simulation in evolutionary game theory (Section 5.6) and the description of punctuated equilibrium in Box 11.2.

17 See Prigogine and Strengers (1984) or Kauffman (1993, 1995). When systems move 'far from equilibrium', that is identical to being 'at the edge of chaos'. The example from Bettis and Prahalad that follows in the main text bears close resemblance to Kauffman's account of how complex, adaptive systems may move through a 'fitness landscape'. For further examples in the fields of strategic management and organizational dynamics, see Beinhocker (2006), Brown and Eisenhardt (1998) and Stacey (2007).

18 This description of the emergence of new markets and their development into maturity closely resembles the findings of population ecology in terms of the development of populations (see Chapter 10). Moreover, it has significant implications for competitive strategy, among others, and the validity of first-mover advantages. See Geroski (2003), Tellis and Golder (1996, 2002), as well as Markides and Geroski (2005) for a discussion of strategic implications.

19 Volberda (2003) calls this competency trap the *renewal trap*. He develops an interesting framework of strategic flexibility. An organization must possess dynamic capabilities that enhance its flexibility to avoid becoming rigid, but must also be sufficiently anchored in order to avoid chaos.

20 See Helfat et al. (2007, pp. 26–7) for a similar perspective on coevolution within the context of dynamic capabilities.

Part III

Applications

12 Mergers and acquisitions

12.1 Introduction

On 10 January 2000, America OnLine (AOL) bid $166 billion for Time Warner in an all-stock offer. AOL was an Internet-based company offering e-mail and messenger services. As such, it was a delivery company with little content. Time Warner, however, was a formidable content company, based on the successes of *Time* magazine, the Warner Brothers movie studio and Turner Broadcasting Systems (owning cable networks).

Steven Case, CEO of AOL, argued that the companies therefore formed a perfect match. They were strongly complementary and could offer the best of both worlds: the 'old world' of content delivered by magazines, books and films and the 'new world' of Internet-based delivery of such content. Jerry Levin, CEO of Time Warner, felt that his company might have missed the Internet revolution and probably saw the merger as a fast route to catch up. Both CEOs promised substantial synergies of the merger at about $1 billion.

After the successful completion of the merger bid, the company renamed itself AOL Time Warner. Shortly thereafter, problems started to emerge.

The new business model did not work as anticipated. Cross-selling Time Warner content to AOL customers proved to be a difficult proposition.

AOL's mail system was largely based on dial-up and not yet on broadband. When the company ordered all employees to switch to AOL e-mail, Time Warner employees rebelled: they complained that the AOL system could not handle large digital files. Executives had to rescind the e-mail mandate.

Another synergy should have come from package deals for advertisers: 'space in *Time* magazine, air time on Turner cable networks, spots on AOL, and licensing opportunities with Warner Brothers film studio'[1] That synergy also failed to materialize.

Perhaps most importantly, the cable system executives in Time Warner resisted carrying AOL on their system, preventing the AOL switchover to broadband.

Problems accumulated to the extent that Jerry Levin stepped down as CEO in December 2001 and Steven Case as chairman in January 2003. In September 2003 the company changed its name back to Time Warner and AOL became one of its divisions. In the process, an enormous amount of 'shareholder value' was first (seemingly) created and then destroyed (Figure 12.1 shows the development of the Time Warner share price from 1996 to 2005). On the merger announcement date of January 7, 2000, AOL and Time Warner had market values of $165 billion and $76 billion respectively – a combined value of $241 billion. By the end of 2004, the combined value of the two firms had slumped to $78 billion, about the same as Time Warner's standalone value at merger.

From this example of Time Warner, it is already clear that mergers and acquisitions (M&A) can be a dangerous route to growth for companies. In this chapter, we will examine the risks from an economic point of view, using the concepts introduced in previous chapters. At the same time, it is also obvious that many successful companies of today have succeeded in executing M&A in an effective way. General Electric (GE) has transformed itself from a lighting company into a broad service and industrial company. M&A has been a very important tool to accomplish this transformation and GE is today still regarded as a skilful acquirer.[2] In the oil industry, Royal Dutch Shell is the result of the successful merger of the Dutch firm Koninklijke Olie with the British firm Shell Transport and Trading Company, while British Petroleum (BP) acquired its American rival Amoco in 1998 and Exxon reacted by acquiring Mobil in 1999. M&A has been instrumental in these oil companies gaining the required scale to compete on a global basis. Apparently, they have also managed to handle the risks involved in such transactions. In this chapter, we will also look at some solutions that have evolved as answers to the risks inherent in M&A.

Acquisition

First, a short introduction to the terminology of M&A.[3] An **acquisition** occurs when one company takes a controlling ownership interest in another firm (or in a subsidiary or selected assets of another firm). Acquisitions may

Takeovers

also be called **takeovers**.

Merger

A **merger** is a combination of two or more firms in which all but one cease to exist, and the combined organization continues under the name of the surviving firm. In practice, the terms 'mergers' and 'acquisitions' are often loosely

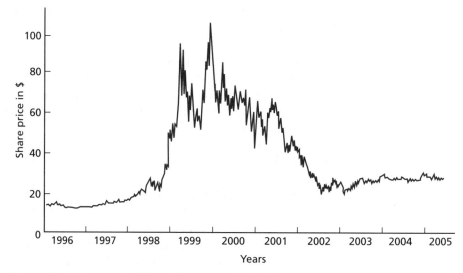

Figure 12.1 Share price Time Warner, 1996–2005

lumped together: acquisitions are often presented as 'mergers' to give them a more equal and friendly appearance.

From an economic point of view, business combinations can also be classified as horizontal, vertical and conglomerate mergers (or acquisitions). A **horizontal merger** is between two competitors in the same industry. A **vertical merger** occurs when two firms combine across the value chain, such as when a firm buys a former supplier (backward integration) or a former customer (forward integration). When there is no strategic relatedness between an acquiring firm and its target, this is called a **conglomerate merger**. Conglomerate mergers are a case of unrelated diversification, as discussed in Chapter 9. Such a classification is used by, for example, the antitrust authorities to evaluate whether or not they can approve M&A in the context of competition policy. In principle, an antitrust authority such as the Federal Trade Commission (FTC) in the USA will disallow any acquisition that has the potential to generate monopoly or oligopoly profits in an industry.

We will discuss the broad field of M&A as follows. We start out by further indicating the significance of M&A and examining the evidence for the success and failure of M&A transactions. We then delineate the M&A process from the buyer's and from the seller's side, pointing out that many M&A transactions are structured as **auctions**. The fundamental problem in such auctions is the **information asymmetry** between the seller and the buyer(s). Such information asymmetry leads to the problems that we encountered in Chapter 4: **hidden information (adverse selection)** and **hidden action (moral hazard)**. There is also the danger that the winner of the auction will experience the **winner's curse**.

Some types of M&A may suffer from problems due to **transaction specificity** and the possibility of **hold-up**.

Finally, we also examine the **agency relationship** between managers and shareholders with respect to incentive alignment for making the right type of M&A transactions and appropriate **corporate governance** after the transaction.

Horizontal merger

Vertical merger

Conglomerate merger

Auctions

Information asymmetry

Hidden information (adverse selection)

Hidden action (moral hazard)

Winner's curse

Transaction specificity

Hold-up

Agency relationship

Corporate governance

12.2 The significance of M&A

The volume and value of M&A are enormous. For 2006, estimates are that almost 8000 M&A transactions took place with a total value of $3.963 billion, nearly 4 trillion. In order to realize the magnitude of that figure let's write it out: $3,963,000,000,000 changed hands in 2006 as a result of mergers and acquisitions. Clearly, this extent to which firms change ownership is of great significance for managers, shareholders, employees and societies alike.

Figure 12.2 gives an overview of the development of M&A in the period 1995–2006. It shows that M&A activity has been cyclical, with peaks (1999–2000 – the Internet boom) and troughs. Indeed, such a pattern has been typical over time. Economists talk of **merger waves** and have identified five such waves in the nineteenth and twentieth centuries. In Box 12.1 Besanko et al. (2004) identify these five waves for the USA and indicate the evolving reasons for such waves over time.

Merger waves

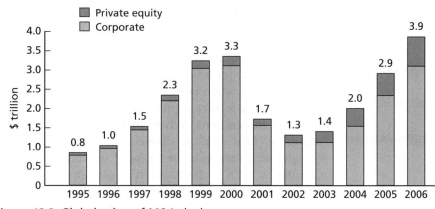

Figure 12.2 Global value of M&A deals

Source: R. Dobbs, M. Goedhart and H. Suonio (2006) 'Are companies getting better at M&A?', *The McKinsey Quarterly*

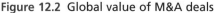

Box 12.1 Merger waves

The first merger wave began after the worldwide depression of 1883, which left many capital-intensive industries with overcapacity, and ended in the early 1900s. This wave involved roughly one-sixth of all US manufacturing firms. Some combinations that arose at this time, such as Standard Oil and United States Steel, were able to monopolize their industries. A second, smaller merger wave occurred in the early 1920s. Antitrust laws, such as the Sherman Act and the Federal Trade Commission Act, discouraged grabs for monopoly power that failed to promote increased efficiency. As a result, many combinations stopped short of achieving 50 per cent market share, and their industries resembled oligopolies instead of monopolies. Other combinations involved vertical, rather than horizontal, integration. The formation and growth of General Motors during this time displayed both types of integration.

The reasons for the first two merger waves are easy to understand. Firms in the same market combined to reduce competition and achieve scale economies. The emergence of manufacturing giants tilted the calculus of the make-or-buy decision in favor of vertical integration. The Great Depression of the 1930s and American participation in World War II put a damper on merger activity until 1950.

By 1960, the pace of merger activity had again quickened. Unlike the previous waves, this third wave featured increased levels of unrelated diversification and produced large conglomerates selling extensive product lines in diverse markets. Mergers in the 1960s resulted in firms such as American Can, which sold cans, clothing and financial services, and ITT, whose business portfolio included life insurance, car rental, hotels and vending machines.

The mergers of the 1980s were different from their predecessors. Many cash-rich firms, lacking solid investments in their own businesses, instead attempted to grow through acquisition. Philip Morris, flush with cash from the tobacco business, bought 7-Up in 1978, General Foods in 1985, and Kraft in 1988. Some economists have argued that the fourth merger wave was a reaction to the poor performance of the conglomerations formed during the third wave. The merger wave of the 1980s also saw the emergence of the 'leveraged buy-out' in which the company was purchased by not another firm, but by a group of private investors (with heavy reliance on debt as a means of financing the transaction).

The fifth merger wave began in the mid-1990s and ended in 2001. Deals made during this period included Exxon-Mobil, Pfizer-Warner Lambert and AOL-Time Warner. It is too early to evaluate these

deals, but they seemed to be motivated by one of two factors: (1) firms desired to establish dominant market shares within specific industries; (2) firms desired access to international markets. In
either case, merging firms were usually 'related' businesses.

Source: Besanko et al. (2004)

As Figure 12.2 shows, a new wave started in the beginning of the twenty-first
century. Probable reasons for this international wave of M&A include the following.

- *Globalization* Many companies found that they were increasingly confronted with global competition. They aspired to obtain global leadership in
  their business areas. This was also fostered by the lowering of trade barriers
  as a result of the cooperation in the World Trade Organisation (WTO).
  Therefore, industry consolidation took place not only at the national or
  regional levels but also on an international scale. The number of cross-
  border and intercontinental deals has been steadily rising.
- *Strong cash flows* After the slump in the years 2001–2003, the global
  economy showed a good performance, generating strong cash flows and
  healthy balance sheets for many companies. Confidence was rising that this
  positive development would continue for some time. Strong demand from
  emerging economies, such as China and India, boosted consumption of
  many products. Even rather mature industries, such as steel, benefited from
  this trend. As a result, the steel industry witnessed its own international
  merger wave with Mittal (India) buying Arcelor (Europe) and Tata (India)
  buying Corus (Europe)
- *Private equity* Figure 12.2 shows that the M&A share of 'private equity' rose.
  In many industries, about 25–30 per cent of all deals in 2006 were done by
  private equity players. Favourable debt markets enabled these acquirers to
  finance their deals with high leverage. We will come back to private equity
  towards the end of this chapter.

In view of the major significance of M&A, it is important to know how successful these transactions are. Failure of major M&A transactions can have
dramatic consequences for the managers and shareholders of the companies
concerned, as we saw in the AOL-Time Warner example discussed in the introduction to this chapter. The consequences may also extend to the employees
of the firm, its suppliers and customers, as well as local communities and
society at large.

So, what do we know about the factors contributing to success and failure
of M&A transactions? The next section attempts to summarize our present
knowledge.

12.3 Success and failure of M&A transactions

The fact that not all M&A transactions are successful has not escaped the notice of the popular press. For example, *Business Week* magazine regularly reviews the success rate of acquisitions, making observations such as, '*Business Week* investigations in 2002 and 2004 showed that 61 per cent of big deals hurt the company's shareholders. Half of them also leave customers dissatisfied'.[4] What, though, do we know about the success and failure of M&A from solid research?

Most empirical M&A research has been done from the perspective of either **corporate finance** or **industrial organization**.[5] Different research tools are used in each tradition. Below we summarize the main findings from both perspectives.

Finance researchers use the research tool of **event studies**. They investigate the movement of share prices when there is an acquisition announcement. If the share price of a company shows an 'abnormal' upward movement, that is interpreted as revealing the shareholders regard the acquisition announcement as good news. If the share price does not move, it is assumed that the acquistion had already been anticipated by the markets. If the share price shows 'abnormal' downward movement, the acquisition is regarded as bad news.[6]

An early survey of such event studies by Jensen and Ruback (1983) showed that the shareholders of target firms typically achieve abnormal returns of 20–30 per cent around the time of an announcement, while shareholders of the bidding companies more or less break even. Overall, the findings have been corroborated in subsequent research. The outcomes were interpreted as demonstrating that acquisitions create value by allocating the assets of the acquired firm to a more efficient management team. If that is the case, then it can be said we observe an efficient market for corporate control.

There is an obvious problem, however, with event studies that concentrate on share price movements around the announcement date. If you look back to Figure 12.1, the problem is clear: the market can be very excited about an acquisition when it is announced, but may be disappointed about the real value of the transaction as it unfolds. Finance researchers have, therefore, tried to lengthen the window of their observations to several years around the announcement date. What they have found is that bidders typically show positive abnormal returns before they make an acquisition announcement and negative abnormal returns thereafter. Tichy (2002) summarized these studies with long windows, quoting Andrade et al. (2001):

> It reveals a clear trend of declining abnormal bidder returns, starting from say +20% five years before the announcement to some −5% two years after and about −10% five years after . . . These results confront the hypothesis of efficient capital markets no less than the hypothesis of value-creating acquisitions: 'In fact, the shareholders of the acquiring firm appear to come dangerously close to actually subsidizing these transactions'.

Corporate finance

Industrial organization

Event studies

All in all, event studies reveal that, around the announcement of a takeover, the target's abnormal returns increase steeply, while the bidder's returns remain unchanged at best. After the acquisition, increasing negative abnormal returns prevail, implying a negative wealth effect on the shareholders of the acquiring company. These findings raise the question as to what the overall net effect of M&A transactions is. Is the gain of the winners higher or lower than the loss of the losers? The overall net economic gain from M&A deals appears to be positive: almost all studies report positive returns for the investors in the combined buyer and target firms. That would imply that M&A *does* create value from an overall economic point of view, presumably by transferring assets to management teams that use them more efficiently (Bruner, 2005).

Outcome studies

Industrial organization researchers use a different research toolbox, named **outcome studies**. Outcome studies compare pre- and post-M&A performance of firms with other firms in their industry, with matching firms or with performance projections. While event studies use a single performance measure (abnormal returns), outcome studies use multiple measures, such as cash flow, profits or performance ratios (return on sales, assets or equity).

Summarizing the results of 36 such outcome studies, Tichy (2002) found that profits come out weaker than in the respective non-merging control group in 58 per cent of the studies and stronger in only 11 per cent. This overall result across outcome studies is consistent with the long-term result of event studies. The combined sales of the two companies are hardly affected in about half of the outcome studies, but are lower in about one third of the cases. That is in spite of the tendency for consumer prices to rise post-acquisition. Investments are not necessarily reduced, but combined R&D may be lowered. Assets are restructured. A few studies report slightly reduced labour costs, but not much is known about lay-offs. Manager turnover, however, is observed in about half of the M&A transactions.

Other research results include the following:[7]

- acquisitions or takeovers are much more prevalent than mergers of 'equals'. Typically, a bidder – large by the standards of its industry – acquires a target that is much smaller, and small by the standards of its industry as well;
- bidder and target are at least as profitable as their respective industries in four out of five cases, but the bidder, generally, is more profitable than the target;
- the bidder tends to grow faster than its industry and faster than the target;
- the shares of the bidder tend towards overvaluation and positive abnormal returns in the year before the acquisition, while those of the target rather tend towards negative abnormal returns;
- focus-increasing acquisitions tend to show relatively the best results, followed by related and horizontal acquisitions, while unrelated acquisitions (diversifications) and conglomerate mergers fare worst;
- cash offers are more likely to have positive returns than share offers;
- returns to buyers will likely be lower if M&A markets are 'hot' (around the peaks of the M&A waves).

From this overview of research results with respect to the success of M&A, it is clear that shareholders of target companies stand to gain most, particularly if they receive cash. If they receive shares of the acquiring company, they may want to consider selling them as the likelihood of abnormal negative returns in the medium term is significant. For the acquiring companies and their shareholders, M&A transactions are clearly risky from the point of view of subsequent performance. For effects on other stakeholders, less robust research results are available, but some evidence suggests that consumers may suffer higher prices and employees slightly reduced labour costs.

Next to the shareholders, it is the stakeholder group of management that is affected most, given the significant likelihood of management turnover. In that sense, our opening example of AOL-Time Warner is illustrative. The transaction led to the departures of both CEOs in a relatively short period of time.

In the next sections, we will further examine M&A transactions mainly from a managerial point of view. We will first ask how buyers and sellers may come to such transactions and which M&A processes are then likely to be employed. Then, we focus on the risks involved in such transactions and the evolution of ways and means to address such risks. From the overview of the M&A research in this section, however, you may conclude that those ways and means are obviously not yet perfect.

12.4 Strategy, acquisitions and hidden information

In Chapter 9, we examined the economic contributions to the field of strategic management. We distinguished between the *competitive strategy* of single business units and the *corporate strategy* of multibusiness firms. In Figure 9.1, we showed the process of strategic planning in a multibusiness firm. In such a process, the firm will have to determine whether or not it can achieve its goals of growth and further

Organic (internal) growth and development

development on its own strength. If so, we say that it can pursue a strategic course of **organic (internal) growth and development**. If organic growth and develop-

External growth and development (through M&A)

ment is insufficient, however, the option of **external growth and development (through M&A)** can be considered. In Chapter 9, we specifically looked at the strategies of vertical integration, diversification and horizontal multinationalization. While such strategies can be pursued organically, in practice they will often be executed via M&A. In such cases, firms will enter the M&A market as buyers.

Divestment

A firm may, alternatively, come to the conclusion that **divestment** is a strategic option to consider. This may apply to the whole firm, such as in the case of a family firm without family members in the next generation to succeed the present owner-managers. Another case might be the national firm that is faced with the choice to either compete with global competitors or sell out to them in time. It may also apply to a multibusiness firm that has come to the conclusion that certain activities no longer belong to its core business. In all these examples, companies enter the M&A market as sellers.

So, there are potential buyers and sellers of business assets. Does that automatically lead to a market for M&A? The answer is no. Buyers and sellers in the

Hidden information

M&A market, in principle, face the same basic difficulty as those in the market for used cars: **hidden information.**

Sellers may have private information as to the assets they are selling. Buyers have private information as to the value they would be willing to attach to those assets. Such private information is unobservable by the other party. As explained in Chapter 4, such information asymmetries may have the consequence that certain transactions are impossible to execute or can only be concluded at a severe discount.

Market for 'lemons'

The classic reference on this subject is to Akerlof's (1970) article on the '**the market for lemons**'. In the article, Akerlof explained the discount that sellers of almost new used cars would have to accept because of the problem of hidden information they might have regarding the quality of the car offered for sale. That discount may be so great that it prevents the successful conclusion of a transaction.

The above problem manifests itself in exactly the same way in the M&A market. The seller of a business may also have hidden information on the quality of the business, its future prospects and its inherent risks. If buyers suspect such hidden information, a transaction will be hindered (see Box 12.2). In Chapter 4, we argued that market participants therefore have an incentive to come up with solutions to those information problems. In the remainder of this chapter we will introduce the solutions that have evolved for problems of asymmetrical information in M&A transactions.

Box 12.2 How M&A targets can be like used cars

In 2001, George Akerlof, Michael Spence and Joseph Stiglitz shared the Nobel Memorial Prize in Economic Sciences for their work on information economics.

The classic 'market for lemons' example offered by Professor Akerlof describes how the market for used cars can fail because of the information asymmetries between a buyer and seller that arise due to the latter's experience of the vehicle. In the absence of appropriate remedies, such as warranties, reputation and so on, buyers will discount their offer prices for all used cars and, as a consequence, the sellers of high-quality vehicles will no longer be willing to trade.

Indeed, information asymmetries crop up in an array of settings, including M&As. During M&A valuation and negotiation processes, an acquirer needs to be able to discern the value of a target and the parties need to agree on a price for the transaction. The acquiring company collects information on the target during the due diligence process, yet it often still remains at an information disadvantage in M&A negotiations. Buyers, therefore, face the risk of 'adverse selection' or overpaying and winding up with a 'lemon'.

Because M&A targets can have attributes that are only understood after purchase, costly surprises emerge during the post-merger integration process. For their part, sellers have an incentive to misrepresent the quality of the company and realize higher gains from the deal.

In short, the seller has a credibility problem that is rooted in the one-shot nature of sell-outs, so its claims will be discounted accordingly. As a result, sellers of good companies run the risk of not receiving fair value for their assets. Therefore, it is in each party's interests to address the problems posed by information asymmetries in M&As. Academics in strategic management and financial economics are now using the insights from information economics to understand when asymmetrical information can adversely affect the efficiency of acquisitions, what remedies might be available and how buyers and sellers can design deals to address these challenges.

Source: Reuer and Ragozzino (2006)

12.5 Auctions

How do the buyers and sellers meet in the M&A market?

A possibility is, of course, that a seller approaches a specific buyer (or a buyer approaches a specific, potential seller) to see whether or not a private negotiation is possible. If both parties agree, they can have an 'exclusive' discussion. That happens, for instance, when two parties want to explore the opportunity for a 'friendly merger of equals'. It is, however, usually to the advantage of sellers to organize some competition for assets to be sold. Therefore, the vast majority of M&A transactions take place through some form of *auction*.

As explained in Chapter 5, auctions are designed to force bidders to reveal their true preferences and their private information as to the valuation of the assets being auctioned. It is therefore a mechanism for promoting the efficient allocation of the assets to be sold to the bidder with the highest private valuation of those assets.

In the auction process, the information asymmetry between buyers and seller can be reduced in order to address uncertainties the buyers may have as to the quality of the assets for sale.

How is such an auction organized? See Box 12.3 for an indication. Usually, the seller engages the services of an investment bank to assist in the auction process. Firms such Goldman Sachs, Morgan Stanley and Rothschild are well-known examples. Together with the investment bank, the seller prepares an **information memorandum**. In the information memorandum (IM), the seller supplies basic data on the company to be sold, such as:

- historic and projected sales, cash flows and profits;
- industry and market data;
- descriptions of assets and technologies;
- profiles of the management team.

The investment bank explores potential interest for the company to be sold (sometimes using condensed information in a 'teaser'). In the first stage of the auction, the IM is sent to potential buyers who have expressed an interest, together with a 'process letter', which outlines the rules and procedures of the auction. The IM can, of course, be understood as the first step towards reducing the information asymmetry between the seller and the potential buyers. It allows interested parties to submit an **indicative bid**.

Indicative bids contain a preliminary price indication, but often also further information required by the buyer and conditions that still have to be fulfilled (such as shareholder approval of the final bid).

On the basis of the indicative bids, the seller can determine which parties are admitted to the second stage of the auction.

Note, however, that an IM contains only basic data. As it may be distributed to several parties, potentially including competitors, the seller will be reluctant to supply sensitive information. Two further steps to reduce the information asymmetry are therefore included in the design of the second stage of a standard auction:

Information memorandum

Indicative bid

Box 12.3 A typical auction process

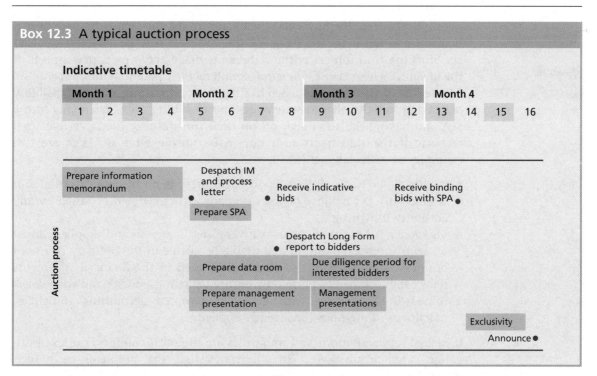

■ the preparation of a **data room**, containing a much wider variety of more detailed data on the business;

■ **management presentations**, allowing potential buyers to interact directly with the management of the company to be sold in a question and answer session.

The data room and the management presentations are elements of the **due diligence process** any serious buyer will have to conduct. Other elements of the due diligence process may include, for example, plant visits and expert meetings (where functional experts can delve deeply into complex topics, such as tax or environmental issues). All elements of the due diligence process together should enable buyers to reach the required 'comfort level' regarding the information obtained on the characteristics of the target company. In all these ways, the auction process is designed to narrow the information gap between buyers and seller.

At the end of the second stage of the auction, buyers submit a **binding bid.** A binding bid is usually based on a **Sales and Purchase Agreement (SPA)**[8] that has been negotiated in the meantime between buyer and seller. The SPA formulates the terms and conditions agreed between the parties in this transaction. Box 12.4 lists a number of typical clauses found in a SPA contract. Such contracts can run to hundreds of pages for complicated deals (and when American lawyers are involved).

Several of the clauses may further address any information problems involved in the transaction. In the 'representations and warranties', for instance, the seller will confirm the veracity of statements made during the sales process. Here the buyer has the chance to list the factors that are of particular importance to the value of the business for the buyer. The seller confirms the truthfulness of the statements made about particular aspects of the business. These clauses therefore counteract the potential for **opportunism** on the part of sellers. As discussed in Chapter 8, opportunism is the possibility of making 'self-disbelieved statements'. By including such statements in the SPA and having the seller sign off on their truthfulness, the buyer has legal recourse if the statements turn out to be untrue after all. Here are two examples of such statements:

■ *Tax liabilities* To the Seller's knowledge, there is no dispute or claim concerning any tax liability of the Company either claimed or raised by any authority in writing.
■ *Inventories*. All of the Company's inventories, materials and supplies consist of items in good condition and usable or salable in the ordinary course of business. The values of the inventories stated in the financial statements reflect the Company's normal inventory valuation policies and were determined in accordance with generally accepted accounting principles, practices and methods consistently applied.

Breached representations and warranties are the most common causes of litigation after acquisitions. This illustrates that the problems of hidden information and opportunism are very real in M&A transactions. In an auction process, such problems can be reduced, but hardly ever completely eliminated. Nevertheless, negotiating and agreeing a SPA can give both parties sufficient comfort to proceed and complete the second stage of the auction process – the buyers submitting binding bids and the seller selecting the best bidder.

Box 12.4 Typical clauses in a Sales and Purchase Agreement (SPA)

■ *Definitions and Interpretation* To avoid confusion regarding terminology.
■ *Scope* Business or assets being sold.
■ *Consideration* Type and amount of payment.
■ *Completion* How to proceed from signing the SPA to closing the transaction.
■ *Closing accounts* How to draw up the financial statements at closing.
■ *Transfer of property* Special clauses as to land or intellectual property (patents), for example.
■ *Business liabilities* How to deal with identified liabilities, such as pensions or claims.
■ *Contracts* How to deal with contracts with other parties, such as change of control clauses.
■ *Representations* Statements about the current status of the business or its operations.
■ *Warranties* Guarantees of the truth of statements made.
■ *Indemnities* Promises by the seller to compensate buyers for specific damages or losses.
■ *Conditions precedent* Conditions that have to be fulfilled before the contract comes into effect (antitrust clearance, for example).

When a seller has received the binding bids of the potential buyers, accompanied by the SPAs outlining the agreed terms and conditions, this provides a basis for making the final selection of the best buyer. As a last stage in the process, a short period of 'exclusivity' may be granted to that buyer. During the exclusivity period, some last items of the most sensitive information may be shared. Examples of such commercially sensitive items are the terms and conditions of the main customer contracts.

The description of the M&A auction process in this section has served to illustrate how its design is geared toward addressing the information asymmetry between the seller and potential buyers. As the auction process proceeds, more detailed and more sensitive information is supplied to an increasingly smaller group of bidders. By gradually narrowing the information gap, buyers can reach a sufficient 'comfort level' to complete the transaction. They form an increasingly solid basis for their bids.

By addressing the specific information needs of the buyers, the seller enables them to assess their value drivers in the deal in a progressively better way. That may lead to upward revisions of their bid range.

By including sufficient competition in the auction (until the very last stage of exclusivity), there is a strong pressure on buyers to reveal their true preference for a price and submit the highest bid they can. The auction process promotes the efficient allocation of the assets to be sold – namely, to the bidder with the highest private valuation.

The widespread use of auctions for M&A transactions can be understood as a way to increase the level of competition in such transactions. Competitive bidding may help to explain why shareholders of target companies do receive abnormal returns on announcement of a deal, while shareholders of the acquiring firm do not. The competitive pressure on the acquiring firm to 'give away' a large part of that private value has been quite high. As a result, they can end up paying 'full value' for the target or more (see Box 12.5 and the next section).

Box 12.5 The Corus auction

In 2007, the UK Takeover Panel took the unusual step of deciding a bidding war for the British-Dutch steelmaker Corus by organizing an auction. The case shows the power auctions have to extract full prices from competitive bidders.

The bidding war had been started off in October 2006 by the Indian group Tata making an all-cash bid of 455 pence per share for Corus, which was recommended by the Corus Board. In November, the Brazilian company CSN announced that it was working on a bid of 475p. Before CSN had a chance to make a formal bid, Tata raised its bid to 500p. CSN struck back and launched an offer of 515p later in December, which was also recommended by the Corus Board.

Rumours circulated about Tata's next move. Worried that the battle would drag on indefinitely, the UK Takeover Panel set a deadline of the end of January and then announced that the outcome would be decided in a ten-hour, nine-round auction.

The auction started at 4.30 p.m. on 30 January and ended at 12 a.m. the next day, when both companies submitted their final sealed bids.

In the meantime, the competitive bidding had driven the price up from 515p to 585p (CSN) and 590p (Tata). CSN's final bid was that it would beat Tata's bid by 5p, up to a maximum of 603p. Tata said that it would top any offer by CSN to an undisclosed maximum above 603p. Therefore, Tata's final winning bid was 608p.

▶

The tit-for-tat bidding war and the subsequent auction had raised the price of Corus' shares from 455p to 608p – an increase of 30 per cent and a cumulative absolute increase of £1.6 billion to £6.7 billion including debt.

Analysts were nearly universally negative about the high price paid. Tata Steel's share price dipped about 10 per cent on the Mumbai stock exchange the following day. Corus' shareholders had enjoyed a 30-fold increase in share price in a four-year period, since Corus had been battling against insolvency.

Reflecting on the process, Ratan Tata, chairman of the Tata group, said that Tata Steel was forced to pay 'very close' to its top price for Corus and almost had to decide between the good of shareholders and India's national pride.

Sources: The Financial Times, January 29 to February 3/4 and *Het Financieele Dagblad,* 1 February 2007

12.6 The winner's curse and hubris

By this time, you may have been thinking about our explanation of the *winner's curse* in Chapter 5. You will recall that this phenomenon is where winners of bidding contests prevail, not because the true valuation is highest to them, but because of their optimistic expectations. We illustrated this phenomenon in Chapter 5 with the examples of MBA students bidding in the jar game and with the outcomes of the 3G mobile spectrum auctions in Europe.

The winner's curse applies in M&A transactions as well. *Business Week* on 14 October 2002, published the results of research conducted in M&A transactions announced between 1 July 1995 and 31 August 2001. *Business Week's* major conclusion was that 'most big deals don't pay off'. Looking at the numbers, 61 per cent of buyers destroyed their own shareholders' wealth. What do the researchers think went wrong? *Business Week* contended that the bidders paid too much, which sounds a lot like the winner's curse. The bidders' CEOs offered an average premium above the target's market price of 36 per cent. 'Executives were brimming with confidence and rich stocks.' It also appears that CEOs were overly optimistic about the synergies that would result from a merger and discounted the difficulties of integrating two companies (Anandalingham and Lucas, 2004, pp. 67–9).

Box 12.6 Hubris and 'Ebbers Rex'

Facing up to 85 years in prison for his part in the $11 billion WorldCom fraud case, former CEO Bernie Ebbers can expect to have plenty of time to read up on his Greek mythology. For the ancient Greeks, the formula of great tragedies such as *Oedipus Rex* and *Antigone* was clear: hubris (pride) leads to ate (an act of arrogance offensive to the gods), which results in nemesis (infamy and death). A more contemporary version is 'pride goes before a fall'.

Corporate fraud and the cycle of hubris, ate and nemesis are much more widespread problems than is often assumed. And the cost is much higher than people realize: from 1978 through 2002, federal regulators initiated 585 enforcement actions for financial misrepresentation by publicly traded companies, naming 2310 individuals and 657 firms as potentially liable parties. The legal penalties imposed on individuals and firms are substantial. For example, individuals were assessed $15.9 billion in fines and civil penalties, and 190 managers received jail sentences for financial reporting violations. Companies were assessed an additional $8.4 billion in fines and damages via class-action lawsuits.

This belies a widespread view that financial misrepresentation is disciplined lightly. To the contrary, the Securities and Exchange Commission historically has pursued many enforcement actions for financial misconduct, resulting in substantial legal penalties but also even higher reputational penalties. Punishment is not a remedy, of course, and it is not clear that we have found a good remedy for a complex problem. Corporate governance – at least as it is measured in corporate governance codes, codes of conduct and Sarbanes-Oxley – is not the cause of most major corporate scandals.

In a survey sponsored by the Dutch Employers' Association, I recently examined 25 cases of corporate fraud, studying incentive compensation paid to top management, the reputations of the CEOs, their growth targets, analysts' expectations and corporate governance. I also looked for evidence of overvaluation and studied price movements around the time the fraud was discovered. All cases were recent (since 2000); they were listed firms where top management was directly or indirectly involved in fraud; the fraud was substantial (at least $10 million and 5 per cent of annual profit) and so were the firms (greater than 1000 employees). Their demise accounted for $25 billion of corporate fraud. Here is what I found: surprisingly, the average governance scores for the 25 fraud firms were exactly the same as the scores of the 25 non-fraud firms they were compared to in the study. The problem, I found, wasn't so much governance, but hubris.

Companies, of course, want successful leaders. Once they find one, the new CEO gets increasingly wealthy (in 2000, the average value of stocks and options for the 25 fraud-CEOs was $1.2 billion versus $150 million for the comparison group). He also acquires icon status. He not only becomes well respected, he becomes a corporate celebrity. Ken Lay of Enron, Joe Nacchio of Qwest, Dennis Kozlowski of Tyco, Rich McGinn of Lucent were all quoted in the press ten times more often than their competitors. Precisely because they are successful, these CEOs set increasingly higher targets, for the following reasons: first, in order to remain successful in the stock market and sustain their icon reputation, they must maintain a profit growth of 15 per cent to 20 per cent per year. Second, because of increasing success and fame, the CEO starts to believe that he can make anything happen and develops 'a little bit of a God syndrome,' as a vice-president of WorldCom put it, referring to Mr Ebbers.

Indeed, one of the most interesting findings of my study was the degree to which the firms found guilty of fraud had committed themselves to unrealistic targets. On average, the 25 firms I looked at had 18 per cent yearly growth targets, that's a whopping 230 per cent growth every 5 years. Meanwhile, the non-fraud firms had on average 7 per cent yearly growth targets, or 40 per cent growth over 5 years. Not surprisingly, the CEOs who set such unrealistic targets resort to fraudulent behavior to sustain the appearance of success.

There is, however, something of a silver lining to this story. On the day the frauds I studied became public, on average 29 per cent of the value of the 25 companies vanished into thin air: $73 billion went up in smoke. Savvy investors, however, anticipated these negative effects well in advance: in the year prior to the uncovering of fraud 40 per cent of the market value of the companies had already been lost.

The moral? It's hard to hide hubris, even if you're a superstar CEO.

Source: K. Cools (2005) 'Ebbers Rex', *The Wall Street Journal,* 22 March 2005

Managerial overconfidence as a potential explanation of the winner's curse in M&A transactions is known as the 'hubris hypothesis'. It was introduced by Richard Roll in 1986.[9] **Hubris** is a word from ancient Greek that today is used to refer to 'exaggerated self-pride or self-confidence, often resulting in fatal retribution' (see Box 12.6). Such overconfidence is not uncommon in decisionmaking, but does it also apply in the context of M&A?

In an investment research report by the bank UBS (2004), this question is answered as follows:

> One of the key findings of decisionmaking theory is overconfidence. People substantially overestimate the precision of their forecasts. A legendary example is a questionnaire in Sweden where one of the questions was: 'on your driving capabilities, compared with the people you encounter on the road, do you consider yourself to be a below-average, average, or an above-average driver?' Of the participants in the questionnaire, 90 per cent considered themselves above-average.
>
> Overconfidence is highest when dealing with difficult tasks, and in contexts where there is a lot of, but not necessarily helpful, information. We think that M&A situations are prime examples of situations that are prone to yield overconfidence. This would cause CEOs to overestimate their knowledge and attribute excessive weight to private relative to public information. It also tends to lead to situations where risk is underestimated. Overconfidence could explain why corporate management engage in M&A deals, despite the difficult odds of generating positive returns for its shareholders.

Indeed, empirical research shows that corporate executives do show overconfidence in M&A contexts. Hayward and Hambrick (1997) investigated the premiums paid in a sample of 106 large acquisitions and found that:

> four indicators of CEO hubris are highly associated with the size of the premium paid: the acquiring company's recent performance, recent media praise for the CEO, a measure of the CEO's self-importance, and a composite factor of these three variables. The relationship between CEO hubris and premiums is further strengthened when board vigilance is lacking—when the board has a high proportion of inside directors and when the CEO is also the board chair.

Malmendier and Tate (2007) use a creative approach to measure CEO overconfidence. They examine the personal decisions of CEOs with respect to the stocks and options they hold in their companies. CEOs are classified as 'overconfident' if they persistently choose to maintain a high degree of exposure to company-specific risk, even if they could diversify that risk by selling some of their company stock and in-the-money options.

Interestingly, their measure of overconfidence is strongly related to press coverage of CEOs as 'confident' or 'optimistic'. Overconfident CEOs are found to conduct more mergers and, particularly, more diversifying acquisitions that are value-destroying.

Outsiders seem to be able to recognize such CEO overconfidence. Using the 'event study' approach, Malmendier and Tate show that the negative market reaction to bids of overconfident CEOs is nearly four times greater than that for non-overconfident CEOs.

Empirical research therefore supports the contention in the popular press that CEO overconfidence or hubris is a significant factor in explaining the winner's curse and value destruction in M&A transactions. Overpayment is quite a common phenomenon in M&A transactions: a 2006 McKinsey analysis showed the proportion of overpayers to be above 50 per cent across the two recent merger waves.[10]

The consultancy firm Accenture published a brochure in 2005 with the title 'Making M&A Pay: Avoiding the winner's curse'. It proudly states:

> With widespread discipline and adherence to M&A best practices, the winner's curse could be stamped out.

The brochure gives a number of admonitions ('separate price from value', 'estimate synergies accurately', 'check their work', 'retain perspective') and maintains that the curse can be staved off by means of proper 'People, Processes, Perspective and Preparation'. Somehow, however, we are less than convinced that we will see no more winner's curses in M&A situations, even when these guidelines are followed.

12.7 Adverse selection: remedies for hidden information

We assume that by now you are convinced M&A provide ample opportunities for the problem of hidden information to occur. As a result, you may run into a situation of adverse selection, where you end up having bought a lemon. In the previous sections we outlined some remedies to the problem of hidden information that have evolved over time. In general, these remedies fall into one of the following two categories.

- *Equalize access to information (or at least come close)* Examples are:
  - auction design with progressive information sharing;
  - due diligence procedures, including data rooms, management presentations and expert meetings.
- *Shift risk to the party with the better information* Examples are:
  - representations and warranties: the seller 'represents' the status of the business and 'warrants' the veracity of that representation;
  - indemnities: the seller undertakes to compensate the buyer for specific damages or losses that could occur in the future (such as historic product liabilities or environmental liabilities);
  - escrow accounts: buyer and seller agree that part of the purchase price is set aside (held 'in escrow') until certain conditions of the deal have been met.

These remedies have evolved as elements of M&A processes and SPA contracts. We will now focus on some other solutions to the problem of hidden information that have been examined in economic research. Interestingly, some of these solutions are organizational and some are market-based. M&A therefore, again, illustrates the basic premise of this book, that markets and organizations represent alternative coordination mechanisms for economic transactions. Also, for M&A transactions, the market/organization mix will primarily depend on the information requirements of the situation, as we will show below.[11]

12.7.1 Organizational solutions

In the late 1980s, Philips NV had determined that its $1.55 billion domestic appliances division was no longer a 'core business'. The division was in need of restructuring. It had plants spread across five European countries. Substantial capital investments were needed to develop selected plants into world-class facilities. The division had 14,000 employees. Performance had been below Philips' standards for some time. Despite such problems, Philips' management knew that the division had potentially valuable assets, including good manufacturing skills, well-known brands, world-class design expertise and a pan-European distribution network, making it number two (behind Electrolux) in European market share.

The Whirlpool Corporation was the obvious buyer. It was looking to expand beyond its US base. It wanted to take over a European position in an industry that was rapidly becoming global. Whirlpool believed that it could radically lower the cost base of the business by rationalizing production, sourcing components globally and coordinating production, sales and distribution across countries. Furthermore, Whirlpool was willing to inject investments and technology into the European operations.

Whirlpool's executives, however, were less convinced than Philips' about the potential of the business. They had concerns about the strength of the consumer franchise behind the brands and the loyalty of the dealer network if the business changed hands. How much time and money would be involved in turning the business around?

Both parties ran the numbers, but their widely different assumptions and information produced valuations that were not even close. A strategically sensible deal was hindered by the issue of price.

Joint Venture (JV)

A **Joint Venture (JV)** proved to be the solution. In 1989, Philips offered Whirlpool a 53 per cent majority stake in its business for $381 million, together with an option to buy the remaining 47 per cent within three years. For Whirlpool, this was an attractive arrangement as it provided an opportunity to learn about the appliances division as an insider and initiate improvement plans before taking over the division entirely.

The JV was created and Whirlpool was able to implement synergies and improvements swiftly. Indeed, the operation was turned around so successfully that Whirlpool exercised its option for the remaining 47 per cent share in 1991 for $610 million. Philips was thus able to exit the business smoothly and on substantially more favourable terms than if it had simply auctioned it in 1989. The price uplift gained by the intermediate step of the JV was estimated at $270 million.

In this example, the organizational solution to the problem of hidden information was to allow Whirlpool to become an 'insider' in Philips' appliance business before fully executing the transaction. It can thus be seen as a mechanism to equalize access to information about the division. Whirlpool was offered access to the private information Philips had about its division. The value of that private information was expressed in the significant price uplift achieved when the option was exercised three years later. To achieve this outcome, both parties were willing to take part of the risks in the JV for the first three years.

Research and case studies note that companies may use such JV-strategies in situations of significant uncertainty and asymmetric information (see Dyer, Kale and Singh, 2004; Reuer and Koza, 2000). Cisco Systems, for example, is widely known to have an acquisition-led strategy, but the company relies on small equity investments as stepping stones for about 25 per cent of its acquisitions. Many other companies have established 'corporate venturing' groups to make such initial small-stake investments in start-up companies before deciding on a full-scale acquisition. These arrangements can be understood as the willingness of the potential acquirers to take some (equity) risk in order to gain access to private information about the target firm and, thus, reduce the information asymmetry.

12.7.2 Market solutions

PayPal is an Internet-based payment system that allows winning buyers to pay sellers in online auctions. It has good antifraud capabilities. These are valuable as fraud is the major concern for participants in online auctions. For that reason, it attracted the attention of eBay.

At the time, PayPal was a privately held start-up. The two parties were, however, unable to agree on price. PayPal subsequently decided to go public in an **initial public offering (IPO)**, which was effected in February 2002. Shares were offered at $13 each and rose sharply after the IPO to levels around $20. A few months later, in July 2002, eBay made a public share offer for PayPal, which valued the PayPal shares at about $23.60. In total, eBay's offer valued PayPal at $1.5 billion.

How should we understand the PayPal–eBay case? Why couldn't eBay and PayPal agree on a price earlier when we now know that PayPal offered its shares for $13 to the public and eBay was willing to buy them for $23.60 a few months later? Did eBay initially just make a big mistake or is there another, more rational explanation?

Economic research has suggested a more rational explanation. While, traditionally, IPOs were merely seen as a means of financing a private company, they are now also recognized as a mechanism for reducing information asymmetries. To understand why that is so, consider the following.

Not a lot of historical, public, certified information about small, privately held firms is available, particularly younger ones. They do not publish their financial statements and they are not followed by the community of investment analysts. Moreover, they may suffer from legitimacy problems and the 'liability of newness' that we discussed in Chapter 10. Finally, the major part of the value of entrepreneurial start-up companies comes from future growth

Initial public offering (IPO)

opportunities and intangible assets, which are notoriously difficult to value. For all those reasons, there is probably a significant information asymmetry between the company and potential acquirers.

Making the private company public can reduce that information gap in two ways.

- There are substantial information requirements to be met in order to obtain approval for public listing. They involve publishing an Offering Memorandum with extensive disclosures about the company. Also the requirements of stock market regulators must be satisfied. In the USA, it would entail substantial documentation to be submitted to the Securities and Exchange Commission (SEC). Those documents are also public information. Finally, investment analysts examine companies going public and publish their findings and recommendations. In all these ways, the gap between private information and public information about the company is reduced.
- By going public, the company also sends signals to potential acquirers. It signals that it is confident that it can pass public scrutiny. It signals that it can bear the costs of going public.[12] It can also signal credibility by selecting reputable investment banks and underwriters to support the IPO. Such institutions then lend their reputation to the firm and bolster its legitimacy by association. All in all, the new issue market can work as a screening device. It helps to screen out credible from less credible private companies.

The market for IPOs of private companies thus serves as a 'market solution' for problems of hidden information and adverse selection. Through their initial public listing, companies can disseminate information in a credible way. Their willingness to do so is a strong signal to potential acquirers. In fact, the value of that signal is recognized as being so strong that many businesses are nowadays sold in a '**dual track**' approach: they are simultaneously prepared for IPO and divestment to a direct acquirer. The seller can determine at the last moment whether the bids received from interested acquirers are sufficiently high to cancel the IPO. Evidence suggests that 'dual tracking' can offer higher premiums to sellers than outright divestments. In a study by Brau and Kohers (2007) two strategies were distinguished.

Dual track approach

- *Dual-track private harvest* The private firm files for an IPO while also courting acquirers. The firm ultimately withdraws the IPO-filing and opts to be taken over directly. Firms using this strategy earned a 22–26 per cent higher premium than single-track divestments.
- *Dual-track public harvest* The private firm first completes the IPO and is then taken over as a newly public firm shortly thereafter (the PayPal case). A 18–21 per cent higher premium was achieved by firms using this strategy rather than single-track sell-outs.

Based on such evidence, we can conclude that there is substantial value in the IPO market solution to reducing information asymmetry, even if used as an option only.

In conclusion, we want to reiterate our observation that markets and organizations offer different solutions to the problem of hidden information in

M&A situations. Which mix of market and organizational remedies will be optimal in any given situation will primarily depend on the information requirements of that specific situation. Is there an obvious buyer who needs to be convinced that he is not buying a lemon? Then it may be optimal to offer a JV as an intermediate step. Alternatively, are there several potential acquirers who may be concerned about the liability of newness of the target? Then, it might be optimal to go through the IPO market as a screening device. It may also be that the optimality of either route can only be determined as the M&A process unfolds. In such a situation, dual-tracking is an effective way for a seller to keep his options open.

The examples given above illustrate that markets and organizations can complement each other in lowering the M&A transaction costs due to hidden information. As discussed in Chapter 4, hidden information is the ex ante information problem. It exists *before* the SPA is written. We next turn our attention to ex post information problems, that is, hidden action *after* parties have agreed to execute a transaction.

12.8 Moral hazard: remedies for hidden action

Now you have signed a deal. There has been a ceremony where the SPA has been signed. Pictures were taken to capture the historic moment. Champagne flowed and all parties congratulated each other on the 'tough but fair' negotiations and on the 'win–win result' (and lawyers from both sides on the fees earned). It is unfortunate that you have to wait some more months before the deal can be executed (called the 'closing'), because the antitrust authorities want to examine the deal first and you also need your shareholders' approval. That evening, you feel a headache coming on. Is it the champagne or might there be another cause?

Another cause could be that there are some nagging questions in your mind. Questions such as, what will happen to your target in the months between signing and closing? Will the value you receive be the value you were expecting? Will managers be motivated to run the company in your best interests? Might they have their own agendas? Questions like these could turn your headache into a true migraine if they are not dealt with properly.

Moral hazard

Hidden action

The issues here are related to **moral hazard** – potential **hidden action** that is unobservable by you as a buyer. These issues originate from post-contractual information asymmetries. Remedies to hidden action usually fall into one of the following categories.

- *Contractual arrangements* Clauses in the SPA that specify (and sanction) post-contractual behaviour.
- *Increased observability* Taking measures to improve the information about post-contractual behaviour.
- *Incentive alignment* Putting incentives in place that align the incentives between current owners (and its management) and the new owners.

The categories are not mutually exclusive. For example, there may be contractual arrangements aimed at improving observability or aligning incentives. Below we give some salient examples of each category.

The *contractual arrangements* in the SPA, which are designed to govern post-contractual behaviour, can cover a wide variety of things. Generally, it will be stated in the contract that the seller and its management should continue to run operations 'in the ordinary course of business'. That general clause provides the norm that seller and management should refrain from exceptional behaviour and should run the business according to customary practices. For example, bonus payments should not suddenly be larger than they have customarily been. Specific clauses may deal with specific situations. Parties may, for instance, agree that investments above a certain specified amount need joint approval. Such a clause makes the behaviour of the seller with respect to the most significant investments observable to buyer.

There are further ways to *increase observability* as a remedy to hidden action. Parties will, for instance, agree to draw up closing statements reflecting the financial status of the company at the time of closing, when the ownership of the business is actually transferred. The closing statements will be audited. Through the auditor, the buyer can ascertain that no hidden action has decreased the value of the business. The purchase price will also be adjusted to allow for certain changes in financial items between signing and closing. Any value decreases that may result from the ordinary course of business can be addressed via such adjustments of the purchase price. Examples are changes in working capital or levels of bad debt.

Finally, there are many ways in which hidden action can be countered by *incentive alignment*. Consider the case of a start-up company with an owner-manager who has successfully built up the firm from scratch. He is the originator of the main technology the company has developed and patented. He has personally supervised the development of the main applications of that technology and the contacts with the main customers for those applications.

When a larger firm buys that start-up company, it can of course buy the patents and the customer contracts, but the value of the start-up resides only partially in those assets. The main asset may be the founder of the company

Tacit knowledge

with his **tacit knowledge**.[13] How do you motivate him to continue to operate in the best interests of the company *and* the new owners?

If the selling of his company has made this entrepreneur seriously rich and if he dislikes working for a larger company, there may be agency problems

Contingent earn-out

ahead. One remedy that has evolved in such situations is the **contingent earn-out**. Under this arrangement, part of the purchase price is made dependent (contingent) upon future performance. By agreeing to a contingent earn-out, the seller can signal his confidence in the future performance of the business to be sold and the buyer is assured that the seller has significant incentives to contribute to the future performance of the company.

In essence, a contingent earn-out shifts part of the risk back to the party with the best information (the seller).

In Section 12.7, we encountered another mechanism that has this virtue: the escrow account. If the buyer and seller agree that part of the purchase price is set aside (held in escrow) until certain conditions of the deal have been met, the seller also agrees to continue to bear part of the risk in the transaction until the firm's performance is clear.

Material adverse change (MAC) clause

The risk that the value of a target firm is materially affected between signing and closing a deal is also covered by another contractual clause: the **material adverse change (MAC) clause**. A standard MAC clause permits the buyer to not close the transaction on the occurrence of 'any change, occurrence or state of facts that is materially adverse to the business, financial condition or results of operations' of the target company. Note that such a clause creates an incentive for the seller to keep the business in good shape. By introducing the threat that the buyer may walk away if the value of the business is materially affected, the seller is encouraged to continue with value-preserving behaviour. The MAC can therefore be seen as a contractual clause aimed at incentive alignment (combining two of our three categories of remedies to hidden action).

Note, however, that the standard MAC clause imposes the risk of break-up of the transaction rather unilaterally on the seller. That is because the value of the business is at risk for two different sets of reasons:

Endogenous risk

Exogenous risk

- **endogenous risk** – risk specific to the transaction, including that from hidden action;
- **exogenous risk** – risk of a generic nature, which means that it would affect all similar transactions.

Examples of exogenous risk include major economic slowdowns, changes in applicable laws and regulations and events impacting all firms in an industry (such as the outbreak of animal diseases affecting all meat producers).

Should buyers be able to walk away from deals that are affected by exogenous risk – risks that neither buyers nor sellers could influence or prevent? Realizing that this is probably too harsh a condition for sellers, MAC clauses have come to contain such exceptions over time. Gilson and Schwartz (2005) document that:

> In 1993, only 18.33% of MAC clauses included one or more event specifications that restricted the buyer's right to exit; more than half of these stated a single event. In 1995, the percentage of clauses with an event specification had increased to 31.74% with an average of 0.67 per transaction. By 2000, event specifications had become mainstream: 83% of the acquisition agreements featured at least one MAC exclusion, with an average of 3.75 per transaction.

Modern MAC clauses (with stated exceptions) thus separate the risks of material adverse changes between sellers and buyers. Buyers can walk away from a deal if endogenous risk (including hidden action) materializes. They cannot simply cancel a deal, however, when exogenous risks arise. The spreading of the modern MAC clause is a nice example of the evolution of an institutional arrangement affecting the execution of economic transactions. Recall that, in Chapter 1, we defined institutions as 'the rules of the game in a society or, more formally, the humanly devised constraints that shape human interaction'. The modern MAC clause is such an institutional arrangement, constraining human interaction specifically to contain the risks of moral hazard.

Interestingly, the market has also developed some complementary solutions to the problems of hidden action. The insurance market has contributed some efficient remedies. It has developed a representations and warranties policy that will cover financial losses from false statements made by sellers in an SPA.[14] Box 12.7 describes a case where this market solution contributed to the successful completion of an acquisition transaction. The example shows that a mix of market solutions and organizational solutions (the contract clauses dealing with the integration into the acquiring organization) together allow agency and transaction costs to be lowered to a level where the transaction can be executed.

Box 12.7 The market solution: M&A insurance

In most deals, buyers ask sellers to put at least 10% of a deal's value in escrow. By offsetting some risk with insurance, bidders can slash their escrow requirements, effectively offering the seller more cash up front.

Such insurance was a dealsaver for Michael Alexander, managing partner of EchoBridge Entertainment. Alexander was close to signing a deal to buy Platinum Disc. Platinum had been profitable for years and its books seemed clean. Nevertheless, Alexander was concerned: 'You worry that there's something the sellers aren't telling you – or something that they don't even know about'.

Alexander asked Platinum's owner, Dave Thompson, to set aside a chunk of the sale proceeds in an escrow account until it was clear that the conditions of the deal had been met. When Thompson balked, Alexander bought a representations and warranties policy and let Thompson put a smaller amount in escrow.

It cost EchoBridge $200,000 to cover the deal, which was worth tens of millions of dollars, and Alexander says it was worth it: 'You get millions of dollars in protection and sleep more comfortably'.

The deal closed in February. So far, there have been no surprises.

Source: 'Deal jitters?', *Inc.* magazine, October 2005

12.9 Transaction specificity and hold-up

Transaction specificity of assets

In Chapter 8, we introduced the concept of **transaction specificity of assets**. An asset is transaction-specific if it cannot be redeployed to an alternative use without a significant reduction in its value. We examined the example of Mr P, who wanted to start a local newspaper in Appropria, and Mrs Q, a printer, who he asks to buy a special printing press for this purpose. The example showed how both parties make transaction-specific investments: Mrs Q in a printing press and Mr P in start-up losses for a new newspaper. As a consequence, they are locked into their relationship.

If either party shows a degree of *opportunism*, it can try to take advantage of that situation by attempting to renegotiate the contract. Economists refer to this possibility as the threat of **hold-up**. Severe threats of hold-up undermine the possibility of even agreeing a transaction.

Hold-up

How can a hold-up problem arise in M&A transactions? Let us return to the AOL-Time Warner deal described at the start of this chapter.

Imagine that you are Jerry Levin, CEO of Time Warner. In October 1999, you receive a phone call from Steven Case, CEO of AOL, proposing a friendly all share merger of equals.[15] You meet with Steven Case several times and, after difficult discussions, an agreement seems within reach, including the terms of the share deal. Both CEOs are to submit this potential agreement to their Boards. It is uncertain how the markets will react to any announcement of the deal.

As Jerry Levin, you should be concerned that AOL could walk away from the deal, perhaps as a result of unfavourable market reactions to the announcement or other target firms offering themselves to AOL on more favourable terms. Even if AOL does not actually walk away, it could try to use the threat of doing so to renegotiate the terms of the deal. Therefore, you will want AOL to make a **credible commitment** to the deal, as agreed. This can be done by agreeing a **break-up fee** to be paid by AOL if it abandons the deal after signing. The break-up fee has to be sizable in order to be credible. It will be a contractual clause in the SPA.

Now imagine that you are Steven Case, CEO of AOL. By bidding for Time Warner you are putting that company 'in play'. Other potential acquirers will examine the terms of the deal and may decide to start a bidding war. You cannot force the Board of Time Warner to stick to your deal because it has a fiduciary duty to consider more favourable bids. You do, however, want a credible commitment from Time Warner that it will not easily succumb to the attractions of a higher bid. Therefore, you ask Time Warner to also agree to a break-up fee in case it walks away from the deal.

In reality, the agreed break-up fees were $5.4 billion for AOL and $3.5 billion for Time Warner. Break-up fees in the USA generally amount to about 3 per cent of the proposed purchase price. They can be understood as a remedy against potential hold-up problems, making it more difficult for parties to renegotiate the terms of the deal or walk away altogether. It is a contractual arrangement mitigating against potential opportunism by having the firms make a credible commitment. Sometimes a break-up fee at least serves the purpose of some consolation for the party that did not see its bid ultimately win (see Box 12.8).

> **Credible commitment**
>
> **Break-up fee**

Box 12.8 Breaking up is hard to do . . .

A boardroom romance that began so sweetly on Valentine's Day may end sourly on Friday. On Feb. 14, Verizon, the former Baby Bell, and MCI, the long-distance company recently revived from bankruptcy, struck a deal in which Verizon would buy MCI for $6.7 billion. Soon after, Qwest jumped into the fray and kicked off a bidding war. Last Friday, MCI's Board, which had plainly favoured walking down the aisle with Verizon, concluded that Qwest's $9.75 billion offer was too good to pass up. Verizon has until Friday to respond.

If MCI ultimately runs off with Qwest, Verizon will be left at the altar with a sizable consolation prize. In March, MCI disclosed that if Verizon were spurned, it would receive a $240 million break-up fee plus reimbursement for up to $10 million in expenses. Who knew parting was such sweet sorrow?

This break-up fee may strike MCI shareholders as both bizarre and unwarranted – the company that submitted the inferior bid still walks away with a few hundred million bucks in pure profit.

But for shareholders of the target company, break-up fees are generally money well-spent. The most recent bid by Qwest is $3.05 billion more than Verizon's original offer. The $250 million MCI may thus pay Verizon if it accepts Qwest's offer is only 8 per cent of the increase; MCI shareholders would pocket the other $2.8 billion.

Source: Daniel Gross, 'Breaking up is hard to do: But less so when you get a $250 million going-away present)', *Slate*, Moneybox, 26 April 2005 (see: www.slate.com/id/2117518)

12.10 Alignment of managers and shareholders

In Section 12.8 above, we encountered the topic of 'incentive alignment' between managers and shareholders. There it was discussed as being a solution to the problem of moral hazard (hidden action) after signing the acquisition contract. Contingent earn-outs, escrow accounts and MAC clauses help to bring the interests of management and the new owners more in line with each other. More generally, the M&A context allows us to illustrate the importance of an alignment of the interests of managers and shareholder-owners by means of appropriate incentives. Such alignment is, of course, the central topic in agency theory, as explained in Chapter 7 of this book.

First, consider the risk that managers will make value-destroying acquisitions. One reason for this is that managers are free to pursue 'their own agenda' in making acquisitions. Jensen (1986) was among the first to point out that, when the interests and incentives of managers and shareholders diverge, managers may grow the company beyond the optimal level for its shareholders. They may do so, for example, to achieve published growth targets that are difficult to reach by organic growth only. They may even be interested in empire building. Managing a large, growing company usually translates into higher salaries and bonuses and a higher standing in the business community. For such 'managerial reasons' companies may be led into acquisitions that destroy value for shareholders. How to prevent this from happening?

Free cash flow

Jensen (1986) proposes that the key concept is **free cash flow**. Free cash flow is defined as cash flow in excess of that required to fund all projects that have positive net present values when discounted at the relevant cost of capital. In other words, it is the cash that remains when managers have made all rational investment decisions, including value-enhancing acquisitions. How a firm deals with free cash flow is crucial, according to Jensen (1989):

A central weakness and source of waste in the public corporation is the conflict between shareholders and managers over the payout of free cash flow. For a company to operate efficiently and maximize value, free cash flow must be distributed to shareholders rather than retained. But this happens infrequently;

senior management has few incentives to distribute the funds, and there exist few mechanisms to compel the distribution.

Leveraged buy-out (LBO)

Jensen explains the rise of the **leveraged buy-out (LBO)** as being a reaction to the inefficiency and waste caused by insufficient disciplining of public corporations to make them distribute free cash flow.

In a LBO transaction, the public company is 'taken private' – that is, delisted from the stock exchange. It is therefore no longer financed by 'public funds' (publically tradable shares). Instead, its financing mix then consists of privately held shares and a much larger portion of debt: the firm's balance sheet becomes highly leveraged. This serves as the required disciplining mechanism on management: free cash flow must now be used to make promised interest and principal payments on the debt as the first priority. The private shareholders benefit from the value created by addressing the inefficiencies in the company and paying down the debt. That value can be realized at 'exit' – when the firm is sold off or again offered through an IPO to the stock market.

In the late 1970s and early 1980s, many specialized buy-out firms were established. The most well-known became Kohlberg Kravis Roberts (KKR) when it acquired RJR Nabisco at a cost of $31.4 billion with only a $3.6 billion equity investment by KKR. That transaction was made famous in the book *Barbarians at the Gate.*

Private equity

Since then, a sizable **private equity** industry has developed, with firms such as KKR, Blackstone, Carlyle and CVC. These firms address the alignment between managers and (private) shareholders differently from public corporations. Their governance model includes the following aspects.

■ High *incentives* for management that are performance-driven and focused on cash generation. Often, management is also required to have some 'skin in the game' – invest its own money alongside that of the private shareholders. By means of such measures, management is offered the chance to become seriously wealthy, but only if the shareholders do well out of their investment, too. In other words, there is a much closer alignment of incentives for managers and shareholders.

■ Very close *monitoring* of management. The Board of a privately held company has the direct participation of the private shareholders. By contrast, the Board of a public company often offers only indirect representation to shareholders through the election of non-executive directors. It is likely that the supervision by such directors is less intense than by active investors. Non-executive directors usually don't have any sizable stake in the company. They are also not supposed to sit on the executives' chairs. Active investors, though, have both the motive and the opportunity to make their presence felt. Indeed, in the context of M&A, McKinsey found that 'active private equity partners devoted half of their time to the company (usually at its premises) during the first three months after the deal' (Beroutsos et al., 2007).

■ Much greater use of debt financing and, therefore, of *financial leverage*. Private equity seeks the limits of financial leverage that banks and debt markets are willing to support. The more debt is financing a transaction, the lower the amount of private equity that is exposed to the risk of the transaction. As a holder of the *residual risk*, the private shareholder can also look forward to higher returns on successful transactions (as the remaining revenue, after the costs of debt have been met, accrue to the shareholders). Finally, the use of debt imposes discipline on managers in their use of free cash flow, as Jensen argued.

Governance model

These are some of the main elements of a different **governance model** applied by private equity firms to their acquisitions. Overall, it has been quite successful. As a consequence, the share of private equity in global M&A transactions has increased significantly, as we saw in Figure 12.2. More specific data are shown in Figures 12.3 and 12.4. They show the rise of private equity financing of M&A transactions and the fact that this phenomenon has initially spread from the USA to Europe and now to Asia.

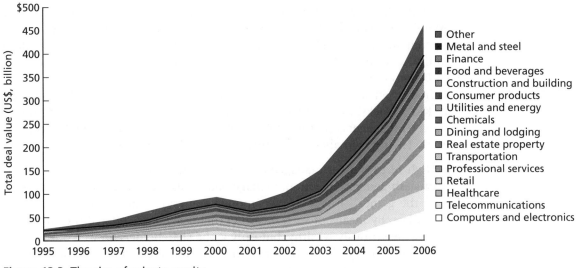

Figure 12.3 The rise of private equity

Source: Dealogic

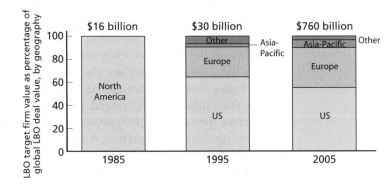

Figure 12.4 The geographical spread of private equity

Source: Thomson Financial; Bain analysis

In 1989, Michael Jensen predicted 'the eclipse of the public corporation'. While overstated, the core of his argument – that substantial value can be created by addressing the potential inefficiencies in public corporations – has proven to be true so far. The rise of the private equity industry has highlighted the choice to be made in appropriate governance models.

Governance by private owners has, of course, always existed. Entrepreneurial firms and family-owned companies have always been governed by private shareholder-owners. Traditionally, however, it was thought that such firms would necessarily become public over time, as their growth and financing needs exceeded the limits of private financing. What is new is that those limits have been stretched beyond recognition by the private equity firms. At the time of writing this fourth edition of our book, the largest private equity deal involved $32 billion.[16] In terms of financing, few large public companies can feel exempt from the pressure this brings to bear on their own performance. The private equity industry is challenging the established model of corporate governance of the public company (see Box 12.9). This situation highlights the importance of appropriate corporate governance, the subject of our next chapter.

Box 12.9 Private equity realignment of owners and managers

In effect, today's successful private equity firms exploit what might be called governance arbitrage rather than the financial engineering or price arbitrage that proved profitable when the industry was less mature. The best private equity firms can find and successfully realign businesses whose governing structures (owners and managers) are misaligned. So big is the opportunity for this type of transaction, we believe, that private equity is likely to maintain, and perhaps to expand, its presence as a parallel system to established public markets.

Source: A. Beroutsos et al. (2007)

12.11 Summary: economic approaches to M&A

In this chapter, we have explored M&A from an economic perspective. We have been able to apply many concepts that were introduced more generally in previous chapters.

We have shown that problems with *information asymmetry* abound. Problems with *hidden information* may prevent transactions in the M&A market in much the same way as described in the used car market in Chapter 4. Problems with *hidden action* may plague M&A transactions after signing.

For these problems, however, remedies have evolved. In part, they are contractual clauses that attempt to address (at least partially) the problem of *incomplete contracting* – the fact that no contract can ever specify *all* potential contingencies upfront. We have seen, too, that market and organizational solutions have also been developed as remedies. Market solutions include the creation of specific insurance markets and the use of the IPO market, also as a *signalling* device. Organizational solutions include the use of joint ventures to allow a potential acquirer to first learn about the business as a JV partner.

Which mix of market and organizational solutions is appropriate for specific transactions, will primarily depend on the nature and severity of the information problems involved.

The M&A process allowed us a practical example of how *auctions* can be designed to both narrow the information asymmetries over time and promote the *efficient allocation* of assets to be sold – namely to the bidder with the highest private valuation. As a result, the winning bidder can end up paying full value for the target firm. Occasionally, the bid may even turn out to be higher than the full value, resulting in the *winner's curse*. It was interesting to review the evidence that especially overconfident CEOs, who suffer from *hubris*, are prone to suffer from this curse. As a result, they are more likely to enter into value-destroying transactions.

On balance, the net economic gain from M&A appears to be positive. It is *not* a *zero-sum game*: the shareholders of target firms win more than the shareholders of acquiring firms tend to lose. Effects on other stakeholder groups are, on average, not very large. That would imply that M&A does create value from an overall economic perspective, presumably by transferring assets to management teams that deploy them more efficiently. In individual cases, however, the value destruction can be quite impressive, as we saw in the case of AOL-Time Warner at the beginning of this chapter. In such cases, there is usually significant management turnover and the companies involved may be destabilized for quite some time. It clearly pays for management to be aware of such risks, take appropriate remedies and avoid becoming trapped in such a situation.

Finally, we discussed the emergence of *private equity* as an alternative governance system to that of public equity markets. Private equity firms address the *alignment between managers and shareholders* differently from that which is customary in public corporations. They restrict management's discretionary use of *free cash flow* by much greater use of debt financing.

The private equity *governance model* includes high performance-driven and cash-based incentives for management, close *monitoring* of management by the shareholders and much greater *financial leverage*. It is a different way in which to address the basic *agency problems* due to the separation of management and ownership.

The rise of private equity is one indication of the importance of *corporate governance*. Recurring problems of misbehaviour, scandal and fraud in corporations is another. We will discuss these issues in Chapter 14, on corporate governance.

Questions

1 During the first stage of an auction process an information memorandum is sent to a number of potential buyers. On the basis of that memorandum, potential buyers make a first estimate of the maximum price they might be willing to pay (they will, of course, not reveal that maximum price to the seller or anyone else).

Do you think that each potential buyer arrives at the same estimate for this maximum price? If not, why not?

2 Transaction costs for M&A transactions are often quite high. In Chapter 8 it was argued that transaction costs depend on three dimensions of transactions (the three critical dimensions of transactions). Which of those three dimensions is, in your opinion, most important for M&A transactions?

3 This chapter argues that information asymmetry is a major problem in many M&A deals. However, the degree of information asymmetry may depend on the characterisics of the deal. Consider the following situations.
  a Two quoted companies consider a merger (such as the merger between AOL and Time Warner).
  b A quoted company is considering the acquisition of another quoted company (an example is the acquisition of Corus by Tata Steel, described in Box 12.5) by making shareholders of the target firm an offer in cash.
  c A quoted company is considering the acquisition of another quoted company by making shareholders of the target firm an offer in shares.
  d A large company wants to sell one of its divisions to another large company (an example is the sale by Philips of its domestic appliances division to Whirlpool).
  e A multibusiness firm wants to sell one of its business units to the manager of that business unit.
  f A multibusiness firm wants to sell one of its business units to a newly formed company in which a private equity firm holds 80 per cent and the manager of the business unit to be sold holds 20 per cent.
  g A large firm in the pharmaceutical industry is considering the acquisition of a small biotech firm from the founders of that company.
  For each of the above situations, discuss if and why information asymmetry is likely to be a problem.

4 You are the CEO of a large pharmaceutical company with a substantial and stable cash flow based on several well-established prescription drugs protected by patents. You know, however, that those patents expire within the next decade. You are now looking at one small biotech firm. The firm is developing a new drug with a huge market potential. The founders and owners of the firm tell you that they need another two years to fully develop and test the new drug in order to get it approved by the authorities. They also tell you that they are prepared to sell for $800 million in cash. Your estimate of the net present value of the cash flow from the new drug is well above $800 million (it could be anywhere between $2 and 5 billion), provided you get approval from the authorities. So, you could make a deal, pay $800 million and hope for the best, or do you see another possibility?

Suggested further reading

Anandalingham, G. and Lucas Jr, H. C. (2004), *Beware the Winner's Curse*, Oxford: Oxford University Press

Besanko, D., Dranove, D., Shanley, M. and Schaefer, S. (2004), *Economics of Strategy*, 3rd edn, New York: John Wiley.

Bruner, R. (2004), *Applied Mergers and Acquisitions*, Hoboken, NJ: John Wiley.

Bruner, R. (2005), *Deals from Hell: M&A lessons that rise above the ashes*, Hoboken, NJ: John Wiley.

DePamphilis, D. (2005), *Mergers, Acquisitions and Other Restructuring Activities,* 3rd edn, Amsterdam: Elsevier.

Dyer, J. H., Kale, P. and Singh, H. (2004), 'When to ally and when to acquire', *Harvard Business Review,* vol. 82 (7/8), pp. 108–15.

Gilson, R. J. and Schwartz, A. (2005), 'Understanding MACs: Moral hazard in acquisitions', *The Journal of Law, Economics and Organization,* vol. 21, pp. 330–58.

Gilson, R. J., Goldberg, V., Klausner, M. and Raff, D. 'Building foundations for a durable deal', *Financial Times* (Supplement), 13 October 2006, reprinted in Mayer, Colin and Franks, Julian, *Mastering Transactions,* Financial Times/Ernst & Young, 2006.

Jensen, M. C. (1989), 'The eclipse of the public corporation', *Harvard Business Review,* Sept/Oct, pp. 61–73.

Nanda, A. and Williamson, P. J. (1995), 'Use joint ventures to ease the pain of restructuring', *Harvard Business Review,* vol. 73 (6), pp. 119–28.

Reuer, J. J. (2005), 'Avoiding lemons in M&A deals', *MIT Sloan Management Review,* vol. 46 (3), pp. 15–17.

Reuer, J. J. and Ragozzino, R. (2006), 'Using IPOs to prove the value of M&A targets', *Financial Times (Supplement),* 6 October, reprinted in Mayer, Colin, and Franks, Julian, *Mastering Transactions,* Financial Times/Ernst & Young, 2006.

Roll, R. (1986), 'The hubris hypothesis of corporate takeovers', *Journal of Business,* vol. 59 (2), pp. 197–216.

Notes

1 *The Wall Street Journal,* July 18, 2002. Based on the case description in Anandalingham and Lucas (2004) and DePamphilis (2005).

2 See http://en.wikipedia.org/wiki/General_Electric_timeline for an overview of GE's major acquisition steps.

3 See DePamphelis (2005) for an extensive classification of types of corporate restructuring, including M&A.

4 'Have dealmakers wised up?', *Business Week,* 21 February 2005.

5 Main source for this section is the excellent overview by Tichy (2002). See also, for example, Besanko et al. (2004), Bruner (2004, 2005), DePamphilis (2005) and Jensen and Ruback (1983).

6 This methodology goes back to the seminal article by Fama et al. (1969). It is based on the 'efficient markets hypothesis', stating that the share price should reflect all publicly available knowledge. The measurement methodology is based on the capital asset pricing model (CAPM).

7 Again, the excellent overview by Tichy (2002) is the main source for this summary. See also Bruner (2005) and DePamphilis (2005). Schleifer and Vishny (2003) offer an interesting model of stock market-driven acquisitions that can explain a number of the observations discussed.

8 We use here the generic term Sales and Purchase Agreement for the SPA. If shares in a company are bought, the SPA may refer to the Share Purchase Agreement. In an 'asset deal' one may speak of an APA: an Asset Purchase Agreement.

9 See Roll (1986). Roll's hubris hypothesis depicts irrational (overconfident) managers operating in rational (efficient) financial markets. An alternative model is proposed by Shleifer and Vishny (2003) in which rational managers exploit inefficiencies in financial markets. In that model, managers of relatively overvalued firms have strong incentives to make a share offer for relatively less (over)valued targets.

10 See Dobbs, Goedhart and Suonio (2006). In their article, the question is raised as to whether or not companies are getting better at M&A as the proportion of overpayers, which rose from 1997 to 2000, was declining from 2000 to 2006. It seems

to us that it is too early to tell. An alternative explanation might be that this proportion rises towards the peak of a merger wave and declines thereafter. Where the peak of the merger wave that started around 2004 will be located remains to be seen. In any case, the article shows the proportion of overpayers to be above 50 per cent across the two recent waves.

11 The following is primarily based on Reuer (2005). See also Reuer and Shen (2004) and Reuer and Ragozzino (2006). The Philips-Whirlpool case is based on Nanda and Williamson (1995).

12 The costs can be substantial. Aside from the direct loss of managerial time, registration and underwriting costs can amount to some 14 per cent of the proceeds raised (Reuer and Ragozzino, 2006).

13 See the discussion of tacit knowledge in Chapter 10. More generally, a firm's value may reside more in its social capital rather than in its physical capital, the more so in cases where its knowledge and social interaction are key to its functioning.

14 Visit the website of insurance company AIG (www.aigmergerrisks.com) for model representations and warranties policies for both buyers and sellers.

15 Although the deal was advertised as a 'merger of equals', in reality, 55 per cent of the ownership of the new firm accrued to AOL's shareholders. The case description here is based on Bruner (2005).

16 In September 2007, a group of private equity investors led by Kohlberg Kravis Roberts and Texas Pacific Group made an offer of $32 billion for TXU, the largest power generator in Texas. The deal was expected to close in the fourth quarter of 2007.

In Chapter 1 we argued that, in *ideal markets*, coordination takes place by using the price mechanism only (prices act as a sufficient statistic) and, in *ideal organizations*, various other forms of coordination are used. We also noted that ideal markets and ideal organizations hardly exist: markets are to some extent organized and within (large) organizations internal markets can exist. That however, is not the full story: there are many governance structures which fall between ideal markets and ideal organizations.

Take as an example franchising. In order to explain what franchising is, consider McDonald's. In 2007, there were more than 30,000 McDonald's restaurants in more than 100 countries. Some 8000 restaurants are owned and operated by the McDonald's Corporation, but the rest (around 21,000) are owned and operated by local entrepreneurs. Those entrepreneurs have a contract with McDonald's Corporation giving them the right to operate under the name McDonald's. Such a contract is called a **franchise contract**. The two parties to such a contract are the franchisor (McDonald's Corporation) and the franchisee (the local entrepreneur owning and operating a McDonald's restaurant).

Franchise contract

The McDonald's Corporation has developed a formula for operating fast-food restaurants. That formula consists of a range of products (including the way those products have to be prepared), a house style (which refers to things such as the furnishing of the restaurant, the clothing of personnel and how customers are treated) and a brand name. Under the franchise contract the franchisees are allowed to use that formula in return for a fee (usually a fixed amount, plus a percentage of sales).

If we first define a hybrid form loosely as a form of governance somewhere between market and organization, then franchising fits that definition. Consider the relationship between franchisor and franchisee. We see that there is certainly an element of a market relation. The franchisee obtains the right to use a brand name owned by the franchisee in return for a fee. That is a market transaction. The franchisee is an entrepreneur who invests in his own establishment. Franchisor and franchisee are best regarded as separate organizations. Coordination between franchisor and franchisee does not take place through the market mechanism only, however. Other coordination mechanisms play an important role: standardization of work processes (for food production), standardization of norms (for the house style) and direct supervision (the franchisor monitors the behaviour of the franchisee in order to protect the value of the brand name). Between franchisor and franchisees, various organizational coordination mechanism are used, as well as the price mechanism.

Hybrid form

We can now give a more precise definition of a **hybrid form**:

> a hybrid form is a set of organizations such that coordination between those organizations takes place by means of the price mechanism and various other coordination mechanisms simultaneously.

Franchising surely fits this definition of hybrid forms. Other examples of hybrid forms are long-term relations between buyers and suppliers, joint ventures, business groups and informal networks.

That hybrid organizational forms exist has also been recognized by Williamson. For him, they occur for intermediate levels of asset specificity. As summarized in Figure 13.1 (see Ménard, 2004), Williamson sees hybrid forms as intermediate forms between markets and organizations. Hybrid forms are efficient (that is, they have the lowest transaction costs) for intermediate levels of asset specificity.

We agree with the basic line of thought behind Figure 13.1: hybrid forms are positioned between markets and hierarchies (or, in our broader approach, organizations). Thus, they can be efficient solutions in cases where neither pure market coordination nor pure organizational coordination would suffice. We find it difficult, however, to assign rather precise levels of asset specificity to the various hybrid forms. From the perspective of this book, we find it more appropriate to discuss the mix of market and organizational coordination mechanisms employed in particular hybrid forms. Some hybrid forms rely more on market than on organizational coordination. For some other hybrid forms, the mix is reversed. Hence, we can construct a picture – Figure 13.2 – in which we position the various hybrid forms somewhere along a continuum with markets at one end and organizations at the other. Towards the left of the

Figure 13.1 Hybrid forms are efficient for intermediate levels of asset specificity

Figure 13.2 Markets, organizations and hybrid forms

picture, market coordination is more prominent in the bundle of coordination mechanisms employed. Towards the right of the picture, organizational coordination is more prevalent in the bundle. In the middle, the mix of coordination mechanisms is quite balanced.

We will return to Figure 13.2 at the end of this chapter to position five examples of hybrid forms that are discussed: long-term relations between buyers and suppliers (Section 13.2), joint ventures (Section 13.3), business groups (Section 13.4), informal networks (Section 13.5), and franchising (Section 13.6). We will show how each of these forms uses market coordination and organizational coordination mechanisms. However, the relative importance of market coordination versus other coordination mechanisms differs for each of these forms. In the concluding section (Section 13.7), apart from positioning the various hybrid forms, we will also summarize some common features shared by hybrid forms. They involve pooling of resources, some joint planning and usually also a level of trust that enables the requisite level of cooperation.[1]

13.2 Long-term relations between buyers and suppliers

Companies offering tangible products often buy materials, parts or components from suppliers. For example, an automobile manufacturer buys tyres, windows, electrical systems, spark plugs, steel and many other items on a regular basis. Some of those intermediate products (dashboards, for example) are designed for a particular car model; other parts or components are not specific to any one car model. A company making a part specifically designed for the Toyota Prius, for example, has only one customer for that part. Its investment in tooling and design for the part are transaction-specific. Because of the high level of asset specificity, transaction cost economics predicts organizational coordination as the optimal choice, which means that the part in question will be manufactured by Toyota itself. In the real world, however, we often see that such parts are manufactured by outside suppliers. The suppliers are independent (in the sense that they are not owned by the automobile company) and usually have long-term relationships, supported by long-term contracts with one or more automobile companies.

Why would an outside supplier place itself in a position where it is vulnerable to its customer(s) choosing to exhibit opportunistic behaviour? There are several answers to this question:

- a long-term contract may offer some legal protection against opportunistic behaviour by the buyer;
- the buyer expects benefits from future cooperation with the supplier that far outweigh any short-term financial gain that may result from opportunistic behaviour;
- the buyer knows that opportunistic behaviour towards one supplier will affect his reputation vis-à-vis other suppliers as a dependable trading partner, so opportunistic behaviour towards one supplier will negatively affect the value of past investments in building that reputation;
- the buyer may pay for and own the design and tooling for the specific part, which reduces the level of asset specificity.

These explanations are perfectly consistent with the assumption of opportunism, which is an important assumption in transaction cost economics.

While these four answers each have an element of truth, we feel that they still fail to fully explain the existence of many successful long-term cooperations between buyers and suppliers. What is that extra element?

The benefits of cooperation are maximized when both parties really trust each other. That is especially true in a dynamic world with important technological developments and volatile markets. When both partners trust each other, they will share their technological know-how (which often means that the buyer transfers technological know-how to the supplier), the buyer and supplier will coordinate their production plans through some form of joint planning and the supplier will share cost data with the supplier and allow the buyer to visit his factory on a regular basis.

Co-makership

Such an intensive cooperation, built on mutual trust, has been termed **co-makership**. In a co-makership relation, buyer and supplier know that the benefits of the relationship are maximized when both of them 'act in good faith'. That means, for example, a supplier will not use technological know-how received from the buyer to produce parts for other customers. It also means that the supplier will be eager to improve efficiency because he knows that the buyer will not try to capture all the benefits of the efficiency improvements. Co-makership relies on both trust and safeguards (such as a long-term contract that can specify the buyer pays for and owns the tooling). Box 13.1 gives an example.

Box 13.1 A clever way to build a Boeing

In July 2007, Boeing produced the first Boeing 787 – a new fuel-saving, medium-sized passenger jet.

The new plane was remarkable for the degree to which Boeing had outscourced development and production around the world. Boeing itself is responsible for about 10 per cent by value – the tail fin and final assembly. The rest is done by 40 partners, with the wings built in Japan, the carbon composite fuselage in Italy and the US and the landing gear in France.

One important reason for doing this was that those partners had state-of-the-art technology – for example, to build wings for commercial aircraft or to build carbon composite fuselages – that Boeing did not have. Those partners, encouraged by Boeing, have developed parts designed specifically for the Boeing 787. In doing so, they extended their expertise, which some of them may use later to

▶

develop and produce parts for others, such as the Airbus. Boeing, however, holds rights to the 787 technology.

In July 2007, Boeing already had $100 billion in orders, which was considered by many to be a big success. Boeing now calls itself a 'systems integrator' rather than a manufacturer.

Source: The Financial Times, 9 July 2007

In a co-makership relation, price negotiations between buyers and suppliers are still important, so price does play a role. Mutual adjustment (through joint production planning and sharing cost data) based on trust also plays a vital role, however.

13.3 Joint ventures

Joint venture

A **joint venture** is established when two existing companies decide to pool resources to set up a new business in a newly formed company. Box 13.2 gives an example of a joint venture, which is, in fact, an international joint venture because it involves companies from two different countries.

The governance structure of two (sometimes more than two) companies acting as parent companies to another company that they jointly own is called a joint venture. A joint venture consists of a subsidiary with (at least two) parent companies. Why do joint ventures exist?

Box 13.2 A joint venture between Telecom Italia Mobile S.p.A. and Is-Bank AS

In March 2001, IS-TIM Telekomunikasyon Hizmetleri AS started its operations as the third mobile operator in Turkey. IS-TIM was set up as a joint venture between Telecom Italia Mobile S.p.A. and Is-Bank AS – a major Turkish bank.

At that time, Turkey already had two mobile operators, but a penetration of only 25 per cent. Prepaid customers accounted for almost 40 per cent of the market. According to *The Wall Street Journal Europe*, IS-TIM hoped to benefit from Telecom Italia's experience in entering a market that already had established competitors. IS-TIM said that it did not intend to discriminate in pricing between subscribers and prepaid customers. Prepaid customers can use Is-Bank automated teller machines to recharge their cards.

IS-TIM's mobile network, named Aria, quickly developed as Turkey's third largest mobile operator. In February 2004, Aria merged with Aycell, Turkey's fourth largest mobile operator. Aycell was a subsidiary of Turk Telecom and had started its operations in 2003. After the merger, the two networks were combined into one: Avea. The combined network, Avea, covers 80 per cent of the Turkish population and has an estimated market share of about 15 per cent (September 2004). The ownership stakes in Avea are 40 per cent Telecom Italia, 40 per cent Turk Telecom and 20 per cent Is-bank.

Source: The Wall Street Journal Europe, 22 March 2001, and website of IFC (International Finance Corporation)

In order to find out why joint ventures exist, let us have a closer look at the example given in Box 13.2.

Apparently, in 2001 there was a business opportunity to set up a third mobile network in Turkey. Telecom Italia and Is-Bank formed a joint venture to grab that opportunity. Telecom Italia did not bid for a licence alone – probably because it knew that operating in a foreign country in which it had no practical experience would not be easy. To set up a new company from scratch can be quite difficult if you are not familiar with local ways of doing things, including labour relations, management practices and how to deal with local authorities. These things can be quite important as a new mobile operator needs all sorts of licences from local authorities (for permission to install transmitters).

So, Telecom Italia needed the experience, know-how and relations of a local partner. Why, though, did Is-Bank not bid alone for a licence? Probably because it lacked the know-how to set up a mobile operator. So, in order to exploit this business opportunity, one needs both technological and managerial know-how (how to run a mobile operator) and local contacts. These are examples of intangible assets. It is quite difficult to buy such intangible assets in the marketplace.

One way to combine intangible assets is to set up a joint venture. The new joint venture in our example benefits from Telecom Italia's dynamic capability to set up a mobile operator in a market with established competitors and from Is-Bank's knowledge of local circumstances.

Another way to combine such intangible assets would be a merger between the two companies or one company acquiring the other company. For example, Telecom Italia could have acquired Is-Bank. That, however, would have given Telecom Italia many assets (such as a network of bank branch offices) that it does not need.

To put what we have learned in more general terms, a joint venture will be the preferred mode of organizing when the following conditions are met.

- There is a business opportunity that requires resources from two existing companies, A and B.
- It is difficult or even impossible to trade those resources. That is often the case with intangible assets (such as Telecom Italia's dynamic capability to set up a mobile operator in a market with established competitors or Is-bank's contacts with local authorities): the resources needed from company A and company B are difficult to trade (if the resource needed from A can be easily bought and sold, B can simply buy the resource from A and set up a wholly owned subsidiary).
- If company A buys company B (or B buys A), it acquires a lot of resources it does not need.

If all three conditions are met, a joint venture will be the preferred organizational form. If the first and second are met but the third is not, a merger or acquisition is an alternative solution.

Intangible assets, such as dynamic capabilities or local contacts, are difficult to trade because of opportunism. It is very difficult to specify in a contract what you buy when you buy 'access to local contacts'. To put it differently, very high transaction costs in the markets for those intangible assets lead to the formation of joint ventures. We want to note that, after the joint venture has been formed, it is still very difficult for one partner to assess whether or not the other partner really contributes the intangible assets expected from him. A certain level of mutual trust is necessary for the joint venture's success.

Joint ventures are usually set up for an indefinite period of time. Despite that, quite often, after a couple of years, changes in the ownership structure occur. Very often one partner buys out the other and the company created as a joint venture continues as a subsidiary of one of the partners. That may happen if the intangible assets provided by one of the partners are no longer needed for the joint venture's success. For example, after a few years, Aria (the mobile telecom company in our example above that was set up in Turkey by Telecom Italia and Is-Bank) was a well-established mobile operator. At that point, Aria itself did have the know-how regarding local circumstances and access to local authorities, as well as the technological and managerial know-how required to run a mobile telecom company. So, it might have been able to continue as an independent company or as a subsidiary of one of its founders if its market share had been substantially higher.

When a joint venture is formed, the companies involved in setting it up usually negotiate about the value of the (intangible) assets that they bring to the joint venture. After it has been set up, there is often a period in which the parent companies assist the subsidiary in various ways. For example, the parent companies often transfer key personnel for a limited period of time. During the period the joint venture is being formed and the first few years after that, prices do play a role in the relations between the subsidiary and its parents. Other coordination mechanisms, such as direct supervision and mutual adjustment, also play important roles. That is why joint ventures also fit our definition of a hybrid form.

13.4 Business groups

Business group

A **business group** is a group of legally independent firms that are nevertheless bound together by one or more formal and informal ties. Formal ties include reciprocal shareholding by members of the group, companies owned in part by the same shareholder (a holding company or an individual shareholder) or group of shareholders, interlocking directors, cross-guarantees of bank loans and trading of parts and supplies between group companies. Informal bonds include family ties between managers of group companies and managers of group companies belonging to the same social or ethnic group.

Business groups play an important role in most emerging markets and in many developed economies. Business groups have different names in different countries: *keiretsu* (Japan), *chaebol* (Korea), *grupos economicos* (Latin and Central America), *jituanqiye* (Taiwan) and *business houses* (India). Box 13.3 gives a description of the origin and nature of business houses in India.

Box 13.3 Business houses in India

Business groups in India (business houses) have caste and provincial origins. The initial activities of most groups can be traced back to certain parts of the country, although, in more recent times, some of the larger groups have assumed a pan-Indian operational character. Groups increased the number of companies under their fold when assets belonging to the erstwhile British companies were acquired. Traditionally, the management of most of these groups was via the *managing agency* system. Under that system, each of the participating firms signs a management contract with a managing agency owned by the group. The *managing agencies*, in turn, run these firms. Several of the largest business groups in India, such as the Tatas and the Birlas, were initially run by managing agencies owned by them.[2] However, that system of managing groups has only historical relevance as the managing agency system was abolished in 1969 as a consequence of amendments in the statute governing corporations in India.

While firms in India are largely focused entities, the business groups tend to be diversified and have certain features similar to a typical Western conglomerate or a Japanese keiretsu. Similarities exist in the sense that, akin to the headquarters of a conglomerate, the controlling family sets the overall strategic direction and regulates financial transfers. An important difference, though, is that, unlike divisions of a typical conglomerate firm, each firm in India has its own unique set of shareholdings comprised of various blockholders (a promoter company, other group companies, domestic and/or foreign financial institutions, foreign corporations) and the general public. Unlike the typical Japanese keiretsu, though, Indian groups do not have an inhouse financial institution.

Control over these group firms is typically exercised through intercorporate equity investments (cross-equity shareholdings), holding companies (pyramidal structures) and interlocking directorates.

Group firms in India generally advertise their affiliation to a particular group and those affiliations remain substantially stable over time. Despite the institution of a takeover code in the 1990s, the practice of group firms interchanging group affiliations is relatively uncommon. Business groups also differ in the extent and diversity of their operations. The largest groups are active in a wide variety of industries, ranging from automobile production to educational publishing. They cover vast tracts of the industrial sector and contribute to a significant chunk of the country's industrial output.[3] Nonetheless, the bulk of the business groups can be categorized as small- and medium-sized, with the scale and scope of their activities being considerably more modest. The firms constituting business groups involve listed as well as unlisted firms. Furthermore, information pertaining to group affiliation is publicly available and it is relatively easy to identify group affiliation in India. Each firm within a group has a separate legal entity and can be listed separately on the stock exchange. Most groups have fewer than five firms listed on stock exchanges such as the Bombay Stock Exchange (BSE). More than 1000 group-affiliated firms are listed on various stock exchanges in India. They belong to a few hundred groups. About 95 per cent of those groups have five or fewer affiliates. In effect, the average business group in India has around two listed firms.

Well-known examples of business groups include Mitsubishi (in Japan – banking, insurance, cars, steel, beer, chemicals), Hyundai (in Korea – sea transport, cars, elevators) and Tata (in India – steel, cars, chemicals, tea, hotels). These three business groups display activities in a wide array of industries, as our lists and a visit to their websites will quickly reveal. That tends to be true for most business groups. Box 13.4 gives more details on the Tata group – a prominent business group in India.

3.4.1 Types of business groups

Horizontal business group

Business groups can be horizontal or vertical as far as their structure is concerned. In a **horizontal business group** there is no central holding company – the group companies are connected through various formal or informal ties, including reciprocal shareholding. Thus, a horizontal business group is a rather loose confederation of firms. Coordination between them is achieved mainly by mutual adjustment and standardization of norms. Mitsubishi is a well-known example of a horizontal business group as are many other keiretsu. Taiwanese and Chinese groups exhibit similar features. Horizontal business groups are also referred to as *associative business groups*.

Vertical business group

A **vertical business group** is a group of companies controlled but not entirely owned by a single investor. Vertical groups are often organized as pyramids of companies controlled by the main investor through a holding company. A unique feature of pyramidal holdings is that it allows the main investor to exert control with a limited amount of capital. Korean chaebols, Indian business houses and most European business groups are vertical in character. Vertical business groups are also referred to as *hierarchical business groups*.

Some business groups do have a main investor and also have extensive cross-holdings of shares in group companies. They thus display the characteristics of both vertical *and* horizontal business groups. One example is the Tata Group (see Box 13.4). Tata clearly has a main investor – Tata Sons – but it rarely owns more than 20 per cent of the Tata Group's companies. There is extensive cross-shareholding between the Tata Group's companies and Mr R. N. Tata, who chairs the Boards of quite a few important Tata companies. Thus, the Tata Group displays characteristics of both horizontal and vertical business groups.

Box 13.4 The Tata Group

The Tata Group is the largest business group in India. It is comprised of approximately 100 operating companies, with activities in more than 50 countries. Some of the Group's companies have a listing on a stock market (in June 2007, 28 Tata Group companies had a stock market listing), while other group companies are not listed on any stock market.

The Tata Group has been founded by Jamsetji Tata in the mid 19th century. In 2006, the combined revenues of the Tata Group's companies was $22 billion. Market capitalization on 21 June 2007 was $59 billion. The Tata Group's companies are active in a wide range of industries, including chemicals, steel, telecom, cars, tea, watches and hotels.

The Tata Group has three important holding companies – Tata Sons, Tata Industries and the Investment Corporation of India. Those companies hold shares in the Group's companies and offer advice and assistance to them. They also take the lead in setting up new companies, which is why they are often referred to as 'promoter' companies. Tata Sons is the main promoter company of the group and can be considered the group headquarters. There is considerable cross-shareholding between the Group's companies. Two-thirds of the equity of Tata Sons is held by various philanthropic trusts endowed by members of the Tata family. Members of the Tata family continue to hold important positions (such as chair of the Board of directors) in the Tata Group.[4]

On 31 January 2007, Tata Steel, a company belonging to the Tata Group, made a successful bid of €6.7 billion for the Anglo-Dutch steelmaker Corus in a competitive auction. In financing this large acquisition, Tata Steel received backing from Tata Sons. See also Box 12.5.

13.4.2 Coordination within business groups

In vertical business groups there is a main investor who exercises control over group companies. Control in a vertical business group involves authority and hierarchy and comes close to the kind of control exercised in an M-form enterprise (see Section 8.6). Coordination between group companies is achieved through a variety of coordination mechanisms, always including direct supervision. The main investor in a vertical business group frequently uses pyramidal structures and/or differential voting rights to exercise control.

Pyramid

To explain the concept of a **pyramid** consider the following example. Suppose a holding company (H) holds a fraction α of the shares of a group company (A), which in turn holds a fraction β of another group company (B). If α and β are smaller than 1, but large enough to exert control, we have a pyramid – in this case, a two-stage pyramid. If, for example $\alpha = .51$ and $\beta = .52$, then holding company H owns, indirectly, only 26.52 per cent of the shares of company B and still has full control over B. A pyramid allows a single investor to control many firms that, collectively, are worth substantially more than his actual wealth. Pyramids effectively lead to a separation of ownership and control.

Pyramidal structures are widely prevalent in several East Asian and European economies. Box 13.5 and Figure 13.3 give an example of a pyramidal construction from Italy. In particular, firms in Indonesia, Singapore, Taiwan and Korea use pyramids extensively (see Claessens, Djankov and Lang (2000); Faccio, Lang and Young (2001)).

Box 13.5 Who controls Fiat?

Fiat S.p.A. (Fiat Group) is the largest industrial group in Italy, employing around 160,000 people, 44 per cent of whom work in Italy. The company is well known for its automobiles (brand names include Fiat, Alfa Romeo, Lancia and Ferrari), but also has important activities in agricultural and construction equipment, commercial vehicles (brand name Iveco), motorcycles, aeronautics, components, metallurgical products, production systems and publishing (for example, the daily newspaper La Stampa).

Fiat S.p.A. is a quoted company that effectively is controlled by the Agnelli family through a cascade of two other quoted companies, IFI and IFIL (see Figure 13.3). Giovanni Agnelli & C is a limited partnership formed by descendants of Fiat's founder. The partnership controls 30.3 per cent of the shares in Fiat S.p.A. In the 2006 shareholders' meeting fewer than half of those entitled to vote did so. As a result, the 30.3 per cent held by IFIL constituted an absolute majority at that meeting.

The partnership Giovanni Agnelli & C is effectively controlled by John Elkan, a grandson and main heir of Gianni Agnelli. Elkan controls a holding company called Dicembre, which has 31.2 per cent of the votes in the limited partnership. None of the other partners/family members has more than 5 per cent of the votes, so one could argue that Dicembre (Elkan) controls Fiat, although it has an effective economic interest of only 3.5 per cent.

Source: The Economist, 17 March 2007

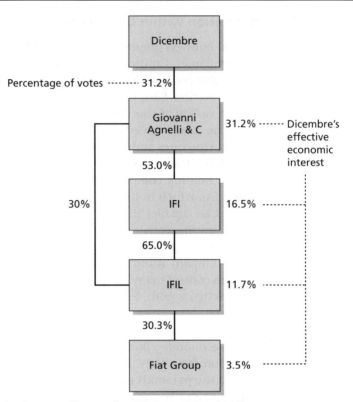

Percentage of votes ········ 31.2%

Figure 13.3 The Agnelli's empire (30 September 2006)

Another way to exert control without (full) ownership is to use shares with different voting rights. They can take the form of two or more classes of shares having the same cash flow rights but with different voting rights. Such **differential voting rights** lead to a considerable separation of ownership and control (DeAngelo and DeAngelo, 1985; De Jong, Kabir, Marra and Roëll, 2001). The main advantage lies in the controlling shareholders being able to raise capital without having to relinquish control, as long as the practice is allowed by law and other shareholders are willing to give up their control rights. Shares with differential voting rights are extremely potent devices, enabling the controlling family to allocate all voting rights associated with a fraction of shares assigned to them, while assigning no or limited voting rights to other shareholders. Such-dual class voting rights are extensively utilized in a number of countries, particularly Brazil, Canada, Denmark, Finland, Germany, Italy, Norway, Korea, Mexico, Sweden and Switzerland (Faccio and Lang, 2002). **Dual-class equity**, therefore, can serve as an ideal device for controlling group-affiliated firms. Shares with superior voting rights usually trade at higher prices than ordinary shares – the premium being 30 per cent or even more.[5]

In horizontal business groups there is no main investor who exercises control over group companies. Coordination in such business groups is achieved mainly by mutual adjustment and standardization of norms. Mutual adjustment is facilitated by cross-holdings between group companies and director interlocks.

Differential voting rights

Dual-class equity

Reciprocal shareholding

Cross-holding of shares

Director interlock

When company A holds shares in company B and vice versa, we say that there is **reciprocal shareholding** between A and B. When company C owns shares in company D, company D owns shares in company E and company E owns shares in company C, we say that there is **cross-holding of shares** between C, D and E. When there is reciprocal shareholding between A and B, A and B have a clear economic motive to cooperate. In such a case we will often see that one of the managing directors of company A sits on the Board of company B and vice versa. Equally, someone may sit as a non-executive Board member on the boards of A and B. In both cases, we say that there is a **director interlock** between A and B. Such a director interlock between A and B facilitates information sharing between them and helps to build trust between the two companies' top management teams. The same mechanisms apply to cross-holdings combined with director interlocks between three or more group companies. Cross-holdings and director interlocks between group companies belonging to a horizontal business group help to reduce opportunistic behaviour and, thus, the cost of transacting between group companies.

Standardization of norms and mutual adjustment in both vertical and horizontal business groups is furthermore fostered by family ties between key managers of group firms or managers having the same cultural or ethnic background. This also facilitates transactions between group companies.

13.4.3 Why do business groups exist?

Business groups will continue to exist if they offer some advantages not available through other organizational arrangements. Alternatives to business groups are a set of independent companies cooperating through market transactions and a set of business units cooperating in a multibusiness firm. If we want to know why business groups exist we have to compare them with these alternatives.

Comparing a business group with a set of independent companies

A business group may have several advantages not available to a group of independent companies cooperating through market transactions.

First, business groups offer opportunities for *reducing transaction costs*. When the quality of institutions (such as intermediaries) or the efficiency of the judicial system is poor, transaction costs may be very high indeed. That may occur in capital markets, markets for consumer goods and managerial labour.

If the rights of minority shareholders are not well protected (which is the case in many countries), investors may prefer to invest in a new company backed by a business group with a reputation of honesty over investing in a similar independent company. In such environments group companies will enjoy a lower cost of capital than independent companies. That situation applies in many developing countries. In many such emerging markets, security analysts, stockbrokers and investment banks are absent or do not offer the same quality as their counterparts in more developed nations. Consequently, potential investors may hesitate to invest in new ventures because they have little reliable information. A business group may develop a reputation for honesty with respect to information disclosure to potential investors. That will help to reduce information asymmetry and lead to a lower cost of capital for that business group's companies.

When consumer protection is poor, a business group may build a reputation for quality of consumer products and a common brand name (the Tata Group has done this). A company belonging to a business group can use the common brand name. Consumers will have more confidence in products under such a business group brand name because the business group puts its reputation at stake if it delivers poor quality. An independent company offering the same quality will have to spend much more to convince potential customers. Thus, business groups may help to overcome a problem of hidden information. This explanation is borne out by the fact that business groups play a very important role in most developing countries.

When well-trained managers are scarce, business groups may hire young management trainees and educate them through a management development programme including a job rotation programme. Independent companies have fewer opportunities for job rotation and weaker incentives to invest in educating management trainees. Business groups may offer more opportunities for promotion and, thus, stronger incentives to young professional managers. At the same time, transaction costs in the managerial labour market are largely avoided by rotating young managers from company to company in the group.

Second, business groups may possess *political clout* that facilitate interaction with key government officials (Pagano and Volpin, 2001), which often leads to preferential access to permits and licences and the preemption of their use by potential entrants (Khanna, 2000). This is an important factor in most emerging markets as, despite liberalization initiatives in several emerging markets, the level of regulation continues to be high, with companies requiring permission for activities such as exiting a business, changing prices and importing raw materials. Bureaucrats exercise a considerable amount of discretion in the application of rules concerning such decisions (Khanna and Palepu, 1997). Realizing this, the largest business houses in India maintain 'industrial embassies' in the capital New Delhi. The embassies serve the purpose of lobbying with the political elite. Independent companies may lack the political clout of such business groups.

Third, business groups may possess *dynamic capabilities* in setting up new ventures. Business groups in emerging markets may have developed dynamic capabilities in setting up joint ventures with foreign partners. The capabilities those groups possess cover the entire spectrum of skills associated with obtaining requisite licences, technology, training of personnel and setting up distribution networks. As that dynamic capability is embodied in the group's owners, managers and routines, it is difficult to trade. Moreover, once a new venture is up and running, that capability lies dormant. There is, therefore, a strong urge for business groups possessing that capability to diversify into a wide range of industries.

While that generic capability represents a vital ingredient in explaining the scope of the activities engaged in by such groups, it is not sufficient to maintain the long-term sustainability of their competitive advantage. To do that, the capability needs to be inimitable as well. Such inimitability could come from the prevailing institutional environment in which these business groups operate. Specifically, the sustainability of the competitive advantage of business groups is hypothesized to be greater in emerging economies with asymmetrical trade and investment conditions as, under these conditions, business groups (vis-à-vis groups of independent companies) are uniquely positioned to exploit their superior ability to combine foreign and domestic resources for repeated industry entry (Guillén, 2000).

Comparing a business group with a multibusiness firm

In the previous section, we mentioned three advantages that a business group may have over a group of independent companies (lower transaction costs, political clout and dynamic capabilities in setting up new ventures). Those advantages are also available to a multibusiness firm. So, why do we observe (at least in many countries) so many business groups and so few multibusiness firms? The answer is that, in certain environments, business groups can have advantages over multibusiness firms.

Private benefits of control

Business groups offer controlling owners an opportunity to appropriate certain **private benefits of control**. Those private benefits involve the transfer of value from firms in which the controlling owners have low cash flow rights to those firms in which they have higher cash flow rights. This phenomenon is referred to as **tunnelling** (Johnson et al., 2000). Value transfers can take place through transactions of intermediate products at non-market prices, provision of capital at artificial prices and inflated payments for intangibles such as patents, brand names and insurance (Morck et al., 2004).

Tunnelling

Propping

Propping (or negative tunnelling) is a related phenomenon wherein controlling owners prop up lower-performing or struggling firms for the benefit of the controlling owners.

Tunnelling and propping can be especially potent devices in countries with low protection of minority shareholder rights. Empirical evidence supports the view that business groups are particularly conducive to practices involving tunnelling, propping or related party transactions, leading to the detriment of the welfare of minority shareholders of the various firms in the group (Bertrand, Mehta and Mullainathan, 2002; Friedman, Johnson and Mitton, 2003; Nam, 2001; Nenova, 2004; Polisiri and Wiwattanakantang, 2004).

The private benefits of control also include providing members of the controlling family with suitable employment opportunities. While it can be argued that a single firm could potentially resolve this problem, the use of multiple firms enables the patriarch to allocate separate businesses to each of his progeny, thereby minimizing thorny control issues in individual firms.

Business groups that extract such private benefits of control make themselves vulnerable vis-à-vis competition from independent companies. They will not be able to build or maintain a reputation for honesty and, thus, will lose certain advantages that they might otherwise have over a group of independent companies.

Business groups do have another advantage over multibusiness firms. They tend to be highly diversified, perhaps because they possess the dynamic capability to set up new ventures quickly and effectively. Highly diversified firms in developed economies tend to perform less well than more focused firms. That is probably because managing a set of business units in widely different industries is a very difficult task for corporate headquarters. At the very least, it requires a control style involving strong incentives for business unit managers. Ideally, those incentives should be tied to creating shareholder value, which is exactly what is achieved by giving the managers an ownership stake. In business groups, managers of group companies often do have an ownership stake. Thus, business groups may be an effective vehicle for obtaining some benefits of cooperation not available to a set of independent companies, while, at the same time, giving strong incentives (through partial ownership) to managers of group companies. To put it differently, just as the private equity governance model competes with the public corporation as an alternative governance model (see Chapter 12), business groups may be regarded as an alternative governance model to that of widely diversified firms. Which governance model is more successful in varying circumstances is an empirical question. Next, we discuss how developments in the institutional context may have an impact on the competitiveness of business groups.

13.4.4 The development of business groups

In the USA and UK, business groups hardly exist, but, in many other countries, they play an important role. Will business groups gradually disappear as a result of globalizing capital markets and institutional reforms in non-Anglo-American countries? To answer that question, let us first discuss recent developments with respect to business groups in one particular country – India.

Developments in the institutional environment in India

When India gained its independence in 1947, it intended to have a planned economy, where all aspects of economic life were controlled by the State and licences to run companies were given to a select few. Under that system – often referred to as the '**Licence Raj**' – the functioning of markets was severely restricted. First, competition in domestic markets for products was restricted by the Industrial Development and Regulation Act of 1956 and the domestic market was shielded from import competition by very high tariff barriers.

Second, a significant proportion of Indian corporations were managed by family members. Professional managers appointed to the highest echelons of the corporate hierarchy were the exception rather than the norm. As a result, the market for managerial labour hardly existed.

Third, M&A were looked on by the Monopolies and Restrictive Trade Practices Commission with disfavour and there were restrictions on the acquisition and transfer of shares. Financial institutions remained dormant and were instructed by their principal shareholder – the government – to not desta-

Licence Raj

bilize existing management. A market for corporate control did not exist under this system.

In this institutional environment, business groups – many of which had existed already under British rule – were able to fill the voids created by those missing markets.

In 1990, India faced an economic crisis and, in 1991, a process of liberalization of the economy began. It entailed the repeal of the Industrial Development and Regulation Act, the Capital Issues Control Act, the Monopolies and Restrictive Trade Practices Act and significant amendments were made to the other acts. This resulted in a more open market ambience. In addition, new bodies and regulations strengthening investor protection measures and furthering the external governance measures were adopted. They included the creation of a Securities and Exchange Board of India (SEBI), along the lines of the Securities and Exchange Commission (SEC) in the USA, the setting up of depositories to facilitate speedier share transactions and mitigate fraudulent ones and the enactment (in 1997) of extensive guidelines for M&A.

Thus, the post-1991 period marked a dramatic shift in the institutional framework in India. Inflow of foreign capital increased dramatically. Financial institutions lost their privileged access to funds from the government and were forced to tap domestic and international markets, which, in turn, fostered a greater sense of accountability with regard to their monitoring roles in Indian corporations. Within the firms themselves, Indian companies realized the necessity to foster professionalism in their management if they were to remain competitive in both product and financial markets, domestically as well as internationally. That led to a new breed of professional managers at the helm of corporate affairs and the beginnings of a vibrant market for managerial labour.

This gradual dismantling of the 'Licence Raj' and the progressive reduction in import tariffs ignited competition in the product market and exposed firms formerly used to a cocooned existence.

As a result of these developments, business groups in India have lost some of their erstwhile advantages. Whether business groups continue to have an advantage in reducing transaction costs in acquiring capital or managerial labour is doubtful. Whether business groups will continue to exist will probably be determined by their relative performance versus independent companies. Also, as competition in the capital market, the market for managerial labour and product markets increases, business groups will lose out in those areas, too.[6]

Developments in some other countries in Asia

In 1997, several countries in East Asia were affected by what has been termed the 'East Asian crisis'. Countries such as South Korea, Malaysia, Indonesia and Thailand faced a major economic crisis and a fall in the value of their currencies against the dollar. The IMF offered to step in on the condition that important institutional reforms would be made.

In South Korea, the government promised to dismantle business groups (the chaebols) in accordance with the IMF-instituted restructuring guidelines. However, the years since the crisis have demonstrated the resilience of business groups as an organizational form and several Korean business groups continue to prosper.

Malaysia, Indonesia and Thailand haven't seen the total disappearance of business groups post-crisis either. Instead, business groups that possessed the requisite political connections with the ruling elite have been able to avoid losses and benefited by acquiring failed businesses.

Japan was not affected to same degree as the other East Asian economies and, in any case, its government made no serious attempt to break up business groups (Chang, 2006).

Developments in the EU

In the EU, business groups continue to play an important role in many countries (such as France, Spain, Italy, Belgium, Sweden). Very few restrictions on competition in product markets remain. Also, there is an increasingly active managerial labour market. As we will discuss more extensively in Section 14.7, however, the market for corporate control is not well developed in many of the EU countries. Despite the adoption of an EU Directive on takeover bids by the EU in 2004, important differences in takeover codes between EU countries still exist (see also Box 14.11). At the time of writing (2007), it is difficult to predict whether or not the role of business groups in the EU will decrease in the near future.

13.5 Informal networks

Informal network

An **informal network** may be thought of as a group of firms bound together by informal ties only. An informal network consists of essentially equal members that have informal relations with one another. The basis of those relations is trust. A network is characterized more by cooperation than competition:[7]

> If it is price competition that is the central co-ordinating mechanisms of the market and administrative orders that of hierarchy, then it is trust and co-operation that centrally articulates networks (Frances et al., 1991, p. 15).

Interlocking directorates

An example of an informal network may be **interlocking directorates** – members of a relatively small number of organizations serving on each others' Boards as outside directors. Such contacts may build an atmosphere of mutual trust and co-operation. Another example is the informal networks that exist in Italy between small- and medium-sized firms, which work together in a sub-contracting mode.

Coordination within informal networks is through mutual adjustment and standardization of norms. Standardization of norms (through self-selection, selection or socialization) probably plays an important role in the case of interlocking directorates. People who come from the same region, who went to the same university or know each other well from 'the old days' sometimes form a closed group, sitting on several Boards and exchanging favours and information with each other. Where such **old boys' networks** exist, outsiders may find it very difficult to penetrate such a network. Companies on whose Boards they sit interact through markets, so market coordination still also plays a role. In our second example, of Italian networks of small- and medium-sized firms, the mechanisms of mutual adjustment and standardization of norms operate as well, combined with market coordination (prices are involved in subcontracting).

Old boys' networks

Networks are important in some developing countries, such as China. In China the rules and institutions that are used in the West to settle disputes are less well developed. That may explain, to some extent, why networks based on personal relations are more of a feature, as suggested by the text in Box 13.6.

Box 13.6 *Guanxi,* transaction costs and rules

Many countries in Eastern Europe and Asia are making a difficult transition to more market-based economies. In Eastern Europe these are mostly replacing former (communist) planning-based systems. In Asia, the economies have often been characterized as more network- or relations-based. Economists around the world have been impressed by the difficulties that such a transition encounters. In particular, the extent to which market-based economies rely on clear and transparent rules, as well as on institutions that safeguard and enforce those rules, has become evident. One particular analysis by Professors Li Shuhe and Li Shaomin of the City University of Hong Kong was summarized as follows in a survey of Asian business in *The Economist*:

The familiar word used to describe the old (Chinese) system is *guanxi.* Usually translated as 'connections', *guanxi* conjures up images of karaoke outings with officials, nods of understanding in smoke-filled rooms, and the invisible hand not of the market, but of influence. *Guanxi* is a cliché, but is only too real.

Western investors tend to assume that Asian tycoons turn to *guanxi* for deep-seated cultural reasons, but in fact they do so out of necessity. Both a rules-based and a *guanxi*-based system of governance incur expenses. For both, these are made up of the fixed costs of keeping the system running – say, training and paying judges, regulators and auditors – and incremental costs, such as the effort and expense of signing one more contract, sealing one more transaction, and so on.

Developed economies have rules-based governance systems that incur enormous fixed, but negligible incremental, costs. The fixed costs, however, are spread over huge numbers of transactions and business relationships, so that the average cost of any single deal is quite low. By contrast, the poor countries of Asia so far have not been able to afford the investment in the high fixed costs of such a system, and have therefore settled on the large incremental costs of a *guanxi*-based system. As long as the number of transactions and business relationships remained comparatively small, the average cost of transactions was bearable.

As *guanxi* economies grow and become more complex, however, the incremental costs of doing business shoot up. What worked with a hundred clients, a dozen suppliers, two creditors and one shareholder no longer works with thousands of all of these. So there comes a point, Messrs Li reckon, when the average cost of doing business in a *guanxi*-based system of governance exceeds that in rules-based systems. When this happens, companies and countries that rely on *guanxi* can no longer compete. Market forces initiate a transition to a rules-based system. This is probably the largest and riskiest step that countries and companies ever have to take.

Source: 'In praise of rules: a survey of Asian business', *The Economist,* 7 April 2001

13.6 Franchising

Franchising is typically found in industries such as fast-food restaurants (McDonald's, Kentucky Fried Chicken), hotels (Hilton, Sheraton, Holiday Inn) and retailing. These industries have two characteristics in common:

- they provide services that have to be 'produced' locally while the customer is present;
- there are large advantages in developing and maintaining a business formula and a brand name.

13.6.1 Why does franchising exist?

Resource scarcity thesis

There are two answers to the question of why franchising exists. The first answer is called the **resource scarcity thesis**. According to this thesis, a firm that has developed a highly successful formula is faced with resource constraints (scarcity of capital and talented managers) if it wants to expand rapidly. Franchising is seen as a means to overcome those constraints.

Administrative efficiency thesis

The second answer is the **administrative efficiency thesis**. In this thesis, franchising is analysed from an agency theory and transaction cost perspective. According to this view franchising, in certain industries, is a more efficient governance structure than either a pure hierarchy or a pure market.

13.6.2 Resource scarcity thesis

Suppose that the owner of a restaurant develops a highly successful formula and she sees an opportunity to open many other restaurants operating with the same formula. If she wants to do so through full ownership, she has to set up and subsequently manage many local units. That requires large amounts of capital and many motivated and capable managers. If she lacks those resources, she is faced with the problem of resource scarcities. That problem can be overcome, it is argued, through franchising.

The franchisee invests in his own local unit, which means that the level of investment by the franchisor is greatly reduced. The franchisee also manages his own local unit. If we suppose that talented managers are eager to work as franchisees but unwilling to work as salaried managers, then franchising also solves the problem of finding capable managers.

The resource scarcity thesis can explain why a small company that happens to find a successful formula in the service sector has little choice but to grow through franchising. It may be very important to grow quickly and a small company may face serious difficulties in attracting large amounts of capital and many talented managers for new local units.

The resource scarcity thesis cannot explain, however, why a large company such as McDonald's Corporation continues to use franchising when it expands still further. Consider first the problem of obtaining additional capital. McDonald's Corporation is a large and highly profitable company. Its shares are listed on the New York Stock Exchange. Such a company is surely not faced with the problem of scarce financial resources. On the contrary, it is quite likely that McDonald's Corporation can acquire additional capital (in the form of both equity and debt) on better conditions than local entrepreneurs.

Let us now consider the problem of hiring talented young managers. It is hard to see why a company like McDonald's Corporation could not attract talented managers working for a salary, while other large multinational companies, such as Unilever and Nestlé, are able to recruit hundreds of talented young managers every year.

To summarize, the resource scarcity thesis can explain why small companies that have found a highly successful formula start to grow through franchising, but it cannot explain why large, established companies continue to use franchising when they expand still further. That brings us to the second view of franchising – the administrative efficiency thesis.

13.6.3 Administrative efficiency thesis

According to the administrative efficiency thesis, franchising exists because, in certain industries, it is a very efficient organizational form. Recall that franchising is found primarily in service industries where production occurs in many local units and there are significant advantages to be gained from operating many local units under the same formula and brand name.

There are, in principle, three organizational arrangements that could be used in that type of industry:

- one company owning and operating all units (a hierarchy);
- franchising;
- a set of independent companies using a common brand name.

In a large company with many dispersed units, the main problem is shirking by local managers. Suppose, first, that local managers receive a fixed level of pay (not related to the sales or profit of the unit they manage). In the language of the theory of principal and agent, that is a wage contract. The theory then predicts that the agent will choose to exert a low level of effort.

One way to reduce shirking by local managers is to monitor them. That requires frequent visits by the district manager to the local units in the district. Another way is to give local managers a share in the profits of their units or offer them career prospects within the company.

In a franchising arrangement, the franchisor usually receives a franchise fee consisting of a percentage of the sales of a local unit plus a fixed annual payment. The profits of the individual unit after payment of the franchise fee are for the franchisee. Thus, although the franchise fee is not a fixed payment (it depends on sales), the risk of variations in profitability is borne by the franchisee. That comes very close to a rent contract. The franchisee, then, has strong incentives to run his unit efficiently. Shirking by the local manager (the main problem in a hierarchy) is not at all a problem here. There are, however, three other problems.

First, there is the problem of **inefficient risk-bearing**. As there are so many restaurants, McDonald's shareholders do not worry about the risk of an individual restaurant. In the agency relationship between franchisor and franchisee, the principal is (almost) risk-neutral and the agent probably risk-averse. We know from Section 7.6.2 that, in that case, the agent should not bear all the risk, yet it seems that in most franchising contracts almost all risk *is* borne by the agent (the franchisee).

The second problem is **free riding by a franchisee** on the common brand name. The franchisee may be tempted to use cheaper inputs for his products. That lowers the quality level. If there are very few repeat customers anyway, perhaps because the restaurant is located at an airport, that can increase local profits. The result, however, is that the value of the general brand name deteriorates. The point is that the decrease in the value of the brand name is borne by the franchisor and all franchisees together. If all other franchisees continue to deliver high quality, then one individual franchisee can deliver a low quality and free ride on the common brand name. In order to reduce this problem, the franchisor usually monitors quality very closely. Doing so is much cheaper than monitoring all aspects of a local operation.

The third problem concerns **appropriability of quasi-rents**. Suppose that the franchisee has to invest in a building that is designed as a McDonald's restaurant and the resale value of that building – should the franchisee's contract with McDonald's Corporation be terminated – is much lower than the original investment. The building is then a transaction-specific investment for the franchisee. The difference between the original investment and the resale value is a quasi-rent that could be appropriated by the franchisor. The problem vanishes if the franchisor owns the building and lets it to the franchisee (as does McDonald's Corporation in many cases).

Consider, finally, an arrangement between, say, 100 hamburger restaurants that have decided to use a common brand name. The main problem here, too, is free riding on the brand name. Such an arrangement can work only if there is a central party to the contract who closely monitors quality levels. That central party should have the right to terminate the contract with an individual company if quality levels are consistently below standard. Then, though, we do not have a contract between 100 hamburger restaurants, but 100 contracts between a central party and 100 hamburger restaurants. That is very much like a franchise arrangement.

The discussion is summarized in Table 13.1. We have looked at three organizational arrangements (one large company, franchising, and a set of independent units) and we have identified four problems: shirking by the local manager, inefficient risk-bearing, free riding on the brand name and appropriation of quasi-rents. The table indicates whether or not a particular problem is really an important issue in a particular organizational arrangement.

In Table 13.1, we have indicated that free riding is not a severe problem in the case of franchising. That is because, in a franchising contract, the franchisor normally has the right to monitor quality levels and terminate the contract if quality is below standard. We have also indicated that appropriation of quasi-rents is not a severe problem in the case of franchising because it is solved if the franchisor owns the building.

Table 13.1 Problems associated with three types of organization arrangement

Problem	Hierarchy	Franchising	Independent companies with common brand name
Shirking	Yes	No	No
Inefficient risk-bearing	No	Yes	Yes
Free riding on brand name	No	No	Yes
Quasi-rent appropriation	No	No	No

By way of a summary of the above, we can conclude that a set of independent companies using a common brand name is not a feasible arrangement: the problem of free riding on the brand name cannot be solved. When comparing franchising with one large company, it seems that franchising is the preferred solution if shirking is a severe problem.

Finally, we want to note that McDonald's Corporation uses a bundle of coordinating mechanisms to organize the actions of the managers of the restaurants it owns: direct supervision, standardization of outputs (products in this case), standardization of work processes and probably also standardization of norms. In its role as franchisor, the McDonald's Corporation uses exactly the same bundle of coordinating mechanisms for the franchisees. The main difference is that, with respect to its franchisees, direct supervision focuses on quality levels, whereas with respect to the managers of its own restaurants, direct supervision includes all aspects of the local manager's job. Another important difference between 'owning' and 'franchising' is the market relation between McDonald's Corporation and its franchisees: the McDonald's Corporation sells the right to use its business formula at a price (the franchise fee). In addition, the franchisee can buy ingredients and equipment from the franchisor.

13.7 Comparing several hybrid forms

From the discussion in the previous sections, it is clear that there are large differences between hybrid forms. There are, however also some common features. The most important common feature is that hybrid forms are based on the necessity to pool resources in order to achieve something. In a co-makership relation, supplier and buyer share know-how, production plans and cost data. Joint ventures are established when two (sometimes more than two) companies pool resources – often intangible as well as tangible assets – to set up a new company. Companies belonging to a business group often use the same brand name, exchange know-how, support an industrial embassy and rotate young managers. In informal networks, information is shared between participating organizations. In franchising, franchisees use the formula, including the brand name, developed and supported by the franchisor. These are all examples of pooling of (intangible) resources.

With pooling of resources often comes joint planning. In a co-makership relation, buyer and supplier often jointly plan production schedules. In a joint venture, the two parent companies jointly make decisions on the strategic direction of their joint subsidiary. Companies belonging to a business group discuss their strategic plans with other group companies. In franchising, the franchisor develops new products in close cooperation with (a selection of) the franchisees.

Pooling of resources and joint planning introduces organizational coordination mechanisms, such as direct supervision, mutual adjustment and standardization of work processes, skills, output and norms. We would place a hybrid form for which these organizational coordinating mechanisms are much more important than the price mechanism to the right side of Figure 13.2. Conversely, when the price mechanism is more important than the organizational coordination mechanisms, we would place a hybrid form to the left side of Figure 13.2. Where exactly each hybrid form should be placed on that line is dependent on the specific arrangements made in particular hybrid forms. Broadly speaking, however, we would say that:

- informal networks should be on the left side;
- long-term buyer–supplier relations (co-makership) should be on the left side;
- vertical business groups should be to the right of horizontal business groups;
- joint ventures, franchising and vertical business groups should be on the right side.

This leads us to the overview as presented in Figure 13.4.

Markets		**Organizations**
Informal networks	Horizontal business groups	Vertical business groups
Long-term buyer–supplier relations		Joint ventures
		Franchising

Figure 13.4 Hybrid forms placed on the line between markets and organizations

13.8 Summary: hybrid forms as governance structures between ideal markets and ideal organizations

We hope that it is clear that there are many types of hybrid forms. They may be seen as intermediate forms between markets and organizations, employing different mixes of market and organizational coordination mechanisms. That conclusion builds on our observations in Chapter 3:

- that it is important analytically to distinguish carefully between market and organizational coordination to determine which is the most efficient in which circumstances;

- when we move from the analytical world (with its sharp distinctions) to the messy real world, we often find bundles of coordination mechanisms operating together.

In previous chapters we often highlighted that many markets are, to a certain extent, 'organized', while many organizations employ internal market mechanisms next to organizational coordination. As this chapter further elucidates, ideal markets and ideal organizations are two ends of a continuum. Between those two ends, many different bundles of coordination mechanisms can be observed. As we move from left to right in Figure 13.4:

- we start with an 'ideal market', utilizing only the price mechanism;
- then markets become increasingly 'organized' (by being regulated, for example);
- they give way to hybrid forms that are first still 'market-like' and then increasingly become 'organization-like';
- organizations then take over – initially, with the price mechanism still playing a role (in the form of transfer pricing, for example);
- finally, we reach 'ideal organizations', entirely utilizing organizational coordination mechanisms.

It is certainly a fascinating world of markets and organizations out there!

Questions

1 Box 13.1 describes how Boeing outsources production and development to its partners around the world.

Referring to the discussion on vertical integration in Section 9.8.2, how would you classify the situation of Boeing and its partners in terms of Figure 9.10?

Do you think Boeing is now vulnerable to opportunistic behaviour by its suppliers? If not, why?

2 In 2001, Telecom Italia entered Turkey by forming a joint venture with a local partner, Is-bank (see Box 13.2). The new company created a new mobile network under the name Aria. In 2001, Telecom Italia needed knowledge of local circumstances and access to local politicians in order to successfully enter Turkey. In 2004, Aria merged with another Turkish mobile network, Aycell (owned by Turk Telecom), to form Avea. After that merger, Telecom Italia owned 40 per cent of Avea. It might have gone otherwise, however. After a couple of years Telecom Italia could have decided that it was sufficiently familiar with local circumstances and therefore no longer needed its local partner. It could have offered to buy the shares of Is-bank. Aria would then have been a subsidiary of Telecom Italia.

What could have been the most important benefits for Telecom Italia of buying out its local partner? Do you expect firms in a high-tech industry to benefit more from buying out their local joint venture partners than firms in industries with a mature technology?

3 In Section 13.4.3, a business group is compared with a set of independent companies. One advantage of a business group mentioned is that business group firms may use a

common brand name. What kind of problem could arise when, say, ten companies belonging to a business group use a common brand name? What could be done to mitigate that problem? How easy (or difficult) would it be to do that if those ten companies offered widely different products?

4 Box 8.7 describes competition between two organizational forms – entrepreneurial firms and farmers' cooperatives. Do you think that the farmers' cooperatives described should be considered as hybrid forms according to the definition of hybrid forms given in this chapter?

5 Box 8.7 describes how competition between two organization forms (entrepreneurial firms and farmers' cooperatives) led to a situation in which one form (farmers' cooperatives) became the dominant form in certain parts of the country, while the other (entrepreneurial firms) came to dominate other parts of the country. According to the scheme presented in this book (Figure 1.7 and 11.1), this should be the result of one or more differences in the environments in which these firms operated. Which difference played a vital role in this respect?

6 Section 12.7 describes how a joint venture can be used as an intermediate stage when overcoming the problem of hidden information at times when a company wants to sell one of its subsidiaries to another company (Section 12.7 discusses how Philips sold its domestic appliances business to Whirlpool in two stages, first forming a joint venture and then selling the remainder of the shares). What differences do you see between the Philips-Whirlpool joint venture and the Telecom Italia-Is Bank joint venture described in Box 13.2?

Suggested further reading

Harrigan, K. (2003), *Joint Ventures, Alliances, and Corporate Strategy*, Washington DC: Beard Books.
Ménard, C. (2004), 'The economics of hybrid organizations', *Journal of Institutional and Theoretical Economics*, pp. 345–76.

Notes

1 While cooperation is required for some dimensions of the hybrid form, competition may remain for other dimensions. In a joint venture, for example, two companies may cooperate regarding production and/or marketing, while each pursues R&D independently to gain a longer-term competitive edge over the JV partner.

2 For a classic treatise on the managing agency system in India, see Lokanathan (1935). See Bagchi (1972) and Goswami (1989) for elaborate accounts of the history of industrialization in India. See also Khanna and Palepu (2004) for discussion on the specifics of Indian business groups.

3 See Hazari (1967) and Encarnation (1989) for exhaustive accounts of the extent of operations of the largest Indian business groups.

4 The description of the structure of the Tata group refers to the situation in 1998. Since then the structure may have changed.

5 Other legal measures for separating ownership and control include voting restrictions and shareholder agreements. A *voting restriction* stipulates that a particular shareholder can vote for only a specified proportion of shares. A *shareholder agreement*

regulates voting behaviour through voting pacts or restricts the sale of superior voting right shares to third parties (see Cronqvist and Nilsson, 2003 for examples on the working of these devices).

6 Douma, George and Kabir (2006) found a negative performance effect resulted from group affiliation, while Khanna and Palepu (2004) using older data found a positive effect. This could indicate that institutional reform in India already erodes the advantages of group firms.

7 The literature on networks is quite diverse. We rely for this discussion on Thompson et al. (1991). For social systems of trust, see Coleman (1990). For sociological analyses of networks see, for example, Burt (1992).

14.1 Introduction

Corporate governance

Corporate governance is the system by which business corporations are directed and controlled. The corporate governance structure specifies the distribution of rights and responsibilities to different participants in the corporation, such as the Board, managers, shareholders and other stakeholders (like employees, customers, suppliers, creditors and society at large). It spells out the rules and procedures for making decisions on corporate affairs. By doing this, it also provides the structure through which the company objectives are set and the means of attaining those objectives and monitoring performance.[1]

In this chapter, we want to focus our attention on the relationship between shareholders and managers. In companies with a separation of ownership and control, there is an agency problem between the shareholders as the principal and the company's top manager or CEO as the agent. The separation of ownership and control noted by Berle and Means in 1932 (discussed in Section 7.2) has been a dominant feature of large companies in the Anglo-American world ever since.

The agency problem arises because, first, there may be a lack of alignment between the desires and objectives of the CEO and those of shareholders (see Section 7.3 for the consequences of such a lack of alignment) and, second, because there is usually information asymmetry between a CEO and the shareholders. Such a lack of alignment may occur for several reasons. Shareholders are interested primarily in obtaining a return on their investment. They will want to make sure that the CEO always makes decisions that maximize shareholder value. A CEO, however, will make decisions that maximize his own utility function, which will not always coincide with maximizing shareholder value.

Free cash flow

First, there is the problem of **free cash flow**. A CEO aiming to maximize shareholder value should invest only in projects with a positive net present value (NPV). If the firm generates more cash flow than the amount it can invest in projects with a positive net present value, the difference is called *free cash flow*. Firms in mature industries often have cash-generating operations and few opportunities to invest these often significant levels of cash in their own industry, simply because, in a mature industry, there are few projects with a positive NPV. According to financial theory, free cash flow should be returned to shareholders, but the CEO may wish to retain it in order to diversify into other lines of business. That may be because managers overestimate their ability to select and subsequently run other companies (a phenomenon referred to as *hubris*: see Section 12.6), their reward scheme is tied to the size of the firm or simply the pure pleasure that comes with empire building. There are many examples of firms in mature industries that have invested heavily in other industries, only to find out much later that those investments did not succeed. One of the problems here is that the *real* NPV of an investment project (such as the acquisition of another firm) may be difficult to determine both ex ante and ex post.

Second, there is the problem of a possible difference in *attitude towards risk*. Many shareholders typically invest only a small proportion of their total wealth in any one firm. If one of their investments fails, that is probably offset by the good performance of their other firms. A CEO, by contrast, works normally for one firm only. The CEO's human capital depends on how well that single firm performs. If the firm fails, the value of the CEO's human capital declines and that human capital (earning power) is probably a large proportion of his or her total wealth. Consequently, the CEO of a widely held firm may be more risk-averse than the shareholders. Of course, this means that a difference in the degree of risk aversion between CEO and shareholders may lead to a situation in which projects that are attractive to shareholders are rejected by the CEO.

Third, there is the problem of different time horizons. Shareholders are entitled to all the company's future cash flows, without any time horizon. Managers, however, serve only for a limited period of time. That may give them a bias for investment projects with high accounting returns in the short term, even if the NPV of such projects is negative. Conversely, they may have a bias against projects with a positive NPV and low or negative accounting returns in the short term. An example of the latter might be investments in R&D.

Finally, there is the problem of on-the-job consumption. This problem has been analysed extensively in Section 7.3.

Any agency problem arises because, first, the principal and agent have different interests and, second, there is information asymmetry between the agent and principal. Consequently, solutions for agency problems aim at:

- narrowing the gap between the interests of principal and agent;
- reducing the information asymmetry between principal and agent.

The gap between the interests of principal and agent can be narrowed by offering the agent an incentive contract (which we would call an organizational solution), but also by improving the functioning of the market for managerial labour and/or the market for corporate control function (which are clearly market solutions).

Information asymmetry can be reduced by monitoring. Monitoring can be done internally (by a large shareholder and/or by the (supervisory) Board), which is an organizational solution. Monitoring can also be done by various parties external to the company in question, such as stock market analysts, credit-rating agencies, private equity firms and other parties possibly interested in acquiring the company. External monitoring helps to reduce information asymmetry in markets, such as the managerial labour market and the market for corporate control. Such measures will improve the functioning of those markets and, consequently, help to reduce the agency problem.

So, we see that the agency problem can be reduced by means of organizational solutions (incentive contracts, internal monitoring) and market solutions (external monitoring and the functioning of various markets). That leads us to the scheme presented in Figure 14.1.

The root of the agency problem between shareholders and managers lies in the separation of ownership and control, as identified by Berle and Means. In a firm led by one owner-manager, agency problems do not exist at the top. However, in many modern firms, management has become a specialized function and ownership is widely dispersed, shared between many shareholders.

In such a modern firm, the first agency problem to be addressed is how to narrow the gap between the interests of the CEO (or top management) and the shareholders. It is a question of **incentive alignment**.

Incentive alignment

The second agency problem is how to reduce the information asymmetry between the shareholders (as principal) and the CEO (as agent). That is a question of effective **monitoring**.

Monitoring

Monitoring can be done and incentives can be given internally (organizational solutions) or externally (market solutions). Information, again, plays a crucial role in this scheme as it facilitates both organizational and market solutions. Corporate governance may be seen as part of the institutional environment in which corporations operate. It consists of rules set by the government or other public bodies (such as the Securities and Exchange Commission – SEC) and companies themselves in their statutes and internal regulations.

The scheme found in Figure 14.1 has a strong resemblance to the scheme of this book, as presented in Figure 1.1. That is no coincidence: corporate governance, in our view, is a special case of the governance of transactions. Figure 14.1 describes corporate governance, while Figure 1.1 portrays the governance of transactions.

In practice, the corporate governance system used in a certain country will most likely involve a mixture of organizational and market solutions. Also, as we will see, it will be influenced by environmental pressure and selection.

In this chapter, we start by examining the evolution of corporate governance from its early beginnings in the first public company to the modern-day struggles to develop and amend corporate governance codes in many countries. We do this by using the VOC – arguably the first public corporation in the world – as an example. This historic example highlights many corporate governance issues that are still prevalent today, especially the divergence of interests between shareholders and managers. We explore the nature of this agency relationship in Section 14.2. We then discuss how the design of incentive contracts can help to reduce (though not eliminate) the agency problem today (Section 14.3). In Section 14.4, we describe how internal monitoring in actual corporations takes place and how it can help to reduce the agency problem. After having discussed organizational solutions, we turn to market

Environment and institutions

Figure 14.1 The corporate governance framework

solutions – first, to external monitoring (Section 14.5) and then to how markets constrain the size of the agency problem (Section 14.6). The next section looks at institutional frameworks in different parts of the world. We then show how, in different parts of the world, different corporate governance systems have evolved, using organizational and market solutions in different proportions (Section 14.8). In the concluding section, we give our views on future developments in corporate governance systems. We also illustrate the relevance of this topic for both organizations and the development of societies. First, though, let's witness the birth of the public corporation and the birth pains of corporate governance issues.

14.2 The first public company

The United East India Company, or Verenigde Oost-Indische Compagnie (VOC),[2] was established in 1602 in the Netherlands. Its purpose was to conduct trade with 'East India' (the area we would now describe as South-east Asia), in competition with the Spanish and Portuguese fleets. It was not the first such trading company to be created, but its predecessors were usually financed in a way that we would nowadays call **'project financing'**. That is to say, entrepreneurs and investors combined in a 'company' to invest money in buying a ship and financing a round trip. On its safe return, the ship and its cargo were sold and the investors were repaid their money together with a

Project financing

handsome profit. If the investors were satisfied with the entrepreneurs, they would consider financing their next project. If not, they would seek alternative projects to finance. Today, we would say that the capital market was acting as disciplining mechanism on the entrepreneurs' activities.

Those projects were not without complexities and risks. A ship had to be built, a crew recruited, a destination in 'The Indies' selected and reached, trade conducted and a safe return accomplished. Risks included pirates underway, shipwrecks and fraudulent behaviour on the part of the captain and/or the crew, who sometimes sold cargoes to parties other than those who had financed the project. In the language of agency theory, the project could be considered as a nexus of contracts (see Section 7.5) between financing parties and project management. Hence, we can observe agency problems such as shirking, which requires monitoring (see Section 7.4). In modern terms, however, we would regard such agency problems as being typical of the contractual relationship between managers and providers of temporary capital. Agency problems were relatively limited because of the financing on a project-by-project basis. Entrepreneurs who built up a doubtful reputation would find the financing of their next project difficult.

The VOC started out this way in 1602, combining 70 entrepreneurs (merchants/shareholders who took the initiative for a trip and had managerial responsibility) with more than a thousand participants/investors with only a passive interest. Gradually, the merchant-shareholders came to feel that it was better to finance the company on a more permanent basis. They sought the approval of the authorities to replace the temporary nature of the financing arrangements with a more permanent structure, allowing participants to trade their shares with each other, so, in effect, creating a stock market.

In 1609, the required approval was granted and trading in the shares started. Through the transformation that resulted, the VOC achieved a permanent, anonymous capital base. It became a **public company**, with a clear separation between (public) ownership and (managerial) control, as later analysed by Berle and Means (see Section 7.2).

Public company

The public invested the enormous sum of 6,424,588 Dutch guilders. The last investor was the 'maid-servant' Neeltje Cornelis, who invested 100 guilders in the shares being issued on 31 August 1602, the day the 'participants book' was closed. Today, we would say that the IPO of VOC shares had been a tremendous success.

Participation in the VOC proved, however, not to be a fast route to high financial returns. The costs for the first fleets exceeded the revenues, partly because they also had the mission to attack the Portuguese in Asia in order to decrease their 'market share' and make room for increasing the share of the Dutch. Only in 1610 were the first dividends paid, albeit largely in kind – the participants received quantities of nutmeg and pepper! Of course, they would have preferred to receive cash. The managers, however, preferred to reinvest the proceeds of projects into the next projects and increasing their market share of the East Indian trade.

The 'outside' shareholders slowly became dissatisfied with this state of affairs. At the same time, they became wary of potential other conflicts of interest between the managers and shareholders. It was rumoured that the managers sometimes sold goods from the cargoes privately and realized substantial private benefits that way. There were also questions about supply contracts: were they sometimes awarded to parties 'befriended' by the managers? Moreover, the remuneration of the managers included fee structures that were not conducive to cost control. Finally, the managers obtained private information on the timing, quality and price of the trade flows that could be very valuable for trading on the domestic goods market. Today we would say that the managers received **inside information** (asymmetrical private information) that created the risk of insider trading.

Inside information

The 'outside' shareholders grew increasingly unhappy. In particular, one shareholder by the name of Isaac le Maire became a vocal protester. Today, we would call him an **activist shareholder**. One of his main objections to the VOC's policy was that it made insufficient use of the charter it was granted by the Dutch government. It focused on the trade with Bantam (Java), the Banda islands and Ambon (all in the present Indonesia), but neglected opportunities in South America, even though its charter permitted it to exploit the Strait of Magellan.

Activist shareholder

The agency problem here was later formulated by Jensen and Meckling (1976, p. 313) as follows:

> Indeed, it is likely that the most important conflict arises from the fact that, as the manager's ownership claim falls, his incentive to devote significant effort to creative activities such as searching out new profitable ventures falls. He may in fact avoid such ventures simply because it requires too much effort on his part to manage or to learn about new technologies. Avoidance of these personal costs and the anxieties that go with them also represent a source of on-the-job utility to him and it can result in the value of the firm being substantially lower than it otherwise could be.

Le Maire calculated that the VOC only generated profits of 2.3 million guilders in the first seven years of its existence. That was insufficient to cover the cost of capital, including a risk premium, set at 8 per cent by Le Maire. Today, we would say that the VOC was destroying **shareholder value** in the first years of its existence.

Shareholder value

In 1622, this led to a published protest containing inter alia the following demands for:

- transparent information on, for example, trading flows, investments and proceeds;
- the right to appoint managers;
- time limits to the managers' tenure;
- adjustments to the remuneration of managers;
- limits to the possibilities of insider trading (for example, with supply contracts).

By threatening to withhold financing for similar companies and exerting pressure on the Dutch government, the outside shareholders achieved extensive adjustments in the corporate governance of the VOC by December 1622, when its charter had to be renewed. This shows how shareholder and environmental pressure led to the adaptation of the institutional framework in which the VOC had to function.

As one can see from the above list of demands, some of the main topics of the discussion regarding corporate governance have remained remarkably constant for the last 400 years. At the same time, the institutional framework has continually evolved to protect the rights of 'outsiders' versus 'insiders' and of minority shareholders versus majority shareholders. Frentrop (2003) shows that stock market crashes and corporate scandals have provided the main triggers for improved protection mechanisms throughout history. The 1720 South Sea Bubble in the UK and the 1873 Panic in the USA were such episodes that led to improved legislation and regulation.

Throughout history, corporations have failed, the reasons for their failure have been examined and those investigations have provided input for adaptations to be made to security laws and regulations. In the USA, for example, the Interstate Commerce Act was adopted in 1887 to bring the American railway companies under federal supervision after several scandals involving fraud and corruption (the directors of the companies were called the *robber barons*). The stock market crash of 1929 led to the Securities and Exchange Act of 1934. More recently, corporate scandals such as Enron and Worldcom triggered renewed legislative efforts, leading to the Sarbanes-Oxley Act. From an evolutionary perspective, in developed economies such as the USA, the institutional framework has therefore been frequently adapted to incorporate the learnings generated by such episodes and scandals. In Section 14.7, we will examine which evolutionary pathways were taken in different environments. Box 14.1 is a reminder of the importance of proper corporate governance for the development of emerging economies and trust in their institutions.

Box 14.1 Corporate governance (or, rather, the lack of it) in Russia and China

Corporate governance is shaped by the institutional framework of the country in which the corporation is domiciled. In some countries, that institutional framework is still inadequate because, for instance, the economy as a whole has only recently been reorientated towards a market economy. That is the case in Russia and China. Joseph Stiglitz discusses how this enabled opportunistic behaviour by some managers (called the oligarchs in Russia):

> For instance, in Russia and other countries, the lack of laws ensuring good corporate governance meant that those who could get control of a corporation had an incentive to steal assets from the minority shareholders; and managers had similar incentives vis-à-vis shareholders. Why expend energy in creating wealth when it was so much easier to steal it? Other aspects of the privatization process, as we have seen, enhanced the incentives as well as opportunities for corporate theft. Privatization in Russia turned over large national enterprises, typically to their old managers. Those insiders knew how uncertain and difficult was the road ahead. Even if they were predisposed to do so, they dared not wait for the creation of capital markets and the hosts of other changes that would be required for them to reap the full value of any investments and restructuring. They focused on what they could get out of the firm in the next few years, and all too often, this was maximized by stripping assets.

The *New York Times* gave the following estimates of the magnitude of the problem in China:

'Corruption is pervasive in China,' Larry Lang, a professor of Finance at the Chinese University of Hong Kong said. 'A lot of State-owned companies have been simply stripped clean.' In the last four years, at least 25 government officials have been sentenced to death for accepting bribes and kickbacks. Hundreds more are serving long prison terms. But every month, the number of fraud cases seems to mushroom. On March 9, the government announced that 58,000 people had been punished for mis-appropriating money or making unauthorized loans at just two of the big four State-owned banks. In 2003 alone, officials said that nearly $8 billion was pilfered from government-owned enterprises.

In both countries, improvements in corporate governance are being actively pursued by govern-ments, also to allow their companies to participate fully in the global economy.

Sources: Stiglitz (2002, pp. 157–8); *'China bank robbers: an inside story, New York Times,* 22 March 2005

14.3 The use of incentive contracts

One way to deal with the agency problem described in Section 14.1 is to offer the CEO an incentive contract. That is, of course, an organizational solution. In the real world, we see three elements in managers' compensation packages that encourage them to act in the interests of shareholders: cash bonuses, share plans and option plans. Many corporate governance codes stipulate that managers should have temporary contracts allowing a renewal of the contract to be based on performance evaluation. We will first describe the elements of managers' compensation packages and the reasons for offering temporary con-tracts. We then discuss a few reasons for the fact that offering incentive contracts or temporary contracts can only partially solve the agency problem.

14.3.1 Cash bonuses

Managers often receive an annual cash bonus if certain specified goals have been met. Those goals are often based on the level or size of the improvement in ratios such as the earnings per share, return on capital employed, return on assets, sales growth or market share. To do so rests on the belief that realizing improvements in these ratios is in the interests of shareholders.

14.3.2 Share plans

A more direct way to ensure that managers will be interested in increasing the share price is to make sure that they own shares. This can be done by giving them shares (or allowing them to buy shares at a reduced price) when they start. That is what private equity firms do (in most cases) when they buy a company and install a new management team. The aim is then to restructure the company and sell it at a later date. It is an effective way to align the interests of the private equity firm (as shareholder and principal) and the manager (as agent).

The remuneration of top managers in listed firms often includes a long-term bonus in the form of a share plan. Under such a plan managers receive shares as part of their compensation package. In a very simple plan, a manager can, for example, receive a salary of $500,000 plus 40,000 shares. That gives the manager an incentive to take actions that increase share price. If the share price goes up, the manager's remuneration increases. In a more complicated plan, a manager may receive a fixed salary plus a *conditional* number of shares. Then, the manager will receive the shares only under certain conditions – when, after three years, a clearly specified goal has been reached, for example. When that goal is an increase in share price of at least X per cent or an increase in earnings per share of at least Y per cent, the manager has a very strong incentive to reach that goal.

We know from the discussion in Section 7.3 that a manager's on-the-job consumption will decrease as a function of α, where α is the fraction of shares he or she owns. So, there is a clear reason to give the manager, or require the manager to buy, a substantial number of shares. If the manager owns a controlling block (more than 50 per cent is a controlling block in any case, but 20 per cent can be if the rest is widely dispersed), however, the problem of **managerial entrenchment** may arise. This occurs when a manager performs poorly and shareholders want to get rid of him. If the manager is also a shareholder, he or she can use his or her voting power as a shareholder to prevent the dismissal. Thus, while some share ownership by the manager may be beneficial, too much share ownership may result in managerial entrenchment.

Managerial entrenchment

14.3.3 Stock options

Stock options

Another possibility is to award **stock options** to managers. A stock option is a right to buy shares at a specified moment in the future against a fixed price. The value of that right will increase when the share price increases, creating a stimulus for managers to maximize the share price.

Stock options can be given to managers as a part of the total compensation package without any further conditions. Options can also can also be given under the condition that, after a certain specified time lag, a precise goal has been reached. For instance, share price performance as compared to a reference group[3] (see Box 14.2). That creates very strong incentives for managers.

14.3.4 Temporary contracts

Many corporate governance codes stipulate that contracts with directors, including the CEO, should be of limited duration. That means their power is limited to a certain timespan, often to a term of four years. After the term has elapsed, the director is up for re-election. The number of times a person can be re-elected may also be limited. This system limits the power of a CEO in a significant way, because he or she cannot be sure of being re-elected. If the CEO ignores the interests of shareholders, the chances of being re-elected decrease. Offering temporary contracts only also mimics the managerial labour market. A disadvantage is that offering temporary contracts increases the problem of different time horizons (see Section 14.1).

14.3.5 Factors outside a manager's control

In order to ensure that a cash bonus gives the manager an incentive to act in the interests of shareholders, the (size of) the bonus should be tied to (the size of) the improvement in one or more (financial) ratios. Share plans are often conditional – tied to improvements in share price or (a number of) ratios. In fact, many corporate governance codes explicitly require that this should be the case. The same is true for stock option plans.

In the real world, profits, financial ratios and share prices are not only determined by managers' actions and decisions but also many other factors outside of a manager's control. Factors such as general macro-economic developments, currency rates and oil prices are at least as important, perhaps more important for share prices, than management performance. Considering that, tying managerial compensation to profits and share prices may produce unsatisfying results. For example, in the general economic peak at the end of the previous century, profits and share prices of almost all companies rose sharply. That meant even managers who had shown only mediocre performance received bonuses and realized huge options profits. In the recessionary years that followed, managers who performed well and limited the decrease of profits and share prices were not rewarded accordingly, as the value of their options suffered under the general economic climate.

Not only does this situation produce unsatisfying results, it also weakens the incentives that variable compensation schemes are designed to give. If managers realize that their level of effort has only a limited influence on their total compensation, they might be motivated only slightly more than if they had just a fixed salary. If that is true, the money spent on the additional variable compensation may be a waste of money from the shareholder's point of view.

To cope with this problem, firms have looked at various ways in which to make a more direct link between management performance and executive compensation.

One of these ways is to measure the performance of the company relative to some of its competitors or companies similar in size and structure. The group

Reference group

of similar companies is called a **reference group**. The performance of the companies in the reference group will be influenced by the same outside factors. This creates an opportunity for a realistic comparison of each companies' performance at the end of each period. Managers of companies that have performed better than those in the reference group are rewarded accordingly. Box 14.2 gives an example of such a compensation scheme.

Box 14.2 ABN AMRO's performance share plan

In 2001, the supervisory Board of ABN AMRO, a large Dutch bank, introduced a new remuneration plan for its top management called the 'performance share plan'.

The company's CEO, Rijkman Groenink, was conditionally awarded 98,000 shares in ABN AMRO. The word 'conditionally' is important here, because Groenink was only to receive the shares under a set of special conditions.

▶

A reference group of 20 similar banks was formed and, after four years, the performance of all the banks, measured as total return to shareholders, was to be evaluated. If ABN AMRO ranked number 1 in this list, 150 per cent of the original number of shares would be awarded to Groenink. In the case of a lower ranking, shares would be awarded on a sliding scale – tenth position would still give Groenink 25 per cent of the original amount of shares.

Early in 2005, ABN AMRO announced that it ranked eleventh in the reference group of 20 banks, as per ultimo 2004. This performance resulted in Groenink not receiving a single share under the performance share plan. That must have been a tough pill to swallow for the CEO as on 31 December 2004, 98,000 shares represented a value of close to €2 million.

Source: Annual Report, ABN AMRO, 2002

14.3.6 Incentives that are too strong

In recent years, we have seen several cases in which managers of very large and respected companies have engaged in fraud. Companies such as Enron, Worldcom and Ahold have been on the front pages of newspapers worldwide after it was discovered that managers had manipulated revenue and profit figures and misled their shareholders in order to increase the share price. In all three cases, criminal charges were brought against those responsible.

What happened? Although it is not exactly clear what triggered the behaviour of those managers, some point at the aggressive reward structures they had. They had a strong incentive to increase the share price in the short term in order to maximize the value of their shares and options. That might have been one of the reasons the managers artificially pumped up the share price by manipulating the figures. Even when the relationship between such behaviour and reward structures cannot be proved, it is clear that the risk of managers giving misleading information can be triggered by their own personal interest in achieving a higher share price. This results in a need for more intensive monitoring of such managers and, ultimately, higher agency costs.

14.3.7 Incentives that lead to wrong decisions

Cash bonuses and share and option plans are often tied to an increase in something – usually a profitability ratio. To show that this can lead to wrong decisions being made, consider the following example.

Suppose a firm has a regular profit level of $1 million. To stimulate management to increase that figure, the firm promises managers a bonus when profits are higher than $1 million in the next year.

Suppose, further, that managers face a decision as to whether or not to undertake a project that , if successful, could result in profits of $2 million. If the project were to fail, it would result in a loss of $5 million. The probability of the project succeeding is 50 per cent. Clearly, it is not in the interests of shareholders to undertake the project: its expected value is negative. For management, however, it might be an attractive prospect: a probability of 50 per cent of a bonus and a probability of 50 per cent of no bonus. If they do *not* undertake the project, they are certain that they will *not* get a bonus, because the net profit will, once again, be $1 million.

Clearly, a bonus tied to an increase in net profit can give a manager the wrong sort of incentive. The problem here, of course, is that the manager is rewarded when the project is a success, but is not punished when it fails.

14.3.8 Ubiquity and usefulness of incentives

Performance pay is now widely used in many parts of the world. Box 14.3 gives some details and outlines significant differences in the levels of performance pay for different environmental contexts.

Box 14.3 Executive compensation

In 1999, Charles Wang, the CEO of Computer Associates (an American company), received $4.6 million in salary, plus $650 million in long-term performance-based compensation. Whether Wang really deserved so much money or not is difficult to know. To some, the amount of compensation paid to American top executives is an indication of corporate plundering. Others may point to the market for managerial labour and argue that managerial compensation is simply the result of supply and demand for managerial talent. Still others argue that one of the ways to motivate middle managers is to let them compete for promotions. To make such competition effective, a promotion should be rewarded with a large increase in compensation. That, too, could explain why the top manager receives such a large amount.

Chief executives in the USA receive far more pay relative to factory floor workers than is the case in other countries. The typical CEO of one of the 500 largest American firms takes home 475 times more than workers in those firms. For European CEOs, the figures are 11–24 times as much as the factory floor workers. In South-east Asia and Latin America the comparable figure is 40–50.

Leaving the amount of compensation that is paid out aside, we still have the question of how to design a pay package for top executives. According to Towers Perrin (a consulting company), there are large differences between countries in this respect. In the USA, for example, long-term performance-based compensation (mainly in the form of stock options) amounts to 111 per cent of base salary. In Europe, that percentage is somewhere between 20 and 30 (see the figure below).

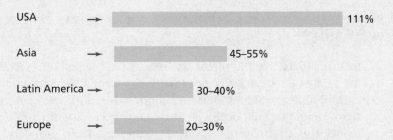

Long-term performance-based compensation as a percentage of base salary for a typical firm with more than $250 million in sales in 2000.

Whatever the differences between countries, it is clear that a significant part of the total compensation of many top managers is based on performance. Quite often managers are given share options. These give the manager a right to buy shares in his or her company at a given price. If the share price rises above that level before the option expires, the manager can pocket the difference.

Sources: The Economist, 30 September, 2000; Towers Perrin press release, 16 October 2000

With compensation schemes based to such a great extent on performance, we would expect that performance-related pay schemes lead to the best results for shareholders. Although there is wide agreement on this in many boardrooms, some doubt remains, as illustrated in Box 14.4.

Box 14.4 Does it pay to pay CEOs for performance?

On the basis of the analysis in this section we would expect that performance-related pay for CEOs yields the best results for shareholders. The Boards of most companies, especially in the USA, expect that to be true, yet some doubt remains.

In 1997, *Across the Board* – the magazine of the Conference Board – interviewed a number of scholars who had done research on the question of whether or not such performance-related incentives are effective as a component of CEOs' pay packages. Here are some of their opinions:

> The issue is largely one of executives' psychological make-up. Sure, some executives' interests lie closer to home than the boardroom, 'But about 70 per cent of executives,' estimates Professor James Davis of the University of Notre Dame, 'are "stewards" rather than "agents", driven by what's good for the company rather than pure self-interest. Stewards treat their company like a football team. If the company wins, they win. The pay just shows that the Board appreciates what they've done. Then there are others, agents, who are in this for the perks, for personal gain. They haven't won unless they've piled up money. The achievement they're looking for is personal success, not group success.'

> Nearly all modern financial economists believe that 'increased stock-based incentives cause managers to take actions that increase shareholder wealth', says Kevin J. Murphy, professor of finance and business economics at the University of Southern California. However, he notes, there's a scarcity of empirical evidence linking stockholdings to shareholder returns. Murphy's own studies have generally found such a link: 'I found that CEOs with higher pay-performance sensitivities have realized significantly higher shareholder returns over the past one year, five years, and 10 years. The issue is simple and my results are clear', Murphy says.

> 'There's been a lot of work on whether managers who hold more equity do better; the evidence is really mixed,' says Professor David Larcker of the Wharton School. 'There's a lot of loose talk, but there's no direct relationship between ownership and performance.'

Source: Based on *Across the Board,* the Conference Board magazine, March 1997

14.4 Internal Monitoring

By using incentive alignment, as discussed in the previous section, agency problems may be reduced, but not totally eliminated. Separation of ownership and control remains. Shareholders remain relative 'outsiders', with less information than the managerial 'insiders'. It remains necessary, therefore, to seek ways to reduce the information asymmetry between shareholders and managers. This can be achieved through monitoring. Monitoring can be done either internally (the subject of this section) or externally (the subject of the next section).

14.4.1 Monitoring by shareholder(s)

Internal monitoring can be done by shareholder(s) themselves. It can be very effective if a firm has one or a few large shareholders, as is often the case for privately held companies (companies owned by members of one family or private equity firms) and for companies belonging to a business group. For public companies with widely distributed shareholding, the situation is different.

Suppose that the largest shareholder (let us call her Mrs Navratilova) owns 6 per cent of all outstanding shares, while the remaining 94 per cent are owned by many smaller investors. Mrs Navratilova knows that if she invests time and money in monitoring, only 6 per cent of the benefits will accrue to her, while 94 per cent of the benefits will go to the other shareholders. This is a **free rider problem**. As a result of this problem, Mrs Navratilova will surely invest less time and money in monitoring than if she were the sole owner of the company.

Free rider problem

In large public companies it may well be that the largest shareholder owns less than 5 per cent of the shares. The incentives for individual shareholders to invest in monitoring in such cases are quite weak. Internal monitoring is then done mainly by the Board.

14.4.2 The role of the Board of directors

In most countries, including the USA and the UK, companies are controlled by a Board of directors that consists of inside directors and outside directors. The **inside directors**, also called executive officers, are full-time managers of the company. The firm's top manager is always a member of the Board. In the USA, the title given to the top manager is chief executive officer or CEO.

Inside directors

The **outside directors**, also called non-executive directors or non-executive officers, are mostly senior managers of other large firms. The Board's chair may be one of the outside or inside directors. Thus, one person can combine the functions of CEO and chair of the Board.

Outside directors

In certain countries in continental Europe (Germany, Switzerland, the Netherlands), large companies are controlled by two Boards: the **executive Board**, which is simply the firm's top management team, and the **supervisory Board**. The supervisory Board consists of outside members only. Such a system of corporate governance is called a **two-tier Board system**.

Executive Board

Supervisory Board

Two-tier Board system

In a two-tier system there are two Boards with a complete separation of executive and supervisory duties. By contrast, the system used in the USA, the UK and many other countries, in which there is only one Board, is called a **one-tier Board system**.

One-tier Board system

14.4.3 Monitoring by non-executive Board members in a one-tier Board

In companies with a one-tier Board, all Board members are appointed by the shareholders' general assembly. They can also be fired by (a majority of) the shareholders. In many countries, including the USA and the UK, Board members are regarded by public opinion and law as fiduciaries for the shareholders. Their main responsibility is to run the company on behalf of the shareholders.

The Board usually consists of executive and non-executive members. While the Board as a whole is responsible for running the company, the non-executive

Board members have the additional task of monitoring their executive colleagues. In a typical Wall Street firm, shareholding is widely dispersed and Board members tend to own very few shares in the company on whose Board they sit.

So, why would they spend time and energy monitoring management? They may want to protect their reputation and be re-elected by the shareholders. For shareholders, however, it is often very difficult to determine how well non-executive directors perform their monitoring role.

If the CEO is also chair of the Board, he or she controls the agenda and the flow of information to the members of the Board to a large extent. That can make it very difficult for Board members, especially outside Board members, to effectively perform their duties as monitors. For that reason, many corporate governance codes require that the roles of CEO and chair of the Board be separated.

14.4.4 The two-tier Board system

In a two-tier Board system, there are two Boards with a complete separation of executive and supervisory duties. The main role of the executive Board is to run the company – that is, to set the strategic direction for the firm, make and implement operational decisions and closely monitor lower-level managers.

The main roles of the supervisory Board are to monitor the (members of) the executive Board and advise it on a broad range of subjects, including the firm's strategic direction. Important decisions, such as large investments, acquisitions, stock issues and choice of the firm's auditor, require the prior approval of the supervisory Board.

Thus, there is a separation of decision management and decision control (see Section 7.5). The executive Board is responsible for decision management, the supervisory Board for decision control. In a one-tier Board system, the Board is responsible for decision management *as well* as decision control.

In Germany 50 per cent of the members of the supervisory Board are designated by the employees, the other 50 per cent by the shareholders. This composition of the supervisory Board recognizes explicitly that the firm's top management team acts as agent for two groups of principals – the employees and shareholders. The members elected by the employees are often union leaders; the members elected by the shareholders are often bankers or (recently retired) executives from other large companies. The members designated by the shareholders elect the chair of the supervisory Board. In the case of a tie in the supervisory Board, the chair may cast a decisive vote.

In Germany, the universal banks own substantial blocks of shares in many large companies and bank managers sit on many supervisory Boards. Members of a supervisory Board can ask for all the information they need to perform their duties as monitors. They are paid by the company to perform the task of monitoring.

Does that mean that members of supervisory Boards in the German system have strong incentives to perform their duties as monitors effectively? Do bank managers who sit on the supervisory Boards of large companies in which their bank has a substantial block of shares have strong incentives to closely monitor the firms' executives? Some would say yes, because their future career at the banks may be at stake. Some would say no because they do not personally reap the rewards of their additional efforts as monitors.

The main task of a supervisory Board is to monitor the members of the executive Board. In the Netherlands, members of a supervisory Board are appointed by the shareholders. Box 14.5 gives details of a typical listed company incorporated under Dutch law.

Box 14.5 The two-tier Board of Accell Group NV

The Accell Group NV is a multinational company listed on the Euronext stock exchange. The company makes and sells bicycles, parts and accessories related to bicycles and fitness equipment, with operations in the Netherlands, Belgium, Germany, France, Finland, Hungary and the USA. The company's HQ are in the Netherlands and the company is incorporated under Dutch law.

The Accell Group has a two-tier Board structure: there is a managing Board (MB) and a supervisory Board (SB). The reward structure of the members of the MB is determined jointly by the SB and the general meeting of shareholders (GMS) as follows. The SB proposes a remuneration policy, including a reward structure (consisting of a base salary and a bonus scheme), for the members of the MB to the GMS. If the GMS approves the remuneration policy, the SB determines the actual levels of pay and actual bonuses for the members of the MB.

Members of the MB are selected and appointed by the SB and can also be fired by the SB. If there is a vacancy on the SB, the SB selects a candidate for that vacancy and proposes the person to the GMS. The GMS appoints the person as a member of the SB. If the GMS disagrees about the candidate, the SB has to come up with another candidate.

The GMS can fire all members of the SB simultaneously, but cannot fire an individual member of the SB.

Members of the SB receive a fixed salary (not dependent on profit, share price or anything else), the level of which is set by the GMS.

The main task of the SB is to monitor the members of the MB, ratify certain important decisions and advise the MB regarding the strategic direction of the company.

Source: Annual Report of Accell Group NV, company law and minutes of GMS

14.5 External monitoring

External monitoring is carried out by parties outside the firm, such as auditors, stock analysts, debt holders and credit-rating agencies. External monitoring helps to reduce information asymmetry in markets and, thus, improves their functioning.

14.5.1 Monitoring by auditing firms

Auditing firms play an important monitoring role. They audit the firm's financial statements and compliance with the law and other regulations. They are appointed (or should be appointed) by the shareholders or perhaps (in a two-tier Board system) by the supervisory Board. Auditors give their stamp of approval on companies' financial statements. For companies and CEOs that is very important because, without approval by an auditor with a good reputation, the firm will soon find access to new capital blocked. It is important that auditing firms are really independent from the companies they audit. Corporate governance codes in many countries as well as the Sarbanes-Oxley Act in the USA require that they do no (or very little) consulting assignments for the firms they audit and also that auditors report not to CEOs but to Boards as a whole or committees from those Boards (**audit committees**). Both requirements help to make auditors less dependent on CEOs. Auditors play a vital role in certifying financial statements and, thus, contribute significantly to the functioning of capital markets.

Audit commitee

Auditors, however, also assist Board members in their monitoring task. They do so through the annual **management letter**, in which an auditor makes suggestions for various improvements, including improvements in the companies' internal bookkeeping systems. So, the activities of auditing firms contain an important element of *internal* monitoring in addition to *external* monitoring.

Management letter

14.5.2 Monitoring by stock analysts

Stock analysts analyse a company's performance and make predictions of the firm's future performance. Reports made by analysts can significantly influence share prices. If the share price drops, the shareholders will start to ask questions. If they are not given satisfactory answers, they may sell their shares (sending the price even further down). Alternatively, they may challenge management and even consider firing the CEO. So, stock analysts play an important role, but it is an indirect one: they help to reduce information asymmetry between shareholders and CEO and overcome the free rider problem mentioned in Section 14.4.1.

14.5.3 Monitoring by debt holders

In companies in mature industries, there is often the problem of free cash flow (Section 14.1).

One way to reduce this problem is to take up large loans and distribute the cash thus obtained to shareholders. That, of course, changes the capital structure of the firm. With a large amount of debt, the cash generated by the firm is necessary to service the debt (interest payments and amortization). Thus, managers can no longer invest in projects with a negative NPV.

Debt covenants

Providers of debt will often attach conditions to the loans they make. Such **debt covenants**, as these conditions are called, often require that the company should maintain a number of financial ratios at or above a certain level. Providers of debt will be keen to monitor management on this point.

14.6 How markets constrain agency costs

Agency costs may be constrained by organizational arrangements such as incentive contracts and monitoring, but also by markets. Each firm deals with many markets – for example, buying raw materials and components, hiring staff and selling products. In such markets, the firm buys inputs or sells its output.

Competition in those markets forces companies to be efficient. In this section, we will discuss how and to what extent competition in markets serves to discipline managers.

14.6.1 Competition in the product market

Consider first the *product market*, which is the market for the firm's products. A firm that sells its products in a perfectly competitive market cannot make an economic profit, as we argued in Section 2.4.3. This also means that the manager cannot engage in on-the-job consumption, simply because that would result in negative profits and the firm would go bankrupt. In a perfectly competitive market, firms have to minimize costs, including agency costs, if they want to survive.

Why doesn't this market mechanism solve all our problems? The answer is that very few markets are perfectly competitive. Remember that a perfectly competitive market assumes, first, a large number of small buyers and sellers, second, no entry or exit barriers and, third, standardized products. In the real world, those assumptions are very often violated: many markets are concentrated and protected by entry barriers. Also, there are few markets with standardized products: most products are branded, so (at least some) buyers do care which company they buy from. Competition in very many markets is far from perfect, which means that companies can make profits without entrants being able to step in and take a share of the market. In such an environment, managers can engage in on-the-job consumption. That will mean lower profits, but, as long as there is sufficient profit left, the firm can continue.

14.6.2 Competition in the managerial labour market

A firm's top manager may also be disciplined by competition in the market for his or her own services – that is to say, the *managerial labour market*.

The CEO of a small firm who creates substantial wealth for her shareholders may be asked to become CEO of a bigger firm. Large firms can offer their CEOs more compensation. Competition between CEOs of small firms for top positions in large firms can possibly motivate CEOs of small firms to act in the interests of shareholders. Consequently some people argue that competition in the managerial labour market also disciplines managers.

For managers it is undoubtedly worthwhile to build up a reputation of successful performance. We submit, however, that competition in the managerial labour market is far from perfect, for the simple reason that, for outsiders, it is very hard to judge a CEO's performance. The CEO acts as an agent for the firm's shareholders. How well he does that job is difficult to determine, for both the firm's shareholders and other firms that might be looking for a new CEO. There is some evidence that only the very poorest performing managers lose their jobs and it takes several years of poor performance before that occurs (Warner et al., 1988; Weisbach, 1988).

14.6.3 Competition in the stock market

Now consider a firm with shares that are traded on the *stock market*. Through this market, investors will put pressure on firms to operate efficiently and maximize the value of the firm. Fast-growing firms in new industries have to attract additional equity capital by issuing new shares. The pricing of new shares is heavily dependent on the firm's prospects, but potential investors also take a good look at its past performance.

14.6.4 Competition in the market for corporate control

Shares held by investors not only represent their right to a certain portion of the firm's profits but also give their owners voting rights. This give shareholders an opportunity to change the management of the firm by, for example, nominating one or more people for the Board even against opposition from incumbent Board members (at least in the USA and many, but not all, other countries). Box 14.6 gives an example.

Box 14.6 ISP versus Hercules: a proxy fight for corporate control

Hercules is an American chemicals company that ran into trouble in the late 1990s. A number of its businesses started underperforming. It then went on to make a very expensive acquisition – buying BetzDearborn, a producer of water treatment chemicals, for $3.1 billion. When that acquisition also failed to bring the anticipated results, trouble started brewing. It intensified when the overall results of Hercules became outright disappointing and its stock price declined month after month. In 2000, Hercules started a process of divestment of parts of the company (BetzDearborn first, if possible) or perhaps even the total sale of the company.

International Specialty Products (ISP) is also an American chemicals company. A small part of it produces 'speciality chemicals' that are similar or related to those produced by Hercules but the major parts of both companies are in different lines of business.

Samuel J. Heyman is chairman of ISP. He has a reputation for taking stakes in companies that are 'in play' (or can be made so). ISP had, for instance, acquired stakes in Dexter Corp. and Life Technologies Inc. and was instrumental in the subsequent sale of the companies. The deals grossed ISP a total profit of $150 million in 1999 and 2000. In July 2000, ISP revealed that it had acquired a 9.9 per cent stake in Hercules (10.7 million shares) for a total of $153.2 million, representing an average cost of around $14.29 per share.

The divestment process at Hercules did not progress well. In March 2001, ISP took the initiative to launch a 'proxy fight', soliciting the shareholders of Hercules to vote for four ISP-backed members of the Hercules Board instead of the nominees put forward by Hercules itself in the following way:

ISP describes the last five years as 'disastrous' for shareholders of Hercules and urges them to place four ISP nominees on the Hercules Board . . . ISP hopes to place its chairman, Sam Heyman, on the Hercules Board together with three others. In a proxy report filed with the US Securities and Exchange Commission (SEC), ISP said its nominees will commit to completing a sale or merger of Hercules 'in the most timely, effective and efficient manner possible'.

ISP cited declines in the Hercules stock price during the last five years as it urged shareholders to vote for the ISP candidates, noting that Hercules shares had lost nearly 80 per cent of their value since reaching a high of $66.25 on 19 March 1996. In addition, ISP also criticized what it called 'the revolving door' of four chief executives during the last 22 months at Hercules. In particular, ISP also attacked the $14.25 million severance package given to R. Keith Elliott when he left the company in May 1999. ISP also chided Hercules for boosting its debt load 11-fold in the last 5 years to $3.2 billion by the end of last year. ISP blamed a lot of the problems on the $3.1 billion acquisition of BetzDearborn in 1998, calling it a 'disaster' for the company.

Hercules countered by appointing the well-respected Bill Joyce, former CEO of Union Carbide, as its new CEO, working together with chairman Tom Gossage.

Analysts at Merrill Lynch said that they remained unclear about the impact of adding Heyman to the Board since he agrees with chairman Tom Gossage about the best goal for the future: a sale of the whole company. Moreover, they note that the company's new chief executive – Union Carbide's Bill Joyce – also has 'significant incentive to sell or merge the company' given the particulars of his compensation package. At the same time, they also note a chilling effect for a company bidding on Hercules with Heyman on the Board. ML analysts said, 'Should Hercules consider a merger or stock-based transaction, a potential suitor might be reluctant to share information about itself with Heyman'.

All four ISP-backed candidates – Sam Heyman, Sunil Kumar, Raymond Troubh and Gloria Schaffer – were elected to Hercules' Board by the shareholders.

Although they don't hold enough seats to control Hercules (which elected a 14-person Board), the ISP candidates said that they will use their positions to lobby for sale of the company or other improvements as best they can.

In 2003, Sam Heyman attempted to take majority control of the 13-person Hercules Board by proposing another four directors to be elected. This time, however, Hercules won the proxy fight and Heyman announced the resignation of all ISP-backed Board members.

Sources: CNI News, 26 March, 24 May, 28 May, 6 June 2001 and 4 August 2003

Managers who perform poorly – perhaps because they do act too much in their own interests as opposed to the interests of the shareholders – must always fear that they may lose their job after the company has been acquired by another firm, as we explained in Section 7.2. Thus, every management team risks being

Hostile takeover

ousted after a **hostile takeover** or, to put it differently, faces the discipline of the market for corporate control (Box 14.7 gives an example).

Box 14.7 The hostile takeover of RJR Nabisco

For this case we go back to 1988. Then, RJR Nabisco was a giant food and tobacco company listed on the New York Stock Exchange and one of America's 20 largest companies.

CEO F. Ross Johnson was famous for his luxurious lifestyle, at the expense of the company. At one point, RJR Nabisco owned ten corporate jets, employed 36 pilots and had its own hangar near cor-

▶

porate headquarters in Atlanta, Georgia. This fleet of planes was made available by Johnson to a range of friends, celebrities and even to Johnson's pets. Meanwhile, RJR Nabisco's shares were valued much lower than those of its competitors.

Investor Henry Kravis of the famous investment company Kohlberg, Kravis and Roberts (KKR) saw an opportunity and launched a bid to gain control of RJR Nabisco through a hostile takeover. Johnson himself launched a competing bid and soon a bidding war started. Eventually, KKR's final bid turned out to be just higher, implying a premium on the initial share price of around 100 per cent and producing the largest buyout so far, with a transaction value of about $25 billion.

Johnson was forced to leave the company after the buyout by KKR. Don't worry about his well-being, though. Before the end of the bidding war, he had arranged a golden parachute for himself should he lose the battle. Under this settlement, Johnson received more than $53 million.

Source: Burrough and Helyar (1990)

If one investor buys all the shares, he or she is simply the owner of the company and, as such, is in a position to fire the top managers of the firm. Depending on the institutional context, that can also be true if one investor holds the majority of the shares.

Now, let's wonder in what cases an investor would be interested in purchasing all the shares in one firm. Note that in the case of a public bid on all the shares, the buyer usually pays a price higher than the current share price (the premium usually amounts to at least 20 per cent and can be as high as 100 per cent, as in the hostile takeover of RJR Nabisco by KKR). Certainly, an investor would not be willing to pay such a premium if the company was run in an efficient way by managers who acted in the shareholders' interests. The investor would not then be able to do a better job managing the company and couldn't earn back that premium.

Now consider a company that is run in an inefficient way. The value of such a firm on the stock market will be low. An investor who buys all the shares, fires the inefficient managers and starts to run the company himself can create a lot of value. If the gap between the actual value (of the inefficiently run firm) and the potential value (of the efficiently managed firm) is large enough, he might be tempted to have a go, even if he has to pay a premium over the current stock price.

Thus, there is a market for not only individual shares but also whole corporations or, to put it differently, for the right to manage corporations. That is the *market for corporate control* introduced in Section 7.2. Please note that it does not have to come to a hostile takeover in order to create an incentive for managers to pursue the right goals. The mere threat of a hostile takeover or even the threat of getting very critical outside directors elected after a proxy fight may be enough as managers know what can happen to them if they do not perform.

What can managers do to avoid the dangers of hostile takeovers, yet still engage in on-the-job consumption? They can, for example, sign a contract with another party that says, in the case of a hostile bid on the company, that party will have the right to buy the firm's most valuable asset (perhaps the firm's most profitable subsidiary) at a price way below the market price. That will certainly prevent an investor from trying to assume control of the firm. In the financial press, such contracts are referred to as **poison pills**.

Poison pills

Another anti-takeover method that works out extremely well for managers is the so-called **golden parachute**. That is a clause in a manager's employment contract holding that, if he is fired because of a takeover of the firm, he will receive a large amount of money. That sum can vary greatly in size, but in some cases, as we have seen, it has amounted to millions of dollars.

Golden parachute

Sometimes managers try to avoid a hostile takeover by arranging a *friendly* takeover by another bidder. The friendly bidder, who has been invited by the managers of the target company, is often referred to as a **white knight**. For example, when, in 2007, the German pharmaceutical firm Merck KGaA made a 'hostile' offer of €77 per share to acquire its rival Schering AG, the management of Schering turned to Bayer AG to be its white knight. Bayer subsequently bid €86 per share and succeeded in a 'friendly' takeover of Schering when Merck walked away.

White knight

The methods mentioned above are contractual forms of protection against hostile takeovers. In some countries, there are also legal restrictions that can make it more difficult for a bidder to take control of a company, such as the limitations on voting powers attached to certain types of shares or rules aiming at protecting minority shareholders against the majority. Those regulations vary strongly from country to country, as we will illustrate in the next section.

14.7 Institutional frameworks: market-orientated and network-orientated systems of corporate governance

We can observe that there are rather different corporate governance systems used in various parts of the world. These can be explained by:

- the features of the societies they are embedded in;
- the economic and political developments that have been incorporated in their institutional frameworks.

For the sake of convenience, we can divide these different systems into two broad categories: *market-orientated systems* and *network-orientated systems*. We introduce both systems below – first by describing their characteristics and then by pointing to some environmental factors that have contributed to their divergent paths of development.

14.7.1 Market-orientated systems of corporate governance

Market-orientated systems

The main characteristics of **market-orientated systems** of corporate governance are the existence of large, efficient stock markets, widely dispersed shareholding, strong legal protection of the interests of minority shareholders and separation of ownership from control. In a typical market-orientated system of corporate governance, all large companies are listed on a stock exchange. Those listed companies have many shareholders and no shareholder holds a controlling block. Managers tend to own only a small percentage of the companies they manage.

Moreover, legal rules designed to protect small individual shareholders limit companies from discussing strategic plans with just a few large institutional investors. That would give those investors inside knowledge about the firm not available to small individual shareholders, which would violate the laws on insider trading. So, in market-orientated systems of corporate governance, long-term relationships between a company listed on a stock exchange and a few institutional investors hardly exist.

That description more or less fits the situation in Anglo-American countries (the USA, the UK, Canada, Australia, New Zealand). In the USA more than 50 per cent of the shares of listed companies are owned by households. The rest are owned mainly by financial institutions, but a single financial institution rarely owns more than 10 per cent of the shares in a non-financial company. Commercial banks in the USA are simply not allowed to hold corporate equity. Mutual funds generally cannot own controlling blocks. Insurance companies can put only a small proportion of their investment portfolio into the stock of any single company. Pension funds are less restricted, but most pension funds are quite small and rarely own more than 1 per cent of a Wall Street firm. Thus, the major financial institutions in the USA (commercial banks, investment banks, mutual funds, insurance companies and pension funds) tend to hold widely diversified portfolios of shares in a large number of companies.

In a typical market-orientated system of corporate governance, each single investor owns a small percentage of a firm's stock. Consequently investors have only weak incentives to monitor the company's managers: they would capture only a very small portion of the benefits thus achieved, other shareholders would be free riders. Thus, investors who are dissatisfied with the financial performance of a company they have invested in tend to sell their shares rather than use their voting power to influence managerial decisions. If many investors do the same, the firm's stock market value will decline and the firm will be an attractive candidate for a takeover, not only by strategic buyers, who can aim to realize synergies, but also by private equity firms. That is what happened to RJR Nabisco in 1988 as we saw earlier and VNU, a media research company, now known as The Nielsen Company, in 2005 (see Box 14.8).

VNU was taken over by a consortium of private equity firms, which immediately started to restructure the company. The consortium probably planned to improve its profitability and growth and then either sell the company to a strategic buyer or float the company again on the stock market. Private equity firms can be said to compete in the market for corporate control for the right to restructure and manage companies. Managers in countries with market-orientated systems of corporate governance know that what happened to VNU's CEO can happen to them. That is why we say that, in a market-orientated system of corporate governance, managers are disciplined mainly by the market for corporate control.

Box 14.8 How VNU lost its independence

In 2005, investors in VNU NV were dissatisfied with the company's management. VNU was a Dutch company, with headquarters in New York and almost all of its activities concentrated in the USA. Its two most important subsidiaries were ACNielsen (it researches consumer behaviour through the collection of data from retailers) and Nielsen Media research (it collects data concerning the behaviour of people using media such as TV and radio). Both Nielsen companies were market leaders in their respective industries, but both were facing difficult times. ACNielsen lost the Wal-Mart account and Nielsen Media research was lagging behind competitors in installing the latest technology. VNU's share price had performed poorly in the years prior to 2005.

When Rob van den Bergh, VNU's CEO, announced plans in July 2005 to acquire IMS Health (a company that collects data about the use of pharmaceutical products in many countries) for $7 billion, shareholders began to revolt. After a group of shareholders led by Knight Vinke and including Fidelity and Templeton had made it clear that they would not support the plan to acquire IMS Health under any circumstance, Rob van den Bergh had to abandon it, which he did in November 2005.

In March 2006, a consortium of six private equity firms made a public offer to buy all the shares in VNU NV for €28.75 (equivalent to $35 at that time). Rob van den Bergh had to step down and was succeeded by David Calhoun. Calhoun started by cutting the number of jobs from 42,000 to 38,000.

Rob van den Bergh received a severance payment of €4.5 million. He soon found other employment as a member of the supervisory Boards of several companies.

In January 2007, VNU decided to change its name to The Nielsen Company.

Sources: Press Release from VNU, Alp Invest, The Blackstone Group, The Carlyle Group, Hellman & Friedman LLC, KKR and THL Partners, Haarlem, the Netherlands, 8 March 2006; Bloomberg.com, 17 January 2006

As the example of VNU shows, hostile takeovers do take place. Even in the USA, however, some managers of public companies are well-protected from the market for corporate control. One example is Google Inc., where a group of three top managers has a controlling block (see Box 14.9).

Box 14.9 Google's corporate governance

Larry Page and Sergey Brin first met when doing a PhD in computer science at Stanford University. They worked on a project called: 'The anatomy of a large-scale hypertextual web search engine'. In 1998, after having developed a search engine that was more efficient than other search engines available at that time, they quit their studies and founded Google Inc. In the beginning they relied on their own funds, but soon had to attract private investments to finance Google's rapid growth.

In 2000, Google introduced ads alongside search results. In that same year, Google made its first profit. In 2001 Eric Schmidt joined the company as chair of the Board and CEO. In 2004, Google became a public company through an IPO. In that IPO, 19.6 million shares were sold to investors, 14.1 million newly issued shares and 5.5 million shares from selling shareholders.

Google has two classes of common stock: class A and class B. The two classes of shares differ only with respect to their voting rights: class A shares have one vote per share while class B shares carry ten votes per share. Class A shares were offered to investors, class B shares are held only by Google's officers and employees. When class B shares are sold, they are automatically converted into class A shares; an exception to this rule is when Page sells to Brin or vice versa.

▶

Immediately after the IPO, Google had 33.6 million class A shares and 237.6 million class B shares outstanding. The investors who bought 19.6 million class A shares obtained an economic interest in Google of 7.2 per cent, for which they paid $1.7 billion, associated with 0.8 per cent of the voting power. Page, Brin and Schmidt, who 'run the company as a triumvirate', controlled 37.6 per cent of the voting power, while the executive management team and directors as a group controlled 61.4 per cent of the voting power.

In a letter to potential investors included in the IPO prospectus, Page makes a comment on the dual class structure: 'Google has prospered as a private company. We believe a dual-class structure will enable Google, as a public company, to retain many of the positive aspects of being private. We understand some investors do not favor dual-class structures. Some may believe that our dual-class structure will give us the ability to take actions that benefit us, but not Google's shareholders as a whole. We have considered this point of view carefully, and we and the Board have not made our decision lightly. We are convinced that everyone associated with Google – including new investors – will benefit from this structure. However, you should be aware that Google and its shareholders may not realize these intended benefits.' In the same letter, Page stresses that Google will optimize for the long term rather than trying to produce smooth earnings for each quarter. Google will support high-risk, high-reward projects and, thus, will be run more like a private company than a public company. That is why a dual-class structure benefits all shareholders, according to Page.

In 2004, shortly before the IPO, Google attracted three additional outside Board members and separated the roles of CEO and chair of the Board.

In February 200,7 Google's class A shares, which had been sold to investors for $85.00, traded at around $480 per share. Larry Page's and Sergey Brin's (then aged 33 and 32 years respectively) net worth at that time was estimated by *Fortune* magazine at $12.8 and $12.9 billion respectively.

Page and Brin continue to work for Google and are regarded by many as technology gurus. They are still too busy to finish their PhDs.

Source: Prospectus issued by Morgan Stanley and Credit Suisse First Boston, 18 August 2004

The example of Google with its dual-class shares illustrates that the environment and institutions (in the case of Google the American environment) codetermine corporate governance but do not completely determine it. Within one institutional environment, degrees of freedom remain for companies to choose their own corporate governance structure.

14.7.2 Network-orientated systems of corporate governance

Network-orientated systems

The main characteristic of **network-orientated systems** of corporate governance is the presence of blockholders. In a typical network-orientated system of corporate governance, large companies may or may not be listed on a stock exchange. Many listed companies have one or a few large shareholders. Those large shareholders do not actively trade their shares. The free float (the number of shares actively traded on the stock market) is significantly less than 100 per cent – for many companies it is even less than 50 per cent. Large shareholders (or their representatives) sit on the Board. They monitor managers and use their voting power if they are dissatisfied with a manager's performance. Managers are disciplined much more by these large shareholders, than by the market for corporate control.

This description more or less fits the situation in most non-Anglo-American countries, in both emerging markets and more developed countries (such as Japan and countries in continental Europe). In those same countries, business groups play an important role, as we noted in Section 13.4.

In a network-based economy, the typical firm has a small number of large shareholders who have a long-term relationship with the firm and its management and are represented on the firm's Board. Those shareholders often have other interests besides maximizing the value of their shares, such as strategic or family ties. If a shareholder is a bank, maybe it has some debt outstanding that it wants to protect. Such shareholders are not very likely to sell their shares to a hostile bidder. In countries with a network-orientated system of corporate governance, the effectiveness of the market for corporate control is limited not only by the institutional setting but also by the typical ownership structure in such countries.

In countries such as Germany, France, Italy, Spain, Japan, Korea and India, shares in large corporations are not as widely distributed as in the USA and UK. In the UK, for example, much more of the country's 100 largest firms are listed on a stock exchange than in Italy. Moreover, for those Italian companies that do have a listing on a stock exchange, shareholdings tend to be more concentrated than in British firms.

In Germany, the so-called universal banks (such as Deutsche Bank, Commerzbank and Dresdner Bank) do not only provide debt capital to large industrial enterprises, they also tend to provide equity capital. The universal banks also advise their clients on which shares to buy or sell. Most private investors deposit their shares with one of these universal banks and allow the bank to vote for them at shareholder meetings. This, together with the shares they own, gives the universal banks considerable voting power at shareholder meetings. Box 14.10 provides an illustration.

Box 14.10 DaimlerChrysler AG and its main shareholder

On Monday 26 February 2001, Juergen Schrempp, chief executive of DaimlerChrysler AG, the German-American auto giant, had some bad news for investors. Chrysler, acquired by Daimler-Benz in 1998, was in deep trouble and had to close six factories in Detroit, cutting 26,000 jobs. Mitsubishi Motors Corporation, of which DaimlerChrysler owned 34 per cent, also announced plans to cut 9500 jobs in Japan. A final piece of bad news was that two leading rating agencies downgraded DaimlerChrysler's credit standing after the plans to restructure Chrysler and Mitsubishi were announced.

When asked by journalists about the consequences for his own position, Schrempp said, 'There is no bigger pressure than the one I put on myself.' However, Deutsche Bank – with 12 per cent, DaimlerChrysler's largest shareholder – issued a statement supporting Schrempp but also making clear that it expected a turnaround within 12 months. A Deutsche Bank spokesman declined to specify what would constitute a sufficient 12-month turnaround in the bank's eyes. Chairman of the supervisory Board of DaimlerChrysler AG was Hilmar Kopper, a retired executive of Deutsche Bank. There were rumours that Deutsche Bank planned to introduce statutory and legal changes in order to prevent competitors acquiring DaimlerChrysler cheaply.

▶

> On 1 January 2006, however, Schrempp was succeeded by Dieter Zetsche. In May, 2007, Daimler unloaded 80 per cent of the troubled Chrysler to the private equity firm Cerberus. It actually paid Cerberus $675 million to take this 80 per cent of a company Daimler had bought in 1998 for $36 billion.
>
> *Source: The Wall Street Journal Europe,* 27 February 2001; 'Daimler gives Chrysler to Cerberus', *Business Week,* 14 May 2007

In the Latin countries of the EU (Italy, Spain, Portugal, France and Belgium) many large companies, even those listed on a stock exchange, have one or a few owners of large blocks of shares. Examples of such large blockholders are financial holding companies, rich families, banks, other industrial corporations and the State. In many listed companies in these countries, one or a few large shareholders together can exercise more than 50 per cent of the voting rights. Those large shareholders may use their power to achieve their own goals, sometimes at the expense of the small private shareholders.

Keiretsu

In Japan, there are many large industrial groups, the so-called **Keiretsu**, such as Mitsubishi and Mitsui. These groups are centred on a bank or insurance company that provides the companies belonging to the group with debt capital as well as equity capital. Companies belonging to the group also commonly hold significant portions of shares in other companies belonging to the group. Thus, a large part of the shares of the companies belonging to a Keiretsu is held by other companies belonging to the Keiretsu.

Chaebol

In Korea and India, business groups are also of paramount importance. In the typical industrial group in Korea (called a **Chaebol**), companies belonging to the group hold shares in other companies belonging to the group and provide guarantees for bank loans taken up by sister companies. The business groups are not structured around a bank. Many business groups are controlled by people belonging to the same family, often the offspring of the founder of a group.

In summary, while there are important differences between the corporate governance systems in the countries mentioned above, there is also a common feature. That is many companies have one or a few owners of large blocks of shares. Companies having the same person or institution as owner of a large block of shares may be seen as forming a network. It is for that reason, the term network-orientated systems of corporate governance has been coined.

In countries with a network-orientated system of corporate governance, laws designed to prevent insider trading are generally not very strict. That allows owners of large blocks of shares to confer with management and, thus, influence managerial decisions. Quite often they sit on the Board. If they are dissatisfied with a top manager's performance, they have the power to fire the manager. Thus, in a network-orientated system of corporate governance, managers are disciplined mainly by organizational arrangements.

14.7.3 A comparison of the two corporate governance systems

In market-orientated systems of corporate governance, severe underperformance by managers is restricted mainly by the fear of a hostile takeover. The

Board of directors is probably less important in this respect because outside directors may lack the incentive to perform their functions as monitors well. That may be especially true when the CEO is also chair of the Board. Thus, the market for corporate control is the most important mechanism for reducing the agency problem between shareholders and managers.

Incumbent managers may spend large amounts of money in the form of fees for lawyers and investment bankers in order to resist a hostile takeover bid. That is a waste of money for the shareholders of the target firm, who may be content with the bid (and the premium above the current share price). To put it differently, transaction costs in the market for corporate control may be very high indeed. As a consequence, incumbent managers have some leeway regarding on-the-job consumption. The market for corporate control is far from frictionless, which is the major disadvantage of market-orientated systems of corporate governance.

In network-orientated systems of corporate governance, monitoring of top managers by outside Board members is probably the most important mechanism for reducing the agency problem. In network-orientated systems, owners of large blocks of shares have the incentives to perform their monitoring role in an effective way. The market for corporate control is of little importance in terms of disciplining managers.

A disadvantage of network-orientated systems is that markets for equity capital, including venture capital, are less well developed. That may hinder the optimal allocation of equity capital in countries in which network-orientated systems prevail. Another disadvantage may arise when the main private shareholders in a company do not act in the best corporate interests for private reasons, such as retaining family influence or prestige.

In a typical network-orientated system of corporate governance, there are virtually no hostile takeovers. This more or less fits the situation in Germany and Japan. In France, Italy and Spain, hostile takeovers are also very rare. The main reason for this is probably that a hostile bidder has to convince owners of large blocks of shares, who are also Board members or are represented on the Board, that selling their shares is in their best interests. It may be quite difficult for General Motors to convince the Agnelli family that selling their shares in Fiat is in their own best interest!

Another reason is that important differences exist in the institutional environment with respect to takeovers. Even within Europe, there are large differences – the UK having the most active market for corporate control. In most countries in continental Europe, corporations have been able to shield themselves from unfriendly takeover threats. Within the EU, there is a lively debate on the need to harmonize the legal framework concerning takeovers. A proposal made by the European Commission has been rejected by the European Parliament, meaning that differences between the UK and other European countries are likely to persist (see also Box 14.11).

> **Box 14.11** The European market for corporatism or corporate control?
>
> In Europe, the notion of a 'market for corporate control' has always been controversial. It is quite readily accepted in the UK, but, on the Continent, the idea generally prevails that corporations lead a life of their own, aimed at continuity and serving all stakeholders equally – not primarily the shareholders. It actively seeks a dialogue with its various stakeholder groups in order to balance their competing claims on the corporation optimally. This idea is referred to as the *stakeholder model* (see also Box 6.1), the Rhineland model or corporatism.
>
> The European Commission worked for 12 years to harmonize takeover codes in Europe in a European directive that would regulate the European market for corporate control. In 2001 it came to the vote and it could not have been closer. On 4 July, the European Parliament split 273 to 273 on plans to push through a new directive establishing a cross-border code for company takeovers in Europe. For a brief, confusing moment, Nicole Fontaine, the Parliament's president, declared that this meant the vote had passed, but she was muddled as to the procedure. After 12 years of work, it looks as if it is back to the drawing Board for the takeover directive.
>
> That failure is a blow for economic liberalizers, who see it as a key part of their strategy for sharpening economic competition within the EU. The thrust of the directive was to make it harder for European corporate bosses to ward off a hostile bid without first consulting shareholders. The idea was that shareholder rights would be strengthened and managers forced to become more efficient. A mere 2 per cent of takeovers in Europe are hostile. Such bids are not by nature good in themselves, but, as Chris Huhne, a British Euro-MP, says, the possibility of them exerts a welcome pressure on managers. Frits Bolkestein, the commissioner in charge of the internal market, called the rejection of the directive a setback to having an integrated capital market in Europe by 2005 and 'making Europe the most competitive economy in the world by 2010'. Both goals were endorsed by the leaders of the 15 members of the EU at a summit in Lisbon in 2000.
>
> The defeat of the directive will not prevent hostile takeovers across European frontiers. After all, Vodafone managed to acquire Mannesmann under the old rules. It will certainly slow corporate restructuring across Europe, however – particularly in Germany. It will also make it harder to establish a genuine European single market. The free flow of goods and a common currency are one thing, but if companies have to deal with 15 different takeover codes when making cross-border acquisitions, a true single market is still an illusion.
>
> *Source: The Economist, 7 July 2001*

Does that mean the managers of companies in continental Europe need not worry about the valuation of their company's stock on the stock market? Not necessarily. So long as the companies have to issue new shares from time to time, they have an interest in the valuation of their shares on the stock market. Moreover, also in Europe the role of 'private equity' has risen, as we discussed in Chapter 12.

14.8 The evolution of different corporate governance systems in the world

What explains the development of these different systems of corporate governance in the world? In the descriptions above, some environmental and institutional factors have already been mentioned. If we try to group some of the important factors, though, they would include the following.

- *Social and cultural values* Social and cultural values differ substantially from one country to another. For example, Anglo-American countries tend to have a more individualistic value set than many other countries. As Hofstede (2001, p. 251) discusses, that translates into social and political systems in which individual interests prevail over collective interests. It may explain why markets (and market-orientated systems of corporate governance) are more important in Anglo-American countries.
- *The concept of the corporation* Is the corporation viewed from the perspective of the 'stakeholder model' or the 'shareholder value' model? In Germany, for instance, the participation of employees in the supervisory Board is explicable from the stakeholder perspective. In the USA and UK, on the other hand, it would be inconceivable as the fiduciary duty of corporate Boards is towards the shareholders as owners.
- *Institutional arrangements* As indicated above, the institutional arrangements in the USA prevented the rise of large institutional blockholdings in individual corporations. In Germany and Japan, however, the large banks were expected to be the major equity investors in large corporations. Whether large blockholdings exist or not is a major determinant of corporate governance, as explained above.
- *Lessons from evolution* The institutional arrangements we observe today have been developed over time and incorporate the lessons of the past. They are path-dependent. As different societies have taken different paths and have accumulated different lessons along the way, we would expect to see those differences reflected in their current institutional frameworks. An extreme example is the learning in many formerly communist nations that State ownership of corporations is usually not a productive and efficient arrangement.

The factors listed above highlight reasons for there being differences in corporate governance systems. Another question is whether such differences are becoming larger or smaller. In other words, do we observe a convergence or divergence of corporate governance systems?

On balance, we would argue that the factors favouring convergence are strong. Those factors are mainly a result of globalization. They include:

- the vast increase in cross-border mergers and acquisitions;
- international standardization of disclosure requirements (such as the International Financial Reporting Standards);
- harmonization of securities regulation and the merger of stock exchanges (the merger of the French, Belgian and Dutch stock exchanges into Euronext and the subsequent merger between the New York Stock Exchange (NYSE) and Euronext, for example);
- the development of corporate governance codes – while these are usually still country-specific, they do tend to incorporate lessons and features from other codes, thereby promoting convergence.

Thus, we would see the environmental and institutional setting as evolving towards further convergence of corporate governance systems of the major economies around the world.

14.9 Summary: how the agency problems of corporate governance can be reduced by organizational and/or market solutions

This chapter has focused on the agency relation between shareholder(s) as principal and manager(s) as agent. This agency problem (as any agency problem) arises because, first, principal and agent have different interests and, second, there is information asymmetry between agent and principal. Consequently, solutions to agency problems aim at:

- narrowing the gap between the interests of principal and agent;
- reducing the information asymmetry between principal and agent.

The gap between the interests of principal and agent can be narrowed by organizational solutions (offering the agent an incentive contract) and/or market solutions (improving the functioning of the market for managerial labour and/or the market for corporate control).

Information asymmetry can also be reduced by organizational solutions (internal monitoring by shareholder(s) and/ or a (supervisory) Board) and/or by market solutions (the managerial labour market and the market for corporate control). The functioning of those markets is improved by external monitoring by, for example, auditors, stock market analysts, credit-rating agencies, private equity firms and other parties possibly interested in acquiring the company.

So, the subject of corporate governance provides an excellent illustration of the framework of the book by showing that the agency problem between shareholder(s) and managers(s) can be reduced by means of organizational solutions (incentive contracts, internal monitoring) and market solutions (external monitoring and the functioning of various markets).

In different parts of the world, different corporate governance systems have evolved – mainly as a result of differences in social and cultural values and historical background. This has resulted in market-orientated systems of corporate governance, which tend to prevail in Anglo-American countries, and network-orientated systems of corporate governance, which tend to prevail elsewhere. We expect that these two systems of corporate governance will converge in the long run as a result of globalization.

Questions

1 Suppose you are a HR consultant specializing on the design of compensation packages for CEOs. Your clients are the remuneration committees of large public companies. You

may assume that those remuneration committees act strictly in the best interests of shareholders. You currently have two different clients. Client A is a large brewery in a Nordic country (Sweden, perhaps) serving the local market only. Demand for beer in that market is relatively stable and so is the company's market share. Profits depend mainly on the efficiency of the production process for the beer. Would you recommend to client A a compensation package including a large or a small amount of variable compensation?

Client B is a trading company, trading in electronic components and consumer products. Company B buys the products in various countries in East Asia, including China, Vietnam, India and Japan, and sells them in Europe. Profits for the company depend on many factors, including exchange rates, changing consumer tastes and the general economic conditions in Europe. Would you recommend to client B a compensation package including a large or a small amount of variable compensation?

2 What do you see as being the main advantages and disadvantages of a two-tier Board system as opposed to a one-tier Board system?

3 Suppose a company has one shareholder and one CEO – shareholder and CEO being two different people. What would be the main functions of the shareholder as principal, according to the theory of principal and agent discussed in Chapter 7?

4 Consider then Accell Group NV (discussed in Box 14.5). The Accel Group's shares are traded on a stock exchange and there are many shareholders. The company has a two-tier Board structure, with a supervisory Board and an executive Board. Who performs the functions you identified in your answer to question 3? Which agency relations do you see? Who monitors whom?

Suggested further reading

Frentrop, P. (2003), *A History of Corporate Governance,* 1602–2002, Amsterdam: Deminor. OECD (2004), 'Principles of corporate governance', OECD.

Notes

1 This is the definition of corporate governance, given by the OECD (1999). It is consistent with, for example, the definition in the Cadbury report on corporate governance in the UK. See www.corpgov.net/library/definitions.html for an extensive, and occasionally amusing, set of various definitions. As explained later, the major dichotomy in these definitions is between those emanating from the stakeholder model and those from the 'shareholder value' model (see also Box 6.1).

2 The primary source for this section is Paul Frentrop (2002), *Ondernemingen en hun aandeelhouders sinds de VOC,* Amsterdam: Prometheus. Translated as (2003) *A History of Corporate Governance, 1602–2002,* Amsterdam: Deminor. See also, for example, Goetzmann and Rouwenhorst (2005), and www.voc-kenniscentrum.nl.

3 Such a reference group is often called a 'peer group' in practice. However, we have already used the term 'peer group' in another well-defined way (see Section 8.4).

Akerlof, G. A. (1970), 'The market for "lemons": qualitative uncertainty and the market mechanism', *Quarterly Journal of Economics*, vol. 84, pp. 488–500.

Alchian, A. A., and Demsetz, H. (1972), 'Production, information costs and economic organization', *American Economic Review*, vol. 62, pp. 777–95.

Aldrich, H. E. (1979), *Organizations and Environments*, Englewood Cliffs, NJ: Prentice Hall.

Alesina, A., and La Ferrara, E. (2002), 'Who trusts others?', *Journal of Public Economics*, vol. 85 (2), pp. 207–34.

Alvesson, M., and Lindkvist, L. (1993), 'Transaction costs, clans and corporate culture', *Journal of Management Studies*, vol. 30, pp. 427–52.

Amit, R., and Shoemaker, P. J. H. (1993), 'Strategic assets and organizational rent', *Strategic Management Journal*, vol. 14, pp. 33–46.

Anandalingham, G., and Lucas Jr, H. C. (2004), *Beware the Winner's Curse*, Oxford: Oxford University Press.

Andrade, G., Mitchell, M., and Stafford, E. (2001), 'New evidence and perspectives on mergers', *Journal of Economic Perspectives*, vol. 15 (2), pp. 103–20.

Ansoff, H. I. (1965), *Corporate Strategy*, Harmondsworth: Penguin.

Arrow, K. J. (1963), 'Uncertainty and medical care', *American Economic Review*, vol. 53, pp. 941–73.

Arrow, K. J. (1973), *Information and Economic Behavior*, Stockholm: Federation of Swedish Industries.

Arrow, K. J. (1985), 'The economics of agency', in J. W. Pratt and R. J. Zeckhauser (eds), *Principals and Agents: The Structure of Business*, Boston, MA: Harvard Business School Press.

Arthur, W. B. (1994a), *Increasing Returns and Path Dependence in the Economy*, Ann Arbor, MI: University of Michigan Press.

Arthur, W. B. (1994b), 'Positive feedbacks in the economy', *McKinsey Quarterly*, no. 1.

Arthur, W. B. (1996), 'Increasing returns and the new world of business', *Harvard Business Review*, vol. 74, July/August, pp. 100–9.

Axelrod, R. (1984), *The Evolution of Cooperation*, New York: Basic Books.

Axelrod, R. (1997), *The Complexity of Cooperation*, Princeton, NJ: Princeton University Press.

Axelrod, R., and Cohen, M. D. (1999), *Harnessing Complexity: Organizational Implications of a Scientific Frontier*, New York: Free Press.

Bagchi, A. K. (1972), *Private Investment in India 1900–1939*, Cambridge: Cambridge University Press.

Barney, J. B. (1989), 'Asset stocks and sustained competitive advantage: a comment', *Management Science*, vol. 35 (12), pp. 1511–13.

Barney, J. B. (1991), 'Firm resources and sustained competitive advantage', *Journal of Management*, vol. 17 (1), pp. 99–120.

Barney, J. B. (1997), *Gaining and Sustaining Competitive Advantage*, Reading, MA: Addison-Wesley.

Barney, J. B., and Hesterly, W. (1996), 'Organizational economics: Understanding the relationship between organizations and economic analysis', in S. R. Clegg, C. Hardy and W. R. Nord (eds), *Handbook of Organization Studies*, London: Sage.

Barney, J. B., and Ouchi, W. G. (eds) (1986), *Organizational Economics*, San Francisco, CA: Jossey-Bass.

Barron, D. N. (2003), 'Evolutionary theories', in D. O. Faulkner and A. Campbell, *The Oxford Handbook of Strategy*, Oxford: Oxford University Press.

Baum, J. A. C. (1996), 'Organizational ecology', in S. R. Clegg, C. Hardy and W. R. Nord (eds), *Handbook of Organization Studies*, London: Sage.

Bazerman M. H., and Samuelson, W. F. (1983), 'I won the auction but don't want the prize', *Journal of Conflict Resolution*, vol. 27, pp. 618–34.

Bazerman, M. H. (2006), *Judgment in Managerial Decision Making*, 6th edn, New York: John Wiley

Becker, G. S., and Elias, J. J. (2003), 'Introducing incentives in the market for live and cadaveric organ donations', at http://home.uchicago.edu/~gbecker/MarketforLiveandCadavericOrganDonations_Becker_Elias. pdf

Beinhocker, E. D. (2006), *The Origin of Wealth: Evolution, complexity and the radical remaking of economics*, Boston, MA: Harvard Business School Press.

Berle, A. A., and Means, G. C. (1932), *The Modern Corporation and Private Property*, New York: Commerce Clearing House.

Beroutsos, A., Freeman, A., and Kehoe, C. F. (2007), 'What public companies can learn from private equity', *McKinsey Quarterly, web exclusive, January 2007*.

Bertrand, M., Metha, P., and Mullainathan, S. (2002), 'Ferreting or tunneling: an application to Indian business groups', *Quarterly Journal of Economics*, vol. 117, pp. 121–48.

Besanko, D., Dranove, D., Shanley, M., and Schaefer, S. (2004), *Economics of Strategy*, New York: John Wiley.

Bettis, R. A., and Prahalad, C. K. (1995), 'The dominant logic: retrospective and extension', *Strategic Management Journal*, vol. 16 (1), pp. 5–14.

Birchler, U., and Bütler, M. (2007), *Information Economics*, London: Routledge.

Boone, C., and van Witteloostuijn, A. (1995), 'Industrial organization and organizational ecology: the potentials for cross-fertilization', *Organization Studies*, vol. 16 (2), pp. 265–98.

Boone, C., de Brabander, B., and van Witteloostuijn, A. (1996), 'CEO locus of control and small firm performance: an integrative framework and empirical test', *Journal of Management Studies*, vol. 33, pp. 667–99.

Boone, C., de Brabander, B., and van Witteloostuijn, A. (1999), 'Locus of control and strategic behavior in a prisoner's dilemma game', *Personality and Individual Differences*, vol. 27, pp. 695–706.

Bose, P. P. (1992), 'Commitment: an interview with Pankaj Ghemawat of the Harvard Business School on new directions in strategic thinking', *McKinsey Quarterly*, no. 3, pp. 121–37.

Bowles, S. (2004), *Microeconomics: Behavior, institutions, and evolution*, Princeton, NJ: Princeton University Press.

Bowman, E. H., and Helfat C. E., (2001), 'Does corporate strategy matter?', *Strategic Management Journal*, vol. 22 (1), pp. 1–23.

Brandenburger, A. M., and Nalebuff, B. J. (1995), 'The right game: use game theory to shape strategy', *Harvard Business Review*, vol. 73, pp. 57–71.

Brau, J. C., and Kohers, N. (2007), 'Dual-track versus single-track sell-outs: An empirical analysis of competing harvest strategies', forthcoming in: *Journal of Business Venturing*.

Brickley, J. A., and Dark, F. H. (1987), 'The choice of organizational form: the case of franchising', *Journal of Financial Economics*, vol. 18, pp. 401–20.

Brown, S. L., and Eisenhardt, K. M. (1998), *Competing on the Edge: Strategy as structured chaos*, Boston, MA: Harvard Business School Press.

Bruner, R. (2004), *Applied Mergers and Acquisitions*, Hoboken, NJ: John Wiley.

Bruner, R. (2005), *Deals from Hell: M&A lessons that rise above the ashes*, Hoboken, NJ: John Wiley.

Burgelman, R. A. (1990), 'Strategy-making and organizational ecology: a conceptual integration', in J. V. Singh, *Organizational Evolution: New Directions*, Newbury Park, CA: Sage.

Burgelman, R. A. (1991), 'Intraorganizational ecology of strategy making and organizational adaptation: theory and field research', *Organization Science*, vol. 2, pp. 239–62.

Burgelman, R. A. (2002), *Strategy is Destiny: How strategy-making shapes a company's future*, New York: Free Press.

Burrough, B., and Helyar, J. (1990), *Barbarians at the Gate: The fall of RJR Nabisco*, New York: Harper & Row.

Burt, R. S. (1992), *Structural Holes: The social structure of competition*, Cambridge, MA: Harvard University Press.

Cameron, S., and Collins, A. (1997), 'Transaction costs and partnerships: the case of rock bands', *Journal of Economic Behavior and Organization*, vol. 32, pp. 171–83.

Carney, M., and Gedajlovic, E. (1991), 'Vertical integration in franchise systems: agency theory and resource explanations', *Strategic Management Journal*, vol. 12, pp. 607–29.

Carroll, G. R. (1987), *Publish and Perish: The organizational ecology of newspaper industries*, Greenwich, CT: JAI Press.

Carroll, G. R. (ed.) (1988), *Ecological Models of Organizations*, Cambridge, MA: Ballinger.

Carroll, G. R., and Hannan, M. T. (1995), *Organizations in Industry: Strategy, structure, and selection*, Oxford: Oxford University Press.

Carroll, G. R., and Hannan, M. T. (2000), *The Demography of Corporations and Industries*, Princeton, NJ: Princeton University Press.

Casson, M. (1997), *Information and Organization: A new perspective on the theory of the firm*, Oxford: Oxford University Press.

Caves, R. E. (1992), *Multinational Enterprise and Economic Analysis*, Cambridge: Cambridge University Press.

Chandler, A. D. (1966), *Strategy and Structure*, New York: Doubleday.

Chang, S-J., (2006) 'The future of business groups in East Asia', in S-J.Chang (ed.) *Business Groups in East Asia: Financial crisis, restructuring and new growth*, Oxford: Oxford University Press.

Chesbrough, H. W. (2003), *Open Innovation: The new imperative for creating and profiting from technology*, Boston, MA: Harvard Business School Press.

Christensen, C. M. (1997), *The Innovator's Dilemma: When new technologies cause great firms to fail*, Boston, MA: Harvard Business School Press.

Christensen, C. M. (2003), *The Innovator's Solution*, Boston, MA: Harvard Business School Press.

Claessens, S., Djankov, S., and Lang, L. H. P. (2000), 'The separation of ownership and control in East Asian corporations', *Journal of Financial Economics,* vol. 58, pp. 81–112.

Clark, K., and Sefton, M. (2001), 'The sequential prisoner's dilemma: evidence on reciprocation', *Economic Journal*, vol. 111, pp. 51–68.

Clarke, R., and McGuinness, T. (eds) (1987), *The Economics of the Firm*, Oxford: Basil Blackwell.

Clegg, S. R., Hardy, C., and Nord, W. R. (eds) (1996), *Handbook of Organization Studies*, London: Sage.

Coase, R. H. (1937), 'The nature of the firm', *Economica*, vol. 4.

Coleman, J. S. (1990), *Foundations of Social Theory*, Cambridge, MA: Harvard University Press.

Coles, J. W., and Hesterly, W. S. (1998), 'The impact of firm specific assets and the interaction of uncertainty: an examination of make or buy decisions in public and private hospitals', *Journal of Economic Behavior and Organization*, vol. 36, pp. 383–409.

Collins, J. C. (2001), *Good to Great*, New York: HarperCollins.

Collins, J. C., and Porras, J. I. (1994), *Built to Last: Successful habits of visionary companies*, London: Century Business.

Collis, D. J., and Montgomery, C. A. (1995), 'Competing on resources: strategy in the 1990s', *Harvard Business Review*, vol. 73 (4), pp. 118–28.

Cronqvist H., and Nilsson, M. (2003), 'Agency costs of controlling minority shareholders', *Journal of Financial and Quantitative Analysis,* vol. 38, pp. 695–719.

Cyert, R. M., and March, J. G. (1963), *A Behavioral Theory of the Firm*, Englewood Cliffs, NJ: Prentice Hall (2nd edn, 1992)

d'Aspremont, C., Gabszewicz, J., and Thisse, J. F. (1979), 'On Hotelling's "stability in competition"', *Econometrica*, vol. 47, pp. 1145–51.

David, P. (1985), 'Clio and the economics of QWERTY', *American Economic Review*, vol. 75, pp. 332–7.

Davis, L. E., and North, D. C. (1971), *Institutional Change and American Economic Growth*, Cambridge: Cambridge University Press.

Dawkins, R. (1986), *The Blind Watchmaker*, Harlow: Longman.

Day, J. D., and Wendler, J. C. (1998), 'The new economics of organization', *McKinsey Quarterly*, 1998, no. 1, pp. 4–17.

DeAngelo H., and DeAngelo, L. (1985), 'Managerial ownership of voting rights: a study of public corporations with dual classes of common stock', *Journal of Financial Economics,* vol. 14, pp. 33–69.

De Jong, A., Kabir, R., Marra, T., and Roëll, A. (2001), 'Ownership and control in the Netherlands', in F. Barca and M. Becgt (eds), *The Control of Corporate Europe*, Oxford: Oxford University Press, pp. 188–206.

Dell, M., with Fredman, Catherine (1999), *Direct from Dell: Strategies which Revolutionized an Industry*, New York: HarperCollins.

Demsetz, H. (1995), *The Economics of the Business Firm: Seven critical commentaries*, Cambridge: Cambridge University Press.

DePamphilis, D. (2005), *Mergers, Acquisitions and Other Restructuring Activities*, Amsterdam: Elsevier, 3rd edn.

Dharwadkar, R., George, G., and Brandes, P. (2000), 'Privatization in emerging economies: an agency theory perspective', *Academy of Management Review*, vol. 25 (3), pp. 650–69.

Dierickx, I., and Cool, K. (1989), 'Asset stock accumulation and sustainability of competitive advantage', *Management Science*, vol. 35 (12), pp. 1504–11.

Dixit, A., and Nalebuff, B.(1991), *Thinking Strategically*, New York: Norton.

Dobbs R., Goedhart, M., and Suonio, H. (2006), 'Are companies getting better at M&A?', *The McKinsey Quarterly*, December 2006.

Doeringer, P., and Piore, M. (1971), *Internal Labor Markets and Manpower Analysis*, Boston, MA: Heath & Co.

Donaldson, T., and Preston, L. (1995), 'The stakeholder theory of the corporation: Concepts, evidence, and implications', *Academy of Management Review*, vol. 20 (1), pp. 65–91.

Douma, S. W. (1997), 'The two-tier system of corporate governance', *Long Range Planning*, vol. 30 (4), pp. 612–14.

Douma, S., George, R., and Kabir, R. (2006), 'Foreign and domestic ownership, business groups, and firm performamnce: evidence from a large emerging market', *Strategic Management Journal*, vol. 27, pp. 637–57.

Dyer, J. H., Kale, P., and Singh, H. (2004), 'When to ally and when to acquire', *Harvard Business Review*, vol. 82 (7/8), pp. 108–15.

Dyer, J. H., and Nobeoka, K. (2000), 'Creating and managing a high-performance knowledge-sharing network: the Toyota case', *Strategic Management Journal*, vol. 21(3), pp. 345–67.

Encarnation, D. (1989), *Dislodging Multinationals: India's Comparative Perspective*, Ithaca, NY: Cornell University Press.

Faccio, L., and Lang, L. H. P. (2002), 'The ultimate ownership of Western European corporations', *Journal of Financial Economics*, vol. 65, pp. 365–95.

Faccio, L., Lang, L. H. P., and Young, L. (2001), 'Dividends and expropriation', *American Economic Review*, vol. 91, pp. 54–78.

Fama, E. F. (1980), 'Agency problems and the theory of the firm', *Journal of Political Economy*, vol. 88, pp. 288–307.

Fama, E. F., Fisher, L., Jensen, M. C., and Roll, R. (1969), 'The adjustment of stock prices to new information', *International Economic Review*, vol. 10 (1), pp. 1–21.

Fama, E. F., and Jensen, M. C. (1983a), 'Separation of ownership and control', *Journal of Law and Economics*, vol. 26, pp. 301–26.

Fama, E. F., and Jensen, M. C. (1983b), 'Agency problems and residual claims', *Journal of Law and Economics*, vol. 26, pp. 327–50.

Ferguson, T. D. (2000), 'Do strategic groups differ in reputation?', *Strategic Management Journal*, vol. 21 (12), pp. 1195–214.

FitzRoy, F. R., Acs, Z. J., and Gerlowski, D. A. (1998), *Management and Economics of Organization*, Harlow: Prentice Hall.

Frances, J. et al. (1991), 'Introduction', in G. Thompson, J. Frances, R. Levacic and J. Mitchell, *Markets, Hierarchies and Networks*, London: Sage.

Freeman, R. E. (1984), *Strategic Management: A stakeholder approach*. Boston, MA: Pitman.

Friedman, E., Johnson, S., and Mitton, T. (2003), 'Propping or tunneling', *Journal of Comparitive Economics*, vol. 31, pp. 732–50.

Frentrop, P. (2003), *A History of Corporate Governance, 1602–2002*, Amsterdam: Deminor.

Galford, R., and Drapeau, A. S. (2003), 'The Enemies of Trust', *Harvard Business Review*, Feb., pp. 89–95.

Gell-Mann, M. (1994), *The Quark and the Jaguar: Adventures in the simple and the complex*, London: Little Brown.

Geroski, P. A. (2003), *The Evolution of New Markets*, Oxford: Oxford University Press.

Gerstner, L. (2002), *Who Says Elephants Can't Dance*, HarperCollins.

Ghemawat, P. (1991), *Commitment: The dynamic of strategy*, New York: Free Press.

Ghemawat, P. (1997), *Games Businesses Play*, Cambridge, MA: MIT Press.

Gibbons, R., and Katz, L. F. (1991), 'Layoffs and lemons', *Journal of Labor Economics*, vol. 9 (4), pp. 351–80.

Gilbert, X., and Strebel, P. (1988), 'Developing competitive advantage', in J. B. Quinn, H. Mintzberg and R. M. James (eds), *The Strategy Process*, Englewood Cliffs, NJ: Prentice Hall.

Gilson, R. J., and Schwartz, A. (2005), 'Understanding MACs: Moral Hazard in Acquisitions', *The Journal of Law, Economics and Organization*, vol. 21, pp. 330–58.

Gilson, R. J., Goldberg, V., Klausner, M., and Raff, D. 'Building foundations for a durable deal', *Financial Times* (Supplement), 13 October 2006, reprinted in Mayer, Colin, and Franks, Julian, *Mastering Transactions*, Financial Times/Ernst & Young, 2006.

Gintis, H. (2000), *Game Theory Evolving*, Princeton, NJ: Princeton University Press.

Glaeser, E. L., Laibson, D. I., Scheinkman, J. A., and Soutter, C. L. (2000), 'Measuring trust', *Quarterly Journal of Economics*, vol. 115 (3), pp. 811–46.

Gleick, J. (1987), *Chaos*, New York: Viking.

Goetzmann, W. N., and Rouwenhorst, K. G. (2005) *The Origins of Value,* Oxford: Oxford University Press.

Goold, M., Campbell, A., and Alexander, M. (1994), *Corporate–level Strategy*, New York: John Wiley.

Goshal, S., and Moran, P. (1996), 'Bad for practice: a critique of the transaction cost theory', *Academy of Management Review*, vol. 21 (1), pp. 13–47.

Goswami, O. (1989), 'Sahibs, babus and Banias: Changes in industrial control in Eastern India 1918–1950', *Journal of Asian Studies*, vol. 48, pp. 289–309.

Gould, S. J. (1989), *Wonderful Life*, New York: Norton.

Granovetter, M. (1985), 'Economic action and social structure: The problem of embeddedness', *American Journal of Sociology*, vol. 91 (3).

Grant, R. M. (1991), 'The resource-based theory of competitive advantage: Implications for strategy formulation', *California Management Review*, vol. 13, pp. 114–35.

Grant, R. M. (2003), 'The knowledge-based view of the firm', in D. O. Faulkner, and A. Campbell (eds), *The Oxford Handbook of Strategy*, Oxford: Oxford University Press.

Grant, R. M. (2005), *Contemporary Strategy Analysis,* Oxford: Blackwell.

Grove, A. S. (1996), *Only the Paranoid Survive,* New York: Doubleday.

Guillén, M. F. (2000), 'Business groups in emerging economies: a resource-based view', *Academy of Management Journal*, vol. 43 (3), pp. 362–81.

Güth, W., Schmittberger, R., and Schwarze, B. (1982), 'An experimental analysis of ultimum bargaining', *Journal of Economic Behavior and Organization*, vol. 3, pp. 367–88.

Hall, R. (1992), 'The strategic analysis of intangible resources', *Strategic Management Journal*, vol. 13, pp. 135–44.

Hall, R. (1993), 'A framework linking intangible resources and capabilities to sustainable competitive advantage', *Strategic Management Journal*, vol. 14, pp. 607–18.

Hannan, M. T., and Freeman, J. (1989a), *Organizational Ecology*, Cambridge, MA: Harvard University Press.

Hannan, M. T., and Freeman, J. (1989b), 'Setting the record straight on organizational ecology: rebuttal to Young', *American Journal of Sociology*, vol. 95 (2), pp. 425–35.

Harrigan, K. (2003), *Joint Ventures, Alliances, and Corporate Strategy*, Washington, DC: Beard Books.

Hatten, K. J., and Hatten, M. L. (1988), *Effective Strategic Management: Analysis and Action*, Englewood Cliffs, NJ: Prentice Hall.

Haugland, S. A. (1999), 'Factors influencing the duration of international buyer–seller relationships', *Journal of Business Research*, vol. 46, pp. 273–80.

Hayek, F. A. (1945), 'The use of knowledge in society', *American Economic Review*, vol. 35 (4).

Hayward, M. L. A., and Hambrick, D. C. (1997), 'Explaining the premiums paid for large acquisitions: evidence of CEO hubris', *Administrative Science Quarterly*, vol. 42 (1), pp. 103–27.

Hazari, R. K. (1967), *The Structure of the Corporate Private Sector: A study of concentration, ownership and control,* London: Asia Publishing House.

Helfat C. E., Finkelstein, S., Mitchell, W., Peteraf, M. A., Singh, H., Teece, D. J., and Winter, S. G. (2007), *Dynamic Capabilities: Understanding strategic change in organizations*, Oxford: Blackwell.

Henrich, J. (2000), 'Does culture matter in economic behavior?: ultimatum game bargaining among the Machiguenga of the Peruvian Amazon', *American Economic Review*, vol. 90, pp. 973–79.

Hennart, J. F., and Reddy, S. (1997), 'The choice between mergers/acquisitions and joint ventures: the case of Japanese investors in the United States', *Strategic Management Journal*, vol. 18 (1), pp. 1–12.

Hill, C. W., and Jones, G. R. (1995), *Strategic Management Theory: An Integrated Approach*, Boston, MA: Houghton Mifflin.

Hillman, A. J., and Keim, G. D. (2001), 'Shareholder value, stakeholder management, and social issues: what's the bottom line?', *Strategic Management Journal*, vol. 22 (2), pp. 125–39.

Hofstede, G. (2001), *Culture's Consequences,* London: Sage.

Holland, J. H. (1998), *Emergence: from Chaos to Order*, Cambridge, MA: Perseus.

Holmstrom, B. R., and Tirole, J. (1989), 'The theory of the firm', in R. Schmalensee and R. Willig (eds), *Handbook of Industrial Organization*, vol. 1, Amsterdam: North Holland.

Hoskisson, R. E., and Hitt, M. A. (1990), 'Antecedents and performance outcomes of diversification: a review and critique of theoretical perspectives', *Journal of Management*, vol. 16 (2), pp. 461–509.

Hotelling, H. (1929), 'Stability in competition', *Economic Journal*, vol. 39, pp. 41–57.

Hurley, R. F. (2006), 'The Decision to Trust', *Harvard Business Review*, Sept., pp. 55–62.

Hymon, D. N. (1986), *Modern Microeconomics: Analysis and applications*, St Louis, MI: Times Mirror/Mosby College Publishing.

Imai, K., and Itami, H. (1984), 'Interpenetration of organization and market', *International Journal of Industrial Organization*, vol. 2, pp. 285–310.

Irvin, R. A., and Michaels III, E. G. (1983), 'Core skills: doing the right things right', *McKinsey Quarterly*, Summer, 4–19.

Jacobides, M. G., and Croson, D. C. (2001), 'Information policy: shaping the value of agency relationships', *Academy of Management Review*, vol. 26 (2), pp. 202–23.

Jensen, M. C. (1986), 'Agency costs and free cash flow, corporate finance, and takeovers', *American Economic Review*, vol. 76, pp. 323–9.

Jensen, M. C. (1989), 'The eclipse of the public corporation', *Harvard Business Review*, September/October, pp. 61–73.

Jensen, M. C. (1998), *Foundations of Organizational Strategy*, Cambridge, MA: Harvard University Press.

Jensen, M. C. (2000), *A Theory of the Firm: Governance, residual claims, and organizational forms*, Cambridge, MA: Harvard University Press.

Jensen, M. C., and Meckling, W. H. (1976), 'Theory of the firm: managerial behavior, agency costs and ownership structure', *Journal of Financial Economics*, vol. 3, pp. 305–60.

Jensen, M. C., and Ruback, R. S. (1983), 'The market for corporate control: the scientific evidence', *Journal of Financial Economics*, vol. 11, pp. 5–50.

Johnson, S. (2001), *Emergence: The connected lives of ants, brains, cities and software*, New York: Scribner.

Johnson, S., La Porta, R., Lopez-de-Silanes, F., and Schleifer, A. (2000), 'Tunneling', *American Economic Review Paper and Proceedings*, vol. 90, pp. 22–7.

Johnson, G., Scholes, K., and Whittington, R. (2005), *Exploring Corporate Strategy: Text and cases*, Harlow: FT Prentice Hall.

Jones, G. R., and Hill, C. W. L. (1988), 'Transaction cost analysis of strategy–structure choice', *Strategic Management Journal*, vol. 9, pp. 159–72.

Kahneman, D. (2002), *Maps of Bounded Rationality*, Nobel Prize Lecture, reprinted in *American Economic Review*, vol 93 (5), pp. 1449–75, 2003.

Katz, M. L., and Rosen, H. S. (1998), *Microeconomics*, Boston, MA: Irwin/McGraw Hill.

Kauffman, S. (1993), *The Origins of Order: Self-organization and selection in evolution*, New York: Oxford University Press.

Kauffman, S. (1995), *At Home in the Universe: The search for laws of complexity*, London: Viking.

Kaufman, A., Wood, C. H., and Theyel, G. (2000), 'Collaboration and technology linkages: a strategic supplier typology', *Strategic Management Journal*, vol. 21 (6), pp. 649–63.

Kay, J. (1993), *Foundations of Corporate Success: How business strategies add value*, Oxford: Oxford University Press.

Kay, J. (1996), *The Business of Economics*, Oxford: Oxford University Press.

Kay, J. (2003), *The Truth about Markets: Their genius, their limits, their follies*, London: Penguin

Kessel, R. A. (1974), 'Transfused blood, serum hepatitis, and the Coase theorem', *Journal of Law and Economics*, vol. 17 (2), pp. 265–89.

Khalil, E. L. (2003), *Trust*, Cheltenham: Elgar.

Khanna, T. (2000), 'Business groups and social welfare in emerging markets: existing evidence and unanswered questions', *European Economic Review*, vol. 44, pp. 748–61.

Khanna, T., and Palepu, K. (1997), 'Why focused strategies may be wrong for emerging markets?', *Harvard Business Review*, vol. 75 (4), pp. 41–54.

Khanna, T., and Palepu, K. (2004), 'The evolution of concentrated ownership in India: broad patterns and a history of the Indian software industry' *Harvard Business School, NBER Working paper W10613.*

Khanna, T., and Rivkin, J. W. (2001), 'Estimating the performance effects of business groups in emerging markets', *Strategic Management Journal*, vol. 22 (1), pp. 45–74.

Klein, B., Crawford, R. A., and Alchian, A. A. (1978), 'Vertical integration, appropriable rents and the competitive contracting process', *Journal of Law and Economics*, vol. 21, pp. 297–326.

Klemperer, P. (2002), 'What really matters in auction design', *Journal of Economic Perspectives*, vol. 16 (1), Winter 2002, pp. 169–89.

Klemperer, P. (2004), *Auctions: Theory and practice*, Princeton, NJ: Princeton University Press.

Kreps, D. M. (2004), *Microeconomics for Managers*, New York: W. W. Norton.

Lafontaine, F. (1992), 'Agency theory and franchising: some empirical results', *RAND Journal of Economics*, vol. 23 (2), pp. 263–83.

Lewin, R. (1995), *Complexity: Life on the edge of chaos*, London: Phoenix.

Li, Shaomin, Li, Shuhe and Zhang, Weiying (2000), 'The road to capitalism: competition and institutional change in China', *Journal of Comparative Economics*, vol 28 (2), pp. 269–92.

Lieberman M. B., and Montgomery, D. B. (1998), 'First-mover (dis)advantages: retrospective and link with the resource-based view', *Strategic Management Journal*, vol. 19 (12), pp. 1111–25

Liebowitz, S., and Margolis, S. (1990), 'The fable of the keys', *Journal of Law and Economics*, vol. 33 (1), pp. 1–25.

Lindgren, K. (1997), 'Evolutionary dynamics in game-theoretic models', in W. B. Arthur, S. N. Durlauf and D. A. Lane, *The Economy as an Evolving Complex System II*, Santa Fe Institute, Reading: Addison-Wesley.

Lokanathan, P. S. (1935), *Industrial Organization in India*, London: Allen and Unwin.

Macaulay, S. (1963), 'Non-contractual relations in business: a preliminary study', *American Sociological Review*, vol. 28 (1).

McColgan, P. (2001), 'Agency and corporate governance: a review of the literature from a UK perspective', part of unpublished PhD dissertation, University of Strathclyde, Glasgow.

McGee, J. (2003), 'Strategic groups: theory and practice', in D. O. Faulkner and A. Campbell, *The Oxford Handbook of Strategy (vol. 1)*, Oxford: Oxford University Press.

McMillan, J. (1991), *Games, Strategies, and Managers*, Oxford: Oxford University Press.

McMillan, J. (2002), *Reinventing the Bazaar: A natural history of markets*, New York: W. W. Norton.

Magretta, Joan (2002), *What Management Is*, New York: Free Press.

Maher, M. E. (1997), 'Transaction cost economics and contractual relations', *Cambridge Journal of Economics*, vol. 21, pp. 147–70.

Malmendier, U., and Tate, G. (2004), 'Who makes acquisitions? CEO overconfidence and the market's reaction', AFA 2004. Available at http://papers.ssrn.com/so13/papers.cfm?abstract_id=470788

March, J. G. (1994), *A Primer on Decision Making: How decisions happen*, New York: Free Press.

March, J. G., and Simon, H. A. (1958), *Organizations*, New York: John Wiley.

Markides, C. C., and Geroski, P. A. (2005), *Fast Second: How smart companies bypass radical innovation to enter and dominate new markets*, San Francisco, CA: Jossey-Bass.

Marshall, A. (1890), *Principles of Economics*, London: Macmillan. (Reprinted 1949.)

Masten, S. E., Meekan Jr, J. W., and Snyder, E. A. (1989), 'Vertical integration in the US auto industry: a note on the influence of transaction specific assets', *Journal of Economic Behavior and Organization*, vol. 12, pp. 265–73.

Maynard Smith, J. and Price, G. (1973), 'The logic of animal conflict', *Nature*, vol. 146, pp. 15–18.

Ménard, C. (1995), 'Markets as institutions versus organizations as markets? Disentangling some fundamental concepts', *Journal of Economic Behavior and Organization*, vol. 28, pp. 161–82

Ménard, C. (2004), 'The economics of hybrid organizations', *Journal of Institutional and Theoretical Economics*, pp. 345–76.

Michael, S. C. (2000), 'Investments to create bargaining power: the case of franchising', *Strategic Management Journal*, vol. 21 (4) pp. 497–514.

Micklethwait, J., and Wooldridge, A. (2003), *The Company: A short history of a revolutionary idea*, London: Weidenfeld & Nicolson.

Milgrom, P., and Roberts, J. (1987), 'Informational asymmetry, strategic behavior, and industrial organization', *American Economic Review*, vol. 77, pp. 184–93.

Milgrom, P., and Roberts, J. (1992), *Economics, Organization and Management*, Englewood Cliffs, NJ: Prentice Hall.

Miller, D. (1990), *The Icarus Paradox*, New York: Harper.

Miller, D. (1994), 'What happens after success: the perils of excellence', *Journal of Management Studies*, vol. 31 (3), pp. 325–58.

Minkler, L. (2004), 'Shirking and motivations in firms: survey evidence on worker attitudes', *International Journal of Industrial Organization*, Vol. 22 (6), pp. 863–84.

Mintzberg, H. (1979), *The Structuring of Organizations*, Englewood Cliffs, NJ: Prentice Hall.

Mintzberg, H. (1983), *Structure in Fives: Designing effective organizations*, Englewood Cliffs, NJ: Prentice Hall.

Mintzberg, H. (1985), 'Of strategies, deliberate and emergent', *Strategic Management Journal*, pp. 257–72.

Mintzberg, H. (1989), *Mintzberg on Management*, New York: Free Press.

Mintzberg, H. and J. B. Quinn (1991), *The Strategy Process: concepts, contexts, cases*, Englewood Cliffs, NJ: Prentice Hall.

Moerland, P. W. (1995), 'Alternative disciplinary mechanisms in different corporate systems', *Journal of Economic Behavior and Organization*, vol. 26, pp. 17–34.

Morck, R., Wolfenzon, D. and Yeung, B. (2004), 'Corporate governance, economic entrenchement and growth', *Harvard Business School, NBER Working paper W10692*.

Morgan, G. (1997), *Images of Organization*, London: Sage.

Moschandreas, M. (1997), 'The role of opportunism in transaction cost economics', *Journal of Economic Issues*, vol. 31 (1), pp. 39–57.

Nair, A., and Kotha, S. (2001), 'Does group membership matter? Evidence from the Japanese steel industry', *Strategic Management Journal*, vol. 22 (3), pp. 221–35.

Nam, S. W. (2001), 'Business groups looted by controlling families, and the Asian crisis', *ADB Institute Research Paper 27*.

Nanda, A., and Williamson, P. J. (1995), 'Use joint ventures to ease the pain of restructuring', *Harvard Business Review*, vol. 73 (6), pp. 119–28.

Nayak, P. R., Garvin, D. A., Maira, A. N., and Bragar, J. L. (1995), 'Creating a learning organization', *Prism*, 3rd quarter.

Nelson, R. R. (1991), 'Why do firms differ and how does it matter?', *Strategic Management Journal*, vol. 12 (special issue), pp. 61–74.

Nelson, R. R., and Winter, S. G. (1982), *An Evolutionary Theory of Economic Change*, Cambridge, MA: Harvard University Press.

Nenova, T. (2004), 'A corporate governance agenda for developing countries' *World Bank working paper*.

Nickerson, J. A., Hamilton, B. H., and Wada T., (2001), 'Market position, resource profile and governance: linking Porter and Williamson in the context of international courier and small package services in Japan', *Strategic Management Journal*, vol. 22 (3), pp. 251–73.

Noorderhaven, N. G. (1995), 'Transaction, interaction, institutionalization: toward a dynamic theory of hybrid governance', *Scandinavian Journal of Management*, vol. 11 (1), pp. 43–55.

North, D. C. (1990), *Institutions, Institutional Change and Economic Performance*, Cambridge: Cambridge University Press.

North, D. C. (2005a), *Understanding the Process of Economic Change*, Princeton, NJ: Princeton University Press.

North, D. C. (2005b), 'Corporate leadership in an uncertain world', New York: Conference Board Annual Report.

O'Donnell, S. W. (2000), 'Managing foreign subsidiaries: agents of headquarters, or an independent network?', *Strategic Management Journal*, vol. 21 (5), pp. 525–48.

OECD (2004), *Principles of corporate governance*, OECD.

Oster, S. (1982), 'Intraindustry structure and the ease of strategic change', *Review of Economics and Statistics*, vol. 64 (3), pp. 376–83.

Ouchi, W. G. (1980), 'Markets, bureaucracies and clans', *Administrative Science Quarterly*, vol. 25, pp. 129–41.

Ouchi, W. G., and Williamson, O. E. (1981), 'The markets and hierarchies perspective: origins, implications, prospects', in A. Van de Ven and W. F Joyce (eds), *Assessing Organizational Design and Performance*, New York: John Wiley.

Pagano, M. and Volpin, P. (2001), 'The political economy of finance', *Oxford Review of Economic Policy*, vol. 17, pp. 502–19.

Park, S. H., and Luo, Y. (2001), 'Guanxi and organizational dynamics: organizational networking in Chinese firms', *Strategic Management Journal*, vol. 22 (5), pp. 455–77.

Parsons, T. (1960), *Structure and Process in Modern Societies*, Glencoe, IL: Free Press.

Perloff, J. M. (2001), *Microeconomics*, Boston, MA: Addison-Wesley.

Peteraf, M. A. (1993), 'The cornerstones of competitive advantage: a resource-based view', *Strategic Management Journal*, vol. 14 (3), pp. 179–91.

Pfeffer, J. (1982), *Organizations and Organization Theory*, Marshfield, MA: Pitman.

Pigou, A. C. (1920), *The Economics of Welfare*, London: Macmillan.

Polanyi, M. (1962), *Personal Knowledge*, New York: Harper.

Polanyi, M. (1967), *The Tacit Dimension*, Garden City, NY: Doubleday.

Polisiri, P., and Wiwattanakantang, Y. (2004), 'Restructuring of family firms after the East Asian financial crisis: shareholder expropriation or alignment?', Working paper, Center for Economic institutions, Institute for Economic Research, Hitotsubashi University, Japan.

Porter, M. E. (1980), *Competitive Strategy: Techniques for Analyzing Industries and Competitors*, New York: Free Press.

Porter, M. E. (1985), *Competitive Advantage: Creating and Sustaining Superior Performance*, New York: Free Press.

Porter, M. E. (2008), 'The five forces that shape strategy', *Harvard Business Review*, vol. 86 (1), pp. 1–17

Powell, J. H. (2003), 'Game Theory in Strategy', in D. O. Faulkner and A. Campbell, *The Oxford Handbook in Strategy (vol. 2)*, Oxford: Oxford University Press

Prahalad, C. K. and Hamel, G. (1994), *Competing for the Future*, Boston, MA: Harvard Business School Press.

Prigogine, I. and Stengers, I. (1984), *Order Out of Chaos*, New York: Bantam.

Putterman, L. (ed.) (1986), *The Economic Nature of the Firm*: A reader, Cambridge: Cambridge University Press.

Quinn, J. B. (1982), *Strategies for Change: Logical incrementalism*, Homewood, IL: Irwin.

Quinn, J. B., Mintzberg, H., and James, R. M. (eds) (1988), *The Strategy Process*, Englewood Cliffs, NJ: Prentice Hall.

Raiffa, H. (1968), *Decision Analysis: Introductory lectures on choices under uncertainty*, Reading, MA: Addison-Wesley.

Rasmusen, E. (1989), *Games and Information: An introduction to the theory of games*, Oxford: Basil Blackwell.

Reuer, J. J. (2001), 'From hybrids to hierarchies: shareholder wealth effects of joint venture partner buy-outs', *Strategic Management Journal*, vol. 22 (1), pp. 27–44.

Reuer, J. J. (2005), 'Avoiding lemons in M&A deals', *MIT Sloan Management Review*, vol. 46 (3), pp. 15–17.

Reuer, J. J., and Koza, M. P. (2000), 'Asymmetric information and joint venture performance: theory and evidence for domestic and international joint ventures', *Strategic Management Journal*, vol. 21 (1), pp. 81–8.

Reuer, J. J. and Ragozzino, R. (2006), 'Using IPOs to prove the value of M&A targets', *Financial Times (Supplement)*, 6 October 2006, reprinted in Mayer, Colin and Franks, Julian, *Mastering Transactions*, Financial Times/Ernst & Young, 2006.

Reuer, J. J., and Shen, J. C. (2004), 'Sequential divestiture through initial public offerings', *Journal of Economic Behavior and Organization*, vol. 54 (2), pp. 249–66.

Roberts, D. J. (2004), *The Modern Firm: Organizational design for performance and growth*, Oxford: Oxford University Press.

Roll, R. (1986), 'The hubris hypothesis of corporate takeovers', *Journal of Business*, vol. 59 (2), pp. 197–216.

Rumelt, R. P. (1974), *Strategy, Structure, and Economic Performance*, Boston, MA: Harvard Business School Press.

Rumelt, R. P., (1984), 'Towards a strategic theory of the firm', in R. B. Lamb, *Competitive Strategic Management*, Englewood Cliffs, NJ: Prentice Hall.

Rumelt, R. P. (1991), 'How much does industry matter?', *Strategic Management Journal*, vol. 12 (3), pp. 167–85.

Sako, M., and Helper, S. (1998), 'Determinants of trust in supplier relations: evidence from the automotive industry in Japan and the United States', *Journal of Economic Behavior and Organization*, vol. 34, pp. 387–417.

Samuelson, P. (1976), *Economics* (10th edn), Tokyo: McGraw-Hill/Kogakusha Ltd.

Saussier, S. (1999), 'Duration: an empirical analysis of EDF coal contracts', *Recherches Economiques de Louvain*, vol. 65 (1), pp. 3–21.

Schelling, T. C. (1960), *The Strategy of Conflict*, Cambridge, MA: Harvard University Press. (Reprinted 1980.)

Schleifer, A., and Vishny, R. W. (1997), 'A survey of corporate governance', *Journal of Finance*, vol. 52, pp. 737–83.

Schleifer, A., and Vishny, R. W. (2003), 'Stock market driven acquisitions', *Journal of Financial Economics*, vol. 70, pp. 295–311

Schreuder, H. (1993a), 'Coase, Hayek, and hierarchy', in S. Lindenberg and H. Schreuder, *Interdisciplinary Perspectives on Organization Studies*, Oxford: Pergamon Press.

Schreuder, H. (1993b), 'Timely management changes as an element of organizational strategy', *Journal of Management Studies*, vol. 30 (5), pp. 723–38.

Schreuder, H., and van Witteloostuijn, A. (1990), *The Ecology of Organizations and the Economics of Firms*, Research Memorandum, University of Limburg.

Schumpeter, J. A. (1934), *The Theory of Economic Development*, Cambridge, MA: Harvard University Press.

Scott, W. R. (1992), *Organizations: Rational, Natural, and Open Systems* (3rd edn), Englewood Cliffs, NJ: Prentice Hall. (5th edn, 2003.)

Sculley, J. with John Byrne (1987), *Odyssey: Pepsi to Apple . . . A Journey of Adventures, Ideas, and the Future*, New York: Harper & Row.

Seabright, P. (2004), *The Company of Strangers: A natural history of economic life*, Princeton, NJ: Princeton University Press.

Simon, H. A. (1961), *Administrative Behavior* (2nd edn), New York: Macmillan.

Simon, H. A. (1991), 'Organizations and markets', *Journal of Economic Perspectives*, vol. 5 (2), pp. 25–44.

Slater, M. (2003), 'The boundary of the firm', in D. O. Faulkner and A. Campbell, *The Oxford Handbook of Strategy*, Oxford: Oxford University Press.

Soeters, J., and Schreuder, H. (1988), 'The interaction between national and organizational cultures in accounting firms', *Accounting, Organizations and Society*, vol. 13 (1), pp. 75–85.

Spence, M. (1973), 'Job market signaling', *Quarterly Journal of Economics,* vol. 87(3), pp. 355–74.

Stacey, R. D. (2007), *Strategic Management & Organisational Dynamics* (5th edn), Harlow: Financial Times/Prentice Hall.

Stigler, G. J., and Friedland, C. (1983), 'The literature of economics: the case of Berle and Means', *Journal of Law and Economics*, vol. 26, pp. 237–68.

Stiglitz, J. (2002), *Globalization and its Discontents,* London: Penguin.

Stuckey, J. and White, D. (1993), 'When and when not to vertically integrate: a strategy as risky as vertical integration can only succeed when it is chosen for the right reasons', *McKinsey Quarterly*, pp. 3–27.

Takeishi, A. (2001), 'Bridging inter- and intra-firm boundaries: management of supplier involvement in automobile product development', *Strategic Management Journal*, vol. 22 (5), pp. 403–33.

Tallman, S. (2003), 'Dynamic capabilities', in D. O. Faulkner and A. Campbell, *The Oxford Handbook of Strategy*, Oxford: Oxford University Press.

Teece, D. J. (1980), 'Economics of scope and scope of the enterprise', *Journal of Economic Behavior and Organization*, vol. 1, pp. 223–47.

Teece, D. J. (1982), 'Towards an economic theory of the multiproduct firm', *Journal of Economic Behavior and Organization*, vol. 3, pp. 39–63.

Teece, D. J., Pisano, G. and Shuen, A. (1997), 'Dynamic capabilities and strategic management', *Strategic Management Journal*, vol. 18, pp. 509–33.

Tellis, G. J., and Golder, P. N. (1996), 'First to market, first to fail? Real causes of enduring market leadership', *MIT Sloan Management Review*, vol. 37 (2), pp. 65–75.

Tellis, G. J., and Golder, P. N. (2002), *Will and Vision: How latecomers grow to dominate markets*, New York: McGraw-Hill

Thompson, G., Frances, J., Levacic, R., and Mitchell, J. (1991), *Markets, Hierarchies and Networks*, London: Sage.

Tichy, G. (2002), 'What do we know about success and failure of mergers?', *Journal of Industry, Competition and Trade*, vol. 1 (4), pp. 347–94.

Titmuss, R. M. (1971), *The Gift Relationship: From human blood to social policy*, New York: Pantheon.

Tversky, A., and Kahneman, D. (1974), 'Judgment under uncertainty: heuristics and biases', *Science*, vol. 185, pp. 1124–31.

UBS (2004), 'Are you prepared for the next wave?', Jullens, D., Cooper, S., and Stillit, D., August. See: www.ubsinvestmentresearch.com

Usher, J. M., and Evans, M. G. (1996), 'Life and death along gasoline alley: Darwinian and Lamarckian processes in a differentiating population', *Academy of Management Journal*, vol. 39 (5), pp. 1428–66.

Volberda, H. W. (2003), 'Strategic flexibility: creating dynamic competitive advantages', in D. O. Faulkner and A. Campbell (2003), *The Oxford Handbook of Strategy*, vol. 2, Oxford: Oxford University Press.

Waldrop, M. M. (1992), *Complexity: The emerging science at the edge of order and chaos*, New York: Simon & Schuster.

Warner, J. B., Watts, R. L., and Wruck, K. H. (1988), 'Stock prices and top management changes', *Journal of Financial Economics*, vol. 20, pp. 461–92.

Weber, Max (1947), *The Theory of Social and Economic Organization* (original edition 1925), A. M. Henderson and T. Parsons (trans.), New York: Free Press.

Weick, K. E. (1979), *The Social Psychology of Organizing* (2nd edn), Reading, MA: Addison-Wesley.

Weisbach, M. S. (1988), 'Outside directors and CEO turnover', *Journal of Financial Economics*, vol. 20, pp. 431–60.

Williamson, O. E. (1975), *Markets and Hierarchies: Analysis and antitrust implications*, New York: Free Press.

Williamson, O. E. (1985), *The Economic Institutions of Capitalism*, New York: Free Press.

Williamson, O. E. (1995), 'Transaction cost economics and organization theory', in O. E. Williamson, *Organization Theory: From Chester Barnard to the present and beyond*', Oxford: Oxford University Press.

Williamson, O. E. (1996), 'Economics and organization: a primer', *California Management Review*, vol. 38, pp. 131–46.

Williamson, O. E. (1998), 'Transaction cost economics: how it works, where it is headed', *De Economist*, vol. 146 (1), pp. 23–58

Williamson, O. E. (1999), 'Strategy research: governance and competence perspectives', *Strategic Management Journal*, vol. 20 (12), pp. 1087–108.

Winter, S. G. (1990), 'Survival, selection, and inheritance in evolutionary theories of organization', in J. V. Singh, *Organizational Evolution: New Directions*, Newbury Park, CA: Sage.

Winter, S. G. (2003), 'Understanding dynamic capabilities', *Strategic Management Journal*, vol. 24, pp. 991–5.

Wu, J., and Axelrod, R. (1995) 'How to cope with noise in the iterated prisoner's dilemma', *Journal of Conflict Resolution*, vol. 39 (1), pp. 183–9

Young, R. C. (1988), 'Is population ecology a useful paradigm for the study of organizations?', *American Journal of Sociology*, vol. 94 (1), pp. 1–24.

Index

Pages numbers in **bold** refer to marginal definitions.